Fodor's

D0367889

NEW MEXICO

6th Edition

**Where to Stay and Eat
for All Budgets**

**Must-See Sights
and Local Secrets**

Ratings You Can Trust

Fodor's Travel Publications   New York, Toronto, London, Sydney, Auckland
www.fodors.com

FODOR'S NEW MEXICO
Editor: Paul Eisenberg

Editorial Production: Tom Holton
Editorial Contributors: Andrew Collins, Georgia de Katona
Maps: David Lindroth, *cartographer*; Robert Blake, Rebecca Baer, *map editors*
Design: Fabrizio La Rocca, *creative director*; Guido Caroti, *art director*; Moon Sun Kim, *cover designer*; Melanie Marin, *senior picture editor*
Production/Manufacturing: Robert B. Shields
Cover Photo (Sand painting, Farmington): Ted Spiegel/Corbis

Sixth Edition

ISBN 978–1–4000–1736–2

ISSN 1526–4734

SPECIAL SALES
This book is available for special discounts for bulk purchases for sales promotions or premiums. Special editions, including personalized covers, excerpts of existing books, and corporate imprints, can be created in large quantities for special needs. For more information, write to Special Markets/Premium Sales, 1745 Broadway, MD 6-2, New York, New York 10019, or e-mail specialmarkets@randomhouse.com.

AN IMPORTANT TIP & AN INVITATION
Although all prices, opening times, and other details in this book are based on information supplied to us at press time, changes occur all the time in the travel world, and Fodor's cannot accept responsibility for facts that become outdated or for inadvertent errors or omissions. So **always confirm information when it matters,** especially if you're making a detour to visit a specific place. Your experiences—positive and negative—matter to us. If we have missed or misstated something, **please write to us.** We follow up on all suggestions. Contact the New Mexico editor at editors@fodors.com or c/o Fodor's at 1745 Broadway, New York, New York 10019.

PRINTED IN THE UNITED STATES OF AMERICA

10 9 8 7 6 5 4 3 2 1

917.8904
FODO

JUL 2 7 2007

3 2530 60626 1848

Be a Fodor's Correspondent

Your opinion matters. It matters to us. It matters to your fellow Fodor's travelers, too. And we'd like to hear it. In fact, we *need* to hear it.

When you share your experiences and opinions, you become an active member of the Fodor's community. That means we'll not only use your feedback to make our books better, but we'll publish your names and comments whenever possible. Throughout our guides, look for "Word of Mouth," excerpts of your unvarnished feedback.

Here's how you can help improve Fodor's for all of us.

Tell us when we're right. We rely on local writers to give you an insider's perspective. But our writers and staff editors—who are the best in the business—depend on you. Your positive feedback is a vote to renew our recommendations for the next edition.

Tell us when we're wrong. We're proud that we update most of our guides every year. But we're not perfect. Things change. Hotels cut services. Museums change hours. Charming cafés lose charm. If our writer didn't quite capture the essence of a place, tell us how you'd do it differently. If any of our descriptions are inaccurate or inadequate, we'll incorporate your changes in the next edition and will correct factual errors at fodors.com *immediately.*

Tell us what to include. You probably have had fantastic travel experiences that aren't yet in Fodor's. Why not share them with a community of like-minded travelers? Maybe you chanced upon a beach or bistro or B&B that you don't want to keep to yourself. Tell us why we should include it. And share your discoveries and experiences with everyone directly at fodors.com. Your input may lead us to add a new listing or highlight a place we cover with a "Highly Recommended" star or with our highest rating, "Fodor's Choice."

Give us your opinion instantly at our feedback center at www.fodors.com/feedback. You may also e-mail editors@fodors.com with the subject line "New Mexico Editor." Or send your nominations, comments, and complaints by mail to New Mexico Editor, Fodor's, 1745 Broadway, New York, NY 10019.

You and travelers like you are the heart of the Fodor's community. Make our community richer by sharing your experiences. Be a Fodor's correspondent.

Happy Traveling!

Tim Jarrell, Publisher

CONTENTS

ABOUT THIS BOOK

Our Ratings

Sometimes you find terrific travel experiences and sometimes they just find you. But usually the burden is on you to select the right combination of experiences. That's where our ratings come in.

As travelers we've all discovered a place so wonderful that its worthiness is obvious. And sometimes that place is so experiential that superlatives don't do it justice: you just have to be there to know. These sights, properties, and experiences get our highest rating, **Fodor's Choice,** indicated by orange stars throughout this book.

Black stars highlight sights and properties we deem **Highly Recommended,** places that our writers, editors, and readers praise again and again for consistency and excellence.

By default, there's another category: any place we include in this book is by definition worth your time, unless we say otherwise. And we will.

Disagree with any of our choices? Care to nominate a place or suggest that we rate one more highly? Visit our feedback center at www. fodors.com/feedback.

Budget Well

Hotel and restaurant price categories from ¢ to $$$$ are defined in the opening pages of each chapter. For attractions, we always give standard adult admission fees; reductions are usually available for children, students, and senior citizens. Want to pay with plastic? **AE, D, DC, MC, V** following restaurant and hotel listings indicate if American Express, Discover, Diners Club, MasterCard, and Visa are accepted.

Restaurants

Unless we state otherwise, restaurants are open for lunch and dinner daily. We mention dress only when there's a specific requirement and reservations only when they're essential or not accepted—it's always best to book ahead.

Hotels

Hotels have private bath, phone, TV, and air-conditioning and operate on the European Plan (aka EP, meaning without meals), unless we specify that they use the Continental Plan (CP, with a continental breakfast), Breakfast Plan (BP, with a full breakfast), or Modified American Plan (MAP, with breakfast and dinner) or are all-inclusive (including all meals and most activities). We always list facilities but not whether you'll be charged an extra fee to use them, so when pricing accommodations, find out what's included.

Many Listings

★ Fodor's Choice
★ Highly recommended
⊠ Physical address
✛ Directions
🕮 Mailing address
☎ Telephone
🖷 Fax
⊕ On the Web
✍ E-mail
🖾 Admission fee
☉ Open/closed times
▶ Start of walk/itinerary
Ⓜ Metro stations
▭ Credit cards

Hotels & Restaurants

🏨 Hotel
↘ Number of rooms
♨ Facilities
🍴 Meal plans
✕ Restaurant
🖾 Reservations
🏛 Dress code
⌕ Smoking
🍺 BYOB
✕🏨 Hotel with restaurant that warrants a visit

Outdoors

🏌 Golf
⛺ Camping

Other

☺ Family-friendly
🄵 Contact information
⇨ See also
⊠ Branch address
☞ Take note

WHAT'S WHERE

ALBUQUERQUE	With the state's international airport, fast-growing Albuquerque is the gateway to New Mexico and the state's business, finance, education, and industry capital. Its residents—like its architecture, food, and art—reflect a confluence of Native American, Hispanic, and Anglo culture.
SANTA FE	On a 7,000-foot-high plateau at the base of the Sangre de Cristo Mountains, Santa Fe is one of the most visited small cities in the United States, with an abundance of museums, one-of-a-kind cultural events, art galleries, first-rate restaurants, and shops.
TAOS	World-famous museums and galleries, stunning views of the desert and Sangre de Cristo Mountains, and charming, cottonwood-shaded streets lined with adobe buildings are a few of the attractions of this town. Nearby historic Taos Pueblo and Ranchos de Taos are other draws.
SIDE TRIPS FROM THE CITIES	Encompassing the stunning mountains and the remnants of a 2,000-year-old Pueblo civilization, this region includes the many artsy and historic villages surrounding Albuquerque, Santa Fe, and Taos. The area is laced with worthy scenic drives.
NORTHWESTERN NEW MEXICO	Red-rock canyons shelter ancient hamlets and high, fortresslike plateaus crowned by Native American villages. Can't-miss places: El Morro National Monument, Chaco Canyon, Zuñi Pueblo, Aztec Ruins, and Acoma Pueblo.
NORTHEASTERN NEW MEXICO	The brilliantly clear light of northeastern New Mexico—the area east of the Sangre de Cristo range that includes parts of Carson National Forest and a large portion of the Santa Fe Trail—illuminates seemingly endless high-desert plains.
SOUTHEASTERN NEW MEXICO	A study in contrasts, this region contains Carlsbad Caverns National Park, one of the largest and most spectacular cave systems in the world; Roswell, which draws UFO enthusiasts from far and wide; the lush, high-elevation Lincoln National Forest; and the surreal gypsum wonderland of White Sands National Monument.
SOUTHWESTERN NEW MEXICO	Shimmering mirages born of desert heat hover here above mesquite-covered sand dunes. Near Silver City, the ore-rich mountains are dotted with old mining ghost towns. Outdoor enthusiasts fish, swim, and boat along the miles of lake water at Elephant Butte Reservoir, near Truth or Consequences.

New Mexico

QUINTESSENTIAL NEW MEXICO

Chile Fever

Nothing sets New Mexican food apart from other cuisines so distinctly as the chile pepper, permutations of which locals will heap upon just about any dish, from blue-corn enchiladas to turkey sandwiches.

Chiles have long been a staple of both Hispanic and indigenous cuisine in the region, and they come in two varieties: red or green. Depending on the restaurant, or even the particular batch, green *or* red may be the hotter variety. Servers always ask which kind you'd prefer, and if you can't decide, try them both by answering "Christmas."

The village of Chimayó produces the best red chiles in the state, while the small town of Hatch, down near Las Cruces, harvests the best green chiles. You can often find fresh roasted green chiles at fairs and festivals—or even by the side of the road, especially during fall harvest time.

Ancient Peoples

Nowhere in the United States will you find communities that have been continuously inhabited for a longer period than the oldest pueblos of New Mexico, Acoma and Taos. Acoma has been a living, working community for more than 1,000 years— the cliff-top city here is perhaps the most dramatically situated pueblo in the state, and a must-see attraction, especially since the tribe opened its stunning new cultural center and museum in 2006. Taos Pueblo, which contains the largest collection of multistory pueblo dwellings in the country, also dates back more than a millennium.

But these are just 2 of the state's 19 pueblos, not to mention the Indian Pueblo Cultural Center in Albuquerque, and outstanding museums on Native American arts and culture in Santa Fe. Ancient, now-deserted sites, such as Chaco and Aztec, offer further opportunities to explore and learn about New Mexico's thriving indigenous culture.

If you want to get a sense of New Mexico culture, and indulge in some of its pleasures, start by familiarizing yourself with the rituals of daily life. These are a few highlights—things you can take part in with relative ease.

The Cradle of Creativity

New Mexico draws all kinds of vibrant spirits, both to visit and relocate, but the state is particularly a magnet for artists. Santa Fe, with its dozens of prestigious galleries and art museums, claims the third largest art market in the nation, after New York City and Los Angeles. The much-smaller town of Taos claims a similarly exciting gallery scene, and countless small villages in the northern Rio Grande Valley—from Abiqui (where Georgia O'Keeffe lived) to Madrid—hold studio tours once or twice a year, when local artists open their home studios to the public.

The state's largest city, Albuquerque, is no slouch when it comes to the arts— galleries have popped up all over the city in recent years. Farther south, places like Las Cruces, Silver City, and Truth or Consequences also boast dynamic art scenes.

Peak Experiences

With nearly 50 peaks towering higher than 12,000 feet, New Mexico is truly a wonderland for people who love to play in the mountains—it's partly this vertiginous topographical feature that gives the state its unparalleled beauty. The southern spine of the Rocky Mountain range, known as the Sangre de Cristos, runs right down through the center of the state, looming over Taos and Santa Fe. The stunning Sandia Mountains face the city of Albuquerque, and similarly beautiful peaks dot the landscape as far south as Cloudcroft.

It's easy to experience the Land of Enchantments high-country. Hiking trails lead to some of the highest points in the state, and several first-rate ski areas have been carved out of New Mexico's mountains, including Taos Ski Valley, Angel Fire, and Ski Santa Fe to the north, and Ski Apache in Ruidoso.

WHEN TO GO

°F ALBUQUERQUE °C

°F LAS CRUCES °C

°F SANTA FE °C

The cool, dry climates of Santa Fe and Taos are a lure in summer, as is the skiing in Taos and Santa Fe in winter. Christmas is a wonderful time to be in New Mexico because of Native American ceremonies as well as the Hispanic religious folk plays, special foods, and musical events. Santa Fe is at its most festive at this time, with incense and piñon smoke sweetening the air and the darkness of winter illuminated by thousands of *farolitos*: these glowing paper-bag lanterns line walkways, doorways, rooftops, and walls. With glowing lights reflected on the snow, Santa Fe is never lovelier.

Most ceremonial dances at the pueblos occur in summer, early fall, and at Christmas and Easter. Other major events—including the Santa Fe Opera, Chamber Music Festival, and Native American and Spanish markets—are geared to the heavy tourist season of July and August. The Santa Fe Fiesta and New Mexico State Fair in Albuquerque are held in September, and the Albuquerque International Balloon Fiesta in October.

Hotel rates are generally highest during the peak summer season but fluctuate less than those in most major resort areas. If you plan to come in summer, **be sure to make reservations in advance.** You can avoid the heaviest crowds by coming in spring or fall.

Climate

Northern New Mexico is significantly cooler on the whole than destinations in the southern part of the state, although colder mountain regions are scattered throughout the South, too. Desert regions can be delightful in late fall and winter months but can surprise you with rare snowfall. Spring weather is unpredictable; it can be mild and cool, or hot and gusty. Certain desert regions in summer months can see temperatures climb above 100°F. Higher elevations are usually within a reasonable drive just about anywhere in New Mexico. October is one of the best months to visit: the air is crisp, and colors are brilliant.

🗂 Forecasts **Weather Channel** (⊕ www.weather.com)

IF YOU LIKE

Historic Sites

There's no state in the Union with a richer historical heritage than New Mexico, which contains not only buildings constructed by Europeans well before the Pilgrims set foot in Massachusetts but also still-inhabited pueblos that date back more than a millennium.

The entire state can feel like one massive archaeological dig, with its mystical Native American ruins and weathered adobe buildings. Stately plazas laid out as fortifications by the Spanish in the 17th century still anchor many communities, including Albuquerque, Las Cruces, Las Vegas, Santa Fe, and Taos. And side trips from these cities lead to ghost towns and deserted pueblos that have been carefully preserved by historians. Here are some of the top draws for history buffs.

- One of the most well-preserved and fascinating ruin sites on the continent, the ancient **Chaco Culture National Historical Park** in Chaco Canyon was home to the forerunners of today's Pueblo Indians more than 1,000 years ago.

- Santa Fe's **San Miguel Mission** is a simple, earth-hue adobe structure built in about 1625—it's the oldest church still in use in the continental United States.

- A United Nations World Heritage Site, the 1,000-year-old **Taos Pueblo** has the largest collection of multistory pueblo dwellings in the United States.

- The oldest public building in the United States, the Pueblo-style **Palace of the Governors** anchors Santa Fe's historic Plaza and has served as the residence for 100 Spanish, Native American, Mexican, and American governors; it's now the state history museum.

Hiking Adventures

At just about every turn in the Land of Enchantment, whether you're high in the mountains or low in a dramatic river canyon, hiking opportunities abound. Six national forests cover many thousands of acres around New Mexico, as do 34 state parks and a number of other national and state monuments and recreation areas. The ski areas make for great mountaineering during the warmer months, and the state's many Native American ruins are also laced with trails.

Hiking is a year-round activity in New Mexico, as you can virtually always find temperate weather somewhere in the state. Consider the following areas for an engaging ramble.

- About midway between Santa Fe and Albuquerque, **Kasha-Katuwe Tent Rocks National Monument** is so-named because its bizarre rock formations look like tepees rising over a narrow box canyon. The hike here is relatively short and only moderately challenging, offering plenty of bang for the buck.

- It's one of the more strenuous hiking challenges in the state, but the 8-mi trek to New Mexico's highest point, **Wheeler Peak** (elevation 13,161 feet), rewards visitors with stunning views of the Taos Ski Valley.

- From the northeastern fringes of Albuquerque, **La Luz Trail** climbs 9 mi (and an elevation of more than 3,000 feet) to Sandia Crest.

- Gila National Forest's short **Catwalk Trail,** in the southwestern corner of the state, is a metal walkway that clings to the sides of the soaring cliffs in White Water Canyon—down below, the mountain stream cascades over huge boulders.

IF YOU LIKE

Burger Joints

In a state with plenty of open ranching land and an appreciation for no-nonsense, home-style eating, it's no surprise that locals debate intensely about where to find the best burger in town.

In New Mexico, the preferred meal is a green-chile cheese burger—a culinary delight that's available just about anyplace that serves hamburgers. Burgers served in tortillas or sopaipillas also earn plenty of kudos, and increasingly, you'll find establishments serving terrific buffalo, lamb, turkey, and even tuna and veggie burgers.

- With about 75 locations throughout the state, the New Mexico chain **Blake's Lotaburger** has become a cult favorite for its juicy Angus beef burgers. Just order at the counter, take a number, and wait for your meal (which is best accompanied by a bag of seasoned fries).

- A friendly and funky little roadhouse about a 15-minute drive south of Santa Fe, **Bobcat Bite** is a much-loved source of outstanding green-chile burgers. Loyalists order them rare.

- Feasting on a burger at the **Mineshaft Tavern** is a big reason to stop in the tiny village of Madrid, as you drive up the fabled Turquoise Trail from Albu-querque to Santa Fe. This rollicking bar serves hefty patties.

- Although it's most famous for its delicious homemade pies, the **Pie-O-Neer Cafe,** in Pie Town along a lonely but beautiful stretch of U.S. 60, serves exceptionally good green-chile cheese-burgers.

Dramatic Photo Ops

New Mexico's spectacular landscapes and crystal-clear atmosphere can help just about any amateur with a decent camera produce professional-quality photos. Many of the common scenes around the state seem tailor-made for photography sessions: terra-cotta-hued adobe buildings against azure blue skies, souped-up low-rider automobiles cruising along wide-open highways, rustic fruit and chile stands by the side of the road.

In summer, dramatic rain clouds contrasted with vermilion sunsets create memorable images. Come fall, shoot the foliage of cottonwood and aspen trees, and in winter, snap the state's snowcapped mountains.

- The **High Road to Taos,** a stunning drive from Santa Fe with a rugged alpine backdrop, encompasses rolling hill-sides studded with orchards and tiny picturesque villages.

- More than 1,000 balloons lift off from the **Albuquerque International Balloon Fiesta,** affording shutterbugs countless opportunities for great photos—whether from the ground or the air. And there are year-round opportunities to soar above the city.

- The dizzyingly high **Rio Grande Gorge Bridge,** near Taos, stands 650 feet above the Rio Grande—the reddish rocks dotted with green scrub contrast brilliantly against the blue sky.

- **White Sands National Monument,** near Alamogordo, is a huge and dramatic expanse of 60-foot-high shifting sand dunes—it's the largest deposit of gypsum sand in the world, and one of the few landforms recognizable from space.

GREAT ITINERARY

ALBUQUERQUE TO TAOS: NEW MEXICO MOUNTAIN HIGH

Day 1: Albuquerque

Start out by strolling through the shops of Old Town Plaza, then visit the New Mexico Museum of Natural History and Science. Also be sure to check out the Albuquerque Museum of Art and History, and also try to make your way over to the Albuquerque Biological Park, which contains the aquarium, zoo, and botanic park. For lunch, try the atmospheric Monica's or the sophisticated St. Clair Winery and Bistro, both near the Old Town center.

Later in the afternoon, you'll need a car to head east a couple of miles along Central to reach the University of New Mexico's main campus and the nearby Nob Hill District. Start with a stroll around the UNM campus with its many historic adobe buildings; if you have time, pop inside either the Maxwell Museum of Anthropology or the University Art Museum. When you're finished here, walk east along Central into Nob Hill and check out the dozens of offbeat shops. If it's summer, meaning that you still have some time before the sun sets, it's worth detouring from Old Town to Far Northeast Heights (a 15-minute drive), where you can take the Sandia Peak Aerial Tramway 2.7 mi up to Sandia Peak for spectacular sunset views of the city. Either way, plan to have dinner back in Nob Hill, perhaps at Graze or Flying Star. If you're still up for more fun, check out one of the neighborhood's lively lounges; head back downtown for a bit of late-night barhopping.

Days 2 & 3: Santa Fe

On Day 2, head to Santa Fe early in the morning by driving up the scenic Turquoise Trail; once you arrive in town, explore the adobe charms of the downtown central Plaza. Visit the Palace of the Governors and browse the wares of the Native American vendors there. At the Museum of Fine Arts you can see works by Southwestern artists, and at the Museum of International Folk Art you can see how different cultures in New Mexico and elsewhere in the world have expressed themselves artistically. Give yourself time to stroll the narrow, adobe-lined streets of this charming downtown, and treat yourself to some fine New Mexican cuisine in the evening, perhaps with a meal at La Choza or Maria's.

On your second day in town, plan to walk a bit. Head east from the Plaza up to Canyon Road's foot, perusing the galleries. Have lunch at one of the restaurants midway uphill, such as Sol or El Farol. From here, you can either continue walking 2 mi up Canyon, and then Upper Canyon, roads to the Randall Davey Audubon Center, or you can take a cab there. If you're up for some exercise, hike the foothills—there are trails within the center's property and also from the free parking area (off Cerro Gordo Road) leading into the Dale Ball Trail Network. You might want to try one of Santa Fe's truly stellar, upscale restaurants your final night in town, either Geronimo on Canyon Road, or the restaurant at the Inn of the Anasazi, a couple of blocks from the Plaza. Later in the evening, enjoy cocktails at the city's swankest lounge, Swig.

Day 4: Abiquiu

From Santa Fe, drive north up U.S. 285/84 through Española, and then take U.S. 84 from Española up to Abiquiu, the fabled community where Georgia O'Keeffe lived and painted for much of the final five decades of her life. On your way up, before you reach Española, make the detour toward Los Alamos and spend the morning visiting Bandelier National Monument. In Abiquiu, plan to tour Georgia O'Keeffe's home (See Tip #2, below).

Days 5 & 6: Taos

Begin by strolling around Taos Plaza, taking in the galleries and crafts shops. Head south two blocks to visit the Harwood Museum. And then walk north on Paseo del Pueblo to the Taos Art Museum at the Fechin House. In the afternoon, drive out to the Rio Grande Gorge Bridge. Return the way you came to see the Millicent Rogers Museum on your way back to town. In the evening, stop in at the Adobe Bar at the Taos Inn and plan for dinner at Joseph's Table. On the second day, drive out to the Taos Pueblo in the morning and tour the ancient village while the day is fresh. Return to town and go to the Blumenschein Home and Museum, lunching afterward at the Dragonfly Café. After lunch drive out to La Hacienda de los Martinez for a look at early life in Taos and then to Ranchos de Taos to see the San Francisco de Asís Church.

Day 7: The High Road

On your final day, drive back down toward Albuquerque and Santa Fe via the famed High Road, which twists through a series of tiny, historic villages—including Peñasco, Truchas, and Chimayó. In the latter village, be sure to stop by El Santuario de Chimayó. Have lunch at Léona's Restaurante or Rancho de Chimayó, and do a little shopping at Ortega's Weaving Shop. From here, it's a 30-minute drive to Santa Fe, where you can spend a final night, or a 90-minute drive to Albuquerque.

Alternatives

On Day 4, as you drive up through Abiquiu, if you're more a fan of historic railroads than Georgia O'Keeffe, continue up U.S. 84 to Chama, and ride the famed Cumbres & Toltec Scenic Railroad in the morning, and then cut east on U.S. 64 to reach Taos. After visiting Taos Pueblo on Day 6, consider doing the Enchanted Circle tour rather than returning to town. This 84-mi loop runs through the scenic villages of Questa, Red River, Eagle Nest, and Angel Fire.

ON THE
CALENDAR

WINTER December	**Christmas Native American Dances** take place at most pueblos. The Spanish-inspired dance-drama *Los Matachines* is performed at Picurís Pueblo. There are also pine-torch processions and kachina dances at Taos Pueblo and Basket, Buffalo, Deer, Harvest, Rainbow, and Turtle dances at Acoma, Cochiti, San Ildefonso, Santa Clara, and Taos pueblos. **Christmas in Santa Fe** is perhaps the city's most festive time of year. During the 10 days of Las Posadas at San Miguel Mission, the story of Mary and Joseph's journey to Bethlehem is reenacted. The Feast Day of Our Lady of Guadalupe, December 12, is grandly celebrated at the Santuario de Guadalupe, and Christmas at the Palace resounds with hours of festive music emanating from the Palace of the Governors in mid-December. The traditional Christmas Eve stroll down Canyon Road, complete with snacks and costumed carolers, is *the* way to celebrate the night before Christmas when in Santa Fe. At **Christmas on the Pecos** in Carlsbad, glittering backyard displays can be viewed from boats that cruise the Pecos River. Tickets usually sell out early and are available beginning in August. With dozens of screenings of provocative, edgy movies over a five-day period, the **Santa Fe Film Festival** (⊕ www.santafefilmfestival. com) has become a highly prestigious event since its inception in 2000.
January	During **Native American New Year's Celebrations** at many pueblos, Comanche, Deer, Turtle, and other traditional dances are performed.
February	Dozens of galleries and restaurants join creative forces during Santa Fe's **ArtFeast** (⊕ www.artfeast.com), which is held along Canyon Road and at several downtown gallery spaces. The galleries show special exhibits of their most popular artists, and guest chefs at each gallery prepare creative foods that reflect the art exhibits. The event culminates with a lavish dinner at an area restaurant, presented by several local star chefs.
SPRING March	The **Fiery Foods Show** (⊕ www.fiery-foods.com/ffshow) held in Albuquerque over one weekend covers the international scope of New Mexico's favorite spicy food. Chile in all its incarnations, from sizzling salsas and dips to unusual beer and chocolate concoctions, is the featured spice here for more than 200 exhibitors from throughout the world.

ON THE CALENDAR

March–April	The **Chimayó Pilgrimage** takes place on Good Friday; thousands of New Mexicans and out-of-state pilgrims trek on foot to the Santuario de Chimayó, a small church north of Santa Fe that is believed to be the scene of miracles. People line U.S. 285/84 for miles en route to this sacred spot.
April	**Frontier Days** (⊕ www.nmculture.org) at Fort Selden State Monument features historic displays and events commemorating the 1865 founding of this remote adobe outpost near Las Cruces. **Gathering of Nations Powwow** (⊕ www.gatheringofnations.com), in Albuquerque, is the largest such gathering in the nation. This popular event attracts Native American dancers from across North America, who are dressed in incredible costumes and compete for large prizes. Arts-and-crafts exhibitions, traditional foods, and a beauty contest are other highlights.
May	The **Taos Spring Arts Celebration** is a two-week festival of contemporary visual arts, music, poetry readings, and dance. Mariachi music and swirling Mexican dancers are among attractions at the **Cinco de Mayo Festival**, May 5, in the Old Mesilla Plaza.
SUMMER June	On the last weekend of the month, Albuquerque's New Mexico State Fairgrounds hosts the **New Mexico Arts and Crafts Fair** (⊕ www.nmartsandcraftsfair.org), at which more than 220 artists and craftspeople come together to display their talents. El Paso's annual musical drama **Viva El Paso!** lights up a canyon amphitheater from June through August. A diverse cast, from flamenco and ballet dancers to guitarists and actors, brings the multicultural history and legends of the region to life.
July	For a small-town Independence Day with glorious fireworks, head to **Las Vegas Fourth of July Fiestas**, which includes several days of fun with a rodeo, kids' programs, games, and parties. Age comes before youthful beauty at the **Magdalena Old-Timers Reunion**, where the queen must be at least 60 years old. The reunion, held on the first weekend after July 4, includes three days of rodeo (one day a kids' rodeo), a big chuckwagon cook-off, and outdoor dancing. The out-of-this-world **UFO Festival** (⊕ www.roswellufofestival.com) celebrates Roswell's notoriety as the home of the 1947 crash of a supposed UFO. Guest lecturers and events like alien costume competitions are part of the fun.

	The **Hatch Chile Festival** (⊕ www.hatchchilefest.com) celebrated in the town that grows the best green chiles in the world, is a great time to save fresh-roasted chiles—there's also live music and a parade.
	Rodeo de Santa Fe (⊕ www.rodeodesantafe.org) brings a taste of the Old West, with calf roping, bull riding, and a traditional rodeo parade. World-champion rodeo competitors come from all parts of the United States and Canada to this four-decades-old event.
	You can smell the burritos, tamales, and chile for blocks around the festive **Spanish Market** (⊕ www.spanishmarket.org) held on the Santa Fe Plaza during the last full weekend of July. Along with the good food, Hispanic arts and crafts are for sale. Many exhibitors are from remote villages, where outstanding works are produced—this is one of the most acclaimed arts events in the Southwest.
July and August	The world-famous indoor-outdoor **Santa Fe Opera** (⊕ www.santafeopera.org) opens for the summer season in a beautiful facility tucked into a hillside. World premieres and classics are presented. Opening night is one of *the* social events of the year in New Mexico.
August	Launched in 1922, Gallup's **Inter-Tribal Indian Ceremonial** is one of the oldest Native American gatherings in the nation. Native American dances, a huge arts-and-crafts fair, several parades, and an all–Native American rodeo are some of the attractions of this event, held outside town in Red Rocks State Park.
	Santa Fe's **Indian Market** (⊕ www.swaia.org) is the world's most prestigious gathering of Native American potters, jewelers, weavers, painters, basket makers, kachina carvers, and other artists and craftspeople. At least 1,200 artists and craftspeople show their work at this event, held on the Plaza on the third weekend in August.
	During **Old Lincoln Days** (⊕ www.oldlincoln.org) this Old West town's early prominence in the violent Lincoln County Wars is depicted in numerous events lasting several days, including performances of the "Last Escape of Billy the Kid" pageant.
FALL September	On Labor Day weekend in Bernalillo, the **New Mexico Wine Festival** (⊕ www.newmexicowinefestival.com) brings dozens of New Mexico artists and representatives from more than 30 New Mexico wineries together in an outdoor event with music and food.
	Las Fiestas de Santa Fe (⊕ www.santafefiesta.org), the city's biggest celebration, begins the first Friday after Labor Day and commemorates the reconquest of Santa Fe from the Pueblos by Don Diego

ON THE CALENDAR

	de Vargas in 1692. A pet parade, dancing, religious observances, ethnic foods, fireworks, and the burning of *Zozobra* (Old Man Gloom) are all part of the event.
	The New Mexico State Fair (⊕ www.exponm.com) takes place at the New Mexico State Fairgrounds in Albuquerque, with arts, crafts, livestock shows, entertainment, and a rodeo.
	If you love pie, head to Pie Town on the second weekend in September for the Pie Festival (⊕ www.pietown.com). Some of the participants arrive a few days early to set up operations and start rolling the crusts of their specialties.
September–November	A number of towns throughout the state, most of them in the northern Rio Grande Valley, host Artists Studio Tours throughout the fall. Typically, they take place over a weekend, during which artists living in these communities throw open their studio doors to the public. It's a great time to meet local talents, peruse and buy artwork, and visit some truly beautiful little villages that many outsiders don't get a chance to see. Towns with especially notable tours include Abiquiu (⊕ www.abiquiustudiotour.org) in early October, the towns along the High Road to Taos (⊕ www.highroadnewmexico.com) in mid- to late September, Dixon (⊕ www.dixonarts.org) in early November, Galisteo (⊕ www.galisteostudiotour.org) in late October, and El Rito (⊕ www.elritostudiotour.org) in mid-October. Although most of these are held in the fall, some towns hold them at other times.
October	The Albuquerque International Balloon Fiesta (⊕www.balloonfiesta.com) is the single most popular event in the state, with about 1 million spectators viewing the mass ascensions of more than 1,000 hot-air and gas balloons. This major event in the world of ballooning—you'll never see anything like it—takes place at Balloon Fiesta Park over 10 days beginning the first full weekend in October.
	The Whole Enchilada Fiesta (⊕ www.twefie.com), in Las Cruces, lasts several days and attracts thousands with food, arts and crafts, and the concoction of the world's largest enchilada—which is shared with the crowd.
	The Taos Mountain Film Festival (⊕ www.mountainfilm.net), as the name suggests, focuses on films about the mountains and the many women and men who have attempted—successfully or not—to climb and live in them.

1

Albuquerque

WORD OF MOUTH

"I always take a ride on the Sandia Peak Tramway. Every time is like the first. You get on at the base, you look up and think to yourself well it couldn't be all that bad . . . then you reach the top of the foothill, and the whole world bursts open like a dream! "

—BeachBoi

"Definitely go to a pueblo! Preferably after visiting the Cultural Center in Albuquerque."

—laurieb_nyny

Updated by
Andrew Collins

AT FIRST GLANCE, ALBUQUERQUE APPEARS TO BE A TYPICAL SUN BELT city, stretching out more than 100 square mi with no grand design, architectural or otherwise, to hold it together. The city's growth pattern seems as free-spirited as all those hot-air balloons that take part in the Albuquerque International Balloon Fiesta every October. With a bit of exploration, however, this initial impression of an asphalt maze softens as you get a sense of Albuquerque's distinctive neighborhoods. The charms of Albuquerque may not jump out to greet you, but the blend of Spanish, Mexican, Native American, Anglo, and Asian influences makes this a vibrant multicultural metropolis well worth exploring. In fact, the city's most distinctive components—first-rate museums and performing arts venues; well-preserved Spanish-colonial, Victorian, and art deco architecture; both sophisticated and funky restaurants and B&Bs; and offbeat shops and galleries—measure up to those you'd find in most U.S. cities this size. You just have to persevere beyond the suburban sprawl and strip-mall excess to find all the good stuff.

An unpretentious, practical city with a metro population nearing 700,000, Albuquerque is the center of New Mexico's educational institutions and financial, business, manufacturing, and medical industries. Its people are easygoing, and the state's three primary cultures rub elbows more comfortably here than anywhere else in New Mexico. Many Albuquerqueans have descended from one or more of three groups: Native Americans, some of whom arrived more than 10,000 years ago; 17th-century Spaniards who came on horseback to conquer and convert; or the European and American trappers, fortune seekers, traders, and merchants who made the arduous journey across the Santa Fe Trail. From its humble beginning as a settlement of Spanish families in what is now known as Old Town, Albuquerque grew into a trade and transportation center. It became an important station on the Spaniards' El Camino Real, or the Royal Road, which wound from Mexico City to Santa Fe and was for centuries New Mexico's primary link to the outside world.

Albuquerque was established in 1706 as a farming settlement near a bend in the Rio Grande. Named for Spain's duke of Alburquerque (the first "r" was later dropped), then viceroy of Mexico, it prospered, thanks to its strategic location on a trade route and its proximity to several Native American pueblos, which were a source of commerce and provided protection from raiding nomadic tribes. The nearby mountains and river forest yielded ample wood, and farming excelled right from the start in the fertile Rio Grande Valley. The settlers built a chapel and then a larger structure, San Felipe de Neri Catholic Church, named after a 16th-century Florentine saint. For protection, the first homes were built around a central plaza like those in other Spanish settlements. The fortresslike community could be entered from the four corners only, making it easier to defend. This four-block area, Old Town, is now the city's tourist hub, filled with shops, galleries, and restaurants.

It would have made sense for the town to simply grow outward, expanding from its central hub. But the Rio Grande gradually changed course, moving farther and farther west, and Albuquerque followed. Albuquerque grew up and down the river valley, with long plots extending along the river to the south and north of the Old Town settlement, each one with a short stretch of river frontage for irrigation. In 1880 the railroad came to central New Mexico, its tracks bypassing Old Town by a good 2 mi and causing another population shift. Old Town wasn't exactly abandoned, but New Town sprouted near the depot and grew until it eventually enveloped Old Town. The city experienced huge growth around the turn of the 20th century, as railroad workers flooded the city.

Then came Route 66. Opened in 1926 and nicknamed "The Mother Road" by John Steinbeck, it sparked much of Albuquerque's modern economic development. Surging through town during the 1930s and '40s, the route had as much impact as the railroad and the river combined. The burgeoning city swelled around the asphalt—motels, gas stations, diners, and truck stops formed a sea of neon that celebrated American mobility. During World War II Albuquerque flourished with the growth of a major air base, Kirtland. It and other military-related facilities such as Sandia National Laboratory remain economic linchpins.

Albuquerque's economy continues to diversify. Intel, the world's largest computer-chip maker, has one of its biggest manufacturing centers here, across the river in the fast-growing northern suburb of Rio Rancho. Intel's presence has stimulated population and housing growth and attracted additional high-tech businesses. That the city has a substantial arts scene is apparent the moment you step off a plane at Albuquerque International Sunport and see the works of New Mexican artists throughout the terminal. The city has significant museums and galleries and is a magnet for artists, writers, poets, filmmakers, and musicians.

Many engaging towns, parks, and Indian pueblos are just outside Albuquerque. The pueblo residents continue to preserve their customs in a changing world. Each pueblo has its own customs, history, art, and design. Visitors are generally welcome, particularly on feast days, which occur throughout the year. For information on the communities and pueblos just outside the city, see the Side Trips from the Cities chapter.

EXPLORING ALBUQUERQUE

Colorful Historic Route 66 is Albuquerque's Central Avenue, unifying, as nothing else, the diverse areas of the city—Old Town cradled at the bend of the Rio Grande; the rapidly rejuvenating downtown business, government, and entertainment center to the east; the University of New Mexico farther east, and the Nob Hill strip of restaurants and shops past the university. The railroad tracks and Central Avenue divide the city into quadrants—Southwest, Northwest, Southeast, and Northeast. ⚠ Although it's generally easy to negotiate the city's gridlike geography, many attractions are a considerable distance apart, making a car a necessity (car-rental rates are quite reasonable here, however).

Albuquerque's terrain is diverse. Along the river in the north and south valleys, the elevation hovers at about 4,800 feet. East of the river, the land rises gently to the foothills of the Sandia Mountains, which rise to higher than 6,000 feet; the 10,378-foot summit is a grand spot from which to view the city below. West of the Rio Grande, where much of Albu-

GREAT ITINERARIES

Most visitors to Albuquerque combine a stay here with some explorations of the entire northern Rio Grande Valley. If you're looking for the perfect regional tour, combine either of the short Albuquerque itineraries here with those provided in the Side Trips from the Cities chapter, which covers several great areas within a 60- to 90-minute drive of Albuquerque as well as covering Isleta Pueblo and the towns of Corrales and Bernalillo, just on the outskirts of Albuquerque.

IF YOU HAVE 1 DAY

One of the best places to kick off the day is the Gold Street Caffe, where you can enjoy breakfast in the heart of downtown before checking out the shops and galleries on Gold and Central avenues. From here, it's a short drive or 30-minute walk west along Central to reach Old Town, where you can explore the shops and museums of the neighborhood. Definitely be sure to check out the Albuquerque Museum of Art and History, and also try to make your way over to the Albuquerque Biological Park, which contains the aquarium, zoo, and botanic park. For lunch, try the atmospheric Monica's or the sophisticated St. Clair Winery and Bistro, both near the Old Town center.

Later in the afternoon, you'll need a car to head east a couple of miles along Central to reach the University of New Mexico's main campus and the nearby Nob Hill District. Start with a stroll around the UNM campus with its many historic adobe buildings; if you have time, pop inside either the Maxwell Museum of Anthropology or the University Art Museum. When you're finished here, walk east along Central into Nob Hill and check out the dozens of offbeat shops. If it's summer, meaning that you still have some time before the sun sets, it's worth detouring from Old Town to Far Northeast Heights (a 15-minute drive), where you can take the Sandia Peak Aerial Tramway 2.7 mi up to Sandia Peak for spectacular sunset views of the city. Either way, plan to have dinner back in Nob Hill, perhaps at Graze or Flying Star. If you're still up for more fun, check out one of the neighborhood's lively lounges or head back downtown for a bit of late-night barhopping.

IF YOU HAVE 3 DAYS

Follow the morning portion of the one-day itinerary above, and then spend the rest of your day exploring Old Town. With the extra time, you can hit the innovative Explora Science Center, the small but fascinating American International Rattlesnake Museum, and the National Hispanic Cultural Center of New Mexico, which is a 10-minute drive away on the southern edge of downtown. At the end of the day, head to one of the trendy, relative new restaurants that have sprung up in the revitalized downtown, such as Slate Street Cafe or Standard Diner.

On your second day, rent a car and drive out to see the more than 25,000 ancient Native American rock drawings at Petroglyph National Monument. From here, follow Coors Boulevard up to Paseo del Norte, heading east to Balloon Fiesta Park, home to the fascinating

Anderson-Abruzzo International Balloon Museum. From here, hop on I-25 north for one exit, getting off onto Tramway Road, which leads east into the foothills to Sandia Peak Aerial Tramway. Here, take the tram 2.7 mi up to Sandia Peak for spectacular views of the city. You can grab lunch up here at High Finance Restaurant, and then walk off your meal with a hike along the crest of the mountain. Depending on how much time you spend on the mountain hiking and exploring and also how exhausted you are, you might either head back to your accommodation to rest a while or drive directly back down Tramway to Sandia Resort & Casino to test your luck on the slots and tables. Either way, when it is time for dinner, head to Bien Shur, the superb restaurant on Sandia Resort's rooftop, where you can first sip cocktails in the open-air lounge while admiring the view of the city before sampling some of the best contemporary food around in the adjacent restaurant.

On your final day, spend the morning checking out the museums at the University of New Mexico, and then enjoy a leisurely afternoon exploring Nob Hill, as described in the one-day itinerary above. If you have some extra time, consider driving north of Old Town to Rio Grande Nature Center State Park, in the North Valley, and then perhaps continue north up Rio Grande Boulevard for some wine-touring at Anderson Valley Vineyards and Casa Rondena Winery. It's not far from here to such appealing dinner options as Casa de Benavidez for great New Mexican fare or Cafe Voila for urbane French bistro cuisine.

WORD OF MOUTH

"Because Albuquerque is at 1 mile in elevation and as far north as Memphis the city has four very distinct seasons. Early October temperatures are usually in the mid 70s during the day and mid to upper 40s at night. Layered clothing is best for a trip to Balloon Fiesta Park."

–daveabq

"Old Town is 'Museum Central' for Albuquerque—you have the Albuquerque Museum (art) the National Atomic Museum, the Natural History Museum, and Explora (hands-on children's museum). . . . You might just enjoy visiting the Rio Grande Nature Center—we always enjoy watching the migrating birds, and there are a couple of fairly easy walking trails. It's peaceful and not too busy."

–ElendilPickle

"My favorite neighborhood is Nob Hill, which is near the University of New Mexico. It's located from approximately Central to Garfield and Yale to Carlisle. . . . There are wonderful shops and restaurants [there], mostly located along Central Ave. Also, Nob Hill is in close proximity to downtown, only a few miles away."

–lovetherain

querque's growth is taking place, the terrain rises abruptly in a string of mesas topped by five volcanic cones. The changes in elevation from one part of the city to another result in corresponding changes in temperature, as much as 10°F at any time. It's not uncommon for snow or rain to fall on one part of town but for it to remain dry and sunny in another.

Old Town & Downtown

Albuquerque's social and commercial anchor since the settlement was established in 1706, Old Town and the surrounding blocks contain the wealth of the city's top cultural attractions, including several excellent museums. The action extends from the historic Old Town Plaza for several blocks in all directions—most of the museums are north and east of the Plaza. In this area you'll also find a number of restaurants and scads of shops. Some of these places are touristy and should be overlooked, but the better ones are included in the Where to Eat and Shopping sections of this chapter. It's a rather drab 1¼-mi walk or drive southeast along Central Avenue to reach Albuquerque's up-and-coming downtown, but it's worth making your way here. Although downtown doesn't have many formal attractions, this bustling neighborhood is one of the West's great urban comebacks—it's a diverting place to wander, shop, and nosh for a couple of hours.

What to See

Albuquerque Biological Park. This city's foremost outdoor attraction and nature center, the park comprises the recently restored Tingley Beach as well as three distinct attractions, Albuquerque Aquarium, Rio Grande Botanic Garden, and Rio Grande Zoo. The garden and aquarium are located together (admission gets you into both facilities), although the zoo is a short drive southeast. You can also ride the scenic *Rio Line* vintage narrow-gauge railroad between the zoo and gardens and aquarium complex; rides cost $2 or are free if you purchase a combination tickets to all of the park's facilities.

Two main components of the Albuquerque Biological Park, **Albuquerque Aquarium and Rio Grande Botanic Garden** (⊠ 2601 Central Ave.) are a huge draw with kids but also draw plenty of adult visitors. At the aquarium, a spectacular shark tank with floor-to-ceiling viewing is among the most popular of the marine exhibits here. A video follows the path of a drop of water as it forms in the Rocky Mountains, enters the upper Rio Grande, and finally spills into the Gulf of Mexico. The Spanish-Moorish garden is one of three walled gardens near the entrance of the 20-acre botanic garden. The glass conservatory has two pavilions, including a seasonal butterfly conservatory open late May through late September. The smaller one exhibits desert plants, and the

> **WORD OF MOUTH**
>
> "How about the . . . Biopark? The Indian Pueblo Cultural Center? Explora Science Center; strolling on Central in Nob Hill; Natural History and Science. . . . I've done or been to all and recommend them!"
>
> –DebitNM

IF YOU LIKE

NIGHTLIFE & THE ARTS

Even more than Santa Fe, Albuquerque claims a bustling, youthful nightlife scene and numerous performing-arts options. Cultural strengths include several first-rate performance venues, a fine symphony, and a handful of excellent theaters. The city also has a nice variety of bars, including a burgeoning club district downtown and some lively collegiate spots in Nob Hill.

SHOPPING

Although visitors to Albuquerque sometimes observe the sprawling shopping-center and strip-mall developments and assume that the Duke City is mostly the domain of chain outlets, you can find some superb, high-quality independent shops in this city, especially in funky Nob Hill and the rejuvenated downtown. Nob Hill, which runs along old Route 66, specializes in offbeat stores carrying vintage clothing, arty home furnishings, and peculiar novelty gifts. Downtown's retail sector is still taking off, as the neighborhood had become rather down-and-out over the years. As with Nob Hill, it's a good bet for unusual stores, from the city's leading chocolatier, Theobroma, to one of the state's favorite Native American trading posts, Skip Maisel. The mother lode for shopaholics, however, is Old Town, which abounds with shops selling Native American and Spanish-colonial arts and crafts, clothing, and the usual array of souvenirs. All three neighborhoods also have an increasing number of art galleries, and the prices here tend to be considerably lower than in Santa Fe.

SPORTS & THE OUTDOORS

You're never far from outdoor diversions in Albuquerque, a city that also follows its professional and college sports teams with great fervor. University of New Mexico's football and men's and women's basketball teams are first-rate and draw huge crowds, as do the Albuquerque Isotopes, the Triple A minor-league baseball team of the Florida Marlins. As for participant sports, there's great biking in several parts of the city as well as the ski area atop Sandia Crest—the parks and recreation department even publishes a highly detailed bike map. Golfing is another favorite pastime, and you'll find excellent municipal courses in town and a highly acclaimed tournament course at the University of New Mexico.

larger houses the Mediterranean collection. Shark Reef Cafe serves breakfast and lunch. Fans of trains enjoy watching the Garden Model Railroad, which runs along a shaded path in two 400-foot loops. In summer there are music concerts given on Thursday at the Botanic Garden. And from late November through late December, the Botanic Garden comes alive each evening from 6 to 9 PM for the River of Lights festival, a walk-through show of holiday lights and decorations.

The 64-acre **Rio Grande Zoo** (⌂ 903 10th St. SW)—an oasis of waterfalls, cottonwood trees, and naturalized animal habitats—is one of the best-managed and most attractive zoos of its kind. More than 250

species of wildlife from around the world live here, including giraffes, camels, polar bears, elephants, zebras, and koalas. The Tropical America exhibit offers a bit of contrast for dry Albuquerque, replicating a jungle rain forest and containing toucans, spider monkeys, and brilliant orchids and bromeliads. In keeping with its mission of wildlife care and conservation, the zoo has established captive breeding programs for more than a dozen endangered species. Concerts are performed on the grounds on summer Friday evenings. There's a café on the premises. The *Thunderbird Express* is a ¾-scale train that runs in a nonstop loop around the zoo, and during the 20-minute ride, conductors talk in depth about the zoo and its environments. It's free with combo tickets, or $2 otherwise (buy tickets onboard or at the Africa exhibit).

The newly renovated **Tingley Beach** (⊠ 1800 Tingley Dr. SW, south of Central Ave. and just east of Central Ave. bridge) is a recreational arm of the biological park that consists of three ponds, created in the 1930s by diverting water from the Rio Grande. The former swimming hole (no swimming or boating is permitted on the ponds these days) had been largely abandoned for many years before being renovated in 2004 and 2005; now it includes a snack bar; a train station for the *Rio Line,* which runs between the Aquarium and garden complex and the zoo; and three

A GOOD TOUR

Numbers in the text correspond to numbers in the margin and on the Albuquerque and Albuquerque Old Town maps.

Soak up the air of history in **Old Town Plaza** ▶ **❶**, and then cross the street and visit **San Felipe de Neri Catholic Church ❷**. Cutting diagonally across the plaza, head south to the corner of San Felipe Street and Old Town Road to drop in on the **American International Rattlesnake Museum ❸**. Walk south on San Felipe and west on Central Avenue to the corner of Rio Grande Boulevard, where in a strip mall you find the **Turquoise Museum ❹**. Farther west on Central, along a historic section of Route 66 lined with shabby vintage motels, is the **Albuquerque Botanical Park ❺**, which consists of the Albuquerque Aquarium, Botanic Garden, Rio Grande Zoo, and Tingley Beach. Then take a five-minute stroll over to two of the city's cultural institutions, the **Albuquerque Museum of Art and History ❻** and the **New Mexico Museum of Natural History and Science ❼**. Kids enjoy the **National Atomic Museum ❽** and the **Explora Science Center ❾**, which are also within walking distance.

You need to hop in your car (or take city Bus 66) to visit the **Indian Pueblo Cultural Center ❿** downtown and the **New Mexico Holocaust & Intolerance Museum ㉔**, and the **National Hispanic Cultural Center ㉓**.

🕐 **TIMING TIPS→** The best time to begin a visit to Old Town is in the morning, before the stores open at 10 and the daily rush of activity begins. In the beaming morning light, the echoes of the past are almost palpable (and you might find parking). Plan to spend an hour and a half at the Old Town sites, an hour in the Albuquerque Museum of Art and History, and two hours in the New Mexico Museum of Natural History and Science. In the afternoon, you can either drive up to the Indian Pueblo Cultural Center or drive downtown, where you can explore this up-and-coming neighborhood, visit the New Mexico Holocaust & Intolerance Museum, or continue driving south to the National Hispanic Cultural Center. It's impractical to see everything in this area in one day, so consider breaking up your tour into two days if you wish to see every attraction.

ponds stocked with trout for fishing (you can buy gear and fishing licenses at a fishing-tackle shop on premises). On the north pond, you can sail your model electric- or wind-powered boats. To the west of the ponds, the cottonwood bosque (wetlands forest) fringes the river, and there are ecological tours of the bosque are given in summer.

✉ *903 10th St. SW, Tingley Park* ☎ *505/764–6200* ⊕ *www.cabq.gov/ biopark* 🎫 *Free Tingley Beach and grounds, $7 Albuquerque Aquarium and Rio Grande Botanic Garden (combined ticket), $7 Rio Grande Zoo, $12 combination ticket for all attractions, which includes unlimited rides on trains* 🕐 *Daily 9–5, until 6 on weekends, June–Aug.*

6 Albuquerque Museum of Art and History. This modern structure, which
Fodor'sChoice underwent a spectacular 40,000-square-foot expansion in 2004, houses
★ the largest collection of Spanish-colonial artifacts in the nation, along
with relics of the city's birth and development. The centerpiece of the
colonial exhibit is a pair of life-size models of Spanish conquistadors in
original chain mail and armor. Perhaps the one on horseback is Francisco Vásquez de Coronado, who, in search of gold, led a small army
into New Mexico in 1540—the turning point in the region's history.
Among the museum's attractions are treasure chests filled with pearls
and gold coins, religious artifacts, and early maps (some dating from
the 15th century and showing California as an island). A multimedia
presentation chronicles the development of the city since 1875. The sculpture garden contains 45 works by 20th-century southwestern artists that
include Glenna Goodacre, Michael Naranjo, and Luís Jiménez. Free tours
of the museum sculpture garden, which contains more than 50 works,
are offered mid-April through mid-October, Tuesday–Saturday at 10 AM.
Across from the museum, Tiguex Park is a tree-shaded, grassy plot that
hosts many events, including arts and crafts fairs and concerts. ✉ *2000
Mountain Rd. NW, Old Town* ☎ *505/243–7255* ⊕ *www.
albuquerquemuseum.com* ⊠ *$4* ⊙ *Tues.–Sun. 9–5.*

3 American International Rattlesnake Museum. Included in the largest collection of different species of living rattlers in the world are such rare
and unusual specimens as an albino western diamondback. The museum's
labels, its engaging staff, and a video supply visitors with the lowdown
on these venomous creatures—for instance, that they can't hear their
own rattles and that the human death rate from rattlesnake bites is less
than 1%. The mission here is to educate the public on the many positive benefits of rattlesnakes, and to contribute to their conservation. ✉ *202
San Felipe St. NW, Old Town* ☎ *505/242–6569* ⊕ *www.rattlesnakes.
com* ⊠ *$3.50* ⊙ *Mon.–Sat. 10–6, Sun. noon–5 (hrs sometimes shorter
in winter, call ahead).*

★ **9 Explora Science Center.** Albuquerque's cultural corridor received another
jewel in 2003, when this imaginatively executed science museum opened
right across from the New Mexico Museum of Natural History and Science. Explora bills itself as an all-ages attraction, but there's no question that many of the hands-on exhibits—from a high-wire bicycle to
kinetic sculpture display—are geared especially to children, with hands-
on exhibits about science, technology, and art. There are also a playground and a freestanding staircase that appears to "float" between floors.
✉ *1701 Mountain Rd. NW, Old Town* ☎ *505/224–8300* ⊕ *www.
explora.mus.nm.us* ⊠ *$7* ⊙ *Mon.–Sat. 10–6, Sun. noon–6.*

★ **10 Indian Pueblo Cultural Center.** The multilevel semicircular design at this
museum was inspired by Pueblo Bonito, the prehistoric ruin in Chaco
Canyon in northwestern New Mexico. Start by watching the museum's
video, which discusses the history of the region's Pueblo culture. Then
move to the upper-level alcove, where each of the state's 19 pueblos has
a space devoted to its particular arts and crafts. Lower-level exhibits trace
the history of the Pueblo people. Youngsters can touch Native American pottery, jewelry, weaving, tools, and dried corn at the Hands-On

Corner and also draw petroglyph designs and design pots. Paintings, sculptures, jewelry, leather crafts, rugs, souvenir items, drums, beaded necklaces, painted bowls, and fetishes are for sale. Ceremonial dances are performed on weekends at 11 and 2, and there are also arts-and-crafts demonstrations each weekend. The Pueblo Harvest Café is a great spot for lunch, where you can try such Native American fare as blue-corn pancakes and Indian tacos. ☒ *2401 12th St. NW, Los Duranes* ☎ *505/843–7270 or 800/766–4405* ⊕ *www.indianpueblo.org* ☒ *$6* ☉ *Daily 9–5.*

🐾 ⑧ **National Atomic Museum.** Currently in a temporary space in Old Town, this popular museum traces the history of the atomic age and how nuclear science has dramatically influenced the course of modern history. Exhibits include replicas of Little Boy and Fat Man (the bombs dropped on Japan at the end of World War II), and there are children's programs and an exhibit about X-ray technology. As of this writing, the museum has plans to move into a larger space and reopen as the National Museum of Nuclear Science and History, but that move appears to be several years off. ☒ *1905 Mountain Rd. NW, Old Town* ☎ *505/245–2137* ⊕ *www.atomicmuseum.com* ☒ *$5* ☉ *Daily 9–5.*

NEED A BREAK?

On the edge of Old Town, toward downtown and near several museums, **Golden Crown Panaderia** (☒ 1103 Mountain Rd. NW, Old Town ☎ 505/243–2424 or 877/382–2924) is an aromatic bakery known for two things: the ability to custom-design and bake unbelievably artful breads that can depict just about any person or place, and hearty green-chile bread (made with tomatoes, cilantro, Parmesan, green chile, and onions). You can also order hot cocoa, cappuccino, bizcochito cookies (the official state cookie), New Mexican wedding cookies topped with powdered sugar, pumpkin-filled empanadas, and plenty of other sweets. There's seating on a small patio. It's closed Sunday and Monday.

㉓ **National Hispanic Cultural Center of New Mexico.** A showcase for Latino culture and genealogy in Albuquerque's old Barelas neighborhood, this dramatic, contemporary space contains several art galleries and performance venues, a 10,000-volume genealogical research center and library, a restaurant, and a television studio. Exhibits include displays of photography and paintings by local artists as well as by internationally known names. The center mounts performances of flamenco dancing, bilingual theater, and traditional Spanish and New Mexican music. This is the largest Latino cultural center in the country, and with a $10 million programming endowment (Rita Moreno and Edward James Olmos are among the notables on the national board), the center provides top-notch entertainment in its stunning Roy E. Disney Center for Performing Arts and smaller Albuquerque Journal Theatre, and it hosts major traveling art exhibits in its first-rate museum, which also houses an esteemed permanent collection. An architectural showpiece, the center

Fodor's Choice ★

> **WORD OF MOUTH**
>
> "National Hispanic Cultural Center = wonderful exhibits in a lovely building."   –Schildc1

Going Downtown

AS ALBUQUERQUE CONTINUES TO GROW and improve as one of the Southwest's most dynamic cities, its downtown continues to undergo a dramatic renaissance, morphing from a somewhat dicey and unquestionably bland district of office buildings into a vibrant, mixed-use neighborhood of upscale condos, historic residential blocks, funky shops, hip if somewhat rowdy nightclubs, and increasingly sophisticated restaurants.

During the four or five decades following World War II, Albuquerque suffered one of the most common civic and planning problems to plague U.S. cities: the death of its downtown. Years ago, it had been a bona fide retail and entertainment district and a true mixed-use neighborhood. But through the 1950s and '60s, demographic patterns shifted. Middle- and upper-income residents moved farther from downtown, and Albuquerque sprawled, with much of the city taking on the almost suburban appearance that prevails today. By the 1980s, most people had stopped shopping and playing downtown, and most of the largely abandoned blocks were razed in favor of office towers and parking garages. Even as recently as the late '90s, downtown was an empty and occasionally unsafe streetscape on weekends and after 6 PM.

Fast-forward to the present. Many U.S. cities have experienced downtown renaissances, and the traditional recipe has been to anchor the neighborhood with a sports and entertainment complex, a few cultural attractions, and a slew of high-profile shopping and restaurant franchises. Albuquerque's downtown planners have largely shunned this quick-fix approach. Rather, local developers have attracted independently owned shops, restaurants, and nightclubs and converted former schools and manufacturing buildings into residential lofts and condos. In 2000, the city introduced "safety ambassadors," who stroll downtown streets and help visitors get around. The old Spanish-colonial-style bus station is being converted into a multipurpose transportation center with car rentals, a taxi stand, Greyhound, Amtrak, and local city buses; and in 2006 the center launched the state's first-ever commuter rail service, the Rail Runner Express, which presently runs from Albuquerque south to Belén and north to Bernalillo, but that will extend to Santa Fe in 2008. Another future component of the transportation center is the planned Wheels Museum, which will interpret Albuquerque's importance as one of the West's leading rail and transportation hubs.

Downtown's transformation has been gradual, but people have begun to notice. Visitors now wander along Central and Gold avenues, checking out bars and restaurants, walking over to the restored KiMo Theater or the snazzy multiplex movie palace. They're no longer warned to stay off downtown streets at night. It's exciting to watch this neighborhood come dramatically back to life.

—Andrew Collins

borrows from a variety of Spanish cultures, from Moorish Spain to the American Southwest. One historic feature is a vintage WPA-era school that now contains a research library and an excellent restaurant, La Fonda del Bosque, which serves excellent New Mexican fare. ⊠ *1701 4th St. SW, at Bridge St., Barelas* ☎ *505/246–2261* ⊕ *www.nhccnm.org* ⊠ *$3* ☉ *Tues.–Sun. 10–5.*

㉔ New Mexico Holocaust & Intolerance Museum. Although it occupies a rather modest storefront in downtown Albuquerque, this moving museum packs plenty of punch with its poignant exhibits that document genocide and persecution against persons throughout history, with special emphasis, of course, placed upon the Holocaust carried out by the Nazis before and during World War II. Exhibits inside touch on child slave labor, the rescue of Bulgarian and Danish Jews, a re-created gate from a concentration camp, the Nuremburg Trials, and many artifacts related to Holocaust survivors and the Nazis. There are also areas that discuss other genocides throughout history, from the Bataan Death March to the extinguishing of indigenous cultures. ⊠ *415 Central Ave. NW, Downtown* ☎ *505/247–0606* ⊕ *www.nmholocaustmuseum.org* ⊠ *Donation suggested* ☉ *Tues.–Sat. 11–3.*

★ ☾ ❼ New Mexico Museum of Natural History and Science. The world of wonders at Albuquerque's most popular museum includes the simulated volcano (with a river of bubbling hot lava flowing beneath the see-through glass floor), the frigid Ice Age cave, and the world-class dinosaur exhibit hall. The Evolator—short for Evolution Elevator—a six-minute high-tech ride, uses video, sound, and motion to whisk you through 35 million years of New Mexico's geological history. A film in the Extreme Screen DynaTheater makes viewers feel equally involved. Arrive via the front walkway, and you'll be greeted by life-size bronze sculptures of a 21-foot-long horned pentaceratops and a 30-foot-long carnivorous albertosaur. The LodeStar Science Center features a state-of-the-art planetarium. ⊠ *1801 Mountain Rd. NW, Old Town* ☎ *505/841–2800* ⊕ *www.nmnaturalhistory.org* ⊠ *Museum $6, DynaTheater $6, planetarium $6; combination ticket for any 2 attractions $11, for any 3 attractions $16* ☉ *Daily 9–5.*

★ ☾ ❶ Old Town Plaza. Don Francisco Cuervo y Valdés, a provincial governor of New Mexico, laid out this small plaza in 1706. No slouch when it came to political maneuvering, he named the town after the duke of Albur-querque, viceroy of New Spain. He hoped flattery would induce the duke to waive the requirement that a town have 30 families before a charter was issued—there were only 15 families living here in 1706. The duke acquiesced. (Albuquerque is

> **DID YOU KNOW?**
>
> New Mexico is officially a bilingual state. One out of three families speaks Spanish at home.

nicknamed "The Duke City," so he's hardly been forgotten.) Today the plaza is an oasis of tranquillity filled with shade trees, wrought-iron benches, a graceful white gazebo, and strips of grass. Roughly 200 shops, restaurants, cafés, galleries, and several cultural sites in *placitas* (small plazas)

A GOOD WALK

The impeccably landscaped grounds of the University of New Mexico surround a central area containing knolls, a duck pond, fountains, waterfalls, and benches. The **Maxwell Museum of Anthropology** ▶ ⓫ is in the Anthropology Building on the western edge of the campus, only a few minutes' walk from the duck pond. From the Maxwell, walk east past Alumni Chapel and turn left. At the duck pond walk north on Yale past University House. You come to a four-way stop at Yale and Las Lomas streets. The **Jonson Gallery** ⓬ is the second building on the northeast corner of this intersection. Walk south past the duck pond, between Zimmerman Library and Ortega Hall. Continue south under a walkway and left, past the Student Union Building, to the **University Art Museum** ⓭, in the Center for the Arts (use the Stanford Drive and Central Av-

enue entrance). At the corner of Central Avenue and Cornell Drive is the sales and exhibition gallery of the **Tamarind Institute** ⓮. Nine blocks south of Central along Girard Boulevard is the **Ernie Pyle Branch Library** ⓯. Back on Central Avenue, you're a 10-minute walk from UNM campus to the edge of **Nob Hill** ⓰, where you can shop, café-hop, and admire the historic residential and commercial architecture. ⊙ **TIMING TIPS→ Seeing the University of New Mexico could take the better part of a day. Spend an hour strolling the grounds, maybe catching some rays by the duck pond. Allot an hour for each subsequent stop. All facilities are open year-round, but some are closed from Saturday to Monday. Save Nob Hill for late afternoon or even the evening, which is when this neighborhood really comes alive.**

and lanes surround Old Town Plaza. The scents of green chile, enchiladas, and burritos hang in the air. During fiestas Old Town comes alive with mariachi bands and dancing señoritas. Event schedules and maps, which contain a list of public restrooms, are available at the **Old Town Visitors Center** (⊠ 303 Romero St. NW, Old Town ☎ 505/243–3215), across the street from the San Felipe de Neri Catholic Church. The center is open daily, typically 9–4:30 but usually a bit later in summer.

❷ **San Felipe de Neri Catholic Church.** More than two centuries after it first welcomed worshippers, this structure, erected in 1793, is still active. The building, which replaced Albuquerque's first Catholic church, has been enlarged and expanded several times, but its adobe walls and other original features remain. Small gardens front and flank the church; the inside is dark and quiet. Next to it is a small museum that displays relics—vestments, paintings, carvings—dating from the 17th century.
⚠ There's a hidden treasure behind the church: inside the gnarled tree is a statue that some speculate depicts the Virgin Mary. ⊠ *2005 Plaza NW, Old Town* ☎ *505/243–4628* ⊙ *Church open to public daily 8* AM*–dusk; museum Mon.–Sat. 1–4. Call ahead to confirm hrs.*

GOOD TERM

Adobe: A brick of sun-dried earth and clay, usually stabilized with straw; a structure made of adobe.

4 Turquoise Museum. A novel attraction, this small museum focuses on the beauty, mythology, and physical properties of turquoise, a semiprecious but widely adored gemstone that many people understandably associate with the color of New Mexico's skies. A simulated mine shaft leads to one-of-a-kind showpieces and examples from more than 60 mines on four continents. Displays show how turquoise is formed and highlight its uses by Native Americans in prehistoric times. At the education center you can learn how to distinguish the real McCoy from plastic. ⊠ *2107 Central Ave. NW, Old Town* ☎ *505/247–8650* ☜ *$4* ⊙ *Weekdays 9:30–5, Sat. 9:30–4.*

NEED A BREAK?

On the east side of town in the historic Huning Highland district, the **Grove Cafe & Market** (⊠ 600 Central Ave. SE, Downtown ☎ 505/248–9800) is a good stop as you continue from this area to the University of New Mexico and Nob Hill districts. Opened in spring 2006, this airy, modern establishment offers such breakfast treats as poached eggs with prosciutto and Parmesan, tuna niçoise, and aged-salami sandwiches with olive tapanade, arugula, and imported provolone on sourdough bread. You can dine on the arbored patio. Or come by for a loose-leaf tea or latte with a cupcake.

University of New Mexico & Nob Hill

Established in 1889, the University of New Mexico is the state's leading institution of higher education, with internationally recognized programs in anthropology, biology, Latin American studies, and medicine. Its many outstanding galleries and museums are open to the public free of charge. The university's Pueblo Revival–style architecture is noteworthy, particularly the old wing of Zimmerman Library and the Alumni Chapel, both designed by John Gaw Meem, a Santa Fe–based architect who was one of the chief 20th-century proponents of the Pueblo style.

What to See

15 Ernie Pyle Library. After several visits to New Mexico, Ernie Pyle, a Pulitzer prize–winning news reporter, built a house in 1940 that now contains the smallest branch of the Albuquerque Public Library. On display are photos, handwritten articles by Pyle, and news clippings about his career as a correspondent during World War II and his death from a sniper's bullet on April 18, 1945, on the Pacific island of Ie Shima. ⊠ *900 Girard Blvd. SE, University of New Mexico* ☎ *505/256–2065* ⊕ *www.cabq. gov/library* ☜ *Free* ⊙ *Tues., Thurs.–Sat. 10–6, Wed. 11–7.*

12 Jonson Gallery. The home and studio of Raymond Jonson (1891–1982) house the abstract, colorful works on paper of this Transcendentalist painter who focused on mass and form. The gallery mounts a major Jonson retrospective each summer and also exhibits works by other contemporary painters. ⊠ *1909 Las Lomas Blvd. NE, University of New Mexico* ☎ *505/277–4967* ⊕ *www.unm.edu/~jonsong* ☜ *Free* ⊙ *Tues.–Fri. 9–4.*

11 Maxwell Museum of Anthropology. Many of the more than 2½ million artifacts at the Maxwell, the first public museum in Albuquerque (estab-

Neon & Nostalgia

MID-20TH-CENTURY AMERICAN motorists came to know their country firsthand via Route 66. Today, frequent flyers enviously wonder about the romance of the open road. Long before the prosperous age of the two-car family, the 2,400 mi of Route 66 opened in 1926 to link eight states, from Chicago to Los Angeles. It came to be known by the nickname John Steinbeck gave it—"The Mother Road." The nation's outlet for movement and change has become enveloped in nostalgia. Today in New Mexico, from the Texas to the Arizona border, it's still possible to experience vestiges of the old Route 66.

Built in part to aid rural communities and the transportation of agricultural goods, Route 66 evolved into a farmer's escape from the Dust Bowl of the 1930s, and then a tryst for the love affair between Americans and their automobiles. The route's other nickname, "America's Main Street," was due to the fact that the road incorporated towns' main streets, and because of this, communities thrived. Along the highway that ran as vividly through the imagination as through the landscape, many discovered their ability to move on beyond the confines of their own hometown. They found places along the road that appeared to offer a better opportunity to prosper and to reinvent their destiny.

The 1940s and '50s were the heyday of the highway, as Nat King Cole crooned the lyrics to Bobby Troup's song of the road. The road's adventure was overplayed in the '60s television series *Route 66*, and by 1970, nearly all of the two-laner was trumped by four-lane interstate highways. Along Route 66, the possibility of connection with America's people and places lived beyond every bend in the road. By contrast, the interstate would dampen travel with franchised monotony. Most of the bypassed Route 66 communities dried up and blew away like tumbleweeds. In many of these ghost towns, only a few crumbling buildings and fading signs remain as markers to a vanished age.

By hopping on and off I-40, it's possible to find the quieter, slower two-laner that's held on to its name. The feeling of adventure still flickers in Tucumcari at twilight, when the neon signs of the Buckaroo Motel, the Westerner Drive-In, and the Blue Swallow light up the cobalt sky. In Santa Rosa, at Joseph's Cafe, the Fat Man continues to beckon. In Albuquerque, you can drive down Central Avenue, stopping at the Route 66 Diner or the Route 66 Malt Shop and heading past the El Vado. And in Gallup, dine at Earl's Restaurant or the Eagle Cafe, and book a room at the stars of yesteryear's hotel, El Rancho Hotel. Between Albuquerque and Gallup, this ribbon of road takes you through dusty towns with names like poetry: Budville, Cubero, McCartys, Thoreau. These places also once offered the traveler the filling stations, motor courts, curio shops, and cafés that gave comfort on a long drive, and every road tripper today hopes to happen upon such an undiscovered (but really just forgotten) place.

For information on dining and lodging along Route 66, contact the **National Historic Route 66 Federation** (☎ 909/336-6131 ⊕ www.national66.com) or contact the **New Mexico Office of Tourism** (☎ 800/545-2040 ⊕ www.newmexico.org) and request the free "Route 66 in New Mexico" brochure.

lished in 1932), come from the Southwest. Two permanent exhibitions chronicle 4 million years of human history and the lifeways, art, and cultures of 11,500 years of human settlement in the Southwest. The photographic archives contain more than 250,000 images, including some of the earliest photos of Pueblo and Navajo cultures. The museum shop sells traditional and contemporary southwestern Native American jewelry, rugs, pottery, basketry, and beadwork, along with folk art from around the world. In the children's section are inexpensive books and handmade tribal artifacts. ⊠ *University of New Mexico, University Blvd., 1 block north of Grand Ave.* ☎ *505/277–4405* ⊕ *www.unm.edu/ maxwell* ⊠ *Free* ☉ *Tues.–Fri. 9–4, Sat. 10–4.*

⑯ Nob Hill. The heart of Albuquerque's Route 66 culture and also its hippest, funkiest retail and entertainment district, Nob Hill is the neighborhood just east of UNM, with its commercial spine extending along Central Avenue (old Route 66). Along this stretch you'll find dozens of offbeat shops, arty cafés, and student hangouts, and on the blocks just north and south of Central Avenue, you'll see a number of historic Pueblo Revival homes, most built during the early 20th century. Most of the hipper and more gentrified businesses are along the stretch of Central between UNM and Carlisle Boulevard, but the activity is gradually moving east. Old art deco strip malls and vintage motels along this stretch are slowly being transformed into new restaurants and shops. The neighborhood was developed during the 1930s and '40s, peaked in prosperity and popularity during the 1950s, and then fell into a state of decline from the 1960s through the mid-'80s. It was at this time that a group of local business and property owners formed a neighborhood group and banded together to help turn the neighborhood around, and Nob Hill has been enjoying great cachet and popularity ever since. ⊠ *Central Ave., from University of New Mexico campus east to Washington St., Nob Hill.*

⑭ Tamarind Institute. This world-famous institution played a major role in reviving the fine art of lithographic printing, which involves working with plates of traditional stone and modern metal. Tamarind certification is to a printer what a degree from Juilliard is to a musician. A small gallery within the facility exhibits prints and lithographs. Guided tours (reservations essential) are conducted on the first Friday of each month at 1:30. ⊠ *108 Cornell Dr. SE, University of New Mexico* ☎ *505/277– 3901* ⊕ *www.unm.edu/~tamarind* ⊠ *Free* ☉ *By appt., Tues.–Fri. 9–5.*

⑬ University Art Museum. A handsome facility inside the UNM Center for the Arts, the museum holds New Mexico's largest collection of fine art. Works of old masters share wall space with the likes of Picasso and O'-Keeffe, and many photographs and prints are on display. Lectures and symposia, gallery talks, and guided tours are regularly scheduled. ⊠ *University of New Mexico Center for the Arts, north of Central Ave. entrance opposite Yale Blvd.* ☎ *505/277–4001* ⊕ *unmartmuseum.unm. edu* ⊠ *Free* ☉ *Tues. 9–4 and 5–8, Wed.–Fri. 9–4, Sun. 1–4.*

NEED A BREAK? The definitive student hangout but also a great place for anybody to satisfy an appetite into the wee hours, **Frontier Restaurant** (⊠ 2400 Central Ave. SE ☎ 505/266–0550) is across from UNM and open 24/7 for inexpensive diner-style American and New Mexican chow. The breakfast burritos in this rambling restaurant are delicious, as are the hefty cinnamon buns.

Elsewhere in Albuquerque

Most of the other attractions in the city lie north of downtown, Old Town, and the University of New Mexico and Nob Hill areas. You can combine some of these attractions into one tour, especially the three wineries (⇨ *see* Great Itineraries for suggestions), but because these attractions lie some distance from one another, it may be most practical to tackle each one on its own.

What to See

㉒ Anderson-Abruzzo International Balloon Museum. Opened in 2005 at Balloon Fiesta Park, the dramatic museum celebrates the city's legacy as the hot-air ballooning capital of the world. This dashing, massive facility is named for Maxie Anderson and Ben Abruzzo, who pioneered ballooning in Albuquerque and were part of a team of three aviators who made the first manned hot-air balloon crossing of the Atlantic Ocean in 1978. You can understand the reason for constructing such a large museum when you examine some of the exhibits inside—these include several actual balloons of important historic note as well as both large- and small-scale replicas of balloons and zeppelins. You'll also see vintage balloon baskets, actual china and flatware used from the ill-fated *Hindenburg* as well as an engaging display on that tragic craft, and dynamic displays that trace the history of the sport, dating back to the first balloon ride, in 1783. Kids can design their own balloons at one particularly creative interactive exhibit. There's a large museum shop offering just about any book or product you could imagine related to hot-air ballooning, and as of this writing, a café was under construction.

★   The museum anchors Albuquerque's Balloon Fiesta Park, home to the legendary **Albuquerque International Balloon Fiesta** (☎ 505/821–1000 or 888/422–7277 ⊕ www.balloonfiesta.com), which began in 1972 and runs for nearly two weeks in early October. Albuquerque's long history of ballooning dates from 1882, when Professor Park A. Van Tassel, a saloon keeper, ascended in a balloon at the Territorial Fair. During the fiesta, which is the largest hot-air-balloon gathering anywhere, you can watch the Special Shapes Rodeo, when hundreds of unusual balloons, including depictions of the old lady who lived in the shoe, the pink pig, and dozens of other fanciful characters from fairy tales and popular culture, soar high above the more than a million spectators. There are night flights, obstacle races, and many other surprising balloon events. Book your hotel far in advance if you plan to attend, and note that hotel rates also rise during the fiesta. ⊠ *9201 Balloon Museum Dr. NE, off Alameda Blvd. west of I–25, Northeast Heights* ☎ *505/768–6020* ⊕ *www.balloonmuseum.com* ⊠ *$4* ☉ *Tues.–Sun. 9–5.*

⓴ Anderson Valley Vineyards. A low-key winery that was established in 1973 and enjoys a dramatic, pastoral North Valley setting not far from the Rio Grande, Anderson Valley specializes in chardonnay and cabernet sauvignon. The staff in the intimate tasting room is friendly and knowledgeable, and you can sip your wine while relaxing on an enchanting patio with wonderful views of the Sandia Mountains in the distance. In this agrarian, tranquil setting, it's hard to imagine that you're just a little more than 3 mi north of the bustle of Old Town and downtown. ✉ *4920 Rio Grande Blvd. NW, North Valley* ☎ *505/344–7266* 💰 *Free* ⊘ *Tues.–Sun. noon–5.*

> ### DID YOU KNOW?
>
> Franciscan monks first planted their grapevines in New Mexico before moving more successfully to northern California.

★ ⑲ **Casa Rondeña Winery.** Perhaps the most architecturally stunning of New Mexico's wineries, Casa Rondeña strongly resembles a Tuscan villa, with its green-tile roof winery and verdant grounds laced with gardens and fountains. The winery produces a superb cabernet franc, one of the most esteemed vintages in New Mexico. Features that you can see during your visit include a vintage oak fermentation tank and a Great Hall with soaring ceilings, where tastings are conducted. The winery hosts a number of events, including a chamber music festival with wine receptions and dinners. ✉ *733 Chavez Rd., North Valley* ☎ *505/344–5911 or 800/706–1699* ⊕ *www.casarondena.com* 💰 *Free* ⊘ *Wed.–Sat. 10–6, Sun. noon–6.*

㉕ **Gruet Winery.** It's hard to imagine a winetasting experience with less curb appeal. Gruet Winery sits along an ugly access road paralleling I–25, sandwiched between an RV showroom and a lawn-furniture store. But behind the vaguely castlelike exterior of this otherwise modern industrial building, you're afforded the chance to visit one of the nation's most acclaimed producers of sparkling wines. Gruet had been famous in France since the 1950s for its champagnes. Here in New Mexico, where the Gruet family has been producing wine since 1984, it's earned similar kudos for its six sparkling wines as well as for impressive pinot noirs and chardonnays. Many of the state's top restaurants now carry Gruet vintages. Tastings include the chance to sample five wines and to take home a souvenir glass. ✉ *8400 Pan American Freeway NE, Northeast Heights* ☎ *505/821–0055 or 888/857–9463* ⊕ *www.gruetwinery.com* 💰 *Free; $5 for a 5-wine tasting* ⊘ *Weekdays 10–5, Sat. noon–5; tours Mon.–Sat. at 2.*

⑰ **Petroglyph National Monument.** Beneath the stumps of five extinct volcanoes, this park encompasses more than 25,000 ancient Native American rock drawings inscribed on the 17-mi-long West Mesa escarpment overlooking the Rio Grande Valley. For centuries, Native American hunting parties camped at the base, chipping and scribbling away. Archaeologists believe most of the petroglyphs were carved on the lava formations between the years 1100 and 1600, but some images at the park may date as far as 1000 BC. Walking trails provide access to them. A paved trail at **Boca Negra Canyon** (north of the visitor center on Unser Boulevard, beyond Montaño Road) leads past several dozen petroglyphs. The trail at **Rinconado Canyon** (south of the visitor center on Unser) is unpaved. ✉ *Visitor center, Unser Blvd. NW at Western Trail Rd., West Side* ☎ *505/899–0205* ⊕ *www.nps.gov/petr* 💰 *$1 weekdays, $2 weekends* ⊘ *Daily 8–5.*

🐾 ⑱ **Rio Grande Nature Center State Park.** Along the banks for the Rio Grande, this year-round 170-acre refuge in a portion of the Bosque is the nation's largest cottonwood forest. If bird-watching is your thing, you've come to the right place: this is home to all manner of birds and migratory waterfowl. Constructed half aboveground and half below the edge of a pond, the park's glass-walled library has viewing windows that provide a look at what's going on at both levels, and speakers broadcast the sounds of the birds you're watching into the room. You may see birds, frogs, ducks, and turtles. The park has active programs for adults and children and trails for biking, walking, and jogging. ⚠ **Keep your eye out for what appears to be a game of jacks abandoned by giants: these jetty jacks were built in the 1950s to protect the Rio Grande levees from flood debris.** ⊠ *2901 Candelaria Rd. NW, North Valley* ☎ *505/344-7240* ⊕ *www.nmparks. com* ⊠ *$1; grounds free* ☉ *Nature Center daily 10–5, park daily 8–5.*

★ 🐾 ㉖ **Sandia Peak Aerial Tramway.** Tramway cars climb 2.7 mi up the steep western face of the Sandias, giving you a close-up view of red rocks and tall trees—it's the world longest aerial tramway. From the observation deck at the 10,378-foot summit you can see Santa Fe to the northeast and Los Alamos to the northwest—all told, you're able to see some 11,000 square feet of spectacular scenery. Cars leave from the base at regular intervals for the 15-minute ride to the top. If you're lucky, you can see birds of prey soaring above or mountain lions roaming the cliff sides. An exhibit room at the top surveys the wildlife and landscape of the mountain, as well as some trails. Narrators point out what you're seeing below, including the barely visible remnants of a 1953 plane crash that killed all 16 passengers onboard.

If you want to tie a meal in to the excursion, there's the upscale **High Finance Restaurant** (☎ 505/243–9742 ⊕ www.highfinancerestaurant. com) on top of the mountain (serving steaks, lobster tail, and good burgers at lunch), and a more casual spot, **Sandiago's** (☎ 505/856–6692 ⊕ www.sandiagos.com), at the tram's base. High Finance affords clear views from every table, making it a favorite destination for a romantic dinner—the food isn't bad, but it's more about the scenic experience here. ⚠ **It's much colder and windier at the summit than at the tram's base, so pack an appropriate jacket, as it would be a shame to spend most of your time at the top huddling inside the visitor center rather than walking around it to drink up the views.** You can also use the tram as a way to reach the Sandia Peak ski and mountain-biking area (⇨ *See* the Sandia Park section *of* the Side Trips from the Cities chapter). ⊠ *10 Tramway Loop NE, Far Northeast Heights* ☎ *505/856–7325* ⊕ *www.sandiapeak.com* ⊠ *$15* ☉ *Memorial Day–Labor Day, daily 9–9; Sept.–May, daily 9–8.*

★ 🐾 ㉑ **Unser Racing Museum.** Albuquerque is home to the illustrious auto-racing family, the Unsers, whose four generations of drivers have dominated the sport since the early 20th century. The most famous of the clan include Bobby Unser Sr. and Al Unser Sr., and their assorted children and grandchildren. Exhibits

---

WORD OF MOUTH

"If you decide to take the Tram in ABQ, go up just before sunset and watch the sun go down from the top! It is really neat."   –DebitNM at this state-of-the-art museum, which opened in fall 2005, include a display on Pikes Peak, Colorado, where the Unsers first began racing; a study of the family's legacy at the Indianapolis 500; memorabilia on the family and the industry; a technological look at race cars; and several vintage autos. ⊠ *1776 Montaño Rd. NW, North Valley* ☎ *505/ 341–1776* ⊕ *www.unserracingmuseum.com* ▨ *$7* ☉ *Daily 10–4.*

WHERE TO EAT

Here's some news that might surprise foodies: when you get right down to it, Albuquerque has nearly as many sophisticated, inspired restaurants as vaunted Santa Fe. The trick is finding them all amid Albuquerque's miles of ubiquitous chain options (most of the better restaurants are on the North Side, along the I–25 corridor) and legions of other less-than-savory dives, but if you look, you'll be rewarded with innovative food, and generally at prices much lower than in Santa Fe or other major Southwestern cities. The Duke City has long been a place for hearty home-style cooking in big portions, and to this day, it's easy to find great steak-and-chops houses, retro diners, and authentic New Mexican restaurants, most them them offering plenty of grub for the price.

Until the early 2000s, it had been a bit more challenging to find truly memorable independent restaurants serving contemporary and creative fare, but the scene has changed a lot since then and continues to evolve. Particularly in Nob Hill, downtown, and Old Town, hip new restaurants have opened, offering swank decor and complex and artful variations on modern Southwest, Mediterranean, Asian, and other globally inspired cuisine. The city has also made tremendous strides with its ethnic cuisine—fine Greek, Japanese, Korean, Persian, Thai, Vietnamese, and South American restaurants continue to open at a rapid rate all over town, making this New Mexico's best destination for ethnic fare.

WHAT IT COSTS				
	$$$$	**$$$**	**$$**	**$**	**¢**
RESTAURANTS	over $30	$24–$30	$17–$24	$10–$17	under $10

Prices are per person for a main course at dinner, excluding 8.25% sales tax.

American–Casual

¢–$ ✗ **66 Diner.** Dining at this '50s-style art deco diner is a must for fans of Route 66 nostalgia, and the upbeat decor and friendly service also make it a hit with families. The specialties here are many: chicken-fried steak, burgers, malted milk shakes, enchiladas. Plenty of breakfast treats are available, too. ⊠ *1405 Central Ave. NE, University of New Mexico* ☎ *505/247–1421* ⊕ *www.66diner. com* ▤ *AE, D, MC, V.*

> **DID YOU KNOW?**
>
> The mean altitude of the entire state of New Mexico is more than a mile above sea level.

Barbecue

¢–$$ ✕ **Quarters BBQ.** All you've ever dreamed of finding in a barbecue joint awaits you when you walk into this dark den. The Albuquerque institution, going strong since the early '70s, serves tender, smoky, falling-off-the-bone ribs and chicken, brisket, and sausage—it's hard to know where to dive in first. You'll need a fistful of napkins, that's for sure. The sauce is more tangy than sweet, and slow smoking with a secret recipe makes for the winning combination. Top steaks and Alaskan king crab legs are also available. ✉ *801 Yale Blvd. SE, University of New Mexico* ☎ *505/843–7505* ▤ *AE, MC, V* ☉ *Closed Sun.*

Brazilian

$–$$ ✕ **Tucanos Brazilian Grill.** There isn't much point in going to Tucanos if you don't love meat. Sure, they serve some vegetables, but the real focus is on *churrascos*, South American–style grilled skewers of beef, chicken, pork, and turkey that parade endlessly out of the open kitchen on the arms of enthusiastic waiters. Carnivority aside, one unexpected treat, if it's available, is the grilled pineapple. The noisy, high-ceiling spot next to the downtown Century 14 Downtown movie theater is a good place to go for drinks, too, and if you're looking for either a stand-alone cooler or a liquid partner for your hearty fare, look no further than a bracing *caipirinha*, the lime-steeped national cocktail of Brazil. ✉ *110 Central Ave. SW, Downtown* ☎ *505/246–9900* ⊕ *www.tucanos.com* ▤ *AE, D, MC, V.*

Cafés

★ ¢–$ ✕ **Flying Star.** Flying Star has become a staple and mini-phenom for many Albuquerqueans, and although it's a chain, each outpost offers something a little different. The cavernous downtown branch opened in 2005, and it's become a favorite for its striking setting inside the historic Southern Union Gas Co. building, designed by John Gaw Meem in 1950. The concept works on many levels: it's a newsstand,

> **WORD OF MOUTH**
>
> "A good, varied local diner chain. Venues fit their surroundings; go to the Central one for the university crowd, the Rio Grande for outdoor seating with pets, the two NE Heights for families."
>
> –Xander on Flying Star

late-night coffeehouse (there's free Wi-Fi), a bakery, and a great restaurant serving a mix of creative Asian, American, and New Mexican dishes (plus several types of wine and beer). Great options include Greek pasta with shrimp, green-chile cheeseburgers, Thai-style tofu salad with tangy lime dressing, turkey and Jack cheese melt sandwiches, and *machacado* (a breakfast casserole of turkey sausage, bacon, eggs, black beans, cheddar-jack cheese, potatoes, onions, tomatoes, and red and green chile). Desserts change often, but there's always a tantalizing array of cakes, pies, cookies, and brownies. For a winning pick-me-up, employ some strong hot coffee to wash down a tall slice of the fantastic coconut cream pie.

The Far Northeast Heights branch has the largest and most attractive patio of the bunch, with great views of the Sandia Mountains. It's a good bet if you're hungry after a visit to the Sandia Peak Aerial Tramway, and this branch also has an especially large work area where you can plug in your laptop and enjoy the free Wi-Fi. The Nob Hill locale is the most atmospheric, drawing college students, yuppies, gays and lesbians, artsy types, and all other walks of life. This branch is open the latest, it's set amid the funky shops along Nob Hill's historic Route 66, and it's not far from the airport, making it perfect for a quick pre- or post-flight meal. The North Valley locale is ideal for a break if you're visiting Rio Grande Nature Center State Park or the North Valley wineries, or you've just gone hot-air ballooning. The Uptown branch is close to a pair of shopping malls and has the same great food and vibe of the other branches, but this one has the smallest dining room of the bunch. Opened in August 2006, the West Side outpost is just south of the Corrales border, perfect if you're exploring the antiques shops and wineries of this funky little town or you've just been to either Petroglyphs National Monument or the Balloon Fiesta Park, which is just a couple of miles to the east. ✉ *723 Silver Ave., Downtown* ☎ *505/244–8099* ✉ *4501 Juan Tabo Blvd., Far Northeast Heights* ☎ *505/275–8311* ✉ *3416 Central Ave. SE, Nob Hill* ☎ *505/255–6633* ✉ *4026 Rio Grande NW, North Valley* ☎ *505/344–6714* ✉ *8001 Menaul Blvd., Uptown* ☎ *505/293–6911* ✉ *10700 Corrales Rd., West Side* ☎ *505/ 938–4717* ⊕ *www.flyingstarcafe.com* ▭ *AE, D, DC, MC, V.*

★ ¢–$ ✕ **Gold Street Caffe.** A culinary cornerstone of downtown Albuquerque's renaissance, this dapper storefront café with exposed-brick walls and high ceilings serves some of the tastiest breakfast fare in town, plus lunch and dinner entrées. In the morning, go with eggs Eleganza (two poached eggs atop a green-chile brioche with local goat cheese), along with a side of honey–red chile–glazed bacon. Later in the day, consider polenta-dusted tilapia with a sundried-tomato cream sauce, or seared-beef chopped salad with fried rice noodles and chile-lime vinaigrette. You can also just hang out among the hipsters and office workers, sipping a caramel latte and munching on one of the tasty desserts. ✉ *218 Gold Ave. SW, Downtown* ☎ *505/765–1633* ▭ *MC, V* ☺ *No dinner Sun. and Mon.*

Contemporary

$$–$$$$ ✕ **Ambrozia Cafe & Wine Bar.** In a modest but charming bungalow on the edge of Old Town, Ambrozia scores raves in part for its exhaustive wine list, but also for its ambitiously creative food. You might begin with the signature lobster "corn dog"—skewered lobster tails with jalapeño corn batter, served with chipotle ketchup, mustard cream, and avocado rémoulade. Next consider citrus-marinated pork loin grilled over charred tomato and chorizo grits with black bean–corn salsa and a

> **WORD OF MOUTH**
>
> "The hostess seated us in the back room which I felt claustrophobic in, so like the three bears, we ended up in the middle room. Very nice." –Dave on the Ambrozia Cafe

sweet plantain crema. Presentation here is just as artful as the food itself. The dining room is clean and simple, the perfect backdrop for such colorful food. There's a popular happy hour on weekdays where discounted wines by the glass are served, and Sunday brunch here is terrific. ☒ *108 Rio Grande Blvd. NW, Old Town* ☎ *505/242–6560* ⊕ *www.ambroziacafe.com* ▤ *AE, D, DC, MC, V* ⊘ *Closed Mon. No dinner Sun.*

$$–$$$$
Fodor'sChoice
★
✕ **Bien Shur.** The panoramic city and mountain views are part of the draw at this fine restaurant on the top floor of the stunning seven-story Sandia Casino complex, but Bien Shur is also one of the most sophisticated restaurants in the city. Even if you're not much for gambling, it's worth coming here for chef Salim Khoury's superbly crafted contemporary fare. You might start with beef carpaccio with marinated Vidalia onions and black-truffle oil, before moving on to Chilean seabass poached in olive oil with spinach risotto, or grilled Rocky Mountain elk chops with smoked corn–and–green chile tamales and blackberry jus. ☒ *Sandia Resort & Casino, Tramway Rd. NE just east of I–25, Far Northeast Heights* ☎ *505/796–7500* ⊕ *www.sandiacasino.com* ▤ *AE, D, MC, V* ⊘ *Closed Mon. and Tues. No lunch.*

$–$$$$
✕ **Seasons Rotisserie & Grill.** Upbeat yet elegant, this Old Town eatery is an easy place to have a business lunch or a dinner date, and it's convenient to museums and shops. The kitchen serves innovative grills and pastas, such as wood-roasted duck breast with Gorgonzola–sweet potato gratin and grilled prime New York strip steak with garlic-mashed potatoes and black-truffle butter; great starters include seared raw tuna with cucumber-ginger slaw, and pecan-crusted three-cheese chiles rellenos with butternut squash coulis. The rooftop patio and bar provides evening cocktails and lighter meals. ☒ *2031 Mountain Rd. NW, Old Town* ☎ *505/766–5100* ⊕ *www.seasonsonthenet.com* ▤ *AE, D, DC, MC, V* ⊘ *No lunch weekends.*

$$–$$$
Fodor'sChoice
★
✕ **Artichoke Cafe.** Locals praise the Artichoke for its service and French, contemporary American, and Italian dishes prepared, whenever possible, with organically grown ingredients. Specialties include house-made ravioli stuffed with ricotta and butternut squash with a white wine, sage, and butter sauce; and pan-seared sea scallops wrapped in prosciutto with red potatoes, haricots vert, and wax beans. The appetizers are so tasty you may want to make a meal out of them. The building is about a century old, in the historic Huning Highland district on the eastern edge of downtown, but the decor is uptown modern. The two-tier dining room spills out into a small courtyard. ☒ *424 Central Ave. SE, Downtown* ☎ *505/243–0200* ⊕ *www.artichokecafe.com* ▤ *AE, D, DC, MC, V* ⊘ *Closed Sun. No lunch Sat.*

★ **$$–$$$**
✕ **Zinc Wine Bar and Bistro.** A snazzy spot in lower Nob Hill, fairly close to UNM, Zinc captures the essence of a San Francisco neighborhood bistro with its high ceilings, hardwood floors, and white tablecloths and dark-wood straight-back café chairs. You can drop in to sample wine from the long list, nosh on tasty contemporary cooking, or listen to live music downstairs in the Blues Cellar. From the kitchen, consider the starter of asparagus-and-artichoke tart with baby greens and spicy dried-fruit tapenade; or the main dish of oven-roasted wild Alaskan halibut with a Parmesan-asparagus risotto cake, braised leek, and fennel, with a

roasted–red pepper vinaigrette. The kitchen uses organic ingredients whenever available. ✉ *3009 Central Ave. NE, Nob Hill* ☎ *505/254–9462* ⊕ *www.zincabq.com* ▤ *AE, D, MC, V* ☾ *No lunch Sat.*

★ **$–$$** ✕ **Slate Street Cafe.** An airy, high-ceiling dining room with a semi-circular central wine bar and modern lighting, this stylish restaurant sits amid pawn shops and bail bond outposts on a quiet, unprepossessing side street downtown. But once inside, you'll find a thoroughly sophisticated, colorful space serving memorable, modern renditions of classic American fare, such as fried chicken and meat loaf. The starters are especially notable, including Japanese-style fried rock shrimp with orange habañero sauce, and bruschetta topped with honey-cured ham and Brie. Banana-stuffed brioche French toast is a favorite at breakfast and Saturday brunch. More than 30 wines by the glass are served. ✉ *515 Slate St. NW, Downtown* ☎ *505/243–2210* ⊕ *www.slatestreetcafe.com* ▤ *AE, D, MC, V* ☾ *Closed Sun.*

¢–$ ✕ **Graze.** Local star-chef Jennifer James helms the kitchen at this bright

Fodor's Choice and informal tapas-inspired restaurant. Here in this airy, high-ceiling

★ dining room you can nosh on small plates of creative and generally healthful ingredients bursting with big flavors. Consider buttermilk-soaked fried calamari with sweet onions, chickpeas, baby tomatoes, and sambal oil; linguini tossed with smoked trout, capers, and preserved lemon; or ancho-barbecue pork spare ribs with corn on the cob—or just nosh on a selection of artisanal cheeses or a few of James's signature deviled eggs. Next door, try a mango margarita in Graze's sexy lounge, Gulp. ✉ *3128 Central Ave. SE, Nob Hill* ☎ *505/268–4729* ⊕ *www.grazejj.com* ▤ *AE, D, MC, V* ☾ *Closed Sun. and Mon.*

¢–$ ✕ **Standard Diner.** In the historic Huning Highland district just east of downtown, the Standard opened in 2006 inside a 1930s Texaco station with high ceilings, massive plate-glass windows, and rich tile floors—it's at once thoroughly elegant yet totally casual, serving upscale yet affordable takes on traditional diner standbys. The long, interesting menu dabbles in meal-size salads (try the chicken-fried-lobster Caesar salad), burgers (including a terrific one topped with crab cakes and hollandaise sauce), sandwiches, and traditional diner entrées given nouvelle flourishes (Moroccan-style

> **GOOD TERM**
>
> If you want both green or red chile peppers with your meal, ask your server for "Christmas."

pot roast, mac and cheese with smoked salmon and green chiles, flatiron steak with poblano cream sauce and bell pepper–ginger puree). Kick everything up with a side of wasabi-mashed potatoes, and save room for the twisted tiramisu (espresso-soaked lady fingers, dulce de leche mascarpone, agave-poached pears, and candied pine nuts. ✉ *320 Central Ave. SE, Downtown* ☎ *505/243–1440* ▤ *AE, D, MC, V.*

Continental

$–$$ ✕ **St. Clair Winery and Bistro.** The state's largest winery, located in the southern New Mexico town of Deming, St. Clair Winery has a charming and affordable restaurant and tasting room in Old Town. It's part

of a small shopping center on the west side of the neighborhood, just south of I–40. You enter a shop with a bar for winetasting and shelves of wines and gourmet goods, which leads into the dark and warmly lighted dining room. There's also a large, attractive patio. At lunch, sample the panini sandwich of New Mexico goat cheese and roasted peppers. Dinner treats include crab-and-artichoke dip, garlic chicken slow-cooked in chardonnay, and pork tenderloin with merlot and raspberry-chipotle sauce. On weekends, St. Clair serves a popular Sunday brunch. ⊠ *901 Rio Grande Blvd., Old Town* ☎ *505/243–9916 or 888/870–9916* ⊕ *www.stclairvineyards.com* ⊟ *AE, D, MC, V.*

French

$–$$$ ✕ **Cafe Voila.** Despite its Northeast Heights setting in a modern shopping center surrounded by sleek, contemporary office parks, Cafe Voila feels thoroughly Parisian in spirit and ambience, thanks in part to the welcoming staff led by owners and hosts Debbie and Christian Tournier. Choose a seat in the romantic, flower- and plant-filled dining room or on the sunny patio. The kitchen prepares everything here from scratch, with specialties that include crepes with leeks and salmon, lobster ravioli in creamy saffron sauce, braised veal shank with red-wine demi glace, and fresh Dover sole with almond-butter sauce. Top everything off with a slice of cheesecake finished with raspberry coulis. ⊠ *7600 Jefferson St. NE, Northeast Heights* ☎ *505/821–2666* ⊕ *www.cafevoila. com/* ⊟ *AE, MC, V* ☉ *Closed Sun. No dinner Mon.*

Greek

$–$$ ✕ **Yanni's Mediterranean Grill and Opa Bar.** Yanni's is a casual, airy place serving marinated grilled lamb chops with lemon and oregano, grilled yellowfin sole encrusted with Parmesan cheese, pastitsio (a Greek version of mac and cheese), and spinach, feta, and roasted garlic pizzas. The popular vegetarian plate includes a surprisingly good meatless moussaka, tabouleh, spanako-

> **WORD OF MOUTH**
>
> "Yanni's Mediterranean is somewhat of a local monument. What started out as a small gyro restaurant has blossomed into one of Albuquerque's top eateries."
> –Natalie Peters

pita, and stuffed grape leaves. There's a huge patio off the main dining room, and next door you can sip cocktails and mingle with locals at Opa Bar. ⊠ *3109 Central Ave. NE, Nob Hill* ☎ *505/268–9250* ⊕ *www. yannisandopabar.com* ⊟ *AE, D, MC, V.*

Italian

★ $–$$$ ✕ **Scalo Northern Italian Grill.** Nob Hill trendsetters have long gathered at this informal art deco eatery to experience well-chosen Italian wines and first-rate pasta, seafood, and grills. Most of the multilevel dining area looks onto the lively bar and an open kitchen. Best bets include roasted wild salmon with warm spinach and bacon salad, and grilled double pork chops with pear-cherry conserves, Gorgonzola-mashed potatoes, and sautéed radicchio. The homemade desserts are mighty fine, among them lemon–goat cheese cheesecake with fresh berry compote. ⊠ *Nob Hill Shopping Center, 3500 Central Ave. SE, Nob Hill* ☎ *505/ 255–8781* ⊟ *AE, DC, MC, V* ⊗ *No lunch Sun.*

Japanese

¢–$ ✗ **Crazy Fish.** A good bet for relatively straightforward sushi and sashimi, Crazy Fish is an attractive, upbeat storefront space with minimal fuss and gimmickry—just clean lines and a black-and-gray color scheme. Friendly young servers whisk out plates of fresh food to a mix of students and yuppies. In addition to sushi, the kitchen prepares such favorites as crispy chicken, and seared-albacore salad with a ginger-soy dressing. Tempura-fried bananas make for a sweet ending. ⊠ *3015 Central Ave. NE, Nob Hill* ☎ *505/232–3474* ⊟ *AE, D, MC, V* ⊗ *Closed Sun. and Mon.*

New Mexican

$–$$ ✗ **Casa de Benavidez.** The fajitas at this sprawling local favorite with a romantic patio are among the best in town, and the chile is faultless; the burger wrapped inside a sopaipilla is another specialty, as are the chimichangas packed with beef. The charming restaurant occupies a late-19th-century Territorial-style house. ⊠ *8032 4th St. NW, North Valley* ☎ *505/898–3311* ⊕ *casadebenavidez.net* ⊟ *AE, D, DC, MC, V* ⊗ *No dinner Sun.*

★ ¢–$$ ✗ **Monica's El Portal.** Locals in the know favor this rambling, assuredly authentic New Mexican restaurant on the west side of Old Town over the more famous, though less reliable, standbys around Old Town Plaza. Monica's has a prosaic dining room plus a cute tiled patio, and the service is friendly and unhurried yet efficient. If you've never had *chicharrones* (fried pork skins), try them here with beans stuffed inside a flaky sopaipilla. Or consider the traditional blue-corn chicken or beef enchiladas, and the savory green-chile stew. This is honest, home-style food, and lunch here may just fill you up for the rest of the day. ⊠ *321 Rio Grande Blvd. NW, Old Town* ☎ *505/247–9625* ⊟ *AE, D, MC, V* ⊗ *Closed Mon. No dinner weekends.*

¢–$ ✗ **El Patio.** A university-area hangout, this sentimental favorite has con-
Fodor'sChoice sistently great food served in the funky patio. Go for the green-chile chicken
★ enchiladas, the best in town, or any of the heart-healthy and vegetarian selections. But watch out for the fiery green chiles served at harvesttime. Note that liquor isn't served, but beer and wine are—they do make decent-tasting "margaritas" using wine. ⊠ *142 Harvard St. NE, University of New Mexico* ☎ *505/268–4245* ⌖ *Reservations not accepted* ⊟ *MC, V.*

¢–$ ✗ **Los Cuates.** A short drive northeast of Nob Hill and UNM, Los Cuates doesn't get as much attention as some of the city's more touristy New Mexican restaurants, but the food here is purely delicious, prepared with pure vegetable oil rather than lard, which is one reason it's never as greasy as at some competitors. Also, the green chile stew is vegetarian (unless you request meat). All the usual favorites are served here, but top picks include the roast-beef burrito covered with melted cheese, and the tostada *compuesta* (a corn tortilla stuffed with beef, beans, rice, potatoes, carne adovada, and chile con queso). ⊠ *5016–B Lomas Blvd. NE, Nob Hill* ☎ *505/268–0974* ⊕ *www.loscuatesrestaurants.com* ⊘ *Reservations not accepted* ⊟ *AE, D, DC, MC, V.*

¢–$ ✕ **Sadie's.** One of the city's longtime favorites for simple but spicy no-nonsense New Mexican fare, Sadie's occupies a long, fortresslike adobe building. Specialties include carne adovada, spicy beef burritos, and chiles rellenos. The service is always prompt, though sometimes there's a wait for a table. While you're waiting, try one of the excellent margaritas. Sadie's salsa is locally renowned and available by the jar for takeout. ⊠ *6230 4th St. NW, North Valley* ☎ *505/345–5339* ⊕ *www.sadiessalsa. com* ⊟ *AE, D, MC, V.*

★ ¢ ✕ **Barelas Coffee House.** Barelas may look like a set in search of a script, but it's the real deal: diners come from all over the city to sup in this old-fashioned chile parlor in the Hispanic Historic Route 66 neighborhood south of downtown. You may notice looks of quiet contentment on the faces of the many dedicated chile eaters as they dive into their bowls of Barelas's potent red. There's also tasty breakfast fare. The staff treats everybody like an old friend—indeed, many of the regulars who come here have been fans of Barelas for decades. ⊠ *1502 4th St. SW, Barelas* ☎ *505/843–7577* ⊘ *Reservations not accepted* ⊟ *D, MC, V* ⊘ *Closed Sun. No dinner.*

¢ ✕ **Duran's Central Pharmacy.** This expanded Old Town lunch counter with a dozen tables and a tiny patio just might serve the best tortillas in town. A favorite of old-timers who know their way around a blue-corn enchilada, Duran's is an informal place whose patrons give their food the total attention it deserves. ⊠ *1815 Central Ave. NW, Old Town* ☎ *505/ 247–4141* ⊟ *No credit cards* ⊘ *No dinner.*

Pizza

¢ ✕ **Il Vicino.** The gourmet pizzas at Il Vicino are baked in a European-style wood-fired oven. If a suitable combination of the 25 possible toppings eludes you, try the rustica pie, a buttery cornmeal crust topped with roasted garlic, artichokes, kalamata olives, and capers. The kitchen also turns out excellent Caesar salad, spinach lasagna, and designer

> **WORD OF MOUTH**
>
> "[It has a] wood oven, variety of fine quality toppings and, surprise, good olive oil to accentuate. And good microbrew to boot."
> —Andrew Mook on Il Vicino

sandwiches. It's also a great place to sample house-brewed beers, including the Wet Mountain India Pale Ale, which consistently wins awards at the Great American Beer Festival. There's another branch, usually less crowded, in a shopping center not too far from Sandia Peak Aerial Tramway. ⊠ *3403 Central Ave. NE, Nob Hill* ☎ *505/266–7855* ⊠ *11225 Montgomery Blvd., Far Northeast Heights* ☎ *505/271–0882* ⊕ *www.ilvicino.com* ⊘ *Reservations not accepted* ⊟ *MC, V.*

Steak

$$–$$$$ ✗ **Gruet Steakhouse.** The acclaimed Gruet winemaking family operates this chic but casual steak house inside the historic Monte Vista Fire Station, a 1930s WPA-built beauty in the heart of Nob Hill. More than a mere showcase for promoting Gruet's outstanding sparkling wines, pinot noirs, and chardonnays, the steak house presents con-

> ### GOOD TERM
>
> Kiva fireplace: A corner fireplace whose round form resembles that of a kiva, a ceremonial room used by Native Americans of the Southwest.

sistently excellent food (including an addictive side dish, lobster-whipped potatoes). Among the apps, try the panfried Dungeness crab cake with a traditional rémoulade sauce. The flat-iron steak topped with chunky Maytag blue cheese is a favorite main dish, along with the rare ahi tuna Wellington with wild mushroom duxelle and seared foie gras. Finish off with a distinctive rose-water-infused ricotta cheesecake topped with candied oranges and toasted-almond sugar. A kiva fireplace warms the patio in back. The same owners run Gruet Grille, a contemporary bistro in Northeast Heights. ⊠ *3201 Central Ave. NE, Nob Hill* ☎ *505/256–9463* ⊕ *www.gruetsteakhouse.com* ☱ *AE, D, MC, V* ☉ *No lunch.*

$$–$$$$ ✗ **Rancher's Club.** Hotel restaurants in Albuquerque aren't generally special dining destinations in and of themselves, but this clubby, old-world steak house in the Albuquerque Hilton earns raves among carnivores for its delicious aged steaks and ribs. The dining room is hung with saddles, mounted bison heads, and ranching-related art. If you're looking to impress a date or clients, order the sublime fillet of Kobe beef with cream spinach, lobster-mashed potatoes, and morel-mushroom jus. Other great standbys include elk chops, fillet of ostrich, porterhouse steak, and the Hunter's Grill of antelope, venison, and wild boar sausage. ⊠ *Albuquerque Hilton, 1901 University Blvd. NE, Midtown* ☎ *505/889–8071* ☱ *AE, D, DC, MC, V* ☉ *No lunch weekends.*

$–$$$ ✗ **Council Room Steakhouse.** Set just off the main lobby of the snazzy Sandia Resort & Casino, the clubby, softly lighted Council Room offers a relaxing alternative to the clattering slot machines of the gaming area, which is safely out of earshot. The kitchen here turns out reasonably priced, classic renditions of old-school steak-house favorites, from the beer-battered megastack of onion rings to a chilled iceberg lettuce wedge topped with beefsteak tomatoes and bacon and slathered in blue cheese dressing. In addition to the usual steak cuts, consider the full rack of smoked baby back ribs, or the Colorado lamb shank braised with tomatoes, raisins, and pine nuts and served with garlic-mashed potatoes. The house margaritas are stellar even by New Mexico standards. Try the green-chile apple pie, a spicy-sweet marriage that works far better than you'd ever expect. ⊠ *Sandia Resort & Casino, Tramway Rd. NE, just east of I-25, Far Northeast Heights* ☎ *505/796–7500* ⊕ *www.sandiacasino.com* ☱ *AE, D, MC, V* ☉ *No lunch.*

$–$$$ ✗ **High Noon Restaurant and Saloon.** In a former woodworking shop in one of Old Town's late-18th-century adobe buildings, touristy but festive High Noon literally exudes warmth with its kiva fireplaces and is accented further by viga ceilings, brick floors, handmade Southwestern furniture, New Mexican art, and a copper-top bar. The kitchen delivers decent steaks and such traditional New Mexico favorites as beef enchiladas and green-chile stew. Among menu highlights are bison rib eye, twin pork medallions encrusted with pine nuts with a red-chile coulis, and flame-broiled fresh salmon. From Thursday to Sunday there's flamenco guitar. ✉ *425 San Felipe St. NW, Old Town* ☎ *505/765–1455* ▤ *AE, D, DC, MC, V.*

> ### WORD OF MOUTH
>
> "We were certainly fooled by the outward appearance of this establishment. Once we ventured into [High Noon], it was one of our best dining experiences in ABQ."
> —Ben Gibson

Thai

¢–$ ✗ **Thai Crystal.** In a state that's sorely lacked good Thai restaurants until recently, this beautiful space filled with Thai artwork and decorative pieces has been a welcome addition to the blossoming Gold Street shopping district. The extensive menu includes a mix of typical Thai specialties (pineapple fried rice, chicken satay, beef panang curry) as well as some less predictable items, such as steamed mussels topped with red coconut curry, and pork sautéed with a spicy mint, chile, and onion sauce. ✉ *109 Gold Ave. SW, Nob Hill* ☎ *505/244–3344* ▤ *AE, MC, V.*

Vietnamese

★ ¢ ✗ **May Cafe.** Few tourists ever make their way to this astoundingly inexpensive and wonderfully authentic Vietnamese restaurant a short drive east of Nob Hill, in an uninspired neighborhood just off old Route 66. Favorites from the extensive menu include rare-beef noodle soup; stir-fried noodles with veggies, fish balls, chicken, barbecue pork, and pork; spicy fish in baked in a hot pot; and catfish with lemongrass sauce. You'll also find plenty of vegetarian options, including knock-out spring rolls. Friendly, prompt service and a simple, attractive dining room add to the experience. ✉ *111 Louisiana Blvd. SE, Nob Hill* ☎ *505/265–4448* ▤ *AE, MC, V* ⊗ *Closed Sun.*

WHERE TO STAY

With few exceptions, Albuquerque's lodging options fall into two categories: modern chain hotels and motels, and distinctive and typically historic inns and B&Bs. Of larger hotels, you won't find many that are independently owned, historic, or especially rife with personality, although Central Avenue—all across the city—is lined with fascinating old motor courts and motels from the 1930s through the '50s, many of them with their original neon signs and quirky roadside architecture. Alas, nearly all of these are run-down and substandard; they should be avoided unless you're extremely adventurous and can't resist the super-low rates (often as little as $18 a night).

If you're seeking charm and history, try one of the many excellent inns and B&Bs (including those in Corrales and Bernalillo, just north of Albuquerque, listed in the Side Trips from the Cities chapter). Although the cookie-cutter chain hotels may appear largely interchangeable, there are several properties that stand out above the rest, and many of these are described below. Two parts of the city with an excellent variety of economic plain-Jane franchise hotels (Hampton Inn, Comfort Inn, Courtyard Marriott, etc.) are the Airport and the north I–25 corridor. As opposed to many other cities, Albuquerque's airport is extremely convenient to attractions and downtown, and the north I–25 corridor also offers easy access to sightseeing and dining as well as the Balloon Fiesta Park. Wherever you end up staying in Albuquerque, you can generally count on finding rates considerably lower than the national average, and much cheaper than in Santa Fe and Taos.

WHAT IT COSTS					
	$$$$	**$$$**	**$$**	**$**	**¢**
HOTELS	over $260	$190–$260	$130–$190	$70–$130	under $70

Prices are for two people in a standard double room in high season, excluding 12%–13% tax.

Downtown & Old Town

$$–$$$ 🖼 **Embassy Suites Hotel Albuquerque.** This swanky new all-suites high-
Fodor's Choice rise with a striking contemporary design sits on a bluff alongside I–40,
★ affording guests fabulous views of the downtown skyline and vast desert mesas to the west, and the verdant Sandia Mountains to the east. Rooms are large, in the Embassy Suites tradition, all with living areas that have pull-out sleeper sofas, refrigerators, dining and work areas, microwaves, and coffeemakers. You'll also find two phones and two TVs in each suite. Included in the rates is a nightly reception with hors d'oeuvres and cocktails, and a full breakfast each morning. With so much living and sleeping space and a great location accessible to downtown, Nob Hill, and the airport, this is a great option if you're staying in town for a while or traveling with a family. ⊠ *1000 Woodward Pl. NE, 87102 Downtown* ☎ *505/245–7100 or 800/EMBASSY* 🖶 *505/247–1083* ⊕ *embassysuites.hilton.com* ⤴ *261 suites* ⚿ *Dining room, refrigerators, cable TV, Wi-Fi, meeting rooms, bar, free parking* ⊟ *AE, D, MC, V* ❢◎❢ *BP.*

$$–$$$ 🖼 **Hyatt Regency Albuquerque.** Adjacent to the Albuquerque Convention Center, the city's most sumptuous hotel comprises a pair of soaring, desert-color towers that figure prominently in the city's skyline. The gleaming art deco–inspired interior is refined and not overbearing. The contemporary rooms in mauve, burgundy, and tan combine Southwestern style with all the amenities you'd expect of a high-caliber business-oriented hotel, including Wi-Fi and plush bathrobes. McGrath's Bar and Grill serves steaks, chops, chicken, and seafood, and there's also a Starbucks on-site. ⊠ *330 Tijeras Ave. NW, 87102 Old Town* ☎ *505/842–1234 or 800/233–1234* 🖶 *505/766–6710* ⊕ *http://albuquerque.hyatt.com* ⤴ *395 rooms, 14 suites* ⚿ *Restaurant, café, cable TV, Wi-Fi, pool, health*

Where to Stay
in Albuquerque

club, massage, 2 bars, shops, business services, meeting rooms, parking (fee) ⊟ *AE, D, DC, MC, V.*

★ **$$–$$$** ⊞ **La Posada de Albuquerque.** Opened in 1939 by Conrad Hilton (who honeymooned here with Zsa Zsa Gabor), this glamorous 10-story hotel on the National Register of Historic Places captures vintage New Mexico's elegance—the lobby bar is one of the classiest places around for cocktails. The tiled lobby fountain, circular balcony, massive vigas, and Native American murals lend the place an easy Southwestern charm. As of this writing, the hotel was closed and in the midst of a massive refurbishment, which is expected to capture the hotel's original splendor but also infuse it with much-needed modern touches and amenities. The new incarnation of the hotel is expected to reopen in spring 2007. Guests have privileges at a health club across the street. ⊠ *125 2nd St. NW, 87102 Old Town* ☎ *505/242–9090 or 800/777–5732* ⊟ *505/242–8664* ⊕ *www.laposada-abq.com* ⇌ *110 rooms, 4 suites* ⚭ *Restaurant, room service, some microwaves, cable TV, massage, 2 bars, laundry service, meeting rooms, parking (fee)* ⊟ *AE, D, DC, MC, V.*

$–$$ ⊞ **Böttger Mansion of Old Town.** Charles Böttger, a German immigrant, built this pink two-story mansion in 1912. The lacy, richly appointed rooms vary greatly in size and decor; some have four-poster beds, slate floors, claw-foot tubs, or pressed-tin ceilings. All have down comforters, fluffy pillows, and terry robes—and a few are said to be haunted by a friendly ghost or two. The Wine Cellar Suite, in the basement, can accommodate up to six guests and has a kitchenette. A grassy courtyard fronted by a patio provides an escape from the Old Town crowds. Breakfast might consist of stuffed French toast or perhaps burritos smothered in green chile, which you can also enjoy in your room. ⊠ *110 San Felipe St. NW, 87104 Old Town* ☎ *505/243–3639 or 800/758–3639* ⊕ *www.bottger.com* ⇌ *7 rooms, 1 2-bedroom suite* ⚭ *Some in-room hot tubs, some kitchenettes, cable TV, in-room VCRs, parking (fee); no smoking* ⊟ *AE, MC, V* ⊠ *BP.*

★ **$–$$** ⊞ **Casas de Suenos.** This historic compound of 1930s- and '40s-era adobe casitas is perfect if you're seeking seclusion and quiet yet seek easy proximity to museums, restaurants, and shops—Casas de Suenos is a few blocks south of Old Town Plaza, but on a peaceful residential street fringing the lush grounds of Albuquerque Country Club. The individually decorated units, which open onto a warren of courtyards and gardens, come in a variety of shapes and configurations. Typical features include Saltillo-tile floors, wood-burning kiva-style fireplaces, leather or upholstered armchairs, skylights, and contemporary Southwestern furnishings. Many rooms have large flat-screen TVs with DVD players and CD stereos, and some sleep as many as four adults. The full breakfast is served outside in the garden when the weather permits, and inside a lovely artists' studio at other times. ⊠ *310 Rio Grande Blvd. SW, 87104 Old Town* ☎ *505/247–4560 or 800/665–7002* ⊟ *505/242–2162* ⊕ *www.casasdesuenos.com* ⇌ *21 casitas* ⚭ *Some kitchens, cable TV, some in-room DVD/VCRs, some in-room hot tubs, free parking* ⊟ *AE, MC, V* ⊠ *BP.*

$–$$ ⊞ **Doubletree Hotel.** A two-story waterfall splashes down a marble backdrop in the lobby of this 15-story downtown hotel, with attractive, classy rooms that contain custom-made Southwestern furniture and complementary art. The restaurant at the foot of the waterfall is called, appropriately, La Cascada (The Cascade). Breakfast, a lunch buffet, and dinner, from fresh seafood to Southwestern specialties, are served. ⊠ *201 Marquette Ave. NW, 87102 Old Town* ☎ *505/247–3344 or 800/ 222–8733* 🖷 *505/247–7025* ⤵ *295 rooms* ♿ *Restaurant, room service, cable TV, pool, bar, laundry service, business services, meeting rooms, parking (fee)* ⊟ *AE, D, DC, MC, V.*

$–$$ 🏨 **Hotel Albuquerque at Old Town.** This modern 11-story hotel rises distinctly above Old Town's ancient structures. The large rooms have desert-color appointments, hand-wrought furnishings, and tile bathrooms with Southwest accents but a slightly dated look; every room has a small balcony with no patio furniture but nice views. Cristobal's serves commendable Spanish-style steaks and seafood, and Cafe Plazuela offers more casual American and New Mexican food. A fine flamenco guitarist entertains in the lounge. Treatments and facials are available at Joseph's Salon & Day Spa. ⊠ *800 Rio Grande Blvd. NW, 87104 Old Town* ☎ *505/843–6300 or 877/901–7666* 🖷 *505/842–8426* ⊕ *www.hotelabq. com* ⤵ *165 rooms, 22 suites* ♿ *2 restaurants, room service, refrigerators, cable TV, pool, gym, spa, hot tub, massage, bar, business services, meeting rooms, free parking* ⊟ *AE, D, DC, MC, V.*

$–$$ 🏨 **Mauger Estate B&B.** This 1897 Queen Anne mansion was the first home
Fodor'sChoice in Albuquerque to have electricity. Oval windows with beveled and
★ "feather-pattern" glass, hardwood floors, high ceilings, a redbrick exterior, and a front veranda are among the noteworthy design elements. Rooms have refrigerators and baskets stocked with munchies, triple-sheeted beds with soft feather duvets, irons and boards, and fresh flowers. There's also a two-bedroom, two-bathroom town house next door. Guests have access to a full-service health club a few blocks away. The same owners run the outstanding Hacienda Antigua B&B in a quiet North Valley neighborhood, not far from the city's wineries and the Balloon Fiesta Park. ⊠ *701 Roma Ave. NW, 87102 Old Town* ☎ *505/242–8755 or 800/719–9189* 🖷 *505/842–8835* ⊕ *www.maugerbb.com* ⤵ *8 rooms, 1 2-bedroom town house* ♿ *Refrigerators, cable TV, free parking, some pets allowed* ⊟ *AE, D, DC, MC, V* ⏀| *BP.*

¢–$ 🏨 **Best Western Rio Grande Inn.** Although part of the Best Western chain, this contemporary four-story low-rise just off I–40—a 10-minute walk from Old Town's plaza—has an attractive Southwestern design and furnishings, plus such modern touches as free high-speed Internet. The heavy handcrafted wood furniture, tin sconces, and artwork in the rooms come from local suppliers and artisans. That locals are familiar with the Albuquerque Grill is a good indicator of the restaurant's reputation. It's a good value. ⊠ *1015 Rio Grande Blvd. NW, 87104 Old Town* ☎ *505/ 843–9500 or 800/959–4726* 🖷 *505/843–9238* ⊕ *www.riograndeinn. com* ⤵ *173 rooms* ♿ *Restaurant, room service, refrigerators, cable TV, Wi-Fi, pool, gym, outdoor hot tub, bar, laundry facilities, business services, meeting rooms, free parking* ⊟ *AE, D, DC, MC, V.*

¢–$ 🏨 **Hotel Blue.** Formerly a bland chain hotel, this 1960s four-story hotel received an art deco makeover in the early 2000s and rebranded itself as a trendy boutique property. In reality, it is intimate and the art deco rooms are fairly attractive (with white walls and furniture and simple black accents), but it would be a serious stretch to call this place hip or truly of the boutique genre. Still, although it's not fancy, the rates are terrific considering the central location and great amenities, such as dual-line phones, free local calls, 25-inch TVs, hair dryers, and irons and ironing boards. It overlooks a small park, is a short stroll from downtown's many lively music clubs and restaurants, and is a short drive or 15-minute walk from Old Town. ⊠ *717 Central Ave. NW, 87102 Old Town* ☎ *505/924–2400 or 877/878–4868* 🖷 *505/924–2465* ⊕ *www. thehotelblue.com* ⊅ *125 rooms, 10 suites* ⚐ *Restaurant, cable TV with movies, pool, gym, bar, meeting rooms, free parking* ▤ *AE, D, DC, MC, V* ⦿*I CP.*

Uptown

$–$$ ▥ **Albuquerque Marriott.** This 17-story upscale uptown property draws a mix of business and leisure travelers; it's close to two shopping malls and not too far from Nob Hill. Kachina dolls, Native American pottery, and other regional artworks decorate the elegant public areas. The rooms are traditional American, with walk-in closets, armoires, and crystal lamps, but have Southwestern touches. Rooms on all but the first few floors enjoy staggering views, either of Sandias to the east or the vast mesas to the west. Ceilo Sandia specializes in steaks and contemporary New Mexican fare. ⊠ *2101 Louisiana Blvd. NE, 87110 Uptown* ☎ *505/881–6800 or 800/228–9290* 🖷 *505/888–2982* ⊕ *www.marriott. com* ⊅ *405 rooms, 6 suites* ⚐ *Restaurant, room service, refrigerators, cable TV with movies, some in-room VCRs, indoor-outdoor pool, gym, hot tub, sauna, bar, laundry facilities, laundry service, concierge floor, business services, meeting rooms, free parking* ▤ *AE, D, DC, MC, V.*

$ ▥ **Sheraton Albuquerque Uptown.** Within easy distance of the airport and a couple shopping malls, this newly renovated property meets the consistent Sheraton standard with a compact but pleasant lobby with a cozy bar area and a tiny gift shop. Earthy and muted reds, oranges, and sand-shaded colors accent the lobby and functional but ample rooms, whose nicer touches include a second sink outside the bathroom, comfy mattresses, and bathrobes. ⊠ *2600 Louisiana Blvd. NE, 87110 Uptown* ☎ *505/881–0000 or 800/252–7772* 🖷 *505/881–3736* ⊕ *www. sheratonuptown.com* ⊅ *294 rooms* ⚐ *Restaurant, room service, refrigerators, cable TV with movies and video games, Wi-Fi, indoor pool, gym, sauna, concierge floor, business services, meeting rooms* ▤ *AE, D, DC, MC, V.*

⚠ **Albuquerque Central KOA.** At town's edge, off Historic Route 66 in the foothills of the Sandia Mountains, this well-equipped campground has expansive views, a dog run, and wireless Internet, but only a few trees. Reservations are essential in October. ⊠ *12400 Skyline NE, Exit 166 off I–40, Uptown* ☎ *505/296–2729 or 800/562–7781* ⊕ *www. koakampgrounds.com* ⚐ *Grills, flush toilets, full hookups, partial hookups (electric and water), dump station, drinking water, guest laundry, showers, fire grates, picnic tables, electricity, public telephone, general store, service station, play area, swimming (pool)* ⊅ *206 sites, 100 with full hookup* ▧ *$38–$62; cabins $47–$70* ▤ *AE, D, MC, V.*

North Side

$$–$$$$
Fodor'sChoice
★
Sandia Resort & Casino. Completed in early 2006 after much antici-
pation, this seven-story casino resort has set the new standard for lux-
ury in Albuquerque. Ceramic bath tiles, walk-in showers with separate
tubs, 32-inch plasma TVs, handcrafted wooden furniture, louvered
wooden blinds, and muted, natural color palettes lend elegance to the
spacious rooms, most of which have sweeping views of the Sandia
Mountains or the Rio Grande Valley. The 700-acre grounds, which are
in the Far Northeast Heights, just across I–25 from Balloon Fiesta Park,
ensure privacy and quiet and include a superb golf course and an am-
phitheater that hosts top-of-the-line music and comedy acts. The fabu-
lous Green Reed Spa offers a wide range of treatments, many of them
using local clay and plantlife. One of the city's best restaurants, Bien
Shur, occupies the casino's top floor, and there are three other places to
eat on-site. The casino is open 24 hours. ⊠ *Tramway Rd. NE just east
of I–25, 87122 Old Town* ☎ *505/796–7500 or 800/526–9366* ⊕ *www.
sandiacasino.com* ➯ *198 rooms, 30 suites* ⚘ *4 restaurants, room serv-
ice, cable TV, Wi-Fi, pool, hot tub, health club, spa, 18-hole golf course,
driving range, amphitheater, 3 bars, casino, laundry service, meeting
rooms, business center, free parking.*

$–$$$
Marriott Pyramid. This curious ziggurat-shape 10-story building fits
in nicely with the other examples of postmodern architecture that have
sprung up in northern Albuquerque in recent years. It's the most upscale of a slew of reputable chain hotels in the area, and it's an excellent base for exploring the North Valley or even having somewhat easier
access to Santa Fe than the hotels downtown or near the airport. Rooms
have sponge-painted walls and dapper country French decor. They open
onto a soaring atrium lobby. Perks include evening turndown service
and newspapers delivered to the room each morning. ⊠ *5151 San Francisco Rd. NE, 87109 Northeast Heights* ☎ *505/821–3333 or 800/466–
8356* ⊟ *505/828–0230* ⊕ *www.marriott.com* ➯ *248 rooms, 54 suites*
⚘ *Restaurant, room service, refrigerators, cable TV, Wi-Fi, pool, gym,
hot tub, bar, laundry facilities, laundry service, meeting rooms, free parking* ⊟ *AE, D, DC, MC, V.*

$$
Fodor'sChoice
★
Los Poblanos Inn. Designed by acclaimed architect John Gaw Meem,
this rambling, historic inn lies outside of Albuquerque's sprawl, on 25
acres of organic farm fields, lavender plantings, and gardens on the town's
north side, near the Rio Grande and just across the street from Ander-
son Valley Vineyards—with all the greenery and the quiet pace of life
here, you'd never know you're in the desert, or in the middle of one of
the Southwest's largest cities. You reach the inn via a spectacular tree-
lined lane. Every accommodation has a private entrance and contains
folk paintings, painted viga ceilings, and high-quality linens. Rooms also
contain bath products made on-site, including lavender soap and oils;
all have kiva fireplaces, too. The property also includes the 15,000-square-
foot La Quinta Cultural Center, a conference space available for meet-
ings that contains a dramatic fresco by Peter Hurd. There's also a library
with beautiful artwork. ⊠ *4803 Rio Grande Blvd. NW, 87107 North
Valley* ☎ *505/344–9297 or 866/344–9297* ⊟ *505/342–1302* ⊕ *www.*

lospoblanos.com 🛏 *3 rooms, 4 suites, 2 guest houses* ⚒ *Some full kitchens, some refrigerators, cable TV in some rooms, some in-room VCR/DVDs, Wi-Fi, massage, meeting rooms, free parking* ⊟ *AE, MC, V* ⑩*BP.*

★ **$–$$** ▦ **Cinnamon Morning B&B.** A private, beautifully maintained, pet-friendly compound set back from the road and a 10-minute drive north of Old Town, Cinnamon Morning is just south of Rio Grande Nature Center State Park and a perfect roost if you want to be close to the city's wineries and the launching areas used by most hot-air-ballooning companies. Three rooms are in the main house, a richly furnished adobe home with colorful decorations and a lush garden patio. Additionally, there's a secluded two-bedroom guest house with a bath, full kitchen, private entrance, living room, and fireplace; and a colorfully painted one-bedroom casita with a private patio, Mexican-style furnishings, a viga ceiling, a living room with a sleeper sofa. The full breakfasts here are filling and delicious, served by a roaring fire in winter or in the courtyard in summer. ⊠ *2700 Rio Grande Blvd. NW, 87104 North Valley* ☎ *505/345–3541 or 800/214–9481* ♁ *505/342–2283* ⊕ *www.cinnamonmorning.com* 🛏 *3 rooms, 1 casita, 1 guest house* ⚒ *Some kitchenettes, cable TV in some rooms, in-room VCRs, Wi-Fi, some pets allowed* ⑩ *BP.*

★ **¢–$** ▦ **Nativo Lodge Hotel.** Although it's priced similarly to a number of generic midrange chain properties on the north side, this five-story property has more character than most, especially in the expansive public areas, bar, and restaurant, which have an attractive Southwestern motif that includes hand-carved panels depicting symbols from Native American lore and river-rock walls. Rooms have wing chairs, work desks, Wi-Fi, and dual-line phones. The hotel is just off I–25, but set back far enough to avoid highway noise; several movie theaters and a bounty of restaurants are nearby. ⊠ *6000 Pan American Freeway NE, 87109 Northeast Heights* ☎ *505/798–4300 or 888/628–4861* ⊕ *www.buynewmexico.com* 🛏*147 rooms, 3 suites* ⚒ *Restaurant, room service, refrigerators, cable TV, Wi-Fi, pool, gym, hot tub, sauna, bar, laundry facilities, business services, meeting rooms, free parking* ⊟ *AE, D, DC, MC, V.*

¢ ▦ **Inn at Paradise.** Near the first tee of the lush Paradise Hills Golf Club, this pleasant, well-priced B&B resort atop the West Mesa is a golfer's dream: the 6,895 yards of bluegrass fairways and bent-grass greens challenge players of all levels. Works by local artists and craftspeople decorate the large rooms, which are filled with attractive, if functional, contemporary furnishings; the two suites have fireplaces. Many rooms have balconies overlooking the golf course. Golf packages are available. It's an outstanding value and a good bet if you want to be close to Petroglyphs National Monument or Corrales. ⊠ *10035 Country Club La. NW, 87114 West Side* ☎ *505/898–6161 or 800/938–6161* ♁ *505/890–1090* ⊕ *www.innatparadise.com* 🛏 *16 rooms, 2 suites, 1 apartment* ⚒ *Kitchens, cable TV, 18-hole golf course, hot tub, massage, free parking* ⊟ *AE, D, MC, V* ⑩ *CP.*

¢ ▦ **Motel 6.** By far one of the cleanest and most pleasant of the dozens of super-cheap budget motels around town, this three-story no-frills cookie cutter sits along the I–25 access road on the north side, close to the Balloon Fiesta Park and Sandia Casino. There's no view and no ambience, but you can't beat the price, and all rooms are off safe interior hallways.

⊠ *8510 Pan American Freeway NE, 87113 Northeast Heights* ☎ *505/821–1472 or 800/466–8356* 🖷 *505/821–7344* ⊕ *www.motel6.com* 🛏 *79 rooms* ⚭ *Cable TV, pool, laundry facilities, free parking, some pets allowed* ☰ *AE, D, DC, MC, V.*

Airport

★ **$–$$** ▦ **Wyndham Albuquerque Hotel.** Only 350 yards from the airport, this 15-story hotel sits up high on a mesa with vast views of the Sandia Mountains to the east and downtown Albuquerque to the northwest. It's handy being so close to the terminal, and the Southwest-accented rooms have large work desks, data ports, and coffeemakers. Rojo Grill ranks among the better hotel restaurants in town. ⊠ *2910 Yale Blvd. SE, 87106 Airport* ☎ *505/843–7000 or 800/996–3426* 🖷 *505/843–6307* ⊕ *www.wyndham.com* 🛏 *276 rooms, 2 suites* ⚭ *Restaurant, room service, cable TV, Wi-Fi, 2 tennis courts, pool, gym, lobby lounge, airport shuttle, free parking* ☰ *AE, D, DC, MC, V.*

$ ▦ **Holiday Inn Select Albuquerque Airport.** Opened just west of the airport in 2006, this upscale, four-story hotel sits high on a bluff, affording nice views of downtown and the western mesa as well as the Sandia Mountains. Some suites have whirlpool tubs. The indoor pool and high-tech fitness room, along with a 24-hour business center, make this a favorite with business travelers. ⊠ *1501 Sunport Pl. SE, 87106 Airport* ☎ *505/944–2255 or 800/315–2621* ⊕ *www.ichotelsgroup.com* 🛏 *110 rooms, 20 suites* ⚭ *Restaurant, room service, cable TV, Wi-Fi, some in-room hot tubs, indoor pool, gym, lobby lounge, laundry facilities, business center, airport shuttle, free parking* ☰ *AE, D, DC, MC, V.*

¢**–$** ▦ **Hampton Inn Airport.** The best of the mid-price options near the airport, the Hampton Inn can be counted on for clean, updated rooms with plenty of handy perks (free Wi-Fi, a pool, on-the-run breakfast bags to take with you to the airport or wherever you're off to that day). ⊠ *2231 Yale Blvd. SE, 87106 Airport* ☎ *505/246–2255 or 800/426–7866* 🖷 *505/246–2255* ⊕ *www.hamptoninn.com* 🛏 *62 rooms, 9 suites* ⚭ *Dining room, cable TV, Wi-Fi, indoor pool, gym, hot tub, lobby lounge, laundry facilities, business services, meeting rooms, airport shuttle, free parking* ☰ *AE, D, DC, MC, V.*

NIGHTLIFE & THE ARTS

For the 411 on arts and nightlife, consult the Sunday editions of the *Albuquerque Journal* (⊕ www.abqjournal.com), the Friday edition of the *Albuquerque Tribune* (⊕ www.abqtrib.com), or the *Weekly Alibi* (⊕ www.alibi.com).

Nightlife

Bars & Lounges
Atomic Cantina (⊠ 315 Gold Ave. SW, Downtown ☎ 505/242–2200), a hip downtown lounge popular for its cool juke box and extensive happy hours, draws a mix of students, yuppies, and music fans. Many nights there's live music, from punk to rockabilly to trance.

Carom Club (⊠ 301 Central Ave. NW, Downtown ☎ 505/243–6520), opened in 2006 by billiards champ Ramona Biddle, is the city's premier billiards facility, with 21 tables plus a variety of TVs showing sports. This swanky lounge also serves up good food, from tuna tartare to blackened rib-eye steaks.

Graham Central Station (⊠ 4770 Montgomery Blvd. NE, Northeast Heights ☎ 505/883–3041), part of a rowdy regional chain of massive nightclubs, consists of four distinct bars under one roof: country-western, rock, dance, and Latin. It's open Wednesday–Saturday.

Kelly's Brew Pub (⊠ 3222 Central Ave. SE, Nob Hill ☎ 505/262–2739) occupies a stylish late-1930s former Ford dealer and service station. Drink house-brewed oatmeal stout or Belgian ale on the sprawling pet-friendly patio (you can get a bowl of dog food for $1.95) or inside the large dining room, and fill up on buffalo burgers, chicken wings, and guac and chips if you're feeling peckish.

Launchpad (⊠ 422 Central Ave. SE, Downtown ☎ 505/255–8295) has long been a venue for some of the city's best rock and alternative bands.

Martini Grill (⊠ 4200 Central Ave. SE, Nob Hill ☎ 505/242–4333) offers live piano in a swank setting; this gay-popular spot is also a respectable restaurant serving burgers, sandwiches, pastas, and salads.

O'Niell's Pub (⊠ 4310 Central Ave. SE, Nob Hill ☎ 505/256–0564) moved into a handsome new space in summer 2006, where it continues to serve good Mexican and American comfort food and present jazz, bebop, and other musicians in a cheery neighborhood bar near the University of New Mexico.

O-PM (⊠ 211 Gold Ave. SE, Downtown ☎ 505/243–0955) brings in a hip, well-dressed crowd for lounge music, live piano on some nights, and rotating art exhibits. The furnishings are cool and comfy, especially in the upstairs bar.

Pulse (⊠ 4100 Central Ave. SE, Nob Hill ☎ 505/255–3334) ranks among the most popular of Albuquerque's handful of gay and lesbian bars, with a busy dance floor and a big patio out back.

Sauce–Liquid Lounge–Raw (⊠ 405 Central Ave. SW, Downtown ☎ 505/242–5839) is really three hipster-infested bars in one. Dark and inviting with big, foofy cocktails and some of the top DJs in town, this cool compound is also a smart bet for curing the late-night munchies. At Raw, you can sample sushi and sake.

Casino

Sandia Casino (⊠ Tramway Rd. NE at I–25, Far Northeast Heights ☎ 505/796–7500 or 800/526–9366 ⊕ www.sandiacasino.com) is a light, open, airy resort with an enormous gaming area brightened up by soaring ceilings and big windows. In addition to 1,700 slot machines, you'll find craps, blackjack, mini baccarat, and several versions of poker.

Comedy Clubs

Laff's Comedy Club (⊠ 6001 San Mateo Blvd. NE, Northeast Heights ☎ 505/296–5653) serves up the live laughs (and dinner) Wednesday–Sunday.

Live Music

In addition to Sandia Casino, listed below, several casinos at Indian pueblos in the metro area book fairly prominent live-music acts.

The 12,000-seat **Journal Pavilion** (⊠ 5601 University Blvd. SE, Mesa del Sol ☎ 505/452–5100 or 505/246–8742 ⊕ www.journalpavilion.com) amphitheater attracts big-name acts such as Green Day, Nine Inch Nails, Stevie Nicks, and the Dave Matthews Band.

Outpost Performance Space (⊠ 210 Yale Blvd. SE, University of New Mexico ☎ 505/268–0044 ⊕ www.outpostspace.org) programs an eclectic slate, from local nuevo-folk to techno, jazz, and traveling East Indian ethnic.

From April through October, the 4,200-seat **Sandia Casino Amphitheater** (⊠ Tramway Rd. NE just east of I–25, Far Northeast Heights ☎ 505/796–7778 ⊕ www.sandiacasino.com) is part of the stunning Sandia Casino Resort & Casino, at the very northern end of the city. It hosts big-name music acts and comedians, such as Bill Cosby, Earth Wind and Fire, and Kenny Rogers.

The Arts

Music

The **New Mexico Symphony Orchestra** (☎ 505/881–8999 or 800/251–6676 ⊕ www.nmso.org) plays pops, Beethoven, and, at Christmas, Handel's *Messiah*. Most performances are at 2,000-seat Popejoy Hall.

Popejoy Hall (⊠ University of New Mexico Arts Center, Central Ave. NE at Stanford Dr. SE ☎ 505/277–4569 or 800/905–3315 ⊕ www.popejoyhall.com) presents concerts, from rock and pop to classical, plus comedy acts, lectures, and national tours of Broadway shows.

Theater

Albuquerque Little Theater (⊠ 224 San Pasquale Ave. SW, Old Town ☎ 505/242–4750 ⊕ www.swcp.com/-alt) is a nonprofit community troupe that's been going strong since 1930. Its staff of professionals teams up with local volunteer talent to produce comedies, dramas, musicals, and mysteries. The company theater, across the street from Old Town, was built in 1936 and designed by John Gaw Meem. It contains an art gallery, a large lobby, and a cocktail lounge.

★ The stunningly restored **KiMo Theater** (⊠ 423 Central Ave. NW, Downtown ☎ 505/768–3522 or 505/768–3544 ⊕ www.cabq.gov/kimo), a 1927 Pueblo Deco movie palace, is one of the best places in town to see anything. Jazz, dance—everything from traveling road shows to local song-and-dance acts—might turn up here. Former Albuquerque resident Vivian Vance of *I Love Lucy* fame once performed on the stage.

La Compania de Teatro de Albuquerque (☎ 505/242–7929), a bilingual theater company based at the KiMo Theater, performs classic and contemporary plays in English and Spanish during April, October, and December. The company also appears at the South Broadway Cultural Center.

Rodey Theater (✉ University of New Mexico Arts Center, Central and Stanford SE ☎ 505/277–4569 or 800/905–3315) stages student and professional plays and dance performances throughout the year, including the acclaimed annual Summerfest Festival of New Plays during July and the June Flamenco Festival.

SPORTS & THE OUTDOORS

Albuquerque is blessed with an exceptional setting for outdoor sports, backed by a favorable, if unpredictable, climate. Usually 10°F warmer than Santa Fe's, Albuquerque's winter days are often mild enough for most outdoor activities. The Sandias tempt you with challenging mountain adventures (⇨ *See* the Sandia Park section *of* the Side Trips from the Cities chapter for details on mountain biking and skiing in the Sandia Mountains above Albuquerque); the Rio Grande and its thick forest, the Bosque, provide settings for additional wilderness pursuits.

Participant Sports

The **City of Albuquerque** (☎ 505/768–5300 ⊕ www.cabq.gov/living. html) maintains a diversified network of cultural and recreational programs. Among the city's assets are more than 20,000 acres of open space, four golf courses, 200 parks, 68 paved tracks for biking and jogging, as well as swimming pools, tennis courts, ball fields, playgrounds, and a shooting range.

Amusement Park

Drive down San Mateo Northeast in summer and you can't help but glimpse a roller coaster smack in the middle of the city. **Cliff's Amusement Park** (✉ 4800 Osuna Rd. NE, off I–25 at San Mateo Blvd. NE, Northeast Heights ☎ 505/881–9373 ⊕ www.cliffsamusementpark. com) is a clean, well-run attraction for everyone from two-year-olds on up. It features a wooden-track roller coaster as well as rides for all ages and state fair–type games of chance. The park also has a large waterplay area. Cliff's is open early April through September, but days and hours vary greatly, so call first.

Ballooning

Albuquerque is blessed with a high altitude, mild climate, and steady but manageable winds, making it an ideal destination for ballooning. A wind pattern famously known as the "Albuquerque Box," created by the city's location against the Sandia Mountains, makes Albuquerque a particularly great place to fly.

If you've never been ballooning, you may have a notion that it's an inherently bumpy experience, where changes in altitude replicate the queasiness-inducing feeling of being in a tiny propeller plane. Rest assured, the experience is far calmer than you'd ever imagine. The balloons are flown by licensed pilots (don't call them operators) who deftly switch propane-fueled flames on and off, climbing and descending to find winds blowing the way they want to go—thus, there's no real "steering" involved, which makes the pilots' control that much more admirable. The norm is for pilots to land balloons wherever the wind dictates—thus creating the need for "chase vehicles" that pick you up and return you to your departure point—but particularly skilled pilots can use conditions created by the "Box" to land precisely where you started. But even without this "door-to-door" service, many visitors rank a balloon ride soaring over the Rio Grande Valley as their most memorable experience while in town.

Fodor's Choice
★
There are several reliable companies around metro Albuquerque that offer tours. A ride will set you back about $160–$180 per person. One of the best outfitters in town is **Rainbow Ryders** (☎ 505/823–1111 or 800/725–2477 ⊕ www.rainbowryders.com), an official Ride Concession for the Albuquerque International Balloon Fiesta. Part of the fun is helping to inflate and, later on, pack away the balloon. And if you thought it best not to breakfast prior to your flight, a continental breakfast and champagne toast await your return.

Bicycling

Albuquerque has miles of bike lanes and trails crisscrossing and skirting the city as well as great mountain-biking trails at Sandia Peak Ski Area (⇨ *See* the Sandia Park section *of* the Side Trips from Albuquerque, Santa Fe & Taos chapter). The city's public works department produces an elaborately detailed **bike map,** which can be obtained free by calling ☎ 505/768–3550 or downloaded from ⊕ www.cabq.gov/bike.

Bikes can be rented at several locations, including **Albuquerque Bicycle Center** (✉ 3330 Coors Blvd. NW, North Valley ☎ 505/831–5739 ⊕ www.albbicyclecenter.com), which has three locations around town. **Two Wheel Drive** (✉ 1706 Central Ave. SE, Old Town ☎ 505/243–8443) is close to UNM, downtown, and Old Town.

Bird-Watching

The Rio Grande Valley, one of the continent's major flyways, attracts many migratory bird species. Good bird-viewing locales include the **Rio Grande Nature Center State Park** (✉ 2901 Candelaria Rd. NW, North Valley ☎ 505/344–7240 ⊕ www.nmparks.com).

Golf

Most of the better courses in the region—and there are some outstanding ones—are just outside of town (⇨ *See* the North-Central New Mexico chapter for details). The four courses operated by the city of Albuquerque actually hold their own pretty nicely, and the rates are extremely fair. Each course has a clubhouse and pro shop, where clubs and other equipment can be rented. Weekday play is first-come, first-served, but reservations are taken for weekends. Contact the **Golf Management Office** (☎ 505/888–8115 ⊕ www.cabq.gov/golf) for details. Of the four city courses, **Arroyo del Oso** (✉ 7001 Osuna Rd. NE, Northeast Heights ☎ 505/884–7505) earns high marks for its undulating 27-hole layout; greens fees are $26 for 18 holes. The 18-hole **Los Altos Golf Course** (✉ 9717 Copper Ave. NE, Northeast Heights ☎ 505/298–1897), one of the region's most popular facilities, has $26 greens fees. There's also a short, par-3, 9-hole "executive course."

★ **Sandia Golf Club** (✉ Tramway Rd. NE just east of I–25, Far Northeast Heights ☎ 505/798–3990 ⊕ www.sandiagolf.com), opened in 2005 at the swanky Sandia Resort & Casino, offers 18 holes set amid lush hilly fairways, cascading waterfalls, and desert brush. Greens fees are $51–$61. The University of New Mexico has two superb courses. Both are open daily and have full-service pro shops, instruction, and snack bars. Greens fees for out-of-staters run about $60 to $70, with cart. **UNM North** (✉ Tucker Rd. at Yale Blvd., University of New Mexico ☎ 505/277–4146) is a first-class 9-hole, par-36 course on the north side of campus.

★ The 18-hole facility at **UNM South** (✉ 3601 University Blvd., just west of airport off I–25, Southeast Heights ☎ 505/277–4546 ⊕ www.unmgolf.com) has garnered countless awards from major golf magazines and hosted PGA and LPGA qualifying events; there's also a short par-3 9-hole course.

Hiking

In the foothills in Albuquerque's Northeast Heights, you'll find great hiking in **Cíbola National Forest,** which can be accessed directly from Tramway Road Northeast, about 4 mi east of I–25 or 2 mi north of Paseo del Norte. Just follow the road into the hillside, and you'll find several parking areas (there's a daily parking fee of $3). This is where you'll find the trailhead for the steep and quiet challenging **La Luz Trail,** which climbs some 9 mi (an elevation of more than 3,000 feet) up to the top of Sandia Crest. You can take the Sandia Peak Aerial Tram to the top and then hike down the trail, or vice versa (keep in mind that it can take up to six hours to hike up the trail, and four to five hours to hike down). Spectacular views of Albuquerque and many miles of desert and mountain beyond that are had from the trail. And you can still enjoy a hike along here without going the whole way—if your energy and time are limited, just hike a mile or two and back. No matter how far you hike, however, pack plenty of water.

Spectator Sports

Baseball

Since 2003, the city has hosted Triple A minor league baseball's **Albuquerque Isotopes** (✉ University Ave. SE at Ave. Cesar Chavez SE, University of New Mexico ☎ 505/924–2255 ⊕ www.albuquerquebaseball. com), the farm club of the Major League Florida Marlins; the season runs April through August.

Basketball

It's hard to beat the excitement of home basketball games of the **University of New Mexico Lobos** (✉ University Ave. at Ave. Cesar Chavez, University of New Mexico ☎ 505/925–5626 ⊕ http://golobos. collegesports.com), when 18,000 rabid fans crowd into the school's arena, "the Pit," from November to March. Both the women's and men's teams enjoy huge success every year.

Football

The competitively ranked **University of New Mexico Lobos** (✉ University Ave. at Ave. Cesar Chavez, University of New Mexico ☎ 505/925–5626) play at 40,000-seat University Stadium in the fall.

SHOPPING

Albuquerque's shopping strengths include a handful of cool retail districts, including Nob Hill, Old Town, and the rapidly gentrifying downtown. These are good neighborhoods for galleries, antiques, and home-furnishing shops, bookstores, and offbeat gift shops. Otherwise, the city is mostly the domain of both strip and indoor malls, mostly filled with ubiquitous chain shops, although you can find some worthy independent shops even in these venues.

Shopping Neighborhoods & Malls

The most impressive of the city's malls, **Cottonwood Mall** (✉ Coors Blvd. NW at Coors Bypass, West Side ☎ 505/899–7467), is anchored by Dillard's, Foley's, Mervyn's, JCPenney, and Sears Roebuck and has about 130 other shops, including Williams-Sonoma, Aveda, Cache, and Abercrombie & Fitch. There are a dozen restaurants and food stalls, plus a 14-screen theater.

Albuquerque's **Downtown** (✉ Central and Gold Aves. from 1st to 10th Sts.) has undergone a stunning revitalization since 2000, and by 2010 the neighborhood should have double—or even triple—the number of shops and restaurants. Local developers have made a point of renting strictly to independent businesses, making an effort to keep downtown from turning into just another collection of chain outlets. In the meantime, stroll along Central and Gold avenues (and neighboring blocks) to admire avant-garde galleries, cool cafés, and curious boutiques.

Funky **Nob Hill** (✉ Central Ave. from Girard Blvd. to Washington St.), just east of University of New Mexico and anchored by old Route 66, pulses with colorful storefronts and kitschy signs. At night, neon-lighted boutiques, galleries, and performing-arts spaces encourage foot traffic. Many of the best shops are clustered inside or on the blocks near Nob Hill Business Center, an art deco structure containing several intriguing businesses and La Montañita Natural Foods Co-op, an excellent spot for a snack.

Old Town (✉ Central Ave. and Rio Grande Blvd.) has the city's largest concentration of one-of-a-kind retail shops, selling clothing, home accessories, and Mexican imports. Also here are a slew of galleries, many exhibiting Native American art.

Art Galleries

Amapola Gallery (✉ 205 Romero St. NW, Old Town ☎ 505/242–4311), west of the plaza near Rio Grande Boulevard, is one of the largest co-op galleries in New Mexico. It has a brick courtyard and an indoor space, both brimming with pottery, paintings, textiles, carvings, baskets, jewelry, and other items.

★ **Coleman Gallery Contemporary Art** (✉ 3812 Central Ave. SE, Nob Hill ☎ 505/232–0224) has emerged as one of Nob Hill's leading art spaces, showing works by a number of the state's top contemporary talents.

DSG (✉ 3011 Monte Vista Blvd. NE, Nob Hill ☎ 505/266–7751 or 800/474–7751), owned by John Cacciatore, handles works by leading regional artists, including Frank McCulloch, Carol Hoy, Leo Neufeld, Larry Bell, Angus Macpherson, Jim Bagley, Nancy Kozikowski, and photographer Nathan Small.

Gowen Arts (✉ 303 Romero St. NW, #114, Old Town ☎ 505/268–6828) specializes in Native American artists, including wonderful jewelry and metal sculpture.

Mariposa Gallery (✉ 3500 Central Ave. SE, Nob Hill ☎ 505/268–6828) sells contemporary fine crafts, including jewelry, sculptural glass, works in mixed media and clay, and fiber arts. The changing exhibits focus on upcoming artists.

Sumner & Dene (✉ 517 Central Ave. NW, Downtown ☎ 505/842–1400), a cool art space in the heart of downtown, sells sleek, retro-cool furnishings; unusual jewelry; and whimsical artwork.

Weems Gallery (✉ 2801–M Eubank Blvd. NE, Northeast Heights ☎ 505/293–6133 ✉ 303 Romero St. NW, Old Town ☎ 505/764–0302) has paintings, pottery, sculpture, jewelry, weaving, stained glass, and original-design clothes.

★ **Weyrich Gallery** (✉ 2935–D Louisiana Blvd. NE, Uptown ☎ 505/883–7410) carries distinctive jewelry, fine art, Japanese tea bowls, woodblocks, hand-color photography, and other largely Asian-inspired pieces.

Specialty Stores

Antiques

FodorśChoice **Classic Century Square Antique Mall** (✉ 4516 Central Ave. SE, Nob Hill
★ ☎ 505/268–8080) is a three-story emporium of collectibles and antiques. The emphasis is on memorabilia from the early 1880s to the 1950s. (When the set designers for the television miniseries *Lonesome Dove* needed props, they came here.) Items for sale include art deco and art nouveau objects, retro-cool '50s designs, Depression-era glass, Native American goods, quilts and linens, vintage clothes, and Western memorabilia.

Cowboys & Indians (✉ 4000 Central Ave. SE, Nob Hill ☎ 505/255–4054) carries Native American and cowboy art and artifacts.

Books

Massive **Page One** (✉ 11018 Montgomery Blvd. NE, Far Northeast Heights ☎ 505/294–2026), arguably the best bookstore in Albuquerque, specializes in technical and professional titles, maps, globes, children's titles, and 150 out-of-state and foreign newspapers. Book signings, poetry readings, and children's events are frequently scheduled.

Gifts, Food & Toys

Beeps (✉ Nob Hill Shopping Center, 3500 Central Ave. SE, Nob Hill ☎ 505/262–1900), a Nob Hill favorite, carries cards, T-shirts, and amusing, if bawdy, novelties.

Candy Lady (✉ Mountain Rd. at Rio Grande Blvd., Old Town ☎ 505/224–9837 or 800/214–7731) is known as much for its scandalous adult novelty candies as for its tasty red- and green-chile brittle, plus the usual fudge, chocolates, piñon caramels, and candies. A small room, to the right as you enter, displays the "adult" candy, so you can easily pilot any kids in your party past it.

La Casita de Kaleidoscopes (⊠ Poco A Poco Patio, 326–D San Felipe St. NW, Old Town ☎ 505/247–4242) carries both contemporary and vintage kaleidoscopes of all styles, by more than 80 top artists in the field.

Martha's Body Bueno (⊠ 3901 Central Ave. NE, Nob Hill ☎ 505/255–1122) is a wonderful, offbeat boutique with sensual bath items, lingerie, jewelry, candles, and other romantic gifts.

Satellite Toys and Coffee (⊠ 3513 Central Ave. SE, Nob Hill ☎ 505/256–0345) is filled with wind-up toys and collector's items for grown-ups.

Theobroma Chocolatier (⊠ 319 Central Ave. NW, Downtown ☎ 505/247–0848 ⊠ 12611 Montgomery Blvd. NE, Far Northeast Heights ☎ 505/293–6545) carries beautifully handcrafted, high-quality chocolates, truffles, and candies (most of them made on premises), as well as Taos Cow ice cream.

Home Furnishings

Fodor's Choice ★ **A** (⊠ 3500 Central Ave. SE, Nob Hill ☎ 505/266–2222) is a Nob Hill stop for housewares, soaps, candles, body-care products, and jewelry.

A branch of a popular regional chain, **El Paso Import Co.** (⊠ 3500 Central Ave. SE, Nob Hill ☎ 505/265–1160) carries distressed and "peely-paint" antique-looking chests and tables loaded with character. If you love the "shabby chic" look, head to this Nob Hill furniture shop.

Hey Jhonny (⊠ 3418 Central Ave. SE, Nob Hill ☎ 505/256–9244) is an aromatic store full of exquisite candles, soaps, pillows, fountains, and other soothing items for the home; there's also a branch that carries more furniture and larger pieces around the corner, at 118 Tulane Street.

★ **Jackalope** (⊠ 6400 San Meteo Blvd. NE, Northeast Heights ☎ 505/349–0955), the favorite Southwestern furniture and bric-a-brac shop in Bernalillo and Santa Fe, opened an Albuquerque branch in 2006. It's a great source of garden furniture, pottery, folk art, and rugs.

Moderno (⊠ 3312 Stanford Dr. NE, Midtown ☎ 505/254–0447) stocks merchandise for contemporary living: handmade steel beds, chairs, mobiles, and modern, locally produced art, rugs, and jewelry.

Objects of Desire (⊠ 3225 Central Ave. NE, Nob Hill ☎ 505/232–3088) is the place to find that special lamp or table from a whimsical and worldly collection of furnishings that appeal to individualized tastes.

Peacecraft (⊠ 3215 Central Ave. NE, Nob Hill ☎ 505/255–5229) supports fair trade and stocks handmade folk art and crafts from all around the world—wooden boxes from Kenya, clothing from Guatemala, hats from Honduras. The store also employs a number of university students on work-study.

Mexican Imports

La Piñata (✉ No. 2 Patio Market, 206 San Felipe St. NW, Old Town ☎ 505/242–2400) specializes in piñatas and papier-mâché products, plus Native American jewelry and leather goods.

Music

Natural Sound (✉ 3422 Central Ave. SE, Nob Hill ☎ 505/255–8295) is an eclectic record store with a large selection of new and used CDs.

Native American Arts & Crafts

Andrews Pueblo Pottery (✉ 303 Romero St. NW, Suite 116, Old Town ☎ 505/243–0414) carries a terrific selection of Pueblo pottery, fetishes, kachina dolls, and baskets for the beginning and seasoned collector.

Bien Mur Indian Market Center (✉ Tramway Rd. NE east of I–25, Northeast Heights ☎ 505/821–5400 or 800/365–5400) in Sandia Pueblo showcases the best of the best in regional Native American rugs, jewelry, and crafts of all kinds. You can feel very secure about what you purchase at this trading post, and prices are fair for what you get.

★ **Gertrude Zachary** (✉ 1501 Lomas Blvd. NW, Old Town ☎ 505/247–4442 ✉ 3300 Central Ave. SE, Nob Hill ☎ 505/766–4700 ✉ 416 2nd St. SW, Old Town ☎ 505/244–1320) dazzles with its selection of Native American jewelry. This may be your best place to shop for a bargain in a good bracelet or ring. Locals buy here, too. A second branch, at 416 2nd Street, carries antiques.

★ **Nizhoni Moses, Ltd.** (✉ 326 San Felipe St. NW, Old Town ☎ 505/842–1808 or 888/842–1808) stocks Pueblo pottery, including the black earthenware pottery of San Ildefonso, as well as the work of potters from Acoma, Santa Clara, Isleta, and Zía. Rare Zuñi and Navajo jewelry is on display, as are Navajo weavings from 1900 to the present.

Skip Maisel Wholesale Indian Jewelry and Crafts (✉ 510 Central Ave. SW, Old Town ☎ 505/242–6526), in business since 1905, has been at this location since 1929. Even its exterior is a piece of art—check out the murals in the entryway alcove. Inside are quality Native American arts and crafts at wholesale prices.

ALBUQUERQUE ESSENTIALS

AIR TRAVEL

See Air Travel *in* New Mexico Essentials.

BUS TRAVEL

For information on reaching Albuquerque by bus, *see* Bus Travel *in* New Mexico Essentials.

Although the city's public bus service, ABQ Ride, provides good coverage, this is still a city where a car is the easiest and most convenient way to get around. Still, buses are fairly practical for getting between downtown, Nob Hill, Old Town, and the airport. The fare is $1 (bills or coins, exact change only). Bus stops are well marked with the line's sunburst signs.
🚌 Sun Tran ☎ 505/243-7433 ⊕ www.cabq.gov/transit/tran.html.

CAR RENTAL

See Car Rental *in* New Mexico Essentials.

CAR TRAVEL

Albuquerque sprawls out in all directions, but getting around town is not difficult, despite growing traffic problems as the city's population steadily increases. Drivers here have a spotty reputation, too, often pushing it through yellow lights and failing to use turn signals. The main highways through the city, north–south I–25 and east–west I–40, converge just northeast of downtown and generally offer the quickest access to outlying neighborhoods and the airport. Rush-hour jams are common in the mornings and late afternoons, but they're still far less severe than in most big U.S. cities.

PARKING Because it's a driving city, most businesses and hotels have free or inexpensive off-street parking, and it's easy to find metered street parking in many neighborhoods. Problems usually arise only when there's a major event in town, such as a concert near University of New Mexico or a festival downtown or in Old Town, when you may want to arrive on the early side to get a space.

EMERGENCIES

In an emergency, dial 911.

🚩 Hospitals **Presbyterian Hospital** ✉ 1100 Central Ave. SE, Downtown ☎ 505/841–1234. **University Hospital** ✉ 2211 Lomas Blvd. NE, University of New Mexico ☎ 505/272–2111.

SIGHTSEEING TOURS

The Albuquerque Museum of Art and History leads free, hour-long historical walks through Old Town at 11 AM except Monday, from March through November.

🚩 **Albuquerque Museum of Art and History** ☎ 505/243–7255 ⊕ www.cabq.gov/museum.

TAXIS

Taxis are metered in Albuquerque, and service is around-the-clock. Given the considerable distances around town, cabbing it can be expensive; figure about $9 from downtown to Nob Hill, and about $20 from the airport to a North Side hotel.

🚩 **Albuquerque Cab** ☎ 505/883–4888. **Yellow Cab** ☎ 505/247–8888.

TRAIN TRAVEL

In summer 2006 the City of Albuquerque launched the state's first-ever commuter train line, the *New Mexico Rail Runner Express.* As of this writing, service is from Bernalillo south through the city of Albuquerque, continuing south through Los Lunas to the suburb of Belén, covering a distance of about 50 mi. The second and final phase of the project, expected to be completed by late 2008, will extend the service north to Santa Fe. For information on Amtrak service, *see* Train Travel *in* New Mexico Essentials.

🚩 Train Information *New Mexico Rail Runner Express* ☎ 505/245–7245 ⊕ www.nmrailrunner.com.

VISITOR INFORMATION

The Albuquerque CVB operates tourism information kiosks at the airport (on the baggage claim level), downtown at the Albuquerque Convention Center (401 2nd St. NW), and in Old Town on Plaza Don Luis, across from San Felipe de Neri church.

🚹 **Albuquerque Convention and Visitors Bureau** ✉ 20 1st Plaza NW, Suite 601, 87125 ☎ 505/842-9918 or 800/284-2282 ⊕ www.itsatrip.org. **State Information Center** ✉ Indian Pueblo Cultural Center, 2401 12th St. NW, 87107 ☎ 505/843-7270 ⊕ www.newmexico.org.

Santa Fe

WORD OF MOUTH

"Santa Fe is a compact and easy town to walk, so I wouldn't worry about a bus tour. Pick up a tourist map and you should be fine."

—beachbum

"June is very hot in NM, even in Santa Fe. Our heat is DRY and some hate it. Why not come in the spring or fall when it is lovely, not scorching. September is still warm, but nice!"

—scsmom

"Don't miss the peddlers on the streets. Makes for good presents, and the numerous galleries (and restaurants) on Canyon Road are not to be missed."

—maria_so

Updated by
Andrew Collins

WITH ITS CRISP, CLEAR AIR AND BRIGHT, SUNNY WEATHER, Santa Fe couldn't be more welcoming. On a plateau at the base of the Sangre de Cristo Mountains—at an elevation of 7,000 feet—the city is surrounded by remnants of a 2,000-year-old Pueblo civilization and filled with reminders of almost four centuries of Spanish and Mexican rule. The town's placid central Plaza, which dates from the early 17th century, has been the site of bullfights, public floggings, gunfights, battles, political rallies, promenades, and public markets over the years. A one-of-a-kind destination, Santa Fe is fabled for its rows of chic art galleries, superb restaurants, and shops selling Southwestern furnishings and cowboy gear.

La Villa Real de la Santa Fe de San Francisco de Asísi (the Royal City of the Holy Faith of St. Francis of Assisi) was founded in the early 1600s by Don Pedro de Peralta, who planted his banner in the name of Spain. In 1680 the region's Pueblo people rose in revolt, burning homes and churches and killing hundreds of Spaniards. After an extended siege in Santa Fe, the Spanish colonists were driven out of New Mexico. The tide turned 12 years later, when General Don Diego de Vargas returned with a new army from El Paso and recaptured Santa Fe.

To commemorate de Vargas's victory, Las Fiestas de Santa Fe have been held annually since 1712. The nation's oldest community celebration takes place on the weekend after Labor Day, with parades, mariachi bands, pageants, the burning of *Zozóbra*—also known as Old Man Gloom— and nonstop parties. "Fiesta" (as it's referred to locally) is but one of many annual opportunities for revelry—from the arrival of the rodeo and the opening week of the Santa Fe Opera in summer to traditional Pueblo dances at Christmastime.

Following de Vargas's defeat of the Pueblos, the then-grand Camino Real (Royal Road), stretching from Mexico City to Santa Fe, brought an army of conquistadors, clergymen, and settlers to the northernmost reaches of Spain's New World conquests. In 1820 the Santa Fe Trail—a prime artery of U.S. westward expansion—spilled a flood of covered wagons from Missouri onto the Plaza. A booming trade with the United States was born. After Mexico achieved independence from Spain in 1821, its subsequent rule of New Mexico further increased this commerce.

The Santa Fe Trail's heyday ended with the arrival of the Atchison, Topeka & Santa Fe Railway in 1880. The trains, and later the nation's first highways, brought a new type of settler to Santa Fe—artists who fell in love with its cultural diversity, history, and magical color and light. Their presence attracted tourists, who quickly became a primary source of income for the largely poor populace.

Santa Fe is renowned for its arts, tricultural (Native American, Hispanic, and Anglo) heritage, and adobe architecture. The Pueblo people introduced adobe to the Spanish, who in turn developed the adobe brick style of construction. In a relatively dry, treeless region, adobe was a suitable natural building material. Melding into the landscape with their earthen colors and rounded, flowing lines, the pueblos and villages were hard to see from afar and thus somewhat camouflaged from raiding no-

GREAT ITINERARIES

Unless you're in Santa Fe for just a few days, you're probably going to explore the rest of the northern Rio Grande Valley. For the best tour, combine either of these itineraries with those in the Albuquerque, Taos, and Side Trips chapters; the latter includes several side trips within a 60- to 90-minute drive of Santa Fe.

IF YOU HAVE 1 DAY

Breakfast in Santa Fe is a social tradition, so consider heading to one of the city's best breakfast spots, such as Cloud Cliff Bakery or Bagelmania. Drive to Museum Hill, spending the morning checking out the area's two best art collections, the Museum of International Folk Art and Museum of Spanish Colonial Art. Return to the Plaza for lunch at the Plaza Café or, nearby, Santacafé. Stroll around the Plaza area, taking in the shops and galleries, and if you'd like, drop by the Georgia O'Keeffe Museum or Museum of Fine Arts.

By later afternoon, saunter east from the Plaza along San Francisco Street, admiring St. Francis Cathedral Basilica; bear right to Alameda Street, turn left and continue to Paseo de Peralta, and then quickly turn right and then left onto Canyon Road to stroll into the leafy foothills. You pass dozens of galleries, several of which stay open into early evening. Finish with a meal at one of the restaurants midway up Canyon Road.

IF YOU HAVE 3 DAYS

Follow the one-day itinerary's morning portion, but allow time to visit another museum on Museum Hill, either the Museum of Indian Arts and Culture or Wheelwright Museum of the American Indian.

Spend the afternoon ambling about the Plaza area, saving additional museum explorations for your last day.

On your second day, plan to walk a bit. Head east from the Plaza up to Canyon Road's foot, perusing the galleries. Have lunch at one of the restaurants midway uphill, such as Sol or El Farol. From here, you can either continue walking 2 mi up Canyon, and then Upper Canyon, roads to the Randall Davey Audubon Center, or you can take a cab there. Alternatively, you could drive from the start, first parking near Canyon Road to check out the galleries (there's a pay lot across from El Farol), then parking at the center. Either way, once you're at the center, you can hike the foothills—there are trails within the center's property and also from the free parking area (off Cerro Gordo Road) leading into the Dale Ball Trail Network. There may be late-afternoon summer thunderstorms and lightning, so check the forecast before you go, and bring at least a liter of water per person, even for a short stroll.

On your final day, spend the morning at the O'Keeffe or Fine Arts museums near the Plaza, and at the Palace of the Governors. In the afternoon, head a few blocks southwest of the Plaza, crossing Alameda Street, and stroll through the Guadalupe District, which abounds with funky design and furniture shops and galleries. End your explorations with a margarita on the patio of the festive Cowgirl restaurant, which has live music most nights.

IF YOU LIKE

ART GALLERIES

Santa Fe's tourism office claims that the city has the third-largest art market in the country, trailing only New York City and Los Angeles. Granted, it's a little difficult to quantify this boast, but it seems absolutely plausible: the city has more than 200 esteemed art galleries, and a significant number of them carry museum-quality art, some of it with museum-quality prices. In few cities in the world are so many paintings, sculptures, photographs, and other artworks by so many iconic artists—dead and living—available. Even if you're not out to buy art, it's worth visiting some of Santa Fe's most esteemed galleries just to admire it. As you might expect, it's easy to find Southwest, Spanish-colonial, Native American, and other art related to the area, but Santa Fe long ago broke out from its regional aesthetic and now represents artists of all genres and styles, from early-20th-century impressionism to African ethnography. Tree-shaded and narrow Canyon Road, which meanders gracefully up a hill on the east side of downtown, contains dozens of the city's galleries—it's great fun to stroll along here, ducking in and out of shops, especially on Friday, when many galleries have openings. However, more than a few locals-in-the-know write off Canyon Road as touristy and predictable and claim that the best galleries in Santa Fe lie elsewhere, mostly on the blocks around the Plaza and on Paseo de Peralta's eastern fringes. Just about any street you wander near the Plaza or east of it, you're likely to encounter acclaimed galleries.

NIGHTLIFE & THE ARTS

Santa Fe, especially come summer, is something of an arts powerhouse, its glittery reputation for performing-arts culture led by the presence of the internationally adored Santa Fe Opera. But the city also has a top-flight chamber music festival, world-class flamenco dancing, a fine ballet, respectable local theater, a couple of venues for arty films, and numerous spots to catch lectures and concerts or to partake of workshops. And although much of the activity takes place in summer, you can find performances of one kind or another year-round. As much as folks rave about the city's arts scene, they often complain about Santa Fe's nightlife options. But for a city its size, and one where visitors and locals head to bed early and get up early the next day, it really does hold its own. Several of the better restaurants in town have inviting bars or lounges, often with live music. And, similarly, some of the nightspots serve pretty good food. You won't find much in the way of massive warehouse discos and all-night revelry, but Santa Fe does have an intriguing mix of nightspots.

SHOPPING

Just as Santa Fe's art scene has grown in focus from regional to international, the city's shopping options have also increased dramatically, with the strongest growth occurring in the hip Guadalupe District, a few blocks southwest of the Plaza. Here you can find minimalls, such as the Design Center and Sanbusco Market Center, filled with stylish boutiques

2

and shops carrying one-of-a-kind antiques, gift, and clothing. Other stores specializing not only in the usual Southwest-influenced decorative items but also housewares and collectibles from Asia, Africa, and South America have also sprung up in this area. Of course, the Plaza and the blocks around it may always be ground zero for retail—here you can find a real mix of authentic Indian and Hispanic arts and clothing, upscale independent and chain clothiers, fine rug and home-furnishings stores, and souvenirs stands of varying quality. Keep strolling east of the Plaza and on up Canyon Road, and you can find more of the same interspersed among the many art galleries. Shopping is a serious sport in this town, and prices tend to be higher than elsewhere in the state, but it's also a city where, with few exceptions, you get what you pay for. And don't be scared to buy something too big or delicate to fit in your suitcase—nearly every shop in Santa Fe ships items all around the globe.

SPORTS & THE OUTDOORS

It's remarkable how many transplants to Santa Fe, when asked why they moved here, reply simply that they appreciate the weather and scenery. For outdoorsy types, this combination of dry, crisp, sunny air and breathtaking mountain and high-desert scenery—all easily accessible from downtown—makes this city a bona fide recreation hub. In winter Santa Fe's a respectable ski town with impressive slopes a 20-minute drive east of downtown; in summer there are terrific off-road mountain biking, hiking, horseback riding, and bird-watching as well as a highly regarded public golf course. Many of the top venues for these activities lie outside city limits, within a half-hour's drive (⇨ see Chapter 4 for specifics).

WORD OF MOUTH

"Found that almost all the hotels in the Plaza area are well-located—everything is pretty much within walking distance of everything else. Spent a fair amount of time just walking, exploring, shopping, absorbing. Visited the Museum of Fine Arts, SITE Santa Fe, Museum Hill (American Indian Museum and Folk Art Museum), Palace of the Governors. Saw about half of Canyon Road in a period of about 3 hours—we stopped into a lot of the galleries. Generally had excellent meals—places I'd recommend: Ristra, The Shed, Guadalupe Cafe, Zia, Plaza Cafe."

–spring212

madic tribes. The region's distinctive architecture no longer repels visitors, it attracts them.

Among the smallest state capitals in the country, Santa Fe has no major airport (Albuquerque's is the nearest). The city's population, an estimated 65,000, swells to nearly double that figure in summer. In winter the skiers arrive, lured by the challenging slopes of Ski Santa Fe and Taos Ski Valley (⇨ Chapter 4). Geared for tourists, Santa Fe can put a serious dent in your travel budget. Prices are highest June–August. Between September and November and between April and May they're lower, and (except for the major holidays) from December to March they're the lowest.

EXPLORING SANTA FE

Humorist Will Rogers said on his first visit to Santa Fe, "Whoever designed this town did so while riding on a jackass, backwards, and drunk." The maze of narrow streets and alleyways confounds motorists, but with shops and restaurants, a flowered courtyard, or an eyecatching gallery at nearly every turn, they're a delight for pedestrians. The trickle of water called the Santa Fe River runs west, parallel to Alameda Street, from the Sangre de Cristo Mountains to the open prairie southwest of town, where it disappears into a narrow canyon before joining the Rio Grande. But in New Mexico there's a *dicho,* or old saying, *"agua es vida"*—"water is life"—be it ever so humble.

There are five state museums in Santa Fe, and purchasing a Museum of New Mexico pass is the most economical way to visit them all. The four-day pass costs $15 and is sold at all five of the museums, which include the Palace of the Governors, Museum of Fine Arts, Museum of Indian Arts and Culture, Museum of International Folk Art, and Museum of Spanish Colonial Art.

Santa Fe Plaza

Much of the history of Santa Fe, New Mexico, the Southwest, and even the West has some association with Santa Fe's central Plaza, which New Mexico governor Don Pedro de Peralta laid out in 1607. The Plaza, already well established by the time of the Pueblo revolt in 1680, was the site of a bullring and of fiestas and fandangos. Freight wagons unloaded here after completing their arduous journey across the Santa Fe Trail. The American flag was raised over the Plaza in 1846, during the Mexican War, which resulted in Mexico's loss of all its territories in the present southwestern United States. For a time the Plaza was a tree-shaded park with a white picket fence. In the 1890s it was an expanse of lawn where uniformed bands played in an ornate gazebo. Particularly festive times on the Plaza are the weekend after Labor Day, during Las Fiestas de Santa Fe, and at Christmas, when all the trees are filled with lights and rooftops are outlined with *farolitos,* votive candles lit within paper-bag lanterns.

Numbers in the text correspond to numbers in the margin and on the Downtown Santa Fe map.

A GOOD WALK

To get started, drop by the information booth at the Plaza's northwest corner, across the street from the clock, where Palace Street meets Lincoln Street (in front of the bank) to pick up a free map. From there, begin your walk around the Plaza. You can get an overview of the history of Santa Fe and New Mexico at the **Palace of the Governors ❶**, which borders the northern side of the Plaza on Palace Avenue. Outside, under the palace portal, dozens of Native American craftspeople sell their wares. From the palace, cross Lincoln Street to the **Museum of Fine Arts ❷**, where the works of regional masters are on display. As you cross Lincoln, note the construction under way on the street's right side—part of the new wing being added to the Palace of the Governors, slated for completion in 2006. The **Georgia O'Keeffe Museum ❸**, on nearby Johnson Street, exhibits the works of its namesake, New Mexico's best known painter. Just down Johnson

Street, the new **Awakening Museum ❹** exhibits the large-scale installation of one-of-a-kind artist Jean-Claude Gaugy.

From the O'Keeffe Museum, return to the Plaza and cut across to its southeast corner to Old Santa Fe Trail, where you can find the town's oldest hotel, **La Fonda ❺**, a good place to soak up a little of bygone Santa Fe. One block east on Cathedral Place looms the imposing facade of **St. Francis Cathedral Basilica ❻**. Across from the cathedral is the **Institute of American Indian Arts, ❼** with its wonderful museum. A stone's throw from the museum is cool, quiet **Sena Plaza ❽**, accessible through two doorways on Palace Avenue.

🕐 **TIMING TIPS➡** It's possible to zoom through this compact area in about five hours—two hours exploring the Plaza and the Palace of the Governors, two hours seeing the Museum of Fine Arts and the Museum of the Institute of American Indian Arts, and an hour visiting the other sites.

What to See

❹ Awakening Museum. This unusual museum celebrates the groundbreaking artwork of Jean-Claude Gaugy, a French-born artist who began work on a large-scale art installation in West Virginia in 1985—it consisted of Gaugy's vibrant, colorful painting on hundreds of wood panels. In 2002, Gaugy moved to Santa Fe and reinstalled his work inside an 11,000-square-foot downtown building. Additionally, the museum contains a meditation garden and an extensive museum shop. Conceptually, it's one of Santa Fe's most fascinating—if rather difficult to describe—museums. ✉ *125 N. Guadalupe St.* ☎ *505/954–4025* ⊕ *www. theawakeningmuseum.org* 🎫*$3* 🕐 *June–Sept., daily 10–5:30; Oct.–May, Thurs.–Mon. 10–5.*

★ **❸ Georgia O'Keeffe Museum.** One of many East Coast artists who visited New Mexico in the first half of the 20th century, O'Keeffe returned to live and paint here, eventually emerging as the demigoddess of Southwestern art. O'Keeffe's innovative view of the landscape is captured in

**See Detail Map
Downtown Santa Fe**

TO TAOS,
ESPANOLA

TO
TESUQUE

84

285

475

N. Guadalupe St.

Old Taos Hwy.

Bishop's Lodge Rd.

Valley Dr.

Paseo de Peralta

Kearney Ave.

Artist Rd.

Hyde Park Rd.

San Francisco St.
W. Alameda St.

**The
Plaza**

E. Water St.

Washington Ave.

Old Fort
Marcy Park

Cathedral

Gonzales Rd.

**Old
Santa Fe
Station**

Guadalupe St.

Sandoval St.

**State
Capitol**

E. Alameda St.

Canyon Rd.

Cerro Gordo Rd.

Santa Fe River

Knox St.

Cerrillos Rd.

Don Diego Ave.

Galisteo St.

Don Gaspar Ave.

Old Santa Fe Trail

Old Pecos Trail

Messenger
Patrick Smith
Park

Upper Canyon Rd.

Cam. Cabra

Cam. del Monte Sol

St. Francis Dr.

Cordova Rd.

Cam. de
Cruz Blanca

**St. John's
College**

Galisteo St.

**Museum of Spanish
Colonial Art**

**Museum of
International
Folk Art**

**Wheelwright Museum
of the American Indian**

St. Michael's Dr.

Butolph Rd.

Zia Rd.

Old Santa Fe Trail

84

285

466

St. Francis Dr.

TO ALBUQUERQUE, I-25

300

TO LAS VEGAS, NM

25

Downtown Santa Fe

From the Plains, inspired by her memory of the Texas plains, and *Jimson Weed,* a study of one of her favorite plants. Special exhibitions with O'Keeffe's modernist peers are on view throughout the year—many of these are exceptional, sometimes even more interesting than the permanent collection. ⊠ *217 Johnson St.* ☎ *505/995–1000* ⊕ *www.okeeffemuseum.org* ⊠ *$8, free Fri. 5–8 PM* ⊙ *Daily Sat.–Thurs. 10–5, Fri. 10–8.*

2

❼ Institute of American Indian Arts. Containing the largest collection of contemporary Native American art in the United States, this museum's paintings, photography, sculptures, prints, and traditional crafts were created by past and present students and teachers. The institute itself, which moved to the College of Santa Fe campus, was founded as a one-room studio classroom in the early 1930s by Dorothy Dunn, a beloved art teacher who played a critical role in launching the careers of many Native American artists. In the 1960s and 1970s it blossomed into the nation's premier center for Native American arts. Artist Fritz Scholder taught here, as did sculptor Allan Houser. Among their disciples was the painter T. C. Cannon. ⊠ *108 Cathedral Pl.* ☎ *505/983–1777* ⊕ *www.iaiancad.org* ⊠ *$4* ⊙ *Mon.–Sat. 10–5, Sun. noon–5.*

❺ La Fonda. A *fonda* (inn) has stood on this site, southeast of the Plaza, for centuries. Architect Isaac Hamilton Rapp, who put Santa Fe style on the map, built this area landmark in 1922. Remodeled in 1926 by architect John Gaw Meem, the hotel was sold to the Santa Fe Railway in 1926 and remained a Harvey House hotel until 1968. Because of its proximity to the Plaza and its history as a gathering place for everyone from cowboys to movie stars (Errol Flynn stayed here), it's referred to as "The Inn at the End of the Trail." Major social events still take place here. Have a drink at the fifth-floor Bell Tower Bar (open late spring–early fall), which offers tremendous sunset views. ⊠ *E. San Francisco St. at Old Santa Fe Trail* ☎ *505/982–5511.*

NEED A BREAK?

Ecco Gelato (⊠ 105 E. Marcy St. ☎ 505/986–9778) has a sleek, minimalist café across from the downtown public library with polished-wood floors, large plate-glass windows, and brushed-metal tables. It's known for its creative gelato flavors (strawberry-habañero, saffon-honey, minty–white grape, chocolate-banana) as well as espressos and coffees, pastries, and sandwiches (roast beef–and–blue cheese, dill-tuna with cucumber and sprouts).

★ **❷ Museum of Fine Arts.** Designed by Isaac Hamilton Rapp in 1917, the museum contains one of America's finest regional collections. It's also one of Santa Fe's earliest Pueblo Revival structures, inspired by the adobe structures at Acoma Pueblo. Split-cedar *latillas* (branches set in a cross-hatch pattern) and hand-hewn vigas form the ceilings. The 8,000-piece permanent collection, of which only a fraction is exhibited at any given

A GOOD WALK

Begin on Paseo de Peralta at the **Gerald Peters Gallery ⑨**, which has an enormous collection. Continue a half block north to Canyon Road. Turn right (east) and follow the road, which unfolds in shadows of undulating adobe walls. Street parking is at a premium, but there's a city-owned pay lot at the corner of Camino del Monte Sol, a few blocks up. Between visits to galleries and shops, take a break at one of the courtyards or fine restaurants. Be sure to stop by the beautiful gardens outside **El Zaguan ⑩**. At the intersection of Upper Canyon and Cristo Rey you'll

find the massive **Cristo Rey Church ⑪**. Wear good walking shoes and watch out for the irregular sidewalks, which are built of stone and can get icy in winter.

🕐 TIMING TIPS➜ A tour of Canyon Road could take a whole day or as little as a few hours. If art is more than a curiosity to you, you may want to view the Gerald Peters Gallery apart from your Canyon Road tour. There's so much to see there that visual overload could hit before you get halfway up the road. Even on a cold day the walk can be a pleasure, with massive, glistening icicles hanging off roofs and a silence shrouding the side streets.

time, emphasizes the work of regional and nationally renowned artists, including the early Modernist Georgia O'Keeffe; realist Robert Henri; the "Cinco Pintores" (five painters) of Santa Fe (including Fremont Elis and Will Shuster); members of the Taos Society of Artists (Ernest L. Blumenschein, Bert G. Philips, Joseph H. Sharp, and E. Irving Couse, among others); and

GOOD TERM

Coyote Fence: A type of wooden fence that surrounds many New Mexico homes; it comprises branches, usually from cedar or aspen trees, arranged vertically and wired tightly together.

the works of noted 20th-century photographers of the Southwest, including Laura Gilpin, Ansel Adams, and Dorothea Lange. Rotating exhibits are staged throughout the year. Many excellent examples of Spanish-colonial–style furniture are on display. An interior *placita* (small plaza) with fountains, WPA murals, and sculpture, and the St. Francis Auditorium are other highlights. Concerts and lectures are often held in the auditorium. ⊠ *107 W. Palace Ave.* ☎ *505/476–5072* ⊕ *www.mfasantafe.org* 🔁 *$8, 4-day pass $18 (good at all 5 state museums in Santa Fe), free Fri. 5–8* PM 🕐 *Tues.–Thurs. and weekends 10–5, Fri. 10–8.*

🕐 ❶ **Palace of the Governors.** A humble-looking one-story adobe on the north
Fodor'sChoice side of the Plaza, the palace is the oldest public building in the United
★ States. Built at the same time as the Plaza, circa 1610 (scholars debate the exact year), it was the seat of four regional governments—those of Spain, Mexico, the Confederacy, and the U.S. territory that preceded New Mexico's statehood, which was achieved in 1912. The building was abandoned in 1680, following the Pueblo Revolt, but resumed its role as government headquarters when Don Diego de Vargas success-

fully returned in 1692. It served as the residence for 100 Spanish, Mexican, and American governors, including Governor Lew Wallace, who wrote his epic *Ben Hur* in its then drafty rooms, all the while complaining of the dust and mud that fell from its earthen ceiling. In 2004, construction began on a brand-new **State History Museum Annex**, behind the palace on Lincoln. It should open in 2008. Simultaneously, the Palace of the

> **WORD OF MOUTH**
>
> "[Buy turquoise] from someone you trust or develop your own expertise. Generally speaking, you can expect natural turquoise to have lots of color variation, and it's usually striated. If it looks uniform in color it's probably not natural."
> –beach_dweller

Governors is being renovated to its original purpose, as a house-museum. Its rooms will contain period furnishings and exhibits that illustrate the building's many functions over the past four centuries. For significant periods throughout the renovation process, the palace is expected to be closed, so call ahead for the latest details.

Dozens of Native American vendors gather daily under the portal of the Palace of the Governors to display and sell pottery, jewelry, bread, and other goods. With few exceptions, the more than 500 artists and craftspeople registered to sell here are Pueblo or Navajo Indians. The merchandise for sale is required to meet Museum of New Mexico standards: all items are handmade or hand-strung in Native American households; silver jewelry is either sterling (92.5% pure) or coin (90% pure) silver; all metal jewelry bears the maker's mark, which is registered with the museum. Prices tend to reflect the high quality of the merchandise. Don't take photographs without permission.

The palace has been the central headquarters of the Museum of New Mexico since 1913, housing the main section of the **State History Museum,** until it moves into its eventual new home behind the palace, on Lincoln Avenue. Permanent exhibits chronicle 450 years of New Mexico history, using maps, furniture, clothing, housewares, weaponry, and village models. The main rooms contain rotating exhibits, such as "Jewish Pioneers of New Mexico," an exploration of the vital role Jewish immigrants played during the late 19th and early 20th centuries in the state's civic, economic, and cultural development. With advance permission, students and researchers have access to the comprehensive **Fray Angélico Chávez Library** and its rare maps, manuscripts, and photographs (more than 120,000 prints and negatives). The palace is also home to the **Museum of New Mexico Press,** which prints books, pamphlets, and cards on antique presses and hosts bookbinding demonstrations, lectures, and slide shows. There's an outstanding gift shop and bookstore. ⊠ *Palace Ave., north side of Plaza* ☎ *505/476–5100* ⊕ *www.palaceofthegovernors.org* ⊒ *$8, 4-day pass $18 (good at all 5 state museums in Santa Fe), free Fri. 5–8* ☉ *Tues.–Thurs. and weekends 10–5, Fri. 10–8.*

★ ❻ **St. Francis Cathedral Basilica.** This magnificent cathedral, a block east of the Plaza, is one of the rare significant departures from the city's ubiquitous Pueblo architecture. Construction was begun in 1869 by Jean Bap-

A GOOD WALK

The **Loretto Chapel** ⓬, facing the Old Santa Fe Trail, behind the La Fonda hotel, is a good place to start your walk. After visiting the chapel, head southeast on Old Santa Fe Trail to the **San Miguel Mission** ⓭. Across from the mission, on De Vargas Street, is the **Oldest House** ⓮. Up and down narrow De Vargas stretches the **Barrio de Analco** ⓯. There are a few galleries worth visiting on De Vargas Street east of Old Santa Fe Trail, and, back across Old Santa Fe Trail on the west side, check out the historic Santa Fe Playhouse. In the early art colony days, literary luminaries like Mary Austin and Witter Bynner would stage shows here. Walk farther away from downtown until you come to the **New Mexico State Capitol** ⓰, which contains some interesting artwork. ☉ **TIMING TIPS→** Plan on spending a half hour at each of the churches and the New Mexico State Capitol and an hour exploring the Barrio de Analco. The entire walk can easily be done in about 3½ hours.

tiste Lamy, Santa Fe's first archbishop, working with French architects and Italian stonemasons. The Romanesque style was popular in Lamy's native home in southwest France. The circuit-riding cleric was sent by the Catholic Church to the Southwest to change the religious practices of its native popu-

DID YOU KNOW?

Two miniseries based on Larry McMurtry novels, *Lonesome Dove* and *Buffalo Girls*, were shot near Santa Fe.

lation (to "civilize" them, as one period document puts it) and is buried in the crypt beneath the church's high altar. He was the inspiration behind Willa Cather's novel *Death Comes for the Archbishop* (1927). In 2005 Pope Benedict XVI declared St. Francis the "cradle of Catholicism" in the Southwestern United States, and upgraded the status of the building from mere cathedral to cathedral basilica—it's one of just 36 in the country.

A small adobe chapel on the northeast side of the cathedral, the remnant of an earlier church, embodies the Hispanic architectural influence so conspicuously absent from the cathedral itself. The chapel's *Nuestra Señora de la Paz* (Our Lady of Peace), popularly known as *La Conquistadora,* the oldest Madonna statue in the United States, accompanied Don Diego de Vargas on his reconquest of Santa Fe in 1692, a feat attributed to the statue's spiritual intervention. Every Friday the faithful adorn the statue with a new dress. Just south of the cathedral, where the parking lot meets Paseo de Peralta, is the **Archdiocese of Santa Fe Museum** (☎ 505/983–3811), a small museum where many of the area's historic, liturgical artifacts are on view. ⊠ *231 Cathedral Pl.* ☎ *505/ 982–5619* ☉ *Mon.–Sat. 6–6, Sun. 7–7, except during mass. Mass Mon.–Sat. at 7 and 5:15 PM; Sun. at 8 and 10 AM, noon, and 7 PM. Museum weekdays 8:30–4:30.*

8 Sena Plaza. Two-story buildings enclose this courtyard, which can be entered only through two small doorways on Palace Avenue. Surrounding the oasis of flowering fruit trees, a fountain, and inviting benches are unique, low-profile shops. The quiet courtyard is a good place for repose. The buildings, erected in the 1700s as a single-family residence, had quarters for blacksmiths, bakers, farmers, and all manner of help. ⊠ *125 E. Palace Ave.*

> **WORD OF MOUTH**
>
> "Food stalls all over the Plaza, entertainment galore. . . . Book early, within walking distance of the Plaza, because parking fills up rapidly."
>
> –Ackislander

Canyon Road

Once a Native American trail and an early-20th-century route for woodcutters and their burros, Canyon Road is now lined with art galleries, shops, and restaurants, earning it the nickname "The Art and Soul of Santa Fe." The narrow road begins at the eastern curve of Paseo de Peralta and stretches for about 2 mi at a moderate incline toward the base of the mountains.

Most establishments are in authentic, old adobe homes with undulating thick walls that appear to have been carved out of the earth. Within many are contemporary and traditional works by artists with internationally renowned names like Fernando Botero to anonymous weavers of ancient Peruvian textiles.

There are few places as festive as Canyon Road on Christmas Eve, when thousands of farolitos illuminate walkways, walls, roofs, and even trees. In May the scent of lilacs wafts over the adobe walls, and in August red hollyhocks enhance the surreal color of the blue sky on a dry summer day.

What to See

11 Cristo Rey Church. Built in 1940 and designed by legendary Santa Fe architect John Gaw Meem to commemorate the 400th anniversary of Francisco Vásquez de Coronado's exploration of the Southwest, this church is the largest Spanish adobe structure in the United States and is considered by many the finest example of Pueblo-style architecture anywhere. The church was constructed in the old-fashioned way by parishioners, who mixed the more than 200,000 mud-and-straw adobe bricks and hauled them into place. The 225-ton stone *reredos* (altar screen) is magnificent. ⊠ *Canyon Rd. at Cristo Rey* ☎ *505/983–8528* ☉ *Daily 8–7.*

10 El Zaguan. Headquarters of the **Historic Santa Fe Foundations (HSFF)**, this 19th-century Territorial-style house has a small exhibit on Santa Fe architecture and preservation, but the real draw is the small but stunning garden abundant with lavender, roses, and 160-year-old trees. You can relax on a wrought-iron bench and take in the fine views of the hills northeast of town. An HSFF horticulturist often gives free tours and lectures in the garden on Thursday at 1 in summer (call to confirm). ⊠ *545 Canyon Rd.* ☎ *505/983–2567* ⊕ *www.historicsantafe.*

Rethinking Santa Fe Style

IN SANTA FE, EVERYTHING FROM THE ANCIENT Palace of the Governors to today's Walgreens is clad in adobe and designed in the Pueblo Revival or Spanish-colonial tradition. Picturesque and charming, this look is not, however, necessarily all that authentic: it dates from the early 20th century, at least as it applies to architecture and urban planning.

Around 1920, less than a decade after New Mexico attained statehood, the city's leaders decided that they could enhance Santa Fe's image, and promote tourism, by instituting urban planning guidelines calling for all new construction in the adobe style. At that time, the Plaza and the blocks around it contained a mix of Italianate, Queen Anne, and other Victorian styles, mixed with Spanish-colonial, and Pueblo Revival buildings.

Some lament that Santa Fe is too uniform, and that the degree to which the city enforces the Santa Fe style verges on the ridiculous. If Santa Fe is going to allow strip malls and tract developments, albeit, thankfully, several miles from the historic district, shouldn't the developers be permitted to design them as they please?

Others argue that Santa Fe, along with much of northern New Mexico's Rio Grande Valley, must rigorously preserve its style, even if it wasn't codified until the 20th century. Aesthetically and architecturally, this part of the country enjoys a singular appearance. The region's buildings may look similar, but they look nothing at all like buildings elsewhere. Besides, an urban design theme developed in the 1920s, based

on regional building traditions of the prior few centuries, can legitimately be called historic at this point.

Although city planners began encouraging a unified style from the 1920s onward, officially, Santa Fe adopted its Historic Zoning Ordinance in 1957. Today, the city's Historic Design Review Board checks that all new development fits within these particular guidelines, and that developers conduct a historical study of the surrounding area before embarking on any new construction.

Regardless of how far back you trace Santa Fe style, the look of the city and the Rio Grande Valley's other communities preserves a distinct amalgam of indigenous, Spanish, and Western architectural traditions. We owe the concept of earthen walls and flat roofs to the region's many centuries of Pueblo Indians, although it was the Spaniards who perfected building with adobe bricks. An increase in trade with U.S. states in the 19th century brought a greater variety of materials to the region, leading to an increasing use of timber and metal in building construction. This led to the development of an architectural style unique to the Southwest, Territorial, which combines American Victorian, frontier, Spanish-colonial, and—to a lesser degree—Pueblo Indian design elements.

For a more thorough examination of Santa Fe's design aesthetic and how it has evolved, take a look at Chris Wilson's book, *The Myth of Santa Fe: Creating a Modern Regional Tradition.*

—Andrew Collins

com ☞ *Free* ☉ *Foundations offices weekdays 9–noon and 1:30–5; gardens Mon.–Sat. 9–5.*

❾ **Gerald Peters Gallery.** While under construction, this 32,000-square-foot building was dubbed the "ninth northern pueblo," its scale rivaling that of the eight northern pueblos around Santa Fe. The suavely designed Pueblo-style gallery is Santa Fe's premier showcase for American and European art from the 19th century to the present. It feels like a museum, but all the works are for sale. Pablo Picasso, Georgia O'Keeffe, Charles M. Russell, Deborah Butterfield, George Rickey, and members of the Taos Society are among the artists represented, along with nationally renowned contemporary ones. ⊠ *1011 Paseo de Peralta* ☎ *505/954–5700* ⊕ *www.gpgallery.com* ☞ *Free* ☉ *Mon.–Sat. 10–5.*

NEED A BREAK?

Locals congregate in the courtyard or on the front portal of **Downtown Subscription** (⊠ 376 Garcia St. ☎ 505/983–3085), a block east of Canyon Road. This café-newsstand sells coffees, snacks, and pastries, plus one of the largest assortments of newspapers and magazines in New Mexico. A delightful spot toward the end of gallery row on Canyon Road, right at the intersection with Palace Avenue, the **Teahouse** (⊠ 821 Canyon Rd. ☎ 505/992–0972) has both a bright dining area and a tranquil outdoor seating area in a rock garden. In addition to teas from all over the world, you can find extremely well-prepared breakfast and lunch fare.

Lower Old Santa Fe Trail

It was along the Old Santa Fe Trail that wagon trains from Missouri rolled into town in the 1800s, forever changing Santa Fe's destiny. This area off the Plaza is one of Santa Fe's most historic.

What to See

⓯ **Barrio de Analco.** Along the south bank of the Santa Fe River, the barrio—its name means "district on the other side of the water"—is one of America's oldest neighborhoods, settled in the early 1600s by the Tlaxcalan Indians (who were forbidden to live with the Spanish near the Plaza) and in the 1690s by soldiers who had helped recapture New Mexico after the Pueblo Revolt. Plaques on houses on East De Vargas Street will help you locate some of the important structures. Check the performance schedule at the **Santa Fe Playhouse** on De Vargas Street, founded by writer Mary Austin and other Santa Feans in the 1920s.

⓬ **Loretto Chapel.** A delicate Gothic church modeled after Sainte-Chapelle in Paris, Loretto was built in 1873 by the same French architects and Italian stonemasons who built St. Francis Cathedral. The chapel is known for the "Miraculous Staircase" that leads to the choir loft. Legend has it that the chapel was almost complete when it became obvious that there

A GOOD WALK

From the Plaza, head west on San Francisco Street, and then take a left onto Guadalupe Street toward **Santuario de Guadalupe** ㉒, a short way farther on your right. After you visit the Santuario, take your time browsing through the shops and eating lunch in one of the restaurants farther down Guadalupe Street or around the corner at the **Sanbusco Market Center,** a massive warehouse. Check out the innovative shops and the photographic history on the walls near the market's main entrance. Back on Guadalupe, head south past the historic Gross Kelly Warehouse, one of the earliest Santa Fe–style buildings. You pass two huge murals on buildings facing Guadalupe Street depicting the magic realism that flavors so much of New Mexico culture. Note Santa Fe's two train depots—one is

now the site of the touristy Tomasita's Restaurant; the other, set farther back, is the Santa Fe Depot, where the **Santa Fe Southern Railway** ㉓ departs. Continue a short distance south on Guadalupe until you reach **SITE Santa Fe** ㉔ gallery and performance space, set inside a former bottling warehouse. Cater-corner from SITE Santa Fe, **El Museo Cultural de Santa Fe** ㉕ is one of the state's more unusual museums, a combination performance space, classroom, gallery, and event venue that promotes Hispanic culture and education in the City Different. ⊙ TIMING TIPS➔ A visit to the Santuario de Guadalupe can take 15 minutes to an hour, depending on whether or not there's an art show in progress. If you like shopping, you might spend hours in this neighborhood.

wasn't room to build a staircase to the choir loft. In answer to the prayers of the cathedral's nuns, a mysterious carpenter arrived on a donkey, built a 20-foot staircase—using only a square, a saw, and a tub of water to season the wood—and then disappeared as quickly as he came. Many of the faithful believed it was St. Joseph himself. The stair-

GOOD TERM

Pueblo Revival: Most homes in this style, modeled after the traditional dwellings of the Southwest Pueblo Indians, are cube or rectangle shaped.

case contains two complete 360-degree turns with no central support; no nails were used in its construction. The chapel closes for services and special events. Adjoining the chapel are a small museum and gift shop. ✉ *211 Old Santa Fe Trail* ☎ *505/982–0092* ⊕ *www.lorettochapel.com* 🖅 *Donation suggested* ⊙ *Mid-Oct.–mid-May, Mon.–Sat. 9–5, Sun. 10:30–5; mid-May–mid-Oct., Mon.–Sat. 9–6, Sun. 10:30–5.*

★ ⑯ **New Mexico State Capitol.** The symbol of the Zía Pueblo, which represents the Circle of Life, was the inspiration for the capitol, also known as the Roundhouse. Doorways at opposing sides of this 1966 structure symbolize the four winds, the four directions, and the four seasons.

Throughout the building are artworks from the outstanding collection of the Capitol Art Foundation, historical and cultural displays, and hand-crafted furniture—it's a superb and somewhat overlooked array of fine art. The **Governor's Gallery** hosts temporary exhibits. Six acres of imaginatively landscaped gardens shelter outstanding sculptures. ⊠ *Old Santa Fe Trail at Paseo de Peralta* ☎ *505/986–4589* ⊕ *http://legis.state. nm.us/lcs* ⊠ *Free* ☉ *Weekdays 7–6; tours weekdays by appt.*

⓮ **The Oldest House.** More than 800 years ago, Pueblo people built this structure out of "puddled" adobe (liquid mud poured between upright wooden frames). This house, which contains a gift shop, is said to be the oldest in the United States. ⊠ *215 E. De Vargas St.*

⓯ **San Miguel Mission.** The oldest church still in use in the United States, this **Fodor'sChoice** simple earth-hue adobe structure was built in the early 17th century by ★ the Tlaxcalan Indians of Mexico, who came to New Mexico as servants of the Spanish. Badly damaged in the 1680 Pueblo Revolt, the structure was restored and enlarged in 1710. On display in the chapel are priceless statues and paintings and the San José Bell, weighing nearly 800 pounds, which is believed to have been cast in Spain in 1356. In winter the church sometimes closes before its official closing hour. Mass is held on Sunday at 5 PM. Next door in the back of the Territorial-style dormitories of the old St. Michael's High School, a **Visitor Information Center** can help you find your way around northern New Mexico. ⊠ *401 Old Santa Fe Trail* ☎ *505/983–3974* ⊠ *$1* ☉ *Mission Mon.–Sat. 10–4, Sun. 3–4:30.*

Upper Old Santa Fe Trail & Museum Hill

What to See

★ ⓱ **Museum of Indian Arts and Culture.** An interactive, multimedia exhibition tells the story of Native American history in the Southwest, merging contemporary Native American experience with historical accounts and artifacts. The collection has some of New Mexico's oldest works of art: pottery vessels, fine stone and silver jewelry, intricate textiles, and other arts and crafts created by Pueblo, Navajo, and Apache artisans. You can also see art demonstrations and a video about the life and work of Pueblo potter Maria Martinez. ⊠ *710 Camino Lejo* ☎ *505/476–1250* ⊕ *www. miaclab.org* ⊠ *$8, 4-day pass $18, good at all 5 state museums in Santa Fe* ☉ *Tues.–Sun. 10–5.*

⓲ **Museum of International Folk Art (MOIFA).** At this museum, the premier institution of its kind in the world, you can find amazingly inventive handmade objects—a tin Madonna, a devil made from bread dough, and all kinds of rag dolls. Florence Dibell Bartlett, who founded the museum in 1953, donated its first 4,000 works. In the late 1970s Alexander and Susan Girard, major folk-art collectors, gave the museum 106,000 items. The Hispanic Heritage Wing contains art dating

> **WORD OF MOUTH**
>
> "This museum is a treat for young and old. Wonderful collections displayed beautifully . . . a most special (and unusual) feast for the eyes!"   –Lynne, on MOIFA

from the Spanish-colonial period (in New Mexico, 1598–1821) to the present. The 5,000-piece exhibit includes religious works—particularly *bultos* (carved wooden statues of saints) and *retablos* (holy images painted on wood or tin). The objects in the Neutrogena Wing are exhibited by theme rather than by date or country of origin—you might, for instance, find a sheer Eskimo parka alongside a Chinese undergarment made of bamboo and cotton webbing. Lloyd's Treasure Chest, the wing's innovative basement section, provides a behind-the-scenes look at more of this collection. You can rummage about storage drawers, peer into microscopes, and, on occasion, speak with conservators and other museum personnel. ⊠ *706 Camino Lejo* ☎ *505/476–1200* ⊕ *www.moifa. org* ⊠ *$8, 4-day pass $18, good at all 5 state museums in Santa Fe* ⊗ *Tues.–Sun. 10–5.*

⑲ Museum of Spanish Colonial Art. Opened in 2002, this 5,000-square-foot
FodorsChoice adobe museum occupies a building designed in 1930 by acclaimed ar-
★ chitect John Gaw Meem. The Spanish Colonial Art Society formed in Santa Fe in 1925 to preserve traditional Spanish-colonial art and culture. The museum, which sits next to the Museum of New Mexico complex, displays the fruits of the society's labor—one of the most comprehensive collections of Spanish-colonial art in the world. The Hale Matthews Library contains a 1,000-volume collection of books relating to this important period in art history. Objects here, dating from the 16th century to the present, include retablos, elaborate santos, tinwork, straw appliqué, furniture, ceramics, and ironwork. There's also a fine collection of works by Hispanic artists of the 20th century. ⊠ *750 Camino Lejo* ☎ *505/982–2226* ⊕ *www.spanishcolonial.org/museum. shtml* ⊠ *$6, 4-day pass $18, good at all 5 state museums in Santa Fe* ⊗ *Daily 10–5.*

⊘ ㉑ Santa Fe Children's Museum. Stimulating hands-on exhibits, a solar greenhouse, oversize geometric forms, and a simulated 18-foot mountain-climbing wall all contribute to this underrated museum's popularity with kids. Puppeteers and storytellers perform often. ⊠ *1050 Old Pecos Trail* ☎ *505/989–8359* ⊕ *www.santafechildrensmuseum.org* ⊠ *$8* ⊗ *Wed.–Sat. 10–5, Sun. noon–5.*

⑳ Wheelwright Museum of the American Indian. A private institution in a building shaped like a traditional octagonal Navajo hogan, the Wheelwright opened in 1937. Founded by Boston scholar Mary Cabot Wheelwright and Navajo medicine man Hastiin Klah, the museum originated as a place to house ceremonial materials. Those items are not on view to the public. What is displayed are 19th- and 20th-century baskets, pottery, sculpture, weavings, metalwork, photography, and paintings, including contemporary works by Native American artists. The Case Trading Post on the lower level is modeled after the trading posts that dotted the southwestern frontier more than 100 years ago. It carries an extensive selection of books and contemporary Native American jewelry, kachina dolls, weaving, and pottery. ⊠ *704 Camino Lejo* ☎ *505/982– 4636 or 800/607–4636* ⊕ *www.wheelwright.org* ⊠ *Free* ⊗ *Mon.–Sat. 10–5, Sun. 1–5; gallery tours weekdays at 2, Sat. at 1.*

Guadalupe District

The historic warehouse and railyard district of Santa Fe is commonly referred to as the Guadalupe District. After the demise of the train route through town, the low-lying warehouses were converted to artists' studios and antiques shops, and bookstores, specialty shops, and restaurants have sprung up. The restored scenic train line puts the town's old depot to use, and eventually this station will be the Santa Fe terminus of the *Railrunner* commuter train service that's planned from Albuquerque sometime in 2008. Presently, the impressive local farmers' market turns the vacant lot at the corner of Guadalupe and Cerrillos into a colorful outdoor fiesta, but as part of a comprehensive redevelopment plan for the neighborhood, this 13-acre lot is slated to be converted into a beautiful, grassy park in the next couple of years. Additional—tentative— plans for the neighborhood include redeveloping much of the dusty parking areas around the old rail depot, building a multiplex cinema, and expanding the neighborhood's retail and entertainment space.

What to See

㉕ El Museo Cultural de Santa Fe. As much an educational and community gathering space as a museum, the Santa Fe Cultural Museum celebrates Santa Fe's—and New Mexico's—rich Hispanic heritage by presenting a wide range of events, from children's theater to musical concerts. The museum also sponsors the Contemporary Hispanic Market on the Plaza each July (held the same time as Spanish Market), and the Contemporary Hispanic Artists Winter Market, held at El Museo Cultural in late November. There's also a gallery that exhibits contemporary art by Hispanic artists. A great resource to visitors are the many classes and workshops, which are open to the public, and touch on everything from guitar and Mexican folkloric dance to children's theater and art. The museum occupies what had been a dilapidated liquor warehouse before El Museo took over the space in the late '90s. ⊠ *1615 Paseo de Peralta* ☎ *505/ 992–0591* ⊕ *www.elmuseocultural.org* ⊠ *Free; prices vary for events and shows* ☉ *Tues.–Fri. 1–5, Sat. 10–5; additionally for events and shows.*

㉓ Santa Fe Southern Railway. For a leisurely tour across the Santa Fe plateau and into the vast Galisteo Basin, where panoramic views extend for up to 120 mi, take a nostalgic ride on the antique cars of the Santa Fe Southern Railway. The train once served a spur of the Atchison, Topeka & Santa Fe Railway. Today the train takes visitors on 36- mi round-trip scenic trips to Lamy, a sleepy village with the region's only Amtrak service, offering picnics under the cottonwoods (bring your own or buy one from the caterer that meets the train) at the quaint rail station. Shorter runs travel down to the scenic Galisteo Basin. Aside from day trips, the railway offers special events such as a Friday-night "High Desert High Ball" cash bar with appetizers and a Saturday Night Barbecue Train. Trains depart from the Santa Fe Depot, rebuilt in 1909 after the original was destroyed in a fire. There's talk of eventually opening a regional transportation and rail museum here, as part of the efforts to redevelop this part of the Guadalupe District. ⊠ *410 S. Guadalupe St.* ☎ *505/989–8600 or 888/989–8600* ⊕ *www.sfsr.*

com ⛵ *Reservations essential* ✉ *Day-trips from $32, dinner trains from $58* ⊙ *Call for schedule.*

㉒ Santuario de Guadalupe. A humble adobe structure built by Franciscan missionaries between 1776 and 1795, this is the oldest shrine in the United States to Our Lady of Guadalupe, Mexico's patron saint. The sanctuary, now a nonprofit cultural center, has adobe walls nearly 3 feet thick. Among the sanctuary's religious art and artifacts is a priceless 16th-century work by Venetian painter Leonardo de Ponte Bassano that depicts Jesus driving the money changers from the Temple. Also of note is a portrait of Our Lady of Guadalupe by the Mexican colonial painter José de Alzíbar. Other highlights are the traditional New Mexican carved and painted altar screen, an authentic 19th-century sacristy, a pictorial-history archive, a library devoted to Archbishop Jean Baptiste Lamy that is furnished with many of his belongings, and a garden with plants from the Holy Land. ✉ *100 Guadalupe St.* ☎ *505/988–2027* ✉ *Donation suggested* ⊙ *May–Oct., Mon.–Sat. 9–4; Nov.–Apr., weekdays 9–4.*

★ ㉔ SITE Santa Fe. The events at this nexus of international contemporary art include lectures, concerts, author readings, performance art, and gallery shows. The facility hosts a biennial exhibition every odd-numbered year. There are always provocative exhibitions here, however, and the immense, open space is ideal for taking in the many larger-than-life installations. ✉ *1606 Paseo de Peralta* ☎ *505/989–1199* ⊕ *www. sitesantafe.org* ✉ *$10, free Fri.* ⊙ *Wed., Thurs., and Sat. 10–5, Fri. 10–7, Sun. noon—5.*

WHERE TO EAT

Eating out is a major pastime in Santa Fe. Several high-profile chefs run restaurants here, but quite a few divey joints also serve highly acclaimed food. People sometimes complain about the steep restaurant prices (often as much as what you pay in New York or San Francisco), and although most of the high-end restaurants are worth it, you can find some great bargains if you look around a bit. Eateries frequented by locals and that serve great cuisine are often outside of downtown and away from the Plaza. Waits for tables are very common during the busy summer season, so it's a good idea to call ahead even when reservations aren't accepted, if only to get a sense of the waiting time.

So-called Santa Fe–style cuisine has so many influences that the term is virtually meaningless. Traditional, old-style Santa Fe restaurants serve New Mexican fare, which combines both Native American and Hispanic traditions and differs markedly from Americanized or even authentic Mexican cooking. Many of the better restaurants in town serve a contemporary regional style of cooking that blends New Mexican ingredients and preparations with those of interior and coastal Mexico, Latin America, the Mediterranean, East Asia, and varied parts of the United States. There are a few respected Italian restaurants in town, and a growing number of commendable Asian eateries, but all in all the city's ethnic culinary diversity is a bit limited.

	WHAT IT COSTS				
	$$$$	**$$$**	**$$**	**$**	**¢**
RESTAURANTS	over $30	$24–$30	$17–$24	$10–$17	under $10

Prices are per person for a main course at dinner, excluding 8.25% sales tax.

American–Casual

$–$$ ✕ **Railyard Restaurant & Saloon.** Set inside a bustling, handsome warehouse in the railyard at the Guadalupe District, this trendy spot operated by the same talented management that runs 315 Restaurant & Wine Bar serves relatively affordable, well-prepared American favorites that have been given nouvelle twists. Good bets include fried buttermilk-chicken strips with Creole rémoulade dipping sauce, sesame-and-panko-crusted tuna with a soy-honey sauce, and barbecued baby back ribs. Many patrons choose to sit in the casual bar, where both the full and lighter menus are available, and sip on pomegranate margaritas or well-chosen wines by the glass. You can also dine on the large patio during the warmer months. ✉ 530 S. Guadalupe St. ☎ 505/989–3300 ▤ AE, D, MC, V ⊘ No lunch Sun.

¢–$$ ✕ **The Cowgirl.** A rollicking, popular bar and grill with several rooms overflowing with Old West memorabilia, Cowgirl has reasonably priced and tasty Southwestern, Tex-Mex, barbecue, and southern fare. Highlights include barbecue, buffalo burgers, bourbon-glaze pork chops, and salmon tacos with tomatillo salsa. So what's the bad news? Consistently subpar service. Nevertheless, knock back a few drinks and catch one of the nightly music acts—usually rock or blues—and you're likely to leave smiling. Grab a seat on the spacious patio in warm weather. Next door, Cowgirl Pickup has an extensive selection of takeout, including what many consider to be the best breakfast burritos in Santa Fe, plus Taos Cow ice cream. ✉ 319 S. Guadalupe St. ☎ 505/982–2565 ▤ AE, D, MC, V.

¢–$ ✕ **Atomic Grill.** Burgers, salads, pizzas, sandwiches, and other light fare are served at this tiny late-night café a block off the Plaza. The food is decent and the service brusque but usually okay. The best attributes are the comfy patio overlooking pedestrian-heavy Water Street, the huge list of imported beers, and the late hours (it's open until 3 most nights)—an extreme rarity in Santa Fe. You'll be glad this place exists when the bars let out and you're famished. ✉ 103 Water St. ☎ 505/820–2866 ▤ MC, V.

¢–$ ✕ **Bagelmania.** Tucked down a side street a few blocks northwest of the Plaza, this always-packed breakfast and lunch spot has a nondescript dining room overlooking a big parking lot, but the food is stellar. Breakfast favorites include the Chesapeake Bay Benedict, topped with blue-crab croquettes, and the Lonestar platter (chicken-fried steak, two eggs, and creamy gravy). At lunch, try the roasted rosemary chicken or char-grilled eggplant sandwich. Yes, they have plenty of New York–style bagels and spreads, too, but there's plenty more to choose from here. ✉ 420 Catron St. ☎ 505/982–8900 ▤ AE, MC, V ⊘ No dinner.

Where to Eat
in Downtown
Santa Fe

¢–$ ✕ **Bobcat Bite.** This divey grill in a tiny roadhouse a 15-minute drive south of town serves steaks and chops but is famous for one thing: the biggest and juiciest burgers in town. Locals prefer them topped with cheese and green chile. Only early dinners are available, as the place closes by 8 most nights. ⊠ *Old Las Vegas Hwy., 4½ mi south of Old Pecos Trail exit off I–25* ☎ *505/983–5319* ⌂ *Reservations not accepted* ▭ *No credit cards* ☉ *Closed Sun.–Tues.*

¢–$ ✕ **San Francisco Street Bar & Grill.** Occupying a sun-filled, second-floor space near the Plaza, this convivial spot offers predictable but inexpensive, well-prepared American fare along with a nice selection of wines, beers, and cocktails. It's a family-friendly, somewhat noisy place with comfy booths and smaller hardwood tables and chairs. Popular starters include fried calamari or pan-seared shrimp salad. The half-pound burger here is superb, along with such reliable standbys as asiago-basil-garlic ravioli and grilled ruby trout with grilled-pineapple salsa. ⊠ *50 E. San Francisco St.* ☎ *505/982–2044* ▭ *AE, D, MC, V.*

¢–$ ✕ **Sol.** Opened in 2004, this casual spot on Canyon Road offers value and convenience to this gallery-studded thoroughfare with few affordable dining options. Another big plus is the cozy patio overlooking the colorful pedestrian traffic. Sol serves mostly burgers and comfort fare, such as mac and cheese, Belgian waffles, catfish sandwiches, and Caesar salads—and there are also 18 kinds of beer. Although it's open for dinner, the restaurant closes early, at 8. The same chef helms the snazzy and more upscale Canyon Restaurant, across the street. ⊠ *802 Canyon Rd.* ☎ *505/989–1949* ▭ *AE, D, MC, V.*

¢–$ ✕ **Tesuque Village Market.** A favorite spot for a snack or a full meal before heading to the opera or after shopping at the Tesuque Pueblo Flea Market, this epicurean grocery and people-watching café has a tiny but lovely patio and a less atmospheric indoor seating area. The kitchen serves up tasty American and New Mexican fare—pork chops verde, posole (stew made with lime hominy, pork, chile, and garlic), French toast, Frito pie. Save room for a fresh-baked brownie or cookie. ⊠ *NM 590 at Bishop's Lodge Rd., Tesuque, 5 mi north of Santa Fe* ☎ *505/988–8848* ⌂ *Reservations not accepted* ▭ *MC, V.*

¢–$ ✕ **Zia Diner.** This slick diner with a low-key, art deco–style interior serves comfort food prepared with the occasional creative enhancement (consider green chile–piñon meat loaf, for example). Stop in for a full meal (ask about the night's blue-plate special, like Friday's fish Vera Cruz style) or just a classic banana split with homemade hot fudge sauce. Zia's Cobb salad is one of the best in town, and the chicken-fried chicken will fill you up for a good long time. Service is friendly but sometimes slow, and the food is fresh. There's a cheerful patio. Breakfast here is a bargain: try the smoked-salmon breakfast pizza. ⊠ *326 S. Guadalupe St.* ☎ *505/988–7008* ⊕ *www.ziadiner.com* ▭ *AE, MC, V.*

Cafés

★ **¢–$** ✕ **Cloud Cliff Bakery.** Breakfast tends to be a big social affair in Santa Fe, and several very good bakeries vie heavily for the morning crowd. Although it's a 10-minute drive south of town, Cloud Cliff Bakery prepares some of the best food, using organic ingredients when possible.

A GOOD TOUR

This museum tour begins 2 mi south of the Plaza, an area known as Museum Hill that's best reached by car or via one of the city buses that leave hourly from near the Plaza. Begin at the **Museum of Indian Arts and Culture ⑰**, which is set around **Milner Plaza,** an attractively landscaped courtyard and gardens with outdoor art installations. Many days the Plaza hosts Native American dances, jewelry-making demonstrations, kids' activities, and other interactive events; there's also the Museum Hill Cafe, which is open for lunch (and Sunday brunch) and serves salads, quiche, burgers, sandwiches and wraps, ice cream, and other light fare. To get here from downtown, drive uphill on Old

Santa Fe Trail to Camino Lejo. Across Milner Plaza is the **Museum of International Folk Art (MOIFA) ⑱**. From Milner Plaza, a bike-pedestrian path leads a short way to the **Museum of Spanish Colonial Art ⑲**. Return to Milner Plaza, from which a different bike-pedestrian path leads a short way to the **Wheelwright Museum of the American Indian ⑳**. To reach the **Santa Fe Children's Museum ㉑** you need to drive back down the hill or ask the bus driver to let you off near it. ⊘ **TIMING TIPS→** Set aside a half to full day to see all the museums on the Upper Santa Fe Trail. Kids usually have to be dragged from the Children's Museum, even after an hour or two.

For lunch, consider smoked Norwegian salmon with herbed cream cheese, spinach, and tomato, or the black-bean chipotle chili. Breakfast favorites include herb-grilled polenta with mozzarella, green chile sauce, and two eggs any style, and blue corn pancakes with granola. This sleek, modern dining room fills up fast on weekends, so expect a wait. ⊠ *1805 2nd St.* ☎ *505/983–6254* ⊟ *MC, V* ⊘ *No dinner.*

¢–$ ✕ **Mission Cafe.** Tucked down an alley off Old Santa Fe Trail, near the capitol, this sunny, art-filled café inside an 1850s adobe serves some of the tastiest breakfast and lunch fare in town. The food is mostly New Mexican–inspired, including excellent breakfast burritos, as well as delicious pies, strong espresso drinks, and locally produced Tara's Organic Ice Cream, which comes in such unusual flavors as blueberry mint and lemongrass. During the warmer months, dine on the big front patio, shaded with leafy trees. ⊠ *237 E. DeVargas St.* ☎ *505/983–3033* ⊟ *MC, V* ⊘ *No dinner.*

¢–$ ✕ **Whole Body Cafe.** This healthful stop is inside Body Santa Fe, a holistically minded center devoted to bodywork and healing where you'll also find a spa offering a full range of treatments, a yoga studio (with classes open to visitors), a child-care center, and boutique selling a wide range of beauty, health, and lifestyle products, plus jewelry, clothing, music, tarot cards, and all sorts of interesting gifts. The café uses mostly organic ingredients and serves three meals a day, including granola or egg scrambles at breakfast. At lunch try soba noodles with peanuts and a ginger-soy vinaigrette, and at dinner there's a very good lasagna layered with basil sunflower pesto, portobello mushrooms, spinach, squash, tomatoes, cheese, and marinara sauce. ⊠ *333 Cordova Rd.* ☎ *505/986–0362* ⊟ *AE, D, MC, V.*

¢ ✕ **Chocolate Maven.** Although the name of this cheery bakery suggests sweets, and you can definitely get a sugar high here, Chocolate Maven produces impressive savory breakfast and lunch fare. Favorite treats include wild mushroom–and–goat cheese focaccia sandwiches, eggs ménage à trois (one each of eggs Benedict, Florentine, and Madison—the latter consisting of smoked salmon and poached egg), and Caprese salad of fresh mozzarella, basil, and tomatoes. Some of the top desserts include Belgian chocolate fudge brownies, mocha-buttercream torte with chocolate-covered strawberries, and perhaps the best carrot cake in New Mexico. ⊠ *821 W. San Mateo St.* ☎ *505/984–1980* ⊟ *AE, D, MC, V* ☉ *No dinner.*

¢ ✕ **Four and Twenty Blackbirds.** Set in a tiny converted 1920s grocery store (it still contains the original deli counter and refrigerator), this café is most famous for its savory and sweet pies, from chicken to gooseberry to coconut cream. But you can drop in at lunchtime to sample such exquisite sandwiches as roast beef with vine-ripened tomatoes and bluecheese cole slaw. There's also a wide selection of kitchen goods, gourmet foods, and fun knickknacks. Parking is at the vintage Texaco station a few doors down. ⊠ *620 Old Santa Fe Trail* ☎ *505/983–7676* ⊟ *MC, V* ☉ *No dinner.*

★ ¢ ✕ **Santa Fe Baking Company.** The large, split-level dining room and expansive patio at this long-running café is usually packed with hungry bargain-minded diners and workers and students pecking away on their laptops, taking advantage of the free Wi-Fi. Breakfast is served all day, and you might try the carne adovada burrito or blue corn pancakes. At lunch consider the grilled ham torta with smoked ham, cheddar, and chipotle mayo, or the big chile dog. Lots of juices, coffees, and teas are served, too. On weekend mornings, expect a wait for a table—this place packs 'em in. It closes at 8 PM nightly. ⊠ *504 W. Cordova St.* ☎ *505/ 988–4292* ⊟ *AE, D, MC, V.*

Chinese

¢–$$ ✕ **Chow's.** A pleasing alternative to the many Americanized Chinese restaurants in town, Chow's occupies a modest but cheerful space in a shopping center a few miles south of the Plaza. The kitchen conjures up imaginative Chinese dishes, including a knockout starter of fried wontons stuffed with crab and Parmesan cheese and tossed with an orangeginger glaze. A worthy entrée is scallops wok-fried with red-chile rings, bok choy, and coconut milk. Green-tea ice cream makes a nice dessert. ⊠ *720 St. Michael's Dr.* ☎ *505/471–7120* ⊟ *AE, MC, V* ☉ *Closed Sun.*

Contemporary

$$$–$$$$ ✕ **The Compound.** Three decades ago, this handsome adobe tucked down an alley off Canyon Road epitomized white-glove fine dining. Its fortunes waxed and waned over the years before acclaimed restaurateurs Brett Kemmerer and Mark Kiffin transformed it into one of the state's

culinary darlings. It's still a fancy place, but dress is a cut below formal, and the staff highly attentive but also easygoing. From Chef Kiffin's oft-changing menu consider a starter of calamari grilled with lime, cilantro, and ginger. Memorable entrées include braised New Mexico lamb shank with fire-roasted tomato risotto; and buttermilk roast chicken with creamed fresh spinach and foie gras pan gravy. ⊠ *653 Canyon Rd.* ☎ *505/ 982–4353* ⊕ *www.compoundrestaurant.com* ⊟ *AE, D, DC, MC, V* ☉ *No lunch weekends.*

$$$–$$$$ ✕ **Coyote Cafe.** Touristy, bold, and presided over by celebrity chef Mark Miller, this is the restaurant lots of people love to bad-mouth. Say what you will, Coyote Cafe manages to produce consistently original Southwest cooking, and the service is surprisingly pleasant considering the high expectations and sometimes overwhelming crowds. Try pecan-grilled New York sirloin with pasilla chile–fig green mole sauce, or rotisserie pheasant with *huitlacoche* (a wild-mushroom fungus that grows on sweet corn) crepe and truffle-whipped cream. The open dining room can be loud and obnoxiously showy. On the wine list are more than 500 vintages. Inventive, delicious, under-$15 fare is served April through October on the open-air Rooftop Cantina, one of Santa Fe's best bargains. ⊠ *132 W. Water St.* ☎ *505/983–1615* ⊕ *www.coyotecafe.com* ⊟ *AE, D, DC, MC, V* ☉ *No lunch except at Rooftop Cantina.*

$$$–$$$$ ✕ **Fuego.** An elegant dining room inside La Posada resort, Fuego lacked pizzazz before current chef Rahm Fama took over in 2003. Now it's one of Santa Fe's top restaurants, albeit with sky-high prices. You might start with seared foie gras with apple pie au poivre, before trying free-range *poussin* (young chicken) over a nest of braised leeks and salsify, or roast rack of Colorado elk with parsnip dumplings and a dried-cherry mole. Perhaps the most astounding dish is the artisanal cheese plate— Fuego has one of the largest selections of cheeses west of the Mississippi. The wine list is similarly impressive. Le Menu Découverte allows you to sample a five-course meal of chef's specialties for $95. ⊠ *330 E. Palace Ave.* ☎ *505/954–9676* ⊕ *www.laposadadesantafe.com* ⊟ *AE, D, DC, MC, V* ☉ *No dinner Mon. and Tues.*

$$$–$$$$ ✕ **Inn of the Anasazi.** Renowned chef Martín Rios has long ranked
Fodor'sChoice among the state's great culinary wizards, and his move in early 2006 to
★ the snazzy Inn of the Anasazi immediately upgraded the hotel's restaurant from merely passable to stellar. The romantic, 90-seat restaurant with hardwood floors, softly indirect lighting, and beam ceilings feels slightly less formal than the other big-ticket dining rooms in town, and Rios's cooking always dazzles. Specialties from the often-changing menu include ahi tuna tartar with artichoke-scallion blinis; pork tenderloin medallions with zinfandel-braised onions, sweet potatoes with piñon nuts, and a red chile–bourbon reduction. The Sunday brunch is terrific. ⊠ *Inn of the Anasazi, 113 Washington Ave.* ☎ *505/988–3030* ⊟ *AE, D, DC, MC, V.*

$$–$$$$ ✕ **Cafe Pasqual's.** This cheerful cubbyhole dishes up Southwestern and
Fodor'sChoice Nuevo Latino specialties for breakfast, lunch, and dinner. Don't be dis-
★ couraged by lines out in front—it's worth the wait. The culinary muse behind it all is Katharine Kagel, who for more than 25 years has been introducing specialties like buttermilk biscuits with sage-bacon gravy,

smoked-trout hash, and poached eggs to diners. Dinner is a more formal affair: char-grilled lamb with pomegranate-molasses glaze, steamed sugar-snap peas, and pan-seared potato cakes is a pleasure; the kicky starter of spicy Vietnamese squid salad with tamarind, garlic, and tomato over arugula is also fantastic. Mexican folk art and colorful tiles and murals by Oaxacan artist Leovigildo Martinez create a festive atmosphere. Try the communal table if you want to be seated in a hurry, although you should still expect a wait. ⊠ *121 Don Gaspar Ave.* ☎ *505/ 983–9340* ⊕ *www.pasquals.com* ⊟ *AE, MC, V.*

$$–$$$$ ✕ **La Casa Sena.** The Southwestern-accented and Continental fare served at La Casa Sena is beautifully presented if not consistently as delicious as it appears. Weather permitting, get a table on the patio surrounded by hollyhocks, flowering shrubs, and centuries-old adobe walls. Typical dishes include the chorizo-stuffed grilled pork tenderloin with roasted sweet-potato puree and peach–prickly pear sauce. There's a knockout lavender crème brûlée on the dessert menu. For a musical meal (evenings only), sit in the restaurant's adjacent, less-pricey Cantina, where the talented staff belt out Broadway show tunes. There's also a wine shop, which sells many of the estimable vintages offered on the restaurant's wine list. ⊠ *Sena Plaza, 125 E. Palace Ave.* ☎ *505/988–9232* ⊕ *www.lacasasena. com* ⊟ *AE, D, DC, MC, V.*

$$–$$$$ ✕ **Geronimo.** Chef Eric DiStefano changes the menu frequently at this **Fodor'sChoice** superb restaurant in the Borrego House, which dates from 1756. A typ-★ ical meal might start with seared Hudson Valley foie gras with candied ginger, sugared pecans, brioche French toast, and sundried-cranberry compote. Entrées are artful, like peppered elk tenderloin with applewood-smoked bacon, garlic-mashed potatoes, snap peas, and a brandy-mushroom sauce. The Sunday brunch is also impressive—try the provolone-and-spinach omelet with prosciutto-wrapped halibut and hollandaise sauce. The intimate, white dining rooms have beamed ceilings, wood floors, fireplaces, and cushioned *bancos*. In summer you can dine under the front portal; in winter the bar with fireplace is inviting. ⊠ *724 Canyon Rd.* ☎ *505/982–1500* ⊕ *www.geronimorestaurant. com* ⊟ *AE, MC, V* ⊗ *No lunch Mon.*

★ **$$–$$$** ✕ **Aqua Santa.** One of Santa Fe's longtime favorite chefs, Brian Knox helms the kitchen at this tiny, informal storefront café that happens to serve some of the finest and most inventive food in town. Diners can watch the chef work his wonders in the open kitchen, where he conjures up such sophisticated, yet simple fare as panfried oysters with bitter honey and a balsamic reduction, Tuscan bean soup with white-truffle oil, and braised organic New Mexico lamb with olives and summer squash. Vanilla panna cotta with chocolate sauce and almonds is a representatively delicious dessert. There's an extensive, pricey wine list, too. ⊠ *451 W. Alameda St. (entrance off Water St.)* ☎ *505/982–6297* ⊟ *MC, V* ⊗ *Closed Sun. and Mon. No lunch Tues. or Sat.*

$$–$$$ ✕ **O'Keeffe Cafe.** This swanky but low-key restaurant at the Georgia O'Keeffe Museum turns out some of the most creative fare in town. This is much more than a typical museum café, although the lunches do make a great break following a jaunt through the museum. Dinner is the main event, however, showcasing such tempting and creative fare as sweetbreads with shallots and cherry demi-glace; cashew-encrusted mahimahi over garlic-mashed potatoes with a mango-citrus–butter sauce; and Colorado lamb chops with red chile–honey glaze; and mint-infused couscous. There's an expansive patio in back shaded by leafy trees. ✉ *217 Johnson St.* ☎ *505/946–1065* ⊕ *www.okeeffecafe.com* ▤ *AE, D, MC, V.*

$$–$$$ ✕ **Ristra.** This unprepossessing restaurant in the trendy Guadalupe District presents a first-rate menu of Southwestern-influenced country French cooking. You might start with chorizo-stuffed calamari with watercress and smoked-tomato sauce; roasted rack of lamb with couscous, minted tomatoes, preserved lemon, and Niçoise olives is a tempting main dish. Top off your meal with an almond-butter cake served with warm spiced apples and a mascarpone-caramel sauce. The wines are well selected, and the service is swift and courteous. Navajo blankets hang on stark white walls, and Pueblo pottery adorns the handful of niches. There's also a trendy cocktail bar with its own menu of lighter dishes. ✉ *548 Agua Fria St.* ☎ *505/982–8608* ⊕ *www.ristrarestaurant.com* ▤ *AE, MC, V* ☾ *No lunch.*

★ **$$–$$$** ✕ **Santacafé.** Minimalist elegance marks the interior of Santacafé, one of Santa Fe's vanguard "food as art" restaurants, two blocks north of the Plaza in the historic Padre Gallegos House. Seasonal ingredients are included in the inventive dishes, which might include Alaskan halibut with English peas, saffron couscous, capers, and preserved lemon. Shiitake-and-cactus spring rolls with ponzu sauce makes a terrific starter, as does the sublime crispy-fried calamari with a snappy lime-chile dipping sauce. The patio is a joy in summer, and the bar makes a snazzy spot to meet friends for drinks just about any time of year. If you're on a tight budget, consider the reasonably priced lunch menu. ✉ *231 Washington Ave.* ☎ *505/984–1788* ⊕ *www.santacafe.com* ▤ *AE, MC, V* ☾ *No lunch Sun.*

$$–$$$ ✕ **315 Restaurant & Wine Bar.** As if it were on a thoroughfare in Paris rather than on Old Santa Fe Trail, 315 has a Continental, white-tablecloth sophistication, but the offbeat wall art gives it a contemporary feel. Chef-owner Louis Moskow prepares refreshingly uncomplicated fare using organic vegetables and locally raised meats. Seasonal specialties on the ever-evolving menu might include basil-wrapped shrimp with apricot chutney and curry sauce, or grilled boneless lamb loin with crispy polenta, spring vegetables, and green peppercorn sauce. The garden patio opens onto the street scene. There's also a wine bar with an exceptional list of vintages. ✉ *315 Old Santa Fe Trail* ☎ *505/986–9190* ⊕ *www.315santafe.com* ▤ *AE, MC, V* ☾ *Closed Sun. No lunch Mon.*

$–$$$ ✕ **Amaya.** One of the better hotel restaurants in town, this handsome space inside the Hotel Santa Fe serves first-rate contemporary Southwestern fare. Consider a starter of panko-crusted calamari with jicama slaw, tequila-lime aioli, and balsamic syrup. Among main courses, try venison osso buco with quinoa risotto, root veggies, and a port wine reduction, or oven-roasted game hen with red-chile-honey glaze and apple-sage stuffing. Amaya also presents several Native American–inspired dishes, including a mixed grill platter featuring marinated elk loin, mint-crusted lamb chop, buffalo sausage, and orange-ginger duck. Dine on the shaded patio in warm weather. ✉ *1501 Paseo de Peralta* ☎ *505/982–1200* ⊕ *www.hotelsantafe.co* ▤ *AE, D, DC, MC, V.*

Eclectic

$–$$$ ✕ **Café San Estevan.** This place is perfect when you're seeking a restaurant with very good New Mexican and Continental fare, all of it prepared simply but with ultrafresh, in many cases organic, ingredients and superb presentation. The small and rather noisy dining room is charming nonetheless, with some tables facing a corner fireplace. The poblano chiles rellenos here are superb, stuffed with cheese and onions and served with rice and *calabacitas* (a kind of squash). Also top-notch is the New Mexico organic lamb loin chops with a rosemary demi-glace and sautéed green beans. Chef-owner Estevan Garcia puts on a great show. ⊠ *428 Agua Fria St.* ☎ *505/995–1996* 🖃 *AE, D, MC, V* ☉ *Closed Mon.*

$–$$$ ✕ **Pink Adobe.** Rosalea Murphy opened her restaurant in 1944, and the place still reflects a time when fewer than 20,000 people lived here. The intimate, rambling rooms of this late-17th-century house have fireplaces and artwork and are filled with conversation made over special-occasion meals. The ambience of the restaurant, rather than the mediocre food and spotty service, accounts for its popularity. The steak Dunigan, smothered in green chile sauce and mushrooms, and the savory shrimp Louisianne—fat and deep-fried crispy—are among the Continental, New Mexican, and New Orleans creole dishes served. The apple pie drenched in rum sauce is a favorite. Particularly strong margaritas are mixed in the adjacent Dragon Room bar. ⊠ *406 Old Santa Fe Trail* ☎ *505/983–7712* ⊕ *www.thepinkadobe.com* 🖃 *AE, D, DC, MC, V* ☉ *No lunch weekends.*

★ **¢–$$** ✕ **Plaza Café.** Run with homespun care by the Razatos family since 1947, this café has been a fixture on the Plaza since 1918. The decor—red leather banquettes, black Formica tables, tile floors, a coffered tin ceiling, and a 1940s-style service counter—hasn't changed much in the past half century. The food runs the gamut, from cashew mole enchiladas to New Mexico meat loaf to Mission-style burritos, but the ingredients tend toward Southwestern. You'll rarely taste a better tortilla soup. You can cool it off with an old-fashioned ice cream treat from the soda fountain. All in all, it's a good stop for breakfast, lunch, or dinner. ⊠ *54 Lincoln Ave.* ☎ *505/982–1664* 🖎 *Reservations not accepted* 🖃 *AE, D, MC, V.*

¢–$ ✕ **Harry's Roadhouse.** This quirky, always-packed adobe compound
Fodor's Choice consists of several inviting rooms, from a diner-style space with counter
★ seating to a cozier nook with a fireplace—there's also an enchanting courtyard out back with juniper trees and flower gardens. The varied menu of contemporary diner favorites, pizzas, New Mexican fare, and bountiful salads is supplemented by a long list of daily specials. Favorites include smoked-chicken quesadillas and grilled-salmon tacos with tomatillo salsa and black beans. Desserts here are a revelation, from the chocolate pudding to the blueberry cobbler. ⊠ *Old Las Vegas Hwy., 1 mi south of Old Pecos Trail exit off I–25* ☎ *505/989–4629* 🖃 *AE, D, MC, V.*

¢ ✕ **Green Canteen.** An airy, art-filled restaurant with a handful of outdoor seats, this cheap and cheerful spot near the College of Santa Fe serves creative, organic food. The enormous salad of cherry tomatoes,

Calamata olives, avocado, Gorgonzola, hardboiled eggs, pumpkin seeds, and greens makes a delicious starter. Follow this with an avocado-Brie-mango quesadilla, or a burger topped with green chile and pepper-Jack cheese. There's also a nice selection of wraps, coffees, wines by the glass, and hot teas, but try the locally beloved (and also organic) Santa Fe Cider. It's right beside an independent film cinema in an otherwise nondescript shopping center. ☒ *1616–A St. Michael's Dr.* ☎ *505/424–6464* ▤ *AE, MC, V* ⊗ *Closed Sun.*

Indian

★ ¢–$$ ✕ **India Palace.** Even seasoned veterans of East Indian cuisine have been known to rate this deep-pink, art-filled restaurant among the best in the United States. The kitchen prepares fairly traditional recipes—tandoori chicken, lamb vindaloo, *saag paneer* (spinach with farmer's cheese), shrimp *biryani* (tossed with cashews, raisins, almonds, and saffron rice)—but the presentation is always flawless and the ingredients fresh. Meals are cooked as hot or mild as requested. Try the Indian buffet at lunch. ☒ *227 Don Gaspar Ave., enter from parking lot on Water St.* ☎ *505/986–5859* ▤ *AE, D, MC, V.*

Italian

$–$$$$ ✕ **Trattoria Nostrani.** This Italian trattoria earns kudos for such stellar fare as steak tartare with shaved asiago, braised baby octopus with soft polenta, and filet mignon with Tuscan vegetable ragu and fried pota-toes. The cozy dining room occupies a late-19th-century Territorial-style house a few blocks from the Plaza. Widespread complaints about the arrogant service seem to be the only drawback. ☒ *304 Johnson St.* ☎ *505/983–3800* ⊕ *www.trattorianostrani.com* ▤ *AE, DC, MC, V* ⊗ *Closed Sun. No lunch.*

★ $–$$ ✕ **Andiamo.** Produce from the farmers' market across the street adds to the seasonal surprises of this intimate northern Italian restaurant set in-side a romantic cottage. Start with the crispy polenta with rosemary and Gorgonzola sauce; move on to the white pizza with roasted garlic, fontina, grilled radicchio, pancetta, and rosemary; and consider such hearty entrées as crispy duck legs with grilled polenta, roasted turnips, and sautéed spinach. ☒ *322 Garfield St.* ☎ *505/995–9595* ⊕ *www.andiamoonline. com* ▤ *AE, DC, MC, V* ⊗ *No lunch.*

$ ✕ **Il Piatto.** Creative pasta dishes like pappardelle with braised duck-ling, caramelized onions, sun-dried tomatoes, and mascarpone-duck au jus, and homemade pumpkin ravioli with pine nuts and brown sage butter grace the menu here. Entrées include grilled salmon with spinach risotto and tomato-caper sauce, and a superb pancetta-wrapped trout with rosemary, wild mushrooms, and polenta. It's a crowded but nev-ertheless enjoyable trattoria with informal ambience, super-low prices, and a snug, urbane bar; the windows are dressed in frilly valances, and a mural of the Italian countryside lines one wall. ☒ *95 W. Marcy St.* ☎ *505/984–1091* ⊕ *www.ilpiattorestaurant.com* ▤ *AE, MC, V* ⊗ *No lunch weekends.*

Japanese

$–$$ ✕ **Izmi Sushi.** Santa Fe's sushi restaurants run the gamut from overpriced to mediocre, an exception being this unassuming strip-mall eatery a 10-minute drive south of the Plaza. Sushi options include surf clam, scallop, eel, toro, and soft-shell crab, but you can also order ginger beef, Korean barbecue, and a wide range of sushi and sashimi "chef's choice" assortments. Don't miss the New Mexico roll, with shrimp tempura, roasted green chile, bell pepper, and crab. ✉ *720 St. Michael's Dr.* ☎ *505/424–1311* ⊕ *www.izmisushi.com* ▤ *AE, D, MC, V* ☻ *Closed Sun. No lunch Sat.*

Latin

$–$$ ✕ **Los Mayas.** Owners Fernando Antillas and Reyes Solano brought the spirit of Latin America with them when they opened this restaurant. They've transformed a nondescript building into a cozy, tile-floored space with a patio. The menu mixes New Mexican, Latin American, and South American recipes. Try the charbroiled skirt steak and cheese rellenos with rice and black beans, or shrimp sautéed with butter and garlic. There's music every night, including flamenco on Saturday. ✉ *409 W. Water St.* ☎ *505/986–9930* ⊕ *www.losmayas.com* ▤ *AE, D, DC, MC, V* ☻ *No lunch.*

¢ ✕ **El Tesoro.** One of the Guadalupe District's better-kept secrets, this small café occupies the high-ceiling foyer of the Sanbusco Center, steps from several boutiques. The tiny kitchen turns out a mix of Central American, New Mexican, and American dishes, all of them using super-fresh ingredients. Grilled tuna tacos with salsa fresca, black beans, and rice; and Salvadorian chicken tamales wrapped in banana leaves are among the tastiest treats. El Tesoro also serves pastries, gelato, lemon bars, hot cocoa, and other snacks, making it a perfect break from shopping. ✉ *Sanbusco Market Center, 500 Montezuma Ave.* ☎ *505/988–3886* ▤ *MC, V* ☻ *No dinner.*

Mexican

¢–$$ ✕ **Bert's la Taqueria.** Salsa fans love this upbeat spot where chips are served with six varieties of the hot stuff. The long-running restaurant moved from a prosaic shopping center off St. Michael's Drive to a charming, historic adobe house in the Guadalupe District in spring 2006, greatly enhancing the dining ambience. Colorful paintings hang on the white-washed walls. The menu mixes the expected Mexican fare—enchiladas, soft tacos—with more unusual regional recipes, such as *chapulines* (grasshoppers—yes, you read that correctly—sautéed with garlic butter). ✉ *416 Agua Fria St.* ☎ *505/474–0791* ▤ *AE, MC, V* ☻ *Closed Sun.*

★ **¢** ✕ **Bumble Bee's Baja Grill.** A bright, new high-ceiling restaurant with closely spaced tables and bumble bee piñatas wafting overhead, Bumble Bee's has quickly delighted locals with its super-fresh Cal-Mex style food, including mahimahi tacos, mammoth burritos with a wide range of fillings, roasted chicken with cilantro-lime rice, and char-grilled trout platters. You order at the counter, grab some snacks from the salsa bar, and wait for your number to come up. There's live jazz on Saturday nights. Beer, wine, and Mexican soft drinks are served. The plastic flatware is a bit off-putting (it breaks easily), but otherwise, this place is a real find. ⊠ *301 Jefferson St.* ☎ *505/820–2862* ⊠ *3701 Cerrillos Rd.* ☎ *505/ 988–3278* ▭ *AE, D, MC, V.*

Middle Eastern

¢–$ ✕ **Cleopatra Cafe.** A quirky, order-at-the-counter Middle Eastern café inside the Design Center home-furnishings mall, Cleopatra serves up ultrafresh Egyptian, Lebanese, and Greek food at bargain prices. You might start with *besara* (fava beans with cilantro, garlic, fried onion, and pita bread). Popular entrées include the falafel plate, with hummus and tabouleh salad, and grilled organic-lamb kebabs with onions, bell peppers, rice, tahini, and Greek salad. Wine, beer, fresh-squeezed lemonade, and Turkish coffee are also offered. ⊠ *418 Cerrillos Rd.* ☎ *505/ 820–7381* ▭ *MC, V* ☾ *Closed Sun.*

New Mexican

$–$$ ✕ **Diego's Cafe.** You have to trek to the north side of downtown to sample some of the most authentic and spicy New Mexican food in Santa Fe. Once inside the cheery, casual dining room, you forget the location, especially when relaxing with one of the potent (even by local standards) margaritas. Best bets here include blue-corn enchiladas, bean-and-chicken-stuffed sopaipilla, posole, and outstanding chile rellenos. Service is typically quick and cheerful. ⊠ *DeVargas Center, 193 Paseo de Peralta* ☎ *505/983–5101* ▭ *MC, V.*

$–$$ ✕ **Gabriel's.** A great option near Pojoaque, perfect before the opera or on your way back to Santa Fe from points north, Gabriel's offers one of the best restaurant settings in the area: a spacious dining room with a Spanish-colonial theme, and a large flower-filled patio with candlelighted tables. The main event here is the guacamole, prepared with great fanfare table-side. The margaritas are also stellar. Main dishes—steak fajitas, crab enchiladas—are less memorable but still usually quite good, and service is friendly but uneven. ⊠ *U.S. 285/84, just north of Camel Rock Casino, 15 mi north of Santa Fe* ☎ *505/455–7000* ⊕ *www. gabrielsrestaurante.com* ▭ *AE, D, DC, MC, V.*

$–$$ ✕ **Maria's New Mexican Kitchen.** Maria's is proud to serve more than 100 kinds of margaritas. All but a few of the tequilas—many of which are quite rare—are 100% agave. This is also a reliable source of authentic New Mexican fare, including chiles rellenos, blue-corn enchiladas, and green-chile tamales. Strolling guitarists serenade the crowds most nights in this rustic space with a kiva fireplace and wood floors. ⊠ *555 W. Cordova Rd.* ☎ *505/983–7929* ⊕ *www.marias-santafe.com* ▭ *AE, D, DC, MC, V.*

¢–$$ ✕ **The Shed.** The lines at lunch attest to the status of this downtown New Mexican eatery. The rambling adobe dating from 1692 is decorated with folk art, and service is downright neighborly. Even if you're a devoted green chile sauce fan, try the locally grown red chile the place is famous for. Specialties include red-chile enchiladas, green-chile stew with potatoes and pork, posole, and charbroiled Shedburgers. The homemade desserts are fabulous. There's a full bar, too. ✉ *113½ E. Palace Ave.* ☎ *505/982–9030* 🍽 *AE, DC, MC, V* ☾ *Closed Sun. No dinner Mon.–Wed.*

¢–$ ✕ **Guadalupe Cafe.** Come to this informal café for hefty servings of New Mexican favorites like enchiladas and quesadillas, topped off with sopaipilla and honey, along with some dishes from other cultures, such as falafel and Asian dumplings stuffed with ginger pork. The seasonal raspberry pancakes are one of many breakfast favorites. Service can be brusque and the wait for a table considerable. ✉ *422 Old Santa Fe Trail* ☎ *505/982–9762* ⚑ *Reservations not accepted* 🍽 *AE, D, DC, MC, V* ☾ *Closed Mon. No dinner Sun.*

¢–$ ✕ **La Choza.** The far-less touristy, harder-to-find, and less expensive sister to the Shed, La Choza arguably serves even better New Mexican fare. **Fodor'sChoice** Chicken or pork *carne adovada* burritos, white clam chowder spiced ★ with green chiles, huevos rancheros, and wine margaritas are specialties. The dining rooms are dark and cozy, with vigas set across the ceiling and local art on the walls. The staff is friendly and competent. ✉ *905 Alarid St., near Cerrillos Rd. at St. Francis Dr.* ☎ *505/982–0909* 🍽 *AE, DC, MC, V* ☾ *Closed Sun.*

Pan-Asian

★ $–$$ ✕ **Kasasoba.** Maybe the best all-around Asian restaurant in Santa Fe, this intimate, classy eatery behind the Sanbusco Center has just a handful of tables and specializes in Japanese small plates and noodle dishes. The *zaru soba* (cold buckwheat noodles with nori, wasabi, spring onions, and a dashi-shoyu dipping sauce) with tempura vegetables and shrimp is heavenly, as is sake-steamed striped bass with enoki mushrooms. Uni-crusted sea scallops and a handful of creative maki sushi rolls round out the menu, and there's a short but well-chosen wine list. ✉ *544 Agua Fria St.* ☎ *505/984–1969* 🍽 *AE, MC, V* ☾ *No lunch.*

$–$$ ✕ **Mu Du Noodles.** This warm and cozy eatery on an unfortunately busy stretch of Cerrillos Road excels both in its friendly and helpful staff and its superb pan-Asian fare. Book ahead on weekends—this place fills up fast. You can count on some great dinner specials each night, too. Sample sweet-and-sour rockfish with water chestnuts, smoked bacon, and jasmine rice; Vietnamese spring rolls with peanut-hoisin sauce; and stir-fried tenderloin beef with whole scallions, sweet peppers, bean sprouts, and fat rice noodles. ✉ *1494 Cerrillos Rd.* ☎ *505/988–1411* ⊕ *www. mudunoodles.com* 🍽 *AE, MC, V* ☾ *Closed Sun. and Mon. No lunch.*

★ ¢–$$ ✕ **Jinja.** Although it's tucked in a shopping center on the north side, a short drive from the Plaza, Jinja is worth the trip for its extremely tasty and creative Asian fare. Specialties include flash-fried calamari with a light mint-lime sauce; Singapore noodles with barbecue pork, chopped peanuts, cilantro, and yellow curry; and Ten Tigers (ten lemongrass-marinated, grilled tiger prawns over fried rice with pineapple salsa and cucumber salad). The sashimi tuna with ginger is another star. The dining room is hip and attractive, and there's a swanky little bar off to one side, perfect for dining alone. A new branch opened in Albuquerque in fall 2006. ✉ *510 N. Guadalupe St.* ☎ *505/982–4321* 🍽 *AE, D, MC, V.*

Pizza

★ ¢–$$ ✕ **Rooftop Pizzeria.** Santa Fe got its first truly sophisticated pizza parlor in 2006 with the opening of this slick indoor-outdoor restaurant atop the Santa Fe Arcade. The kitchen here scores high marks for its rich and imaginative pizza toppings: consider the one topped with lobster, shrimp, mushrooms, apple-smoked bacon, caramelized leeks, truffle oil, Alfredo sauce, and four cheeses on a blue-corn crust. Antipasti and salads are impressive, too, as there's a wonderful smoked-duck confit–and–peppercorn spread, or the smoked-salmon Caesar salad. There's also an extensive beer and wine list. Although the Santa Fe Arcade's main entrance is on the Plaza, it's easier to access the restaurant from the arcade's Water Street entrance, a few doors up from Don Gaspar Avenue. ✉ *60 E. San Francisco St.* ☎ *505/984–0008* ▭ *AE, D, MC, V.*

Seafood

¢–$ ✕ **Mariscos la Playa.** Yes, even in landlocked Santa Fe, it's possible to find incredibly fresh and well-prepared seafood served in big portions. This no-frills restaurant surrounded by strip malls is just a short hop south of downtown and serves up absolutely delicious shrimp wrapped in bacon with Mexican cheese. One of the most famous dishes is *caldo vuelve a la vida,* a hearty soup of shrimp, octopus, scallops, clams, crab, and calamari. There's also shrimp soup in a tomato broth, fresh oysters on the half shell, and grilled salmon with pico de gallo. ✉ *537 W. Cordova St.* ☎ *505/982–2790* ▭ *AE, D, MC, V* ☻ *Closed Tues.*

Southwestern

$–$$ ✕ **Señor Lucky at the Palace.** The owners and chef of Geronimo operate this celebration of cowboy kitsch and Santa Fe chic—the dining room is painted with dramatic cowboy murals and filled with Western Americana. Specialties from the lengthy menu range from the light and simple (Caesar salad with achiote grilled chicken, sweet-corn tortilla soup) to the hearty and complex (two sweet-and-hot-grilled quail with jicama cabbage slaw, grilled red-chile pork chops with cheddar-mashed potatoes). There's also a lavish cocktail menu, great desserts (try the ice cream sandwich version of a peanut-butter-and-jelly sandwich), and extensive wine list. Señor Lucky's is nothing if not original. ✉ *142 W. Palace Ave.* ☎ *505/982–9891* ⊕ *www.senorluckys.com* ▭ *AE, D, DC, MC, V.*

Spanish

$$–$$$$ ✕ **El Farol.** In this crossover-cuisine town, owner David Salazar sums up his food in one word: "Spanish." Order a classic entrée like paella or make a meal from the nearly 30 different tapas—from tiny fried squid to wild mushrooms. Dining is indoors and out. Touted as the oldest continuously operated restaurant in Santa Fe, El Farol (built in 1835) has a relaxed ambience, a unique blend of the western frontier and contemporary Santa Fe. People push back the chairs and start dancing at around 9:30. The restaurant books outstanding live entertainment,

mostly blues and jazz, and there's usually a festive flamenco performance weekly. ✉ *808 Canyon Rd.* ☎ *505/983–9912* ⊟ *D, DC, MC, V* ☺ *No lunch Mon. and Tues.*

★ **$$–$$$** ✕ **El Mesón.** This place is as fun for having drinks and tapas or catching live music (from tango nights to Sephardic music) as for enjoying a full meal. The dignified dining room with an old-world feel has simple

> **WORD OF MOUTH**
>
> "Great music, great food, great wine list. Eat as much or as little as you want! You can have tapas or a full entree. Great for trying a bunch of different things."
> –Annie, on Mesón

dark-wood tables and chairs, white walls, and a wood-beam ceiling—unpretentious yet elegant. Livelier but still quite handsome is the Chispa bar. Tapas include Serrano ham and fried red potatoes with garlic aioli. Among the more substantial entrées are a stellar paella as well as cannelloni stuffed with veal, smothered with béchamel sauce, and served with manchego cheese au gratin. ✉ *213 Washington Ave.* ☎ *505/983–6756* ⊟ *AE, MC, V* ☺ *Closed Sun. and Mon. No lunch.*

Steak

$–$$$$ ✕ **Vanessie.** This classy, lodgelike space with high ceilings and a tremendously popular piano cabaret serves hefty portions of well-prepared chops and seafood. New Zealand rack of lamb, tenderloin of elk, and dry-aged steaks are among the specialties. There's lighter fare—burgers, onion loaf, salads—served in the piano bar, where noted musicians Doug Montgomery and Charles Tichenor perform classical and Broadway favorites well into the evening (no cover). ✉ *434 W. San Francisco St.* ☎ *505/982–9966* ⊕ *www.vanessiesantafe.com* ⊟ *AE, DC, MC, V* ☺ *No lunch.*

Thai

¢–$ ✕ **Thai Cafe.** Thai restaurants haven't enjoyed a great deal of success in Santa Fe over the years, but this intimate, warmly lighted space a few blocks from the Plaza has earned consistent praise since it opened in 2005. The aroma of authentic spices fills this art-filled adobe dining room with wide-plank floors, orange walls, and beam ceilings. Here patrons savor such tempting starters as *Tom Ka Gai* (coconut-milk soup with chicken, lemongrass, galangal) and Thai beef salad. Stars among the main dishes include grilled salmon with sweet-and-sour sauce, the seafood mix stir-fried with red curry and pineapple sauce, and stir-fried broccoli with garlic. The kitchen is quite liberal with spices, so ask them to tone down the heat if you're sensitive to such things. ✉ *329 W. San Francisco St.* ☎ *505/982–3886* ⊟ *AE, DC, MC, V* ☺ *Closed Mon.*

WHERE TO STAY

In Santa Fe you can ensconce yourself in quintessential Santa Fe style or anonymous hotel-chain decor, depending on how much you want to spend—the city has costlier accommodations than anywhere in the

Where to
Stay & Eat in
Greater Santa Fe

0   1/2 mile

0   1 km

See Detail Maps:
Where to Stay in
Downtown Santa Fe
Where to Eat in
Downtown Santa Fe

TO
TAOS, ESPAÑOLA

84/
285

1 ①

N. Guadalupe St.

Paseo

San Francisco St.

W. Alameda St.

Old
Santa Fe
Station

Sandoval St.

Guadalupe St.

Galisteo St.

Hickox St.

Cerrillos Rd.

Don Diego Ave.

St. Francis Dr.

Cordova Rd.

Don C

W. Alameda St.

Santa Fe River

Agua Fria St.

3

Osage Rd.

5

Galisteo St.

14

7

8

9

4 5

6

College
of Santa Fe

6 7

St. Michael's Dr.

10

11

8

St. Michael's Dr.

Butoph Rd.

Llano St.

Calle Lorca

84/
285

TO TURQUOISE TRAIL

Siringo Rd.

St. Francis Dr.

Calle Pintora

Yucca St.

Zia Rd.

TO ALBUQUERQUE

Restaurants ▼

Hotels & Campgrounds ▼

Southwest. Cheaper options are mostly on the southern reaches of Cerrillos (pronounced sah-*ree*-yos) Road, a dreadful, traffic-clogged strip. Quality varies greatly on Cerrillos, but some of the best-managed, most attractive properties are (from most to least expensive) the Holiday Inn, the Courtyard Marriott, and the Motel 6. You pay more the closer you are to the Plaza, but for many visitors it's worth it to be within walking distance of many attractions. Some of the best deals are offered by B&Bs—many of those near the Plaza offer much better values than the big, touristy hotels. Rates drop, often from 30% to 50%, from November to April (excluding Thanksgiving and Christmas).

In addition to the usual array of inns and hotels here, Santa Fe has a wide range of **long- and short-term vacation rentals,** some of them available through the **Management Group** (☎ 866/982–2823 ⊕ www.santaferentals.com). Rates generally range from $100 to $300 per night for double-occupancy units, with better values at some of the two- to four-bedroom properties. Most have fully stocked kitchens. Another route is to rent a furnished condo or casita at one of several compounds geared to travelers seeking longer stays. The best of these is the luxurious **Campanilla Compound** (☎505/988–7585 or 800/828–9700 ⊕www.campanillacompound.com), on a hill just north of downtown; rates run from about $1,400 to $1,800 per week in summer. Another good, similarly priced bet is **Fort Marcy Suites** (☎ 505/988–2800 or 888/600–4990 ⊕ www.fortmarcy.com), on a bluff just northeast of the Plaza with great views. The individually furnished units accommodate two to six guests and come with full kitchens, wood fireplaces, VCRs, and CD stereos—these can be rented nightly or weekly.

WHAT IT COSTS				
$$$$	$$$	$$	$	¢
HOTELS over $260	$190–$260	$130–$190	$70–$130	under $70

Prices are for a standard double room in room in high season, excluding 13.5%–14.5% tax.

Downtown Vicinity

$$$$
Fodor'sChoice
★

▣ **Inn of the Anasazi.** Unassuming from the outside, this first-rate boutique hotel is one of Santa Fe's finest, with superb architectural detail. The prestigious Rosewood Hotel group took over the property in 2005, carefully upgrading the already sumptuous linens and furnishings. Each room has a beamed viga-and-latilla ceiling, kiva-style gas fireplace, antique Indian rugs, handwoven fabrics, and organic toiletries (including sunblock). Other amenities include full concierge services, twice-daily maid service, exercise bikes upon request, and a library. An especially nice

> **WORD OF MOUTH**
>
> "The rooms (keep in mind that we are very picky) are very nice, upscale, cozy and have very authentic New Mexico charm. The kiva fireplaces are great."
>
> –Dawn, on Inn of the Anasazi

2

touch in this desert town are the humidifiers in each guest room. A few deluxe rooms have balconies. The staff is thorough, gracious, and highly professional. The restaurant, under the helm of acclaimed chef Martín Rios, is one of the best in New Mexico. ⊠ *113 Washington Ave., 87501* ☎ *505/988–3030 or 800/688–8100* ☒ *505/988–3277* ⊕ *www. innotheanasazi.com* ⬅ *57 rooms* ⚒ *Restaurant, in-room safes, mini-bars, cable TV, in-room VCRs, Wi-Fi, bar, library, business services, park-ing (fee), some pets allowed (fee)* ⊟ *AE, D, DC, MC, V.*

$$$$
Fodor's Choice
★
🏨 **Inn of the Five Graces.** The Garrett hotel group took over what had been a fading property in 2003 and transformed it into a sumptuous hotel with an East-meets-West design that pleases most guests but dif-fers from the usual, ubiquitous Santa Fe style. The suites have Asian and Latin American antiques and art, kilim rugs, jewel-tone throw pillows, and mosaic-tile bathrooms; most have fireplaces, and many have soak-ing tubs or walk-in steam showers. The personal service really stands out: dream catchers and ghost stories are left on your pillow, refriger-ators are stocked, and afternoon margarita and wine-and-cheese spreads, an exquisite breakfast, and even daily walking tours are all available. ⊠ *150 E. DeVargas St., 87501* ☎ *505/992–0957 or 866/992–0957* ☒ *505/955–0549* ⊕ *www.fivegraces.com* ⬅ *22 suites* ⚒ *Some kitch-enettes, refrigerators, cable TV, Wi-Fi, massage, free parking, some pets allowed (fee)* ⊟ *AE, MC, V* ⦿ *BP.*

$$$–$$$$
🏨 **Inn at Loretto.** This plush, oft-photographed, ancient pueblo–inspired property attracts a loyal clientele, many of whom swear by the friendly staff and high decorating standards. The lobby opens up to the gardens and pool, and leather couches and high-end architectural details make the hotel a pleasure to relax in. Rooms are among the largest of any down-town property and contain vibrantly upholstered handcrafted furnish-ings and sumptuous slate-floor bathrooms—many have large balconies overlooking downtown. The restaurant, Baleen, serves estimable, cre-ative Southwestern fare. SpaTerre offers a wide range of Balinese and Thai-style treatments and services. ⊠ *211 Old Santa Fe Trail, 87501* ☎ *505/988–5531 or 800/727–5531* ☒ *505/984–7988* ⊕ *www. hotelloretto.com* ⬅ *134 rooms, 5 suites* ⚒ *Restaurant, cable TV, pool, health club, spa, lounge, shops, business services, meeting rooms, park-ing (fee)* ⊟ *AE, D, DC, MC, V.*

$$$–$$$$
🏨 **La Fonda.** History and charm are more prevalent in this sole Plaza-front hotel than first-class service and amenities. The pueblo-inspired structure was built in 1922 and enlarged many times. Antiques and Na-tive American art decorate the tiled lobby, and each room has hand-dec-orated wood furniture, wrought-iron light fixtures, beamed ceilings, and high-speed wireless. Some suites have fireplaces. The 14 rooftop rooms are the most luxurious and include Continental breakfast and private concierge services; there's also an exercise room, garden, and outdoor hot tub there. La Plazuela Restaurant, with its hand-painted glass tiles, serves good and creative

> **WORD OF MOUTH**
>
> "A great historic hotel. We had a basic room for one night and it was fine."
>
> –Sheila on La Fonda

Where to Stay in Downtown Santa Fe

TO TAOS, ESPAÑOLA

National Cemetery

Fort Marcy Park

84/285

Guadalupe St.

Paseo de Peralta

Bishop's Lodge Rd.

Artist Rd. 475

Kearney Ave.

Old Taos Hwy.

S. Federal

W. San Francisco St.

McKenzie St.

Otero St.

W. Alameda St.

Johnson St.

W. Water St.

Grant St.

Sheridan St.

Lincoln Ave.

Washington Ave.

E. Marcy Ave.

Nussbaum St.

E. San Francisco St.

E. Water St.

Cathedral Pl.

Paseo de Peralta

Palace Ave.

Agua Fria

W. De Vargas

Aztec St.

Montezuma Ave.

Sandoval St.

E. Alameda St.

Santa Fe River

Garfield St.

S. Capitol St.

E. De Vargas

Delgado St.

Guadalupe St.

Read St.

Hickox St.

Old Santa Fe Trail

Acequia Madre Rd.

Cerrillos Rd.

Galisteo St.

Buena Vista St.

Don Gaspar Ave.

Garcia St.

Don Diego Ave.

E. Berger St.

0   500 yards

0   500 meters

Southwestern food. Folk and Latin jazz bands rotate nightly in the bar. ⊠ *100 E. San Francisco St., 87501* ☎ *505/982–5511 or 800/523–5002* 🖷 *505/988–2952* ⊕ *www.lafondasantafe.com* ➲ *143 rooms, 24 suites* ♨ *Restaurant, cable TV, Wi-Fi, pool, gym, 3 hot tubs, pool, massage, 2 bars, laundry service, concierge, business services, meeting rooms, parking (fee)* ☰ *AE, D, DC, MC, V.*

$$$–$$$$ 🏨 **La Posada de Santa Fe Resort and Spa.** Rooms here vary, from cozy to high-ceiling to dark and simple, although ongoing renovations and upgrades continue to enhance all rooms, many of which have fireplaces, flat-screen TVs, CD players leather couches, Spanish-tile bathrooms, and Navajo-inspired rugs. Many accommodations are in an adobe complex surrounding the main building; those in the older casitas, though capturing vintage Santa Fe's artsy charm, lack the newer units' plush feel. The main building contains a handful of high-ceiling Victorian rooms with marble-accent bathrooms. The real stars here are the bar, spa, and common areas, including the Staab House Lounge. The hotel's location, just blocks from the Plaza, is ideal. Fuego restaurant specializes in excellent world-beat contemporary fare. ⊠ *330 E. Palace Ave., 87501* ☎ *505/986–0000 or 866/331–7625* 🖷 *505/982–6850* ⊕ *www. laposadadesantafe.com* ➲ *120 rooms, 39 suites* ♨ *Restaurant, cable TV, Wi-Fi, pool, health club, spa, bar, business services, meeting rooms, parking (fee)* ☰ *AE, D, DC, MC, V.*

$$$– 🏨 **Las Palomas.** It's a pleasant 10-minute walk west of the Plaza to reach this property, which consists of two historic, luxurious compounds, one of them Spanish Pueblo–style adobe, the other done in the Territorial style, with a Victorian ambience. A network of brick paths shaded by mature trees leads past the casitas, connecting them with secluded courtyards and flower gardens. Each casita has a bedroom, full kitchen, living room with pull-out sofa, and fireplace, and each opens onto a terrace or patio. Locally handcrafted wooden and leather sofas, desks, and tables fill these spacious accommodations, along with Native American artwork and sculptures. It's an elegant alternative to the city's upscale full-service hotels, affording guests a bit more privacy and the feel of a private cottage rental. ⊠ *460 W. San Francisco St., 87501* ☎ *505/982–5560 or 877/982–5560* 🖷 *505/982–5562* ⊕ *www. laspalomas.com* ➲ *38 units* ♨ *Kitchens, cable TV, in-room VCRs, Wi-Fi, health club, playground* ℗ *CP.*

$$–$$$$ 🏨 **Eldorado Hotel & Spa.** Because it's the closest thing Santa Fe has to a convention hotel, the Eldorado sometimes gets a bad rap, but it's actually quite inviting, with individually decorated rooms, a generally helpful staff, and stunning mountain views. Rooms are stylishly furnished with carved Southwestern-style desks and chairs, large upholstered club chairs, and art prints; many have terraces or kiva-style fireplaces. The rooftop pool and gym are great fun, and there's music nightly, from classical Spanish guitar to piano, in the comfortable lobby lounge. A full slate of treatments, from Vichy rain showers to High Mesa salt scrubs, are offered by the hotel's luxe Nidah Spa. The hotel also rents out a number of casitas and suites in a pair of smaller, nearby buildings, the Casapueblo Inn and Zona Rosa—these are more intimate and private, and some have full kitchens. ⊠ *309 W. San Francisco St., 87501* ☎ *505/988–4455 or 800/955–4455* ᵬ *505/995–4555* ⊕ *www.eldoradohotel.com* ⇨ *201 rooms, 18 suites, 41 apartments, 10 condos* ⚫ *2 restaurants, room service, some kitchens, cable TV with movies, Wi-Fi, pool, health club, hot tub, massage, sauna, spa, bar, lounge, shops, laundry service, concierge, business services, meeting rooms, parking (fee)* ⊟ *AE, D, DC, MC, V.*

★ **$$–$$$$** 🏨 **Inn on the Alameda.** Near the Plaza and Canyon Road is one of the Southwest's best small hotels. Alameda means "tree-lined lane," and this one perfectly complements the inn's location by the gurgling Santa Fe River. The adobe architecture and enclosed courtyards strewn with climbing rose vines combine a relaxed New Mexico country atmosphere with the luxury and amenities of a top-notch hotel, from afternoon wine and cheese to free local and toll-free calls to triple-sheeted beds with 300-count Egyptian bedding. Rooms have a Southwestern color scheme, handmade armoires and headboards, and ceramic lamps and tiles—many have patios and kiva fireplaces. The solicitous staff is first-rate. ⊠ *303 E. Alameda St., 87501* ☎ *505/984–2121 or 888/984–2121* ᵬ *505/986–8325* ⊕ *www.innonthealameda.com* ⇨ *59 rooms, 10 suites* ⚫ *Some refrigerators, cable TV, gym, hot tubs, massage, bar, library, laundry facilities, concierge, meeting rooms, free parking, some pets allowed (fee)* ⊟ *AE, D, DC, MC, V* ⏐❴⏐ *CP.*

> **WORD OF MOUTH**
>
> "The third floors rooms that opened out onto an adjoining balcony were perfect for our group. The staff was unbelievably helpful and friendly."
>
> –Linda on Inn on the Alameda

$$–$$$ 🏨 **Dancing Ground of the Sun.** This attractive compound of 1930s adobe casitas and guest rooms has saltillo-tile floors and handsome, locally made furnishings—aspen-and-willow chairs, Native American drums, and driftwood tables are among the many pieces that recall the region's Native American and Hispanic legacy. The casitas have fully stocked kitchens, and many other units have refrigerators, microwaves, and coffeemakers; many rooms have fireplaces. The inn is on the curve of a busy road that loops around the historic center of town—somewhat noisy, but ideal for access to both the Plaza and Canyon Road. ⊠ *711 Paseo de Peralta, 87501* ☎ *505/986–9797 or 888/600–4990* ᵬ *505/986–8082* ⊕ *www.dancingground.com* ⇨ *6 rooms, 5 casitas* ⚫ *Some kitchens, cable TV; no smoking* ⊟ *AE, MC, V* ⏐❴⏐ *CP.*

$$–$$$ 🏨 **El Farolito.** All the beautiful Southwestern and Mexican furniture in this small, upscale compound is custom-made, and all the art and photography original. Rooms are spacious with fireplaces and separate entrances; some are in their own little buildings. El Farolito has a peaceful downtown location, just steps from the capitol and a few blocks from the Plaza, and rooms are spacious and pleasant. Some have CD players. The same owners run the smaller Four Kachinas inn, which is close by and has one handicapped-accessible room (rare among smaller Santa Fe properties). The continental breakfast here is a real treat, featuring a tempting range of delicious baked goods. ⊠ *514 Galisteo St., 87501* ☎ *505/988–1631 or 888/634–8782* ⊕ *www.farolito.com* ⇆ *7 rooms, 1 suite* ⚲ *Cable TV, some in-room VCRs; no smoking* ⊟ *AE, D, MC, V* ⎮◎⎮ *CP.*

★ **$$–$$$** 🖳 **Inn of the Governors.** This rambling hotel by the Santa Fe River received a major makeover in 2004, and is staffed by a polite, enthusiastic bunch. Rooms have a Mexican theme, with bright colors, hand-painted folk art, feather pillows, Southwestern fabrics, and handmade furnishings; deluxe rooms also have balconies and fireplaces. Perks include a complimentary tea and sherry social each afternoon and a quite extensive breakfast buffet along with free Wi-Fi and newspapers. New Mexican dishes and lighter fare like wood-oven pizzas

> **WORD OF MOUTH**
>
> "The location was great. The breakfast buffet was also wonderful. A friendly place."
> –Nancy on Inn of the Governors

are served in the restaurant, Del Charro, which also books first-rate entertainers. ⊠ *101 W. Alameda St., 87501* ☎ *505/982–4333 or 800/234–4534* 🖷 *505/989–9149* ⊕ *www.innofthegovernors.com* ⇆ *100 rooms* ⚲ *Restaurant, room service, refrigerators, cable TV, Wi-Fi, pool, bar, concierge, business services, meeting rooms, free parking* ⊟ *AE, D, DC, MC, V* ⎮◎⎮ *BP.*

$$–$$$ 🖳 **Lodge at Santa Fe.** Rooms at this former Radisson have pleasant Southwestern furnishings and earth-tone fabrics, and higher-end condo units have full kitchens and one or two bedrooms. Renovations in recent years greatly enhanced the hotel's appearance, although service can be hit-or-miss. The hilltop location offers spectacular views cast toward the Sangre de Cristo Mountains and south toward the Sandias—but only from certain rooms, so ask when reserving. The Plaza is a five-minute drive, the Santa Fe Opera just a bit farther. Las Mañanitas restaurant serves decent Spanish and Southwestern fare, and the adjacent cabaret is home in summer to flamenco dancer Maria Benitez. Guests have free access to the Santa Fe Spa next door, which has a full health club. ⊠ *750 N. St. Francis Dr., 87501* ☎ *505/992–5800 or 888/563–4373* 🖷 *505/842–9863* ⊕ *www.buynewmexico.com* ⇆ *137 rooms, 4 suites, 6 condos* ⚲ *Restaurant, room service, cable TV, pool, hot tub, bar, meeting rooms, free parking* ⊟ *AE, D, DC, MC, V.*

$$–$$$ 🖳 **Water Street Inn.** The large rooms in this restored adobe 2½ blocks from the Plaza are decorated with reed shutters, antique pine beds, viga-beam ceilings, hand-stenciled artwork, and a blend of cowboy, Hispanic, and Native American art and artifacts. Most have fireplaces, and all have flat-screen TVs with DVD players and CD stereos. Afternoon hors d'oeuvres are served in the living room. A patio deck is available for relaxing. The one negative is that the inn overlooks a parking lot. ⊠ *427 W. Water St., 87501* ☎ *505/984–1193 or 800/ 646–6752* ⊕ *www.waterstreetinn.com* ⇆ *8 rooms, 4 suites* ⚲ *Cable TV, in-room DVDs, Wi-Fi, outdoor hot tub, free parking* ⊟ *AE, DC, MC, V* ⎮◎⎮ *CP.*

$–$$$ ☒ **Alexander's Inn.** This two-story 1903 Craftsman-style house in the Eastside residential area, a few blocks from the Plaza and Canyon Road, exudes the charm of an old country inn. Rooms are cozy and warm, with American country–style wooden furnishings, family heirlooms, skylights and tall windows, hand-stenciled walls, and dried-flower arrangements. The grounds are dotted with tulips, hyacinths,

and lilac and apricot trees. There's also a pair of two-story cottages with kitchens. The owners also run the seven-room Hacienda Nicholas ($$–$$$), a small adobe house done in Southwestern style and with a more upscale look, and the Madeleine Inn ($–$$$), a lacy Queen Anne house with eight rooms. Guests receive full access to El Gancho Health Club, a 15-minute drive away. ☒ *529 E. Palace Ave., 87501* ☎ *505/986–1431 or 888/321–5123* ⊕ *www.alexanders-inn.com* ☜ *5 rooms, 2 with shared bath; 2 cottages* ♿ *Some kitchens, cable TV, outdoor hot tub, free parking, some pets allowed (fee); no TV in some rooms, no kids under 12 (except in cottage)* ☐ *D, MC, V* ♱ *CP.*

★ **$–$$$** ☒ **Don Gaspar Inn.** One of the city's best-kept secrets, this exquisitely landscaped and decorated compound is on a pretty residential street a few blocks south of the Plaza. Its three historic houses have three distinct architectural styles: Arts and Crafts, Pueblo Revival, and Territorial. Floral gardens and aspen and cottonwood trees shade the tranquil paths and terraces, and both Southwest and Native American paintings and handmade furnishings enliven the sunny rooms and suites. The Arts and Crafts main house has two fireplaces, two bedrooms, and a fully equipped kitchen. Considering the setting and amenities, it's a great value. ☒ *623 Don Gaspar Ave., 87505* ☎ *505/986–8664 or 888/986–8664* 🖷 *505/986–0696* ⊕ *www.dongaspar.com* ☜ *5 rooms, 5 suites, 1 cottage* ♿ *Cable TV, some in-room hot tubs, some kitchens, refrigerators, free parking; no smoking* ☐ *AE, MC, V* ♱ *CP.*

$–$$$ ☒ **Hotel St. Francis.** Listed on the National Register of Historic Places, this three-story building, parts of which were constructed in 1923, has walkways lined with turn-of-the-20th-century lampposts and is one block south of the Plaza. The simple, elegant rooms with high ceilings, casement windows, brass-and-iron beds, marble and cherry antiques, and original artworks suggest a refined establishment, but the service can be spotty and many of the rooms (and especially bathrooms) are quite tiny. Afternoon tea, with scones and finger sandwiches, is served daily (not complimentary) in the huge lobby, which rises 50 feet from a floor of blood-red tiles. The hotel bar is among the few places in town where you can grab a bite to eat until midnight. ☒ *210 Don Gaspar Ave., 87501* ☎ *505/983–5700 or 800/529–5700* 🖷 *505/989–7690* ⊕ *www.hotelstfrancis.com* ☜ *80 rooms, 2 suites* ♿ *Restaurant, room service, refrigerators, cable TV, Wi-Fi, bar, gym, laundry service, concierge, business services, meeting rooms, parking (fee)* ☐ *AE, D, DC, MC, V.*

2

★ **$–$$$** ☒ **Inn of the Turquoise Bear.** In the 1920s, poet Witter Bynner played host to an eccentric circle of artists and intellectuals, as well as some wild parties in his mid-19th-century Spanish–Pueblo Revival home, which is now a B&B. Rooms are simple but have plush linens. The inn's style preserves the building's historic integrity, and there's plenty of ambience and a ranchlike lobby. You might sleep in the room where D. H. Lawrence slept, or perhaps Robert Oppenheimer's room. The terraced flower gardens provide plenty of places to repose, away from the traffic on Old Santa Fe Trail, which borders the property. This is the quintessential Santa Fe inn. ☒ *342 E. Buena Vista, 87501* ☎ *505/983– 0798 or 800/396–4104* 🖷 *505/988–4225* ⊕ *www.turquoisebear.com* ➟ *8 rooms, 2 with shared bath; 2 suites* ⚹ *Cable TV, in-room VCRs, library, free parking* ▤ *AE, D, MC, V* ⦿ *CP.*

$–$$$ ☒ **La Tienda Inn and Duran House.** This is an offbeat but charming lodging option that comprises a former neighborhood market and adjacent Territorial-style abode house (which together make up La Tienda) as well as second Territorial-style house down the street (Duran House). Rooms throughout are exquisitely furnished with well-chosen country, folk, Southwestern, and Victorian antiques and fine linens and Navajo rugs—the look is refreshingly uncluttered, and some rooms have private patios and kiva fireplaces. The substantial Continental breakfast is served in a flowery garden courtyard in warm weather and in the common room fashioned out of the old market during the cooler months. ☒ *445–447 W. San Francisco St., 87501* ☎ *505/989–8259 or 800/889–7611* ⊕ *www.latiendabb.com* ➟ *11 rooms* ⚹ *Refrigerators, cable TV, free parking* ▤ *MC, V* ⦿ *CP.*

$$ ☒ **Hotel Santa Fe.** Picurís Pueblo has controlling interest in this handsome Pueblo-style three-story hotel on the Guadalupe District's edge and a short walk from the Plaza. The light, airy rooms and suites are traditional Southwestern, with locally handmade furniture, wooden blinds, and Pueblo paintings; many have balconies. The hotel gift shop, Santa Fe's only tribally owned store, has lower prices than many nearby retail stores. The 35 rooms and suites in the posh Hacienda wing have corner fireplaces and the use of a London-trained butler. Amaya is one of the better hotel restaurants in town. Informal talks about Native American history and culture are held in the lobby, and Native American dances take place May–October. ☒ *1501 Paseo de Peralta, 87505* ☎ *505/ 982–1200 or 800/825–9876* 🖷 *505/984–2211* ⊕ *www.hotelsantafe.com* ➟ *40 rooms, 91 suites* ⚹ *Restaurant, some microwaves, cable TV, pool, outdoor hot tub, massage, bar, laundry service, concierge, meeting rooms, free parking* ▤ *AE, D, DC, MC, V.*

Fodor's Choice
★

$$ ☒ **Pueblo Bonito B&B Inn.** Rooms in this 1873 adobe compound have handmade and hand-painted furnishings, Navajo weavings, brick and hardwood floors, sand paintings and pottery, locally carved santos, and Western art. All have kiva fireplaces and private entrances, and many have kitchens. Breakfast is served in the main dining room. Afternoon tea also offers complimentary margaritas. The Plaza is a five-minute walk away. ☒ *138 W. Manhattan Ave., 87501* ☎ *505/984–8001 or 800/461– 4599* 🖷 *505/984–3155* ⊕ *www.pueblobonitoinn.com* ➟ *13 rooms, 5 suites* ⚹ *Dining room, some kitchens, some refrigerators, cable TV, hot tub, laundry facilities, free parking; no smoking* ▤ *AE, DC, MC, V* ⦿ *CP.*

$–$$ ⊞ **Garrett's Desert Inn.** This sprawling, U-shape motor court may surround a parking lot and offer relatively little in the way of ambience, but it's well maintained and has an outstanding location a few blocks from the Plaza, smack in the middle of historic Barrio de Analco. The clean, no-frills rooms are done in earthy tones with a smattering of Southwest touches, and there's a pleasant pool and patio as well as an inviting bar that serves cocktails and light food and has a pool table. For the price and location, this is a real find. ⊠ *311 Old Santa Fe Trail, 87501* ☎ *505/982–1851 or 800/888–2145* ⊕ *www.garrettsdesertinn.com* ➾ *83 rooms* ♿ *Restaurant, cable TV, pool, billiards, lounge, car rental, meeting rooms, free parking* ⊟ *AE, DC, MC, V* ⑩ *CP.*

$–$$ ⊞ **Inn on the Paseo.** This inn is on a busy road, but at least this stretch of Paseo de Peralta is two lanes wide and is in a semi-residential neighborhood a short walk from the Plaza. Rooms are fairly simple but clean and light, some with hardwood floors and all with pleasing Southwestern furnishings and color schemes—some have fireplaces and private patios. The staff is laid-back and friendly. Try to get a room away from the road to avoid traffic noise. The two historic main buildings are joined by a modern lobby with a pitched ceiling, where continental breakfast is served—in warm weather you can dine on the sundeck. ⊠ *630 Paseo de Peralta, 87501* ☎ *505/984–8200 or 800/457–9045* 🖷 *505/989–3979* ⊕ *www.innonthepaseo.com* ➾ *16 rooms, 2 suites* ♿ *Cable TV, free parking; no kids under 8, no smoking* ⊟ *MC, V* ⑩ *CP.*

★ **$–$$** ⊞ **Old Santa Fe Inn.** About four blocks south of the Plaza, in the hip Guadalupe District, this contemporary inn, which opened in 2001 and looks like an attractive, if fairly ordinary, adobe motel, has stunning and spotless rooms with elegant Southwestern furnishings. Tile baths, high-quality linens, and upscale furnishings fill every room, along with two phone lines and CD stereos; many have kiva fireplaces, or balconies and patios. It may not have the staff and all of amenities of a full-service hotel, but the rooms themselves are more inviting than several more-expensive downtown hotels, and the small business center and gym are open 24 hours. Most rooms open onto a gravel parking lot, although chile ristras hanging outside each unit brighten things up. The make-your-own-breakfast-burrito buffet is a nice touch. ⊠ *320 Galisteo St., 87501* ☎ *505/995–0800 or 800/745–9910* 🖷 *505/995–0400* ⊕ *www.oldsantafeinn.com* ➾ *34 rooms, 9 suites* ♿ *Some in-room hot tubs, some microwaves, some refrigerators, cable TV, in-room VCRs, Wi-Fi, gym, business services, free parking* ⊟ *AE, D, DC, MC, V* ⑩ *CP.*

¢–$ ⊞ **Santa Fe Sage Inn.** On the southern edge of the Guadalupe District, this motel offers affordable low-frills comfort and surprisingly attractive (given the low rates) Southwestern decor within walking distance of the Plaza (six blocks). Special packages are available for three- and four-day stays during peak-season events. Get a room in one of the rear buildings for the most privacy and quiet. There's an informal New Mexico restaurant on premises. ⊠ *725 Cerrillos Rd., 87501* ☎ *505/982–5952 or 866/433–0335* 🖷 *505/984–8879* ⊕ *www.santafesageinn.com* ➾ *162 rooms* ♿ *Restaurant, cable TV, Wi-Fi, pool, free parking, some pets allowed* ⊟ *AE, DC, MC, V* ⑩ *CP.*

South of Downtown

$$–$$$ ⊞ **Residence Inn.** This compound consists of clusters of three-story adobe town houses with pitched roofs and tall chimneys. Best bets for families or up to four adults traveling together are the one-room suites, which each have a loft bedroom and then a separate sitting area (with a curtain divider) that has a Murphy bed. All units have wood-burning fireplaces. It's right off a major intersection about 3 mi south of the Plaza, but it's set back far enough so that there's no traffic noise. Complimentary full breakfast, evening socials, and grocery-shopping service are provided. Ask for one of the second-floor end units for the best mountain views. ⊠ *1698 Galisteo St., 87505* ☎ *505/988–7300 or 800/331–3131* 🖷 *505/988–3243* ⊕ *www.residenceinn.com* ⇄ *120 suites* ⚶ *Dining room, kitchens, cable TV, Wi-Fi, meeting rooms, free parking* ☲ *AE, D, DC, MC, V* ⦿ *BP.*

$–$$ ⊞ **El Rey Inn.** The kind of place where Lucy and Ricky might have
Fodor'sChoice stayed during one of their cross-country adventures, the El Rey was built
★ in 1930s but has been brought gracefully into the 21st century, its rooms handsomely made over. Rooms are individually decorated and might include antique television armoires, beamed ceilings, upholstered wing chairs and sofas; some have kitchenettes. Bathrooms have been handsomely updated with glass brick and tile. Each unit has a small covered front patio with wrought-iron chairs. Towering shade trees loom over the parking lot, and there's a landscaped courtyard with tables and chairs by the pool. ⊠ *1862 Cerrillos Rd., 87505* ☎ *505/982–1931 or 800/521–1349* 🖷 *505/989–9249* ⊕ *www.elreyinnsantafe.com* ⇄ *79 rooms, 8 suites* ⚶ *Some kitchenettes, cable TV, pool, hot tubs, sauna, exercise equipment, playground, laundry facilities, free parking; no smoking* ☲ *AE, DC, MC, V* ⦿ *CP.*

> **WORD OF MOUTH**
>
> "El Rey is very charming and there's a nice free breakfast. I usually stay there, but you do have to drive down to the plaza area, find a place to park."   –jayne1973

$–$$ ⊞ **Santa Fe Courtyard by Marriott.** Of the dozens of chain properties along gritty Cerrillos Road, this is the only bona fide gem, even though it looks like all the others: clad in faux adobe and surrounded by parking lots and strip malls. Don't fret—it's easy to forget about the morose setting once inside this glitzy miniature resort, which comprises several buildings set around a warren of lushly landscaped interior courtyards. Rooms have the usual upscale-chain doodads: mini-refrigerators, coffeemakers, hair dryers, clock radios—there's also high-speed Internet. Aesthetically, the rooms look Southwestern, with chunky carved-wood armoires, desks, and headboards reminiscent of a Spanish-colonial hacienda. ⊠ *3347 Cerrillos Rd., 87505* ☎ *505/473–2800 or 800/777–3347* 🖷 *505/473–4905* ⊕ *www.santafecourtyard.com* ⇄ *213 rooms* ⚶ *Restaurant, room service, refrigerators, cable TV, Wi-Fi, pool, gym, hot tub, lounge, shop, laundry facilities, laundry service, business services, free parking* ☲ *AE, D, DC, MC, V.*

★ $ ▣ **Bobcat Inn.** A delightful, affordable, country hacienda that's a 15-minute drive southeast of the Plaza, this adobe B&B sits amid 10 secluded acres of piñon and ponderosa pine, with grand views of the Sangre de Cristos and the area's high-desert mesas—it's right beside the popular Bobcat Bite restaurant. John and Amy Bobrick run this low-key retreat and prepare expansive full breakfasts as well as high tea on Saturday during the summer high season (these are by reservation only). Arts and Crafts furniture and Southwest pottery fill the common room, in which breakfast is served and guests can relax throughout the day. The unpretentious rooms are brightened by Talvera tiles, folk art, and colorful blankets and rugs; some have kiva fireplaces. The Lodge Room is outfitted with handcrafted Adirondack furniture, and its bathroom has a whirlpool tub. ⊠ *442 Old Las Vegas Hwy., 87505* ☎ *505/988–9239* ⊕ *www.nm-inn.com* ➷ *5 rooms* ⚴ *Some in-room hot tubs, Wi-Fi, massage, free parking; no room TVs* ▭ *D, MC, V* ¶◎¶ *BP.*

$ ▣ **Camel Rock Suites.** Although this modern, affordable, all-suites property is operated by the Tesuque Pueblo north of Santa Fe, it's situated about 3 mi south of the Plaza, close to I–25 and behind a small shopping center with an Alberton's grocery store (handy, given the rooms' self-catering facilities). The curb appeal is nil, but it's still more pleasant in this part of town than along traffic-clogged Cerrillos Road, and the reasonable rates and pleasant rooms make this a great bet. Each unit has a separate sitting area, attractive hand-carved wood furniture, fully equipped kitchen, and either two double beds or a queen bed and twin pull-out sofa. An expanded breakfast buffet and organic coffee are included, and you can use the health club and pool at Genoveva Chavez Community Center, which is a 10-minute drive away. ⊠ *3007 St. Francis Dr. (entrance off Zia Rd.), 87505* ☎ *505/989–3600 or 877/989–3600* ▭ *505/989–1058* ⊕ *www.camelrocksuites.com* ➷ *120 suites* ⚴ *Kitchens, cable TV, laundry facilities, business services, some pets allowed, free parking* ▭ *AE, D, MC, V* ¶◎¶ *CP.*

¢ ▣ **Silver Saddle Motel.** Something of an exception to the mostly seedy and sketchy motels along Cerrillos Road, this low-slung adobe property transcends the genre, if barely. Sure, the carpets are a bit faded, the walls thin, the staff less than responsive, and Santa Fe's only strip club is across the street. But there's a kitschy, fun-loving swagger about the place. Most rooms are named for icons of the West (Annie Oakley, Wyatt Earp) and contain related plaques with colorful biographies. Furnishings range from motel drab to quirky Southwest: Talavera-tile bathrooms, serape tapestries, built-in bancos, and equipale chairs. The wildly popular home-furnishings and gift emporium, Jackalope, is next door. ⊠ *2810 Cerrillos Rd., 87505* ☎ *505/471–7663* ➷ *27 rooms* ⚴ *Some kitchenettes, cable TV, free parking* ▭ *AE, D, MC, V* ¶◎¶ *CP.*

North of Santa Fe

$$$–$$$$ ▣ **Bishop's Lodge Resort and Spa.** In a bucolic valley at the foot of the Sangre de Cristo Mountains, this 1918 resort is five minutes from the Plaza. Behind the main building is a chapel that was once Archbishop Jean Baptiste Lamy's retreat. Unfortunately, despite the interesting history, the resort has slipped in quality and service in recent years and could

greatly stand an overhaul, especially given the high rates. Outdoor activities include hiking, horseback riding, skeet-shooting, and trapshooting. The two lodge buildings have antique and reproduction Southwestern furnishings—shipping chests, Mexican tinwork, and Native American and Western art; most of the rooms, in the property's other buildings, have less character, though some have fireplaces. The lodge has fitness facilities and is home to the excellent ShàNah Spa. The serviceable but overpriced restaurant, specializing in inventive Nuevo Latino fare, serves Sunday brunch. ⊠ *Bishop's Lodge Rd., 2½ mi north of downtown, 87501* ☎ *505/983–6377 or 800/419–0492* ⊕ *www.bishopslodge.com* ⇨ *92 rooms, 19 suites* ☼ *2 restaurants, some refrigerators, cable TV, 2 tennis courts, pool, gym, hot tub, massage, spa, fishing, hiking, horseback riding, bar, children's programs (ages 4–12), business services, meeting rooms, airport shuttle, free parking* ☰ *AE, D, MC, V.*

$$$–$$$$
Fodor'sChoice
★

🏨 **Ten Thousand Waves.** Devotees appreciate the Zenlike atmosphere of this Japanese-style health spa and small hotel above town. Nine light and airy hillside cottages tumble down a piñon-covered hill below the first-rate spa, which is tremendously popular with day visitors. The sleek, uncluttered accommodations have marble or stone wood-burning fireplaces, CD stereos, fine woodwork, low-slung beds or futons, and courtyards or patios; two come with full kitchens. There's also a cozy, vintage Airstream Bambi trailer available at much lower rates ($99–$109 nightly)—it's a kitschy, fun alternative to the much pricier cottages. The facility has private and communal indoor and outdoor hot tubs and spa treatments. Overnight guests can use the communal tubs for free. The snack bar serves sushi and other healthful treats, and a restaurant is planned, somewhat tentatively, for the next few years, along with additional hotel rooms. ⊠ *3451 Hyde Park Rd., 4 mi northeast of the Plaza* ✉ *Box 10200, 87501* ☎ *505/982–9304* 🖷 *505/989–5077* ⊕ *www. tenthousandwaves.com* ⇨ *12 cottages, 1 trailer* ☼ *Snack bar, some kitchens, refrigerators, cable TV, some in-room VCRs, some Wi-Fi, outdoor hot tubs, spa, shop, free parking, some pets allowed (fee); no a/c, no TV in some rooms* ☰ *D, MC, V.*

Camping

🏕 **Los Campos RV Resort.** The only full-service RV park in town lies between a car dealership on one side and open vistas on the other. Poplars and Russian olive trees, a dry riverbed, and mountains rise in the background. ⊠ *3574 Cerrillos Rd.* ☎ *505/473–1949 or 800/852–8160* ☼ *Grills, flush toilets, full hookups, dump station, drinking water, guest laundry, picnic tables, electricity, public telephone, play area, swimming (pool)* ⇨ *95 sites* 🖻 *$30–$37* ☰ *MC, V.*

★ 🏕 **Rancheros de Santa Fe Campground.** This 22-acre camping park is on a hill in the midst of a piñon forest. Bring your tent or RV, or rent a cabin. You can get LP gas service here. Amenities include free Wi-Fi and cable TV hookups, nightly movies in summer, a hiking trail, a fenced-in dog run, and a recreation room. ⊠ *Old Las Vegas Hwy., Exit 290 from I–25, 10½ mi south of the Plaza* ☎ *505/466–3482 or 800/426–9259* ⊕ *www.rancheros.com* ☼ *Grills, flush toilets, full hookups, dump* station, drinking water, guest laundry, showers, picnic tables, electricity, public telephone, general store, play area, swimming (pool) 🏊 37 tent sites, 95 RV sites, 5 cabins 🏕 Tent sites $18–$20, water and electric hookups $24–$27, full hookups $28–$36, cabins $38–$44 ▤ MC, V ☉ Mid-Mar.–Oct.

🏕 **Santa Fe KOA.** In the foothills of the Sangre de Cristo Mountains, 20 minutes southeast of Santa Fe, this large campground with tent sites, RV sites, and cabins is covered with piñons, cedars, and junipers. Wi-Fi is available; activities include basketball, ring toss, video games, and free movies. ✉ Old Las Vegas Hwy., Box 95–A, 87505 ☎ 505/466–1419 or 800/562–1514 ⊕ www.koa.com/where/nm/31159.htm ⚿ Flush toilets, partial hookups (electric), drinking water, guest laundry, showers, fire grates, fire pits, picnic tables, electricity, public telephone, general store 🏊 44 RV sites, 26 tent sites, 10 cabins 🏕 Tent sites $25, RV sites $32–$38, cabins $42–$45 ▤ D, MC, V ☉ Mar.–Oct.

NIGHTLIFE & THE ARTS

Santa Fe ranks among America's most cultured small cities. Gallery openings, poetry readings, plays, and dance concerts take place year-round, not to mention the famed opera and chamber-music festivals. Check the arts and entertainment listings in Santa Fe's daily newspaper, the *New Mexican* (⊕ www.santafenewmexican.com), particularly on Friday, when the arts and entertainment section, "Pasatiempo," is included, or check the weekly *Santa Fe Reporter* (⊕ www.sfreporter.com) for shows and events. Activities peak in the summer.

Nightlife

Culturally endowed though it is, Santa Fe has a pretty mellow nightlife scene, its key strength being live music, which is presented at numerous bars, hotel lounges, and restaurants. Austin-based blues and country groups and other acts wander into town, and members of blockbuster bands have been known to perform unannounced at small clubs while vacationing in the area. But on most nights your best bet might be quiet cocktails beside the flickering embers of a piñon fire or under the stars out on the patio.

Catamount Bar (✉ 125 E. Water St. ☎ 505/988–7222) is popular with the postcollege set; jazz and blues-rock groups play on weekends and some weeknights. The dance floor is small, but there's a enjoyable second-story balcony with seating. This is the best place in town to shoot pool.

★ The **Cowgirl** (✉ 319 S. Guadalupe St. ☎ 505/982–2565) is one of the most popular spots in town for live blues, country, rock, folk, and even comedy, on occasion.

Dragon Room (✉ 406 Old Santa Fe Trail ☎ 505/983–7712), at the Pink Adobe restaurant, has been the place to see and be seen in Santa Fe for decades; flamenco and other light musical fare entertain at the packed bar.

Eldorado Court and Lounge (✉ 309 W. San Francisco St. ☎ 505/988-4455), in the lobby of the classy Eldorado Hotel, is a gracious lounge where classical guitarists and pianists perform nightly. It has the largest wines-by-the-glass list in town.

★ **El Farol** (✉ 808 Canyon Rd. ☎ 505/983-9912) restaurant is where locals like to hang out. The roomy, somewhat ramshackle bar area has an old Spanish–Western atmosphere, but you can order some fine Spanish brandies and sherries. On most nights you can listen to live flamenco, country, folk, or blues.

Evangelo's (✉ 200 W. San Francisco St. ☎ 505/982-9014) is an old-fashioned, smoky street-side bar, with pool tables, 200 types of imported beer, and rock bands on many weekends.

Rodeo Nites (✉ 2911 Cerrillos Rd. ☎ 505/473-4138) attracts a country-western crowd and lots of singles on the make. It can get a bit rough in the wee hours, so get here on the early side for line dancing and some very hot two-stepping.

Second Street Brewery (✉ 1814 2nd St. ☎ 505/982-3030), a short drive south of downtown, packs in an eclectic bunch for outstanding microbrewed ales, pretty good pub fare, and live rock and folk. There's an expansive patio, and the staff is friendly.

★ **Swig** (✉ 135 W. Palace Ave., Level 3 ☎ 505/955-0400), Santa Fe's trendiest upscale lounge, has developed a loyal following for its chichi postmodern decor, rooftop patio, small but swanky disco, and well-dressed crowd. The kitchen serves sublime pan-Asian bar food, including panko-crusted calamari and Szechuan duck breast—a few of these tapas-style dishes make a memorable meal.

Tiny's (✉ Cerrillos Rd. and St. Francis Dr. ☎ 505/983-9817), a retro-fabulous restaurant serving excellent steaks and New Mexican fare, is a legend in this town with politicos, reporters, and deal-makers. The real draw is the kitsch-filled '50s cocktail lounge.

WilLee's Blues Club (✉ 401 S. Guadalupe St. ☎ 505/982-0117) presents poundin' blues and some jazz several nights a week in an intimate, often-packed space in the Guadalupe District.

The Arts

The performing arts scene in Santa Fe blossoms in summer. Classical or jazz concerts, Shakespeare on the grounds of St. John's campus, experimental theater at Santa Fe Stages, or flamenco—"too many choices!" is the biggest complaint. The rest of the year is a bit more quiet, but an increasing number of off-season venues have developed in recent years.

The city's most interesting multiuse arts venue, the **Center for Contemporary Arts (CCA)** (✉ 1050 Old Pecos Trail ☎ 505/982-1338 ⊕ www.ccasantafe.org) presents indie and foreign films, art exhibitions, provocative theater, and countless workshops and lectures.

Concert Venues

A 10-minute drive north of town, **Camel Rock Casino** (✉ U.S. 285/84 ☎ 800/462–2635 ⊕ www.camelrockcasino.com) presents relatively inexpensive pop and rock (Neil Sedaka, Pat Benatar, etc.) concerts.

Santa Fe's vintage downtown movie house was fully restored and converted into the 850-seat **Lensic Performing Arts Center** (✉ 211 W. San Francisco St. ☎ 505/988–1234 ⊕ www.lensic.com) in 2001. The grand 1931 building, with Moorish and Spanish Renaissance influences, hosts the Santa Fe Symphony, theater, classic films, lectures and readings, noted pop and jazz musicians, and many other noteworthy events.

On the campus of the Santa Fe Indian School, the **Paolo Soleri Outdoor Amphitheater** (✉ 1501 Cerrillos Rd. ☎ 505/989–6318) hosts pop, blues, rock, reggae, and jazz concerts spring–fall; past performers have included Bonnie Raitt, Tracy Chapman, and Chris Isaak.

The **St. Francis Auditorium** (✉ Museum of Fine Arts, northwest corner of Plaza) is the scene of cultural events such as theatrical productions and varied musical performances.

Dance

The esteemed **Aspen Santa Fe Ballet** (☎ 505/983–5591 or 505/988–1234 ⊕ www.aspensantafeballet.com) presents several ballet performances throughout the year at the Lensic Performing Arts Center.

Fans of Spanish dance should make every effort to see **Maria Benitez Teatro Flamenco** (✉ Lodge at Santa Fe, 750 N. St. Francis Dr. ☎ 505/955–8562 or 888/435–2636 ⊕ www.mariabenitez.com), who performs from late June through August at the Lodge at Santa Fe. Maria Benitez is one of the world's premier flamenco dancers, and her performances often sell out well in advance.

Film

The intimate **Jean Cocteau** (✉ 418 Montezuma Ave. ☎ 505/988–2711) shows art films and has a pleasant little café.

Music

The acclaimed ★ **Santa Fe Chamber Music Festival** (☎ 505/983–2075 ⊕ www.sfcmf.org) runs mid-July through late August, with performances nearly every night at the St. Francis Auditorium, or, occasionally, the Lensic Performing Arts Center. There are also free youth-oriented concerts given on several summer mornings. You can also attend many rehearsals for free; call for times.

Performances by the **Santa Fe Desert Chorale** (☎ 505/988–2282 or 800/244–4011 ⊕ www.desertchorale.org) take place throughout the summer at a variety of intriguing venues, from the Cathedral Basilica St. Francis to Loretto Chapel. This highly regarded singing group, which was begun in 1982, also performs a series of concerts during the December holiday season.

Fodor'sChoice ★ **Santa Fe Opera** (☎ 505/986–5900 or 800/280–4654 ⊕ www.santafeopera.org) performs in a strikingly modern structure—a 2,126-seat, indoor-outdoor amphitheater with excellent acoustics and sight lines. Carved into the natural curves of a hillside 7 mi north of the city on U.S. 285/ 84, the opera overlooks mountains, mesas, and sky. Add some of the most acclaimed singers, directors, conductors, musicians, designers, and composers from Europe and the United States, and you begin to understand the excitement that builds every June. The company, which celebrated its 50th anniversary in 1956, presents five works in repertory each summer—a blend of seasoned classics, neglected masterpieces, and world premieres. Many evenings sell out far in advance, but inexpensive standing-room tickets are often available on the day of the performance. A favorite pre-opera pastime is tailgating in the parking lot before the evening performance—many guests set up elaborate picnics of their own, but you can also preorder picnic meals ($30 per meal) by calling ☎ 505/983–2433 24 hours in advance; pick up your meal up to two hours before the show, at the Angel Food Catering kiosk on the west side of the parking lot. Or you can dine at the Preview Buffet, set up 2½ hours before each performance by the Guilds of the Santa Fe Opera. These meals include a large spread of very good food along with wine, held on the opera grounds. During dessert, a prominent local expert on opera gives a talk about the evening's performance. The Preview Buffet is by reservation only, by calling the opera box office number listed above, and the cost is $48 per person.

Orchestra and chamber concerts are given at St. Francis Auditorium and the Lensic Performing Arts Center by the **Santa Fe Pro Musica** (☎ 505/ 988–4640 or 800/960–6680 ⊕ www.santafepromusica.com) from September through April. Baroque and other classical compositions are the normal fare; the annual Christmas performance is a highlight.

The **Santa Fe Symphony** (☎ 505/983–1414 or 800/480–1319 ⊕ www. sf-symphony.org) performs seven concerts each season (from October to April) in the Lensic Performing Arts Center.

Theater

The **Greer Garson Theatre Company** (✉ College of Santa Fe, 1600 St. Michael's Dr. ☎ 505/473–6511 or 800/456–2673 ⊕ www.csf.edu) stages student productions of comedies, dramas, and musicals from October to May.

The oldest extant theater company west of the Mississippi, the **Santa Fe Playhouse** (✉ 142 E. De Vargas St. ☎ 505/988–4262 ⊕ www. santafeplayhouse.org) occupies a converted 19th-century adobe stable and has been presenting an adventurous mix of avant-garde pieces, classical drama, and musical comedy since 1922. The Fiesta Melodrama— a spoof of the Santa Fe scene—runs late August–mid-September.

Theaterwork (✉ 1336 Rufina Circle ☎ 505/471–1799 ⊕ www. theaterwork.org) is a well-respected community theater group that performs five plays each season, which runs from September through May.

SPORTS & THE OUTDOORS

The Santa Fe National Forest is right in the city's backyard and includes the Dome Wilderness (5,200 acres in the volcanically formed Jémez Mountains) and the Pecos Wilderness (223,333 acres of high mountains, forests, and meadows at the southern end of the Rocky Mountain chain). The 12,500-foot Sangre de Cristo Mountains (the name translates as "Blood of Christ," for the red glow they radiate at sunset) fringe the city's east side, constant and gentle reminders of the mystery and power of the natural world. To the south and west, sweeping high desert is punctuated by several less formidable mountain ranges. The dramatic shifts in elevation and topography around Santa Fe make for a wealth of outdoor activities. Head to the mountains for fishing, camping, and skiing; to the nearby Rio Grande for kayaking and rafting; and almost anywhere in the area for bird-watching, hiking, and biking.

Participant Sports

For a report on general conditions in the forest, contact the **Santa Fe National Forest Office** (✉ 1474 Rodeo Rd., 87505 ☏ 505/438–7840 ⊕ www. fs.fed.us/r3/sfe). For a one-stop shop for information about recreation on public lands, which includes national and state parks, contact the **New Mexico Public Lands Information Center** (✉ 1474 Rodeo Rd., 87505 ☏ 505/438–7542 ⊜ 505/438–7582 ⊕ www.publiclands.org). It has maps, reference materials, licenses, permits—just about everything you need to plan an adventure in the New Mexican wilderness.

The state-of-the-art **Genoveva Chavez Community Center** (✉ 3221 Rodeo Rd. ☏ 505/955–4001 ⊕ www.chavezcenter.com) is a reasonably priced (adults $4 per day), top-notch facility with a regulation-size ice rink, an enormous gymnasium, indoor running track, 50-meter pool, leisure pool with waterslide and play structures, aerobics center, state-of-the-art fitness room, two racquetball courts, and a child-care center.

For gear related to just about any outdoors activity you can think of, check out **Sangre de Cristo Mountain Works** (✉ 328 S. Guadalupe St. ☏ 505/984–8221), a well-stocked shop that both sells and rents hiking, climbing, camping, trekking, snowshoeing, and skiing equipment. The staff here can also advise you on the best venues for these activities.

Bicycling

You can pick up a map of bike trips—among them a 30-mi round-trip ride from downtown Santa Fe to Ski Santa Fe at the end of NM 475—from the New Mexico Public Lands Information Center. One excellent place to mountain-bike is the Dale Ball Trail Network, which is accessed from several points, including the road to the ski valley and the east end of Canyon Road.

Bike N' Sport (✉ 530 W. Cordova Rd. ☏ 505/820–0809) provides rentals and information about guided tours. **Sun Mountain** (✉ 102 E. Water St. ☏ 505/982–8986) rents mountain bikes and offers a wide range of bike tours. The shop will also deliver to your hotel, any day, year-round.

Bird-Watching

At the end of Upper Canyon Road, at the mouth of the canyon as it wends into the foothills, the 135-acre **Randall Davey Audubon Center** harbors diverse birds and other wildlife. Guided nature walks are given many weekends; there are also two major hiking trails that you can tackle on your own. The home and studio of Randall Davey, a prolific early Santa Fe artist, can be toured on Monday afternoons in summer. There's also a nature bookstore. ✉ *1800 Upper Canyon Rd.* ☎ *505/983–4609* ⊕ *www. audubon.org/chapter/nm/nm/rdac* ✆ *$2, house tour $5* ⊙ *Weekdays 9–5, weekends 10–4; grounds daily dawn–dusk; house tours Mon. at 2.*

For a knowledgeable insider's perspective, take a tour with **WingsWest Birding** (☎ 800/583–6928 ⊕ http://home.earthlink.net/~wingswestnm/). Guide Bill West leads four- to eight-hour early-morning or sunset tours that venture into some of the region's best bird-watching areas, including Santa Fe Ski Basin, Cochiti Lake, the Jémez Mountains, the Upper Pecos Valley, and Bosque del Apache National Wildlife Refuge.

Fishing

There's excellent fishing spring through fall in the Rio Grande and the mountain streams that feed into it, as well as a short drive away along the Pecos River. **High Desert Angler** (✉ 451 Cerrillos Rd. ☎ 505/988–7688 or 888/988–7688 ⊕ www.highdesertangler.com) is a superb fly-fishing outfitter and guide service. This is your one-stop shop for equipment rental, fly-fishing tackle, licenses, and advice.

Golf

Marty Sanchez Links de Santa Fe (✉ 205 Caja del Rio Rd., off NM 599, the Santa Fe Relief Rte. ☎ 505/955–4400 ⊕ www.linksdesantafe.com), an outstanding municipal facility with beautifully groomed 18- and 9-hole courses, sits on high prairie west of Santa Fe with fine mountain views. It has driving and putting ranges, a pro shop, and a snack bar. The greens fees are $31 for the 18-hole course, $22 on the par-3 9-holer.

Hiking

Hiking around Santa Fe can take you into high-altitude alpine country or into lunaresque high desert as you head south and west to lower elevations. For winter hiking, the gentler climates to the south are less likely to be snow packed, while the alpine areas will likely require snowshoes or cross-country skis. In summer, wildflowers bloom in the high country, and the temperature is generally at least 10° cooler than in town. The mountain trails accessible at the base of the Ski Santa Fe area (end of NM 475) stay cool on even the hottest summer days. Weather can change with one gust of wind, so be prepared with extra clothing, rain gear, food, and lots of water. Keep in mind that the sun at 10,000 feet is very powerful, even with a hat and sunscreen. See the Side Trips from the Cities chapter (Chapter 4) for additional hiking areas near Santa Fe.

For information about specific hiking areas, contact the New Mexico Public Lands Information Center. The **Sierra Club** (⊕ www.riogrande. sierraclub.org/santafe/home.html) organizes group hikes of all levels of difficulty; a schedule of hikes is posted on the Web site.

Aspen Vista is a lovely hike along a south-facing mountainside. Take Hyde Park Road (NM 475) 13 mi, and the trail begins before the ski area. After walking a few miles through thick aspen groves you come to panoramic views of Santa Fe. The path is well marked and gently inclines toward Tesuque Peak. The trail becomes shadier with elevation—

snow has been reported on the trail as late as July. In winter, after heavy snows, the trail is great for intermediate-advanced cross-country skiing. The round-trip is 12 mi and sees an elevation gain of 2,000 feet, but it's just 3½ mi to the spectacular overlook. The hillside is covered with golden aspen trees in late September.

A favorite spot for a ramble, with a vast network of trails, is the **Dale Ball Foothills Trail Network,** a network of some 20 mi of paths that winds and wends up through the foothills east of town and can be accessed at a few points, including Hyde Park Road (en route to the ski valley) and the far end of Canyon Road, at Cerro Gordo. There are trail maps and signs at these points, and the trails are very well marked.

★ Spurring off the Dale Ball trail system, the steep but rewarding (and dog-friendly) **Atalaya Trail** runs from the visitor parking lot of St. John's College (off of Camino de Cruz Blanca, on the East Side) up a winding, ponderosa pine–studded trail to the peak of Mt. Atalaya, which affords incredible 270-degree views of Santa Fe. The nearly 6-mi round-trip hike climbs a nearly 2,000 feet (to an elevation of 9,121 feet), so pace yourself. The good news: the return to the parking area is nearly all downhill.

Horseback Riding

New Mexico's rugged countryside has been the setting for many Hollywood westerns. Whether you want to ride the range that Gregory Peck and Kevin Costner rode or just head out feeling tall in the saddle, you can do so year-round. Rates average about $20 an hour. See the Side Trips from the Cities chapter (Chapter 4) for additional horseback listings in Cerrillos, Galisteo, and Ojo Caliente.

Bishop's Lodge (✉ Bishop's Lodge Rd. ☎ 505/983–6377) provides rides and guides year-round. Call for reservations.

Jogging

Because of the city's altitude (7,000–7,500 feet), you may feel heavy-legged and light-headed if you start running shortly after you arrive. Once you become acclimated, though, you can find that this is a great place to run. There's a jogging path along the Santa Fe River, parallel to Alameda, and another at Fort Marcy on Washington Avenue. The winding roads and paths up near the scenic campus of St. John's College are also ideal, although the terrain is quite hilly. Pick up gear and running advice at **Running Hub** (✉ 333 Montezuma Ave., No. 6 ☎ 505/820–2523); the store sponsors informal group runs many days—these are open to anybody.

River Rafting

If you want to watch birds and wildlife along the banks, try the laid-back Huck Finn floats along the Rio Chama or the Rio Grande's

WORD OF MOUTH

"When we go to Santa Fe, my husband usually runs on the trails in and around St. John's College which is up above Santa Fe. I don't know where you live but remember Santa Fe is at 7,000 ft elevation."

–martym

White Rock Canyon. The season is generally between April and September. Most outfitters have overnight package plans, and all offer half- and full-day trips. Be prepared to get wet, and wear secure water shoes. For a list of outfitters who guide trips on the Rio Grande and the Rio Chama, write the **Bureau of Land Management (BLM), Taos Resource Area Office** (⊠ 226 Cruz Alta Rd., Taos 87571 ☎ 505/758–8851 ⊕ www.nm.blm.gov), or stop by the BLM visitor center along NM 68 16 mi south of Taos.

Kokopelli Rafting Adventures (⊠ 551 W. Cordova Rd. ☎ 505/983–3734 or 800/879–9035 ⊕ www.kokopelliraft.com) specializes in trips through the relatively mellow White Rock Canyon as well as white water. **New Wave Rafting** (⊠ 1101 Cerrillos St. ☎ 505/984–1444 or 800/984–1444 ⊕ www.newwavecrafting.com) conducts full-day, half-day, and overnight river trips, with daily departures from Santa Fe. **Santa Fe Rafting Company and Outfitters** (⊠ 1000 Cerrillos Rd. ☎ 505/988–4914 or 800/467–7238 ⊕ www.santaferafting.com) customizes rafting tours. Tell them what you want—they'll do it.

Skiing

To save time during the busy holiday season you may want to rent skis or snowboards in town the night before hitting the slopes, or early in the morning so you don't waste any time paid for by your pricey lift ticket. **Alpine Sports** (⊠ 121 Sandoval St. ☎ 505/983–5155 ⊕ www.alpinesports-santafe.com) rents downhill and cross-country skis and snowboards. **Cottam's Ski Rentals** (⊠ Hyde Park Rd., 7 mi northeast of downtown, toward Ski Santa Fe ☎ 505/982–0495 or 800/322–8267) rents the works, including snowboards, sleds, and snowshoes.

Ski Santa Fe (⊠ End of NM 475, 18 mi northeast of downtown ☎ 505/982–4429, 505/983–9155 conditions ⊕ www.skisantafe.com), open roughly from late November through early April, is a fine, mid-size operation that receives an average of 225 inches of snow a year and plenty of sunshine. It's one of America's highest ski areas—the 12,000-foot summit has a variety of terrain and seems bigger than its 1,700 feet of vertical rise and 660 acres. There are some great powder stashes, tough bump runs, and many wide, gentle cruising runs. The 44 trails are ranked 20% beginner, 40% intermediate, and 40% advanced; there are seven lifts. Snowboarders are welcome, and there's the Norquist Trail for cross-country skiers. Chipmunk Corner provides day care and supervised kids' skiing. The ski school is excellent. Rentals, a good restaurant, a ski shop, and Totemoff Bar and Grill round out the amenities.

Snowshoeing

You can always snowshoe on your own in Santa Fe National Forest, which also has fine cross-country ski trails, by renting poles and shoes at **Alpine Sports** (*see above*), but it's more fun and interesting to take a guided tour. **Outspire Santa Fe** (☎ 505/660–0394 ⊕ www.outspire.com) offers guided snowshoe tours in Santa Fe National Forest. No experience is necessary to enjoy this relaxing, wintertime version of hiking.

SHOPPING

Santa Fe has been a trading post for eons. A thousand years ago the great pueblos of the Chacoan civilizations were strategically located between the buffalo-hunting tribes of the Great Plains and the Indians of Mexico. Native Americans in New Mexico traded turquoise and other valuables with Indians from Mexico for metals, shells, parrots, and other exotic items. After the arrival of the Spanish and the West's subsequent development, Santa Fe became the place to exchange silver from Mexico and natural resources from New Mexico for manufactured goods, whiskey, and greenbacks from the United States. With the building of the railroad in 1880, Santa Fe had access to all kinds of manufactured goods as well as those unique to the region via the old trade routes.

The trading legacy remains, but now downtown Santa Fe caters almost exclusively to those looking for handcrafted goods. Sure, T-shirt outlets and major retail clothing shops have moved in, but shopping in Santa Fe consists mostly of one-of-a-kind independent stores. Canyon Road, packed with art galleries, is the perfect place to find unique gifts and collectibles. The downtown district, around the Plaza, has unusual gift shops, clothing, and shoe stores that range from theatrical to conventional, curio shops, and art galleries. The funky, laid-back Guadalupe District, less touristy than the Plaza, is on downtown's southwest perimeter and includes the Sanbusco Market Center and the Design Center.

Farther out on Cerrillos Road, a traffic-jammed strip of shopping centers and chain motels, a new clutch of modern superstores has sprung up alongside Santa Fe's rather ordinary Villa Linda shopping mall. All the usual suspects are out here, around the intersection with Rodeo Road. On Cerrillos out by the I–25 exit, the inevitable **Santa Fe Premium Outlets** (✉ 8380 Cerrillos Rd., at I–25 ☎ 505/474–4000) contains about 40 shops, including Bass, Coach, Dansk, Eddie Bauer, Jones New York, and Brooks Brothers.

Art Galleries

The following are only a few of the nearly 200 galleries in greater Santa Fe—with the best of representational, nonobjective, Native American, Latin American, cutting-edge, photographic, and soulful works that defy categorization. The Santa Fe Convention and Visitors Bureau (⇨ Visitor Information *in* Santa Fe Essentials, *below*) has a more extensive listing. *The Wingspread Collectors Guide to Santa Fe and Taos* is a good resource and is available in hotels and at some galleries, as well as on the Web at ⊕ www.collectorsguide.com. Check the "Pasatiempo" pullout in the *Santa Fe New Mexican* on Friday for a preview of gallery openings.

Andrew Smith Gallery (✉ 203 W. San Francisco St. ☎ 505/984–1234) is a significant photo gallery dealing in works by Edward S. Curtis and other 19th-century chroniclers of the American West. Other major figures are Ansel Adams, Edward Weston, O. Winston Link, Henri Cartier-

Bresson, Eliot Porter, Laura Gilpin, Dorothea Lange, Alfred Stieglitz, Annie Liebowitz, and regional artists like Barbara Van Cleve.

Bellas Artes (⊠ 653 Canyon Rd. ☎ 505/983–2745), a sophisticated gallery and sculpture garden, has ancient ceramics and represents internationally renowned artists like Judy Pfaff, Phoebe Adams, and Olga de Amaral.

Carole LaRoche (⊠ 415 Canyon Rd. ☎ 505/982–1186) displays the owner's striking, archetypal paintings depicting wolves, warriors, and other primeval figures.

Charlotte Jackson Fine Art (⊠ 200 W. Marcy St. ☎ 505/989–8688) focuses primarily on monochromatic "radical" painting. Florence Pierce, Joe Barnes, William Metcalf, Anne Cooper, and Joseph Marioni are among the artists producing minimalist works dealing with light and space.

Cline Fine Art (⊠ 135 W. Palace Ave. ☎ 505/982–5328) specializes in contemporary paintings and sculpture, especially modernism and regionalism, from Southwestern to European works.

FodorśChoice ★ **Gerald Peters Gallery** (⊠ 1011 Pasco de Peralta ☎ 505/954–5700) is Santa Fe's leading gallery of American and European art from the 19th century to the present. It has works by Max Weber, Albert Bierstadt, the Taos Society, the New Mexico Modernists, and Georgia O'Keeffe, as well as contemporary artists.

LewAllen Contemporary (⊠ 129 W. Palace Ave. ☎ 505/988–8997) is a leading center for a variety of contemporary arts by both Southwestern and other acclaimed artists, among them Judy Chicago; sculpture, photography, ceramics, basketry, and painting are all shown in this dynamic space.

FodorśChoice ★ **Monroe Gallery** (⊠ 112 Don Gaspar Ave. ☎ 505/992–0800) showcases works by the most celebrated black-and-white photographers of the 20th century, from Margaret Bourke-White to Alfred Eisenstaedt.

★ **Nedra Matteucci Galleries** (⊠ 1075 Paseo de Peralta ☎ 505/982–4631 ⊠ 555 Canyon Rd. ☎ 505/983–2731) exhibits works by California regionalists, members of the early Taos and Santa Fe schools, and masters of American Impressionism and Modernism. Spanish-colonial furniture, Indian antiquities, and a fantastic sculpture garden are other draws of this well-respected establishment.

Niman Fine Arts (⊠ 125 Lincoln Ave. ☎ 505/988–5091) focuses on the prolific work of contemporary Native American artists–Hopi painters Arlo Namingha and Michael Namingha.

Peyton Wright (⊠ 237 E. Palace Ave. ☎ 505/989–9888), tucked inside a charming cottage, represents some of the most talented emerging and established contemporary artists in the country, as well as antique and even ancient Chinese, pre-Columbian, Russian, and Latin works.

Photo-eye Gallery (⊠ 376–A Garcia St. ☎ 505/988–5159) shows contemporary photography that includes the beautiful and sublime; there's also a stellar bookstore.

The Art of Santa Fe

THE ARTISTIC ROOTS OF SANTA FE stretch back to the landscape and the devotion of those who roamed and settled here long before the Santa Fe Trail transplanted goods and people from the East. The intricate designs on Native American pottery and baskets, the embroidery on the ritual dance wear, the color and pattern on Rio Grande weavings, and the delicate paintings and carvings of devotional images called santos all contributed to the value and awareness of beauty that Santa Fe holds as its cultural birthright. The rugged landscape, the ineffable quality of the light, and the community itself continue to draw to Santa Fe a plethora of musicians, writers, and visual artists. The spell of beauty is so powerful here that some people call the town "Fanta Se," but for those who live in Santa Fe the arts are very real (as are economic realities; most artists hold additional jobs—ask your waiter).

With wide-eyed enchantment, visitors often buy paintings in orange, pink, and turquoise that are perfect next to the adobe architecture, blue sky, and red rocks of the New Mexican landscape. When they get home, however, the admired works sometimes end up in a closet simply because it's so hard to integrate the Southwestern look with the tone of the existing furnishings and artwork. Taking the risk is part of the experience. Rather than suffering from buyer's remorse, those who make the aesthetic leap can take the spirit of northern New Mexico home with them. Although it may shake up the home decor, the works are a reminder of a new way of seeing and of all the other values that inspire one to travel in the first place.

Most galleries will send a painting (not posters or prints) out on a trial basis for very interested clients. If looking at art is new to you, ask yourself if your interest is in bringing home a souvenir that says "I was there" or in art that will live in the present and inspire the future, independent of the nostalgia for the "land of enchantment." Santa Fe has plenty of both to offer—use discrimination while you look so you don't burn out on the first block of Canyon Road.

Santa Fe, while holding strong in its regional art identity, emerged in the late 1990s as a more international art scene. Native American and Hispanic arts groups now include the work of contemporary artists who have pressed beyond the bounds of tradition. Bold color and the oft-depicted New Mexico landscape are still evident, but you're just as likely to see mixed-media collages by a Chinese artist currently living in San Francisco. A few Santa Fe outlets, such as the Riva Yares Gallery and evo gallery, are dedicated to representing artists with Latin American roots. "The world is wide here," Georgia O'Keeffe once noted about northern New Mexico. And just as Santa Fe welcomed early Modernist painters who responded to the open landscape and the artistic freedom it engendered, contemporary artists working with edgier media, such as conceptual, performance, and installation art, are finding welcoming venues in Santa Fe, specifically at SITE Santa Fe museum.

Puskin Gallery (✉ 550 Canyon Rd. ☎ 505/982–1990) is yet more evidence that Santa Fe's art scene is about so much more than regional work—here you can peruse works by some of Russia's leading 19th- and 20th-century talents, with an emphasis on impressionism.

Riva Yares Gallery (✉ 123 Grant St. ☎ 505/984–0330) specializes in contemporary artists of Latin American descent. There are sculptures by California artist Manuel Neri, color field paintings by Esteban Vicente, and works by Santa Feans Elias Rivera, Rico Eastman, and others—plus paintings by such international legends as Hans Hofman, Milton Avery, and Helen Frankenthaler.

Santa Fe Art Institute (✉ 1600 St. Michael's Dr. ☎ 505/424–5050), a nonprofit educational art organization that sponsors several artists in residence and presents workshops, exhibitions, and lectures, has a respected gallery whose exhibits change regularly. The institute is set inside a dramatic contemporary building. Past artists in residence have included Richard Diebenkorn, Larry Bell, Moon Zappa, Henriette Wyeth Hurd, and and Judy Pfaff.

★ **Shidoni Foundry and Galleries** (✉ Bishop's Lodge Rd., 5 mi north of Santa Fe, Tesuque ☎ 505/988–8001) casts work for accomplished and emerging artists from all over North America. On the grounds of an old chicken ranch, Shidoni has a rambling sculpture garden and a gallery. Self-guided foundry tours are permitted Saturday 9–5 and weekdays noon–1, but the sculpture garden is open daily during daylight hours; you can watch bronze pourings most Saturday afternoons.

Specialty Stores

Antiques & Home Furnishings

Artesanos (✉ 222 Galisteo St. ✉ 1414 Maclovia St. ☎ 505/471–8020) is one of the best Mexican-import shops in the nation, with everything from leather chairs to papier-mâché *calaveras* (skeletons used in Day of the Dead celebrations), and tinware. The location on Maclovia Street specializes in Talavera and other tiles.

At **Asian Adobe** (✉ 530 S. Guadalupe St. ☎ 505/992–6846) browse porcelain lamps, silk scarves, red-lacquer armoires, and similarly stunning Chinese and Southeast Asian artifacts and antiques.

★ **Bosshard Fine Art Furnishings** (✉ 340 S. Guadalupe St. ☎ 505/989–9150) deals in African ethnographica, which complement the vast selection of tapestries, architectural elements, statues, and ceramics from the Southwest as well as Asia.

Casa Nova (✉ 530 S. Guadalupe St. ☎ 505/983–8558) sells functional art from around the world, deftly mixing colors, textures, and cultural icons—old and new—from stylish pewter tableware from South Africa to vintage hand-carved ex-votos (votive offerings) from Brazil.

★ The **Design Center** (✉ 418 Cerrillos Rd.), which occupies an art deco former Chevy dealership in the Guadalupe District, contains some of the most distinctive antique and decorative arts shops in town, plus a couple of small restaurants. Be sure to browse the precious Latin American antiques at **Claiborne Gallery** (☎ 505/982–8019), along with the artful contemporary desks, tables, and chairs created by owner Omer Claiborne. **Gloria List Gallery** (☎ 505/982–5622) specializes in rare 17th- and 18th-century devotional and folk art, chiefly from South America, Italy, Spain, and Mexico. And at **Sparrow & Magpie Antiques** (☎ 505/982–1446), look mostly for East Coast and Midwest folk art and textiles, although the shop carries some Southwestern pieces, too.

Design Warehouse (✉ 101 W. Marcy St. ☎ 505/988–1555), a welcome antidote to Santa Fe's preponderance of shops selling Spanish-colonial antiques, stocks super-hip and mod sofas, kitchenware, lamps, and other sleek knickknacks.

Doodlet's (✉ 120 Don Gaspar Ave. ☎ 505/983–3771) has an eclectic collection of stuff: pop-up books, bizarre postcards, tin art, hooked rugs, and stringed lights. Wonderment is in every display case, drawing the eye to the unusual. Note that the store is closed through early 2007 for remodeling.

Foreign Traders (✉ 202 Galisteo St. ☎ 505/983–6441), a Santa Fe institution founded as the Old Mexico Shop in 1927 and still run by the same family, stocks handicrafts, antiques, and accessories from Mexico and other parts of the world.

Jackalope (✉ 2820 Cerrillos Rd. ☎ 505/471–8539), a legendary if somewhat overpriced bazaar, sprawls over 7 acres, incorporating several pottery barns, a furniture store, endless aisles of knickknacks from Latin America and Asia, and a huge greenhouse. There's also an area where craftspeople, artisans, and others sell their wares—sort of a mini–flea market.

Montez Gallery (✉ Sena Plaza Courtyard, 125 E. Palace Ave. ☎ 505/982–1828) sells Hispanic works of religious art and decoration, including retablos (holy images painted on wood or tin), bultos (carved wooden statues of saints), furniture, paintings, pottery, weavings, and jewelry.

★ **Nambé Outlets** (✉ 104 W. San Francisco St. ☎ 505/988–3574 ✉ 924 Paseo de Peralta ☎ 505/988–5528) carries the classic metal bowls, vases, and candlesticks made by the acclaimed artisans of the Nambé Pueblo, just north of town; lead crystal, lighting, and porcelain are also sold.

Pachamama (✉ 223 Canyon Rd. ☎ 505/983–4020) carries Latin American folk art, including small tin or silver *milagros,* the stamped metal images used as votive offerings. The shop also carries weavings and Spanish-colonial antiques.

Sequoia (✉ 201 Galisteo St. ☎ 505/982–7000) shows the imaginative, almost surreal, furniture creations of its owner, who was born in India. Curvaceous glass shelves, lamps, and candlesticks mix with paintings and fine linens.

Books

More than a dozen shops in Santa Fe sell used books, and a handful of high-quality shops carry the latest releases from mainstream and small presses.

ALLÁ (⊠ 102 W. San Francisco St., upstairs ☎ 505/988–5416) is one of Santa Fe's most delightful small bookstores. It focuses on hard-to-find Spanish-language books and records, including limited-edition handmade books from Central America. It also carries Native American books and music, as well as English translations.

Collected Works Book Store (⊠ 208B W. San Francisco St. ☎ 505/988–4226) carries art and travel books, including a generous selection of books on Southwestern art, architecture, and general history, as well as the latest in contemporary literature.

Garcia Street Books (⊠ 376 Garcia St. ☎ 505/986–0151) is an outstanding independent shop strong on art, architecture, cookbooks, literature, and regional Southwestern works—it's a block from the Canyon Road galleries.

Nicholas Potter (⊠ 211 E. Palace Ave. ☎ 505/983–5434) specializes in used, rare, and out-of-print books. The quixotic shop also stocks used jazz and classical CDs.

Photo-eye Books (⊠ 376 Garcia St. ☎ 505/988–5152) stocks new, rare, and out-of-print photography books.

Travel Bug (⊠ 839 Paseo de Peralta ☎ 505/992–0418) has a huge array of travel tomes and guidebooks, and USGS and other maps. There's also a cozy coffeehouse with high-speed wireless.

Clothing & Accessories

Women have been known to arrive here in Liz Claiborne and leave in a broomstick skirt and Navajo velvet shirt, but function dictates form in cowboy fashions. A wide-brim hat is essential in open country for protection from heat, rain, and insects, and the pointed toes of cowboy boots slide easily in and out of stirrups, while the high heels help keep feet in the stirrups. Tall tops protect ankles and legs on rides through brush and cactus country and can protect the wearer from a nasty shin bruise from a skittish horse.

Some Western fashion accessories were once purely functional. A colorful bandanna protected an Old West cowboy from sun- and windburn and served as a mask in windstorms, when riding drag behind a herd or, on occasions far rarer than Hollywood would have us believe, when robbing trains. A cowboy's sleeveless vest enhanced his ability to maneuver during roping and riding chores and provided pocket space that his skintight pants—snug to prevent wrinkles in the saddle area—didn't. Belt buckles are probably the most sought-after accessories—gold ones go for as much as $1,000.

Back at the Ranch (⊠ 209 E. Marcy St. ☎ 505/989–8110 or 888/962–6687) is an attractive old shop stocked with handmade cowboy boots, from red leather to turquoise snakeskin, along with funky furniture, 1950s blanket coats, jewelry, and buckles. Some things get better with age, especially cowboy boots.

★ **O'Farrell Hats** (✉ 111 E. San Francisco St. ☎ 505/989–9666) is the domain of America's foremost hatmaker, Kevin O'Farrell. This quirky shop custom-crafts one-of-a-kind beaver-lined cowboy hats that make the ultimate Santa Fe keepsake. This level of quality comes at a cost, but devoted customers—who have included everyone from cattle ranchers to U.S. presidents—swear by O'Farrell's artful creations.

★ **Double Take at the Ranch** (✉ 321 S. Guadalupe St. ☎ 505/820–7775) ranks among the best consignment stores in the West, carrying elaborately embroidered vintage cowboy shirts, hundreds of pairs of boots, funky old prints, and one-of-a-kind jewelry. The store adjoins Santa Fe Pottery, which carries the works of more than 70 local artists.

Lucchese (✉ 203 W. Water St. ☎ 505/820–1883) has been crafting some of the West's finest handmade cowboy boots since 1883.

Mirá (✉ 101 W. Marcy St. ☎ 505/988–3585) clothing for women is slick, eclectic, and funky, combining the adventurous spirit of Mexico with global contemporary fashion. The shop has accessories and collectibles from Latin America, hemp apparel, and knockout vintage-inspired dresses.

Origins (✉ 135 W. San Francisco St. ☎ 505/988–2323) borrows from many cultures, carrying pricey women's wear like antique kimonos and custom-dyed silk jackets. One-of-a-kind accessories complete the spectacular look that Santa Fe inspires.

Food & Cookery
In the DeVargas shopping center, **Las Cosas Kitchen Shoppe** (✉ N. Guadalupe St. at Paseo de Peralta ☎ 505/988–3394 or 877/229–7184) carries a fantastic selection of cookery, tableware, and kitchen gadgetry and gifts. The shop is also renowned for its cooking classes, which touch on everything from high-altitude baking to Asian-style grilling.

★ **Todos Santos** (✉ 125 E. Palace Ave. ☎ 505/982–3855) is a tiny candy shop in an 18th-century courtyard, carrying seen-to-be-believed works of edible art, including chocolate milagros and altar pieces gilded with 23-karat gold or silver leaf. Truffles come in exotic flavors, like rose caramel and lemon verbena.

Jewelry
Karen Melfi Collection (✉ 225 Canyon Rd. ☎ 505/982–3032) sells high-quality yet moderately priced handmade jewelry and other wearable art.

Primavera (✉ 209 W. San Francisco St. ☎ 505/995–8552) is highly regarded not only for its imaginative goldsmithing but also for its brightly colored glass–and–wrought-iron lamps, which seem surreally inspired by Louis Tiffany.

Markets

Browse through the vast selection of local produce, meat, flowers, honey, and cheese—much of it organic—at the **Santa Fe Farmers Market** (✉ Gualadupe St. and Cerrillos Rd. ☎ 505/983–4098 ⊕ www.

santafefarmersmarket.com), which is held Tuesday and Saturday mornings from 7 until noon, late April–early November; in winter, a smaller indoor version is held just on Saturday mornings nearby at El Museo Cultural, in the Railyard on Guadalupe Street. It's a great people-watching event, and there's storytelling for kids as well as a snack bar selling terrific breakfast burritos and other goodies. Additionally, on Thursday afternoons in summer, the market sets up at the Rodeo Fairgrounds on Rodeo Road.

★ **Tesuque Pueblo Flea Market** (⊠ U.S. 285/84, 7 mi north of Santa Fe ☎ 505/995–7767 ⊕ www.tesuquepuebloflea market.com) was once considered the best flea market in America by its loyal legion of bargain hunters. The Tesuque Pueblo took over the market in the late '90s and raised vendor fees, which increased the presence of predictable, often pricey goods brought in by professional flea-market dealers. In recent years, however, the pueblo has brought in a nice range of vendors, and this market with as many as 500 vendors in peak season is again one of the best shopping events in town. The 12-acre market is next to the Santa Fe Opera and is open Friday–Sunday, mid-March–December.

Native American Arts & Crafts

Frank Howell Gallery (⊠ 103 Washington Ave. ☎ 505/984–1074) stocks lithographs, serigraphs, prints, and posters of the late Frank Howell as well as works by other Native American artists.

Morning Star Gallery (⊠ 513 Canyon Rd. ☎ 505/982–8187) is a veritable museum of Native American art and artifacts. An adobe shaded by a huge cottonwood tree houses antique basketry, pre-1940 Navajo silver jewelry, Northwest Coast Native American carvings, Navajo weavings, and art of the Plains Indians.

Packard's on the Plaza (⊠ 61 Old Santa Fe Trail ☎ 505/983–9241), the oldest Native American arts-and-crafts store on Santa Fe Plaza, sells Zapotec Indian rugs from Mexico and original rug designs by Richard Enzer, old pottery, saddles, kachina dolls, and an excellent selection of coral and turquoise jewelry. Prices are quite high, but so are the standards. There's also an extensive clothing selection.

★ The **Rainbow Man** (⊠ 107 E. Palace Ave. ☎ 505/982–8706), established in 1945, does business in the remains of a building that was damaged during the 1680 Pueblo Revolt. The shop carries early Navajo, Mexican, and Chimayó textiles, along with photographs by Edward S. Curtis, vintage pawn jewelry, Day of the Dead figures, Oaxacan folk animals, and kachinas.

Shush Yaz (⊠ 1048 Paseo de Peralta ☎ 505/992–0441), in the tradition of the great trading posts of Gallup, has been dealing in fine turquoise jewelry, fine baskets, kachina dolls, and pottery—much of it from the early 20th century—for more than 120 years.

Trade Roots Collection (⊠ 411 Paseo de Peralta ☎ 505/982–8168) sells Native American ritual objects, such as fetish jewelry and Hopi rattles. The store is a good source of crafts materials.

SANTA FE ESSENTIALS

AIR TRAVEL
Most visitors to Santa Fe fly into the state's main airport in Albuquerque, about an hour away. There's no air service between Albuquerque and Santa Fe. Great Lakes Aviation flies three or four times daily from Denver to Santa Fe and has code sharing with United and Frontier airlines.
🚹 **Great Lakes Aviation** ☎ 800/554-5111 ⊕ www.greatlakesav.com.

AIRPORTS
Tiny Santa Fe Municipal Airport offers limited services, although there's some talk of expanding the facility and its runways to help lure additional airlines. The airport is 9 mi southwest of downtown.
🚹 **Santa Fe Municipal Airport (SAF)** ✉ Airport Rd. and NM 599 ☎ 505/473-4118.

BUS TRAVEL
Bus service on Texas, New Mexico & Oklahoma Coaches, affiliated with Greyhound Lines, is available to Santa Fe from major cities and towns throughout the region.

The city's bus system, Santa Fe Trails, covers 10 major routes through town and is useful for getting from the Plaza to some of the outlying attractions. Route M is most useful for visitors, as it runs from downtown to the museums on Old Santa Fe Trail south of town, and Route 2 is useful if you're staying at one of the motels out on Cerrillos Road and need to get into town (still a car is a much more practical way to get around). Individual rides cost $1, and a daily pass costs $2. Buses run about every 30 minutes on weekdays, every hour on weekends. Service begins at 6 AM and continues until 11 PM on weekdays, 8–8 on Saturday, and 10–7 (limited routes) on Sunday.
🚹 **Greyhound/Texas, New Mexico & Oklahoma Coaches** ☎ 505/243-4435 or 800/231-2222 ⊕ www.greyhound.com. **Santa Fe Trails** ☎ 505/955-2001 ⊕ www.santafenm.gov/public-works.

CAR RENTAL
Santa Fe is served by several national rental car agencies, including Avis, Budget, and Hertz. Additional agencies with locations in Santa Fe include Advantage, Classy Car Rentals (which specializes in luxury and sports vehicles), Enterprise, Sears, and Thrifty. *See* Car Rental *in* New Mexico Essentials for national rental agency phone numbers.
🚹 **Advantage** ☎ 505/983-9470. **Enterprise** ☎ 505/473-3600. **Sears** ☎ 505/984-8038. **Thrifty** ☎ 505/474-3365 or 800/367-2277.

CAR TRAVEL
South–north–running I–25 actually curves in almost an west–east direction as it cuts just south of Santa Fe, which is 62 mi northeast of Albuquerque. U.S. 285/84 runs north–south through the city. The Turquoise Trail (Chapter 4) is a scenic, two-lane approach to Santa Fe from Albuquerque. The NM 599 bypass, also called the Santa Fe Relief Route, cuts around the city from I–25's Exit 276, southwest of the city, to U.S. 285/

84, north of the city; it's a great shortcut if you're heading from Albuquerque to Española, Abiquiu, Taos, or other points north of Santa Fe.

PARKING Parking in Santa Fe is difficult, but public and private lots can be found throughout the city. Parking meters are well monitored. There are parking garages near the Plaza on San Francisco and Water streets. On weekends, you can park for free in the lots of some of the government buildings near the capitol, which is within walking distance of the Plaza (check signs carefully for specific parking rules).

EMERGENCIES

In an emergency, dial 911.

🏥 Hospital **St. Vincent Hospital** ⊠ 455 St. Michael's Dr. ☎ 505/983-3361.
🏥 24-hour Pharmacy **Walgreens** ⊠ 1096 St. Francis Dr. ☎ 505/982-4643 ⊠ 3298 Cerrillos Rd. ☎ 505/474-3523.

SIGHTSEEING TOURS

GENERAL   Aboot About has been walking groups through the history, art, and ar-
INTEREST chitecture of Santa Fe since the late 1970s. Tours leave daily at 9:30 and 1:30 from the Eldorado Hotel, 9:45 and 1:45 from the Hotel St. Francis, and Saturday and Monday at 9:45 from La Posada Resort. Tours take about two hours. No reservations are required. The company also offers a variety of additional tours on everything from ghosts and legends to Georgia O'Keeffe Country to local culinary rambles. Great Southwest Adventures conducts guided mountain hikes and 7- to 35-passenger van and bus excursions to Bandelier, Abiquiu, Taos, and elsewhere in the region; it also provides a shuttle service to and from downtown hotels and the Santa Fe Opera. Santa Fe Detours conducts bus, river, rail, horseback, and walking tours and organizes rafting and ski packages. This is an excellent choice if you're looking for a general overview of the city and some of the nearby attractions. The walking tours are offered daily at 9:30 and 1:30 from the northeast corner of the Plaza. Custom Tours by Clarice are guided open-air tram excursions that run five times a day from the corner of Lincoln Avenue and West Palace Avenue. These 90-minute tours offer a nice overview of downtown; the company also gives bus and shuttle tours of Bandelier and Taos, and shuttle services from town to the Santa Fe Opera.

Rojo Tours designs specialized trips—to view wildflowers, pueblo ruins and cliff dwellings, galleries and studios, Native American arts and crafts, and private homes—as well as adventure activity tours. Santa Fe Guides is an organization of about 15 respected independent tour guides—their Web site lists each member and his or her specialties.

For an unforgettable bird's-eye view of the region, book a helicopter tour with HeliNM, which offers several different trips, costing from about $75 and up per person—popular destinations include the Turquoise Trail, Tent Rocks and Los Alamos, Pecos Wilderness, and O'Keeffe Country. These tours depart from Santa Fe Municipal Airport, and charters are also available.

🏥 **Aboot About** ☎ 505/988-2774 or 866/614-8404 ⊕ www.abootabout.com. **Custom Tours By Clarice** ☎ 505/438-7116 ⊕ www.santafecustomtours.com. **Great Southwest**

Adventures ☎ 505/455-2700 ⊕ www.swadventures.com. HeliNM ☎ 866/995-1058 ⊕ www.helinm.com. Rojo Tours ☎ 505/474-8333 ⊕ www.rojotours.com. Santa Fe Detours ☎ 505/983-6565 or 800/338-6877 ⊕ www.sfdetours.com. Santa Fe Guides ☎ 505/466-4877 ⊕ www.santafeguides.org.

LEARNING EXPERIENCES Art Adventures in the Southwest takes you into the New Mexico landscape for outdoor art classes with Jane Shoenfeld. All materials are supplied, and all experience levels are welcome. Santa Fe Art Institute is housed in the Visual Arts Center designed by Mexican architect Ricardo Legorreta (a Modernist break from Santa Fe style). The institute (not part of the College of Santa Fe) offers weeklong workshops that have been led by such renowned artists as Phoebe Adams and Richard Diebenkorn. Dormitory quarters are available and studio space is provided. Workshops are offered year-round.

Santa Fe Photographic Workshops offers workshops in photographic processes, including digital imaging, platinum, and travel photography. The workshops have an excellent reputation, and many instructors return year after year. Santa Fe School of Cooking holds night and day classes in regional New Mexican fare.
🔢 **Art Adventures in the Southwest** ☎ 505/986-1108 ⊕ www.skyfields.net. **Santa Fe Art Institute** ✉ 1600 St. Michael's Dr., College of Santa Fe campus ☎ 505/424-5050 ⊕ www.sfai.org. **Santa Fe Photographic Workshops** ☎ 505/983-1400 ⊕ www.sfworkshop.com. **Santa Fe School of Cooking** ☎ 505/983-4511 or 800/982-4688 ⊕ www.santafeschoolofcooking.com.

TAXIS
Capital City Cab Company controls all the cabs in Santa Fe. The taxis aren't metered; you pay a flat fee based on how far you're going, usually $6–$10 within the downtown area. There are no cab stands; you must phone to arrange a ride.
🔢 **Capital City Cab** ☎ 505/438-0000.

BY TRAIN
Amtrak's *Southwest Chief* stops in Lamy, a short drive south of Santa Fe, on its route from Chicago to Los Angeles via Kansas City; other New Mexico stops include Raton, Las Vegas, Albuquerque, and Gallup daily. In summer 2006, the City of Albuquerque launched the state's first-ever commuter train line, the *New Mexico Rail Runner Express*. As of this writing, service is from Bernalillo south through the city of Albuquerque, continuing south through Los Lunas to the suburb of Belén, covering a distance of about 50 mi. The second and final phase of the project, expected to be completed by late 2008, will extend the service north to Santa Fe.
🔢 **Amtrak** ☎ 800/872-7245 ⊕ www.amtrak.com. *New Mexico Rail Runner Express* ☎ 505/245-7245 ⊕ www.nmrailrunner.com.

VISITOR INFORMATION
🔢 **New Mexico Department of Tourism visitor center** ✉ Lamy Bldg., 491 Old Santa Fe Trail, 87503 ☎ 505/827-7400 or 800/733-6396 Ext. 0643 ⊕ www.newmexico.org. **Santa Fe Convention and Visitors Bureau** ✉ 201 W. Marcy St., Box 909, 87501 ☎ 505/955-6200 or 800/777-2489 ⊕ www.santafe.org.

Taos

WORD OF MOUTH

"We both loved Taos—small, but so unassuming. We managed to take in the plaza, Kit Carson Home, Millicent Rogers Museum, Rio Grande Gorge Bridge, Hacienda de los Martínez (hard to find, but worth it!), San Francisco de Asís Church, and, the highlight I think, Taos Pueblo."

—Chele60

"The Taos Pueblo is larger than most, and it does offer some little shops, but it's definitely not a shopping destination. It's more of a place to see how the Indians live/lived."

—JackOneill

Updated by
Andrew Collins

TAOS CASTS A LINGERING SPELL. Set on a rolling mesa at the base of the Sangre de Cristo Mountains, it's a place of piercing light and spectacular views, where the desert palette changes almost hourly as the sun moves across the sky. Adobe buildings—some of them centuries old—lie nestled amid pine trees and scrub, some in the shadow of majestic Taos Mountain. The smell of piñon wood smoke rises from the valley in winter; in spring and summer, it gives way to fragrant sage.

The magic of the area has drawn people here for hundreds of years. The earliest inhabitants were Native Americans of the Taos–Tiwa tribe; their descendants still live and maintain a traditional way of life at Taos Pueblo, a 95,000-acre reserve 3 mi north of what is now the town's commercial center. Spanish settlers, who arrived in the 1500s, brought both farming and Catholicism to the area; their influence can still be seen today at Ranchos de Taos, 4 mi south of town, and at the San Francisco de Asís Church, whose massive adobe walls and *camposanto* (graveyard) are among the most photographed in the country.

In the early 20th century, another population—artists—discovered Taos and began making the pilgrimage here to write, paint, and take photographs. The early adopters of this movement were painters Bert Phillips and Ernest Blumenschein, who were traveling from Denver on a planned painting trip into Mexico in 1898 when they stopped to have a broken wagon wheel repaired in Taos. Enthralled with the earthy beauty of the region, they abandoned their plan to journey farther south, settled, and eventually formed the Taos Society of Artists in 1915. Over the following years, many illustrious artists, including Georgia O'Keeffe, Ansel Adams, and D. H. Lawrence also took up residence in the area, and it is still a mecca for creative types today. The downtown area is now filled with galleries and shops that display the work of local artists, and museums that document Taos's artistic history.

These days, Taos has a variable population of about 6,500 (the 2000 U.S. Census officially places it at 4,700, but there's always an influx during the summer and the winter ski season, and these numbers don't include Arroyo Seco, Taos Ski Valley, and other neighboring villages). Many come here for a break from the urban sprawl of larger U.S. cities; among the escapees are actress Julia Roberts and U.S. Secretary of Defense Donald Rumsfeld.

EXPLORING TAOS

Taos is small and resolutely rustic, and the central area is highly walkable. Sociable Taoseños make the town a welcoming place to explore. You need a car to reach the Rio Grande Gorge and other places of interest beyond Taos proper. Traffic can be heavy in the peak summer and winter seasons (an accident on the main route through town, Paseo del Pueblo, can back up traffic for miles); ask locals about back roads that let you avoid the busy street.

The Museum Association of Taos includes six properties. Among them are the Harwood Museum, Taos Art Museum at the Fechin House, the

GREAT ITINERARIES

IF YOU HAVE 1 DAY

Begin by strolling around **Taos Plaza ❶**, taking in the galleries and Native American crafts shops. Take Ledoux Street south from the west Plaza and go two blocks to visit the **Harwood Museum ❸**. Walk back to the Plaza and cross over to Kit Carson Road, where you can find more shops and galleries as well as the **Kit Carson Home and Museum ❹**. Continue north on Paseo del Pueblo to the **Taos Art Museum at the Fechin House ❽**. In the afternoon, get in the car and head north on Paseo del Pueblo to the traffic light, where you turn left on U.S. 64. to the **Rio Grande Gorge Bridge ❽**. If you're feeling peppy, you can climb down to the river, or just gaze down into the breathtaking chasm from the bridge. Return the way you came, turning right at the light, and drive the short distance to Millicent Rogers Road. Turn right and proceed to the **Millicent Rogers**

Museum ❷, where you can easily spend the rest of the afternoon. If you're in town for the evening, stop in at the Adobe Bar at the Taos Inn for music and people-watching.

IF YOU HAVE 2 DAYS

Spend the first day doing the one-day tour above. On the second day, drive out to the **Taos Pueblo ⓫** in the morning and tour the ancient village while the day is fresh. Return to town and go to the **Blumenschein Home and Museum ❷**. Lunch at the nearby Dragonfly Café. After lunch drive out to **La Hacienda de los Martinez ❾** for a look at early life in Taos and then to **Ranchos de Taos ❿** to see the beautiful San Francisco de Asís Church. If it's dinnertime, eat at Joseph's Table or the Trading Post Café. If it's still early, drive back to town and browse in the shops on Bent Street and the adjacent John Dunn House Shops.

Millicent Rogers Museum, and buildings in the Kit Carson Historic Museum consortium that include the Blumenschein Home and Museum, the Kit Carson Home and Museum, and La Hacienda de los Martínez. Each of the museums charges $5–$7 for admission, but you can opt for a combination ticket—$20 for all five, valid for one year.

Numbers in the text correspond to numbers in the margin and on the Taos map.

Downtown Taos

More than four centuries after it was laid out, Taos Plaza remains the center of commercial life in Taos. Bent Street, where New Mexico's first American governor lived and died, is an upscale shopping area and gallery enclave.

What to See

❷ **Blumenschein Home and Museum.** For an introduction to the history of the Taos art scene, start with Ernest L. Blumenschein's residence, which provides a glimpse into the cosmopolitan lives led by the members of the

Taos Society of Artists, of which Blumenschein was a founding member. One of the rooms in the adobe-style structure dates from 1797. On display are the art, antiques, and other personal possessions of Blumenschein and his wife, Mary Greene Blumenschein, who also painted, as did their daughter Helen. Several of Ernest Blumenschein's vivid oil paintings hang in his former studio, and works by other early Taos artists are also on display. ☒ *222 Ledoux St.* ☎ *505/758–0505* ⊕ *taoshistoricmuseums. com/blumenschein.html* ✉ *$6, $20 with Museum Association of Taos combination ticket* ☉ *Apr.–Oct., daily 9–5; Nov.–Mar., daily 10–4.*

❻ Firehouse Collection. More than 100 works by well-known Taos artists like Joseph Sharp, Ernest L. Blumenschein, and Bert Phillips hang in the Taos Volunteer Fire Department building. The exhibition space adjoins the station house, where five fire engines are maintained at the ready and an antique fire engine is on display. ☒ *323 Camino de la Placita* ☎ *505/758–3386* ✉ *Free* ☉ *Weekdays 9–4:30.*

❺ Governor Bent Museum. In 1846, when New Mexico became a U.S. possession as a result of the Mexican War, Charles Bent, a trader, trapper, and mountain man, was appointed governor. Less than a year later he was killed in his house by an angry mob protesting New Mexico's annexation by the United States. Governor Bent was married to María Ignacia, the older sister of Josefa Jaramillo, the wife of mountain man Kit Carson. A collection of Native American artifacts, western Americana, and family possessions is squeezed into five small rooms of the adobe building where Bent and his family lived. ☒ *117 Bent St.* ☎ *505/758–2376* ✉ *$2* ☉ *Apr.–Oct., daily 9–5; Nov.–Mar., daily 10–4.*

★ ❸ Harwood Museum. The Pueblo Revival former home of Burritt Elihu "Burt" Harwood, a dedicated painter who studied in France before moving to Taos in 1916, is adjacent to a museum dedicated to the works of local artists. Traditional Hispanic northern New Mexican artists, early art-colony painters, post–World War II modernists, and contemporary artists such as Larry Bell, Agnes Martin, Ken Price, and Earl Stroh are represented. Mabel Dodge Luhan, a major arts patron, bequeathed many of the 19th- and early-20th-century works in the Harwoods' collection, including *retablos* (painted wood representations of Catholic saints) and *bultos* (three-dimensional carvings of the saints). In the Hispanic Traditions Gallery upstairs are 19th-century tinwork, furniture, and sculpture. Downstairs, among early-20th-century art-colony holdings, look for E. Martin Hennings's *Chamisa in Bloom*, which captures the Taos landscape particularly beautifully. A tour of the ground-floor galleries shows that Taos painters of the era, notably Oscar Berninghaus, Ernest Blumenschein, Victor Higgins, Walter Ufer, Marsden Hartley, and John Marin, were fascinated by the land and the people linked to it. An octagonal gallery exhibits works by Agnes Martin. Martin's seven large canvas panels (each 5 feet square) are

> **WORD OF MOUTH**
>
> "Contemporary to classic, great place to see art."
> –Gary Miller on the Harwood Museum

IF YOU LIKE

ARTS & CRAFTS

If your idea of fun is museum-going and gallery-hopping, you'll love Taos. The creative spirit is strong here, and it's contagious. Even if you begin by just browsing, you might find that you can't go home without a certain painting or pot that captures the unique enchantment of the place. When browsing for art, you often have the opportunity to meet the artists themselves, an eclectic and almost universally free-thinking collection of individuals, some of whom might wear cowboy boots and speak with drawl. You can even join in the flow of creative energy by participating in art workshops yourself. It's easy to visit a lot of galleries in a short time; many are side by side on a few streets around the Plaza. Southwestern landscapes and Native American themes are frequent subjects. Look for outstanding weaving, jewelry, tinwork, and other crafts, too.

NEW MEXICAN CUISINE

Taos is a great place for New Mexican fare, prepared with locally grown chiles and homemade tortillas, but the town also draws raves for outstanding contemporary restaurants with award-winning wine lists. The many New Agers who live in and frequent the area mean that fresh organic and vegetarian dishes abound here. Pan-Asian and Middle Eastern flavors are also influences in the increasingly sophisticated cuisines finding their way to this small town with a big attitude.

OUTDOOR ACTIVITIES & SPORTS

The glorious landscape around Taos draws serious athletes as well as those who just want to wander under the huge skies and gaze at the mountains. Cycling is popular, with rallies and races held in late summer. The vast Carson National Forest is an excellent spot for most any outdoor pursuit. The rivers and lakes are excellent for trout fishing; you can arrange for outings with local expert guides. The waters also invite rafters, especially when spring runoff fills the rivers with white water. There are innumerable trails for hiking for all levels of fitness, up into alpine reaches and down into rocky gorges. If you're really after a thrill or something different, try a hot-air balloon ride into the Rio Grande Gorge or llama trekking in the wilderness. And of course winter brings skiers from all over to the world-class slopes of Taos Ski Valley and other nearby resorts.

studies in white, their precise lines and blocks forming textured grids. Operated by the University of New Mexico since 1936, the Harwood is the second-oldest art museum in the state. ✉ *238 Ledoux St.* ☎ *505/758–9826* ⊕ *www.harwoodmuseum.org* ✑ *$7, $20 with Museum Association of Taos combination ticket* ☉ *Tues.–Sat. 10–5, Sun. noon–5.*

4 Kit Carson Home and Museum. Kit Carson bought this low-slung 12-room adobe home in 1843 for his wife, Josefa Jaramillo, the daughter of a powerful, politically influential Spanish family. Three of the museum's rooms

A GOOD WALK

Begin at the gazebo in the middle of **Taos Plaza** ▶ **①**. After exploring the Plaza, head south from its western edge down the small unmarked alley (its name is West Plaza Drive). The first cross street is Camino de la Placita. Across it, West Plaza Drive becomes Ledoux Street. Continue south on Ledoux to the **Blumenschein Home and Museum ②** and, a few doors farther south, the **Harwood Museum ③**. (If you're driving, the parking area for the Harwood Foundation is at Ledoux and Ranchitos Road.)

From the Harwood Foundation, walk back north on Ranchitos Road a few blocks, make a left on Camino de la Placita, and go right onto Don Fernando Road. Follow it east along the north side of the Plaza to Paseo del Pueblo Norte (NM 68), which is the main street of Taos. As you cross NM 68, Don Fernando Road changes to Kit Carson Road. On the north side of Kit Carson Road is the **Kit Carson Home and Museum ④**. After visiting the home, head back to Paseo del Pueblo Norte and walk north past the Taos Inn to browse through Bent Street's shops, boutiques, and galleries.

In a tiny plaza is the **Governor Bent Museum ⑤**, the modest home of the first Anglo governor of the state. Across the street is the John Dunn House. Once the homestead of a colorful and well-respected Taos gambling and transportation entrepreneur, the Dunn House is now a small shopping plaza. At the western end of Bent Street, head north on Camino de la Placita. In about 2½ blocks you'll come to the Taos Volunteer Fire Department building, which doubles as a fire station and the **Firehouse Collection ⑥** exhibition space.

Head east on Civic Plaza and cross Paseo del Pueblo Norte. To the north will be **Kit Carson Park ⑦** and the **Taos Art Museum at the Fechin House ⑧**, named for the iconoclastic artist Nicolai Fechin.

🕓 **TIMING TIPS→→ The entire walk can be done in a half day, a whole day if you stop to lunch along the way and browse in the shops and galleries. The Taos Art Museum at the Fechin House is closed Monday. Hours vary by season, but visits by appointment are welcomed. Some museums are closed on the weekend, so you may want to do this walk on a Wednesday, Thursday, or Friday. You can tour each of the museums in less than an hour.**

are furnished as they were when the Carson family lived here. The rest of the museum is devoted to gun and mountain-man exhibits, such as rugged leather clothing and Kit's own Spencer carbine rifle with its beaded leather carrying case, and early Taos antiques, artifacts, and manuscripts. ✉ *Kit Carson Rd.* ☎ *505/758–0505* 💬 *$5, $20 with Museum Association of Taos combination ticket* 🕙 *May–Oct., daily 9–5; Nov.–Apr., daily 10–4.*

NEED A BREAK?

Let the aroma of fresh-ground coffee draw you into the tiny **World Cup** (✉ 102 Paseo del Pueblo Norte ☎ 505/737–5299), where you can sit at the counter or wander outside to a bench on the porch. Locals engage in political rhetoric here, often slanted toward the left, so be prepared for a rousing debate if you dare to dissent.

⑦ Kit Carson Park. The noted pioneer is buried in the park that bears his name. His grave is marked with a *cerquita* (a spiked wrought-iron rectangular fence), traditionally used to outline and protect burial sites. Also interred here is Mabel Dodge Luhan, the pioneering patron of the early Taos art scene. The 32-acre park has swings and slides for recreational breaks. It's well marked with big stone pillars and a gate. ✉ *211 Paseo del Pueblo Norte* ☎ *505/758–8234* ✆ *Free* ☾ *Late May–early Sept., daily 8–8; early Sept.–late May, daily 8–5.*

⑧ Taos Art Museum at the Fechin House. The interior of this extraordinary adobe house, built between 1927 and 1933 by Russian émigré and artist Nicolai Fechin, is a marvel of carved Russian-style woodwork and furniture that glistens with an almost golden sheen. Fechin constructed it to showcase his daringly colorful paintings. The house has hosted the Taos Art Museum since 2003, with a collection of paintings from more than 50 Taos artists, including founders of the original Taos Society of Artists, among them Joseph Sharp, Ernest Blumenschein, Bert Phillips, E.I. Couse, and Oscar Berninghaus. ✉ *227 Paseo del Pueblo Norte* ☎ *505/ 758–2690* ⊕ *www.taosartmuseum.org* ✆ *$8, $20 with Museum Association of Taos combination ticket* ☾ *Tues.–Sun. 10–5.*

Fodor's Choice ★

① Taos Plaza. The first European explorers of the Taos Valley came here with Captain Hernando de Alvarado, a member of Francisco Vásquez de Coronado's expedition of 1540. Basque explorer Don Juan de Oñate arrived in Taos in July 1598 and established a mission and trading arrangements with residents of Taos Pueblo. The settlement developed into two plazas: the Plaza at the heart of the town became a thriving business district for the early colony, and a walled residential plaza was constructed a few hundred yards behind. It remains active today, home to a throng of gift and coffee shops. The covered gazebo was donated by heiress and longtime Taos resident Mabel Dodge Luhan. On the southeastern corner of Taos Plaza is the **Hotel La Fonda de Taos.** Some infamous erotic paintings by D. H. Lawrence that were naughty in his day but are quite tame by present standards can be viewed ($3 entry fee) in the former barroom beyond the lobby.

> **WORD OF MOUTH**
>
> "Very nice shops, but don't expect the average person to afford much in any of them. If you love window shopping this is the place to go."
> —Jodie on Taos Plaza

NEED A BREAK? Join the locals at the north or south location of the **Bean** (✉ 900 Paseo del Pueblo Norte ☎ 505/758–7711 ✉ 1033 Paseo del Pueblo Sur ☎ 505/758–5123). The Bean roasts its own coffee, and the south-side location (where you can dine on an outside patio) offers good breakfast and lunch fare. The north location, in an adobe building, displays local artwork and is the most atmospheric of the two.

A GOOD DRIVE

Head south 3 mi on NM 240 (also known as Ranchitos Road) to **La Hacienda de los Martínez** ▶ ❾. As you pass by the adobe cottages and modest homes dotting the landscape, you get a sense of the area's rural roots. From the hacienda continue south and east another 4 mi to NM 68 and the small farming village of **Ranchos de**

Taos ❿. Watch for signs for **San Francisco de Asís Church,** which is on the east side of NM 68. The small plaza here contains several galleries worth checking out.

🕙 **TIMING TIPS➔** Set aside about two hours to tour the hacienda, a bit of Ranchos de Taos, and San Francisco de Asís Church.

3

South of Taos

The first Spanish settlers were farmers who faced raids by non-Pueblo Native Americans like the Comanches. Aspects of this history come alive on this meandering drive south through fields and farmland to a restored hacienda and into a former farming village with its famous, fortresslike church.

What to See

❾ **La Hacienda de los Martínez.** Spare and fortlike, this adobe structure built between 1804 and 1827 on the bank of the Rio Pueblo served as a community refuge during Comanche and Apache raids. Its thick walls, which have few windows, surround two central courtyards. Don Antonio Severino Martínez was a farmer and trader; the hacienda was the final stop along El Camino Real (the Royal Road), the trade route the Spanish established between Mexico City and New Mexico. The restored period rooms here contain textiles, foods, and crafts of the early 19th century. There's a working blacksmith's shop, usually open to visitors on Saturday, and weavers create beautiful textiles on reconstructed period looms. ✉ *Ranchitos Rd., NM 240* ☎ *505/758–1000* ⊕ *www. taoshistoricmuseums.com/martinez.html* 💲 *$6, $20 with Museum Association of Taos combination ticket* 🕙 *Apr.–Oct., daily 9–5; Nov.–Mar., daily 10–4.*

❿ **Ranchos de Taos.** A few minutes' drive south of the center of Taos, this village still retains some of its rural atmosphere despite the highway traffic passing through. Huddled around its famous adobe church and dusty plaza are cheerful, remodeled shops and galleries standing shoulder to shoulder with crumbling adobe shells. This ranching, farming, and budding small-business community was an early home to Taos Native Americans before being settled by Spaniards in 1716. Although many of the adobe dwellings

GOOD TERM

Retablo: Holy image painted on wood or tin.

have seen better days, the shops, modest galleries, taco stands, and two fine restaurants point to an ongoing revival.

★ The massive bulk of **San Francisco de Asís Church** (⊠ NM 68, 500 yards south of NM 518, Ranchos de Taos ☎ 505/758–2754) is an enduring attraction. The Spanish Mission–style church was erected in 1815 as a spiritual and physical refuge from raiding Apaches, Utes, and Comanches. In 1979 the deteriorated church was rebuilt with traditional adobe bricks by community volunteers. Every spring a group gathers to re-mud the facade. The earthy, clean lines of the exterior walls and supporting bulwarks have inspired generations of painters and photographers. The late-afternoon light provides the best exposure of the heavily buttressed rear of the church—though today's image-takers face the challenge of framing the architecturally pure lines through rows of parked cars and a large, white sign put up by church officials; morning light is best for the front. Bells in the twin belfries call Taoseños to services on Sunday and holidays. Monday through Saturday from 9 to 4 you can step inside. In the parish hall nearby (and for a $3 fee) you can view a 15-minute video presentation every half hour that describes the history and restoration of the church and explains the mysterious painting *Shadow of the Cross,* on which each evening the shadow of a cross appears over Christ's shoulder (scientific studies made on the canvas and the paint pigments cannot explain the phenomenon). The fee also allows you to view the painting. ⊠ *Paseo del Pueblo Sur, NM 68, about 4 mi south of Taos Plaza.*

> **WORD OF MOUTH**
>
> "Gorgeous building (a former home), exquisite Indian Jewelry as well as blankets and Maria Martinez pottery. You feel like you are visiting someone's home that has REALLY GOOD taste in art of the region. I never miss it when in Taos."
> –Marjorie on the Millicent Rogers Museum

Taos Pueblo to Rio Grande Gorge

What to See

⑫ **Millicent Rogers Museum.** More than 5,000 pieces of spectacular Native
Fodor's Choice American and Hispanic art, many of them from the private collection
★ of the late Standard Oil heiress Millicent Rogers, are on display here. Among the pieces are baskets, blankets, rugs, kachina dolls, carvings, paintings, rare religious artifacts, and most significantly, and jewelry (Rogers, a fashion icon in her day, was one of the first Americans to appreciate the turquoise-and-silver artistry of Native American jewelers). Other important works include the pottery and ceramics of Maria Martinez and other potters from San Ildefonso Pueblo (23 mi north of Santa Fe). Docents conduct guided tours by appointment, and the museum hosts lectures, films, workshops, and demonstrations. ⊠ *1504 Millicent Rogers Rd., from Taos Plaza head north on Paseo del Pueblo Norte and left at sign for CR BA030, also called Millicent Rogers Rd. or Museum Rd.* ☎ *505/758–2462* ⊕ *www.millicentrogers.com* ☞ *$7, $20 with Museum Association of Taos combination ticket* ☉ *Apr.–Sept., daily 10–5; Nov.–Mar., Tues.–Sun. 10–5.*

A GOOD DRIVE

Drive 2 mi north on Paseo del Pueblo Norte (NM 68), and keep your eyes peeled for the signs on the right, beyond the post office, directing you to **Taos Pueblo** ▶ ⑪. To reach the **Millicent Rogers Museum** ⑫ next, return to NM 68 to head north and make a left onto County Road BA030. If you find yourself at the intersection with U.S. 64 and 150, you've gone too far. Continue down the county road to the big adobe wall; the sign for the museum is on the right. This rural road eventually connects back onto Upper Ranchitos Road. After exploring the museum, return to NM 68 north; then make a left on U.S. 64 west to the **Rio Grande Gorge Bridge** ⑬, a stunning

marriage of natural wonder and human engineering. Bring along sturdy hiking shoes and plenty of water and snacks for an invigorating walk down into the gorge. But remember, what goes down must come up, and it's an arduous path. ⊙ **TIMING TIPS→**
Plan on spending 1½ hours at the pueblo. Taos can get hot in summer, but if you visit the pueblo in the morning, you'll avoid the heat and the crowds. Winters can be cold and windy, so dress warmly. If your visit coincides with a ceremonial observance, set aside several hours, because the ceremonies, though they are worth the wait, never start on time. Two hours should be enough time to take in the museum and the grandeur of the Rio Grande Gorge Bridge.

★ ☺ ⑬ **Rio Grande Gorge Bridge.** It's a dizzying experience to see the Rio Grande 650 feet underfoot, where it flows at the bottom of an immense, steep rock canyon. In summer the reddish rocks dotted with green scrub contrast brilliantly with the blue sky, where you might see a hawk lazily floating in circles. The bridge is the second-highest expansion bridge in the country. Hold on to your camera and eyeglasses when looking down, and watch out for low-flying planes. The Taos Municipal Airport is close by, and daredevil private pilots have been known to challenge one another to fly under the bridge. Shortly after daybreak, hot-air balloons fly above and even inside the gorge. ⊠ *U.S. 64, 12 mi west of town.*

☺ ⑪ **Taos Pueblo.** For nearly 1,000 years the mud-and-straw adobe walls of FodorśChoice Taos Pueblo have sheltered Tiwa-speaking Native Americans. A United ★ Nations World Heritage Site, this is the largest collection of multistory pueblo dwellings in the United States. The pueblo's main buildings, Hlauuma (north house) and Hlaukwima (south house), are separated by a creek. These structures are believed to be of a similar age, probably built between 1000 and 1450. But the entire site is covered in the UN World Heritage designation. The dwellings have common walls but no connecting doorways—the Tiwas gained access only from the top, via ladders that were retrieved

WORD OF MOUTH

"Taos Pueblo is worth the price of the tour. Our guide grew up in the pueblo and returned to live there after college. She gave many cultural and spiritual insights on the tour."   –eileenleft after entering. Small buildings and corrals are scattered about.

The pueblo today appears much as it did when the first Spanish explorers arrived in New Mexico in 1540. The adobe walls glistening with mica caused the conquistadors to believe they had discovered one of the fabled Seven Cities of Gold. The outside surfaces are continuously maintained by replastering with thin layers of mud, and the interior walls are frequently coated with thin washes of white clay. Some walls are several feet thick in places. The roofs of each of the five-story structures are supported by large timbers, or vigas, hauled down from the mountain forests. Pine or aspen *latillas* (smaller pieces of wood) are placed side by side between the vigas; the entire roof is then packed with dirt.

Even after 400 years of Spanish and Anglo presence in Taos, inside the pueblo the traditional Native American way of life has endured. Tribal custom allows no electricity or running water in Hlauuma and Hlaukwima, where varying numbers (usually fewer than 100) of Taos Native Americans live full-time. About 2,000 others live in conventional homes on the pueblo's 95,000 acres. The crystal-clear Rio Pueblo de Taos, originating high above in the mountains at the sacred Blue Lake, is the primary source of water for drinking and irrigating. Bread is still baked in *hornos* (outdoor domed ovens). Artisans of the Taos Pueblo produce and sell (tax-free) traditionally handcrafted wares, such as mica-flecked pottery and silver jewelry. Great hunters, the Taos Native Americans are also known for their work with animal skins and their excellent moccasins, boots, and drums.

Although the population is about 80% Catholic, the people of Taos Pueblo, like most Pueblo Native Americans, also maintain their native religious traditions. At Christmas and other sacred holidays, for instance, immediately after Mass, dancers dressed in seasonal sacred garb proceed down the aisle of St. Jerome Chapel, drums beating and rattles shaking, to begin other religious rites.

The pueblo **Church of San Geronimo,** or St. Jerome, the patron saint of Taos Pueblo, was completed in 1850 to replace the one destroyed by the U.S. Army in 1847 during the Mexican War. With its smooth symmetry, stepped portal, and twin bell towers, the church is a popular subject for photographers and artists (though the taking of photographs inside is discouraged).

The public is invited to certain ceremonial dances held throughout the year: January 1, Turtle Dance; January 6, Buffalo or Deer Dance; May 3, Feast of Santa Cruz Foot Race and Corn Dance; June 13, Feast of San Antonio Corn Dance; June 24, Feast of San Juan Corn Dance; second weekend in July, Taos Pueblo Powwow; July 25 and 26, Feast of Santa Ana and Santiago Corn Dance; September 29 and 30, Feast of San Geronimo Sunset Dance; December 24, Vespers and Bonfire Pro-

CLOSE UP

Festivals of Tradition

SEVERAL YEARLY FESTIVALS CELEBRATE the Native American and Hispanic roots of Taos. During the last weekend in September, La Hacienda de los Martínez hosts the **Old Taos Trade Fair,** a reenactment of autumn gatherings of the 1820s, when Plains Indians and trappers came to Taos to trade with the Spanish and the Pueblo Indians. The two-day event includes demonstrations of blacksmithing, weaving, and other crafts, a chili cook-off, native foods, music, and dancing.

The **Wool Festival** (⊕ www.taoswoolfestival.org), held in early October in Kit Carson Park, commemorates the long tradition of wool growing and weaving begun

in the 16th century, when Spanish settlers brought the tough little churro sheep to northern New Mexico. Every aspect of the craft "from sheep to shawl" is demonstrated, including shearing, spinning, and weaving. Handmade woolen items are for sale, and you can taste favorite lamb dishes.

During the second weekend of July, the **Taos Pueblo Powwow** (⊕ www.taospueblopowwow.com) attracts Native Americans from many Indian nations. Visitors are welcome to watch the traditional drumming and dancing, shop at the arts-and-crafts market, and partake of fry bread, mutton, green chile sauce, and other local delicacies.

---

cession; December 25, Deer Dance or Matachines. While you're at the pueblo, respect the RESTRICTED AREA signs that protect the privacy of residents and native religious sites; do not enter private homes or open any doors not clearly labeled as curio shops; do not photograph tribal members without asking permission; do not enter the cemetery grounds; and do not wade in the Rio Pueblo de Taos, which is considered sacred and is the community's sole source of drinking water.

The small, rather prosaic, and smoke-free Taos Mountain Casino (open daily) is just off Camino del Pueblo after you turn right off Paseo del Pueblo on your way to the main pueblo. ⊠ *Head to right off Paseo del Pueblo Norte just past Best Western Kachina Lodge* ☎ *505/758–1028* ⊕ *www.taospueblo.com* ▧ *Tourist fees $10. Guided tours by appt. Still-camera permit $5; note: cameras that may look commercial, such as those with telephoto lenses, might be denied a permit; video-camera permit $5. Commercial photography, sketching, or painting only by prior per-*

> **DID YOU KNOW?**
>
> The privilege of setting up an easel and painting all day at a pueblo will cost you as little as $35 or as much as $150 (at Taos Pueblo).

mission from governor's office (505/758–1028); fees vary; apply at least 10 days in advance ☉ *Mon.–Sat., 8–4:30, Sun. 8:30–4:30. Closed for funerals, religious ceremonies, and for 2-month "quiet time" in late win-*

ter or early spring, and last part of Aug.; call ahead before visiting at these times.

■ NEED A BREAK?

Look for signs that read FRY BREAD on dwellings in the pueblo: you can enter the kitchen and buy a piece of fresh bread dough that's flattened and deep-fried until puffy and golden brown and then topped with honey or powdered sugar. You also can buy delicious bread that's baked daily in the clay hornos (outdoor adobe ovens) that are scattered throughout the pueblo.

WHERE TO EAT

For a place as remote as Taos, the dining scene is surprisingly varied. You can find the usual coffee shops and Mexican-style eateries but also restaurants serving creatively prepared Continental, Italian, and Southwestern cuisine.

WHAT IT COSTS				
$$$$	$$$	$$	$	¢
AT DINNER over $32	$24–$32	$17–$24	$10–$17	under $10

Prices are for a main course, excluding 8.25% sales tax.

Downtown Taos

American

$-$$$ ✗ **Ogelvie's Taos Grill and Bar.** On the second floor of an old two-story adobe building, touristy but festive Ogelvie's is the perfect spot for people-watching from on high, especially from the outdoor patio in summer. You won't find any culinary surprises here, just dependable meat-and-potato dishes. The sure bets are filet mignon with brandy-cream sauce, lamb sirloin with rosemary aioli, and blue-corn enchiladas stuffed with beef or chicken. There's live music many nights. ✉ *East side of Taos Plaza* ☎ *505/758–8866* ⊕ *www.ogelvies.com* ⌕ *Reservations not accepted* ☰ *AE, D, DC, MC, V.*

$-$$ ✗ **Bravo!** This restaurant and full bar inside an upscale grocery, beer, and wine shop, is a great stop for gourmet picnic fixings or an on-site meal on the outdoor patio. You can feast on anything from a turkey sandwich to lobster-, and-shrimp ravioli to well-prepared pizzas. The beer and wine selection is formidable. ✉ *1353–A Paseo del Pueblo Sur* ☎ *505/758–8100* ⊕ *www.bravotaos.com* ⌕ *Reservations not accepted* ☰*AE, MC, V* ☾ *Closed Sun.*

¢-$ ✗ **Eske's Brew Pub.** This casual dining and quaffing pub is favored by off-duty ski patrollers and river guides. The menu mostly covers hearty sandwiches (try the grilled

WORD OF MOUTH

"This had to be one of our best experiences of our trip to Taos. We ate breakfast there and had wonderful café mochas. The food was hot, fresh, and service was done with a smile."

–Jodie on Bent Street Café

Where to Eat in Taos

bratwurst and sauerkraut sandwich), soups, and salads. The microbrewery downstairs produces everything from nutty, dark stout to light ales, but you shouldn't leave without sampling the house specialty—Taos green-chile beer. There's live music on weekends, and in good weather you can relax on the patio. ⊠ *106 Des Georges La.* ☎ *505/758–1517* ⊕ *www.eskesbrewpub.com* ▤ *MC, V.*

¢–$ ✕ **Michael's Kitchen.** This casual, homey restaurant serves up a bit of everything—you can order a hamburger while your friend who can't get enough chile sauce can order up vegetarian cheese enchiladas garnished with lettuce and tomatoes. Brunch is popular with the locals (dig into a plate of strawberry-banana-pecan pancakes), and amusing asides to the waitstaff over the intercom contribute to the energetic buzz. Breakfast, lunch, and dinner are served daily, but you must order dinner by 8:30 PM. ⊠ *304 Paseo del Pueblo Norte* ☎ *505/758–4178* ⊕ *www.michaelskitchen.com* ⟲ *Reservations not accepted* ▤ *AE, D, MC, V.*

Cafés

★ ¢–$ ✕ **Bent Street Cafe & Deli.** Try for a seat on the cheery, covered outdoor patio next to giant sunflowers. You can enjoy a breakfast croissant sandwich, smoked turkey for lunch, or a fancier organic New York steak for dinner. Great food can be topped off with a chocolate nut brownie and washed down with beer, wine, and gourmet coffees. There's something on the menu for all budget ranges, even a peanut butter and jam sandwich. Cheerful service is rendered in an old-fashioned country kitchen atmosphere, complete with frilly curtains. Breakfast is served until 11 AM. ⊠ *120 Bent St.* ☎ *505/758–5787* ▤ *MC, V* ☉ *Closed Sun.*

¢–$ ✕ **Dragonfly Café.** This charming breakfast and lunch café bakes its own bread and serves large and tasty omelets (the best one if packed with house-cured gravlax, cream cheese, red onion, and tomato), Swedish pancakes, udon noodle bowls, Vietnamese chicken salad, and panini sandwiches. You can sit out front on a shaded outdoor patio with a fountain when it's warm and watch the tourists go by. Dragonfly also does a brisk mail-order business with its red chile–infused truffles, delicious granola, and many other tasty products. ⊠ *402 Paseo del Pueblo Norte* ☎ *505/737–5859* ⊕ *www.dragonflytaos.com* ▤ *MC, V* ☉ *No dinner.*

¢ ✕ **Taos Wrappers.** A loyal clientele visits this place for take-out lunch, or to eat in a cozy space with tiny tables. Pesto chicken, roasted veggies, and curried tuna are among the healthful ingredients inside flavored tortilla wraps. There are soups, salads, and desserts, too. Breakfast is available on weekends. ⊠ *616 Paseo del Pueblo Sur* ☎ *505/751–9727* ▤ *No credit cards* ☉ *No dinner.*

Contemporary

$$–$$$$ ✕ **Joseph's Table.** Locally renowned chef Joseph Wrede has moved
Fodor'sChoice around the area a bit in recent years, but has settled into what he does
★ best—overseeing his own swank yet friendly restaurant in the La Fonda Hotel on the Taos Plaza. Amid artful surroundings of giant flowers handpainted on walls, you can sample some of the most innovative and masterfully prepared cuisine in the state. You might start with lobster tamales served with roasted-corn puree and trout caviar, before moving on to pistachio-crusted halibut with tarragon butter, strawberries,

and fresh spinach. But the master-piece here is pepper-crusted elk ten-derloin with foie gras and truffle demi-glace. Lighter fare, including addictive duck-fat fries, are avail-able at the bar, and there's an as-tounding wine list. ⊠ *108–A S. Taos Plaza, La Fonda Hotel* ☎ *505/ 751–4512* ⊕ *www.josephstable. com* ☐ *AE, D, DC, MC, V.*

WORD OF MOUTH

"I took my boyfriend here to cele-brate his 36th birthday and it was perfect. We started with the duck-fat fries and proceeded with lovely wines and entrees. The 'cubbies' are very romanic (all we did was ask!). I can't wait to return."
–Cat on Joseph's Table

★ $$–$$$ ✕ **Byzantium.** Off a grassy court-yard near the Blumenschein and Harwood museums, this tradi-tional-looking adobe restaurant offers an eclectic menu. Asian, Euro-pean, and Middle Eastern influences can be tasted in dishes like seafood cakes, duck curry, and vegetable potpie. Service is friendly, and the vibe is low-key—this is a spot relatively few tourists find out about. ⊠ *Ledoux St. and La Placita* ☎ *505/751–0805* ☐ *AE, MC, V* ☺ *Closed Tues. and Wed. No lunch.*

★ $$–$$$ ✕ **De La Tierra.** A dashing, dramatic, high-ceiling restaurant inside the fancifully plush El Monte Sagrado resort, this chic spot presents daring globally influenced cuisine. Top starters include smoked trout with horseradish-cognac cream, and blue-corn calamari with grilled-pineap-ple salsa and chipotle-lime vinaigrette. Among the mains, you can't go wrong with the molasses-marinated quail with a parsnip cake and dried-blueberry sauce, or pan-roasted lamb with asiago, grilled asparagus, and sage bread pudding. Tequila-lime pie with white-chocolate–ancho chile crust and prickly pear syrup makes for a happy ending. It's dressy by Taos standards, but you'll still fit in wearing smartly casual threads. ⊠ *317 Kit Carson Rd., El Monte Sagrado Resort* ☎ *505737–9855* ⊕ *www. elmontesagrado.com* ☐ *AE, D, DC, MC, V.*

$$–$$$ ✕ **Doc Martin's.** The restaurant of the Historic Taos Inn takes its name from the building's original owner, a local physician who saw patients in the rooms that are now the dining areas. The creative menu includes Dungeness crab salad with asparagus, jicama, and avocado-lime vinai-grette, blue-crusted boneless trout with pumpkin-mole, and organic fil-let of beef with heirloom tomatoes, blue cheese, and roasted-tomato demi-glace. There's an extensive wine list, and the adjoining Adobe Bar serves up some of the best margaritas in town. In winter ask for a table near the cozy kiva fireplace. ⊠ *Historic Taos Inn, 125 Paseo del Pueblo Norte* ☎ *505/758–1977* ⊕ *www.taosinn.com* ☐ *AE, D, MC, V.*

★ $–$$$ ✕ **Trading Post Cafe.** Colorful paintings of Southwest scenes, a covered, fenced-in patio, impeccable service and an imaginative menu have made the Trading Post a favorite spot in Ranchos. The beef carpaccio appe-tizer and signature chicken-noodle soup are both exceptional, and the oven-roasted half duck and New Zealand lamb chops with tomato-mint sauce both make superb main dishes. Flan or homemade raspberry sor-bet makes a fine finish. To park, turn east onto NM 518 (Talpa Road) just north of the restaurant, and then walk back along Talpa Road to get to the entrance. ⊠ *4179 Paseo del Pueblo Sur, NM 68, Ranchos de*

Taos ☎ *505/758–5089* ▤ *AE, D, DC, MC, V* ☺ *Closed Mon. No lunch Sun.*

Continental

$$–$$$$ ✕ **Lambert's of Taos.** In what was once an elegant family home, this lace-curtained restaurant looks over lushly cultivated grounds 2½ blocks south of the Plaza. The signature dishes here include Dungeness crab cakes with Thai curry, pepper-crusted lamb with a red-wine demi-glace, and fillet of beef over a potato cake with grilled spinach and horseradish cream. The lengthy wine list includes some of California's finest vintages. ✉ *309 Paseo del Pueblo Sur* ☎ *505/758–1009* ▤ *AE, D, DC, MC, V* ☺ *No lunch.*

Eclectic

★ **$–$$$** ✕ **Apple Tree.** Named for the large tree in its umbrella-shaded courtyard, this terrific lunch and dinner spot is in a historic adobe just a block from the Plaza. Among the well-crafted dishes are barbecued duck fajitas, Baja fish tacos, chipotle-shrimp over corn cakes, and mango-chicken enchiladas. The restaurant has an outstanding wine list. Sunday brunch is great fun here—dig into a plate of Papas Tapadas (two eggs any style over

> **WORD OF MOUTH**
>
> "The menu is a delightful mix of old favorites with a new twist—e.g., the duck fajitas. My wife raved over their baked brie. The ambiance was casual, relaxed, but as you would expect on a Saturday night, busy."
>
> —Steve on Apple Tree

seasoned homefries, with red or green chile, and topped with white cheddar. Expect a bit of a wait if you don't have a reservation. ✉ *123 Bent St.* ☎ *505/758–1900* ⊕ *www.appletreerestaurant.com* ▤ *AE, D, DC, MC, V.*

Mexican

¢–$ ✕ **Guadalajara Grill.** Tasty regional Mexican cuisine, served quickly from these open, spotless kitchens, is popular enough with local patrons that there's a location on both the north and south ends of town. It's ultracasual here (you select your own beer from a cooler, and order from the counter). You can hear Spanish banter from the kitchen while you watch your chicken tacos or green-chile cheese enchiladas being prepared. ✉ *822 Paseo del Pueblo Norte* ☎ *505/737–0816* ✉ *1384 Paseo del Pueblo Sur* ☎ *505/751–0063* ▤ *MC, V.*

Middle Eastern

¢–$ ✕ **Sheva Café.** The Israeli owners here have created an authentic menu that includes delectable falafel, eggplant salad, and stuffed grape leaves served with homemade pita bread. You can dine on organic lamb kebobs served with Israeli salad, or sample one of many vegetarian-friendly (and often kosher) items such as zucchini paté and eggplant-lemon salad. Middle Eastern music and art set the scene, along with works of local artists. An outdoor patio is a lovely place to linger over coffee or one of the many organic desserts prepared by the restaurant's bakery, Magic Flavors. Breakfast is available until 11 daily. ✉ *Overland Ranch, 1405 Paseo del Pueblo Norte* ☎ *505/737–9290* ▤ *D, MC, V.*

New Mexican

★ ¢ ✕ **Orlando's.** This family-run local favorite may be packed during peak hours, while guests wait patiently to devour favorites such as *carne adovada* (red chile–marinated pork), blue-corn enchiladas, and scrumptious shrimp burritos. You can eat in the cozy dining room, outside on the front patio, or call ahead for takeout if you'd rather avoid the crowds. ⊠ *114 Don Juan Valdez La., off Paseo del Pueblo Norte* ☎ *505/751–1450* ☐ *No credit cards* ⊘ *Closed Sun.*

Steak

$$–$$$$ ✕ **Stakeout Grill and Bar.** On Outlaw Hill in the foothills of the Sangre
Fodor'sChoice de Cristo Mountains, this old adobe homestead has 100-mi-long views
★ and sunsets that dazzle. The outdoor patio encircled by a piñon forest has kiva fireplaces to warm you during cooler months. The decadent fare is well-prepared, fully living up to the view it accompanies—try filet mignon, buffalo rib eye with jalapeño sauce, duck with apple-raisin chutney, or—if you're truly up for a challenge—the grilled 32-ounce cowboy steak with chipotle barbecue sauce. Don't miss the tasty desserts, such as Kentucky bourbon pecan pie and crème brûlée with toasted coconut. ⊠ *Stakeout Dr., 8½ mi south of Taos Plaza, east of NM 68, look for cowboy sign* ☎ *505/751–3815* ☐ *AE, D, DC, MC, V* ⊘ *No lunch.*

Arroyo Seco & Vicinity

Cafés

¢–$ ✕ **Gypsy 360°.** Set back from the main road in the tiny village of Arroyo Seco, cheap and cheerful Gypsy 360° is a favorite spot for a filling lunch or breakfast, especially on warm days, when you can dine on the patio. The menu borrows from all around the world, with everything from hearty curries to bountiful salads to Japanese sushi rolls, plus some of the juiciest burgers in the area. Organic coffees are served as well as beer and wine. There's a popular brunch on Sunday. ⊠ *480 NM 150* ☎ *505/776–3166* ☐ *MC, V* ⊘ *Closed Mon. No dinner.*

¢ ✕ **Abe's Cantina y Cocina.** Family-owned and -operated since the 1940s, Abe's is both store and restaurant. You can have your breakfast burrito, rolled tacos, or homemade tamales at one of the small tables crowded next to the canned goods, or take it on a picnic. ⊠ *489 NM 150, Taos Ski Valley Rd., Arroyo Seco* ☎ *505/776–8643* ☐ *AE, D, MC, V* ⊘ *Closed Sun.*

★ ¢ ✕ **Taos Cow.** Locals, travelers headed up to Taos Ski Valley, and visitors to funky Arroyo Seco rejoiced when the famed Taos Cow ice-cream company opened this cozy storefront café in 2005. This isn't merely a place to sample amazing homemade ice cream (including such innovative flavors as piñon-caramel, lavender, and Chocolate Rio Grande, which consists of chocolate ice cream packed with cinnamon-chocolate chunks). You can also nosh on French toast, omelets, turkey-and-Brie sandwiches, black bean–and–brown rice bowls, organic teas and coffees, natural sodas, homemade granola, and more. The friendly but zoned-out staff and burning incense lend a hippie-dippie vibe to the place. ⊠ *485 NM 150* ☎ *505/776–5640* ⊕ *www.taoscow.com* ☐ *MC, V* ⊘ *No dinner.*

Hostess of Taos

MABEL DODGE LUHAN, a progressive-minded socialite from Buffalo, New York, arrived on the scene in 1917, fell in love with Taos, and stayed. In the high-desert landscape and in the Taos Pueblo culture she found a purpose and unity that she firmly believed ought to be extended to American society at large. When she walked away from her "old, mythical life," aiding her as soul mate and spiritual mainstay was a statuesque Taos Pueblo man, Antonio Luhan, who became her fourth, and last, husband. In the house they built together next to Pueblo land, they hosted many of the era's great artists, writers, philosophers, psychologists, anthropologists, and social reformers. Mabel's friends and acquaintances

included Martha Graham, Aldous Huxley, and Carl Jung. Mabel wrote to D. H. Lawrence many times and even tried to send him psychic messages until finally he, too, came to Taos and was profoundly affected by what he found. Although he stayed less than two years all together, some of his finest writing, including *The Plumed Serpent* and several novelettes, essays, and poems, grew out of his experiences in Taos and Mexico. Mabel herself penned several books; *Edge of Taos Desert: An Escape to Reality* (1937) is a part of her autobiography that vividly describes her life in Taos. She and her beloved Tony died within months of each other in 1970. Their house is now a conference center and B&B.

Contemporary

★ $-$$$ ✕ **Sabroso.** Reasonably priced, innovative cuisine and outstanding wines are served in this 150-year-old adobe hacienda, where you can also relax in lounge chairs near the bar, or on a delightful patio surrounded by plum trees. The Mediterranean-influenced contemporary menu changes regularly, but an evening's entrée might be wood-grilled shrimp skewers with clam-broth, risotto cakes, and ratatouille, or New York strip steak with gnocchi and Gorgonzola cream. There's live jazz and cabaret in the piano bar several nights a week. Order from the simpler bar menu if you're seeking something light—the antipasto plate and white-truffle-oil fries are both delicious. ✉ *470 NM 150, Taos Ski Valley Rd.* ☎ *505/776–3333* ⊕ *www.sabrosotaos.com* ⊟ *AE, MC, V* ⊘ *Closed Mon. No lunch.*

New Mexican

$-$$$ ✕ **Old Blinking Light.** Just past the landmark "old blinking light" (now a regular stoplight at Mile Marker 1), this rambling adobe is known for its steaks, ribs, and enormous (and potent) margaritas. There's also a long list of tasty apps, such as posole stew and chipotle-shrimp quesadillas. Several huge burgers are available, plus first-rate chicken mole. In summer you can sit out in the walled garden and take in the spectacular mountain view. There's a wineshop on the premises. ✉ *Taos Ski Valley Rd., between El Prado and Arroyo Seco* ☎ *505/776–8787* ⊕ *www. oldblinkinglight.com* ⊟ *AE, MC, V* ⊘ *No lunch.*

WHERE TO STAY

The hotels and motels along NM 68 (Paseo del Pueblo Sur and Norte) suit every need and budget; with a few exceptions, rates vary little between big-name chains and smaller establishments. Make advance reservations and expect higher rates during the ski season (usually from late December to early April) and in the summer. Skiers have many choices for overnighting, from accommodations in the town of Taos to spots snuggled up right beside the slopes, although several of the hotels up at Taos Ski Valley have been converted to condos in recent years, eroding the supply of overnight accommodations. Arroyo Seco is a good alternative if you can't find a room right up in the Ski Valley.

The best deals in town are the bed-and-breakfasts. Mostly family-owned, they provide personal service, delicious breakfasts, and many extras that hotels charge for. The B&Bs are often in old adobes that have been refurbished with style and flair. Many have "casitas," private cabins or lodges separate from the main building.

WHAT IT COSTS					
	$$$$	**$$$**	**$$**	**$**	**¢**
FOR 2 PEOPLE	over $260	$190–$260	$130–$190	$70–$130	under $70

Prices are for a standard double room in high season, excluding 10%–12% tax.

Downtown Taos

$$$$　🏨 **El Monte Sagrado.** Pricey but classy (although the resort has lowered
Fodor'sChoice　its rates a bit in recent years), El Monte Sagrado is an eco-sensitive New
★　Age haven offering all manner of amenities, from alternative therapies like milk-and-honey body wraps to cooking and wine classes. A short drive away, the property has an expansive ranch property that's available for you to explore on horseback or on foot. Suites and casitas are accented with exotic themes, ranging from Native American designs to foreign flourishes from faraway lands including Japan or Tibet. A popular outdoor area dubbed the Sacred Circle is a patch of grassy land encircled by cottonwoods. The on-site restaurant, De la Tierra, serves daring cuisine. ⊠ *317 Kit Carson Rd., 87571* ☎ *505/758–3502 or 800/828–8267* 🖶 *505/737–2980* ⊕ *www.elmontesagrado.com* 🛏 *18 suites, 18 casitas* ⚒ *2 restaurants, picnic area, room service, some in-room hot tubs, some kitchenettes, minibars, some refrigerators, cable TV, in-room VCRs, Wi-Fi, indoor pool, pond, fitness classes, gym, outdoor hot tubs, Japanese baths, massage, sauna, spa, steam room, bicycles, mountain bikes, archery, billiards, hiking, horseback riding, cross-country skiing, ski storage, snowmobiling, bar, library, piano, recreation room, shop, babysitting, children's programs (ages 4–12), dry cleaning, laundry service, concierge, business services, meeting rooms, some pets allowed (fee)* 🖃 *AE, D, DC, MC, V.*

★ **$$$–$$$$**　🏨 **Casa de las Chimeneas.** Tile hearths, French doors, and traditional viga ceilings grace the "House of Chimneys" B&B, 2½ blocks from the Plaza

Where to Stay
in Taos

and secluded behind thick walls. Each room in the 1912 structure has a private entrance, a fireplace, handmade New Mexican furniture, bathrooms with Talvera tiles, and a bar stocked with complimentary beverages. All rooms overlook the gardens, and facilities include a small but excellent spa offering a wide range of treatments. Two-course breakfasts are included, as are full evening meals. ⊠ *405 Cordoba Rd., Box 5303, 87571* ☎ *505/758–4777 or 877/758–4777* 📠 *505/758–3976* ⊕ *www.visittaos.com* 🛏 *6 rooms, 2 suites* ♻ *Picnic area, minibars, some microwaves, some refrigerators, some in-room hot tubs, cable TV, in-room VCRs, gym, outdoor hot tub, sauna, spa, laundry facilities, laundry service, no-smoking rooms; no kids* ⊟ *AE, D, DC, MC, V* ⭢❙ *MAP.*

★ **$$–$$$$** ⛰ **Hacienda del Sol.** Art patron Mabel Dodge Luhan bought this house in the 1920s and lived here with her husband, Tony Luhan, while building their main house. It was also their private retreat and guesthouse for visiting notables; Frank Waters wrote *People of the Valley* here— other guests have included Willa Cather and D. H. Lawrence. Most of the rooms contain kiva fireplaces, Southwestern handcrafted furniture, and original artwork, and all have CD players. Certain adjoining rooms can be combined into suites. Breakfast is a gourmet affair that might include banana pancakes or stuffed French toast. Perhaps above all else, the "backyards" of the rooms and the secluded outdoor hot tub have a view of Taos Mountain so idyllic it can evoke tears of joy from even the most cynical of travelers. ⊠ *109 Mabel Dodge La., Box 177, 87571* ☎ *505/758–0287 or 866/333–4459* 📠 *505/758–5895* ⊕ *www. taoshaciendadelsol.com* 🛏 *11 rooms* ♻ *Some refrigerators, some in-room hot tubs, hot tub; no room TVs* ⊟ *AE, D, MC, V* ⭢❙ *BP.*

★ **$$–$$$$** ⛰ **Inn on La Loma Plaza.** The walls surrounding this Pueblo Revival building date from the early 1800s; the inn itself is listed on the National Register of Historic Places. The rooms have kiva fireplaces, CD stereos, coffeemakers, and Mexican-tile bathrooms, and many have private patios or decks. The living room has a well-stocked library with books on Taos and art. Owners Jerry and Peggy Davis provide helpful advice about the area and serve a generous breakfast, afternoon snacks, and evening coffee. Guests have privileges at the nearby health club (but the inn has its own hot tub). ⊠ *315 Ranchitos Rd., Box 4159, 87571* ☎ *505/758–1717 or 800/530–3040* 📠 *505/751–0155* ⊕ *www. vacationtaos.com* 🛏 *5 rooms, 2 studios* ♻ *Some kitchenettes, cable TV, in-room VCRs, Wi-Fi, outdoor hot tub, library* ⊟ *AE, D, MC, V* ⭢❙ *BP.*

★ **$$–$$$** ⛰ **Touchstone Inn.** D. H. Lawrence visited this house in 1929; accordingly, the inn's owner, Taos artist Bren Price, has named many of the antiques-filled rooms after famous Taos literary figures. The grounds overlook part of the Taos Pueblo lands, and this makes for a quiet stay within a mile of Taos Plaza. Some rooms have fireplaces. The enormous Royale Suite has a second-story private deck and large bathroom with Jacuzzi, walk-in shower, and skylight. Early-morning coffee is available in the living room, and breakfasts with inventive vegetarian presentations (such as blueberry pancakes with lemon sauce) are served in the glassed-in patio. The adjacent Riverbend Spa offers a wide range of beauty and skin treatments. ⊠ *110 Mabel Dodge La., Box 1885, 87571* ☎ *505/ 758–0192 or 800/758–0192* 📠 *505/758–3498* ⊕ *www.touchstoneinn.*

com 🖥 *6 rooms, 3 suites* ⚫ *Cable TV, in-room VCRs, hot tub, spa* ⊟ *MC, V* ⫶◎⫶ *BP.*

★ **$–$$$** ⊞ **American Artists Gallery House Bed & Breakfast.** Each of the immaculate adobe-style rooms and suites here is called a "gallery," and owners LeAn and Charles Clamurro have taken care to decorate them with local arts and crafts. Some have Jacuzzis and all have kiva fireplaces; one family-friendly suite has a full kitchen; and all have private entrances, wood-burning fireplaces, and front porches where you can admire the view of Taos Mountain. Sumptuous hot breakfasts—along with conversation and suggestions about local attractions—are served up at a community table in the main house each morning, where you can often see the resident peacock, George, preening outside the windows. ⊠ *132 Frontier La., Box 584, 87571* ☎ *505/758–4446 or 800/532–2041* 🖷 *505/758–0497* ⊕ *www.taosbedandbreakfast.com* 🖥 *7 rooms, 3 suites* ⚫ *Fans, some in-room hot tubs, some kitchens, some microwaves, some refrigerators, some cable TV, some in-room VCRs, Wi-Fi, outdoor hot tub, some pets allowed (fee)* ⊟ *AE, D, DC, MC, V* ⫶◎⫶ *BP.*

★ **$–$$$** ⊞ **Historic Taos Inn.** Mere steps from Taos Plaza, the inn is listed on the National Register of Historic Places. Spanish-colonial-style architecture including decorative alcoves in rooms provides an authentic feel to this atmospheric property that consists of four buildings, including the upscale Helen's House, which was added in 2006 and contains eight posh rooms. Many units have thick adobe walls, viga ceilings, and other elements typical of vintage Taos architecture. In summer there's dining alfresco on the patio. The lobby, which also serves as seating for the Adobe Bar, is built around an old town well from which a fountain bubbles forth. Many shops and eateries are within walking distance of the inn, and the restaurant, Doc Martin's, is popular with locals. ⊠ *125 Paseo del Pueblo Norte, 87571* ☎ *505/758–2233 or 888/518–8267* 🖷 *505/ 758–5776* ⊕ *www.taosinn.com* 🖥 *41 rooms, 3 suites* ⚫ *Restaurant, cable TV, bar* ⊟ *AE, DC, MC, V.*

★ **$$** ⊞ **Fechin Inn.** Artistically savvy guests from other parts of the world journey here just to soak up the atmosphere of grounds once owned by internationally renowned artist Nicolai Fechin (Fechin's home, now converted to the Taos Art Museum, is in front of the inn). You're also likely to spot artists earnestly participating in various workshops the inn sponsors. Many guests are immediately awed by the intricacy of hand-carved woodwork throughout the Fechin, which was created by 52 wood-carvers during a three-year span. Rooms have modern Southwestern furnishings, and suites have separate living rooms with fireplaces. The Fechin is the perfect combination of warmth and gracious sophistication; you can fit in here whether you prefer to wear evening dress or cowboy boots to dinner. It's on a 6-acre tree-shaded plot on the north side of downtown, an easy

> **WORD OF MOUTH**
>
> "My husband and I stayed at the Fechin Inn for five nights. Our suite was nicely decorated and comfortable. It had a fireplace and huge balcony. We had a slight problem during our stay and the staff went out of their way to accommodate us."
>
> –Heide on Fechin Inn

walk from dining and shopping. ⊠ *227 Paseo del Pueblo Norte, 87571* ☎ *505/751–1000 or 800/811–2933* 🖷 *505/751–7338* ⊕ *www.fechininn. com* ☞ *70 rooms, 14 suites* ⚹ *Dining room, cable TV, in-room VCRs, gym, hot tub, massage, ski storage, lounge, dry cleaning, laundry facilities, laundry service, concierge, meeting rooms, some pets allowed (fee)* ═ *AE, D, DC, MC, V* |◯| *CP.*

$$ 🏨 **La Posada de Taos.** A couple of blocks from Taos Plaza, this family-friendly inn has beam ceilings, a decorative arched doorway, and the intimacy of a private hacienda. Five guest rooms are in the main house; the sixth is a separate cottage with a king-size bed in a separate bedroom, sitting room, and fireplace. The rooms all have mountain or courtyard garden views, and some open onto private patios almost all have kiva-style fireplaces. Breakfasts are hearty; if you're lucky, they might include baked apple French toast. ⊠ *309 Juanita La., Box 1118, 87571* ☎ *505/758–8164 or 800/645–4803* 🖷 *505/751–4694* ⊕ *www. laposadadetaos.com* ☞ *5 rooms, 1 cottage* ⚹ *Some in-room hot tubs, cable TV, in-room VCRs; no phones in some rooms* ═ *AE, MC, V* |◯| *BP.*

$–$$ 🏨 **Adobe & Pines Inn.** Native American and Mexican artifacts decorate the main house of this B&B, which has expansive mountain views. Part of the main building dates from 1830. The rooms and suites contain Mexican-tile baths, kiva fireplaces, and fluffy goose-down pillows and comforters, plus such modern touches as flat-screen TVs, DVD players, Wi-Fi, and CD players. Separate casitas and suites are more spacious and offer plenty of seclusion, with private entrances and courtyard access. The owners serve gourmet breakfasts in a sunny glass-enclosed patio. ⊠ *NM 68 and Llano Quemado* ⊕ *Box 837, Ranchos de Taos 87557* ☎ *505/751–0947 or 800/723–8267* 🖷 *505/758–8423* ⊕ *www. adobepines.com* ☞ *4 rooms, 2 suites, 2 casitas* ⚹ *Some in-room hot tubs, cable TV, in-room DVDs, Wi-Fi, sauna, steam room, some pets allowed (fee)* ═ *MC, V* |◯| *BP.*

$–$$ 🏨 **Best Western Kachina Lodge & Meeting Center.** Just north of Taos Plaza, this two-story Pueblo-style adobe carries the theme of the kachina (a figure representing a masked ancestral spirit) throughout. Guest rooms sustain the Native American motif, with handmade and hand-painted furnishings and colorful bedspreads. From Memorial Day to Labor Day a troupe from Taos Pueblo performs nightly ritual dances outside by firelight. Rates include a wine-and-cheese welcome reception in the early evening. ⊠ *413 Paseo del Pueblo Norte, Box NN, 87571* ☎ *505/ 758–2275 or 800/522–4462* 🖷 *505/758–9207* ⊕ *www.kachinalodge. com* ☞ *113 rooms, 5 suites* ⚹ *Restaurant, coffee shop, cable TV, in-room VCRs, Wi-Fi, pool, hot tub, bar, shop, laundry facilities, meeting rooms* ═ *AE, D, DC, MC, V* |◯| *BP.*

$–$$ 🏨 **Brooks Street Inn.** An elaborately carved corbel arch, the handiwork of Japanese carpenter Yaichikido, spans the entrance to a shaded, walled garden. Fluffy pillows, fresh flowers, CD stereos, and paintings by local artists are among the grace notes in the rooms; some have fireplaces. Blue-corn pancakes with pineapple salsa, stuffed French toast with an apricot glaze, and other home-baked delights are served at breakfast. ⊠ *119 Brooks St., Box 4954, 87571* ☎ *505/758–1489 or 800/758–1489* ⊕ *www.brooksstreetinn.com* ☞ *6 rooms* ⚹ *Refrigerators, cable TV, in-room VCRs* ═ *AE, MC, V* |◯| *BP.*

$–$$ ⌾ **Casa Europa.** This 17th-century estate on 6 acres, with views of pastures and mountains, is furnished with European antiques and Southwestern pieces. The two main guest areas are light and airy, with comfortable chairs to relax in while the fireplace crackles. Breakfasts are elaborate, and complimentary homemade afternoon baked treats are served, except during ski season, when they're replaced by evening hors d'oeuvres. ✉ *840 Upper Ranchitos Rd.* ⌂ *HC 68, Box 3F, 87571* ☎ *888/758–9798* 🖷 *505/758–9798* ⊕ *www.casaeuropanm.com* ⇌ *5 rooms, 2 suites* ⌂ *Some in-room hot tubs, some cable TVs, some in-room VCRs, outdoor hot tub, sauna, 2 lounges, some pets allowed (fee); no kids under 14* ⊟ *AE, D, MC, V* ¶⊙¶ *BP.*

$–$$ ⌾ **Comfort Suites.** Mexican hand-crafted furniture gives these basic but large units (technically they're not full suites but rather rooms with large sitting areas) a sense of Southwestern style. You can enjoy lounging in front of the kiva fireplace in the lobby area, surrounded by *nichos*—enclaves where statues are placed. The property adjoins the popular Sagebrush Inn and is run by the same owners, and guests have access to the Sagebrush facilities. It's one of the better chain options in town. ✉ *1500 Paseo del Pueblo Sur, Box 1268, 87571* ☎ *505/751–1555 or 888/751–1555* ⊕ *www.taoshotels.com/comfortsuites* ⇌ *60 rooms* ⌂ *Refrigerators, cable TV, pool, hot tub* ⊟ *AE, D, DC, MC, V* ¶⊙¶ *CP.*

$–$$ ⌾ **Sagebrush Inn.** Georgia O'Keeffe once lived and painted in one of the third-story rooms here, and this adobe-style inn, built in 1929, has retained much of its charm since then. It's not as upscale—or expensive—as many other lodging options in Taos, but it has a comfortable shaded patio with large trees, a good restaurant, and a substantial art collection including antique Navajo rugs, rare pottery, and paintings by Southwestern masters such as R. C. Gorman. Many of the guest rooms have kiva-style fireplaces; some have balconies looking out to the Sangre de Cristo Mountains. There's country-western music nightly. ✉ *1508 Paseo del Pueblo Sur, Box 557, 87571* ☎ *505/758–2254 or 800/428–3626* 🖷 *505/758–5077* ⊕ *www.sagebrushinn.com* ⇌ *68 rooms, 32 suites* ⌂ *2 restaurants, cable TV, pool, hot tubs, bar, lounge, meeting rooms* ⊟ *AE, D, DC, MC, V* ¶⊙¶ *BP.*

$–$$ ⌾ **San Geronimo Lodge.** Built in 1925, this lodge sits on 2½ acres that front majestic Taos Mountain and adjoin the Carson National Forest. A balcony library, attractive grounds, many rooms with fireplaces, two rooms designed for people with disabilities, and a room for guests with a pet are among the draws. Hanging Navajo-style rugs, Talvera-tile bathrooms, and beam ceilings lend an authentic Southwestern feel to the rooms. The hotel staff can arrange ski packages. ✉ *1101 Witt Rd., 87571* ☎ *505/751–3776 or 800/894–4119* 🖷 *505/751–1493* ⊕ *www.sangeronimolodge.com* ⇌ *16 rooms* ⌂ *Cable TV, some in-room VCRs, pool, outdoor hot tub, massage, some pets allowed (fee)* ⊟ *AE, D, MC, V* ¶⊙¶ *BP.*

$ ⌾ **Don Fernando de Taos Hotel.** The accommodations at this Pueblo-style hotel are grouped around central courtyards and connected by walkways. Appointed with hand-carved New Mexican furnishings, some rooms have fireplaces. A glassed-in atrium with sliding side doors and roof panels surrounds the pool. There's a free shuttle to take guests to the town center. ✉ *1005 Paseo del Pueblo Sur, 87571* ☎ *505/758–4444 or 800/*

759–2736 🖷 *505/758–0055* 🌐 *www.donfernandodetaos.com* 🖘 *110 rooms, 14 suites* ⚬ *Restaurant, some refrigerators, cable TV, indoor-outdoor pool, hot tub, bar, lounge, dry-cleaning, meeting rooms* ▤ *AE, D, DC, MC, V.*

$ 🏨 **Mabel Dodge Luhan House.** This National Historic Landmark was once home to the heiress who drew literati—including D. H. Lawrence and Willa Cather—to Taos. The main house, which has kept its simple, rustic feel, has nine guest rooms; there are eight more in a modern building, as well as a two-bedroom cottage. You can sleep in Mabel's own hand-carved bed; you can also stay in the O'Keeffe Room, which has twin beds, Southwest furnishings, and its own courtyard entrance, or the Ansel Adams Room with its bright white walls and view of nearby Taos Pueblo land. The inn is frequently used for artistic, cultural, and educational workshops. ✉ *240 Morada La., Box 558, 87571* 🕾 *505/751–9686 or 800/846–2235* 🖷 *505/737–0365* 🌐 *www.mabeldodgeluhan. com* 🖘 *16 rooms, 2 with shared bath; 1 suite, 1 guest house* ⚬ *Meeting rooms; no room phones, no room TVs* ▤ *AE, MC, V* ⦿ *BP.*

$ 🏨 **Old Taos Guesthouse B&B.** Once a ramshackle adobe hacienda, this homey B&B on 7½ acres has been completely and lovingly outfitted with the owners' hand-carved doors and furniture, Western artifacts, and antiques. Some rooms have the smallest bathrooms you'll ever encounter but have private entrances, and some have fireplaces. There are 80-mi views from the outdoor hot tub, and it's a five-minute drive to town. The owners welcome families. Breakfasts are healthy and hearty. ✉ *1028 Witt Rd., Box 6552, 87571* 🕾 *505/758–5448, or 800/758–5448* 🌐 *www. oldtaos.com* 🖘 *7 rooms, 2 suites* ⚬ *Some kitchens, some cable TV, some in-room VCRs, Wi-Fi, outdoor hot tub, some pets allowed (fee); no phones in some rooms* ▤ *D, MC, V* ⦿ *BP.*

$ 🏨 **Orinda.** Built in 1947, this adobe estate has spectacular views and country privacy. The rustic rooms have separate entrances, kiva-style fireplaces, traditional viga ceilings, and Mexican-tile baths. Some of the rooms can be combined with a shared living area into a large suite. One has a Jacuzzi. The hearty breakfast is served family-style in the soaring two-story sun atrium amid a gallery of artworks, all for sale. ✉ *461 Valverde, Box 4451, 87571* 🕾 *505/758–8581 or 800/847–1837* 🖷 *505/751–4895* 🌐 *www.orindabb.com* 🖘 *5 rooms* ⚬ *Refrigerators, some in-room hot tubs, cable TV, some in-room VCRs, some pets allowed (fee); no a/c in some rooms, no smoking* ▤ *AE, MC, V* ⦿ *BP.*

¢–$ 🏨 **El Pueblo Lodge.** This low-to-the-ground, pueblo-style adobe a few blocks north of Taos Plaza has traditional Southwestern furnishings including colorful blankets spread across wooden floors, along with solid viga crossbeams in the ceilings. Fireplaces in some rooms add to a homey feel. A number of more expensive but well-equipped condominiums also are available as rentals. ✉ *412 Paseo del Pueblo Norte, Box 92, 87571* 🕾 *505/758–*

> **WORD OF MOUTH**
>
> "The most quiet and comfortable place to stay . . . within walking distance of the plaza and little shops along the way. . . . Service is excellent."
>
> –Fidel on El Pueblo Lodge

8700 or 800/433–9612 🖥 *505/758–7321* ⊕ *www.elpueblolodge.com*
🖘 *61 rooms* �б *Some kitchenettes, refrigerators, cable TV, pool, hot tub,
laundry facilities, some pets allowed (fee)* ⊟ *AE, D, MC, V* ⬤ *CP.*

¢ 🖫 **Sun God Lodge.** Though inexpensive, this motel has old-fashioned adobe
charm with basic amenities; some rooms have kitchenettes and fireplaces.
Right on the main highway, the Sun God is convenient to restaurants
and historic sites. ✉ *919 Paseo del Pueblo Sur, 87571* ☎ *505/758–3162
or 800/821–2437* 🖥 *505/758–1716* ⊕ *www.sungodlodge.com* 🖘 *45
rooms, 11 suites* �б *Some kitchenettes, cable TV, some in-room VCRs,
outdoor hot tub, laundry facilities, some pets* ⊟ *AE, D, MC, V* ⬤ *CP.*

★ ⚠ **Orilla Verde Recreation Area.** You can hike, fish, and picnic among trees
and sagebrush at this beautiful area along the banks of the Rio Grande,
10 mi south of Ranchos de Taos, off NM 68 at NM 570. The area has
four developed campgrounds with running water, flush toilets, and
showers costing $1 for four minutes. Three primitive campgrounds have
vault toilets only. To pay the camping fee, leave cash in an envelope provided, drop it in a tube, and the rangers will collect it (or a volunteer
sometimes is on hand to collect payments). ⚲ *Bureau of Land Management, 226 Cruz Alta Rd., Taos 87571* ☎ *505/758–4060* ⚬ *Flush toilets, drinking water, fire grates, picnic tables* 🖘 *9 RV sites with hookups,
70 developed sites (tent and RV)* 🖾 *$15 (RV with electric and water
hookups), $7 (developed campsites), $5 (primitive campsites), $3 (day
use)* ⊟ *No credit cards.*

⚠ **Taos Valley RV Park.** The sites are grassy, with a few shade trees, in
this park 2½ mi from Taos Plaza near the junction of NM 68 and NM
518. A recreation room has video games, TV, and a pool table. Some
RV supplies are for sale. There are horseshoes, billiards, and a kitchen
area. ✉ *120 Estes Rd., off Paseo del Pueblo Sur, behind Rio Grande
Ace Hardware* ⚲ *Box 7204, Taos 87571* ☎ *505/758–2524 or 800/999–
7571* ⊕ *www.newmex.com/rv* ⚬ *Flush toilets, full hookups, drinking
water, showers, picnic tables, electricity, public telephone, general store,
play area* 🖘 *60 RV sites, 4 tent sites* 🖾 *RV sites $31–$38, tent sites
$22* ⊟ *D, MC, V.*

Arroyo Seco

★ $$$ 🖫 **Alma del Monte.** Mountain views
abound from the rooms and court-
yard of this B&B on the high plain
between Taos and the ski valley.
The 4-acre property is private; the
only neighbors you have are friendly
horses from adjoining farms. Some
rooms have private outside entry-
ways and fenced gardens, where
you can languish in seclusion.
Heated saltillo-tile floors, kiva fire-
places, whirlpool baths, Bose
stereos, Victorian antiques, gener-
ous breakfasts (which feature such creative fare as hazelnut-lemon–cream
cheese French toast), and afternoon wine with hors d'oeuvres make it

> **WORD OF MOUTH**
>
> "The inn has 360-degree views of
> the mountains and the furnishings
> are superb and immaculate. Each
> of the 5 rooms has great views and
> are quiet and private. The owners
> offer a wealth of information on
> area restaurants and attractions."
> –Gail on Alma del Monte

CLOSE UP

The Taos Hum

INVESTIGATIONS INTO WHAT CAUSES A MYSTERIOUS low frequency sound dubbed the "Taos Hum" are ongoing, although the topic was more popular during a worldwide news media frenzy in the 1990s. Taos isn't the only place where the mysterious "hum" has been heard, but it's probably the best known locale for the phenomenon. (The Taos Hum, for example, now has been officially documented in Encyclopaedia Britannica.)

Scientists visited Taos during the 1990s in unsuccessful good faith efforts to trace the sound, which surveys indicated were heard by about 2% of the town's population. Described as a frequency similar to the low, throbbing engine of a diesel truck, the Taos Hum has reportedly created disturbances among its few hearers from mildly irritating to profoundly disturbing. In the extreme, hearers say they experience constant problems including interrupted sleep and physical effects such as dizziness and nosebleeds.

Speculation about the Taos Hum abounds. Conspiracy theorists believe the sound originates from ominous secret government testing,

possibly emanating from the federal defense establishment of Los Alamos National Laboratory 55 mi southwest of Taos. The theory correlates with reports of some hearers that the sound began suddenly, as though something had been switched on.

Some investigators say the hearers may have extraordinary sensitivity to low frequency sound waves, which could originate from all manner of human devices (cell phones, for one) creating constant sources of electromagnetic energy. Still other theorists postulate that low frequency sound waves may originate in the Earth's lower atmosphere. One intriguing theory says that the "hum" could be explained by vibrations deep within the Earth, as a sort of precursor to earthquakes (although earthquakes are extremely rare in New Mexico).

Although many believe there's something to the mysterious Taos Hum, less kindly skeptics have dismissed the phenomenon as New Age nonsense linked to mass hysteria. But while you're here, you may as well give it a try (no one need know what you're up to). Find yourself a peaceful spot. Sit quietly. And listen.

a hard place to leave, even for skiing. ⊠ *372 Hondo Seco Rd., Box 1434, Taos 87571* ☎ *505/776–2721 or 800/273–7203* 🖷 *505/776–8888* ⊕ *www.almaspirit.com* ➾ *5 rooms* ⚸ *Picnic area, in-room hot tubs, outdoor hot tub, massage, laundry service, kennel; no room TVs, no kids under 15* ⊟ *AE, MC, V* ⦿ *BP.*

★ **$–$$** 🎏 **Little Tree B&B.** In an authentic adobe house in the open country between Taos and the ski valley, Little Tree's rooms are built around a garden courtyard and have magnificent views of Taos Mountain and the high desert that spans for nearly 100 mi to the west. Some have kiva fireplaces and Jacuzzis, and all are decorated in true Southwestern style. ✉ *226 County Rd. B143, Arroyo Hondo* ⬩ *Box 509, 87571* ☎ *505/ 776–8467 or 800/334–8467* ⊕ *www.littletreebandb.com* ➲ *4 rooms* ⬩ *Some cable TV, some in-rooms VCRs, some in-room hot tubs; no TV in some rooms* ⊟ *MC, V* ⎮◎⎮ *BP.*

$–$$ 🖼 **Salsa del Salto.** Rooms at this handsome compound set back from the road to the Ski Valley, just a short drive up from the funky village of Arroyo Seco, are either in the sunny, contemporary main inn building or in separate units with private entrances and a bit more seclusion. The master suite affords panoramic views of the mountains and has a huge bathroom. The Lobo and Kachina rooms are a great value, not as large as some but with romantic glass-brick showers, high beam ceilings, Saltillo-tile floors with radiant heating. Friendly and helpful owners Pam and Jim Maisey worked for Marriott hotels for 25 years, and it shows. Breakfast is a substantial affair, where you might enjoy a shrimp, mushroom, and provolone omelet or salmon eggs Benedict, and there's always a hearty soup or snack presented in the afternoon. ✉ *543 NM 150, Box 1468, El Prado 87529* ☎ *505/776–2422 or 800/530– 3097* 🖨 *505/776–5734* ⊕ *www.bandbtaos.com* ➲ *10 rooms* ⬩ *Some cable TV, some in-room DVDs, some in-room hot tubs, Wi-Fi, pool, hot tub* ⊟ *AE, MC, V* ⎮◎⎮ *BP.*

NIGHTLIFE & THE ARTS

Evening entertainment is modest in Taos. Some motels and hotels present solo musicians or small combos in their bars and lounges. Everything from down-home blues bands to Texas two-step dancing blossoms on Saturday and Sunday nights in winter. In summer things heat up during the week as well. For information about what's going on around town pick up *Taos Magazine.* The weekly *Taos News,* published on Thursday, carries arts and entertainment information in the "Tempo" section. The arts scene is much more lively, with festivals every season for nearly every taste.

Nightlife

FodorsChoice The **Adobe Bar** (✉ Taos Inn, 125 Paseo del Pueblo Norte ☎ 505/758– ★ 2233), a local meet-and-greet spot known as "Taos's living room," books talented acts, from solo guitarists to small folk groups and, two or three nights a week, jazz musicians.

★ **Alley Cantina** (✉ 121 Teresina La. ☎ 505/758–2121) has jazz, folk, and blues—as well as shuffleboard and board games for those not moved to dance. It's housed in the oldest structure in downtown Taos.

Caffe Tazza (✉ 122 Kit Carson Rd. ☎ 505/758–8706) presents free evening performances throughout the week—folk singing, jazz, belly dancing, blues, poetry, and fiction readings.

Fernando's Hideaway (✉ Don Fernando de Taos Hotel & Suites, 1005 Paseo del Pueblo Sur ☎ 505/758–4444) occasionally presents live entertainment—jazz, blues, hip-hop, R&B, salsa, and country music. Complimentary happy-hour snacks are laid out on weekday evenings, 5–7.

The **Kachina Lodge Cabaret** (✉ 413 Paseo del Pueblo Norte ☎ 505/758–2275) usually brings in an area radio DJ to liven up various forms of music and dancing.

The **Sagebrush Inn** (✉ 1508 Paseo del Pueblo Sur ☎ 505/758–2254) hosts musicians and dancing in its lobby lounge. There's usually no cover charge for country-western dancing.

The piano bar at **Sabroso** (✉ CR 150, Arroyo Seco ☎ 505/776–3333) often presents jazz and old standards.

The Arts

Long a beacon for visual artists, Taos is also becoming a magnet for touring musicians, especially in summer, when performers and audiences are drawn to the heady high desert atmosphere. Festivals celebrate the visual arts, music, poetry, and film.

The **Taos Center for the Arts** (✉ 133 Paseo del Pueblo Norte ☎ 505/758–2052 ⊕ www.taoscenterforthearts.org), which encompasses the Taos Community Auditorium, presents films, plays, concerts, dance shows, and the like.

The **Taos Fall Arts Festival** (☎ 505/758–3873 or 800/732–8267 ⊕ www.taosfallarts.com), from late September to early October, is the area's major arts gathering, when buyers are in town and many other events, such as a Taos Pueblo feast, take place.

The **Taos Spring Arts Celebration** (☎ 505/758–3873 or 800/732–8267 ⊕ www.taoschamber.org), held throughout Taos in May, is a showcase for the visual, performing, and literary arts of the community and allows you to rub elbows with the many artists who call Taos home. The Mother's Day Arts and Crafts weekend during the festival always draws an especially large crowd.

Music

From mid-June to early August the Taos School of Music fills the evenings with the sounds of chamber music at the **Taos School of Music Program and Festival** (☎ 505/776–2388 ⊕ www.taosschoolofmusic.com). Running strong since 1963, this is America's oldest chamber music summer program and possibly the largest assembly of top string quartets in the country. Concerts are presented a couple of times a week from mid-June to August, at the Taos Community Auditorium and at Taos Ski Valley. Tickets cost $10–$20. The events at Taos Ski Valley are free.

Solar energy was pioneered in this land of sunshine, and each year in late June the flag of sustainability is raised at the three-day **Taos Solar Music Festival** (⊕ www.solarmusicfest.com). Top-name acts appear, and booths promote alternative energy, permaculture, and other ecofriendly technologies.

SPORTS & THE OUTDOORS

Whether you plan to cycle around town, jog along Paseo del Pueblo Norte, or play a few rounds of golf, keep in mind that the altitude in Taos is higher than 7,000 feet. It's best to keep physical exertion to a minimum until your body becomes acclimated to the altitude—a full day to a few days, depending on your constitution.

Ballooning

Hot-air ballooning has become nearly as popular in Taos as in Albuquerque, with a handful of outfitters offering rides, most starting at about $200 per person. **Paradise Balloons** (☎ 505/751–6098 ⊕ www. taosballooning.com) will thrill you with a "splash and dash" in the Rio Grande River as part of a silent journey through the 600-foot canyon walls of Rio Grande Gorge. **Pueblo Balloon Company** (☎ 505/751–9877 ⊕ www.puebloballoon.com) conducts balloon rides over and into the Rio Grande Gorge.

Bicycling

Taos-area roads are steep and hilly, and none have marked bicycle lanes, so be careful while cycling. The West Rim Trail offers a fairly flat but view-studded 9-mi ride that follows the Rio Grande canyon's west rim from the Rio Grande Gorge Bridge to near the Taos Junction Bridge.

Gearing Up Bicycle Shop (✉ 129 Paseo del Pueblo Sur ☎ 505/751–0365) is a full-service bike shop that also has information about tours and guides. **Native Sons Adventures** (✉ 1033–A Paseo del Pueblo Sur ☎ 505/758–9342 or 800/753–7559) offers guided tours on its mountain bikes.

Fishing

Carson National Forest has some of the best trout fishing in New Mexico. Its streams and lakes are home to rainbow, brown, and native Rio Grande cutthroat trout.

In midtown Taos, **Cottam's Ski & Outdoor** (✉ 207–A Paseo del Pueblo Sur ☎ 505/758–2822 or 800/322–8267 ⊕ www.cottamsoutdoor.com) provides equipment rentals and half- and full-day fly-fishing tours. Shuttles are available to area trails that lead to fishing waters. Free fly-fishing clinics from **Los Rios Anglers** (✉ 126 W. Plaza Dr. ☎ 505/758–

> ### DID YOU KNOW?
>
> Anyone over the age of 12 who wishes to fish must buy a New Mexico fishing license. Many sporting goods stores in the state sell them.

2798 or 800/748–1707 ⊕ www.losrios.com) are offered weekly between May and August. **Solitary Angler** (✉ 204–B Paseo del Pueblo Norte ☎ 505/758–5653 or 866/502–1700 ⊕ www.thesolitaryangler.com) guides fly-fishing expeditions that search out uncrowded habitats. Well-known area fishing guide Taylor Streit of **Taos Fly Shop & Streit Fly Fishing** (✉ 308–B Paseo del Pueblo Sur ☎ 505/751–1312 ⊕ www.taosflyshop.com) takes individuals or small groups out for fishing and lessons.

Golf

The greens fees at the 18-hole, PGA-rated, par-72 championship course at **Taos Country Club** (⊠ NM 570, Ranchos de Taos ☎ 505/758–7300) are $65–$78.

> **DID YOU KNOW?**
>
> Although faced with water-shortage obstacles, New Mexico does have a growing and quite vital golf scene.

3

Health Clubs & Fitness Centers

The **Northside Health & Fitness Center** (⊠ 1307 Paseo del Pueblo Norte ☎ 505/751–1242) is a spotlessly clean facility with indoor and outdoor pools, a hot tub, tennis courts, and aerobics classes. Nonmembers pay $10 per day. The center provides paid child care with a certified Montessori teacher. The **Taos Youth and Family Center** (⊠ 407 Paseo del Cañon E ☎ 505/758–4160) has an outdoor Olympic-size ice arena, where rollerblading, volleyball, and basketball take place in summer. There's also a large swimming pool. Admission is $3 per day.

Llama Trekking

As one of the most offbeat outdoor recreational activities in the Taos area, llama trekking is offered by **Wild Earth Llama Adventures** (☎ 505/586–0174 or 800/758–5262 ⊕ www.llamaadventures.com) in a variety of packages, from one-day tours to excursions lasting several days in wilderness areas of the nearby Sangre de Cristo Mountains. Llamas, relatives of the camel, are used as pack animals on trips that begin at $89 for a day hike. Gourmet lunches eaten on the trail are part of the package, along with overnight camping and meals for longer trips.

River Rafting

The Taos Box, at the bottom of the steep-walled canyon far below the Rio Grande Gorge Bridge, is the granddaddy of thrilling white water in New Mexico and is best attempted by experts only—or on a guided trip—but the river also offers more placid sections such as through the Orilla Verde Recreation Area. Spring runoff is the busy season, from mid-April through June, but rafting companies conduct tours March to November. Shorter two-hour options usually cover the fairly tame section of the river. The **Bureau of Land Management, Taos Resource Area Office** (⊠ 226 Cruz Alta ☎ 505/758–8851) has a list of registered river guides and information about running the river on your own.

Big River Raft Trips (☎ 505/758–9711 or 800/748–3760 ⊕ www.bigriverrafts.com) offers dinner float trips and rapids runs. **Far Flung Adventures** (☎ 505/758–2628 or 800/359–2627 ⊕ www.farflung.com) operates half-day, full-day, and overnight rafting trips along the Rio Grande and the Rio Chama. **Los Rios River Runners** (☎ 505/776–8854 or 800/544–1181 ⊕ www.losriosriverrunners.com) will take you to your choice of spots—the Rio Chama, the Lower Gorge, or the Taos Box. **Native Sons Adventures** (⊠ 1033A Paseo del Pueblo Sur ☎ 505/758–9342 or 800/753–7559 ⊕ www.nativesonsadventures.com) offers several trip options on the Rio Grande.

SHOPPING

Retail options in Taos Plaza consist mostly of T-shirt emporiums and souvenir shops that are easily bypassed, though a few stores, like Blue Rain Gallery, carry quality Native American artifacts and jewelry. The more upscale galleries and boutiques are two short blocks north on Bent Street, including the John Dunn House Shops. Kit Carson Road, also known as U.S. 64, has a mix of the old and the new. There's metered municipal parking downtown, though the traffic can be daunting. Some shops worth checking out are in St. Francis Plaza in Ranchos de Taos, 4 mi south of the Plaza near the San Francisco de Asís Church. Just north of Taos off NM 522 you can find Overland Ranch (including Overland Sheepskin Co.), which has gorgeous sheepskin and leather clothing, along with other shops, galleries, restaurants, and an outdoor path winding through displays of wind sculptures.

Art Galleries

For at least a century, artists have been drawn to Taos's natural grandeur. The result is a vigorous art community with some 80 galleries, a lively market, and an estimated 1,000 residents producing art full- or part-time. Many artists explore themes of the western landscape, Native Americans, and adobe architecture; others create abstract forms and mixed-media works that may or may not reflect the Southwest. Some local artists grew up in Taos, but many—Anglo, Hispanic, and Native Americans—are adopted Taoseños.

Blue Rain Gallery (✉ 117 S. Plaza ☎ 505/751–0066) carries some of the finest examples of Pueblo pottery and Hopi kachina dolls to be found anywhere, ranging in price from several hundred to several thousand dollars. The owner, Leroy Garcia, takes time to explain the materials and traditions. The gallery also sells Native American–made jewelry and art.

Clay and Fiber Gallery (✉ 201 Paseo del Pueblo Sur ☎ 505/758–8093) has exhibited first-rate ceramics, glass, pottery, and hand-painted silks and weavings by local artists for the past quarter century.

Envision Gallery (✉ Overland Ranch Complex, NM 522 north of Taos ☎ 505/751–1344) has contemporary art and an outdoor exhibit of wind sculptures.

Farnsworth Gallery Taos (✉ 1129 Paseo del Pueblo Norte ☎ 505/758–0776). Best known for his finely detailed paintings of horses, the work of artist John Farnsworth also includes colorful local landscapes, large-scale still-lifes, and scenes of Native American kiva dancers.

Fenix Gallery (✉ 208–A Ranchitos Rd. ☎ 505/758–9120) is a showcase for contemporary art, exhibiting paintings, sculpture, ceramics, and lithography by established Taos artists.

Gallery Elena (✉ 111 Morada La. ☎ 505/758–9094) shows the symbolic and impressionistic works of Veloy, Dan, and Michael Vigil.

Inger Jirby Gallery (✉ 207 Ledoux St. ☎ 505/758–7333) displays Jirby's whimsically colored landscape paintings.

★ **J.D. Challenger Gallery** (✉ 221 Paseo del Pueblo Norte ☎ 505/751–6773 or 800/511–6773) is the home base of personable painter J. D. Challenger, who has become famous for his dramatically rendered portraits of Native Americans from tribes throughout North America.

Las Comadres (✉ 228–A Paseo del Pueblo Norte ☎ 505/737–5323) is a women's cooperative gallery showing arts and crafts.

Lumina Fine Art & Sculpture Gardens (✉ 11 NM 230 ☎ 505/776–0123 or 877/558–6462) exhibits paintings by worldwide artists and has 3 acres of sculpture gardens, including works of Japanese stone carvers.

Michael McCormick Gallery (✉ 106–C Paseo del Pueblo Norte ☎ 505/758–1372 or 800/279–0879) is home to the sensual, stylized female portraits of Miguel Martinez and the architectural paintings of Margaret Nes. The gallery also has an extensive collection of Rembrandt etchings.

Mission Gallery (✉ 138 E. Kit Carson Rd. ☎ 505/758–2861) carries the works of early Taos artists, early New Mexico Modernists, and important contemporary artists. The gallery is in the former home of painter Joseph H. Sharp.

> **DID YOU KNOW?**
>
> For more than a century, clear mountain light, sweeping landscapes, and a soft desert palette have drawn artists to Taos.

Navajo Gallery (✉ 210 Ledoux St. ☎ 505/758–3250) shows the works of the internationally renowned Navajo painter and sculptor R. C. Gorman, who died in 2005 and who was known for his ethereal imagery—especially his portraits of Native American women.

Nichols Taos Fine Art Gallery (✉ 403 Paseo del Pueblo Norte ☎ 505/758–2475) has exhibits of oils, watercolors, pastels, charcoal, and pencils from artists representing many prestigious national art organizations. The gallery cooperates with the nearby Fechin Inn to provide art programs and workshops.

Parks Gallery (✉ 127–A Bent St. ☎ 505/751–0343) specializes in contemporary paintings, sculptures, and prints. Mixed-media artist Melissa Zink shows here, as well as painter Jim Wagner.

R. B. Ravens Gallery (✉ 4146 NM 68, Ranchos de Taos ☎ 505/758–7322 or 866/758–7322) exhibits paintings by the founding artists of Taos, pre-1930s weavings, and ceramics.

Robert L. Parsons Fine Art (✉ 131 Bent St. ☎ 505/751–0159 or 800/613–5091) shows Southwest paintings, antiques, and authentic antique Navajo blankets.

Six Directions (✉ 129B N. Plaza ☎ 505/758–5844) has paintings, alabaster and bronze sculpture, Native American artifacts, silver jewelry, and pottery. Bill Rabbit and Robert Redbird are among the artists represented here.

Spirit Runner Gallery (✉ 303 Paseo del Pueblo Norte ☎ 505/758–1132) exhibits colorful acrylic and gold-leaf paintings by Taos native Ouray Meyers.

Studio de Colores Gallery (✉ 115 Quesnel, El Prado near Taos ☎ 505/751–3502 or 888/751–3502) is home to the work of two artists, Ann Huston and Ed Sandoval, who are married to one another but have extremely distinctive styles. Sandoval is known for his trademark *Viejito* (Old Man) images and swirling, vibrantly colored landscapes; Ann specializes in soft-hue still lifes and scenes whose stillness evokes the work of Edward Hopper.

Specialty Stores

Books
Brodsky Bookshop (✉ 226–A Paseo del Pueblo Norte ☎ 505/758–9468) has new and used books—contemporary literature, Southwestern classics, children's titles—piled here and there, but amiable proprietor Rick Smith will help you find what you need.

G. Robinson Old Prints and Maps (✉ John Dunn House, 124–D Bent St. ☎ 505/758–2278) stocks rare books, maps, and prints from the 16th to 19th century.

Moby Dickens (✉ John Dunn House, 124–A Bent St. ☎ 505/758–3050), great for browsing, is a bookstore for all ages. It carries many books on the Southwest as well as a large stock of general-interest books.

Mystery Ink (✉ 121 Camino de la Placita ☎ 505/751–1092) specializes in high-quality used books—mainly mysteries, but also contemporary books, science fiction, and children's books. The shop also carries some foreign-language literature.

Sustaining Cultures (✉ 114 Doña Luz ☎ 505/751–0959) stocks spiritual and new-age books and tapes and offers tarot readings.

Clothing
Aventura (✉ Overland Ranch, 4 mi north of Taos ☎ 505/758–2144), which opened in 2005, produces stylish (and super-warm) contemporary blanket "wraps" as well as other winter-oriented outdoor wear.

Overland Sheepskin Company (✉ NM 522, Overland Ranch, 4 mi north of Taos ☎ 505/758–8820 or 888/754–8352) carries high-quality sheepskin coats, hats, mittens, and slippers, many with Taos beadwork.

Collectibles & Gifts
Horse Feathers (✉ 109–B Kit Carson Rd. ☎ 505/758–7457) is a fun collection of cowboy antiques and

---

DID YOU KNOW?

In New Mexico shops, it's acceptable to ask for a certificate of authenticity, written verification of a piece's origin, or a receipt that lists the materials that make up an item.

vintage western wear—boots, hats, buckles, jewelry, and all manner of paraphernalia.

Twining Weavers & Contemporary Crafts (⊠ 129 Kit Carson Rd. ☎ 505/758–9000) sells stunning textiles, blankets, table runners, throws, and the like, using colorful fabrics from Guatemala, as well as a wide range of decorative crafts.

Home Furnishings

Abydos (⊠ 7036 SR 518, Talpa ☎ 505/758–0483 or 888/900–0863) sells fine handmade New Mexican–style furniture.

Alhambra (⊠ 124 Paseo del Pueblo Sur ☎ 505/758–4161) carries a lovely collection of antiques, Oriental rugs and textiles, and South Asian artifacts.

Casa Cristal Pottery (⊠ 1306 Paseo del Pueblo Norte ☎ 505/758–1530), 2½ mi north of the Taos Plaza, has a huge stock of stoneware, serapes, clay pots, Native American ironwood carvings, fountains, sweaters, ponchos, clay fireplaces, Mexican blankets, tiles, piñatas, and blue glassware from Guadalajara.

★ **Country Furnishings of Taos** (⊠ 534 Paseo del Pueblo Norte ☎ 505/758–4633) sells folk art from northern New Mexico, handmade furniture, metalwork lamps and beds, and colorful accessories.

La Unica Cosa (⊠ 117 Paseo del Pueblo Norte ☎ 505/758–3065) has a striking collection of Zapotec Indian rugs and hangings.

Lo Fino (⊠ 201 Paseo del Pueblo Sur ☎ 505/758–0298) carries the works—hand-carved beds, tables, chairs, *trasteros* (free-standing cupboards), and benches—of the 10 top Southwestern furniture and lighting designers, as well as some Native American alabaster sculpture, basketry, and pottery.

Los Ancestros (⊠ 66 St. Francis Plaza, Ranchos de Taos ☎ 505/737–5053) stocks Spanish-colonial reproductions and accessories.

Taos Blue (⊠ 101–A Bent St. ☎ 505/758–3561) carries jewelry, pottery, and contemporary works by Native Americans (masks, rattles, sculpture), as well as Hispanic *santos* (bultos and retablos).

The **Taos Company** (⊠ 124–K Bent St. ☎ 800/548–1141) sells magnificent Spanish-style furniture, chandeliers, rugs, and textiles; Mexican *equipal* (wood and leather) chairs; and other accessories.

Taos Tin Works (⊠ 1204–D Paseo del Pueblo Norte ☎ 505/758–9724) sells handcrafted tinwork such as wall sconces, mirrors, lamps, and table ornaments by Marion Moore.

Weaving Southwest (⊠ 216–B Paseo del Pueblo Norte ☎ 505/758–0433) represents 25 tapestry artists who make beautiful rugs, blankets, and pillows. The store also sells supplies for weavers, including hand-dyed yarn.

Native American Arts & Crafts

Buffalo Dancer (⊠ 103–A E. Plaza ☎ 505/758–8718) buys, sells, and trades Native American arts and crafts, including pottery, belts, kachina dolls, hides, and silver-coin jewelry.

El Rincón Trading Post (⊠ 114 E. Kit Carson Rd. ☎ 505/758–9188) is housed in a large, dark, cluttered century-old adobe. Native American items of all kinds are bought and sold here: drums, feathered headdresses, Navajo rugs, beads, bowls, baskets, shields, beaded moccasins, jewelry, arrows, and spear-

> **DID YOU KNOW?**
>
> Your best guarantee of authenticity, particularly involving Navajo blankets, is to purchase directly from a reputable reservation outlet.

heads. The packed back room contains Native American, Hispanic, and Anglo Wild West artifacts.

Taos Drums (⊠ NM 68, 5 mi south of Plaza ☎ 505/758–9844 or 800/424–3786) is the factory outlet for the Taos Drum Factory. The store, 5 mi south of Taos Plaza (look for the large tepee), stocks handmade Pueblo log drums, leather lamp shades, and wrought-iron and Southwestern furniture.

Taos General Store (⊠ 223–C Paseo del Pueblo Sur ☎ 505/758–9051) stocks a large selection of furniture and decorative items from around the world, as well as American Indian pots, rugs, and jewelry.

Sporting Goods

Cottam's Ski & Outdoor (⊠ 207–A Paseo del Pueblo Sur ☎ 505/758–2822) carries hiking and backpacking gear, snowboarding and skateboarding equipment, maps, fishing licenses and supplies, and ski equipment, along with related clothing and accessories.

Los Rios Anglers (⊠ 226–C Paseo del Pueblo Norte ☎ 505/758–2798 or 800/748–1707) is a fly-fisherman's haven for fly rods, flies, clothing, books, instruction, and guide service to local streams.

Mudd 'n' Flood Mountain Shop (⊠ 134 Bent St. ☎ 505/751–9100) has gear and clothing for rock climbers, backpackers, campers, and back-country skiers.

Taos Mountain Outfitters (⊠ 114 S. Plaza ☎ 505/758–9292) has supplies for kayakers, skiers, climbers, and backpackers, as well as maps, books, and handy advice.

TAOS SKI VALLEY

🔟 *NM 150, 22 mi northeast of Taos.*

A trip to Taos Ski Valley begins at the traffic light where you turn right onto NM 150 (Taos Ski Valley Road) from U.S. 64. Along the way, the hamlet of Arroyo Seco, some 5 mi up NM 150 from the traffic light, is worth a stop for lunch (try Gypsy 360° café) and a look at crafts and antiques shops. Beyond Arroyo Seco the road crosses a high plain, then plunges into the Rio Hondo Canyon to follow the cascading brook upstream through the forest to Taos Ski Valley, where NM 150 ends. (It does not continue to Red River, as some disappointed motorists discover.)

Skiers from around the world return to the slopes and hospitality of the Village of Taos Ski Valley every year. This world-class area is known for its alpine village atmosphere, perhaps the finest ski school in the country, and the variety of its 72 runs—it's also slowly but surely becoming more of a year-round destination, as the valley attracts outdoors enthusiasts with spectacular, and often challenging, hiking in summer and fall. Many of the few hotels at the ski valley have been converted to ski-in ski-out condos since the early 2000s, further evidence that the once funky ski area is becoming more of a Colorado-style full-scale resort town. Some of the best trails in Carson National Forest begin at the Village of Taos Ski Valley and go though dense woodland up to alpine tundra. There aren't many summer visitors, so you can have the trails up to Bull-of-the-Woods, Gold Hill, Williams Lake, Italianos, and Wheeler Peak nearly all to yourself. Easy nature hikes are organized by the Bavarian hotel, guided by Shar Sharghi, a botanist and horticulturist. Special events like barn dances and wine tastings occur throughout the nonskiing seasons.

WHERE TO STAY & EAT

$–$$ ✕ **Rhoda's Restaurant.** Rhoda Blake founded Taos Ski Valley with her husband, Ernie. Her slope-side restaurant serves pasta, burgers, and sandwiches for lunch. Dinner fare is a bit more substantive, such as veal medallions with pancetta and seafood chile rellenos with ancho-chile sauce. There's also a kids' menu. ⊠ *Resort Center, on the slope.* ☎ *505/ 776–2005* ▤ *AE, MC, V.*

¢–$$ ✕ **Tim's Stray Dog Cantina.** This wildly popular spot occupies a chalet-style building in the heart of the Taos ski area, and it's a favorite spot not only for breakfast, lunch, and dinner but for après-ski cocktails. Favorites include rainbow trout with lemon butter, chile rellenos, green-chile burgers (both beef and veggie), and—at breakfast—blueberry blue-corn pancakes. ⊠ *105 Sutton Pl.* ☎ *505/776–2894* ▤ *MC, V.*

★ $$$$ ✕▦ **The Bavarian.** This luxurious, secluded re-creation of a Bavarian lodge has the only mid-mountain accommodations in the Taos Ski Valley. The King Ludwig suite has a dining room, kitchen, marble bathroom, and two bedrooms with canopied beds. Three suites have whirlpool tubs, and there's a three-bedroom, three-bath apartment. The restaurant ($$–$$$$) serves contemporary Bavarian-inspired cuisine, such as baked artichokes and Gruyère, and braised pork loin with garlic-mashed potatoes and red cabbage. Summer activities include hiking, touring with the resident botanist, horseback riding, rafting, and fishing. Seven-night ski packages are offered. ⊠ *Twining Rd. off NM 150* ⬡ *Box 653, Taos Ski Valley 87525* ☎ *505/776–8020* 🖷 *505/776–5301* ⊕ *www. thebavarian.net* ⇋ *4 suites* ⬥ *Restaurant, kitchenettes, cable TV, in-room VCRs, fishing, hiking, horseback riding* ▤ *AE, MC, V* ⊙ *Closed May and early Nov.* ⊗⊙ *BP.*

$$$$ ✕▦ **Inn at Snakedance.** This modern resort hotel is right on the slopes. The inn has a handsome library where guests can enjoy an après-ski coffee or after-dinner drink next to a fieldstone fireplace. Some rooms have fireplaces. In summer the hotel offers weeklong vacation packages, including a cooking school and fitness adventure

> **DID YOU KNOW?**
>
> Compared with other notable ski areas, New Mexico is more susceptible to extended periods of dry weather that can create meltdowns.

courses. Hondo Restaurant ($$–$$$; no dinner Sunday–Thursday in summer), a frequent winner of the *Wine Spectator* Award of Excellence, turns out esteemed contemporary American cooking, such as curry-crusted lamb chops with blackberry coulis and wild-rice pilaf. ⊠ *Off Taos Ski Valley Rd.* ⌂ *NM 150; Box 89, Village of Taos Ski Valley 87525* ☎ *505/776–2277 or 800/322–9815* 🖶 *505/776–1410* ⊕ *www. innsnakedance.com* ➥ *60 rooms, 1 condo* ⌂ *Restaurant, minibars, refrigerators, cable TV, exercise equipment, hot tub, massage, sauna, library; no smoking* ▤ *AE, DC, MC, V* ☉ *Closed mid-Apr.–Memorial Day* ⦿ *BP.*

$$–$$$ 🏨 **Thunderbird Lodge and Chalet.** This two-story wood-frame inn is only 150 yards from the main lifts, on the sunny side of Taos Ski Valley. A large conference room has board games and a library. There are supervised children's activities during holiday seasons. Lodge rooms are cozy and functional; the six rooms in the adjacent chalet are a bit larger and have king-size beds. Sumptuous breakfast buffets and family-style dinners, which are included in the rates, are served in the pine-panel dining room. Ski-week packages are available. ⊠ *3 Thunderbird Rd., off Taos Ski Valley Rd.* ⌂ *NM 150; Box 87, Village of Taos Ski Valley 87525* ☎ *505/776–2280 or 800/776–2279* 🖶 *505/776–2238* ⊕ *www. thunderbird-taos.com* ➥ *30 rooms* ⌂ *Restaurant, cable TV, hot tub, massage, sauna, bar, library, recreation room, meeting room* ▤ *AE, MC, V* ⦿ *MAP.*

★ $–$$ 🏨 **Austing Haus.** Owner Paul Austing constructed much of this handsome, glass-sheathed building, 1½ mi from Taos Ski Valley, along with many of its furnishings. The breakfast room has large picture windows, stained-glass paneling, and an impressive fireplace. Aromas of fresh-baked goods, such as Paul's apple strudel, come from the kitchen. Guest rooms are pretty and quiet with harmonious, peaceful colors; some have four-poster beds and fireplaces. In winter the inn offers weeklong ski packages. ⊠ *NM 150* ⌂ *Box 8, Village of Taos Ski Valley 87525* ☎ *505/776–2649 or 800/748–2932*

> **DID YOU KNOW?**
>
> Major ski resorts have snow machines, but you should check conditions first to avoid disappointment.

🖶 *505/776–8751* ⊕ *www.austinghaus.net* ➥ *22 rooms, 3 chalets* ⌂ *Dining room, cable TV, hot tub, meeting rooms* ▤ *AE, DC, MC, V* ⦿ *CP.*

NIGHTLIFE & THE ARTS **Thunderbird Lodge** (⊠ 3 Thunderbird Rd. ☎ 505/776–2280) in the Taos Ski Valley has free jazz nights and country-and-western swing dancing. The Taos School of Music gives free weekly summer concerts and recitals from mid-June to early August at the **Hotel Saint Bernard** (☎ 505/776–2251), at the mountain base (near the lifts) of Taos Ski Valley.

SPORTS & THE OUTDOORS **Wheeler Peak** is a designated wilderness area of Carson National Forest, where travel is restricted to hiking or horseback riding. Part of the Sangre de Cristo Mountains, this 13,161-foot peak is New Mexico's highest. The 8-mi trail to the top begins at the Village of Taos Ski Valley. Only experienced hikers should tackle this strenuous trail. Dress warmly even in summer, take plenty of water and food, and pay attention to *all* warnings and instructions distributed by the forest rangers. Quite a few shorter and less taxing trails also depart from the ski valley and points nearby; trailheads are usually marked with signs. ✉ *Twining Campground, next to ski area parking lot* ☎ *505/758–6200.*

Fodor's Choice ★ With 72 runs—more than half of them for experts—and an average of more than 320 inches of annual snowfall, **Taos Ski Valley** ranks among the country's most respected—and challenging—resorts. The slopes tend to be tough here (the ridge chutes, Al's Run, Inferno), but 25% (e. g., Honeysuckle) are for intermediate skiers, and 24% (e.g., Bambi, Porcupine) for beginners. It's one of the nation's handful of resorts that still, controversially, bans snowboarding. Taos Ski Valley is justly famous for its outstanding ski schools, one of the best in the country—if you're new to the sport, this is a terrific resort to give it a try. ✉ *Village of Taos Ski Valley* ☎ *505/776–2291* ⊕ *www.skitaos.org* ✉ *Lift tickets $61* ☉ *Late Nov.–early Apr.*

SHOPPING **Andean Softwear** (✉ 118 Sutton Pl. ☎ 505/776–2508) carries exotic clothing, textiles, and jewelry. Note the deliciously soft alpaca sweaters from Peru. You can bring your ski boots up to the pros at the **Boot Doctor** (✉ 103 Sutton Pl. ☎ 505/776–2489)—if anyone can make 'em fit, they can; if not, they'll find a pair that does. A demo program lets you try skis out. Ski clothing and accessories fill out the store in winter, and in summer you can get hiking clothing, sandals, and clogs.

TAOS ESSENTIALS

AIRPORTS & TRANSFERS
Albuquerque International Sunport is the nearest (130 mi) major airport to Taos. Taos Municipal Airport is 12 mi west of the city but ceased offering commercial service in 2005 and is just open to charters and private planes.

Faust's Transportation offers shuttle service between Albuquerque's airport and Taos, as well as to Taos Ski Valley, Angel Fire, and Red River. The cost is $40 to $50 per person, and the ride takes 2¾–3 hours.
🚌 **Faust's Transportation** ☎ 505/758–3410 or 888/830–3410 ⊕ www.newmexiconet.com/trans/faust/faust.html.

BUS TRAVEL
Texas, New Mexico & Oklahoma Coaches, a subsidiary of Greyhound Lines, runs buses twice a day from Albuquerque to Taos.
🚌 **Texas, New Mexico & Oklahoma Coaches** ☎ 800/231–2222 ⊕ www.greyhound.com.

CAR RENTAL
Cottam Walker rents cars by the day, week, and month.
🚌 **Cottam Walker Ford** ✉ 1320 Paseo del Pueblo Sur ☎ 505/751–3200 ⊕ www.forddetaos.com.

CAR TRAVEL
The main route from Santa Fe to Taos is NM 68, also known as the Low Road, which winds between the Rio Grande and red-rock cliffs

before rising to a spectacular view of the plain and river gorge. You can also take the wooded High Road to Taos (⇨ Side Trips from Santa Fe *in* Chapter 4). From points north of Taos, take NM 522; from points east or west, take U.S. 64.

PARKING   Major hotels have ample parking. Metered parking areas are all over town; in peak seasons—summer and winter—traffic and parking can be a headache. There's a metered parking lot between Taos Plaza and Bent Street and a free lot on Kit Carson, two blocks east of Paseo del Pueblo.

EMERGENCIES

In an emergency, dial 911.

🚻 **Hospital Holy Cross Hospital** ⊠ 1397 Weimer Rd. ☎ 505/758-8883 ⊕ www. taoshospital.org.

LODGING

Taos has a handful of useful reservation and vacation-rental services.

🚻 **Taos Central Reservations** ☎ 505/758-9767 or 800/821-2437 ⊕ www. taoscentralreservations.com. **Taos Lodging** ☎ 505/751-1771 or 800/954-8267 ⊕ www. taoslodging.com.

TAXIS

Taxi service in Taos is sparse, but Faust's Transportation, based in nearby El Prado, has a fleet of radio-dispatched cabs.

🚻 **Faust's Transportation** ☎ 505/758-3410 or 505/758-7359.

TOURS

ORIENTATION   Historic Taos Trolley Tours conducts daily narrated tours of Taos, in-
TOUR   cluding stops at the San Francisco de Asís Church, Taos Pueblo, Millicent Rogers Museum, and La Hacienda de los Martínez. Separate history and culture tours also are available. Tours run from May to October and cost $33 each, which covers entry fees to all sights.

SPECIAL-   Native Sons Adventures organizes biking, backpacking, rafting, snow-
INTEREST TOURS   mobiling, and horseback and wagon expeditions. Taos Indian Horse Ranch conducts two-hour trail rides, as well as old-fashioned horse-drawn sleigh rides through the Taos Pueblo backcountry—winter weather permitting—complete with brass bells, a Native American storyteller, toasted marshmallows, and green-chile roasts. Tours are by reservation only; no alcohol is permitted. The ranch closes for 42 to 48 days each year to observe the Taos Pueblo Sweats Ceremony; call the Taos Pueblo Governor's Office for the exact dates.

🚻 **Historic Taos Trolley Tours** ☎ 505/751-0366 or 800/753-7559 ⊕ www.taostrolleytours. com. **Native Sons Adventures** ⊠ 1033A Paseo del Pueblo Sur, Taos ☎ 505/758-9342 or 800/753-7559. **Taos Indian Horse Ranch** ⊠ 1 Miller Rd., Taos Pueblo ☎ 800/659-3210. **Taos Pueblo Governor's Office** ☎ 505/758-9593.

VISITOR INFORMATION

🚻 **Taos Chamber of Commerce** ⊠ 1139 Paseo del Pueblo Sur ⌖ Drawer I, Taos 87571 ☎ 505/758-3873 or 800/732-8267 ⊕ www.taosguide.com. **Taos Ski Valley Chamber of Commerce** ☎ 505/776-1413 or 800/517-9816 ⊕ www.taosskivalley.com.

Side Trips from the Cities

WORD OF MOUTH

"One of my favorite things to do near ABQ is the Jemez Mountain Trail. You can spend anywhere from 3–4 hours to a whole day driving this 200-mile (or so) loop. The scenery is constantly changing and there are plenty of worthwhile stops along the way. Bandelier is one of them, but I would recommend at least a half a day for that alone. "

—travel_addict

"We really got a kick out of the Tinkertown Museum. What was most fun for us was finding the things that seemed most out of place."

—moldyhotelsaregross

By Andrew
Collins

IF YOU'RE PLANNING A TRIP to any of north-central New Mexico's three most important destinations—Albuquerque, Santa Fe, or Taos—it's worth spending an extra day or even just a half day to explore the surrounding area. It's by venturing out of town that you really come to appreciate and understand northern Rio Grande Valley's exceptionally diverse and visually stunning scenery, from dramatic river gorges with sheer basalt walls to the evergreen- and aspen-coated slopes of the highest mountain range in New Mexico, the Sangre de Cristos. Within an hour's drive of Albuquerque, Santa Fe, or Taos are nearly a dozen Indian pueblos, the countryside that inspired Georgia O'Keeffe's artwork, some of the West's finest ski resorts, an emerging crop of prestigious wineries, several insular villages famous for both contemporary and traditional arts and crafts, two villages famous for their curative hot springs, and some of the best hiking, rafting, fly-fishing, and biking terrain you'll ever lay eyes on.

There are at least three road routes to get from Albuquerque to Santa Fe, and then three more from Santa Fe up to Taos. And they all have their charms, even the seemingly mundane trek up I–25 from Albuquerque to Santa Fe. Traveling among the region's three key towns, and opting when time allows for the most scenic and circuitous routing, is one way to experience north-central New Mexico's most alluring off-the-beaten-path scenery. Another is simply to plan a few day trips from Albuquerque, Santa Fe, or Taos, or even to consider spending the night in one of the out-of-the-way communities described in this chapter—the region offers a wealth of lodging options, from funky to five-star elegant, and prices out in the country tend to be considerably lower than in Santa Fe and Taos.

However you go about experiencing the region's smaller communities and less-traveled byways, venture out into the hinterlands as often as you can. You haven't really been to north-central New Mexico until you've explored the cave dwellings at Bandelier National Monument, driven over the dramatic mountain passes of the Enchanted Circle and High Road to Taos, or checked out the acclaimed galleries and funky shops of Madrid and Chimayó. As the old travel cliché goes, in New Mexico, getting there is half the fun.

Exploring North-Central New Mexico

You need a car to embark on any of the side trips described in this chapter, and you should generally allow yourself an extra hour or two to complete most of these journeys. Distances aren't as vast in north-central New Mexico as in the rest of the state: the Turquoise Trail extends only about 70 mi from Albuquerque to Santa Fe and can be managed, if you hustle, in roughly 90 minutes, but to truly appreciate the scenery and attractions along the way, you should really allow anywhere from three to six hours. Same goes for driving the High Road to Taos, the Enchanted Circle, Jémez Country, and Abiquiu. Roads in this part of the state can be windy and even a bit treacherous, espe-

GREAT ITINERARIES

As you tour north-central New Mexico, it's best to mix your explorations of the destinations in this chapter with stops in the region's three main bases: Albuquerque, Santa Fe, and Taos.

IF YOU HAVE 3 DAYS

With just three days, you can make the three most popular driving tours in this chapter with relative ease. Begin your travels in Albuquerque, and drive up the Turquoise Trail on Day 1. Plan to make the side trip up NM 536 to Sandia Crest, and also to take some time admiring the galleries and shops in **Madrid** ❼. There are a handful of overnight accommodations along this route, but you can also just spend your first night in Santa Fe. Make Day 2 your most ambitious one for driving. Start off in Santa Fe and take the Low Road up to Taos, perhaps stopping at Embudo Station for lunch along the way. Once you reach Taos, continue north of town and embark on the Enchanted Circle tour, which loops around the majestic mountains north of town. You can spend the night in **Angel Fire** ❸❺, along the Enchanted Circle, or back in Taos. On Day 3, you can return to Santa Fe (continuing on back down to Albuquerque if need be), by taking the High Road from Taos, passing through the charming villages of **Truchas** ❸❶ and **Chimayó** ❷❾.

IF YOU HAVE 5 DAYS

With an extra two days, you can complete all of the tours described above while allowing some time to make several additional side trips. For Day 1, repeat the itinerary described above, ending your day either at the north end of Turquoise Trail or in Santa Fe. The following day, drive north from Santa Fe, and at **Española** ❷❷, hang a left and continue north along U.S. 84 into the heart of Georgia O'Keeffe Country. You can spend the night in **Abiquiu** ❷❸; at Rancho de San Juan, just north of Española; or at **Ojo Caliente** ❷❼. Whatever you decide, plan to head north up U.S. 285 on the morning of Day 3, turning east on U.S. 64 (in Tres Piedras), which takes you into Taos. Alternatively, if you're more a fan of historic railroads than you are of Georgia O'Keeffe, plan to spend your second day up in **Chama** ❷❺, and ride the famed Cumbres & Toltec Scenic Railroad in the morning, and then cut east on U.S. 64 to reach Taos. From here, embark on the Enchanted Circle tour, spending the night either in **Angel Fire** ❸❺ or back in Taos. Make the drive back down toward Santa Fe along the High Road on Day 4; however, after you reach **Pojoaque** ❶❸ (where you might stop and spend a couple of hours), make the turn (just north of Pojoaque) onto NM 502 and follow this road up into **Los Alamos** ❶❼, where you can tour some of the museums or check out **Bandelier National Monument** ❶❽. Spend your fourth night here in Los Alamos. The following day, continue west from Los Alamos along NM 4, passing through the Jémez Valley and stopping in **Jémez Springs** ❷⓿. This leads you to U.S. 550, onto which a left turn leads south and into the northern Albuquerque suburbs of **Bernalillo** ❹ and **Corrales** ❸, where more exploring, restaurants, and lodging options await you.

4

cially in snowy winter weather, so take your time and avoid racing around on roads unfamiliar to you.

That being said, virtually every attraction and community covered here can be visited as part of a day trip from Albuquerque, Santa Fe, and/or Taos. If you have only two or three hours, stick with manageable and nearby jaunts. From Albuquerque, head to Isleta Pueblo or the North Valley. From Santa Fe, visit some of the towns just south of town or some of the pueblos to the north—you can even visit Los Alamos or Bandelier in a half day if you're quick. From Taos, it's possible to cover part of the Enchanted Circle, and to drive up to the ski valley, in just two or three hours.

Keep in mind that many of the recreation areas, museums, campgrounds, and even restaurants and lodgings covered in this chapter keep seasonal or limited hours. As it can take a bit of driving to reach some of these places, it's *always* best to phone ahead to avoid disappointment. And if you're unfamiliar with the area, always ask about driving times and current weather conditions. A little planning goes a long way when exploring some of the region's more remote towns and villages.

About the Restaurants

Somehow, just about any meal tastes a little better when it follows a long, windy road trip through magnificent scenery. North-central New Mexico has no shortage of tantalizing "road food"—simple and honest New Mexican fare, diner snacks, juicy burgers, and the like. But in these parts you can also find one of the Southwest's most acclaimed restaurants, Rancho de San Juan, along with several other fine eateries. A number of the restaurants in these parts are informal and operate with seasonal or less than regular hours, so it's always best to call first. Most of them serve dinner on the early side, too, so don't expect to find a restaurant open after 9 PM—or even 8 PM on weeknights. Casual attire is always the norm around here.

About the Hotels

There are several good reasons to consider spending a night in one of the towns covered in this chapter, rather than in Albuquerque, Santa Fe, and Taos. First, distinctive B&Bs and inns are the norm when you get out into the countryside—these properties tend to be more personal than big chain hotels, which predominate in Albuquerque and to a lesser extent in Santa Fe and Taos. Also, you pay higher prices for the same amenities in Santa Fe and Taos, if not Albuquerque, which has quite low hotel rates. If you prefer the sounds of coyotes howling and a pitch-black sky illuminated only by bright stars, you're more likely to appreciate one of the off-the-beaten-path lodgings described in this chapter than a place right in the heart of busy and bustling Albuquerque, Santa Fe, or even Taos. What you may lose in convenience to shopping, dining, and nightlife, you often gain in proximity to great outdoorsy attractions, such as ski resorts and hiking trails.

IF YOU LIKE

ART GALLERIES

Where do artists and arts patrons open galleries when they can't afford the exorbitant rents of Santa Fe and Taos, but they prefer a more scenic setting than Albuquerque? Quite a few of them have chosen to set up galleries in the many alluring, small, and inexpensive villages of north-central New Mexico. The region's arts hub, Madrid—along the Turquoise Trail—continues to grow in eminence, with new galleries opening on a regular basis. Other communities with a strong arts presence include Corrales, Jémez Springs, Abiquiu (the site of Georgia O'Keeffe's artists' studio), Chimayó, and Truchas. Finally, most of the Indian Pueblos in this region have galleries and shops selling pottery, jewelry, crafts, and other fine artworks made by pueblo members.

HIKING

You see them from the historic plazas and bustling downtowns of Albuquerque, Santa Fe, and Taos: towering, often snowcapped, mountains. Travel the side roads and rural highways of north-central New Mexico, and you reach the trailheads leading to amazing hikes through the state's rugged, 12,000- to 13,000-foot mountain peaks. If you're looking for a lot of bang for your buck, hike the ridge along Sandia Crest, reached via the Turquoise Trail, or make the relatively easy but spectacular jaunt through Kasha-Katuwe Tent Rocks National Monument, south of Santa Fe. Wild Rivers Recreation Area, along the Enchanted Circle tour, can also be managed easily as a day hike. You can find more substantial hiking throughout this area, but especially in Kit Carson National Forest, which surrounds Taos—some of the best hikes depart from Taos Ski Valley.

SKIING

Even more than explaining to outsiders that, yes, New Mexico is actually a U.S. state and not a foreign country (seriously, it happens more than you might imagine), New Mexicans tire of insisting that their state has huge mountains, cold winters, and tons of snow—in other words, it's one of the West's prime venues for both downhill and cross-country skiing. The most famous facility in the region, often cited among the greatest ski challenges in the country in polls and ski magazines, is Taos Ski Valley, a 30-minute drive from downtown Taos. But nearby Angel Fire is another first-rate ski resort. Other fine options include Red River (which also offers exceptional cross-country skiing) and Pajarito Mountain.

WHAT IT COSTS					
	$$$$	**$$$**	**$$**	**$**	**¢**
RESTAURANTS	over $30	$24–$30	$17–$24	$10–$17	under $10
HOTELS	over $260	$190–$260	$130–$190	$70–$130	under $70

Restaurant prices are per person for a main course at dinner, excluding the 8.25% sales tax. Hotel prices are for two people in a standard double room in high season, excluding 11%–14% tax.

SIDE TRIPS FROM ALBUQUERQUE

It takes only a few minutes of driving in either direction to leave urban Albuquerque behind and experience some of New Mexico's natural and small-town beauty. Rivers, valleys, canyons, and peaks are just outside the city's limits, and amid them are many villages worth a stop. If you're headed up to Santa Fe, definitely consider traveling there by way of the rambling and tortuous Turquoise Trail, a charming alternative to speedy I–25.

South of Albuquerque

When Francisco Vásquez de Coronado arrived in what is now New Mexico in 1540, he found a dozen or so villages along the Rio Grande in the ancient province of Tiguex, between what is now Bernalillo to the north of Albuquerque and Isleta to the south. Of those, only Sandia and Isleta survive today. The Salinas Pueblo Missions ruins, about 65 mi southeast of Albuquerque, remain a striking example of the Spanish penchant for building churches on sites inhabited by native people.

Isleta Pueblo

❶ *13 mi south of Albuquerque, via I–25 (Exit 213) and NM 47.*

Of the pueblos in New Mexico when the Spanish first arrived, Isleta Pueblo is one of two Tiwa-speaking communities left in the middle of the Rio Grande Valley. It was also one of a handful of pueblos that didn't participate in the Pueblo Revolt of 1680, during which Isleta was abandoned. Some of the residents fled New Mexico with the Spanish to El Paso, where their descendants live to this day on a reservation called Ysleta del Sur. Other members went to live with the Hopi of Arizona but eventually returned and rebuilt the pueblo.

Facing the quiet plaza is Isleta's church, **St. Augustine,** built in 1629. One of the oldest churches in New Mexico, it has thick adobe walls, a viga-crossed ceiling, and an austere interior. Legend has it that the ground beneath the floor has the odd propensity to push church and community figures buried under the floor back up out of the ground; bodies have been reburied several times, only to emerge again.

Polychrome pottery with red and black designs on a white background is a specialty here. The pueblo celebrates its feast days on August 28 and September 4, both in honor of St. Augustine. The tribal government maintains picnicking and camping facilities, several fishing ponds, and a renowned 18-hole golf course. It also runs the **Isleta Casino and Resort** (✉ 11000 Broadway SE ☎ 505/724–3800 or 877/747–5382 ⊕ www.isletacasinoresort.com), which ranks among the state's most popular gaming facilities. It's a large and handsome space with 1,600 slots and myriad gaming tables; the concert hall hosts a mix of oldies, pop stars, and country-western acts—past numbers have included Tom Jones, Vince Gill, and Tony Bennett, but competition from improved casino resorts elsewhere in the region has pulled away many of the big-name acts that used to favor Isleta. There's also boxing held throughout the year. Currently there's no hotel at Isleta, but the tribe is planning

Albuquerque Side Trips

Kasha-Katue Tents Rocks National Monument

El Rancho de las Golondrinas

Santa Fe

Jémez Pueblo

5 Santo Domingo Pueblo

8 Cerrillos

Santa Ana Pueblo

San Félipe Pueblo

7 Madrid

CIBOLA NATIONAL FOREST

Rio Puerco

Rio Grande

550

25

14

Bernalillo

4 165

Golden

Sandía Park

Sandia Crest

Corrales

3 448

530

Sandia Park

6 306 344

Albuquerque

Laguna Pueblo

Tijeras

40 66

LAGUNA INDIAN RESERVATION

66 40 25

Albuquerque International Sunport

Moriarty

Isleta Pueblo 1

Acoma Pueblo

ISLETA INDIAN RESERVATION

337

41

6

47

Los Lunas

55

CIBOLA NATIONAL FOREST

Belen

47

Willard

60

0   25 miles

0   50 km

Salinas Pueblo Missions National Monument 2

Mountainair

55

---

a full-service, upscale hotel and expanded resort facilities so that it can better compete with other high-profile Native American resorts that have opened around the state in recent years, including Sandia, Santa Ana, and Pojoaque.

Although Isleta is wonderfully picturesque—beehive ovens stand beside adobe homes bedecked with crimson chiles—camera use is restricted here. Only the church may be photographed. ✉ *Tribal Rd. 40* ☎ *505/869–3111* ⊕ *www.isletapueblo.com* ✂ *Free.*

SPORTS & THE OUTDOORS One of the most esteemed facilities in the state, **Isleta Eagle Golf Course** (✉4001 NM 47 ☎505/869–0950 or 888/293–9146 ⊕www.isletaeagle. com) consists of three 9-hole layouts set around three lakes; greens fees are $40–$55 for 18 holes.

Salinas Pueblo Missions National Monument

2 *58 mi (to Punta Agua/Quarai) from Albuquerque, east on I-40 (to Tijeras Exit), south on NM 337 and NM 55; 23 mi from Punta Agua to Abó, south on NM 55, west (at Mountainair) on U.S. 60, and north on NM 513; 34 mi from Punta Agua to Gran Quivira, south on NM 55.*

Salinas Pueblo Missions National Monument is made up of three sites— **Quarai, Abó, and Gran Quivira**—each with the ruins of a 17th-century

Spanish-colonial Franciscan missionary church and an associated pueblo. The sites represent the convergence of two Native American peoples, the Anasazi and the Mogollon, who lived here for centuries before the Spanish arrived. Quarai, the nearest to Albuquerque, was a flourishing Tiwa pueblo whose inhabitants' pottery, weaving, and basket-making techniques were quite refined. On the fringe of the Great Plains, all three of the Salinas pueblos were vulnerable to raids by nomadic Plains Indians. Quarai was abandoned about 50 years after its mission church, **San Purísima Concepción de Cuarac,** was built in 1630. The church's sandstone walls still rise 40 feet out of the earth. At Abó are the remains of the three-story church of San Gregorio and a large unexcavated pueblo. (The masonry style at Abó bore some similarity to that at Chaco Canyon, which has led some archaeologists to speculate that the pueblo was built by people who left the Chaco Canyon area.) A video about Salinas Pueblo can be viewed at Gran Quivira, which contains two churches and some excavated Native American structures. The monument headquarters is in the town of Mountainair. ✉ *N. Ripley Ave. at W. Broadway (U.S. 60), Mountainair* ☎ *505/847–2585* ⊕ *www.nps.gov/sapu* ✉ *Free* ⊙ *Late May–early Sept., daily 9–6; early Sept.–late May, daily 9–5.*

WHERE TO STAY ⛺ **Shaffer Hotel.** One of the nation's few remaining structures built in
$ the Pueblo–art deco style, the Shaffer was restored and reopened as a hotel in 2005 after many years of neglect. The 1923 building, in the heart of historic—if modest—downtown Mountainair, offers a wide range of accommodations. The simple "cowboy rooms" share a community bathroom, but all others have private baths, some with original clawfoot tubs. All are done with 1920s and '30s deco antiques and tile bathrooms. Some suites have two bedrooms, and the Wedding Suite has a romantic glass-brick double shower. A festively decorated restaurant serves decent, country-style American and New Mexican fare. Also on-site is Pop's Curio Shop, which carries a quirky mix of jewelry, decorative arts, gifts, and musical instruments. ✉ *103 W. Main St., Mountainair 87036* ☎ *505/847–2888 or 888/595–2888* ✉ *505/847–0299* ⊕ *www. shafferhotel.com* ⇆ *11 rooms, 9 with bath; 8 suites* ⇆ *Restaurant, cable TV, Wi-Fi, shop, meeting room* ⊟ *AE, D, MC, V.*

North Valley & Beyond

The land north of Albuquerque is a little bit cooler, a little bit greener, and a lot more pastoral than the city. Drive slowly through Bernalillo and Corrales, and you're bound to see lots of horses, cows, and llamas.

Corrales

➌ *2 mi north of Albuquerque. Take Paseo Del Norte (NM 423) or Alameda Blvd. (NM 528) west from I–25 and head north on Corrales Rd. (NM 448).*

Serene Corrales is an ancient agricultural community now inhabited by artists, craftspeople, and the affluent—plus a few descendants of the old families. Small galleries, shops, and places to eat dot the town, and in fall, roadside fruit and vegetable stands open. Bordered by Albuquerque and Rio Rancho, Corrales makes a pleasant escape to winding dirt roads, fields of corn, and apple orchards. On summer weekends visit the Corrales Farmers' Market; in October, the village holds a Harvest Festival. The village's main drag, NM 448, is one of New Mexico's official scenic byways, lined with grand estates and haciendas and shaded by cottonwoods. Just off the byway, you can break for a stroll through Corrales Bosque Preserve, a shaded sanctuary abutting the Rio Grande that's a favorite spot for bird-watching—some 180 species pass through here throughout the year.

WHERE TO STAY & EAT $–$$$ ✕ **Casa Vieja.** Set in a rambling early-18th-century compound along the Corrales Scenic Byway and helmed by charismatic chef and local TV personality Jim White, this supposedly haunted hacienda has inspired a devoted following. The menu mixes classic American and New Mexican fare and includes both lighter options and rather rich and lavish entrées. Top picks include crab cakes with mild poblano-chile crème, shrimp sautéed in tequila and lime juice, filet mignon au poivre, and carne adovada burritos. Desserts are made on the premises and include an obscenely rich cinnamon-bun bread pudding with caramel sauce. ✉ *4541 Corrales Rd.* ☎ *505/898–7489* ⊕ *www.chefwhite.com* ▤ *AE, D, DC, MC, V.*

¢–$ ✕ **Village Pizza.** A Chicago native with a knack for baking runs this ordinarily named joint that serves extraordinarily good pizza. Crusts come in different styles (including Chicago-style deep dish), and a wide range of toppings are offered, including such gourmet fixings as artichoke hearts and smoked oysters. The Corrales calzone is packed with mozzarella and ricotta and slathered with pesto sauce. Locals love the all-you-can-eat buffets (available daily for lunch, Monday and Tuesday for dinner). In back is a rambling courtyard with a couple of big leafy trees and lots of seating. You get a 10% discount if you ride in on horseback. ✉ *4266 Corrales Rd.* ☎ *505/898–0045* ▤ *AE, D, MC, V.*

★ $ ⌂ **Chocolate Turtle B&B.** Hosts Nancy and Dallas Renner run this light-filled four-room hideaway in a quiet neighborhood in West Corrales. It's a short drive from the massive Intel plant in the nearby suburb of Rio Rancho and a 20-minute from downtown Albuquerque, but the setting is as peaceful as can be, this Territorial-style home's large windows and neatly landscaped grounds affording sweeping views of the Sandia Mountains. Fresh flowers and chocolates brighten the rooms, which range from a cozy room with single beds to three more substantial doubles, the most desirable with its own private terrace. All contain well-chosen Southwestern art and furnishings. ✉ *1098 W. Meadowlark La., Corrales 87048* ☎ *505/898–1800 or 877/298–1800* ⊕ *www. chocolateturtlebb.com* ⌁ *4 rooms* ⌂ *Wi-Fi, business services; no room phones, no room TVs* ▤ *AE, D, DC, MC, V* ⍑ *BP.*

Bernalillo

❹ *17 mi north of Albuquerque via I–25, 8 mi north of Corrales via NM 448 to NM 528.*

Once a rather tranquil Hispanic village, Bernalillo is today one of New Mexico's fastest-growing towns—it's increasingly absorbing the suburban growth northward from Albuquerque. The town holds a Wine Festival each Labor Day weekend, but the most memorable annual event is the Fiesta of San Lorenzo, which has honored the town's patron saint for nearly 400 years. On August 10, San Lorenzo Day, the entire town takes to the streets to participate in the traditional masked *matachine* dance. Matachines, of Moorish origin, were brought to this hemisphere by the Spanish. In New Mexico various versions are danced to haunting fiddle music, in both Native American pueblos and old Spanish villages at different holidays. Though interpretations of the matachines are inexact, one general theme is that of conquest. One dancer, wearing a devil's mask and wielding a whip, presides over the others. A young girl, dressed in white, is also present.

The town's leading attraction, **Coronado State Monument**, is named in honor of Francisco Vásquez de Coronado, the leader of the first organized Spanish expedition into the Southwest, from 1540 to 1542. The prehistoric **Kuaua Pueblo**, on a bluff overlooking the Rio Grande, is believed to have been the headquarters of Coronado and his army, who were caught unprepared by severe winter weather during their search for the legendary Seven Cities of Gold. A worthy stop, the monument has a museum in a restored kiva, with copies of magnificent frescoes done in black, yellow, red, blue, green, and white. The frescoes depict fertility rites, rain dances, and hunting rituals. The original artworks are preserved in the small visitor center. Adjacent to the monument is **Coronado State Park**, which has campsites and picnic grounds, both open year-round. In autumn the views at the monument and park are especially breathtaking, with the trees turning russet and gold. There's also overnight camping at the adjacent Coronado Campground (505/980–8256). ⊠ *485 Kuaua Rd., off NM 44/U.S. 550* ☎ *505/867–5351* ⊕ *www.nmstatemonuments.org* ▦ *$3* ☉ *Wed.–Mon. 8:30–5.*

WHERE TO STAY & EAT
★ **$$–$$$$**

✕ **Prairie Star.** Albuquerque residents often make the drive to this 1920s Pueblo Revival hacienda, renowned for the sunset views from its patio. The menu combines contemporary American, Southwestern, and classical cuisine, including duck-confit crepes with red-chile-infused blueberries, lemon chèvre, mint, and pistachios, and dry-aged prime New York steak with black truffle potatoes, cheesy collard greens, and roasted garlic–tomato confit. The culinary quality has become consistently outstanding over the years, and the setting is gorgeous. Prairie Star is on the Santa Ana reservation, right beside the Santa Ana Golf Club. ⊠ *288 Prairie Star Rd., Santa Ana Pueblo* ☎ *505/867–3327* ⊕ *www. santaanagolf.com* ▤ *AE, D, DC, MC, V* ☉ *Closed Mon. No lunch.*

¢–$$
Fodor's Choice
★

✕ **Range Cafe & Bakery.** Banana pancakes, giant cinnamon rolls, Asian spinach salad, grilled portobello burgers, homemade meat loaf with garlic mashed potatoes, steak-and-enchilada platters, and the signature dessert, Death by Lemon, are among the highlights at this quirky spot known for down-home fare with creative touches. All the above, plus a full complement of rich, decadent Taos Cow ice cream, is served in a refurbished mercantile building with a dead-center view of the Sandia Mountains. You can order breakfast fare until 3 PM. There are also two newer branches in Albuquerque, but the original has the best ambience. ⊠ *925 Camino del Pueblo* ☎ *505/867–1700* ⊕ *www.rangecafe.com* ▥ *Reservations not accepted* ▤ *AE, D, MC, V.*

$$-$$$$ ✕▣ **Hyatt Regency Tamaya.** This spectacular large-scale resort, on 500
Fodor's Choice acres on the Santa Ana Pueblo, includes a top-rated golf course, state-
★ of-the-art spa, and cultural museum and learning center. Most rooms,
swathed in natural stone, wood, and adobe and filled with pueblo-in-
spired textiles and pottery, overlook the Sandia Mountains or cotton-
wood groves; many have balconies or patios. Cultural events include
bread-baking demonstrations (in traditional adobe ovens), storytelling,
and live tribal dance and music performances. Other amenities include
waterslides over two of the outdoor pools, atmospheric bars, guided na-
ture walks, and hot-air ballooning nearby. The Hyatt's outstanding
Corn Maiden restaurant (⊘ Closed Sun. and Mon. No lunch) serves out-
standing contemporary fare that mixes New Mexican, Asian, regional
American influences and ingredients. Try buffalo topped with foie gras
and a truffle demi-glace, or crispy-skin duck served with an apple–green
chile pancake and orange-whiskey sauce. The Santa Ana Star Casino is
a free shuttle ride away. And if you're looking for an exceptional horse-
back ride, arrange one with the Tamaya stables. As you drink in eye-
fuls of the spectacular pueblo backcountry and weave among trees and
plantings, you'll wonder why you ever settled for the dull nose-to-butt
riding experiences of yesteryear. If you're too suave to wear the helmet
or gloves offered, by all means do not forego a heavy layer of sunscreen,
especially on your face, ears, and neck. ⊠ *1300 Tuyuna Trail, Santa Ana
Pueblo, 87525* ☎ *505/867–1234 or 800/633–7313* 🖷 *505/771–6180*
⊕ *www.tamaya.hyatt.com* ⬮ *331 rooms, 19 suites* ⅋ *3 restaurants,
room service, refrigerators, cable TV with movies, driving range, 18-
hole golf course, 2 tennis courts, 3 pools, health club, spa, basketball,
horseback riding, 3 bars, children's programs (ages 2–14), concierge,
business services, meeting rooms* ▤ *AE, D, DC, MC, V.*

⚠ **Albuquerque North Bernalillo KOA.** Cottonwoods, pines, evergreens,
and willows shade this park, where morning brings a free pancake
breakfast and in summer free outdoor movies are screened. You can play
badminton, basketball, croquet, horseshoes, and video games. ⊠ *55 S.
Hill Rd., 87004* ☎ *505/867–5227 or 800/562–3616* ⊕ *www.koa.com*
⅋ *Grills, snack bar, laundry facilities, flush toilets, full hookups, show-
ers, picnic tables, swimming (pool)* ⬮ *57 RV sites, 36 tent sites, 6 cab-
ins* ☒ *$21–$51; cabins $37–$56* ▤ *D, MC, V.*

SHOPPING **Jackalope** (⊠ 834 NM 44/U.S. 550 ☎ 505/867–9813) has acres of im-
ported pottery, crafts, table linens, jewelry, clothing, glass, tinwork,
and furniture from Mexico as well as India, Eastern Europe, and China.
This is a good place to hunt for gifts and a great place to spend an hour
(at least) browsing.

Santo Domingo Pueblo

❺ *40 mi northeast of Albuquerque via I–25; exit on NM 22 and drive 4½
mi west.*

Santo Domingo Pueblo craftspeople sell outstanding *heishi* (shell) jew-
elry and pottery, along with other traditional arts and crafts, year-
round, but the pueblo's three-day Labor Day Arts and Crafts Fair brings
out artists and visitors in full force. The colorful, dramatic Corn Dance,

held in honor of St. Dominic, the pueblo's patron saint, on August 4, attracts more than 2,000 dancers, clowns, singers, and drummers. Painter Georgia O'Keeffe supposedly said the Corn Dance was one of the great events in her life. Still and video cameras, tape recorders, and sketching materials are prohibited. It's quite easy to visit the pueblo as part of a trip to Tent Rocks, covered in the South of Santa Fe section. ⊠ *Off NM 22, 4½ mi west of I–25* ☎ *505/465–2214* 🏷 *Donations encouraged* ⊙ *Daily dawn–dusk.*

The Turquoise Trail

Fodor'sChoice ★ Etched out in the early 1970s and still well traveled is the scenic Turquoise Trail, which follows an old route between Albuquerque and Santa Fe that's dotted with ghost towns now being restored by writers, artists, and other urban refugees. This 70 mi of piñon-studded mountain back road is a gentle roller coaster of panoramic views of the Ortiz, Jémez, and Sangre de Cristo mountains. It's believed that 2,000 years ago Native Americans mined turquoise in these hills. The Spanish took up turquoise mining in the 16th century, and the practice continued into the early 20th century, with Tiffany & Co. removing a fair share of the semiprecious stone. In addition, gold, silver, tin, lead, and coal have been mined here. There's plenty of opportunity for picture-taking and picnicking along the way. The pace is slow, the talk is about the weather, and Albuquerque might as well be on another planet. The entire loop of this trip takes a day, the drive up the Sandia Crest a half day.

Sandia Park

6 *7 mi north of Tijeras. From Tijeras, take I–40 east and exit north on the Turquoise Trail (NM 14); proceed 6 mi and turn left onto NM 536.*

☾ At the **Sandia Ranger Station** you can pick up pamphlets and maps, and—if there are enough kids in the audience—witness a fire-prevention program with a Smokey the Bear motif. From here you can also embark on a short self-guided tour to the nearby **fire lookout tower** and **Tijeras Pueblo ruins;** the ranger station has maps and can provide details on how to do this. Here you can also pick up information on trails in Cibola National Forest, which encompasses the Sandia Mountains. ⊠ *11776 NM 337, south of I–40* ☎ *505/281–3304* ⊕ *www.fs.fed.us/r3/cibola/districts/ sandia.shtml* 🏷 *Free, $3 for parking in Cibola National Forest* ⊙ *Weekdays 8–5, weekends 8:30–5.*

☾ It may take months for this odyssey of a place to completely sink in: Fodor'sChoice ★ quirky and utterly fascinating, **Tinkertown Museum** contains a world of miniature carved-wood characters. The museum's late founder, Ross Ward, spent more than 40 years carving and collecting the hundreds of figures that populate this cheerfully bizarre museum, including an animated miniature Western village, a Boot Hill cemetery, and a 1940s circus exhibit. Ragtime piano music, a 40-foot sailboat, and a life-size general store are other highlights. The walls surrounding this 22-room museum have been fashioned out of more than 50,000 glass bottles pressed into cement. This homage to folk art, found art, and eccentric kitsch tends to strike a chord with people of all ages. As you might expect, the gift shop offers plenty of fun oddities. ⊠ *121 Sandia Crest Rd., take Cedar Crest* *exit off I–40 east and follow signs to Sandia Crest turnoff* 🖾 *505/281–5233* ⊕ *www.tinkertown.com* 🖾 *$3* ⊙ *Apr.–Oct., daily 9–6.*

In Cedar Crest, just off NM 14 a couple of miles south of Sandia Park, the modest but nicely laid-out **Museum of Archaeology & Material Culture** chronicles archaeological finds and contains artifacts dating from the Ice Age to the Battle of Wounded Knee. Exhibits shed light on prehistoric man, buffalo hunting, a history of turquoise mining in north-central New Mexico, and the 1930s excavations of a cave about 15 mi away that offered evidence of some of the earliest human life in North America. 🖾 *22 Calvary Rd.* 🖾 *505/281–4745* ⊕ *www.museumarch.org* 🖾 *$3* ⊙ *May–Oct., daily noon–7.*

★ For awesome views of Albuquerque and half of New Mexico, take NM 536 up the back side of the Sandia Mountains through Cibola National Forest to **Sandia Crest.** At the 10,378-foot summit, explore the foot trails along the rim (particularly in summer) and take in the breathtaking views of Albuquerque down below, and of the so-called Steel Forest—the nearby cluster of radio and television towers. Always bring an extra layer of clothing, even in summer—the temperature at the crest can be anywhere from 15 to 25 degrees cooler than down in Albuquerque. If you're in need of refreshments or are searching for some inexpensive souvenirs, visit the **Sandia Crest House Gift Shop and Restaurant** (🖾 505/243–0605), on the rim of the crest.

As you continue north up NM 14 from Sandia Park, after about 12 mi you pass through the sleepy village of **Golden,** the site of the first gold rush (in 1825) west of the Mississippi. It has a rock shop and a mercantile store. The rustic adobe church and graveyard are popular with photographers. Be aware that locals are very protective of this area and aren't known to warm up to strangers.

WHERE TO STAY
★ $–$$

🖾 **Elaine's, A Bed and Breakfast.** This antique-filled three-story log-and-stone home is set in the evergreen folds of the Sandia Mountain foothills. Four acres of wooded grounds beckon outside the back door. The top two floors have rooms with balconies and big picture windows that bring the lush mountain views indoors. The third-floor room also has cathedral ceilings and a brass bed; some rooms have fireplaces, and one has its own outside entrance. Breakfast, served in a plant-filled room or outside on a patio with a fountain, often includes fresh fruit, pancakes, or waffles with sausage. 🖾 *Snowline Estate, 72 Snowline Rd.* 🖾 *Box 444, Cedar Crest 87008* 🖾 *505/281–2467 or 800/821–3092* ⊕ *www.elainesbnb.com* 🖘 *5 rooms* 🖾 *Some in-room hot tubs, outdoor hot tub; no room phones, no room TVs, no smoking* 🖾*AE, D, DC, MC, V* 🖾*BP.*

🖾 **Turquoise Trail Campground and RV Park.** Pine and cedar trees dot this 14-acre park in the Sandias, which has hiking trails with access to the Cibola National Forest. Adjacent to the premises is the Museum of Archaeology & Material Culture. Campsite rates are calculated per person; you will need reservations in October. 🖾 *22 Calvary Rd., 5 mi north of I-40 Exit 175 in Cedar Crest* 🖾 *505/281–2005* 🖾 *debswe@earthlink.com* 🖾 *Grills, laundry facilities, flush toilets, full hookups, partial hookups (electric and water), dump station, drinking water, showers,* *fire grates, fire pits, picnic tables, electricity, public telephone, general store, play area ⬅ 57 sites, 45 with hookups ⬌ $15–$25; cabins $29–$58.*

SPORTS &
THE OUTDOORS

The 18-hole **Paa-Ko Ridge Golf Course** (⬌ Sandia Park, 1 Club House Dr. ☎ 505/281–6000 or 866/898–5987 ⊕ www.paakoridge.com) has been voted "The Best Place to Play Golf in New Mexico" by *Golf Digest*. Golfers enjoy vistas of the mesas and the Sandia Mountains from any of five tee placements on each hole. Greens fees are $60–$75. The course is just off NM 14, 3½ mi north of the turnoff for Sandia Crest (NM 536).

Although less extensive and challenging than the ski areas farther north in the Sangre de Cristos, **Sandia Peak** (⬌ NM 536 ☎ 505/242–9052, 505/857–8977 snow conditions ⊕ www.sandiapeak.com) is extremely popular with locals from Albuquerque and offers a nice range of novice, intermediate, and expert downhill trails; there's also a ski school. Snowboarding is welcome on all trails, and there's cross-country terrain as well, whenever snow is available. Snowfall can be sporadic, so call ahead to check for cross-country; Sandia has snow-making capacity for about 30 of its 200 acres of downhill skiing. The season runs from mid-December to mid-March, and lift tickets cost $43. Keep in mind that you can also access the ski area year-round via the Sandia Peak Aerial Tramway (*see* Chapter 1, Albuquerque), which is faster from Albuquerque than driving all the way around. In summer, the ski area converts into a fantastic mountain-biking and hiking terrain. The ski area offers a number of packages with bike and helmet rentals and lift tickets. Other summer activities at Sandia Peak include sand-pit volleyball, horseshoes, and picnicking.

Madrid

❼ *37 mi northeast of Albuquerque, 12 mi northeast of Golden on NM 14.*

Totally abandoned when its coal mine closed in the 1950s, Madrid has gradually been rebuilt and is now—to the dismay of some longtime locals—on the verge of trendiness. The entire town was offered for sale for $250,000 back then, but there were no takers. Finally, in the early 1970s, a few artists fleeing big cities settled in and began restoration. Weathered houses and old company stores have been repaired and turned into boutiques and galleries, some of them selling high-quality furniture, paintings, and crafts. Big events here include Old Timers Days on July 4 weekend, and the Christmas open house, held weekends in December, when galleries and studios are open and the famous Madrid Christmas lights twinkle brightly.

NEED A
BREAK?

Aged hippies, youthful hipsters, and everyone in between congregate at **Java Junction** (⬌ 2855 NM 14 ☎ 505/438–2772) for lattes, chai, sandwiches, pastries, and other toothsome treats. Upstairs there's a pleasantly decorated room for rent that can sleep up to three guests.

☺ Madrid's **Old Coal Mine Museum** is a remnant of a once-flourishing industry. Children can explore the old tunnel, climb aboard a 1900 steam train, and poke through antique buildings full of marvelous relics. Museum tickets are available at the Mine Shaft Tavern out front. On weekends at 3 PM from late May to mid-October you can cheer the heroes and hiss the villains of the old-fashioned melodramas performed at the **Engine House Theater.** The theater, inside a converted roundhouse machine shop, has a full-size steam train that comes chugging onto the stage. ⊠ *2814 NM 14* ☏ *505/438–3780* ⊕ *www.oldcoalminemuseum.com* ▧ *Museum $4, melodrama $10* ⊙ *Late May–mid-Oct., weekdays 9:30–5, weekends 9:30–6; mid-Oct.–late May, daily 10–4.*

WHERE TO EAT ✕ **Mineshaft Tavern.** A rollicking old bar and restaurant adjacent to the
★ ¢–$ Old Coal Mine Museum, this boisterous place was a miners' commissary back in the day. Today it serves what many people consider to be the best green-chile cheeseburger in New Mexico, along with ice-cold beer and a selection of other pub favorites and comfort foods. ⊠ *2846 NM 14* ☏ *505/473–0743* ▤ *D, MC, V* ⊙ *No dinner Mon., Tues., and Thurs.*

SHOPPING The town of Madrid has only one street, so the three-dozen-or-so shops and galleries are easy to find.

You can watch live glassblowing demonstrations at **Al Leedom Studio** (☏ 505/473–2054); his vibrant vases and bowls are sold alongside the beautiful handcrafted jewelry of wife Barbara Leedom. The Leedoms' friendly cat and dancing dog are also big crowd pleasers. In a pale-blue cottage in the center of town, the **Ghost Town Trading Post** (☏ 505/471–7605) is a great bet for fine Western jewelry fashioned out of local gemstones (not just turquoise but opal, amber, and onyx). **Johnsen & Swan** (☏ 505/473–1963) stocks fine leather belts, bags, and wallets; beadwork; custom-made chaps; and Western-inspired jewelry and gifts. **Johnsons of Madrid** (☏ 505/471–1054) ranks among the most prestigious galleries in town, showing painting, photography, sculpture, and textiles created by some of the region's leading artists. You could spend hours browsing the fine rugs and furnishings at **Seppanen & Daughters Fine Textiles** (☏ 505/424–7470), which stocks custom textiles from Oaxaca, Navajo weavings, Tibetan carpets, and fine Arts and Crafts tables, sofas, and chairs.

Cerrillos

❽ *3 mi northeast of Madrid on NM 14.*

Cerrillos was a boomtown in the 1880s—its mines brimmed with gold, silver, and turquoise, and eight newspapers, four hotels, and 21 taverns flourished. When the mines went dry the town went bust. Since then, Cerrillos has served as the backdrop for feature-film and television westerns, among them *Young Guns* and *Lonesome Dove*. Today, it might easily be mistaken for a ghost town, which it's been well on the way to becoming for decades. Time has left its streets dry, dusty, and almost deserted, although the occasional passing Amtrak or freight train roaring through town serves as a reminder of what century you're in.

Casa Grande (⊠ 17 Waldo ☏ 505/438–3008), a 21-room adobe (several rooms of which are part of a shop), has a small museum ($2) with a display of early mining exhibits. There's also a petting zoo ($2) and a scenic overlook. Casa Grande is open daily 8 AM–sunset.

Pack rats and browsers alike ought not to miss the **What-Not Shop** (✉ 15B 1st St. ☎ 505/471–2744), a venerable secondhand–antiques shop of a half-century's standing packed floor to ceiling with Native American pottery, cut glass, rocks, political buttons, old postcards, clocks, and who knows what else.

WHERE TO
STAY & EAT
¢–$
Fodor'sChoice
★

✕ **San Marcos Cafe.** In Lone Butte, north of Cerrillos, this restaurant is known for its creative fare and nontraditional setting—an actual feed store, with roosters, turkeys, and peacocks running about outside. In one of the two bric-a-brac–filled dining rooms, sample rich cinnamon rolls and such delectables as burritos stuffed with roast beef and potatoes and topped with green chile, and the classic eggs San Marcos, tortillas stuffed with scrambled eggs and topped with guacamole, pinto beans, melted Jack cheese, and red chile. Hot apple pie à la mode with rum sauce is a favorite. Expect a wait on weekends unless you make a reservation. ✉ *3877 NM 14* ☎ *505/471–9298* ▤ *MC, V* ☺ *No dinner.*

$$

🏨 **High Feather Ranch.** A grand adobe homestead opened as a B&B in 2001, plush High Feather Ranch anchors 65 wide-open acres with breathtaking views of the Ortiz, Jémez, and Sangre de Cristo mountains. It feels completely removed from civilization but is, in fact, within an hour's drive of both Santa Fe and Albuquerque. Although newly built, the sprawling inn contains reclaimed 19th-century timber, antique gates, and fine vintage furnishings. Rooms have high ceilings and plenty of windows, and you're never far from a portal or patio; one room has an outdoor shower in a private courtyard. Rates include an impressive full breakfast. ✉ *29 High Feather Ranch, off CR 55, 87010* ☎ *505/424–1333 or 800/757–4410* ⊕ *www.highfeatherranch-bnb.com* ⤴ *2 rooms, 1 suite* ♿ *Some in-room hot tubs, massage, hiking, horseback riding, some pets allowed; no room phones, no room TVs, no smoking* ▤ *AE, D, MC, V* ◑ *BP.*

SPORTS &
THE OUTDOORS
★

Rides with **Broken Saddle Riding Co.** (✉ Off NM 14, Cerrillos ☎ 505/424–7774 ⊕ www.brokensaddle.com) take you around the old turquoise and silver mines the Cerrillos area is noted for. On a Tennessee Walker or a Missouri Fox Trotter you can explore the Cerrillos hills and canyons, 23 mi southeast of Santa Fe. This is not the usual nose-to-tail trail ride.

SIDE TRIPS FROM SANTA FE

You can hardly grasp the profundity of New Mexico's ancient past or its immense landscape without journeying into the hinterland. Each of the excursions below can be accomplished in a day or less, but in the cases of Abiquiu and Los Alamos it's worth considering an overnight. The High Road to Taos is a very full day, so start early or plan to spend the night near or in Taos, or along the way in Chimayó.

South of Santa Fe

The most prominent side trip south of the city is along the fabled Turquoise Trail, an excellent—if leisurely—alternative route to Albuquerque that's far more interesting than I–25; it's covered earlier in this chapter under the Side Trips from Albuquerque section. Although the drive down I–25 offers some fantastic views of the Jémez and Sandia mountains, the most interesting sites south of town require hopping off the interstate. From here you can uncover the region's history at El Rancho de las Golondrinas and enjoy one of New Mexico's most dramatic day hikes at Tent Rocks canyon. Conversely, if you leave Santa Fe via I–25 north and then cut down in a southerly direction along U.S. 285 and NM 41, you come to tiny Galisteo, an engaging little hamlet steeped in Spanish-colonial history.

Pecos National Historic Park

★ ❾ *25 mi east of Santa Fe on I–25.*

Pecos was the last major encampment that travelers on the Santa Fe Trail reached before Santa Fe. Today the little village is mostly a starting point for exploring the Pecos National Historic Park, the centerpiece of which is the **ruins of Pecos,** once a major Pueblo village with more than 1,100 rooms. Twenty-five hundred people are thought to have lived in this structure, as high as five stories in places. Pecos, in a fertile valley between the Great Plains and the Rio Grande Valley, was a trading center centuries before the Spanish conquistadors visited in about 1540. The Spanish later returned to build two missions.

The Pueblo was abandoned in 1838, and its 17 surviving occupants moved to the Jémez Pueblo. Anglo travelers on the Santa Fe Trail observed the mission ruins with a great sense of fascination (and relief—for they knew it meant their journey was nearly over). A couple of miles from the ruins, **Andrew Kozlowski's Ranch** served as a stage depot, where a fresh spring quenched the thirsts of horses and weary passengers. The ranch now houses the park's law-enforcement corps and is not open to the public. You can view the mission ruins and the excavated pueblo on a ¼-mi self-guided tour in about two hours.

The pivotal Civil War battle of Glorieta Pass took place on an outlying parcel of parkland in late March 1862; a victory over Confederate forces firmly established the Union army's control over the New Mexico Territory. The Union troops maintained headquarters at Kozlowski's Ranch during the battle. Check out the park visitor center for information about guided park tours (in summer only) and to see exhibits on the region's checkered history. ⊠ *NM 63, off I–25 at Exit 307, Pecos* ☎ *505/757–6414* ⊕ *www.nps.gov/peco* ⊠ *$3* ☉ *Late May–early Sept., daily 8–6; early Sept.–late May, daily 8–5.*

Galisteo

❿ *25 mi south of Santa Fe via I–25 north to U.S. 285 to NM 41 south.*

South of Santa Fe lie the immense open spaces of the sublime Galisteo Basin and the quintessential New Mexican village of Galisteo—a harmonious blend of multigenerational New Mexicans and recent migrants who protect and treasure the bucolic solitude of their home. The drive from Santa Fe takes about 30 minutes and offers a panoramic view of the surreal, sculpted landscape of the Galisteo Basin, which is an austere contrast to the alpine country of the Sangre de Cristos. It's a good place to go for a leisurely lunch or a sunset drive to dinner, maybe with

Santa Fe Side Trips/ High and Low Roads to Taos

Chama 25 17

64/ 84

26 Los Ojos
Brazos

Tierra Amarilla

64

CARSON NATIONAL FOREST

Questa

San Cristobal 522

Arroyo Hondo

Cebolla

El Vado

Canjilon

Vallecitos

519

Rio Grande

Taos

Rancho de Taos

Pilar

Rio Chama

24 Ghost Ranch

El Rito 554

111 La Madera

27 Ojo Caliente

285

Dixon

28

32 Peñasco

Chamisal

23 Abiquiu

84 Medanales

Velarde

Alcade

31 Truchas

Cordova

30

SANTA FE NATIONAL FOREST

126

Española

22

Santa Cruz

Chimayó

29

Santa Clara Pueblo 16

San Ildefonso Pueblo 15

Nambé Pueblo

13 14

Pojoaque Pueblo

SANTA FE NATIONAL FOREST

Baldy Peak

Hyde Memorial State Park

Valle Caldera National Preserve

19 17 Los Alamos

4

Bandelier National Monument 18

84/ 285

475

Santa Fe Ski Area

Jémez Springs 20

Kasha-Katuwe Tent Rocks National Monument 12

4

Cañon

21 Jémez Pueblo

San Isidro

Tesuque

El Rancho de las Golondrinas 11

599

Santa Fe

Pecos National Historic Park

9 Pecos

La Cienaga

Glorieta

25

25

Cerrillos

Madrid

14

Lamy

Rowe

Galisteo

10

285

41

Golden

Rio Grande

0   10 miles

0   20 km

horseback riding. Galisteo is probably most famous for **Vista Clara Ranch** (⊠ NM 41 ☎ 505/466–4772 or 888/663–9772 ⊕ www.vistaclara. com), an ultraposh spa resort known for its holistic approach and incredibly fancy digs. The 140-acre resort closed in 2004 and is, as of this writing, undergoing a complete refurbishment and transformation into a residential condo resort. It's expected to reopen again in mid-2007, with rates beginning at $250 per person, per night.

Founded as a Spanish outpost in 1614 and built largely with rocks from nearby Pueblo ruins, Galisteo has many artists and equestrians (trail rides and rentals are available at local stables). Cottonwoods shade the low-lying pueblo-style architecture, a premier example of vernacular use of adobe and stone. The small church is open only for Sunday services.

WHERE TO STAY & EAT
★ $–$$$

✕🖪 **The Galisteo Inn.** This rambling old adobe hacienda has been transformed into an idyllic inn. Worn pine floors and massive wood beams rich in patina and vistas and patios from which to enjoy them add to the privacy and romance of this upscale refuge, which also has two cozy, economical rooms that share a bath. Many rooms, including one of the inexpensive ones, have fireplaces, and all are decorated with tasteful, understated antiques and hand-crafted newer pieces. The acclaimed La Mancha Restaurant ($–$$$; no dinner Sunday and Monday, reservations essential) serves superb contemporary, Latin-infused cuisine and is well worth a visit whether or not you're staying at the inn. The often-changing menu might feature pistachio-crusted Dungeness crab cakes with pineapple-caper tartar sauce, and an unusual "mac-and-cheese" with orzo pasta, black truffles, oyster mushrooms, goat cheese, and white-truffle essence. There's also a wonderful Sunday brunch as well as a lighter tapas menu. ⊠ 9 La Vega St. 🕭 HC 75, Box 4, Galisteo 87540 ☎ 505/ 466–8200 or 866/404–8200 🖨 505/466–4008 ⊕ www.galisteoinn. com ⇨ 11 rooms, 9 with bath; 1 suite ⌂ Restaurant, cable TV, Wi-Fi, pool, hot tub, massage, sauna, horseback riding; no kids under 10, no smoking ⊟ D, MC, V ⋔⋔ BP.

SPORTS & THE OUTDOORS

Galarosa Stable (⊠ NM 41, Galisteo ☎ 505/466–4654 or 505/670–2467 ⊕ www.galarosastables.com) provides rentals by the half- or full day south of Santa Fe in the panoramic Galisteo Basin.

El Rancho de las Golondrinas

★ ⑪ 15 mi south of Santa Fe off I–25's Exit 276 in La Cienega.

The "Williamsburg of the Southwest," El Rancho de las Golondrinas ("the ranch of the swallows") is a reconstruction of a small agricultural village with buildings from the 17th to 19th century. Travelers on the El Camino Real would stop at the ranch before making the final leg of the journey north, a half-day ride from Santa Fe in horse-and-wagon time. By car, the ranch is only a 25-minute drive from the Plaza. From I–25, the village is tucked away from view, frozen in time. Owned and operated by the Paloheimo family, direct descendants of those who owned the ranch when it functioned as a *paraje,* or stopping place, the grounds maintain an authentic character without compromising history for commercial gain. Even the gift shop carries items that reflect ranch life and the cultural exchange that took place there.

Self-guided tours survey Spanish-colonial lifestyles in New Mexico from 1660 to 1890: you can view a molasses mill, threshing grounds, and wheelwright and blacksmith shops, as well as a mountain village and a *morada* (meeting place) of the order of Penitentes (a religious fraternity known for its reenactment during Holy Week of the tortures suffered by Christ). Farm animals roam through the barnyards on the 200-acre complex. Wool from the sheep is spun into yarn and woven into traditional Rio Grande–style blankets, and the corn grown is used to feed the animals. During the spring and harvest festivals, on the first weekends of June and October, respectively, the village comes alive with Spanish-American folk music, dancing, and food and crafts demonstrations. ⊠ *334 Los Pinos Rd.* ☎ *505/471–2261* ⊕ *www.golondrinas. org* ⌑ *$5* ⊗ *June–Sept., Wed.–Sun. 10–4; some additional weekends for special events.*

WHERE TO STAY & EAT
$–$$

✕⌑ **Sunrise Springs Inn.** Down the road from Las Golondrinas, this miniresort offers guests holistic-based rest and rejuvenation. The sleek, minimalist accommodations are either in private casitas, with kitchenettes and fireplaces, or in a standard room; four rooms and two suites are located near the Samadhi Spa, which specializes in Far Eastern body work. Other amenities at this lush retreat with ponds and gardens are a Japanese-style teahouse and the Sages Art Center, which holds a raku-pottery studio and offers classes in raku, yoga, and tai chi. You can enjoy fine, globally inspired cuisine at the Blue Heron restaurant ($$–$$$); try the duck confit hot pot with noodles and ginger broth, or house-smoked tofu with sesame-sautéed greens, coconut sweet potatoes, and fresh garden vegetables. ⊠ *242 Los Pinos Rd., Santa Fe 87507* ☎ *505/471– 3600 or 800/955–0028* ☎ *505/471–7365* ⊕ *www.sunrisesprings.com* ⌑ *38 rooms, 20 casitas, 2 suites* ⌑ *Restaurant, some kitchenettes, some refrigerators, cable TV, some in-room DVDs, hot tubs, spa, bar, meeting rooms; no TV in some rooms* ⊟ *AE, D, MC, V.*

Kasha-Katuwe Tent Rocks National Monument

⑫
Fodor'sChoice
★

40 mi south of Santa Fe via I–25, Exit 264.

This is a terrific hiking getaway, especially if you have time for only one hike. The sandstone rock formations look like stacked tents in a stark, water- and wind-eroded box canyon. Located 45 minutes south of Santa Fe, near Cochiti Pueblo, Tent Rocks offers excellent hiking year-round, although it can get hot in summer, when you should bring extra water. The drive to this magical landscape is equally awesome, as the road heads west toward Cochiti Dam and through the cottonwood groves around the pueblo. It's a good hike for kids. The round-trip hiking distance is only 2 mi, about 1½ hours, but it's the kind of place where you'll want to hang out for a while. Take a camera. There are no facilities here, just a small parking area with a posted trail map and a self-pay admission box; you can get gas and pick up picnic supplies and bottled water at Cochiti Lake Convenience Store. ⊠ *I–25 south to Cochiti Exit 264; follow NM 16 for 8 mi, turning right onto NM 22; continue approximately 3½ more mi past Cochiti Pueblo entrance; turn right onto BIA 92, which after 2 mi becomes Forest Service Rd. 266, a rough road of jarring, washboarded gravel that leads 5 mi to well-marked parking area*

☎ *505/761–8700* ⊕ *www.nm.blm.gov* ✉ *$5 per vehicle* ✆ *Apr.–Oct., daily 7–7; Nov.–Mar., daily 8–5.*

SPORTS &
THE OUTDOORS

The 18-hole, par-72 **Pueblo de Cochiti Golf Course** (✉ 5200 Cochiti Hwy., Cochiti Lake ☎ 505/465–2239 ⊕ www.pueblodecochiti.org/golfcourse. html), set against a backdrop of steep canyons and red-rock mesas, is a 45-minute drive southwest of Santa Fe. Cochiti was designed by Robert Trent Jones Jr. and offers one of the most challenging and visually stunning golfing experiences in the state. Greens fees are $45–$55.

Pueblos near Santa Fe

A pleasant side trip is to visit several of the state's 19 pueblos, including San Ildefonso, one of the state's most picturesque, and Santa Clara, whose lands harbor a dramatic set of ancient cliff dwellings. Between the two reservations sits the ominous landmark called Black Mesa, which you can see from NM 30 or NM 502. The solitary butte has inspired many painters, including Georgia O'Keeffe. Plan on spending one to three hours at each pueblo, and leave the day open if you're there for a feast day, when dances are set to an organic rather than mechanical clock. Pueblo grounds and hiking areas do not permit pets.

Pojoaque Pueblo

⓭ *17 mi north of Santa Fe on U.S. 285/84.*

There's not much to see in the pueblo's plaza area, but the state visitor center and adjoining **Poeh Cultural Center and Museum** on U.S. 285/84 are worth a visit. The latter is an impressive complex of traditional adobe buildings, including the three-story Sun Tower; the facility comprises a museum, a cultural center, and artists' studios. The museum holds some 8,000 photographs, including many by esteemed early-20th-century photographer Edward S. Curtis, as well as hundreds of works of both traditional and contemporary pottery, jewelry, textiles, and sculpture. There are frequent demonstrations by artists, exhibitions, and, on Saturday from May through September, traditional ceremonial dances. By the early 20th century the pueblo was virtually uninhabited, but the survivors eventually began to restore it. Pojoaque's feast day is celebrated with dancing on December 12. The visitor center is one of the friendliest and best stocked in northern New Mexico, with free maps and literature on hiking, fishing, and the area's history. The crafts shop in the visitor center is one of the most extensive among the state's pueblos; it carries weaving, pottery, jewelry, and other crafts by both Pojoaque and other indigenous New Mexicans.

The pueblo also operates the adjacent **Cities of Gold Casino Resort** (☎ 505/455–3313 or 800/455–3313 ⊕ www.citiesofgold.com), which comprises a 40,000-square-foot casino with the only poker room in northern New Mexico, sports bar and simulcast, Towa Golf Resort, and several shops and restaurants. Additionally, beside Towa Golf Resort, is a 79-room Homewood Suites hotel, which opened in 2005. And as of this writing, construction was underway on a new upscale resort accommodation to be operated by Hilton, called the Buffalo Thunder Resort. This property—which will be similar in scope to the Hyatt Tamaya and

CLOSE UP

Pueblo Etiquette

WHEN VISITING PUEBLOS AND RESERVATIONS, you're expected to follow a certain etiquette. Each pueblo has its own regulations for the use of still and video cameras and video and tape recorders, as well as for sketching and painting. Some pueblos, such as Santo Domingo, prohibit photography altogether. Others, such as Santa Clara, prohibit photography at certain times; for example, during ritual dances. Still others allow photography but require a permit, which usually costs from $10 to $20, depending on whether you use a still or video camera. The privilege of setting up an easel and painting all day will cost you as little as $35 or as much as $150 (at Taos Pueblo). Associated fees for using images also can vary widely, depending on what kind of reproduction rights you might require. Be sure to **ask permission before photographing anyone in the pueblos**; it's also customary to give the subject a dollar or two for agreeing to be photographed. Native American law prevails on the pueblos, and violations of photography regulations could result in confiscation of cameras.

Specific restrictions for the various pueblos are noted in the individual descriptions. Other rules are described below.

• Possessing or using drugs and/or alcohol on Native American land is forbidden.

• Ritual dances often have serious religious significance and should be respected as such. Silence is mandatory—that means no questions about ceremonies or dances while they're being performed. Don't walk across the dance plaza during a performance, and don't applaud afterward.

• Kivas and ceremonial rooms are restricted to pueblo members only.

• Cemeteries are sacred. They're off-limits to all visitors and should never be photographed.

• Unless pueblo dwellings are clearly marked as shops, don't wander or peek inside. Remember, these are private homes.

• Many of the pueblo buildings are hundreds of years old. Don't try to scale adobe walls or climb on top of buildings, or you may come tumbling down.

• Don't litter. Nature is sacred on the pueblos, and defacing land can be a serious offense.

• Don't bring your pet or feed stray dogs.

• Even off reservation sites, state and federal laws prohibit picking up artifacts such as arrowheads or pottery from public lands.

Sandia resorts near Albuquerque, adjoins the casino and will comprise 400 upscale rooms, an expanded casino, a 35,000-square-foot convention center, and a high-caliber performing arts center. The project is expected to be completed in 2008. Sketching, cameras, and video cameras are prohibited, except during Saturday Native American dances. ⊠ *78 Cities of Gold Rd., off U.S. 285/84, 17 mi north of Santa Fe* ☎ *505/455–*

3334 ⊕ *www.poehmuseum.com* ⌨ *Donation suggested* ⊙ *Apr.–Dec., Mon.–Sat. 9–5, Sun. 10–4; Jan.–Mar., Mon.–Sat. 9–5:30, Sun. 10–4.*

WHERE TO STAY
$–$$$

⊞ **Homewood Suites Santa Fe–North.** Opened in 2005 on the Pojoaque Pueblo, right by the Cities of Gold Casino and nearly adjacent to Towa Golf Resort, this all-suites extended-stay property is a good bet even if you're not planning to spend much time at Pojoaque—it's a practical base for exploring Los Alamos, the High Road to Taos, Española, and even Taos, and it's just a 20-minute drive north of Santa Fe. All of the brightly furnished units in this immaculately kept three-story adobe hotel have full kitchens, large work areas, and great views of the golf course and surrounding mountains. Rates include full breakfast and an evening snack and cocktail receptions Monday through Thursday nights. The top rooms have fireplaces, and some have two bedrooms. ⊠ *18 Buffalo Trail, Santa Fe 87506* ☎ *505/455–9100 or 800/225–5466* 🖷 *505/455–9111* ⊕ *www.santafenorth.homewoodsuites.com* ⏎ *79 suites* ⚭ *Kitchens, cable TV, in-room VCRs, Wi-Fi, gym, pool, 18-hole golf course, putting green, driving range, laundry facilities, business services, meeting rooms, some pets allowed* 🖃 *AE, D, MC, V* ⦿ *BP.*

SPORTS &
THE OUTDOORS

The **Towa Golf Resort** (⊠ Cities of Gold Casino Resort, 17746 U.S. 285/84, Pojoaque ☎ 505/455–9000 or 877/465–3489 ⊕ www.towagolf.com) was designed by pro legend Hale Irwin and sits in the foothills of the Sangre de Cristos, with stunning views of the Santa Fe ski basin and the Jémez Mountains over Los Alamos. The challenging 18-hole course opened in 2001; another 9 holes were added in 2003, and plans call for the unveiling of yet another 9 holes down the road, once the new hotel and resort is completed. Greens fees are $64.

Nambé Pueblo

⓮ *4 mi east of Pojoaque on NM 503, 20 mi north of Santa Fe.*

Nambé Pueblo has no visitor center, so the best time to visit is during the October 4 feast day of St. Francis celebration or the very popular July 4 celebration. If you want to explore the landscape surrounding the pueblo, take the drive past the pueblo until you come to **Nambé Falls and Nambé Lake Recreation Area** (☎ 505/455–2304). There's a shady picnic area and a large fishing lake that's open March–November (the cost is $10 for fishing, and $20 for boating—no gas motors are permitted). The waterfalls are about a 15-minute hike in from the parking and picnic area along a rocky, clearly marked path. The water pours over a rock precipice—a loud and dramatic sight given the river's modest size. Overnight RV ($35) and tent ($25) camping are also offered. ⊠ *Nambé Pueblo Rd. off NM 503* ☎ *505/455–4444* ⊕ *www.nambefalls.com* ⌨ *$8 per car.*

San Ildefonso Pueblo

⓯ *23 mi north of Santa Fe via U.S. 285/84 to NM 502 west.*

Maria Martinez, one of the most renowned Pueblo potters, lived here. She first created her exquisite "black on black" pottery in 1919 and in doing so sparked a major revival of all Pueblo arts and crafts. She died in 1980, and the 26,000-acre San Ildefonso Pueblo remains a major center for pottery and other arts and crafts. Many artists sell from their homes, and there are trading posts, a visitor center, and a museum where some of Martinez's work can be seen on weekdays. San Ildefonso is also one of the more visually appealing pueblos, with a well-defined plaza core and a spectacular setting beneath the Pajarito Plateau and Black Mesa. The pueblo's feast day is January 23, when unforgettable buffalo, deer, and Comanche dances are performed from dawn to dusk. Cameras are not permitted at any of the ceremonial dances but may be used at other times with a permit. ⊠ *NM 502* ☎ *505/455–3549* 🖼 *$5 per vehicle, still-camera permit $10, video recorder permit $20, sketching permit $15* ⊙ *Daily 8–5; museum weekdays 8–4:30.*

Santa Clara Pueblo

🔟 *27 mi northwest of Santa Fe, 10 mi north of San Ildefonso Pueblo via NM 30.*

Santa Clara Pueblo, southwest of Española, is the home of a historic treasure—the awesome **Puyé Cliff Dwellings,** believed to have been built in the 13th to 14th centuries. They can be seen by driving 9 mi up a gravel road through a canyon, south of the village off NM 502. The pueblo also contains four ponds, miles of stream fishing, and picnicking and camping facilities. You can tour the cliff dwellings, topped by the ruins of a 740-room pueblo, on your own or with a guide. Permits for the use of trails, camping, and picnic areas, as well as for fishing in trout ponds, are available at the sites; recreation areas are open April–October, dawn–dusk.

The village's shops sell burnished red pottery, engraved blackware, paintings, and other arts and crafts. All pottery is made via the coil method, not with a pottery wheel. Santa Clara is known for its carved pieces, and Avanyu, a water serpent that guards the waters, is the pueblo's symbol. Other typical works include engagement baskets, wedding vessels, and seed pots. The pueblo's feast day of St. Claire is celebrated on August 12. ⊠ *Off NM 502 on NM 30, Española* ☎ *505/753–7326* 🖼 *Pueblo free, cliff dwellings $5, video and still-camera permits $15* ⊙ *Daily 8–4:30.*

Jémez Country

In the Jémez region, the 1,000-year-old Anasazi ruins at Bandelier National Monument present a vivid contrast to Los Alamos National Laboratory, birthplace of the atomic bomb. You can easily take in part of Jémez Country in a day trip from Santa Fe.

On this tour you can see terrific views of the Rio Grande Valley, the Sangre de Cristos, the Galisteo Basin, and, in the distance, the Sandias. There are places to eat and shop for essentials in Los Alamos and a few roadside eateries along NM 4 in La Cueva and Jémez Springs. There are also numerous turnouts along NM 4, several that have paths leading down to the many excellent fishing spots along the Jémez River.

The 48,000-acre Cerro Grande fire of May 2000 burned much of the pine forest in the lower Jémez Mountains, as well as more than 250 homes in Los Alamos. Parts of the drive are still scarred with charcoaled remains, but most of the vegetation has returned, and many homes have been rebuilt in the residential areas.

Los Alamos

17 *35 mi from Santa Fe via U.S. 285/84 north to NM 502 west.*

Look at old books on New Mexico and you rarely find a mention of Los Alamos, now a busy town of 19,000 that has the highest per capita income in the state. Like so many other Southwestern communities, Los Alamos was created expressly as a company town; only here the workers weren't mining iron, manning freight trains, or hauling lumber— they were busy toiling at America's foremost nuclear research facility, Los Alamos National Laboratory (LANL). The facility still employs some 8,000 full-time workers, most who live in town but many others who live in the Española Valley and even northern Santa Fe. The lab has experienced some tough times in recent years, from the infamous Wen Ho Lee espionage case in the late '90s to a slew of alleged security breaches in 2003 and 2004. The controversies have shed some doubt on the future of LANL; at the very least, it's possible that the University of California, which has managed the lab on behalf of the U.S. Department of Energy, may cease its operations of LANL.

A few miles from ancient cave dwellings, scientists led by J. Robert Oppenheimer built Fat Man and Little Boy, the atom bombs that in August 1945 decimated Hiroshima and Nagasaki, respectively. LANL was created in 1943 under the auspices of the intensely covert Manhattan Project, whose express purpose it was to expedite an Allied victory during World War II. Indeed, Japan surrendered—but a full-blown Cold War between Russia and the United States ensued for another four and a half decades.

Despite the negative publicity of recent years, LANL works hard today to promote its broader platforms, including "enhancing global nuclear security" but also finding new ways to detect radiation, fighting pollution and environmental risks associated with nuclear energy, and furthering studies of the solar system, biology, and computer sciences. Similarly, the town of Los Alamos strives to be more well rounded, better understood, and tourist-friendly.

The **Bradbury Science Museum** is Los Alamos National Laboratory's public showcase, and its exhibits offer a balanced and provocative examination of such topics as atomic weapons and nuclear power. You can experiment with lasers; witness research in solar, geothermal, fission, and fusion energy; learn about DNA fingerprinting; and view exhibits about World War II's Project Y (the Manhattan Project, whose participants developed the atomic bomb). ⊠ *Los Alamos National Laboratory, 15th St. and Central Ave.* ☎ *505/667–4444* ⊕ *www.lanl. gov/museum* ⊠ *Free* ⊙ *Tues.–Fri. 9–5, Sat.–Mon. 1–5.*

New Mexican architect John Gaw Meem designed **Fuller Lodge,** a short drive up Central Avenue from the Bradbury Science Museum. The massive log building was erected in 1928 as a dining and recreation hall for a small private boys' school. In 1942 the federal government purchased the school and made it the base of operations for the Manhattan Project. Part of the lodge contains an art center that shows the works of northern New Mexican artists; there's a picturesque rose garden on the grounds. ✉ *2132 Central Ave.* ☎ *505/662–9331* ⊕ *www.artfulnm. org* ✆ *Free* ☉ *Mon.–Sat. 10–4.*

NEED A BREAK?   Join the ranks of locals, Los Alamos National Laboratory employees, and tourists who line up each morning at **Chili Works** (✉ 1743 Trinity Dr. ☎ 505/662–7591) to sample one of the state's best breakfast burritos. This inexpensive, simple take-out spot is also worth a stop to grab lunch before heading off for a hike at Bandelier.

The **Los Alamos Historical Museum,** in a log building beside Fuller Lodge, displays exhibits on the once-volatile geological history of the volcanic Jémez Mountains, the 700-year history of human life in this area, and more on—you guessed it—the Manhattan Project. It's rather jarring to observe ancient Anasazi potsherds and arrowheads in one display and photos of an obliterated Nagasaki in the next. ✉ *1921 Juniper St.* ☎ *505/662–4493* ⊕ *www.losalamoshistory.org* ✆ *Free* ☉ *Mon.–Sat. 9:30–4:30, Sun. 1–4.*

WHERE TO STAY & EAT

$–$$ ✕ **Blue Window Bistro.** Despite its relative wealth, Los Alamos has never cultivated much of a dining scene, which makes this cheerful and elegant restaurant all the more appreciated by foodies. The kitchen turns out a mix of New Mexican, American, and Continental dishes, from a first-rate Cobb salad to steak topped with Jack cheese and green chile to double-cut pork chops with mashed potatoes, applewood-smoked bacon, and red-onion marmalade. In addition to the softly lighted dining room with terra-cotta walls, there are several tables on a patio overlooking a lush garden. ✉ *813 Central Ave.* ☎ *505/662–6305* ☰ *AE, D, DC, MC, V* ☉ *Closed Mon.*

$ ✕▣ **Quality Inn Los Alamos.** Rooms in this one-story hotel, which became part of the Quality Inn chain following a significant renovation in 2005, have modern Southwestern decor, large work desks, attractive white-tile bathrooms, and sweeping canyon views. A full hot breakfast buffet is included. The hotel's Trinity Beverage Company ($–$$$) serves commendable American fare with contemporary accents, such as pistachio-crusted salmon with pineapple beurre blanc, and seared duck breast with chipotle sauce. There's live music many nights, and a nice selection of microbrew beers. ✉ *2201 Trinity Dr., 87544* ☎ *505/662–7211 or 877/424–6423* ☐ *505/661–7714* ⊕ *www.qualityinnlosalamos.com* ⤵ *115 rooms* ⌂ *Restaurant, BBQs, some kitchenettes, refrigerators, cable TV, Wi-Fi, pool, bar, business services, meeting rooms, some pets allowed* ☰ *AE, D, DC, MC, V* �.

$ ▣ **Best Western Hilltop House Hotel.** Minutes from the Los Alamos National Laboratory, this well-kept three-story hotel hosts both vacationers and scientists. Rooms are done with contemporary, functional furniture and have microwaves, refrigerators, and coffeemakers; deluxe ones have kitchenettes. The very good Blue Window Bistro is next door. ✉ *400 Trinity Dr., Box 250, 87544* ☎ *505/662–2441 or 800/462–0936*

📠 *505/662–5913* ⊕ *www.bestwesternlosalamos.com* 🛏 *87 rooms, 13 suites* ⚴ *Restaurant, room service, some kitchenettes, refrigerators, cable TV, Wi-Fi, indoor pool, gym, hot tub, sauna, lounge, laundry facilities, meeting rooms, some pets allowed* ▤ *AE, D, DC, MC, V* ⟋◯⟋ *CP.*

SPORTS &
THE OUTDOORS

Tsankawi Trail (pronounced sank-ah-*wee*) will take you through the Pajarito Plateau's ancient rock trails, near Bandelier National Monument. The Pueblo people created the trails in the 1400s as they made their way from their mesa-top homes to the fields and springs in the canyon below. In the 1½ mi loop you can see petroglyphs and south-facing cave dwellings. Wear good shoes for the rocky path and a climb on a 12-foot ladder that shoots between a crevasse in the rock and the highest point of the mesa. This is an ideal walk if you don't have time to explore Bandelier National Monument in depth. It's on the way to Los Alamos, about a 35-minute drive from Santa Fe. ✉ *From NM 502, take turnoff for White Rock, NM 4; continue west for about 10 mi to sign for Tsankawi on left; trail is clearly marked* ☎ *505/672–3861.*

Pajarito Mountain Ski Area (✉ 397 Camp May Rd., off NM 501, just west of downtown Los Alamos ☎ 505/662–5725 ⊕ www.skipajarito. com), a small, low-key area near Los Alamos, has some excellent long runs and a good selection of wide-open, intermediate mogul runs, plus a terrain park; the base elevation is 9,200 feet, and there's a vertical rise drop of 1,410 feet. There's no artificial snowmaking, so the slopes are barely open during dry winters and the season runs according to conditions (usually about mid-December through April). But there's never a wait for the five lifts. In summer there's mountain biking on Pajarito's trails.

Bandelier National Monument

⑱ *10 mi south of Los Alamos via NM 501 south to NM 4 east; 40 mi north of Santa Fe via U.S. 285/84 north to NM 502 west to NM 4 west.*

Seven centuries before the Declaration of Independence was signed, compact city-states existed in the Southwest. Remnants of one of the most impressive of them can be seen at **Frijoles Canyon** in Bandelier National Monument. At the canyon's base, beside a gurgling stream, are the remains of cave dwellings, ancient ceremonial kivas, and other stone structures that stretch out for more than a mile beneath the sheer walls of the canyon's tree-fringed rim. For hundreds of years the Anasazi people, relatives of today's Rio Grande Pueblo Indians, thrived on wild game, corn, and beans. Suddenly, for reasons still undetermined, the settlements were abandoned.

Wander through the site on a paved, self-guided trail. If you can climb steep wooden ladders and squeeze through narrow doorways, you can explore some of the cave dwellings and cell-like rooms.

Bandelier National Monument, named after author and ethnologist Adolph Bandelier (his novel *The Delight Makers* is set in Frijoles Canyon), contains 23,000 acres of backcountry wilderness, waterfalls, and wildlife. Sixty miles of trails traverse the park. A small museum in the visitor center focuses on the area's prehistoric and contemporary Native American cultures, with displays of artifacts from 1200 to modern times as well as displays on the forest fires that have devastated parts of the park in recent years. ☎ 505/672–0343 ⊕ *www.nps.gov/band* ☒ *$10 per vehicle, good for 7 days* ☉ *Late May–early Sept., daily 8–6; early Sept.–Oct. and Apr.–late May, daily 8–5:30; Nov.–Mar., daily 8–4:30.*

Valles Caldera National Preserve

⑲ *15 mi southwest of Los Alamos via NM 4.*

A high-forest drive brings you to the awe-inspiring Valles Grande, which at 14 mi in diameter is one of the world's largest calderas and which became Valles Caldera National Preserve in summer 2000. You can't imagine the volcanic crater's immensity until you spot what look like specks of dust on the lush meadow floor and realize they're cows. Since 2003, the Valles Caldera Trust has managed this 89,000-acre multiuse preserve with the aim to "protect and preserve the scientific, scenic, geologic, watershed, fish, wildlife, historic, cultural, and recreational values of the Preserve, and to provide for multiple use and sustained yield of renewable resources within the Preserve."

The preserve is open to visitors for hiking, cross-country skiing, horseback riding, horse-drawn carriage rides, van wildlife photography tours, mountain-bike tours, bird-watching, and fly-fishing. Most of the activities require reservations and a fee, although there are two free, relatively short hikes signposted from the parking area along NM 4, and no reservations are needed for these. Other self-guided hikes are about 7 mi and cost $10; there's also a guided hike that's 7 mi and costs $15. Shuttle buses take you from the parking area to the trailheads and pick you up again later in the day. Horseback riding is self-guided and costs $20. Fly fishing costs $25, for which you (and up to three friends) are entitled to cast a line into your own designated 1-mi stretch of San Antonio Creek; only 10 fishing permits are issued each day. The season runs late May through late October, and these permits are awarded on a lottery system (lottery tickets cost $5 each). Contact the preserve or visit the Web site for information on other kinds of tours and events. Elk hunting is also offered each fall, again on a lottery basis. ☒ *NM 4* ☎ *505/ 661–3333 or 866/382–5537* ⊕ *www.vallescaldera.gov.*

Jémez Springs

⑳ *20 mi west of Valles Caldera on NM 4.*

The funky mountain village of Jémez Springs draws outdoorsy types for hiking, cross-country skiing, and camping in the nearby U.S. Forest Service areas. The town's biggest tourist draws are Jémez State Monument and Soda Dam, but many people come here for relaxation at the town's bathhouse.

The geological wonder known as **Soda Dam** was created over thousands of years by travertine deposits—minerals that precipitate out of geothermal springs. With its strange mushroom-shape exterior and caves split by a roaring waterfall, it's no wonder the spot was considered sacred by Native Americans. In summer it's popular for swimming. ☒ *NM 4, 1 mi north of Jémez State Monument.*

Jémez State Monument contains impressive Spanish and Native American ruins set throughout a 7-acre site and toured via an easy ⅓ mi loop trail. About 700 years ago ancestors of the people of Jémez Pueblo built several villages in and around the narrow mountain valley. One of the villages was Guisewa, or "Place of the Boiling Waters." The Spanish colonists built a mission church beside it, San José de los Jémez, which was abandoned by around 1640. ✉ *NM 4, Jémez Springs* ☎ *505/829–3530* ⊕ *www.nmstatemonuments.org* ✑ *$3* ☯ *Wed.–Mon. 8:30–5.*

The original structure at the **Jémez Spring Bath House** was erected in the 1870s near a mineral hot spring. Many other buildings were added over the years, and the complex was completely renovated into an intimate Victorian-style hideaway in the mid-1990s. It's a funky, low-key spot that's far less formal and fancy than the several spa resorts near Santa Fe. You can soak in a mineral bath for $10 (30 minutes) or $15 (60 minutes). Massages cost between $40 (30 minutes) and $95 (90 minutes). An acupuncturist is available with advance notice. Beauty treatments include facials, manicures, and pedicures. The Jémez Package ($100) includes a half-hour bath, an herbal blanket wrap, and a one-hour massage. You can stroll down a short path behind the house to see where the steaming-hot springs feed into the Jémez River. ✉ *NM 4* ☎ *505/829–3303 or 866/204–8303* ⊕ *www.jemezspringsbathhouse.com* ☯ *July–early Sept., daily 10–8; early Sept.–June, daily 10–7:30.*

WHERE TO STAY & EAT

★ ¢ ✕⊞ **Laughing Lizard Inn and Cafe.** Consisting of a simple four-room motel-style inn and a cute adobe-and-stone café with a corrugated-metal roof, the Laughing Lizard makes for a sweet and cheerful diversion—it's right in the center of the village. Rooms are cozy and simple with white linens, dressers, books, and porches that look out over the rugged mesa beyond the river valley. Healthful, eclectic fare—apple-walnut sandwiches, sweet potato–and–spinach salads, raspberry-chipotle-chicken burritos, veggie pizzas, herbal teas, offbeat beers, homemade desserts—is served in the homey café (limited hours off-season; call first), which has a saltillo-tile screened porch and an open-air wooden deck. ✉ *NM 4, 87025* ☎ *505/829–3108* ⊕ *www.thelaughinglizard.com* ➴ *4 rooms* ⎔ *Café, cable TV, some pets allowed* ➳ *D, MC, V.*

$ ⊞ **Cañon del Rio.** On 6 acres along the Jémez River beneath towering mesas, this light-filled, contemporary adobe inn (formerly called the Riverdancer) has rooms with cove ceilings, tile floors, and Native American arts and crafts. All have French doors and open onto a courtyard with a natural-spring fountain. Wellness packages include massage, acupuncture, and aromatherapy. ✉ *16445 NM 4, 87025* ☎ *505/829–4377* ⊕ *www.canondelrio.com* ➴ *6 rooms, 1 suite* ⎔ *Some kitchens, Wi-Fi, hot tub, massage, hiking; no room TVs* ⑂ *CP* ➳ *AE, D, MC, V.*

Jémez Pueblo

21 *12 mi south of Jémez Springs via NM 4; 85 mi west of Santa Fe via U.S. 285/84 and NM 4; 50 mi north of Albuquerque via I–25, U.S. 550, and NM 4.*

As you continue southwest along NM 4, the terrain changes from a wooded river valley with high mesas on either side to an open red-rock valley, the home of the Jémez Pueblo, which is set along the Jémez River. After the pueblo at Pecos (⇨ Chapter 6) was abandoned in 1838, Jémez was the state's only pueblo with residents who spoke Towa (different from Tiwa and Tewa). The Jémez Reservation encompasses 89,000 acres, with two lakes, Holy Ghost Springs and Dragonfly Lake (off NM 4), open for fishing by permit only, April to October on weekends and holidays. The only part of the pueblo open to the public is the **Walatowa Visitor Center,** a fancy Pueblo Revival building that contains a small museum, an extensive pottery and crafts shop, and rotating art and photography exhibits; there's a short nature walk outside. The pueblo is sometimes open to the public for special events, demonstrations, and ceremonial dances—call for details. On weekends April–mid-October (10–6) when weather permits, arts and crafts and traditional foods are sold across the street at the **Jémez Red Rocks Open-Air Market.** The pueblo is noted for its polychrome pottery. The Walatowa gas and convenience store, on NM 4 next to the visitor center, is one of the few such establishments between Los Alamos and Bernalillo. Photographing, sketching, and video recording are prohibited. ⊠ 7413 NM 4 ☎ 505/834–7235 ⊕ www. jemezpueblo.org ☜ Free ☉ Daily 8–5.

Georgia O'Keeffe Country

It's a 20-minute drive north of Santa Fe to reach the Española Valley, which leads to the striking mesas, cliffs, and valleys that so inspired the artist Georgia O'Keeffe—she lived in this area for the final 50 years of her life. You first come to the small, workaday city of Española, a major crossroads from which roads lead to Taos, Chama, and Abiquiu. The other notable community in this area is tiny Ojo Caliente, famous for its hot-springs spa retreat.

Española
㉒ 20 mi north of Santa Fe via U.S. 285/84.

This small but growing city midway along the Low Road from Santa Fe to Taos is a little rough around the edges—it was founded in the 1880s as a stop on the Denver & Rio Grande Railroad, and it lacks the colonial charm of either Santa Fe or Taos. Española is rather busy today and has many cheap burger joints, New Mexican–food restaurants, and a few chain motels, but few reasons to stick around for more than a quick meal. One of the city's modern trademarks are lowriders, which you'll see cruising the streets. They're mostly classic cars that have been retrofitted with lowered chassis and hydraulics that often allow the cars to bump and grind; the cars are often painted with spectacular murals, from religious art to scenes of the region's landscape.

All of the main arteries converge in the heart of town in a confusing, unpleasant maze of drab shopping centers, so watch the signs on the town's south side. Traffic moves slowly, especially on weekend nights when cruisers bring car culture alive.

The region is known for its longstanding weaving traditions, and one place you can learn about this heritage is the **Española Valley Fiber Arts Center** (⊠ 325 Paseo de Oñate ☎ 505/747–3577 ⊕ www.evfac.org

🎨 Free ☉ Mon. 9–8, Tues.–Sat. 9–5), a nonprofit facility set inside an adobe building in the city's historic section. Here you can watch local weavers working with traditional materials and looms and admire (and purchase) their works in a small gallery. There are also classes offered on spinning, weaving, and knitting, which are open to the public and range from one day to several weeks. Emphasis here is placed on the styles of weaving that have been practiced here in the northern Rio Grande Valley since the Spaniards brought sheep and treadle looms here in the late 16th century. The center also celebrates the ancient traditions of New Mexico's Navajo and Pueblo weavers.

Set along NM 68 2 mi north of town, en route to Taos, **Ohkay Casino Resort** (⊠ NM 68 ☎ 505/747–1668 or 877/829–2865 ⊕ www.ohkay. com) comprises a casino with 700 slots, numerous blackjack tables, a 101-room hotel, two restaurants, a lounge with live music and comedy, a gift shop with Pendleton blankets and Native American jewelry, and a sporting clays shooting club.

WHERE TO
STAY & EAT
★ ¢ $$

✕ **El Paragua Restaurant.** With a dark, intimate atmosphere of wood and stone, this historic place started out as a lemonade-cum-taco stand in the late 1950s but is now known for some of the state's most authentic New Mexican and regional Mexican cuisine. Steaks and fish are grilled over a mesquite-wood fire; other specialties include chorizo enchiladas, panfried breaded trout amadine, and menudo. ⊠ 603 Santa Cruz Rd., NM 76 just east of NM 68 ☎ 505/753–3211 or 800/929–8226 ⊕ www. elparagua.com ⊟ AE, DC, MC, V.

$$$$
Fodor$Choice
★

✕🏨 **Rancho de San Juan.** This secluded 225-acre Relaix & Châteaux compound hugs Black Mesa's base. Many of the inn's rooms are self-contained suites, some set around a courtyard and others amid the wilderness. All rooms have Southwestern furnishings, Frette robes, Aveda bath products, and CD stereos; nearly all have kiva fireplaces. The top units have such cushy touches as two bedrooms, 12-foot ceilings, Mexican marble showers, kitchens, Jacuzzis, and private patios. A spectacular four-course, prix-fixe, contemporary-cuisine dinner is available (by reservation only) in the restaurant Tuesday through Saturday. Past fare has included Texas quail stuffed with corn bread, green chiles, and linguica sausage, and Alaskan halibut with tomatillo-lime salsa, caramelized butternut squash, and creamed spinach. You can hike up to a sandstone shrine on a bluff above the property. In-suite spa and massage services are available. ⊠ U.S. 285, 3½ mi north of U.S. 84 ☜ Box 4140, Española 87533 ☎ 505/753–6818 ⊕ www.ranchodesanjuan.com ⤴ 9 rooms, 6 suites ⚑ Restaurant, some in-room hot tubs, some kitchens, massage, hiking; no a/c in some rooms, no room TVs, no kids under 8, no smoking ⊟ AE, D, DC, MC, V.

Abiquiu

㉓ *24 mi northwest of Española via U.S. 84.*

This tiny, very traditional Hispanic village was home to *genizaros,* people of mixed tribal backgrounds with Spanish surnames that came from Spanish families who used Native Americans as servants. Many descendants of original families still live in the area, although since the late 1980s

Abiquiu and its surrounding countryside have become a nesting ground for those fleeing big-city lifestyles, among them actresses Marsha Mason and Shirley MacLaine. Abiquiu—along with parts of the nearby Española Valley—is also a hotbed of organic farming, with many of the operations here selling their goods at the Santa Fe Farmers Market and to restaurants throughout the Rio Grande Valley. A number of artists have moved to Abiquiu in recent years, with several studios open regularly to the public and many others open each year over Columbus Day weekend for the **Annual Abiquiu Studio Tour** (☎ 505/685–4454 ⊕ www. abiquiustudiotour.org). A feeling of insider versus outsider and old-timer versus newcomer still prevails. Newcomers or visitors may find themselves resented; it's best to observe one very important local custom: no photography is allowed in and around the village.

You can visit **Georgia O'Keeffe's home** through advance reservation (four months recommended) with the **Georgia O'Keeffe Foundation** (☎ 505/685–4539 ⊕ www.abiquiuinn.com), which conducts one-hour tours Tuesday, Thursday, and Friday, mid-March–November, for $25. In 1945 Georgia O'Keeffe bought a large, dilapidated late-18th-century Spanish-colonial adobe compound just off the Plaza. Upon the 1946 death of her husband, photographer Alfred Stieglitz, she left New York City and began dividing her time permanently between this home, which figured prominently in many of her works, and the one in nearby Ghost Ranch. She wrote about the house, "When I first saw the Abiquiú house it was a ruin . . . As I climbed and walked about in the ruin I found a patio with a very pretty well house and a bucket to draw up water. It was a good-sized patio with a long wall with a door on one side. That wall with a door in it was something I had to have. It took me 10 years to get it—three more years to fix the house up so I could live in it—and after that the wall with the door was painted many times." The patio is featured in *Black Patio Door* (1955) and *Patio with Cloud* (1956). O'Keeffe died in 1986 at the age of 98 and left provisions in her will to ensure that the property's houses would never be public monuments.

Bode's (⊠ U.S. 84 ☎ 505/685–4422 ⊕ www.bodes.com), across from the Abiquiu post office, is much more than a gas station. It's a popular stop for newspapers, quirky gifts, cold drinks, supplies, and hearty green chile stew, sandwiches, and other short-order fare. The station serves as general store and exchange post for news and gossip.

The **Dar al Islam** (⊠ CR 155 at sign 42 ☎ 505/685–4515 ⊕ www. daralislam.org) adobe mosque was built by Egyptian architect Hassan Fathy, and visitors are welcome. The annual North American Muslim Powwow is held here each June. To reach the mosque from Bode's, drive ¼ mi north, turn right onto unpaved County Road 155, and proceed 3 mi, and make a left at the main entrance sign.

WHERE TO
STAY & EAT
$–$$

×🏠 **Abiquiu Inn and Cafe Abiquiu.** Deep in the Chama Valley, the inn has a secluded, exotic feel—almost like an oasis—with brightly decorated rooms, including several four-person casitas, with woodstoves or fireplaces and tiled baths; some units have verandas with hammocks and open views of O'Keeffe Country. The café (¢–$$) serves commendable

CLOSE UP

Studio Tours

NORTH-CENTRAL NEW MEXICO IS A REGION of artists' colonies, and from the last weekend of September through the first weekend of December artisans in the villages of Galisteo, the Pecos Valley, El Rito, Abiquiu, Dixon, Jémez Springs, and Madrid take turns hosting studio-tour weekends. Homes and studios are open for browsing, shopping, and conversing; maps are provided to guide you to the open houses, where you can find reasonably priced arts and crafts. Wares include everything from pottery and paintings to wreaths, ristras, and dried-flower arrangements; homemade jellies, pestos, and chile sauces; and other food items; and wood carvings, religious paintings, clothing, and handmade furniture.

The quality varies, but bargains are abundant. Of course for many the real fun is the opportunity to experience village life and to get inside those charming old adobes that you can only pass by at other times of the year. Many of the villagers provide refreshments, and you're encouraged to wander at a leisurely pace.

Because studio-tour planning passes from one chairperson to another each year, there's no central number to call for information. But if you're in the Santa Fe area during the fall season, check "Pasatiempo," the Friday supplement of the *Santa Fe New Mexican*, for a report about which village is open for touring and what items are for sale. There are also a few tours held annually, such as the High Road Arts Tour, which runs from Chimayo to Peñasco in mid-September; and the Dixon tour, which takes place every year on the first weekend in November. About a half hour south of Taos, Dixon was the first village to host a studio tour, and its version still has the largest number of participating artists and the greatest variety of merchandise.

New Mexican, Italian, and American fare, from blue-corn tacos stuffed with grilled trout to lamb–and–poblao chile stew; it's also known for its seasonal fresh-fruit cobblers. The inn is owned and operated by the Dar al Islam mosque and is the departure point for O'Keeffe-home tours. It has an exceptional art gallery, crafts shop, and gardens. ⊠ *U.S. 84* ⬧ *Box 120, Abiquiu 87510* ☎ *505/685–4378 or 888/735–2902* 🖷 *505/685–4931* ⊕ *www.abiquiuinn.com* 🛏 *14 rooms, 5 casitas* ⚭ *Restaurant, some kitchens, cable TV, Wi-Fi, shops, meeting room* ▭ *AE, D, DC, MC, V.*

Ghost Ranch

24 *10 mi northwest of Abiquiu on U.S. 84.*

For art historians, the name Ghost Ranch brings to mind Georgia O'-Keeffe, who lived on but a small parcel of this 20,000-acre dude and cattle ranch. The ranch's owner in the 1930s—conservationist and publisher of *Nature Magazine*, Arthur Pack—first invited O'Keeffe here to visit in 1934; Pack soon sold the artist the 7-acre plot on which she lived summer through fall for most of the rest of her life.

In 1955 Pack donated the rest of the ranch to the Presbyterian Church, which continues to use Pack's original structures and about 55 acres of land as a conference center.

The **Ghost Ranch Education and Retreat Center** (✉ U.S. 84 ☎ 505/685–4333 or 877/804–4678 ⊕ www.ghostranch.org), open year-round, is busiest in summer, when the majority of workshops take place. Subjects range from poetry and literary arts to photography, horseback riding, and every conceivable traditional craft of northern New Mexico. These courses are open to the public, and guests camp or stay in semirustic cottages or casitas. After registering at the main office, you may come in and hike high among the wind-hewn rocks so beloved by O'Keeffe. Ghost Ranch offers guided tours of the ranch's landscape, which show the vistas that O'Keeffe painted during the five decades that she summered here. Her original house is not part of the tour and is closed to the public. These one-hour tours, which have nothing to do with the O'Keeffe studio tours offered in Abiquiu, are available mid-March through mid-November, on Tuesday, Thursday, Friday, and Saturday at 1:30; the cost is $25, and you must call first to make a reservation.

The **Ghost Ranch Piedra Lumbre Education and Visitor Center** has a gallery with rotating art presentations, exhibits on New Mexico's natural history, a gift shop, and two museums. The **Florence Hawley Ellis Museum of Anthropology** contains Native American tools, pottery, and other artifacts excavated from the Ghost Ranch Gallina digs. Pioneer anthropologist Florence Hawley Ellis conducted excavations at Chaco Canyon and at other sites in New Mexico. Adjacent to the Ellis Museum, the **Ruth Hall Museum of Paleontology** exhibits the New Mexico state fossil, the coelophysis, also known as "the littlest dinosaur," originally excavated near Ghost Ranch. ✉ *U.S. 84, just north of main Ghost Ranch entrance* ☎ *505/685–4312* ⊕ *www.ghostranch.org* 🏷 *Donation $3* ☉ *Visitor Center: Mar.–Oct., daily 9–5. Hawley and Hall museums: Late May–early Sept., Tues.–Sat. 9–5, Sun. and Mon. 1–5; early Sept.–late May, Tues.–Sat. 9–5.*

**OFF THE
BEATEN
PATH**

MONASTERY OF CHRIST IN THE DESERT – Designed by renowned Japanese-American architect and wood-carver George Nakashima, this remote rock-and-adobe church—with one of the state's most spectacular natural settings—can be visited for daily prayer or silent overnight retreats (if requested in advance by mail or e-mail); there are basic accommodations for up to 16 guests (10 single and 3 double rooms), and there's a two-night minimum, with most visitors staying for several days. A suggested per-night donation of $50 to $125 is requested, depending on the room, and none have electricity. Day visitors can come anytime and stroll the grounds, visit the gift shop, and participate in different prayer services throughout the day. The road is rutted in places and becomes impassable during rainy weather—you can definitely get stuck here for a day, or even a few days, during particularly wet periods, such as summer monsoon season. Check weather forecasts carefully if you're only intending to visit for the day. ✉ *Guestmaster, Christ in the Desert; pass Ghost Ranch Visitor's Center and turn left on Forest Service Rd. 151;*

follow dirt road 13 mi to monastery ⬦ Box 270, Abiquiu 87510 ☏ No phone ⊕ www.christdesert.org.

EN ROUTE

★ The best and most interesting way to reach Ojo Caliente from Ghost Ranch is to return down U.S. 84 just past Abiquiu and then make a left turn (north) onto NM 554 toward El Rito, 12 mi away. This small, rural community known for its crafts making (especially weaving) has a funky general store and the **El Farolito** (✉ 1212 Main St. ☏ 505/581–9509), a minuscule dinner restaurant on the town's tree-shaded Main Street that serves State Fair blue-ribbon green chile and other New Mexican specialties, including a terrific posole. This place has a cult following, so expect a wait some evenings. The ride here offers a stunning view back east toward the Sangre de Cristos.

4

Chama

㉕ *30 mi east of Jicarilla Apache Reservation and 95 mi west of Taos on U.S. 64, 59 mi north of Abiquiu on U.S. 84.*

A railroad town nestled at the base of 10,000-foot Cumbre Pass, lush and densely wooded Chama offers year-round outdoor activities, as well as a scenic railroad. From there, U.S. 84 hugs the Rio Chama and leads southward through monumental red rocks and golden sandstone spires that inspired Georgia O'Keeffe's vivid paintings of creased mountains, stark crosses, bleached animal skulls, and adobe architecture.

The booms and busts of Chama have largely coincided with the popularity of train transportation. The town's earliest boom, which precipitated its founding, occurred in the 1880s when workers piled into town to construct the Denver & Rio Grande Railroad. In those days, narrow-gauge trains chugged over the high mountain tracks carrying gold and silver out from the mines of the San Juan Mountains, which straddle the nearby Colorado–New Mexico border. Gambling halls, moonshine stills, speakeasies, and brothels were a fixture along the main drag, Terrace Avenue. The lumber industry also thrived during the early years, and the town still has quite a few houses and buildings fashioned out of spare hand-hewn railroad ties.

Chama's outdoor recreation opportunities are hard to beat. Vast meadows of wildflowers and aspen and ponderosa pines blanket the entire region. Hunters are drawn here by the abundant wildlife. There's cross-country skiing and snowmobiling in winter; camping, rafting, hiking, and fishing in summer, all in a pristine, green, high-mountain setting that feels like the top of the world. The temperate mountain air means that most lodgings in the area neither have nor need air-conditioning.

All directions are given in terms of "the Y," the town's only major intersection (of U.S. 64/84 and NM 17).

★ The big attraction in Chama is the historic **Cumbres & Toltec Scenic Railroad,** the narrow-gauge coal-driven steam engine that runs through the San Juan Mountains and over the Cumbres Pass. You chug over ancient trestles, around breathtaking bends, and high above the Los Pinos River—if the terrain looks at all familiar, you may have seen this railroad's "performance" in *Indiana Jones and the Last Crusade*. Midway through the trip you break for lunch and can switch to a waiting Colorado-based train to complete the 64 mi to Antonito, Colorado (from which you'll be shuttled back by bus), or return from this point on the same train. Train trip packages including stays at area lodgings are also available. ⊠ *15 Terrace Ave.* ☎ *505/756–2151 or 888/286–2737* ⊕ *www.cumbresandtoltec.com* 🖾 *$59–$115* ⊘ *Late May–mid.-Oct., daily departures at 10* AM.

WHERE TO
STAY & EAT
¢–$

✕ **Elkhorn Cafe.** Here is the place for a plate of true-blue, stacked New Mexican enchiladas with posole (a New Mexican specialty of hominy slow-cooked in an herbed broth, often with chunks of pork), and beans nestled happily under tasty red chile. The *carne adovado* (pork marinated in red chile and slow-cooked until tender) is songworthy. The salad bar is simply stocked with fresh ingredients. Locals fill the place for breakfast, which starts at 6 AM, as well as lunch and dinner. ⊠ *2663 U.S. 64/ 84, on south end of town* ☎ *505/756–2229* ⚬ *Reservations not accepted* ▤ *DC, MC, V.*

$$$$

▦ **The Lodge and Ranch at Chama Land & Cattle Company.** If you're looking for an outdoor-oriented vacation that's also luxurious, this is the place for you. The lodge and working ranch, owned by the Jicarilla Apache tribe, is on 32,000 idyllic acres on the Colorado border, at an elevation between 9,000 and 11,000 feet, with 10 lakes. Horseback riding, trophy fishing and hunting, touring the ranch, and sitting by the huge stone fireplace ought to relax the most stressed-out executive. The luxe 27,000-square-foot lodge is lavishly furnished. Gourmet meals and drinks from the bar are included in your room rate, and packages are available that include all ranch activities. The lodge also offers day-packages for fly-fishing (which include a guide and lunch), and fly-fishing school. ⊠ *16253 U.S. 84, Box 127, 87520* ☎ *505/756–2133* 🖶 *505/756– 2519* ⊕ *www.lodgeatchama.com* ⇨ *9 rooms, 2 suites* ⚬ *Dining room, cable TV, hot tub, sauna, gym, fishing, horseback riding, bar, meeting rooms; no TV in some rooms* ▤ *D, MC, V* ⏐⊘⏐ *AI.*

★ $–$$

▦ **Gandy Dancer B&B Inn.** A five-minute walk from the rail depot in the center of town, this handsomely furnished pale-yellow Victorian inn offers the most charming accommodations in town, plus a well-prepared full breakfast. From the tree-shaded deck in back, watch hummingbirds feast at feeders all summer long, and enjoy the sight of countless other birds throughout the year. Rooms have railroad-related names (Cinders & Smoke, Caboose, Golden Spike) and contain a mix of Victorian and early-20th-century antiques, original artwork, and plush quilts and linens. ⊠ *299 Maple Ave., Box 810, 87520* ☎ *505/756–2191 or 800/424–6702* ⇨ *7 rooms* ⚬ *Cable TV, in-room VCRs, Wi-Fi, hot tub* ▤ *MC, V* ⏐⊘⏐ *BP.*

$

▦ **Branding Iron Motel.** A spotless, old-time motel with rooms that have been attractively updated over the years, the Branding Iron lies a mile south of the railroad depot, along the main highway through town. There's nothing special about the decor, but the rooms do have all the basics, including coffeemakers and alarm clocks. Pine trees dot the peaceful grounds. ⊠ *1511 NM 17, 87520* ☎ *505/756–2162 or 800/446–2650* ⇨ *39 rooms* ⚬ *Restaurant, cable TV, Wi-Fi, some pets allowed* ▤ *AE, D, MC, V.*

$ ⌂ **River Bend Lodge.** This comfortable, basic lodge has one of the few hot tubs in town. It's right on the Chama River, so you can walk out your door and cast a fly (just keep an eye out for black bears; you might see one meandering by). Management here is especially solicitous and accommodating, particularly for groups or family reunions. It also offers train packages. Cabins have kitchenettes and fireplaces. ⊠ *U.S. 84, Box 593, 87520* ☎ *505/756–2264 or 800/288–1371* ⊟ *505/756–2664* ⊕ *www.chamariverbendlodge.com* ⤳ *14 rooms, 7 cabins* ⚭ *Cable TV, hot tub, meeting room* ⊟ *AE, D, DC, MC, V.*

SPORTS & THE OUTDOORS
Plenty of outfitters are here to help out with equipment and tours. **Nordic Adventures** (☎ 888/660–9878 ⊕ www.yurtsogood.com) provides snowmobiles and yurts for rent and offers backcountry snowmobile and ski tours.

Looking to get on the water? You've got a few options for rafting and guided fishing trips. **Far Flung Adventures** (☎ 800/359–2627 ⊕ www.farflung.com) runs half-day, one-day, and multiday trips along the Rio Grande. **Los Rios** (☎ 800/544–1181 ⊕ www.losriosriverrunners.com) offers Rio Grande day trips and also overnight trips in Rio Chama. If you have your own boat, the folks at **Canyon REO** (☎ 800/637–4604 ⊕ www.canyonreo.com) will pick you and your equipment up in a shuttle, and even pack food for you to take along.

SHOPPING
Local Color Gallery (⊠ 567 Terrace Ave. ☎ 505/756–2604) carries photography and jewelry of local artisans. The sales of many goods at **Trackside Emporium** (⊠ 611 Terrace Ave. ☎ 505/756–1848) support the preservation of the railroad; here you can find books, signs, and other memorabilia pertaining to the trains. **Chama Valley Supermarket** (⊠ 2451 U.S. 84 ☎ 505/756–2545) at the "Y" intersection sells groceries and fishing supplies.

Los Ojos
㉖ *13 mi south of Chama on U.S. 64/84.*

Los Ojos, midway between Tierra Amarilla and Chama, could well serve as a model for rural economic development worldwide. The little town has experienced an economic revival of sorts by returning to its ancient roots—the raising of churro sheep (the original breed brought over by the Spanish, prized for its wool) and weaving. Ganados del Valle, the community-based, nonprofit economic development corporation headquartered here, has created jobs and increased prosperity by returning to the old ways, with improved marketing. You can also find a smattering of artists' studios, most of them in rustic buildings with corrugated metal roofs.

★ The cooperative **Tierra Wools** produces some of the finest original weavings in the Southwest. Designs are based on the old Rio Grande styles, and weavers make rugs and capes of superb craftsmanship entirely by hand, using old-style looms. Weaving workshops are offered. ⊠ *91 Main St.* ☎ *505/588–7231 or 888/709–0979* ⊕ *www.handweavers.com* ☉ *June–Oct., Mon.–Sat. 9–6, Sun. 11–4; Nov.–May, Mon.–Sat. 10–5.*

WHERE TO STAY
$

🏨 **Cooper's El Vado Ranch.** This old-time hunting camp with simple, wood-paneled, gas-heated cabins on the river is a launch site for rafters and a favorite haunt of fishermen. They're still bragging over here about the state-record brown trout they caught in 1946. ⊠ *3150 NM 112* 🖃 *Box 129, Tierra Amarilla 87575* ☎ *505/588–7354* ⊕ *www.elvado.com* ⇨ *9 cabins* ⚫ *Kitchenettes, some pets allowed; no room TVs* ⊟ *AE, D, MC, V* ⊗ *Closed mid-Dec.–mid-Mar.*

⌐ EN ROUTE

Heading south on U.S. 84 from Los Ojos, you can reach the small town of **Tierra Amarilla**, from which you can access two state parks. Both parks have developed campsites. Eleven miles west of town, **Heron Lake State Park** (⊠ NM 95 and U.S. 64 ☎ 505/588–7470 ⊕ www.emnrd.state. nm.us) is a designated "quiet lake" (powerboats may not exceed no-wake speed) ideal for sailing and trout fishing. Seventeen miles southwest of Tierra Amarilla is **El Vado Lake State Park** (⊠ NM 112 ☎ 505/ 588–7247 ⊕ www.emnrd.state.nm.us), where you can water-ski, fish, and watch for bald eagles, osprey, and other birds in winter. From Heron Lake, the 5½-mi **Rio Chama Trail** crosses the Rio Chama, winds along the south slope of the canyon, goes up to a mesa top, and descends to the shore of El Vado Lake.

Ojo Caliente

㉗ *28 mi northeast of Abiquiu by way of El Rito via NM 554 to NM 111 to U.S. 285, 50 mi north of Santa Fe on U.S. 285.*

Ojo Caliente is the only place in North America where five different types of hot springs—iron, lithia, arsenic, salt, and soda—are found side by side. The town was named by Spanish explorer Cabeza de Vaca, who visited in 1535 and believed he had stumbled upon the Fountain of Youth. Modern-day visitors draw a similar conclusion about the restorative powers of the springs. The spa itself, built in the 1920s, is a no-frills establishment that has seen better days but has received some much needed renovations in the past couple of years; it comprises a hotel and cottages, a restaurant, a gift shop, massage rooms, men's and women's bathhouses, a chlorine-free swimming pool, and indoor and outdoor mineral-water tubs. The hotel, one of the original bathhouses, and the springs are all on the National Register of Historic Places, as is the adjacent and recently restored Round Barn (the only adobe one in the nation), from which visitors can take horseback tours and guided hikes to ancient Pueblo dwellings and petroglyph-etched rocks. Spa services include wraps, massage, facials, and acupuncture. The setting at the foot of sandstone cliffs topped by the ruins of ancient Indian pueblos is nothing short of inspiring.

WHERE TO STAY
$–$$

🏨 **Ojo Caliente Mineral Springs Spa and Resort.** Accommodations here run the gamut from spartan in the unfussy 1916 hotel (no TVs, simple furnishings) to rather upscale in the elegant suites, which were added in summer 2006. Rooms in the hotel have bathrooms but no showers or tubs—bathing takes place in the mineral springs (it's an arrangement that pleases most longtime devotees but doesn't sit well with others). The cottages are quite comfy, with refrigerators and TVs; some have kitchenettes, and as of this writing tile showers had been added to some and were planned for the rest by 2007. In summer 2006, Ojo opened 12 spacious suites, which have such luxury touches as kiva fireplaces and patios; half of these have private double soaking tubs outside, which are filled with Ojo mineral waters. All lodgers have complimentary access to the mineral pools and *milagro* (miracle) wraps, and the bathhouse has showers. Horseback tours can be prearranged. The Artesian Restaurant serves world-beat fare in a charming dining room. Four-day and overnight packages are available, from $700 per person. There's also camping on-site, beside the cottonwood-shaded Rio Ojo Caliente—double-occupancy camping rates are $20 for tents, $40 for RVs. ⊠ *50 Los Baños Dr., off U.S. 285, 30 mi north of Española* ⌒ *Box 68, 87549* ☎ *505/583–2233 or 800/222–9162* 🖶 *505/583–2464* ⊕ *www. ojocalientespa.com* ➪ *19 rooms, 19 cottages, 12 suites, 3 3-bedroom houses* ⌓ *Restaurant, some kitchenettes, some refrigerators, spa, horseback riding, meeting rooms; no a/c, no room phones, no TV in some rooms* ▭ *AE, D, DC, MC, V.*

Low Road to Taos

Widely considered to be the less scenic route to Taos, the Low Road actually offers plenty of dazzling scenery once you get through traffic-clogged Española and down into the Rio Grande Gorge. As you emerge from the gorge roughly 25 minutes later, NM 68 cuts up over a plateau that affords stupendous views of Taos and the surrounding mountains. Note that whether you take the Low Road or the High Road (described below), you first follow U.S. 285/84 north from Santa Fe for about 20 mi—this somewhat dull stretch of road was vastly improved in 2004 with a major road widening project. Whereas you exit the highway just north of Pojoaque in order to travel the High Road, you remain on U.S. 285/84 all the way to Española to follow the Low Road; once there, you pick up NM 68 north. Just before you descend into the Rio Grande Gorge, where you parallel the river for several scenic miles, you pass through tiny Velarde, which has a number of fruit and vegetable stands worth checking out. Without stops, it takes 80 to 90 minutes to make it from Santa Fe to Taos via the Low Road, whereas the High Road takes 2 to 2½ hours.

Dixon

28 *45 mi north of Santa Fe via U.S. 285/84 and NM 68, 20 mi south of Taos via NM 68.*

The small village of Dixon and its surrounding country lanes are home to a surprising number of artists. Artistic sensitivity, as well as generations of dedicated farmers, accounts for the community's well-tended fields, pretty gardens, and fruit trees—a source of produce for restaurants and farmers' markets such as the one in Santa Fe. It's simple to find your way around; there's only one main road.

The Dixon Arts Association has some four dozen members, many represented in a cooperative gallery attached to **Métier Weaving & Gallery** (⊠ NM 75 ☎ 505/579–4111), which also has also has a showroom that sells the textiles and weavings of artists and owners Irene Smith and Le-

zlie King. Dixon also hosts a popular studio tour (⊕ www.dixonarts.
org) the first weekend in November, when area artists open up their home
studios to the public.

WHERE TO
STAY & EAT
¢–$$

✕ **Embudo Station.** Set inside an 1880s railroad station, historic Embudo
Station comprises a casual restaurant with a riverside patio; a smoke-
house that cures delicious ham, turkey, pheasant, and rainbow trout; a
winery open for tastings; and a cabin available for nightly or weekly
rentals. The restaurant serves traditional New Mexican fare and bar-
becue; many dishes incorporate the house-smoked meats. Limited sand-
wich fare, beers, and wine are available on weekends during the
off-season, but it's always best to call first. ⊠ NM 68, Embudo ☎ 505/
852–4707 or 800/852–4707 ⊕ www.embudostation.com ⊟ AE, MC,
V ⊙ Closed Nov.–Mar. and Mon.

$

🏠 **Rock Pool Gardens.** A private guesthouse with two warmly furnished
two-bedroom suites, Rock Pool is one of the few accommodations be-
tween Española and Taos, and it's also a good value. One suite has a
kitchenette and a bathroom connecting the bedrooms, each of which
has its own access and patio. The other has a full kitchen. The rustic
walls, Mexican tile work, and willow twig furniture lend a country air
to these otherwise contemporary suites, and lush gardens surround the
building. There's a Jacuzzi under the trees and a heated pool set in nat-
ural rock. Each unit comes stocked with breakfast items. ⊠ NM 75,
87527 ☎ 505/579–4602 ▷ 2 suites � BBQ, kitchens, refrigerator, cable
TV, in-room VCRs, indoor pool, hot tub, some pets allowed ⊟ No credit
cards ⫯⫯ CP.

The High Road to Taos

Fodor'sChoice
★

The main highway (NM 68) to Taos along the Rio Grande Gorge pro-
vides dramatic close-ups of the river and rocky mountain faces, but if
you have an extra hour or two, the High Road to Taos is worth choos-
ing for its views of sweeping woodlands and traditional Hispanic vil-
lages. The High Road follows U.S. 285/84 north to NM 503 (a right
turn just past Pojoaque), to County Road 98 (a left toward Chimayó),
to NM 76 northeast to NM 75 east, to NM 518 north. The drive
through the rolling foothills and tiny valleys of the Sangre de Cristos,
dotted with orchards, pueblos, and picturesque villages, is stunning. And
although most of these insular, largely Hispanic communities offer lit-
tle in the way of shopping and dining, the region has steadily become
more of a haven for artists. From Chimayó to Peñasco, you can find
mostly low-key but often high-quality art galleries, many of them run
out of the owners' homes. And during the final two weekends in Sep-
tember, more than 100 artists in these parts show their wares during
the **High Road Art Tour** (☎ 866/343–5381 ⊕ www.highroadnewmexico.
com); call or visit the Web site for a studio map.

Depending on when you make this drive, you're in for some of the state's
most radiant scenery. In mid-April the orchards are in blossom; sum-
mer turns the valleys into lush green oases; and in fall the smell of piñon
adds to the sensual overload of golden leaves and red-chile ristras hang-
ing from the houses. In winter the fields are covered with quilts of

snow, and the lines of homes, fences, and trees stand out like bold pen-and-ink drawings against the sky. But the roads can be icy and treacherous—if in doubt, stick with the Low Road to Taos. If you decide to take the High Road just one way between Santa Fe and Taos, you might want to save it for the return journey—the scenery is best enjoyed when traveling north to south.

Chimayó

29 *28 mi north of Santa Fe, 10 mi east of Española on NM 76.*

From U.S. 285/84 north of Pojoaque, scenic NM 503 winds past horse paddocks and orchards in the narrow Nambé Valley, then ascends into the red-sandstone canyons with a view of Truchas Peaks to the northeast before dropping into the bucolic village of Chimayó. Nestled into hillsides where gnarled piñons seem to grow from bare bedrock, Chimayó is famed for its weaving, its red chiles, and its two chapels.

Fodor'sChoice
★ **El Santuario de Chimayó**, a small frontier adobe church, has a fantastically carved and painted wood altar and is built on the site where, believers say, a mysterious light came from the ground on Good Friday in 1810 and where a large wooden crucifix was found beneath the earth. The chapel sits above a sacred *pozito* (a small hole), the dirt from which is believed to have miraculous healing properties. Dozens of abandoned crutches and braces placed in the anteroom—along with many notes, letters, and photos—testify to this. The Santuario draws a steady stream of worshippers year-round—Chimayó is considered the Lourdes of the Southwest. During Holy Week as many as 50,000 pilgrims come here. The shrine is a National Historic Landmark, and its altar and artwork underwent an ambitious and much needed restoration in 2004. It's surrounded by commercialism in the way of small adobe shops selling every kind of religious curio imaginable. ✉ *Signed lane off CR 98* ☎ *505/ 351–4889* ⊕ *www.archdiocesesantafe.org/AboutASF/Chimayo.html* 🎫 *Free* ⊙ *June–Sept., daily 9–5; Oct.–May, daily 9–4.*

A smaller chapel 200 yards from El Santuario was built in 1857 and dedicated to **Santo Niño de Atocha**. As at the more famous Santuario, the dirt at Santo Niño de Atocha's chapel is said to have healing properties in the place where the *Santo Niño* was first placed. The little boy saint was brought here from Mexico by Severiano Medina, who claimed Santo Niño de Atocha had healed him of rheumatism. San Ildefonso pottery master Maria Martinez came here for healing as a child. Tales of the boy saint's losing one of his shoes as he wandered through the countryside helping those in trouble endeared him to the people of northern New Mexico. It became a tradition to place shoes at the foot of the statue as an offering. 🎫 *Free* ⊙ *Daily 9–5.*

WHERE TO STAY & EAT
$–$$ ✕ **Rancho de Chimayó.** In a century-old adobe hacienda tucked into the mountains, with whitewashed walls, hand-stripped vigas, and cozy dining rooms, the Rancho de Chimayó is still owned and operated by the family that first occupied the house. There's a fireplace in winter and, in summer, a terraced patio shaded by catalpa trees. Good, if predictable New Mexican fare is served, but the ambience is the real draw here. You can take an after-dinner stroll on the grounds' paths. Reservations are

essential in summer. The owners also operate the seven-room **Hacienda de Chimayó B&B** (☎ 505/351–2222) just across the road. ⊠ *CR 98* ☎ *505/351–4444* ⊕ *www.ranchodechimayo.com* ▤ *AE, D, DC, MC, V* ⊘ *Closed Mon. Nov.–May.*

★ ¢ ✗ **Léona's Restaurante.** This fast-food-style burrito and chili stand under a massive catalpa tree at one end of the Santuario de Chimayó parking lot has only a few tables, and in summer it's crowded. The specialty is flavored tortillas—everything from jalapeño to butterscotch. Other treats include homemade posole stew, carne adovada, and green-chile cheese tamales. The tortillas have become so legendary that owner Léona Medina-Tiede opened a tortilla factory in Chimayó's Manzana Center and now does a thriving mail-order business. ⊠ *Off CR 98, behind Santuario de Chimayó* ☎ *505/351–4569 or 888/561–5569* ⊕ *www. leonasrestaurante.com* ▤ *AE, D, DC, MC, V* ⊘ *Closed Tues. and Wed. No dinner.*

$–$$ ▥ **Casa Escondida.** Intimate and peaceful, this adobe inn has sweeping views of the Sangre de Cristo range. The setting makes it a great base for mountain bikers. The scent of fresh-baked strudel wafts through the rooms, which are decorated with antiques and Native American and other regional arts and crafts. Ask for the Sun Room, in the main house, which has a private patio, viga ceilings, and a brick floor. The separate one-bedroom Casita Escondida has a kiva-style fireplace, tile floors, kitchenette, and a sitting area. A large hot tub is hidden in a grove behind wild berry bushes. ⊠ *CR 0100, off NM 76* ① *Box 142, 85722* ☎ *505/ 351–4805 or 800/643–7201* 🖷 *505/351–2575* ⊕ *www.casaescondida. com* ⑤ *Some kitchenettes, Wi-Fi, outdoor hot tub, some pets allowed; no room phones, no room TVs, no smoking* ⇝ *7 rooms, 1 suite* ▤ *MC, V* ⑩ *BP.*

SHOPPING **Centinela Traditional Arts-Weaving** (⊠ NM 76, 1 mi east of junction with CR 98 ☎ 505/351–2180 or 877/351–2180 ⊕ www.chimayoweavers. com) continues the Trujillo family weaving tradition, which started in northern New Mexico more than seven generations ago. Irvin Trujillo and his wife, Lisa, are both award-winning master weavers, creating Rio Grande–style tapestry blankets and rugs, many of them with natural dyes that authentically replicate early weavings. Most designs are historically based, but the Trujillos contribute their own designs as well. The shop and gallery carries these heirloom-quality textiles, with a knowledgeable staff on hand to demonstrate or answer questions about the weaving technique.

Ortega's Weaving Shop (⊠ NM 76 at CR 98 ☎ 505/351–2288 or 877/ 351–4215 ⊕ www.ortegasdechimayo.com) sells Rio Grande–and Chimayó-style textiles made by the family whose Spanish ancestors brought the craft to New Mexico in the 1600s. The Galeria Ortega, next door, sells traditional New Mexican and Hispanic and contemporary Native American arts and crafts. In winter the shop is closed on Sunday.

In the plaza just outside the Santuario, **Highroad Marketplace** (⊠ Off CR 98 ☎ 505/351–1078 or 866/343–5381) stocks a variety of arts and crafts created all along the High Road, from Chimayó to Peñasco.

Cordova

30 *4 mi east of Chimayó via NM 76.*

A minuscule mountain village with a small central plaza, a school, a post office, and a church, Cordova is the center of the regional wood-carving industry. The town supports more than 30 full-time and part-time carvers. Many of them are descendants of José Dolores López, who in the 1920s created the village's signature unpainted "Cordova style" of carving. Most of the *santeros* (makers of religious images) have signs outside their homes indicating that santos are for sale. The pieces are fairly expensive, a reflection of the hard work and fine craftsmanship involved—prices range from several hundred dollars for small ones to several thousand for larger figures. There are also affordable and delightful small carvings of animals and birds. The St. Anthony of Padua Chapel, which is filled with handcrafted retablos and other religious art, is worth a visit.

Truchas

31 *4 mi northeast of Cordova via NM 76.*

Truchas (Spanish for "trout") is where Robert Redford shot the movie *The Milagro Beanfield War* (based on the novel written by Taos author John Nichols). This village is perched dramatically on the rim of a deep canyon beneath the towering Truchas Peaks, mountains high enough to be almost perpetually capped with snow. The tallest of the Truchas Peaks is 13,102 feet, the second-highest point in New Mexico. This is an insular town, and locals don't always take a shine to visitors, so be discreet and try not to wave your camera around, snapping photos of residents or their property. Truchas has been developing increased cachet with artsy, independent-minded folks from Santa Fe and Taos, who have been lured here in part because of the cheaper real estate and also the breathtaking setting. There are several galleries throughout town, most open by chance, as well as a small general store that sells a variety of snacks and even a few gifts. Continue 7 mi north on NM 76, toward Peñasco, and you come to the marvelous San José de Gracia Church in the village of Trampas. It dates from at least 1760.

SHOPPING In the heart of Truchas, **Cordovas Handweaving Workshop** (⊠ Village center ☎ 505/689–2437) produces vibrant and colorful contemporary rugs.

Peñasco

32 *15 mi north of Truchas on NM 76.*

Although still a modest-size community, Peñasco is one of the larger towns along the High Road and a good bet if you need to fill your tank with gas or pick up a snack at a convenience store.

WHERE TO EAT ✕ **Sugar Nymphs Bistro.** It's taken a little time for folks to learn about, ★ ¢–$ let alone find, this delightful little place set inside a vintage theater in sleepy Peñasco. In fact, it's right along the tourist-trodden High Road, and it's the best restaurant along this route. Chef-owner Kai Harper earned her stripes at San Francisco's famed vegetarian restaurant, Greens, and presents an eclectic menu of reasonably priced, inspired food: creatively topped pizzas, bountiful salads, juicy bacon cheeseburgers, butternut-squash ravioli. Desserts are also memorable—consider the chocolate pecan pie. You can dine on the patio in warm weather. The Sunday brunch is excellent. ⊠ *15046 NM 75* ☎ *505/587–0311* ≡ *MC, V* ✆ *Closed Mon.*

SPORTS &
THE OUTDOORS
About 10 mi east of Peñasco, **Sipapu Lodge and Ski Area** (⊠ NM 518, Vadito ☎ 505/587–2240 or 800/587–2240) is a low-key, family-friendly compound with skiing and snowboarding in winter, and fishing, rafting, disc golf, hiking, mountain biking, and camping the rest of the year. There's a modest lodge with inexpensive rooms, camping, and a restaurant.

SIDE TRIPS FROM TAOS

Surrounded by thousands of acres of pristine Carson National Forest and undeveloped high desert, Taos makes an ideal base for road-tripping. Most of the nearby adventures involve the outdoors, from skiing to hiking to mountain biking, and there are several noteworthy campgrounds in this part of the state. Although these side trips can be done in a day, several of the ski-resort communities mentioned in this section have extensive overnight accommodations.

The Enchanted Circle

Fodor'sChoice
★
The Enchanted Circle, an 84-mi loop north from Taos and back, rings Wheeler Peak, New Mexico's highest mountain, and takes you through glorious panoramas of alpine valleys and the towering mountains of the lush Carson National Forest. You can see all the major sights in one day, or take a more leisurely tour and stay overnight.

From Taos, head north about 15 mi via U.S. 64 to NM 522, keeping your eye out—after about 15 mi—for the sign on the right that points to the D. H. Lawrence Ranch and Memorial. You can visit the memorial, but the other buildings on the ranch are closed to the public. Continue north a short ways to reach Red River Hatchery, and then go another 5 mi to the village of Questa. Here you have the option of continuing north on NM 522 and detouring for some hiking at Wild Rivers Recreation Area, or turning east from Questa on NM 38 and driving for about 12 mi to the rollicking ski town of Red River. From here, continue 16 mi east along NM 38 and head over dramatic Bobcat Pass, which rises to a tad under 10,000 feet. You'll come to the sleepy old-fashioned village of Eagle Nest, comprising a few shops and down-home restaurants and motels. From here, U.S. 64 joins with NM 38 and runs southeast about 15 mi to one of the state's fastest-growing communities, Angel Fire, an upscale ski resort that's popular for hiking, golfing, and mountain biking in summer. It's about a 25-mi drive west over 9,000-foot Palo Flechado Pass and down through winding Taos Canyon to return to Taos.

Leave early in the morning and plan to spend the entire day on this trip. During ski season, which runs from late November to early April, you may want to make it an overnight trip and get in a day of skiing. In spring, summer, and fall your drive should be free of snow and ice. A sunny winter day can yield some lovely scenery (but if it's snowy, don't forget your sunglasses).

Carson National Forest surrounds Taos and spans almost 200 mi across northern New Mexico, encompassing mountains, lakes, streams, villages, and much of the Enchanted Circle. Hiking, cross-country skiing, horseback riding, mountain biking, backpacking, trout fishing, boating, and wildflower viewing are among the popular activities here. The forest is home to big-game animals and many species of smaller animals and songbirds. For canyon climbing, head into the rocky Rio Grande Gorge. The best entry point into the gorge is at the Wild Rivers Recreation Area, north of Questa. You can drive into the forest land via NM 522, NM 150, NM 38, and NM 578. Carson National Forest also has some of the best trout fishing in New Mexico. Its streams and lakes are home to rainbow, brown, and native Rio Grande cutthroat trout.

The forest provides a wealth of camping opportunities, from organized campgrounds with restrooms and limited facilities to informal roadside campsites and sites that require backpacking in. If mountains, pines, and streams are your goal, stake out sites in Carson National Forest along the Rio Hondo or Red River; if you prefer high-desert country along the banks of the Rio Grande, consider Orilla Verde or Wild Rivers Recreation Area. Backcountry sites are free; others cost up to $7 per night.

If you're coming from a lower altitude, you should take time to acclimatize, and all hikers should follow basic safety procedures. Wind, cold, and wetness can occur any time of year, and the mountain climate produces sudden storms. Dress in layers and wear sturdy footwear; carry water, food, sunscreen, hat, sunglasses, and a first-aid kit. Contact the Carson National Forest's visitor center for maps, safety guidelines, camping information, and conditions (it's open weekdays 8–4:30). ⊠ *Forest Service Bldg., 208 Cruz Alta Rd., Taos 87571* ☎ *505/758–6200* ⊕ *www.fs.fed.us/r3/carson.*

The Enchanted Circle Bike Tour takes place in mid-September. The rally loops through the entire 84-mi Enchanted Circle, revealing a brilliant blaze of fall color. In summer you can head up the mountainside via ski lift in Red River and Angel Fire.

Questa

🗿 *25 mi north of Taos via U.S. 64 to NM 522.*

Literally "hill," in the heart of the Sangre de Cristo Mountains, Questa is a quiet village nestled against the Red River itself and amid some of New Mexico's most striking mountain country. **St. Anthony's Church,** built of adobe with 5-foot-thick walls and viga ceilings, is on the main street. Questa's **Cabresto Lake,** in Carson National Forest, is about 8 mi from town. Follow NM 563 northeast to Forest Route 134, then 2 mi of a primitive road (134A)—you'll need a four-wheel-drive vehicle. You can trout fish and boat here from about June to October.

Although it's only a few miles west of Questa as the crow flies, you have to drive about 15 mi north of Questa via NM 522 to NM 378 to reach **Wild Rivers Recreation Area,** which offers hiking access to the dramatic confluence of two national wild and scenic rivers, the Rio Grande and

Red River. There are some fairly easy and flat trails along the gorge's rim, including a ½ mi interpretive loop from the visitor center out to La Junta Point, which offers a nice view of the river. But the compelling reason to visit is a chance to hike down into the gorge and study the rivers up close, which entails hiking one of a couple of well-marked but steep trails down into the gorge, a descent of about 650 feet. It's not an especially strenuous trek, but many visitors come without sufficient water and stamina, have an easy time descending into the gorge, and then find it difficult to make it back up. There are also 10 basic campsites, some along the rim and others along the river. ⊠ *NM 522, follow signed dirt road from highway, Cerro* ☎ *505/770–1600, 505/758–8851 camping information* 🖃 *$3 per vehicle; camping $7 per vehicle* ⊙ *Daily 6 AM–10 PM; visitor center late May–early Sept., daily 10–4.*

NEED A BREAK? Hip coffeehouses are something of a rarity in rural New Mexico, but funky **Paloma Blanca** (⊠ 2255 S. NM 522 ☎ 505/586–2261) is a hit, not only because of its excellent coffee drinks but owing to the excellent sandwiches, salads, pastries, and Taos Cow ice cream. It's the perfect place to stock up on food before hiking at Wild Rivers Recreation Area.

At the **Red River Hatchery,** freshwater trout are raised to stock waters in Questa, Red River, Taos, Raton, and Las Vegas. You can feed them and learn how they're hatched, reared, stocked, and controlled. The visitor center has displays and exhibits, a fishing pond, and a machine that dispenses fish food. The self-guided tour can last anywhere from 20 minutes to more than an hour, depending on how enraptured you become. There's a picnic area and camping on the grounds. ⊠ *NM 522, 5 mi south of Questa* ☎ *505/586–0222* 🖃 *Free* ⊙ *Daily 8–5.*

The influential and controversial English writer David Herbert Lawrence and his wife, Frieda, arrived in Taos at the invitation of Mabel Dodge Luhan, who collected famous writers and artists the way some people collect butterflies. Luhan provided them a place to live, Kiowa Ranch, on 160 acres in the mountains. Rustic and remote, it's now known as the **D. H. Lawrence Ranch and Memorial,** though Lawrence never actually owned it. Lawrence lived in Taos on and off for about 22 months during a three-year period between 1922 and 1925. He wrote his novel *The Plumed Serpent* (1926), as well as some of his finest short stories and poetry, while in Taos and on excursions to Mexico. The houses here, owned by the University of New Mexico, are not open to the public, but you can enter the small cabin where Dorothy Brett, the Lawrences' traveling companion, stayed. You can also visit the D. H. Lawrence Memorial, a short walk up Lobo Mountain. A white shedlike structure, it's simple and unimposing. The writer fell ill while in France and died in a sanatorium there in 1930. Five years later Frieda had Lawrence's body disinterred and cremated and brought his ashes back to Taos. Frieda Lawrence is buried, as was her wish, in front of the memorial. ⊠ *NM 522, follow signed dirt road from highway, San Cristobal* ☎ *505/776–2245* 🖃 *Free* ⊙ *Daily dawn–dusk.*

Red River

�

12 mi east of Questa via NM 38.

Home of a major ski resort that has a particularly strong following with
folks from Oklahoma and the Texas panhandle, Red River (elevation
8,750 feet) came into being as a miners' boomtown during the 19th century, taking its name from the river whose mineral content gives it a rosy
color. When the gold petered out, Red River died, only to be rediscovered in the 1920s by migrants escaping the dust storms in the Great Plains.
An Old West flavor remains: Main Street shoot-outs, an authentic melodrama, and square dancing and two-stepping are among the diversions.
Because of its many country dances and festivals, Red River is affection-
ately called "The New Mexico Home of the Texas Two-Step." The bustling
little downtown area contains souvenir shops and sportswear boutiques, casual steak and barbecue joints, and a number of motels, lodges,
and condos. There's good fishing to be had in the Red River itself, and
excellent alpine and Nordic skiing in the surrounding forest.

**NEED A
BREAK?**
In Red River stop by the **Sundance** (✉ 401 High St. ☎ 505/754–2971) for Mexican food or a fresh-fruit sangria. The stuffed sopapillas here are particularly
good. **Texas Red's Steakhouse** (✉ 111 E. Main St. ☎ 505/754–2964) has char-
broiled steaks, chops, buffalo burgers, and chicken. There's also a branch
down in Eagle Nest, in the heart of downtown.

About 16 mi southeast of Red River, NM 38 leads to the small village
of Eagle Nest, the home of New Mexico's most recently designated state
park, **Eagle Nest Lake State Park** (✉ NM 38/U.S. 64, just south of town
☎ 505/377–1594 ⊕ www.emnrd.state.nm.us ✉ $5), which became
part of the park system in 2004. This 2,400-acre lake is one of the state's
top spots for kokanee salmon and rainbow trout fishing as well as a favorite venue for boating; there are two boat ramps on the lake's northwest side. You may also have the chance to spy elk, bears, mule deer,
and even reclusive mountain lions around this rippling body of water,
which in winter is popular for snowmobiling and ice-fishing. The park
is open 6 AM–9 PM, and camping is not permitted.

Thousands of acres of national forest surround rustic Eagle Nest, population 189, elevation 8,090 feet. The shops and other buildings here
evoke New Mexico's mining heritage, while a 1950s-style diner, Kaw-
Lija's, serves up a memorable burger; you can also grab some take-out
food in town and bring it to Eagle Nest Lake for a picnic.

WHERE TO STAY   🏕 **Roadrunner Campground.** The Red River runs right through this
woodsy mountain campground set on 25 rugged acres. There are two
tennis courts and a video-game room. ✉ *1371 E. Main St., Box 588,
Red River 87558* ☎ *505/754–2286 or 800/243–2286* ⊕ *www.redrivernm.
com/roadrunnerrv* ⚬ *Laundry facilities, flush toilets, full hookups,
drinking water, showers, picnic tables, electricity, public telephone, general store, play area, swimming (river)* 🚐 *155 RV sites, 6 cabins* 💲 *$33
sites, $94 cabins* ⊙ *Closed mid-Sept.–Apr.*

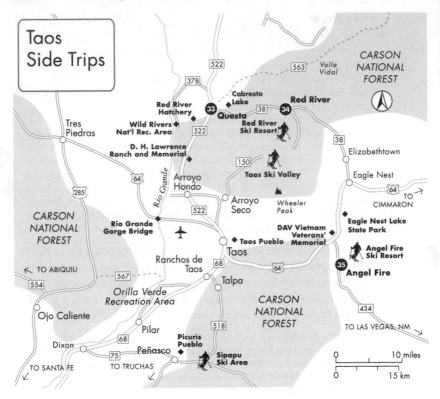

Taos
Side Trips

SPORTS & At the **Enchanted Forest Cross-Country Ski Area,** 24 mi of groomed trails
THE OUTDOORS loop from the two warming huts, stocked with snacks and hot cocoa,
★ through 600 acres of meadows and pines in Carson National Forest, 3
mi east of Red River. ⊠ *417 W. Main St.* ☎ *505/754–2374 or 800/966–
9381* ⊕ *www.enchantedforestxc.com* ⊡ *$12* ☉ *Late Nov.–Easter,
weather permitting.*

The **Red River Ski Area** is in the middle of the historic gold-mining town
of Red River, with lifts within walking distance of restaurants and hotels. Slopes for all levels of skiers make the area popular with families,
and there's a snowboarding park. There are 58 trails served by seven
lifts, and the vertical drop is about 1,600 feet. Red River has plenty of
rental shops and accommodations. ⊠ *400 Pioneer Rd., off NM 38*
☎ *505/754–2223, 505/754–2220 snow conditions* ⊕ *www.
redriverskiarea.com* ⊡ *Lift tickets $50* ☉ *Late Nov.–late Mar.*

Angel Fire

③⑤ *30 mi south of Red River and 13 mi south of Eagle Nest via NM 38
and U.S. 64.*

Named for its blazing sunrise and sunset colors by the Ute Indians who
gathered here each autumn, Angel Fire is known these days primarily
as a ski resort, generally rated the second-best in the state after Taos.

In summer there are arts and music events as well as hiking, river raft-ing, and ballooning. A prominent landmark along U.S. 64, just north-east of town, is the **DAV Vietnam Veterans Memorial**, a 50-foot-high wing-shaped monument built in 1971 by D. Victor Westphall, whose son David was killed in Vietnam.

WHERE TO STAY   ☷ **Angel Fire Resort.** The centerpiece of New Mexico's fastest-growing

$$–$$$ and most highly acclaimed four-season sports resort, this upscale hotel is set at the mountain's base, a stone's throw from the chairlift. Indeed, winter is the busiest season here, but during the warmer months it's a popular retreat with hikers, golfers, and other outdoorsy types who ap-preciate retiring each evening to cushy and spacious digs. Even the stan-dard rooms are a whopping 500 square feet, and the larger deluxe units have feather pillows, ski-boot warmers, and fireplaces. The resort also manages a variety of privately owned condo units, from studios to three-bedrooms, which are available nightly or long-term. ⊠ *10 Miller La., Box Drawer B, 87710* ☎ *505/377–4282 or 800/633–7463* ☎ *505/ 377–4200* ⊕ *www.angelfireresort.com* ↴ *139 rooms* ♨ *4 restaurants, refrigerators, cable TV, 18-hole golf course, 6 tennis courts, fishing, moun-tain bikes, basketball, hiking, horseback riding, cross-country skiing, downhill skiing, ski shop, sleigh rides, snowmobiling, 2 bars, play-ground, business services, meeting rooms* ☰ *AE, D, MC, V.*

▲ **Enchanted Moon Campground.** In Valle Escondido, off U.S. 64 near Angel Fire, this wooded area with a trout pond has views of the Sangre de Cristos. Features include horse stalls, a chuckwagon, and an indoor recreation area with video games. ⊠ *7 Valle Escondido Rd., Valle Es-condido 87571* ☎ *505/758–3338* ⊕ *www.emooncampground.com* ♨ *Grills, flush toilets, full hookups, drinking water, showers, picnic ta-bles, electricity, public telephone, play area* ↴ *44 RV sites, 25 tent sites* ☲ *RV sites $22, tent sites $15* ☉ *Closed mid-Oct.–Apr.*

NIGHTLIFE &   **Music from Angel Fire** (☎ *505/377–3233 or 888/377–3300* ⊕ www.

THE ARTS   musicfromangelfire.org) is a nightly series of classical (and occasional jazz) concerts presented at venues around Angel Fire and Taos for about three weeks from late August to early September. Tickets cost $18–$25 per concert, and the festival—begun in 1983—continues to grow in pop-ularity and esteem each year.

SPORTS &   The 18-hole golf course at the **Angel Fire Country Club** (⊠ Country Club

THE OUTDOORS   Dr. off NM 434 ☎ 505/377–3055), one of the highest in the nation, is open May to mid-October, weather permitting. The challenging front 9 runs a bit longer than the back and takes in great views of aspen- and pine-shaded canyons; the shorter back 9 has more water play and some-what tighter fairways. Greens fees are $41–$58.

★   The fast-growing and beautifully maintained **Angel Fire Resort** is a busy ski destination, with 70 runs for all levels of skiers, five lifts, 19 mi of cross-country trails, and four terrain parks; the vertical drop is about 2,100 feet. Other amenities include a 1,000-foot snow-tubing hill, a well-respected ski and snowboard school, snowbiking (also taught at the school), ice fishing, a children's ski-and-snowboard center, and superb snowmaking capacity. ⊠ *N. Angel Fire Rd. off NM 434* ☎ *505/377–*

6401 or 800/633–7463, 505/377–4222 snow conditions ⊕ www.
angelfireresort.com ☒ Lift tickets $50 ⊙ Mid-Dec.–early Apr.

SIDE TRIPS ESSENTIALS

See the Essentials sections of the Albuquerque, Santa Fe, and Taos chapters for additional information on regional transportation, guided tours, visitor information, and other helpful travel resources in north-central New Mexico.

CAR TRAVEL

As there's virtually no public transportation that covers the towns and recreation areas covered in this chapter, a car is absolutely indispensable. Most of the major regions covered are accessed via well-paved and clearly marked two-lane state and U.S. highways, but a few off-the-beaten path attractions and recreation areas are along rutted dirt roads that can become impassable during rainy or snowy weather. If you're planning extensive side trips and forays into forests and outdoorsy areas, it's advisable to use a four-wheel-drive vehicle. Detailed maps showing most of the routes covered in this chapter can be obtained from the relevant visitor information centers listed below.

TOURS

Begun in New Mexico in 2004, **Audio CD Road Trips** (☎ 505/988–7016 ⊕ www.gallopinggalleries.com) produces extremely informative and engaging audio CDs that cover different unusual roads throughout north-central New Mexico. The three CDs cover the Turquoise Trail, Camino Real (I–25 from Albuquerque to Santa Fe), and the High Road to Taos. Each CD costs $19.50 and contains about an hour of stories and tour highlights, along with music by local New Mexico artists.

VISITOR INFORMATION

🛈 Albuquerque Convention and Visitors Bureau ☒ 20 1st Plaza NW, Suite 601, 87102 ☎ 505/842–9918 or 800/284–2282 ⊕ www.itsatrip.org. **Angel Fire Chamber of Commerce** ⌂ Box 547, 87110 ☎ 505/377–6900 or 800/446–8117 ⊕ www.angelfirenm.com. **Chama Valley Chamber of Commerce** ☒ 499 S. Terrace Ave., 87520 ☎ 505/756–2306 or 800/477–0149 ⊕ www.chamavalley.com. **Española Valley Chamber of Commerce** ☒ 710 Paseo de Oñate ⌂ Box 190, Española 87532 ☎ 505/753–2831 ⊕ www.espanolanmchamber. com. **Los Alamos Chamber of Commerce** ☒ 109 Central Park Sq., 87544 ☎ 505/661–4844 or 800/444–0707 ⊕ www.visit.losalamos.com. **Red River Chamber of Commerce** ☒ Off NM 38 ⌂ Box 870, 87558 ☎ 505/774–2366 or 800/348–6444 ⊕ www.redrivernewmex.com. **Santa Fe Convention and Visitors Bureau** ☒ 201 W. Marcy St. ⌂ Box 909, Santa Fe 87501 ☎ 505/955–6200 or 800/777–2489 ⊕ www.santafe.org. **Taos County Chamber of Commerce** ☒ 1139 Paseo del Pueblo Sur ⌂ Drawer I, Taos 87571 ☎ 505/758–3873 or 800/732–8267 ⊕ www.taoschamber.com.

Northwestern New Mexico

WORD OF MOUTH

"I'm interested in visiting Chaco Culture National Park, but have read it is accessible only by dirt road."

—Dema

"We drove it in June in an SUV, but we saw many regular cars on the way in and out. You should have no problem. The road was very rough, but in a washboard sense, not potholes."

—richbutnot

"The road was not badly rutted, nor full of canyons large enough to swallow a VW Beetle. Right after a rain, or during one, I can see where that clay like surface might get very slick."

—bob_brown

Updated by
Georgia
de Katona

WHEN NEW MEXICANS SAY THEY ARE "ON INDIAN TIME," they're refer-ring to a certain relaxed approach to schedules and numbers that is sim-ply part of the way of life in their home state. But once you leave the urban areas of Albuquerque or Santa Fe and start winding your way through the red canyons of the northwestern New Mexican desert, the phrase seems to take on a new significance. The enormous, silent sweep of plateaus and sky really does seem to form a landscape that's impervious to time—one that conjures the spirits of those who lived here long before recorded his-tory. As you stand on the edge of a sandstone cliff overlooking the San Juan River, enter the restored Great Kiva at the Aztec Ruins, or study the pattern of a handwoven Navajo rug, don't be surprised if you sense the presence of the ancient cultures that inhabited these places, and lived their lives based on the cycles of nature rather than the clock.

The countryside here has a stark and powerful beauty that has been rec-ognized for centuries. The Anasazi people (whose name in Navajo means "Ancient Enemies") first built their cities and roads here more than 1,000 years ago. Today, the region is dominated by the Navajo in the northwest, and the Puebloan descendants of the Anasazi, who live closer to the Rio Grande. The two largest cities in the northwest, Gallup and Farmington, are the legacy of later arrivals—the traders, soldiers, home-steaders, and prospectors who made this area their home beginning in the 19th century. Today Gallup is a prime destination for Native Amer-ican art and jewelry, and Farmington is a hub of energy exploration.

Exploring Northwestern New Mexico

This region covers an immense territory—give yourself five to seven days for a reasonably thorough exploration. Begin by heading west out of Albuquerque on I–40, planning a night or two in the Indian Country, and then heading north toward Farmington for another night in the Four Corners region. Allow most of a day for touring Chaco Canyon. On your way back to Albuquerque, take an hour or so to visit the Jémez area. If you're daunted by squeezing so much into a short period, re-member that it's easy to visit Acoma, Laguna, and Grants at other times as day trips from Albuquerque or Santa Fe. Some folks tackle Chaco as a day trip from the Rio Grande Valley, but it's far more practical to spend the night closer by, if not in Cuba then in Abiquiu, Farmington, or even Grants or Gallup (the last two towns being relatively near Chaco's southern entrance).

Timing

Weatherwise, the best months to tour the ruins of Anasazi Country are from April to early June and from late August to October, but there's no bad time. On rare occasions the roads to Chaco Canyon are closed be-cause of snow or mud in winter, and cold winds can make the going rough in late fall and early spring. The best seasons for attending Pueblo In-dian dances are summer and fall, when harvest celebrations take place, and from Thanksgiving through early January. Late June through July are the hottest months, but by August afternoon thunderstorms, called monsoons, begin cooling things down. The trick, like elsewhere in the Southwest, is to simply slow down and relax, Zen-like, into the dry heat.

GREAT ITINERARIES

IF YOU HAVE 2 OR 3 DAYS

The only way to tour this region adequately in two days is if you're incorporating your trip into a journey west into Arizona (via Gallup or Farmington), northwest into Utah (via Farmington), or north into Colorado (via Farmington). In three days, however, you can make a nice loop of the region's top sites: drive west from Albuquerque on I-40, stopping in **Acoma Pueblo ②** before continuing west to 🚉 **Gallup ⑦**. Spend the late afternoon shopping the old trading posts there, have dinner at Earl's, and stay overnight at the atmospheric El Rancho—or, if it's not too late, head south to spend a night in Zuñi at the stellar **Inn at Halona**. On Day 2, head south on NM 602 to 🚉 **Zuñi**, before heading on to **El Morro National Monument ⑤** and then the **Ice Cave and Bandera Volcano ④**. If you've got a third day, spend the night in **Grants ③**, get up early and head north to spend as much time as you can manage in **Chaco Culture**

National Historical Park ⑫ before heading back to **Albuquerque.**

IF YOU HAVE 5 TO 7 DAYS

In five to seven days you can get a real sense for the past and present of northwestern New Mexico. On Day 1, drive west on I-40 to **Acoma Pueblo ②**, then loop down along NM 53 for short hikes at the **Ice Cave and Bandera Volcano ④**, and stay the night at one of the B&Bs in the area. The next day, explore **El Morro National Monument ⑤** before stopping at 🚉 **Zuñi Pueblo ⑥** en route to 🚉 **Gallup ⑦**. Spend the remainder of the day wandering the trading posts and book a night at **El Rancho**. Next, follow NM 371 to 🚉 **Farmington ⑧**, visiting the Bisti Wilderness Area en route. Plan to spend at least a day exploring **Chaco Culture National Historical Park ⑫** from your base in Farmington, and you may find it surprisingly easy to go back for another day or more.

5

When visiting pueblos and reservations you are expected to follow a certain etiquette (*see* the "Pueblo Etiquette" feature *in* Chapter 4). Check the pueblos and monuments for dates of feast-day celebrations and fairs; some pueblos are open only on specific days.

About the Restaurants

Fast-food and familiar franchise restaurants thrive in this region, but there are also lots of reputable homegrown establishments. The B&Bs here serve uniformly delicious, homemade breakfasts (and some serve equally tasty dinners). Western favorites like rib-eye steak and barbecue pork and chicken are common menu items and, as elsewhere in New Mexico, the specialty is red and green chile sauce, commonly referred to as "chile." Vegetarians take note: chile is often cooked with pork in its green incarnation, and beef with red; ask about it when you order. Posole is another dish in which it is more common to find pork than not. Other local specialties include Navajo fry bread, which can be served plain, or topped with honey and powdered sugar, or taco-style with beans, lettuce, and cheese; and mutton stew such as you would be served at a pueblo's feast day. Delicious bread and pies, baked in beehive-shape outdoor *hornos* (ovens), are sold at roadside stands at some pueblos.

About the Hotels

Farmington, Grants, and Gallup are well supplied with chain motels; Cuba also has a couple decent mo-

> **CHILE IS A SAUCE**
>
> Throughout this book and on menus throughout the state you'll see variations on "red chile" or "green chile," which refer to any sauce made with a chile pepper.

tels. There are several appealing B&Bs in the region. Rooms in the areas surrounding Chaco Canyon can fill quickly during the busy spring and fall seasons when weather is ideal, but otherwise are not a problem. Book in advance if attending a special event.

WHAT IT COSTS					
	$$$$	**$$$**	**$$**	**$**	**¢**
RESTAURANTS	over $30	$23–$30	$16–$22	$10–$15	under $10
HOTELS	over $250	$176–$250	$121–$175	$70–$120	under $70

Restaurant prices are per person for a main course at dinner. Hotel prices are for two people in a standard double room in high season, excluding 5%–12% tax.

PUEBLO COUNTRY

The scent of smoldering piñon, the hypnotic chant of dancers, and the mood of reverence and joy that comes over a pueblo on a feast day leave lasting impressions on visitors to Pueblo country. The sense of long history and calm that pervades a pueblo like Acoma, secluded on an imposing mesa that served as a lookout for "the people of the white rock" (as the name translates in the Keresan language), is unmistakable. Unlike other spots where travelers have felt a certain spiritual pull—Peru's Machu Picchu, for example, or England's Stonehenge—New Mexico's Indian pueblos are still inhabited. They are alive, their residents carrying on traditions, arts, and ways of living as vibrant today as they were centuries ago. Much but not all of Pueblo country lies within northern New Mexico. Among the region's important pueblos are Acoma, Laguna, and Zuñi. Sacred grounds include portions of El Malpais and El Morro national monuments.

Laguna Pueblo

❶ *50 mi west of Albuquerque on I–40.*

Laguna Pueblo, which was established in 1697 by refugees from Zía, Cochiti, and Santo Domingo pueblos, is one of the youngest of New Mexico's pueblos. Scattered about the reservation are six villages, but most visitors are drawn to **Old Laguna,** capped by the eye-catching white facade of San José de Laguna Church, which is visible from I–40. The church, built in 1699, is a National Historic Landmark. In shops and artists' homes (the latter identified by signs) you can buy fine pottery

IF YOU LIKE

ARTS & CRAFTS

Although most visitors to this part of New Mexico tend to buy Native American arts and crafts, there's also a rich selection of traditional Hispanic art to choose from. Although they may not market themselves as such, many of the small communities have a strong artistic tradition, and many artisans living there today still create weaving, pottery, jewelry, iron- and tinwork, woodcarvings, and other crafts much as their ancestors did. Wandering around these little villages can result in some surprising and delightful folk art finds.

FISHING

No question about it, fishing is a big draw in northwestern New Mexico—and the San Juan River is fishable year-round. In fact, some of the best fishing happens in winter. Trout here are routinely over 20 inches long, but experienced fly-fishers will tell you it takes tiny flies, fine tippets, and knowing how to sneak up on the wily fish to catch them. If you have always wondered about fly-fishing but never tried it, this is the place to satisfy your curiosity. There are numerous guides in the region and they all share a unique passion for the sport.

TRACES OF THE ANASAZI

Called Anasazi or "ancient enemies" by the Navajo, and Hisatsinom or "the ones who came before" by the Hopi, the people who built the amazing villages that can still be seen in the Four Corners were ahead of their time in many ways. Their culture is thought to have flowered between AD 900 and 1250, after the construction of large villages and trade roads. Cultivation of "the holy trinity," beans, corn, and squash was responsible for feeding thousands of people. Pottery was utilitarian and artful. Trade goods came from southern Mexico and the Great Plains. Studies of burials have raised new questions the Anasazi way of life, but archaeologists are still putting together the clues about this fascinating culture.

decorated with traditional geometric designs. The pueblo's villages celebrate many feast days and dances, including St. Joseph (March 19), Virgin Mary (September 8), and Sts. Margaret and Mary (October 17). Most of the pueblo's residents gather at Old Laguna on September 19 to honor St. Joseph with a fair. Photography rules vary; contact the governor's office for information. ⊠ *Off I–40* ☎ *505/552–6654 governor's office* ☎ *Free* ☉ *Daily 8–4:30, village tours by appt.*

Acoma Pueblo

★ ❷ *63 mi west of Albuquerque on I–40 and NM 22 south.*

Atop a 367-foot mesa that rises abruptly from the valley floor, Acoma Pueblo's terraced, multistory, multiunit Sky City is like no other pueblo structure. It's one of the oldest continually inhabited spots in North America, with portions believed to be more than 1,500 years old. Captain

Hernando de Alvarado, a member of Francisco Vásquez de Coronado's Expedition of 1540, was the first European to see Acoma. He reported that he had "found a rock with a village on top, the strongest position ever seen in the world." The Spanish eventually conquered the Acoma people and brutally compelled them to build **San Estéban del Rey,** the immense adobe church that stands to this day. Native American laborers cut the massive vigas for the church's ceiling 30 mi away on Mt. Taylor and physically carried them back to the mesa.

About a dozen families live at the mesa-top pueblo full time, with most other Acomas living on Native American land nearby and returning only in summer and for celebrations, such as the feast day of St. Stephen (September 2), and Christmas mass (both are open to the public). Acoma's artisans are known for their thin-walled pottery, hand-painted with intricate black-and-white geometrical patterns. Visitation is by an hour-long guided tour; you're whisked by van up a steep road from the visitor center and then led about the mesa community on foot. Allow time to walk back down to the visitor center via the ancient staircase carved into the side of the mesa (ask your guide to point it out). There's no electricity or running water in the village, but you can see cars parked outside many homes—one wonders what it must have been like to visit Acoma before the road was constructed in 1969. Open hours vary slightly, depending on the weather. Videotaping, sketching, and painting are prohibited, and a permit is required for still photography. Note that the pueblo prohibits photography of the church interior and exterior as well as the adjoining cemetery. As a general rule, it's best to ask permission before photographing pueblo residents or their artwork. ⊠ *Off NM 22* ☎ *505/552–6604 or 800/747–0181* ⩘ *$10* ⊙ *Early Apr.–late Oct., daily 8–6, tours daily 8–4:30; late Oct.–early Apr., daily 8–4, tours daily 8–3:30. Closed certain periods; call first.*

> ## WORD OF MOUTH
>
> "You cannot just park [at Acoma] and go in on your own as at Taos and others. They take you via bus and if you are going to visit, be sure to do it earlier rather than later during the day. If you get there too late, they simply will not have a bus to take you up."
> —Debi

Grants

❸ *34 mi west of Laguna Pueblo, 29 mi northwest of Acoma via NM 38 north and I–40 west.*

The largest community on old Route 66 between Albuquerque and Gallup, little Grants has an intriguing museum and enough chain hotels and inexpensive restaurants to make it a fair base for exploring the eastern half of this region. The night skies here are said to be some of the clearest in the world, making it a worthwhile stop for stargazers. The seat of Cibola County, Grants started out as a farming and ranching center, grew into a rail transport hub, and boomed during the 1950s when uranium was discovered in the nearby mountains. The city has struggled since then to find its economic niche.

In the center of sleepy downtown Grants, the small **New Mexico Mining Museum** shares quarters with the chamber of commerce off Santa Fe Avenue. On the ground level are charts, photos, gems, and minerals, and depictions of uranium-mining life in the region—this area is free. After paying admission, you can ride the elevator down into an amazingly realistic, re-created mine in the building's basement, where you can make a self-guided tour of the equipment and exhibits. ⊠ *100 N. Iron Ave.* ☎ *505/287–4802* ✐ *Museum free, mine exhibit $3* ☉ *Mon.–Sat. 9–4.*

Looming 11,301 feet above Grants to the northeast, **Mt. Taylor** is the highest peak in northwestern New Mexico. You can drive fairly far up the mountain for fine views and hop out to hike on marked trails. On the main road to the peak, Coal Mine Canyon campground, at 7,444 feet elevation, offers restrooms and drinking water amidst ponderosa pines. The campground is closed September 30–May 15; call the ranger station for information at ☎ 505/287–8833. The annual **Mt. Taylor Winter Quadrathlon** (☎ 505/287–4802 or 800/748–2142 ⊕ www. mttaylorquad.org) takes place mid-February, when 600 unbelievably fit athletes compete in a highly challenging bicycle, foot, ski, and snowshoe race near the summit.

Where to Stay & Eat

$–$$$ ✕ **Monte Carlo.** A fixture in town since the 1940s, this old New Mexican eatery with no-frills decor is best known for its rich red chile, and the unusual *chile relleno del mar* (a green chile pepper stuffed with cheese, bay shrimp, and crabmeat). Fodors.com users say that they do steaks rather well. ⊠ *721 W. Santa Fe Ave.* ☎ *505/287–9250* ☐ *MC, V.*

¢ ✕ **El Cafecito.** Nothing fancy, just big helpings of tasty regional favorites like enchiladas, stuffed sopaipillas, burgers, and the breakfast of Southwest champions: huevos rancheros. Chile is rich and hot. Kids are welcome and happily accommodated. ⊠ *820 E. Santa Fe Ave.* ☎ *505/285–6229* ☐ *AE, DC, MC, V.*

¢–$ ✕▥ **Ancient Way Outpost.** This pleasant oasis is made up of log cabins, a campground, and a café with a great front porch overlooking a gorgeous valley. The café, which serves breakfast, lunch, and dinner—including vegetarian plates such as their divine lasagna—is one of the best eateries in the Grants area. Log cabins provide comfortable and cozy shelter with private baths, and camping is available for tents and RVs. ⊠ *4018 Ice Caves Rd., on NM 53, 1 mi east of El Morro Nat'l Monument, not in Grants, 87020* ☎☎ *505/783–4612* ⊕ *www. elmorro-nm.com* ⇙ *6 cabins* ⚷ *Cable TV, full hookups, showers* ☐ *AE, DC, MC, V.*

$$ ▥ **The Mission at Riverwalk.** How about sleeping in the former parsonage, now guest house, of the first Protestant church built in this heavily Catholic region (1920)? Fact is, despite all the intriguing historical tidbits, interesting architecture (adobe, but not Pueblo style), on-site gallery, *and* coffeehouse (coffee-addicts rejoice, the joe is good, and guests get a free coffee drink of their choice each day), the Mission is a gracious and comfortable B&B. A complimentary bottle of wine awaits your arrival and a Jacuzzi tub will soak travel-tired muscles. The guest house is perfect for families, and management will roll extra beds (up to two,

no charge) into the living room at your request. Artist workshops are offered by one of the proprietors, Michael, who is a well-regarded painter, and a stay in the guesthouse is included in the workshop rate, which also includes painting instruction and marketing advice. ⊠ *422 W. Santa Fe Ave., 87020* ☎ *505/285–4632* ⊕ *www.grantsmission.com* ⌄ *1 room* ⚮ *King-size bed, walk-in shower, full kitchen, cable TV* ⊟ *AE, D, MC, V* ⊠ *BP.*

$–$$ ⌖ **Cimarron Rose.** Rustic Southwestern comfort is the specialty of the house at this B&B, on 20 ponderosa pine-laden acres. Proprietor Sheri McWethy has created a "green" inn, with natural-fiber sheets, no perfumes or dyes in the cleaning products, and a conscientious approach to water use. Full breakfasts are delivered to your door each morning and special dietary requests are accommodated with notice. Day packs and picnic baskets are supplied for those wanting to explore the area. Reservations are required. ⊠ *689 Oso Ridge Rte., 30 mi southwest of Grants on NM 53, 87020* ☎☎ *505/783–4770 or 800/856–5776* ⊕ *www. cimarronrose.com* ⌄ *3 rooms* ⚮ *In-room VCRs; no room phones* ⊟ *No credit cards* ⊠ *BP.*

$ ⌖ **Zuni Mountain Lodge.** Airy and tranquil, this Federal-style lodge lies at the edge of the Zuñi Mountain Range, 1 mi from Bluewater Lake State Park, south of Thoreau (pronounced "through"). Simply furnished rooms with private baths are quiet and surrounded by views of the lake and Cibola National Forest. The proprietor is a wellspring of area history and suggestions for places to explore. Included in your stay are a full breakfast and delicious dinners of hearty home-style favorites. ⊠ *40 Perch Dr., between Grants and Gallup; from I–40 Exit 53, head south 13 mi on NM 612* ✉ *Box 5114, Thoreau, 87323* ☎ *505/862–7769* 🖶 *505/862–7616* ⌄ *7 rooms* ⚮ *Internet, some pets allowed; no room phones, no room TVs* ⊟ *No credit cards* ⊠ *MAP.*

EN ROUTE   As you head toward El Morro National Monument on NM 53, you pass through the stark, volcanic rock–strewn **El Malpais National Monument and Conservation Area** (⊠ NM 53, 23 mi south of Grants ☎ 505/783–4774). The conservation area contains New Mexico's largest natural arch and has miles of hiking trails. The monument is popular for hiking as well as caving in the miles of lava tubes. Some 40 volcanoes dot 114,000 acres. There are no tourist facilities here, but a visitor center has maps and knowledgeable staff. El Malpais is not much of an attraction for the pass-through visitor, but it's well worth spending a full day or two exploring the park in depth. Backcountry camping permits are available at the visitor center, though camping is *very* primitive—no facilities exist. A quick snapshot of the volcanic landscape and terrain is best gained from the Ice Cave and Bandera Volcano.

Ice Cave & Bandera Volcano

☾ ❹ *25 mi southwest of Grants, 1 mi west of El Malpais via NM 53.*

Despite its unabashed commercialism (announced by its many somewhat-over-the-top, retro-style billboard advertisements), this roadside curiosity, set squarely on the Continental Divide, easily merits an hour of your time—the short trail from the 1930s trading post (now the gift shop) just off NM 53 affords unusual vistas of blackened lava fields and gnarled juniper and ponderosa stands. It's about a 20-minute moderately strenuous jaunt up to the 1,200-foot-diameter crater of **Bandera Volcano,** which last unleashed a torrent of lava 10,000 years ago. An even shorter walk leads to an old wooden staircase that descends 100 feet into the bowels of a collapsed lava tube, where the **Ice Cave** remains 31°F year-round and has a perpetual floor of blue-green ice. The ice remains year after year because of the combination of the air flow patterns in the lava tube and the insulating properties of the lava itself. ⊠ *12000 Ice Caves Rd.* ☎ *888/423–2283* 🖼 *$9* ⊙ *Late May–early Sept., daily 8–7; early Sept.–late May, daily 8–5.*

**OFF THE
BEATEN
PATH**

WILD SPIRIT WOLF SANCTUARY – The mystique of wolves is powerful and Wild Spirit is one of the few places where you can see them up close, in large enough enclosures that allow them to behave somewhat naturally. The staff at Wild Spirit are focused on educating the public about the dangers of trying to keep these animals, even hybrid wolf–dogs, as pets. Camping is allowed on the premises, if you have a hankering to listen to wolf howls; it's primitive and only $10 a night. The gift shop closes after the last tour, about 4:30. If you'll arrive later than that, you *must* call ahead to make arrangements. ⊠ *50 mi southwest of Grants, or 10 mi east of Ramah on NM 53, turn south onto BIA 125. Follow BIA 125 8 mi south through Mountainview. Turn right onto BIA 120. Sanctuary is 4 mi down on left.* ☎ *505/775–3304* ⊕ *www.inetdesign.com/candykitchen* 🖼 *$5* ⊙ *Thurs.–Sun., tours at 11, 1, and 3; Wed. by appt. only.*

El Morro National Monument

★ **⑤** *43 mi southwest of Grants, 15 mi west of Ice Cave and Bandera Volcano via NM 53.*

When you see the imposing 200-foot-high sandstone bluff that served as a rest stop for explorers, soldiers, and pioneers, you can understand how El Morro ("the Headlands") got its name. The bluff is the famous **Inscription Rock,** where wayfarers, beginning with Juan de Oñate in 1605, stopped to carve their names and leave messages. Petroglyphs mark the passage of travelers from earlier times. The **Inscription Trail** makes a quick ½-mi round-trip from the visitor center. While El Morro is justly renowned for Inscription Rock, try to allow an extra 90 minutes or so to venture along the spectacular, moderately strenuous 2-mi (round-trip) **Mesa Top Trail,** which meanders past the excavated edge of an extensive field of pueblo ruins, cuts along the precarious rim of a deep box canyon, and affords panoramic views of the region. The monument's **museum** chronicles 700 years of human history in this region. ⊠ *Visitor center: NM 53* ☎ *505/783–4226* 🖼 *$3 per person* ⊙ *Late May–early Sept., daily 8–7; early Sept.–late May, daily 9–5. Trails close 1 hr before monument.*

Where to Stay

⚠ **El Morro National Monument.** The park has a primitive campground amid the trees ¼ mi from the visitor center. Tap water is turned off between approximately November and March; at those times camping is free. ✉ *NM 53* ☎ *505/783–4226* ⛏ *Pit toilets, drinking water, picnic tables, public telephone* ⛺ *9 sites* 💲 *$5* ⛔ *Reservations not accepted.*

Zuñi Pueblo

❻ *35 mi west of El Morro National Monument on NM 53.*

Zuñi Pueblo has been occupied continuously since at least the year 700, and its language is unrelated to that of any other pueblo. Hawikuh, a Zuñi-speaking settlement now 12 mi south of the pueblo, was the first contacted by the Spaniards, in 1539. Francisco Vásquez de Coronado came here seeking one of the Seven Cities of Gold. He'd been tipped off by his guide, Estéban, who had seen the setting sun striking the walls of the dwellings and thought the multistoried villages were made of gold.

With a population of more than 10,000, Zuñi Pueblo is the largest of New Mexico's 19 Indian pueblos. Zuñi has a mix of buildings; modern ones in addition to traditional adobes, along with some beautifully hewn red sandstone structures more than 100 years old. The artists and craftspeople here are renowned for their masterful stone inlay, Zuñi "needlepoint" turquoise and silver jewelry, carved stone animal fetishes, pottery, and kachina figures. Weavings are becoming increasingly difficult to find as old weavers pass on and younger Zuñis don't take up the craft, but it's fine work and worth looking for if textiles are your passion.

> ### WORD OF MOUTH
>
> "It's a good couple hundred miles from Santa Fe to the Zuni Pueblo. It's all interstate driving but it's going to take you three hours. I think it would be possible to see both the pueblo and visit El Morro but it's going to be one long day."
> –obxgirl

The original **Our Lady of Guadalupe Mission,** built in 1629, was destroyed during the Pueblo Revolt of 1680 when Native Americans ousted the Spanish. In 1699 the mission was rebuilt, and in 1966 it was excavated and reconstructed in the simple late-colonial adobe style prevalent throughout New Mexico. ✉ *Old Mission Dr.* ☎ *505/782–4403* 💲 *Free* 🕐 *Weekdays 9–noon; hrs sometimes vary, call ahead.*

A:shiwi A:wan Museum and Heritage Center, which celebrates Zuñi history and culture, was built with traditional materials. The museum gives a basic orientation to the Zuñi culture, which tends to be lesser known than other pueblos because of its remoteness in the region. Artifacts, baskets, and pottery are displayed, as well as a beautiful mural depicting the peoples' history. ✉ *1222 NM 53* ☎ *505/782–4403* 💲 *Free* 🕐 *Nov.–Apr., weekdays 9–5:30; May–Oct., Mon.–Sat. 9–5:30.*

The **Zuñi Tourism Office,** staffed by helpful folks who will tell you what your options are for exploring Zuñi (as well as any special events that might be going on), is also a great source for free area maps. ✉ *1203C NM 53, in Zuñi Tribal Government complex* ☎ *505/782–7238* 🌐 *www.experiencezuni.com* 🕐 *Weekdays 9–5.*

Buying Smart: Native Arts & Crafts

WHEN YOU VISIT NORTH-WESTERN NEW MEXICO, you'll have numerous opportunities to buy Native American arts, crafts, and souvenirs. But how can you be sure the pieces you buy are "the real McCoy"—in other words, authentically Native American-made? There's a lot of fake merchandise out there, and it's sold by Native Americans and non-Native Americans alike.

Although quality arts and crafts aren't necessarily expensive, if a price for a piece seems too good to be true, it probably is. Still, knowing what you're looking for—and most important, what questions to ask—can help you determine what's worth buying and what isn't. Here are some good rules of thumb:

When buying jewelry, ask the vendor to tell you about the stones you're looking at and where they came from. Ask if the turquoise is stabilized, from block, or injected. Hand-polished American turquoise is more costly if it hasn't been stabilized or injected with dye to enhance the color, and is uniquely beautiful. Matrix, the brown or black veins in turquoise, is not a flaw, but it often provides clues as to the quality of the stone. Also ask if the jewelry settings are hand-fabricated or precast; the former will be more expensive.

If you're interested in pottery, start looking at the wares offered by the renowned potters at Acoma, although the Laguna and Zuñi pueblos also have fine potters. Ask whether you're looking at "greenware," precast commercial ceramics that come ready for the artist to apply paint, or hand-coiled pottery. Hand-coiled pots start as coils of hand-gathered clay and are built from the bottom up; feel inside a pot and for the tell-tale unevenness that distinguishes a hand-coiled pot. You can also ask what kind of paintbrush was used to embellish the pottery; traditionally, yucca-fiber brushes are used for this intricate work.

In the market for a rug? Beware of imported, foreign-made rugs with Navajo designs. These rugs may be nicely made, but they are entirely different from handwoven Navajo textiles. Authentic pieces usually have tags that identify the weaver; but you can also ask if the yarn is hand spun, hand dyed, and what types of dye were used (commercial or natural or both). A rug that is entirely hand-processed will be the most expensive, but it will also be an heirloom. And before complaining about the $5,000 price of a Two Gray Hills rug, remember that it probably took several months to weave.

Where to Stay

$
Fodor'sChoice
★

🖪 **Inn at Halona.** Your only opportunity to stay right in the heart of Zuñi, this bright and cheery inn is decorated with handwoven rugs, fine Zuñi arts and crafts, and locally made furniture. Six of the rooms have private baths, two share a bath. Outside you can relax in the tree-shaded enclosed flagstone courtyard or walk a short distance to the village plaza and several art galleries. Limited room service is available if you order ahead, or you may purchase ingredients at the grocery store next door and prepare a meal in the communal kitchen. The breakfasts are not to be missed. Between the host, the staff, and the super comfortable rooms, this is a real Southwestern standout. ✉ *23B Pia Mesa Rd., off NM 53* ✆ *Box 446, Zuñi, 87327* ☎ *505/782–4118 or 800/752–3278* 📠 *505/ 782–2155* ⊕ *www.halona.com* ⇌ *8 rooms* � *Internet, meeting rooms; no room TVs, no smoking* ☰ *MC, V* ᛏⵔᛚ *BP.*

Shopping

Zuñi Arts & Crafts (✉ 1222 NM 53, on southside of the road as you enter pueblo from east ☎ 505/782–5531) is a tribally operated shop that carries authentic Zuñi products of all kinds. In addition to an excellent selection of books on Zuñi history, arts, and culture, you can find jewelry, fetishes, and pottery. Also sold here are beautifully crafted furnishings from the Zuñi Furniture Enterprise, a woodworking cooperative on the pueblo. Handcrafted from pine and exotic woods like wormwood maple, and decorated with distinctive, highly stylized traditional motifs, these pieces are different from anything you'll find in mainstream furniture stores.

Gallup

❼ *42 mi north of Zuñi on NM 602, 138 mi west of Albuquerque on I–40.*

Known as both the Heart of Indian Country and the Indian Jewelry Capital of the World, with more than 100 trading posts that deal in Native American jewelry, pottery, rugs, and all manner of other arts and crafts, Gallup might just be the best place to acquire that concho belt or squash-blossom necklace you've always wanted. Prices are often better than those you can find in Santa Fe, and the selection is just short of overwhelming. Many of the Navajos selling their wares are from Window Rock, Arizona, the Navajo Nation's capital, 25 mi northwest of town. As elsewhere, you should be careful when buying in Gallup. Generally, if a deal seems too good to be true, it is. To assure yourself of authenticity and quality, shop at a reputable, established dealer and ask lots of questions. See "Buying Smart: Native Arts & Crafts."

Gallup originated in the 1880s as a coal-mining town, and the railroad that followed encouraged a boom. Long strings of freight cars still rumble along the tracks paralleling Historic Route 66, and train whistles hoot regularly. During the late 1920s and '30s, Gallup became a fabled stop along Route 66. When you drive down its neon-illuminated main street, you enter a retro world of pop-culture nostalgia.

The 12-block downtown section bounded by Historic Route 66, 1st Street, Hill Avenue, and 4th Street is best explored on foot. You can browse through the trading posts and get a glimpse of 19th-century architecture. The small but lively contemporary arts scene is best enjoyed on the first Saturday of every month during the **Arts Crawl** (☎ 505/863–3841), held in the evening on West Coal Avenue. Galleries such as **Crashing Thunder** (✉ 226 W. Coal Ave.) open their doors with new shows, while coffeehouses and shops offer snacks and entertainment.

The newly renovated 1928 "Pueblo Deco" **El Morro Theater** (✉ 207 W. Coal Ave. ☎ 505/726–0050) is a shining example of a unique regional building style. El Morro tends to be open sporadically for events and the occasional film fest, call to find out what's on the schedule. Walk one block south of Route 66 to have a look.

NEED A BREAK? The **Coffee House** (⊠ 203 W. Coal Ave., 1 block south of Rte. 66 ☎ 505/726–0291) serves delicious coffees, teas, and Italian sodas in addition to salads, sandwiches, and sweet treats. This friendly, family-run community house of sorts is also a gallery, with exhibits of local artists' works changing monthly. On weekend evenings you're likely to catch a poetry reading or an open-mike night.

Clothing, furniture, tools, and typewriters are among the artifacts of the coal-mining era on display at the **Rex Museum**, operated by the Gallup Historical Society inside the former Rex Hotel. ⊠ *300 W. Historic Rte. 66* ☎ *505/863–1363* ⊠ *$2* ☉ *Weekdays 9–3:30, Sat. 9–3, later in summer.*

Part of the **Gallup Cultural Center,** a project of the Southwest Indian Foundation, is inside the restored 1927 Atchison, Topeka & Santa Fe Railway station, a gem of a building designed by Mary E. Coulter. Buses and trains still run in and out of the station. The cultural center includes a café (where you can lunch or sip coffee out of replicas of the china used on AT&S trains), a cinema that screens documentaries about the Southwest, and two dozen dioramas that relate the history of area native peoples, western expansion, and the building of the railroads. In summer there are Native American dances in the courtyard at 7 every night. ⊠ *201 E. Historic Rte. 66* ☎ *505/863–4131* ⊠ *Free* ☉ *Late May–early Sept., daily 9–9; early Sept.–late May, daily 9–4.*

In spring, summer, and early fall, wildflowers add brilliance to the landscape of **Red Rock State Park,** which has a small nature trail, and campgrounds.

The park's red-rock amphitheater holds Gallup's premier event, the **Inter-Tribal Indian Ceremonial** (☎ 800/233–4528), each August. About 50,000 people come to see the dances of more than 30 tribes, watch rodeo events and parades, and stroll the marketplaces. The **Red Rocks Museum** contains exhibits of jewelry, pottery, rugs, architecture, and tools of the Anasazi, Zuñi, Hopi, and Navajo. ⊠ *NM 566, Exit 31 from I–40, 7 mi east of Gallup* ☎ *505/722–3829* ⊠ *Park free, museum $1* ☉ *Park Nov.–Feb., daily 8–4:30; Mar.–mid-May, daily 8–6; mid-May–mid-Sept., daily 7:30 AM–10 PM; mid-Sept.–Oct., daily 7:30–6. Museum Mon.–Sat. 8:30–4:30.*

OFF THE BEATEN PATH **CANYON DE CHELLY NATIONAL MONUMENT** – Ninety-eight miles northwest of Gallup, past Window Rock on AZ Route 264, Canyon de Chelly—pronounced de-*shay*—is well worth the drive and a day of exploring. Amid its fascinating pueblo ruins, Navajo residents farm and raise sheep in the canyon. The

WORD OF MOUTH

"To go into the canyon at Canyon de Chelly you are only allowed to take the Whitehouse ruins trail on your own. If you want to do any more exploring of the canyon, it has to be with a Navajo guide."

–utahtea

visitor center and museum are open all year, and from there you can book canyon tours with Navajo guides or drive the canyon rim and take the self-guided hikes. A guide will cost about $15 per hour, per vehicle, and is well worth doing if your budget allows. ⊠ *AZ Rte. 264, 3 mi east of AZ Rte. 191, Chinle, AZ* ☎ *520/674–5500* 🎫 *Free* ⊙ *May–Sept., daily 8–6; Oct.–Apr., daily 8–5.*

Where to Stay & Eat

★ **$-$$** ✕ **Earl's Restaurant.** If you have time for only one meal in Gallup, do as most folks do and head to Earl's. The home-style rib-sticking daily specials here include meat loaf and fried chicken with mashed potatoes, as well as some of the best green chile in all New Mexico. This is a classic Southwestern diner, down to the Naugahyde booths and the Western Americana objects hanging on the walls. It's a custom here for Native American jewelry vendors to go table-to-table displaying their wares. Simply say "No, thank you" if you're not interested and the vendor will leave. ⊠ *1400 E. Historic Rte. 66* ☎ *505/863–4201* ⌘ *Reservations not accepted* ▭ *AE, D, DC, MC, V.*

<table>
<tr><td>

> **WORD OF MOUTH**
>
> "We really liked Earl's. The food was Tex Mex and yummy, and it was fun to see the different beads, silver, and other items that children/adults carried table to table for sale. It had a sort of old-time diner feel."   –sfamylou

</td></tr>
</table>

¢–$ ✕ **Coal Street Pub.** Gallup's first pub has arrived at long last. There are plenty of bars in this town, for sure, but this is a friendly, relaxed pub, locally owned by the Chavez family. A good selection of beer is backed up with tasty Western favorites: burgers, bratwurst, steaks, salads, fish, and crispy, gooey appetizers. ⊠ *303 W. Coal Ave.* ☎ *505/722–0117* ▭ *AE, D, MC, V.*

¢ ✕ **Eagle Cafe.** Not much has changed through the years at this 80-year-old diner. For a taste of the past, slide into a red-vinyl booth and watch trains chug by as you munch on mutton stew, enchiladas, or a burger. ⊠ *220 W. Historic Rte. 66* ☎ *505/722–3220* ⌘ *Reservations not accepted* ▭ *No credit cards* ⊙ *Closed Sun.*

★ **$** ✕🖾 **El Rancho.** Book a night in the Katharine Hepburn or Ronald Reagan room—all units at this National Register historic property are named for vintage movie stars, many of whom stayed here back when Hollywood westerns were shot in the region—for a combination of aging '50s-era nostalgia and Old West glamour. Rooms are basic, accented with Western prints and a few other flourishes. The restaurant (¢–$$$), open all day, serves acceptable American and Mexican food. You can browse through the respected on-site art gallery for pottery, kachinas, and sand paintings. ⊠ *1000 E. Historic Rte. 66, 87301* ☎ *505/863–9311 or 800/543–6351* 🖶 *505/722–5917* 🛏 *73 rooms, 3 suites* ⌘ *Restaurant, bar, no-smoking rooms* ▭ *AE, D, MC, V.*

¢ 🖾 **Sleep Inn.** Sleep here and you can get a reasonably priced motel room with all the basics: chairs, a dresser, TV with remote, and a phone. The pool offers a wonderful, wet respite from the dry desert climate. ⊠ *3820 E. Historic Rte. 66, 87301* ☎ *505/863–3535 or 800/753–3746* 🖶 *505/*

722–3737 ⟴ 61 rooms ♨ In-room data ports, indoor pool, hot tub, no-smoking rooms ☰ AE, D, DC, MC, V.

⚠ **Canyon de Chelly National Monument.** Rustling cottonwood trees shade campsites that serve both RVs and tents. ⊠ AZ Rte. 264, 3 mi east of AZ Rte. 191, Chinle, AZ ☎ 520/674–5500 ♨ Flush toilets, dump station, drinking water, fire pits, picnic tables, public telephone ⟴ 104 tent and RV sites ▨ Free ⚱ Reservations not accepted.

⚠ **Red Rock State Park.** Red rocks loom 500 feet over the park's paved campsites, which are surrounded by red sand and shady trees. ⊠ NM 566, Exit 31 from I–40, 7 mi east of Gallup ☎ 505/722–3829 ♨ Flush toilets, partial hookups, dump station, drinking water, showers, fire pits, picnic tables, public telephone, ranger station ⟴ 160 RV sites ▨ $14 ☰ MC, V.

Shopping

Kiva Gallery (⊠ 202 W. Historic Rte. 66 ☎ 505/722–5577) exhibits art of the American Indian, including many original paintings.

At **Richardson's Trading Company** (⊠ 222 W. Historic Rte. 66 ☎ 505/ 722–4762), the great-granddaddy of trading posts, the wooden floors creak under your feet as you gawk at the knockout array of Navajo and Zuñi turquoise and silver earrings, squash blossoms, concho belts, bracelets, natural-dye handwoven rugs, and beadwork. Richardson's is also a veritable museum of old pawn (the often valuable, unclaimed items pawned by local Native Americans). The fourth generation of the Tanner trading family runs **Shush Yaz Trading Co.** (⊠ 1304 W. Lincoln Ave. ☎ 505/722–0130), which stocks all manner of Native American arts and crafts, including locally made Navajo squaw skirts. The store sells traditional and contemporary jewelry and is a great source of old pawn. The on-site restaurant serves native foods. **Tobe Turpen's Indian Trading Post** (⊠ 1710 S. 2nd St. ☎ 505/722–3806) has been in business for more than 80 years, selling kachinas, sand paintings, jewelry, folk art, and more.

▌ EN
ROUTE

Held the third Friday of (most) every month, the **Crownpoint Rug Auction** (⊠ Crownpoint Elementary School, NM 371, 26 mi north of Thoreau at I–40, Exit 53 ☎ 505/786–7386 ⊕ www.crownpointrugauction.com) is the foremost place to buy handwoven Navajo rugs—you're bidding with a mix of collectors and dealers, so prices on the some 300 to 400 rugs are sometimes well below what you'd pay at a store. Viewing begins at 4, with the actual auction running from 7 usually until midnight or later. Keep in mind there are no overnight facilities in Crownpoint, though there is a food and drink concession at the auction. Call ahead to confirm auction dates. Cash, traveler's checks, personal checks only; no credit cards.

ANASAZI COUNTRY

To gain a sense of the beauty, power, and complexity of the ancient civilizations of the Americas, you can do no better than to travel to Chaco Canyon, sometimes called the "Stonehenge of the West," and the more

INTO THE WILDERNESS

Dinosaurs roamed the Bisti and De-Na-Zin Wilderness areas when they were part of a shallow sea some 70 million years ago. Hoodoos (mushroom-shape rock formations in subtle shades of brown, gray, and white) lend the 45,000 acres an eerie, lunarlike appearance. De-Na-Zin (pronounced duh-*nah*-zen and named for a petroglyph found nearby) is the much larger and less visited of the two sections, and here you can find hillier and more challenging terrain, plus numerous fossils and petrified logs. At Bisti (pronounced *biss*-tye), you can encounter deeply eroded hoodoos whose striations represent layers of sandstone, shale, mudstone, coal, and silt. In many spots you'll climb over mounds of crumbly clay and silt that looks a bit like the topping of a coffee cake (but gray). Both sections are ideal for photography, and backcountry camping is permitted—and not to be missed during a full moon, if your timing is good. The Bureau of Land Management, which administers the land, asks that you remove nothing from either area, preserving its magical appearance for those who follow. The most fascinating terrain is 2 to 3 mi from the parking areas, and there are no trails, so bring a compass and be alert about your surroundings and where you are in relation to the sun—it's relatively easy to get lost in this vast, incredible place. And how 'bout bringing some more water? ✉ *Bisti: NM 371, 36 mi south of Farmington; De-Na-Zin: unpaved CR 7500, off either NM 371 8 mi south of Bisti entrance or NM 44 at Huerfano, 34 mi south of Bloomington* ☎ *505/599-8900.*

accessible Salmon Ruins and Aztec Ruins. Discoveries of the past 30 years, notably the Sun Dagger, which appears at a particular point in Chaco Canyon on each summer solstice, have increased interest in the science of archaeoastronomy—the study of the ways in which ancient peoples surveyed the skies, kept track of the movement of the planets and stars, and marked their passage within the construction of elaborate stone structures. But Anasazi Country is more than ancient ruins. Spectacular hiking, camping, and fishing can be had here, and you can poke through small towns that are the products of northwestern New Mexico's homesteading era. The best shopping is for antiques and Native American jewelry and pottery.

Farmington

❽ *142 mi north of Gallup via I–40 east to NM 371 north.*

A rough-and-tumble, unpretentious town full of pickup trucks, whose radio dial is loaded with country-and-western stations, Farmington sits in the heart of the Four Corners region (so called because four different states all intersect here). Archaeological, recreational, and scenic wonders are within easy driving distance, and its reasonable prices and friendly ways make it an ideal base for exploring the area.

The Navajo gave the name *Totah* ("among the waters") to the land around what is now Farmington, which lies at the confluence of three rivers—the Animas, La Plata, and San Juan. For both travelers and locals, the presence of these flowing waters gives welcome respite from the surrounding region's dry mesas. Homesteaders began planting farms and orchards on the fertile land in 1879, and the "farming town" eventually became Farmington.

The agricultural economy shifted to one based on oil and gas in the late 1940s, beginning a boom-and-bust cycle tied to the fluctuation of fuel prices. Diversification didn't come until the past decade or so, when Farmington began promoting its historic past with more gusto. Even more revitalizing was the creation of a regional shopping center, which swells the population by thousands on weekends. People from miles around make their weekly or monthly trip to town to stock up on supplies.

You can get an inkling of what the Four Corners area was like during the trading-post days at the **Farmington Gateway Museum and Visitors Center,** in a spectacular modern sandstone building whose stonework closely resembles the Aztec and Chaco ruins. Landscaped grounds behind the building, where the Farmington Convention and Visitors Bureau is, extend down to the Animus River—an ideal spot for a picnic. The museum contains a permanent trading post exhibit and also presents art, science, Native American, and regional history exhibits throughout the year. Occasionally a traveling exhibit will require an entrance fee; otherwise, admission is free. There's a summertime music series on the terrace; 6–7:30 PM, call for dates and performers. ⊠ *3041 E. Main St.* ☎ *505/ 599–1174* 🖅 *Free, $2 donation requested* ☉ *Mon.–Sat. 9–5, Sun. noon–5* ⊕ *www.farmingtonmuseum.org.*

☺ If the kids are getting restless, try stopping by the **E3 Children's Museum.** The interactive exhibits here include a shadow room, a magnet table, giant floor puzzles, and a role-play area. It's a great spot to rest and regroup. ⊠ *302 N. Orchard Ave.* ☎ *505/599–1425* 🖅 *Free* ☉ *Tues.–Sat. noon–5.*

The **River Corridor,** a 5-mi walkway between Scott Avenue and U.S. 64 along the Animas River, winds alongside Berg Park. The corridor contains trails for walkers, runners, cyclists, and wildlife- and bird-watchers, as well as a man-made, 300-yard-long white-water course.

**OFF THE
BEATEN
PATH**

SHIPROCK PINNACLE – West of Farmington, at U.S. 666 and U.S. 64, the 1,700-foot Shiprock Pinnacle rises from the desert floor like a massive schooner. It's sacred to the Navajo, who call it Tse'Bit'Ai, or "rock with wings." No climbing or hiking is permitted. The pinnacle is composed of igneous rock flanked by upright walls of solidified lava.

FOUR CORNERS MONUMENT – About 30 mi west of Shiprock you can reach the only place in the United States where you can stand in four states at the same time—at the intersection of New Mexico, Arizona, Colorado, and Utah. There's no view to speak of at this popular attraction, though Native American artisans do sell their wares here nearly every day of the year. ⊠ *U.S. 160, north from U.S. 64* ☎ *928/871–6647* 🖅 *$3* ☉ *May–Aug., daily 7 AM–8 PM; Sept.–Apr., daily 8–5.*

Where to Stay & Eat

$$–$$$$ ✕ **K. B. Dillon's.** The punched tin ceiling and dark wood furnishings feed the appeal of this clubby steak house, but it's the food that keeps people coming back to splurge on really fine beef, fish, and pasta creations. Ask for the local, grass-fed beef; it's a taste revelation for steak aficionados. There's live music on weekend nights. ⊠ *101 W. Broadway* ☎ *505/325–0222* ▤ *AE, MC, V* ☉ *Closed Sun.*

★ **$–$$** ✕ **Three Rivers Eatery & Brewhouse.** In a historic downtown building with a gorgeous pressed-tin ceiling, exposed air ducts, and walls lined with historic photos, this microbrewery whips up more than 10 kinds of beer (also available to go) with names like Power Plant Porter and Chaco Nut Brown Ale. The brews go well with the enormous portions of tasty soups, salads, burgers, ribs, and other pub grub served here (although Mandarin Tilapia hardly qualifies as "typical"–delicious, nonetheless). The staff is friendly and inclined to get you something special from the kitchen if you ask nicely. ⊠ *101 E. Main St.* ☎ *505/324–2187* ⊕ *www. threeriversbrewery.com* ⚇ *Reservations not accepted* ▤ *AE, D, MC, V* ☉ *Closed Sun.*

¢ ✕ **El Charro Cafe.** Don't be put off by El Charro's out-of-the-way location or slightly tattered decor. Locals who demand authentic Mexican fare head here for lunch. The red chile is hot and terrific, and the combination plate—including a tamale, an enchilada, a burrito, and guacamole, rice, and beans—might be the only meal you need all day. ⊠ *737 W. Main St.* ☎ *505/327–2464* ⚇ *Reservations not accepted* ▤ *AE, D, DC, MC, V* ☉ *No dinner Sun.*

¢ ✕ **The Spare Rib.** The decor here is nothing fancy—just plastic tablecloths over picnic tables—but the whole family can fill up on generous portions of delicious smoked pork and beef barbecue. Ribs and brisket are as tender as they come, all slow-cooked in house-made sauce. ⊠ *1700 E. Main St.* ☎ *505/325–4800* ⚇ *Reservations not accepted* ▤ *AE, D, MC, V* ☉ *Closed Sun.*

★ **$$$** 🏨 **Kokopelli's Cave.** Carved into the cliff-side 250 feet above La Plata River and adjoining a wildlife refuge, this spacious one-bedroom cave's exposed sandstone walls trace 70 million years of erosion history. The cave has fireplace, full kitchen (stocked with Continental breakfast supplies), and a stone shower with a waterfall trickling into a hot tub. Two terraces afford breathtaking views, and a trail on the cliff face runs some 70 vertical feet to the parking area. The cave accommodates up to six people and remains a temperate 72°F year-round. It's recommended that you book at least one month in advance. ⊠ *206 W. 38th St., 87401* ☎ *505/325–7855* 🖷 *505/325–9671* ⊕ *www.bbonline.com/nm/kokopelli* ⤴ *1 unit* ⚿ *In-room VCR; no a/c, no kids under 12, no smoking* ▤ *AE, MC, V* ⵔ *CP.*

$$ 🏨 **Casa Blanca Inn.** Luxury without pretense is the trademark at this Mission-style inn, which stands atop a bluff overlooking Farmington. You can relax in the Southwestern-style den or near the patio's fountain, or watch city lights twinkle from the solarium. One room has a two-person hot tub, another has a fireplace, and all receive turn-down service. Breakfast is a gourmet affair, and fresh-baked goodies are served in the afternoon. Business travelers seeking a homey atmosphere make it a point

5

to stay in this little oasis. ⊠ *505 E. La Plata St., 87401* ☎ *505/327–6503 or 800/550–6503* 🖶 *505/326–5680* ⊕ *www.4cornersbandb.com* ⇨ *4 rooms, 1 suite* ♤ *Cable TV, Internet, meeting rooms; no smoking* ▤ *AE, D, MC, V* ⏏ *BP.*

$–$$ 🔲 **Silver River Adobe Inn.** Take a deep breath and relax at this red-roof adobe sitting on a sandstone cliff 30 feet above where the San Juan River meets La Plata, at the west end of town. Rough-hewn timbers, fluffy quilts, and complete privacy make this rustic getaway ideal for romance or rumination, though the property and the proprietors are definitely kid-friendly. The proprietors, Diana Ohlson and David Beers, are excellent sources of information about adventures and explorations in the area. The Inn's organic, home-style breakfasts are a great start to the day. ⊠ *3151 W. Main St., Box 3411, 87499* ☎ *505/325–8219 or 800/382–9251* ⊕ *www.silveradobe.com* ⇨ *2 rooms, 1 suite* ♤ *Some kitchenettes, meeting room; no room TVs* ▤ *AE, MC, V* ⏏ *BP.*

$ 🔲 **Comfort Inn.** Though a chain hotel, this lodging stands out for the gracious and helpful staff. Modern, comfortable rooms and a very generous Continental breakfast make it a bargain. ⊠ *555 Scott Ave., 87401* ☎ *505/325–2626 or 800/341–1495* 🖶 *505/325–7675* ⇨ *42 rooms, 18 suites* ♤ *Cable TV with movies, pool, meeting rooms* ▤ *AE, D, DC, MC, V* ⏏ *CP.*

Nightlife

Several of the restaurants in Farmington and Aztec are popular for cocktails, notably K. B. Dillon's and Three Rivers Eatery & Brewhouse. Both have music on weekend nights. From Wednesday to Saturday, regional history and other plays are performed at the **Outdoor Summer Theater** (⊠ Lion's Wilderness Park, College Blvd. at Piñon Hills Blvd. ☎ 505/327–9336 or 800/448–1240) between mid-June and mid-August at 8 in a sandstone amphitheater. An optional Southwestern-style dinner is served prior to each performance. **San Juan College Theater** (⊠ 4601 College Blvd. ☎ 505/326–3311 Ext. 364) presents concerts, student recitals, lectures, and theatrical performances.

Sports & the Outdoors

FISHING   The rivers in this region are a great place to learn fly-fishing, and Harry Lane of **San Juan Troutfitters** (☎ 505/324–8149 ⊕ www.sanjuantroutfitters. com) is the guy to teach you. He conducts private and group classes and runs guided fishing trips—a great activity for a family vacation. A three-day course starts at $300 per person; rates drop significantly with each additional person. Call ahead to make arrangements.

WATER SPORTS   **Farmington Aquatic Center** (⊠ 1151 N. Sullivan St. ☎ 505/599–1167), a public water wonderland, has a 150-foot-long waterslide and three pools. Prices for the pool and slide are $5 for adults, $3.25–$4.50 for children; those under 2 get in free. Open 1–7:30.

Shopping

The historic trading-post district along Main Street downtown is a good place to look for antiques, especially 20th-century Southwestern Americana. Stores at the gargantuan **Animas Valley Mall** (⊠ 4601 E. Main St. ☎ 505/326–5465) include Dillard's, Sears Roebuck, JCPenney, and Western Warehouse, plus specialty shops like Home Sweet Home. The debut of the ubiquitous Gap clothing chain a few years back was a sign of the region's steadily growing prosperity.

It's easy to while away an afternoon at the **Dusty Attic** (⊠ 111 W. Main St. ☎ 505/327–7696), a 17,000-square-foot downtown mall where you can find antiques, arts, crafts, and gifts. **Fifth Generation Trading Co.** (⊠ 232 W. Broadway ☎ 505/326–3211), an old trading post run by the Tanner family since 1875, has a wealth of Native American wares and is known for sand paintings. Creaky wooden floors add to the charm of **Foutz Indian Room** (⊠ 301 W. Main St. ☎ 505/325–9413), which sells superb Navajo folk art and old pawn. About a half-hour drive west of town is the **Hogback Trading Co.** (⊠ 3221 U.S. 64 ☎ 505/598–5154), a trading post known for fine, handwoven Navajo rugs.

Salmon Ruins

9 *10 mi east of Farmington on U.S. 64.*

Salmon (pronounced *sol*-mon) Ruins, which dates from the 11th century, is a large Chacoan Anasazi living complex on the northern edge of the San Juan River. A stunning example of pre-Columbian Pueblo architecture and stonework, the site is named for a homesteader whose family protected the ruins for nearly a century. **Heritage Park** contains the restored Salmon Homestead, a root cellar, bunkhouse, sweat lodge, hogan, and other types of Native housing structures. ⊠ 6131 U.S. 64 ☎ 505/632–2013 🖾 $3 ⊘ Apr.–Oct., daily 9–5; Nov.–Mar., Mon.–Sat. 8–5, Sun. noon–5.

Aztec

10 *14 mi northeast of Farmington on U.S. 550, 10 mi north of Bloomfield on NM 544.*

The many Victorian brick buildings and quaint outlying residential blocks give charming Aztec, the seat of San Juan County, the feeling of a picture-book hometown. Adding to the allure are the views of the far-distant snowcap mountains north of Durango, Colorado, toward Telluride. The village part of the **Aztec Museum, Pioneer Village and Oil Field Exhibit** contains more than a dozen late-19th-century buildings—a blacksmith shop, a schoolhouse, a wooden oil derrick, and a log cabin, among others—that convey a sense of life as it used to be lived in these parts. ⊠ 125 N. Main St. ☎ 505/334–9829 🖾 Free ⊘ Late May–early Sept., Mon.–Sat. 9–5; early Sept.–late May, Mon.–Sat. 10–4.

★ Dating from the early 1100s, North America's largest reconstructed Great Kiva (a partially submerged, circular earthen structure used for ceremonial and community-wide activities) and a pueblo dwelling that once contained more than 500 rooms, **Aztec Ruins National Monument and Museum,** makes for a fun and interesting stop. The Ruins have been designated a World Heritage Site because of their significance in what is known as the Chaco Phenomenon, the extensive multitribal social and economic system that reached far beyond Chaco Canyon. This pueblo was abandoned by the mid-1200s. Early homesteaders thought they'd come across an ancient Aztec ruin, hence the odd name. You only need an hour or so to tour the ruin, which is less spectacular but considerably more accessible than those at Chaco. The reconstructed kiva here offers a rare chance to get inside one of these multipurpose structures and get a real feeling for what it might have been like to have been one of the participants at the time. The breadth of uses for kivas is still not entirely understood, even today. ⊠ *84 Ruins Rd., ¾ mi north of U.S. 550* ☎ *505/334–6174* ✍ *$4* ☉ *Late May–early Sept., daily 8–6; early Sept.–late May, daily 8–5.*

Where to Stay & Eat

¢–$ ✕ **Hiway Grill.** There's a '50s era car stuck in the facade of the building; inside, the vintage car photos, art deco tables, red vinyl booths, and superfriendly staff give this place the feel of a '50s malt shop. Many of the American and New Mexican dishes, like the Mustang Melt (a burger with grilled onions and melted Swiss on rye with Thousand Island dressing), are named for classic cars. Only order a shake if you've really got an appetite or someone to share it with; vanilla is a favorite. ⊠ *401 N.E. Aztec Blvd.* ☎ *505/334–6533* 🖃 *AE, D, DC, MC, V* ☉ *Closed Sun.*

¢ 🍴 ✕ **Main Street Bistro.** When just the thought of one more plate of heavy food in hot weather makes you want to *cry,* forestall a meltdown by coming here. Quiches, soups, fritattas, and delicious sandwiches will set you straight, as will their excellent coffee. The Bistro Special is a grilled portobello mushroom sandwich with mixed greens, tomato, sprouts, and a homemade Italian feta dressing. Also quite worthy is the Ultimate, a croissant with thin sliced turkey, avocado, greens, red onion, crispy bacon, provolone, and creamy avocado dressing. Fresh pastries and desserts are available daily. ⊠ *122 N. Main St., across from Aztec Museum* ☎ *505/ 334–0109* 🖃 *D, MC, V* ☉ *No dinner.*

$ ✕🖼 **Miss Gail's Inn.** On Main Street just steps from the town's best antiquing (and the Aztec Museum), this rambling redbrick Victorian has charming rooms enlivened with quilts, antiques, and collectibles. Delicious home-cooked breakfasts are a super way to start the day. ⊠ *300 S. Main St., 87410* ☎ *505/334–3452 or 888/534–3452* 🖶 *505/334–9664* 🛏 *8 rooms* ᗙ *Some kitchenettes, cable TV* 🖃 *AE, D, MC, V* ⦁⦿⦁ *CP.*

$ 🖼 **Step Back Inn.** Though technically a modern motor hotel, this Victorian-style clapboard structure on the north edge of downtown offers a considerably more memorable experience than you can have at any of the countless chain properties in nearby Farmington, and at similar prices. The public areas are inviting, and individually decorated rooms have a mix of newer pieces and reproduction antiques, floral wallpaper, and cozy chenille bedspreads. ⊠ *U.S. 550 at NM 544, 87410* ☎ *505/334– 1200 or 800/334–1255* 🖶 *505/334–9858* 🛏 *40 rooms* 🖃 *AE, MC, V* ⦁⦿⦁ *CP.*

⛰ **Angel Peak Recreation Area.** Get the feel of the canyon rim country and enjoy a hike through badlands formed by an ancient seabed before you pitch your tent. The last 6 mi of road leading to this primitive site are gravel. ⊠ *Rte. 7175, 20 mi south of Bloomfield* ☎ *505/599–8900* ᗙ *Pit toilets, picnic tables* 🛏 *7 sites* ✍ *Free.*

MY ROUTE 66

Georgia de Katona
Writer, avid motorist

So much has been written about Route 66 that I'm almost embarrassed to admit my fascination with it. Almost involuntarily I turn onto its crumbling asphalt, cruising slowly past countless broken-down establishments in remote parts of New Mexico and beyond. From my abiding curiosity grows a hope that I'll see signs of life reemerging in some of the sweetest old towns you're ever likely to see.

I'm happy to report that Albuquerque's stretch of Route 66 is, for the most part, a treasure trove of vitality and variety. Hip restaurants and shops, the huge University of New Mexico, brew pubs, groovy thrift stores, and art galleries populate the route across the city. Multiple lifestyles, ethnicities, and eccentricities are on full display. Route 66 as it exists in Albuquerque today is the one place in the state that might possibly live up to the nostalgic language referring to the route as the "embodiment of all that makes this nation great." But, wow, that's a lot to live up to.

The stretch of 66 from Albuquerque through most of eastern New Mexico is a reminder that the transition from highway to freeway was rough on many little towns whose lifeblood were the motorists themselves. Places like San Jon (pronounced "hone"), Montoya, Cuervo, San Fidel, and Bluewater provide homes for just a few remaining residents these days. This is where the Route is missed.

Tucumcari's lovely old downtown, just a few blocks north of Route 66, is all but abandoned, it's ornate and intriguing early-20th-century buildings succumbing to age and neglect.

At many points on the road, the memory of what's no longer there is less troubling than what is: in Gallup, Santa Rosa, and parts of Albuquerque the road is sprinkled with pedestrian big box stores, an almost boundless variety of mediocre restaurants, vendors of pseudo-Western and "Indian" trinkets made in China, and other schlock that's bound to make passing motorists and born-and-bread Westerners (like yours truly) lament the state of an American icon.

In such moments of despair about Route 66, there is often a simple antidote: neon. Amid the decay and blandness is an abundance of neon in crazy, kitschy themes and otherworldy colors. It outlives the attention span of property owners, tourists, and highway planners. Its glow draws folks like Connie and Jean (who I met at the Blue Swallow in Tucumcari, and again in Santa Rosa when they saved me from a terrible restaurant). It tempts them with the allure of driving from Chicago all the way to Santa Monica on a road that really has shaped the American psyche.

Navajo Dam

⑪ *26 mi east of Aztec on NM 173.*

Navajo Dam is the name of a tiny town a few miles below Navajo Lake State Park, as well as the name of the dam itself. At the base of the dam lie the legendary trout waters of the San Juan River. One of the country's top five trophy-trout streams, the San Juan has year-round fishing for rainbow, brown, and cutthroat trout. Many areas are catch-and-release only. The San Juan carves a scenic gorge of stepped cliffs along cottonwood-lined banks that attract elk, Barbary sheep, golden and bald eagles, blue herons, and not a few fly-fisherfolk in waders.

As you drive up over the dam you can be rewarded with panoramic views down into the valley. **Navajo Lake State Park** is a popular boating and fishing spot; you can rent boats at two marinas. Short trails lead to the lakeshore, and the 3-mi-long cottonwood-shaded San Juan River Trail parallels the river down below the dam. Driving the narrow road across the top of the dam, with no guardrails, is a slightly hair-raising, memorable experience. ⊠ *1448 NM 511, off NM 173* ☎ *505/632–2278* ⊠ *$4 per vehicle.*

Where to Stay

$–$$$ ⊞ **Soaring Eagle Lodge.** A haven for fly-fishers who want casual but upscale accommodations, this lodge houses guests in cabins that are fully furnished, complete with kitchenettes and rod-and-wader racks. You can step out of your cabin to a mile and a half of private river access, or take advantage of the on-site guide service and full fly shop. The food here is excellent, so the package that includes breakfast and dinner is a good choice. ⊠ *NM 511, 2 mi south of Navajo Dam, 87419* ☎ *505/632–3721 or 800/866–2719* ⊕ *www.soaringeaglelodge.net* ⇨ *11 cabins* ⚇ *Kitchenettes, cable TV with movies, Internet, meeting rooms* ⦿⃝ *MAP.*

⚠ **Navajo Lake State Park.** At the park's three campgrounds some sites sit among piñon and juniper trees and overlook the lake. Hot showers are available at Sims Mesa and Pine campgrounds but not at Cottonwood Campground. ⊠ *1448 NM 511, off NM 173* ☎ *505/632–2278* ⚇ *Flush toilets, dump station, drinking water, fire pits, picnic tables* ⇨ *200 sites* ▣ *Tent sites $10, RV sites $14 with electricity, $18 with full hookup.*

Sports & the Outdoors

Stop by **Abe's Motel & Fly Shop/Born-n-Raised on the San Juan** (⊠ 1791 NM 173 ☎ 505/632–2194 ⊕ www.sanjuanriver.com) to find out what flies you need to snare the wily San Juan rainbows, book a wade or float trip, or just to pick up a cold drink and snacks. There's also lodging here, although it's nothing fancy ($64 per room; 59 rooms in all). If you're hungry for more than chips, El Pescador's Restaurant & Lounge is next door. At the revered **Rizuto's Fly Shop** (⊠ 1796 NM 173 ☎ 505/632–3893), you can pick up fishing tips or book a guide.

Chaco Culture National Historical Park

⑫ *144 mi west of Abiquiu via NM 96 to NM 44/U.S. 550 to (unpaved)*
Fodor's Choice *NM 57 south; 90 mi south of Farmington via NM 44/U.S. 550 to (un-*
★ *paved) NM 57 south; 78 mi north of Grants via I–40 west to (unpaved)*
NM 57 north.

The roads accessing **Chaco Canyon,** home to Chaco Culture National Historical Park, do a fine job of deterring exploration: They are dirt roads and can be very muddy and/or icy during inclement weather (particularly Route 57 from the south). The silver lining is that the dirt roads leading in—and the lack of gas stations, food concessions, or hotels once you get off the highway—keep this archaeological treasure free from the overcrowding that can mar other national park visits: only about 85,000 people visit annually, compared with at least 10 times that number to Canyon de Chelly, which is 80 mi away as the crow flies.

Once past the rough roads you'll see one of the most amazingly well-preserved and fascinating ruin sites on the continent. The excavations here have uncovered what was once the center of a vast multitribal community—the locus of a system of ancient roads that radiated 400 mi outward from Chaco Canyon. The majority of these roads, and the buildings and dwellings that make up the canyon site, were constructed between 900 and 1,150 years ago. Several of the ancient structures—such as Pueblo Bonito, which once stood five stories tall and held 800 rooms—are astounding, although there's still a shroud of mystery surrounding them. Did 5,000 people really once live here, as some archaeologists believe? Or was Chaco maintained as a ceremonial and trade center? The more that's learned about such phenomena as the Sun Dagger—a petroglyph that's bisected by the same spear of sunlight at each summer solstice—the more questions arise about the sophistication of the people that created them.

At the **visitor center** you can meander through a small museum on Chaco culture, peruse the bookstore, and buy bottled water (but no food). From here you can drive along the paved loop road to the various trailheads for the ruins; at each you can find a small box containing a detailed self-guided tour brochure (a 50¢ donation per map is requested). Many of the 13 ruins at Chaco require a significant hike, but a few of the most impressive are just a couple hundred yards off the road. The stargazing here is spectacular: there is a small observatory and numerous telescopes, which are brought out for star parties; ask about the schedule at the front desk.

Pueblo Bonito is the largest and most dramatic of the Chaco Canyon ruins, a massive semicircular "great house" that once stood five stories in places and encompasses many kivas and interconnected cells. The park trail runs alongside the outer mortar-and-sandstone walls, up a hill that allows a great view over the entire canyon, and then right through the ruin and several rooms. It's the most substantial of the structures—the ritualistic and cultural center of a Chacoan culture that may once have comprised some 150 settlements. Pueblo Bonito was used from AD 850 to about 1150, longer than any other area ruin. ✉ *Take U.S. 550 3 mi east of Nageezi, then turn south onto CR 7900, follow signs* ☎ *505/ 786-7014* ✉ *$8 per vehicle* ☉ *Late May–early Sept., daily 8–6; early Sept.–late May, daily 8–5.*

Where to Stay

⚠ **Chaco Culture National Historical Park.** Not far from the visitor center is a park service–operated campground. The site's primitiveness is its greatest asset: at night the skies come alive with stars, and the only noises you can hear are those of nature. The primary advantage of staying here is waking up in the canyon and having a full day to explore the ruins and perhaps hike some of the backcountry trails. Camping is limited to seven days; vehicles up to 30 feet can park here. Drinking water is available at the visitor center. Starting in early May it's best to arrive as early in the day as possible; the campground fills quickly. ✉ *Take U.S. 550 3 mi east of Nageezi, then turn south onto CR 7900, follow signs* ☎ *505/786-7014* ⚫ *Flush toilets, fire grates, picnic tables* ⇆ *47 sites* ✉ *$10* ⚫ *Reservations not accepted, except for groups.*

EN ROUTE Whether you're coming or going from Chaco, **Cuba** is a good place to stop for gas and, depending on your inclination and the season, hot coffee or a cold soda. There are gas stations, a convenience store, and **El Bruno's** (✉ NM 44/U.S. 550 at NM 126 ☎ 505/289–9429), a decent Mexican restaurant that's right on the highway, plus a handful of inexpensive motels; your best bet in this regard is the **Cuban Lodge** (✉ 6332 NM 44/U.S. 550 ☎ 505/289–3475). If you've got some time to spare, visit nearby **Pueblo Pintado** on NM 197. The village is little more than a few houses and a convenience store, but the Chacoan ruins are spectacular and easy to find.

Jicarilla Apache Reservation

⓭ *55 mi east of Navajo Dam on U.S. 64.*

The Spanish named the Jicarilla tribe (pronounced "hick-uh-*ree*-ya," meaning little basket), for their beautiful basketry. For centuries before the arrival of the Spanish, these Native Americans, who were related to the Navajo and Apache, were a nomadic people who roamed across northeastern New Mexico, southeastern Colorado, and the Oklahoma and Texas panhandles. Their tribe of 10,000 was decimated to 330 by 1897. The federal government relocated the tribe to this isolated area of almost a million acres a century ago. Since then, the tribe has made something of a comeback with the sale of timber, oil, and gas development, casino gambling, and savvy investing.

Dulce (pronounced "*dull*-say," meaning "sweet" in Spanish) on U.S. 64 is the capital of the reservation. The free **Arts & Crafts Museum** (✉ ¼ mi west of downtown, U.S. 64 ☎ 505/759–3242 Ext. 274) remains the best place to see the fine historic Jicarilla baskets, beadwork, and pottery. It's also the place to inquire about tours, events, and any tourism restrictions in place because of ceremonial activities. The **Cultural Center** (✉ Basket La. and U.S. 64 ☎ 505/759–1343) is a small gift shop that sells mostly beadwork and some basketry.

This country is known for fishing, particularly at Stone Lake, and for hunting; contact the **Game & Fish Department** (☎ 505/759–3442) for information. You may also hike and camp. As on many other pueblos in New Mexico, the casino has become a big draw as well. Some Jicarilla celebrations are open to the public. The Little Beaver Roundup, the third weekend in July, entails a rodeo, powwow, and carnival and draws participants from Native American tribes and pueblos throughout the United States.

Where to Stay

$ 🏨 **Best Western Jicarilla Inn.** This is the only place to stay in Dulce. The room furnishings preserve the flavor of the cultural and natural setting, with dark woods, Native American art, and stone fireplaces. The restaurant, the Hill Crest, is a favorite gathering spot for celebration dinners. ⊠ *U.S. 64, 12 mi west of Junction 84* ⌂ *Box 233, Dulce 87528* ☎ *505/759–3663 or 800/528–1234* 🖷 *505/759–3170* 🖵 *42 rooms* ♿ *Restaurant, some kitchenettes, cable TV, Internet, meeting rooms, some pets allowed* ▭ *AE, D, DC, MC, V.*

NORTHWESTERN NEW MEXICO ESSENTIALS

AIR TRAVEL

Most major airlines provide service to the state's main airport in Albuquerque, 145 mi east of Gallup and 185 mi southeast of Farmington. Some regional carriers fly in and out of Four Corners Regional Airport in Farmington; Great Lakes Aviation flies from Denver. There are currently no airlines flying into Gallup. *See* Air Travel *in* New Mexico Essentials for national airline phone numbers.

🛫 **Airports Four Corners Regional Airport** ⊠ 1300 W. Navajo St., Farmington ☎ 505/599-1285. **City of Gallup Airport** ⊠ 2111 W. NM 66, Gallup ☎ 505/722-4896.

🛫 **Regional Airlines Great Lakes Aviation** ☎ 800/554-5111 ⊕ www.greatlakesav.com. **Mesa Airlines** ☎ 800/637-2247 ⊕ www.mesa-air.com.

BUS TRAVEL

Texas, New Mexico & Oklahoma Coaches, affiliated with Greyhound Lines, provides service to Grants, Gallup, Farmington, and other towns in northwestern New Mexico.

🚌 **Texas, New Mexico & Oklahoma Coaches** ☎ 505/325-1009 or 800/231-2222.

CAR RENTAL

You can rent a car from Avis, Budget, or Hertz at the Farmington airport. Budget and Enterprise have offices at the Gallup airport. *See* Car Rental *in* New Mexico Essentials for national rental agency phone numbers.

CAR TRAVEL

A car is your best bet for getting to and around the region. Interstate 40 heads due west from Albuquerque toward Arizona. U.S. 64 leads west from Taos into northwestern New Mexico and east from Arizona. NM 44/U.S. 550 travels to the northwest from I–25 (15 mi north of Albuquerque), intersecting with U.S. 64 at Bloomfield, 14 mi east of Farmington. Road conditions vary with the seasons. Winter can create snowy, icy roads; summer can bring ferocious thunderstorms, hailstorms, and flash flood warnings.

EMERGENCIES

In an emergency, dial 911.

🖪 Hospitals **Rehoboth McKinley Christian Health Care Services** ✉ 1901 Red Rock Dr., Gallup ☎ 505/863-7141. **San Juan Regional Health Center** ✉ 801 W. Maple St., Farmington ☎ 505/325-5011.

🖪 Late-Night Pharmacies **Walgreens** ✉ Main and 30th Sts., Farmington ☎ 505/325-1749 ✉ 1626 Historic Rte. 66, Gallup ☎ 505/722-9499. **Wal-Mart** ✉ 1650 W. Maloney Ave., Gallup ☎ 505/722-2226 ✉ 4600 E. Main St., Farmington ☎ 505/326-1100.

TRAIN TRAVEL

Amtrak has daily service between Gallup and Albuquerque, as well as service from Lamy, near Santa Fe, on the *Southwest Chief*. Taking a train into Gallup and renting a car there to explore western New Mexico is an alternative.

🖪 **Amtrak** ☎ 800/872-7245 ⊕ www.amtrak.com.

VISITOR INFORMATION

🖪 **Farmington Convention and Visitors Bureau** ✉ 3041 E. Main St., 87402 ☎ 505/326-7602 or 800/448-1240 ⊕ www.farmingtonnm.org. **Gallup Convention and Visitors Bureau** ✉ 701 Montoya St., 87301 ☎ 505/863-3841 or 800/242-4282 ⊕ www.gallupnm.org. **Grants/Cibola County Chamber of Commerce** ✉ 100 N. Iron Ave., 87020 ☎ 800/748-2142 ⊕ www.grants.org. **Tourism Department, Jicarilla Apache Tribe** ✉ Box 507, Dulce 87528 ☎ 505/759-3242 ⎙ 505/759-3005. **Navajo Nation Tourism Office** ✉ Box 633, Window Rock, AZ 86515 ☎ 520/871-6436 or 520/871-7371 ⎙ 520/871-7942 or 520/871-7381.

Northeastern New Mexico

WORD OF MOUTH

"We spent time in Cimarron and Las Vegas, which were fascinating in an old west kind of way."

　　　　　　　　　　　　　　　　　　　—McShane

"If you want to stay in Las Vegas, the Plaza hotel is one of the oldest in northern NM and it's been featured in many movies set in the southwest. They have an attached restaurant and bar. The Inn on the Santa Fe Trail is another favorite for movie stars when filming in the area."

　　　　　　　　　　　　　　　　　　　—jbee

Updated by
Georgia
de Katona

YOU'LL BATTLE NEITHER CROWDS NOR HYPE in northeastern New Mexico, truly one of the best-kept secrets in the state. You can have a wildflower-strewn trail through alpine meadows and forests of aspen and ponderosa pine all to yourself, or step back in time in small towns that treasure their past but do not exploit it. The sheer variety of terrain and climate, and the combination of natural and social history, make the region an ideal destination, whether as a short side trip or part of a journey from New Mexico toward the Plains states.

The northeastern region of New Mexico has been inhabited for centuries by such Native American tribes as the Apaches, Comanches, and Utes, but it wasn't until about 1835 that non-Native American populations moved in in any significant numbers. Hispanic settlers moved up into the area at that time from San Miguel del Vado, which is just south of I–25, and established the Las Vegas Land Grant; Las Vegas has remained a Hispanic stronghold ever since. William Becknell had established Las Vegas as the Mexican port of entry when he brought the first packtrain west from Missouri to Santa Fe in 1821, in turn creating a pathway for Americans to spread west. The railroad's arrival in the 1870s and '80s brought streams of people and goods into northeastern New Mexico, as did the coal mines. Italians, Mexicans, Greeks, Slavs, Spaniards, and Irish all headed to Raton to harvest coal in mines that first opened in 1879. German-Jewish merchants opened shops in Las Vegas to serve the miners, the railroads, and the local Hispanic population.

In 1908, an African-American cowboy named George McJunkin found a collection of arrowheads in an arroyo near Folsom where he was looking for lost cattle. They looked different from the other arrowheads he'd seen—and indeed they were. Archaeologists eventually determined that the arrowheads had been made by ancient hominids, now known as Folsom Man, who inhabited northeastern New Mexico at least 10,000 years ago.

During the railroad heyday, Civil War veterans homesteaded in the region, some working for Lucien Maxwell, onetime mountain man and fur trader who came to control the largest landholding (1,714,765 acres) in the western hemisphere. Many of New Mexico's large ranches date from the era of the Maxwell Land Grant, territory awarded to the father of Maxwell's wife and another man by the Mexican government in 1841. Modern-day land baron Ted Turner now owns an enormous chunk of open land in these parts. The historic Bell Ranch near Solano still maintains an active cattle operation (as well as a beautiful guest *hacienda*) on 292,000 acres near Solano, though it originally held 655,468 acres as the Pablo Montoya Land Grant of 1824.

History is very much alive in northeastern New Mexico, in the stories and the way of life of the people who live here, in the architecture, and in the landscape itself. Exploring this land of vast plains, rugged mesas, and wild, crystalline streams may well be the best way to immerse yourself in the American West.

GREAT ITINERARIES

IF YOU HAVE 2 DAYS

Stroll around the Plaza and Bridge Street in **Las Vegas ❶**. After you've walked the town, drive north on I-25 to 🚗 **Raton ❺** and visit the Raton Museum and Historic First Street. Take a picnic up to Lake Maloya in Sugarite Canyon State Park and hike or go fishing. The next day, drive west on U.S. 64 to 🚗 **Cimarron ❽**, exploring the heart of yesteryear's Wild West. Spend the night in the allegedly haunted St. James Hotel. In the morning continue west on U.S. 64, stopping off to fish or walk along the Cimarron River in Cimarron Canyon, and then head south on NM 434 at Angel Fire, stopping off for a visit to Victory Ranch in **Mora ❾**, before continuing back toward Santa Fe.

IF YOU HAVE 4 TO 5 DAYS

The main routes through northeastern New Mexico follow the path of the original Santa Fe Trail and its shortcut, the Cimarron Route (which passed near Clayton and Springer), enabling you to retrace the steps of the pioneers. Begin in 🚗 **Las Vegas ❶**, where you can stay at the Plaza Hotel. Detour for an hour or two to **Fort Union National Monument ❷**. Back at I-25, continue north to 🚗 **Raton ❺**. On Day 3 head east on NM 72 over starkly captivating Johnson Mesa and visit Capulin Volcano National Monument. After viewing four states from the rim of the volcano, have lunch at the Capulin Country Store, at the junction of U.S. 64/87 and NM 325. If you have an extra day, head east to 🚗 **Clayton ❼** to view the dinosaur tracks at Clayton Lake State Park. Have dinner and stay at the Eklund Hotel Dining Room & Saloon. The following day drive west on U.S. 56 toward Springer, detouring first to Dorsey Mansion. **Springer ❹** is a good place to have lunch and browse in the antiques shops downtown. With or without the Clayton detour, continue west to 🚗 **Cimarron ❽** (via U.S. 64 from Capulin, or NM 58 from Springer), and from here repeat the last day of the two-day itinerary given above.

6

Exploring Northeastern New Mexico

Interstate 25 heading north from Santa Fe is the fastest route through the region, but you'll want to sample as many local roads as possible to catch the area's true flavor. The destinations below are arranged in a loop from Las Vegas, Springer, and Raton (with an optional side loop over Johnson Mesa to Folsom, Capulin, and Clayton). Either way, the tour continues by heading west to Cimarron and then along U.S. 64 west through Cimarron Canyon; past Eagle Nest Lake and Angel Fire; and then south on NM 434 through stunning Guadalupita Canyon to Mora. Here you can either continue south toward Santa Fe back through Las Vegas or opt for the more dramatic mountain route, skirting over the east face of the Sangre de Cristo range.

Timing

In a region where the weather is close to perfect, the only months to consider avoiding are March and April, when "Texas blows through" and you find yourself dodging tumbleweeds, though this is applicable to the flatter regions rather than the mountains, which are still quite cool. From late spring, when the wildflowers begin to bloom, into late summer is a wonderful time to visit—an occasional afternoon thunderstorm, or "monsoon," often followed by a rainbow, punctuates days that are mostly sunny. Fall brings the gold of aspens, and fishing and hiking are especially spectacular. Temperatures can remain mild through Thanksgiving, and a crisp winter with good snow is a blessing for cross-country skiers. The wide vistas on snowy days are unforgettable. Roads are well maintained throughout the year, but be alert to storm warnings.

About the Restaurants

Food in the northeast is heavily New Mexican and American and dining is casual, just like the region itself. You can continue on the chile tour of the West, but vegetarians should ask whether there is beef in the red or pork in the green before diving in. Reservations are almost unheard of here, but seasonal closings during winter months are common.

About the Hotels

Chain hotels, privately operated lodges and B&Bs are abundant. Choose a B&B when you can—you can get a real taste of regional character, and delicious breakfasts to boot. Given the amazing natural beauty and generally easy weather from May through late September, it's also no surprise that many visitors to the area choose to camp.

WHAT IT COSTS				
	$$$$	**$$$**	**$$**	**$**	**¢**
RESTAURANTS	over $30	$23–$30	$16–$22	$10–$15	under $10
HOTELS	over $250	$176–$250	$121–$175	$70–$120	under $70

Restaurant prices are per person for a main course at dinner. Hotel prices are for two people in a standard double room in high season, excluding 5%–12% tax.

SANTA FE TRAIL COUNTRY

Native American tribes of the Great Plains and Southwest lived and thrived in resource rich northeastern New Mexico. Throughout the region you can find reminders of them and the pioneers who traveled the Santa Fe Trail, two sections of which passed through the area. The Mountain Route entered New Mexico from southeastern Colorado, crossed through Raton Pass, and passed Cimarron and Rayado before heading on to Fort Union. Because it was so arduous, this route was less subject to attack from the Comanches and Apaches, who were on the defensive warpath because their land was being usurped. The quicker, flatter Cimarron Route (aka Cimarron Cutoff), entering New Mexico from Oklahoma and passing across the dry grasslands, left travelers much more vulnerable. The Mountain Route, which William Becknell followed 900 mi from

IF YOU LIKE

FESTIVALS

Las Vegas is the place to be for the 4th of July. The town's wildly popular parade begins on the Plaza around 9 AM and proceeds down Bridge Street. Proud veterans, civic groups, high school bands, even "low riders," whose elaborately painted cars with amazing hydraulics lift, tilt, and bounce, all join in. There is a craft fair with local artists selling everything from food to tie-dyed clothing, to traditional Hispanic arts.

FISHING

Whether you prefer lake or stream fishing, gray hackle peacocks or PowerBait, some of your greatest fishing dreams might just come true in northeastern New Mexico. Idyllic clear mountain streams and alpine lakes are regularly stocked with rainbows; in Cimarron Canyon State Park you can catch your limit on German browns. Numerous operators arrange fishing trips.

VIEWING WILDLIFE

Early morning and late afternoon are the best times to grab your binoculars and head out to spot wildlife—elk, deer, wild turkey, bears, and bobcats—in the Raton area, or on the road to Sugarite Canyon State Park, Yankee Canyon, or York Canyon. But it's possible to catch a glimpse of antelope any time of day, especially on the open range.

Franklin, Missouri, during his first successful navigation, also provided an excellent source of water—the Arkansas River—while the Cimarron Route was deathly dry.

Las Vegas

🟠 *64 miles northeast of Santa Fe on I-25.*

The antithesis of the Nevada city that shares its name, Las Vegas, elevation 6,470, is a town of 16,000 that time appears to have passed by. For decades, Las Vegas was actually two towns: East Las Vegas, the Hispanic community anchored by the Spanish-style plaza, and West Las Vegas, where German Jews and Midwesterners have established themselves around a proper town square. Once an oasis for stagecoach passengers en route to Santa Fe, it became—for a brief period after the railroad arrived in the late 19th century—New Mexico's major center of commerce, and its largest town, where more than a million dollars in goods and services were traded annually.

The 1870s were a decade of booming business and near-total lawlessness. Famous characters on both sides of the law passed through the town—including Doc Holliday (who practiced dentistry here), Billy the Kid, and Wyatt Earp. Fierce battles for land—often swindled out of the hands of illiterate Hispanic land grant holders by ruthless American businessmen—and water rights ensued, with the *Gorras Blancos*("white hoods") appearing in 1889 to begin their campaign of cutting fences and setting fire to buildings on lands that had once been community property of the many land grants of the area. Today, the town is positively sedate, though ethnic tensions still occasionally arise.

The seat of San Miguel County, Las Vegas lies where the Sangre de Cristo Mountains meet the high plains of New Mexico, and its name, meaning "the meadows," reflects its scenic setting. Bookstores, Western-wear shops, restaurants, boutiques, and coffeehouses line the streets near the downtown Plaza and Bridge Street. More than 900 structures here are listed on the National Register of Historic Places, and the town has nine historic districts, many with homes and commercial buildings of ornate Italianate design (a welcome relief if you're experiencing adobe overload). Many of these buildings can be seen easily by taking a walk around town. Exploring on foot will give you a sense of some of the area's rough-and-tumble history—Butch Cassidy is rumored to have tended bar here. You may also recognize some of the streets and facades from films; Las Vegas is where scenes from *Wyatt Earp, The HiLo Country,* and *All the Pretty Horses* were shot, and where Tom Mix shot his vintage westerns.

To gain an appreciation of the town's architecture, try some of the walking tours described in brochures available at the **Las Vegas Chamber of Commerce** (⊠ 727 Grand Ave. ☎ 505/425–8631 or 800/832–5947).

Best bets include Stone Architecture of Las Vegas; the Carnegie Park Historic District, with the Carnegie Library; and the business district of Douglas–6th Street and Railroad Avenue, which includes the famous Harvey House hotel of the railroad chain, La Casteneda, where the grand lobby and dining room are still intact. Open 9–5, weekdays.

Las Vegas City Museum & Rough Riders Memorial houses historical photos, medals, uniforms, and memorabilia from the Spanish-American War, documents pertaining to the city's history, and Native American artifacts. Theodore Roosevelt recruited many of his Rough Riders— the men the future president led into battle in Cuba in 1898—from northeastern New Mexico, and their first reunion was held here. ⊠ *725 Grand Ave.* ☎ *505/454–1401 Ext. 283* ☞ *Free* ☺ *Weekdays 9–noon and 1–4, Sat. 10–3.*

A favorite fishing hole for rainbow and German brown trout is **Storrie Lake State Park.** The 1,200-acre lake also draws water-skiers, sailboarders, and windsurfers. You can camp in the area. ⊠ *NM 518, 4 mi north of Las Vegas* ☎ *505/425–7278* ⊕ *www.emnrd.state.nm.us* ☞ *$5 per vehicle.*

Las Vegas National Wildlife Refuge has the best bird-watching around, with 271 known species—including eagles, sandhill cranes, hawks, and prairie falcons—that travel the Central Flyway to this 18,750-acre area of marsh, wetlands, native grasslands, and timber. Here, where the Sangre de Cristo Mountains meet the Great Plains, a ½-mi-long nature trail winds beside sandstone cliffs and ruins. You can get oriented by dropping by the visitor center. ⊠ *Rte. 1, 1 mi east of Las Vegas on NM 104, then 4 mi south on NM 281* ⬠ *Box 399, Las Vegas 87701* ☎ *505/425–3581.*

Las Vegas is the home of **New Mexico Highlands University** (⊠ 901 University Ave. ☎ 800/338–6648 ⊕ www.nmhu.edu), which puts on concerts, plays, sporting events, and lectures. Its tree-shaded campus of largely Spanish-colonial and Romanesque Revival buildings anchors the eastern side of downtown. It houses Depression-era murals by painter Lloyd Moylan.

About 5 mi northwest of town in Montezuma, students from around the world study language and culture at the **Armand Hammer United World College of the American West** (⊠ NM 65 ☎ 505/454–4200 ⊕ www. uwc-usa.org). Looming over the school property is the fantastically ornate, vaguely Queen Anne–inspired Montezuma Castle, a former resort hotel developed by the Santa Fe Railroad and designed by the famous Chicago firm of Burnham and Root. The structure that stands today was the third incarnation of the Montezuma Hotel, which opened in 1886. Weekly tours of the castle are available, and you can wander the school's majestic, rolling grounds. Check in with the guard booth at the campus entrance.

If you continue another ½ mi past the turnoff of the campus on NM 65, you can see the signs to the right for the **hot springs** that inspired Montezuma's tourist boom in the 1880s. Soaking in these relaxing, lithium-laced pools is free, as long as you follow basic rules: no nude bathing, no alcohol, and bathing only between 5 AM and midnight. If crowds allow, try soaking in several different pools; temperatures vary significantly but the view of the Castle and the creek are equally lovely.

OFF THE
BEATEN
PATH

MADISON VINEYARDS & WINERY – If you're driving to or or from the northeast on I–25, a side trip down NM 3 is well worth your while. Scenic and loaded with history, the road will also take you to the proud producers of some very fine New Mexico wines, including the crisp, sweet white "Pecos Wildflower." Madison has picked up quite a few awards over the years. The tasting room in El Barranco is open Monday–Saturday 10–4:30, Sunday noon–5. ☒ *NM 3, 6 mi south of I–25, Exit 323, 23 mi southwest of Las Vegas* ☎ *505/421–8028.*

Where to Stay & Eat

¢–$$ ✕ **El Rialto Restaurant & Lounge.** The margaritas here will put you in the right mood for fried oyster dinners, huge steaks, stuffed sopaipillas, and tamales. American dishes, seafood, and the salad bar are other options. The antique bar and historic photos, in addition to good drinks and an eclectic jumble of friendly locals, make the attached Rye Lounge a fun spot for drinks. ☒ *141 Bridge St.* ☎ *505/454–0037* ⊟ *AE, D, MC, V* ✆ *Closed Sun.*

★ ¢–$ ✕ **Estella's Restaurant.** An old-fashioned storefront café with a high pressed-tin ceiling, vintage photos, and a Formica counter with swivel stools, Estella's serves simple, spicy New Mexican fare—huevos rancheros, stacked enchiladas—plus a few American favorites like burgers. Pescado Veracruz, snapper simmered in a piquant sauce of spices, tomato, red chile, and onion, is a good choice for dinner. ☒ *148 Bridge St.* ☎ *505/ 454–0048* ⊟ *No credit cards* ✆ *Closed Sun. No dinner Mon.–Wed.*

¢ ✕ **Charlie's Bakery & Café.** Huevos rancheros and burritos smothered with spicy salsa top the list in this large, simply furnished room that rings with friendly greetings among locals and is a good bet for either breakfast or lunch. You can also pick up cookies, donuts, and pastries from the on-site bakery, or a stack of freshly made corn tortillas from the *tortilleria.* ☒ *715 Douglas* ☎ *505/426–1921* ⊟ *AE, DC, MC, V* ✆ *Mon.–Sat. 6:30 AM–5:30 PM, Sun. 6:30 AM–3 PM.*

★ $–$$ ✕▦ **Plaza Hotel.** Rooms at this three-story Italianate hotel balance the old and the new—they're not fancy, but they've got plenty of space, painted molding, and high stamped-tin ceilings, and a sprinkling of charming antiques. Each room also has a modern bath, coffeemaker, TV, phone, and continental breakfast included in the rate. Reasonably priced packages include dinner at the Landmark Grill ($$–$$$), which serves, among other dishes, filet mignon, piñon-crusted trout, and Mexican specialties. ☒ *230 Old Town Plaza, 87701* ☎ *505/425–3591 or 800/328– 1882* ☐ *505/425–9659* ⊕ *www.plazahotel-nm.com* ➲ *32 rooms, 4 suites* ⟁ *Restaurant, room service, cable TV, bar, Internet, meeting rooms, some pets allowed (fee)* ⊟ *AE, D, DC, MC, V* ❏ *CP.*

¢–$ ▦ **Inn on the Santa Fe Trail.** A lovely central courtyard and a friendly staff grace this well-kept, hacienda-style motel. The grounds are well manicured, there's a nice pool area, and the rooms are comfortably outfitted with Southwestern wood furnishings created by area artisans. Attached to the Inn is Blackjack's Grill ($–$$), where fine dining comfortably mixes with the town's casual sensibility. Generally, the style is

Continental, but the food is prepared wonderfully, and daily specials are offered based on seasonally available ingredients. If you've got steak on your mind, Blackjack's will treat you right. The dining room is small, so reservations are recommended. A cozy patio is open for dining during the summer months. ⊠ *1133 N. Grand Ave., 87701* ☎ *505/ 425–6791 or 888/448–8438* 🖷 *505/425–0417* ⊕ *www. innonthesantafetrail.com* ⌖ *28 rooms, 2 suites* ⚲ *Restaurant, cable TV, in-room data ports, pool, hot tub, business services* ⊟ *AE, D, DC, MC, V* ⎮⊚⎮ *CP.*

¢–$ ⊞ **Pendaries Village.** The mood here (where the name is pronounced "panda-ray") is Holiday Inn meets Kit Carson, but the hotel and the surrounding mountain hamlet of Rociada provide a relaxing place to enjoy some high altitude golfing. The **Pendaries Golf Course** (☎ 505/ 425–8890) begins at 7,500 feet with a par 73, set smack at the eastern edge of the Sangre de Cristo Mountains. Special golf packages are offered. Greens fees are $32 weekdays, $40 weekends; optional golf cart rental is $22. The rooms here have standard motel-room decor, but are clean and comfortable; the on-site restaurant is usually crowded with locals who come for the steaks and Southwestern food. ⊠ *1 Lodge Rd., off NM 105, 26 mi northwest of Las Vegas* 🖅 *Box 820, Rociada 87742* ☎ *505/425–3561 or 800/733–5267* 🖷 *505/425–3562* ⊕ *www.pendaries. net* ⌖ *18 rooms* ⚲ *Restaurant, cable TV, 18-hole golf course, bar, meeting rooms* ⊟ *MC, V.*

⛺ **Las Vegas New Mexico KOA.** Five miles south of Las Vegas you can camp and cook out near a piñon-juniper hillside with beautiful views. There's a recreation room, as well as outdoor areas for playing volleyball and horseshoes. The pool feels fantastic after a dry, dusty day of exploring. In addition to the usual KOA accommodations, this site has a one bedroom apartment available above the main office. ⊠ *I–25, Exit 339, at U.S. 84* 🖅 *HCR 31, Box 1, Las Vegas 87701* ☎ *505/454–0180 or 800/562–3423* ⊕ *www.koa.com* ⚲ *Pool, playground, laundry facilities, flush toilets, full hookups, drinking water, showers, picnic tables, general store* ⌖ *5 cabins, 50 tent sites, 54 hookups* 🖾 *RV sites $32–$34, tent sites $22, cabins $45, apartment $55* ⊟ *D, MC, V.*

Sports & the Outdoors

Brazos River Ranch and Outfitters (☎ 505/425–1509) can take you on jeep tours, trail rides, and hunting and fishing trips—and they'll do it with the friendliest service this side of the Pecos.

Shopping

Shops are located mainly on Bridge Street, off the Plaza. **Meadowland Antiques and Spice Co.** (⊠ 131 Bridge St. ☎ 505/425–9502) sells gourmet foods, candies, a huge selection of spices, and distinctive furnishings and has a little espresso bar in back. **New Moon Fashions** (⊠ 132 Bridge St. ☎ 505/454–0669) has a well-chosen selection of natural fiber and imported women's clothing, and comfortable shoes. **Plaza Antiques** (⊠ 1805 Old Town Plaza ☎ 505/454–9447) contains several dealers offering a wide range of antiques from different periods; it's in a stunningly restored hip-roof adobe 1870s Victorian. **Rough Rider Trading Co.** (⊠ 158 Bridge St. ☎ 505/425–0246) sells Western wear, handcrafted furniture, and handwoven, wood, and metal crafts. **Tome on the Range** (⌧ 116 Bridge St. ☏ 505/454–9944) is a well-appointed bookstore with good Southwestern and kids' sections.

Right across the street from Tome on the Range is its offshoot, **Second Tome Around** (⌧ 131 Bridge St. ☏ 505/454–8511). Aside from a large selection of used books and cozy chairs to read them in, there's a bright little café in the back serving the best coffee in town. Among the yummy offerings are pastries, salads with nuts and sprouts, quiche made with green chile and calabacitas (squash), and green chile-and-cheese corn chowder.

Fort Union National Monument

❷ *26 mi from Las Vegas, north on I–25 and (past Watrous) northwest on NM 161; 94 mi northeast of Santa Fe on I–25.*

The ruins of New Mexico's largest American frontier–era fort sit on an empty windswept plain. It still echoes with the isolation surely felt by the soldiers stationed here between 1851 and 1890, when the fort was established to protect travelers and settlers along the Santa Fe Trail. It eventually became a military supply depot for the Southwest, but with the "taming" of the West it was abandoned. The visitor center provides historical background about the fort and the Santa Fe Trail; guided tours are available when volunteers are on hand. ⌧ *Off NM 161, Watrous* ☏ *505/425–8025* ☞ *$3* ☉ *Early Sept.–late May, daily 8–5; late May–early Sept., daily 8–6.*

Wagon Mound

❸ *40 mi north of Las Vegas on I–25.*

As you drive up I–25 from Las Vegas and Fort Union, the high prairie unfolds before you to the east, an infinite horizon of grassland that's quite breathtaking when the sun sets. Soon interrupting this view is a butte shaped like a covered wagon that was a famous Santa Fe Trail landmark, Wagon Mound. The butte is where travelers crossed over from the Cimarron Cutoff to journey south to Fort Union. Local lore tells of mysterious lights, ghosts, and murders committed on top of the butte. The town serves a free barbecue at noon on Labor Day to celebrate its bean-growing heritage. Other events—horseshoe tournaments, a rodeo, and a parade—take place that same weekend in this otherwise sleepy village.

Springer

❹ *25 mi north of Wagon Mound on I–25.*

A stroll under the shady oaks of Springer's main street is a journey into the past; if it weren't for the modern-day cars driving by, you might think Harry Truman was still president. More than a few locals here still seem a bit rankled about losing the title of county seat to Raton—in 1897. The main industry of this town of 1,262 is the Springer Boys School, an incarceration facility for minors. Long a shipping center for cattle, sheep, and mining machinery, Springer was founded in 1870 when land baron Lucien Maxwell deeded 320 acres to his lawyer, Frank Springer, for handling the sale of the Maxwell Land Grant to the Dutch East India Company.

Crammed with everything you'd expect to find at a five-and-dime, **Springer Drug** is a local hangout and the site of an ongoing gabfest. The highlight is the old (not old-fashioned, this is the original article) soda fountain, where you can order a sundae, malt, shake, or cone. The root-beer float comes in a glass so big you could dive into it. In winter home-made chili is served on Wednesday. ⊠ *825 4th St.* ☎ *505/483–2356.*

When Springer was the Colfax County seat, the 1883 structure that houses the **Santa Fe Trail Museum** served as a courthouse. The museum has a curious jumble of documents, maps, memorabilia, and other artifacts. The setup is not particularly sophisticated—it takes a bit of patience to wade through the assorted bits and pieces of the past. ⊠ *606 Maxwell St.* ☎ *505/483–2998* 🖭 *$2* ☉ *Late May–early Sept., Mon.–Sat. 9–4; limited hrs early fall to late spring, call ahead.*

OFF THE
BEATEN
PATH

DORSEY MANSION – In the middle of nowhere (about 35 mi northeast of Springer) stands this curious 36-room log-and-masonry castle built in 1880 by Stephen Dorsey, a U.S. senator from Arkansas. Its grand furnishings include a cherrywood staircase from Chicago, statuary depicting Dorsey family members, a dining room that seats 60, and a swank billiard room. It was once a social gathering place for the rich and powerful. The career of the ambitious senator, who owned the mansion for 15 years, dissolved in a mail-fraud scandal. You must make reservations by phone to visit the mansion. ⊠ *Off U.S. 56, 25 mi east of Springer; turn north (left) at rest stop at Mile Marker 24 and take dirt road 12 mi* ☎ *505/375–2222* ⊕ *www.dorseymansion.com* 🖭 *$3* ☉ *Daily, by appt.*

MAXWELL NATIONAL WILDLIFE REFUGE – More than 300 species of migratory waterfowl, including many geese and ducks in fall and winter, stop for a spell at this low-key 2,800-acre prairie refuge 12 mi north of Springer. Sightings of great blue herons are not uncommon in mid-winter, and bald eagles are fairly plentiful at this time. Sandhill cranes usually drop by in early fall, Canada geese around December. Deer, prairie dogs, long-tail weasels, jackrabbits, coyotes, bears, and elk live here. The fishing season (Lake 13 is a fabled spot to catch rainbows) is between March and October. You can camp (no fee, no facilities) near the fishing areas. ⊠ *Off I–25, take Maxwell Lakes exit at Mile Marker 426; follow NM 445 north ¾ mi, then NM 505 west 2½ mi to unmarked gravel road to refuge* ☎ *505/375–2331* 🖭 *Free* ☉ *Daily.*

Where to Stay & Eat

¢ ✕🏨 **Brown Hotel & Cafe.** Granny's parlor circa 1924 is the best way to describe the Brown Hotel, where the lobby furnishings include a rocking chair by the fireplace and hooked rugs and doilies. Antiques decorate the basic rooms, some of which have chenille bedspreads. The café's (¢–$) claims to fame include the baked goods and made-from-scratch soups (try the yummy broccoli–cheddar); both New Mexican and standard American dishes are on the menu. ⊠ *302 Maxwell Ave., 87747* ☎ *505/483–2269* ⊷ *11 rooms* ₺ *Café* ⊟ *MC, V* ⦿ *BP.*

Shopping

Jespersen's Cache (✉ 403 Maxwell Ave. ☎ 505/483–2349), a pack rat's paradise, is a place to get lost for a morning or afternoon. The sheer mass of stuff is astounding—boxed Barbies, railroad lanterns, Depression-era glass, carousel horses. If you've got a collector's eye, you could make your lucky find here. Call if the doors are locked between 9 and 5; the proprietor may be around the corner at her house and she'll come right down.

Raton

❺ *39 mi north of Springer on I–25, 100 mi northeast of Taos on U.S. 64.*

Generally underrated as a destination, Raton occupies an appealing spot at the foot of a lush mountain pass and offers wide-open views of stepped mesas and sloping canyons from the higher points in town. Midway between Albuquerque and Denver, it's an ideal base for exploring northeastern New Mexico. Because Raton was a racetrack town from the 1940s through the early '90s, motels are plentiful. There's always talk of bringing back horse racing.

As it has for more than a century, Raton (population 8,500), the seat of Colfax County, runs on ranching, railroading, and the industry for which it's most famous, mining. In the early 1900s there were about 35 coal camps around Raton, most of them occupied by immigrants from Italy, Greece, and Eastern Europe. It was hard-living in these camps and a tough road out, but a close-knit familial interdependence grew out of mining life—a spirit that still prevails in Raton today. People here are genuinely friendly and have great pride in their town.

Originally a Santa Fe Trail forage station called Willow Springs, Raton was born in 1880 when the Atchison, Topeka & Santa Fe Railway established a repair shop at the bottom of Raton Pass. The town grew up around 1st Street, which paralleled the railroad tracks. Much of the Raton Downtown Historic District, which has 70-odd buildings on the National Register of Historic Places, lies along Historic First Street, which consists of several restored blocks of antiques shops, galleries, and everyday businesses. Much of historic downtown is closed on Sunday; some businesses are closed Monday as well.

The Historic First Street area provides a fine survey of western architecture from the 1880s to the early 1900s. In the early 20th century the **Mission Santa Fe Depot** (✉ 1st St. and Cook Ave.), a 1903 Spanish Mission Revival structure, serviced several dozen trains daily (Amtrak still stops here). The **Wells Fargo Express Building** (✉ 145 S. 1st St.), also designed in the Spanish Mission Revival style, was erected in 1910. The building houses the **Old Pass Gallery** (☎ 505/445–2052), which presents exhibits of regional art, books, and jewelry. Garlands and female figureheads adorn the 1906 **Abourezk Building** (✉ 132 S. 1st St.), originally a drugstore, later a dry-goods and grocery store, and now the home of the Heirloom Shop.

The tiny storefront **Raton Museum,** inside the 1906 Coors Building (the beer manufacturer once used it as a warehouse), brims with artifacts of the coal camps, railroading, ranch life, and the Santa Fe Trail. The museum, which has a large and interesting photo collection, is a good first stop on a visit to the area. The docents enjoy explaining local history. ⊠ *218 S. 1st St.* ☎ *505/445–8979* ⊠ *Free* ☉ *May–Sept., Tues.–Sat. 10–5; Oct.–Apr., Thurs.–Sat. 10–3.*

Just down a couple of blocks from the train station, the **Scouting Museum,** devoted to all things Boy Scout, is a must-see for anyone planning a visit to Philmont Scout Ranch in Cimarron. Amiable curator Dennis Downing has amassed an exhaustive collection of scouting-related books, badges, films of old jamborees, buttons, and *Boys Life* magazines. ⊠ *400 S. 1st St.* ☎ *505/445–1413* ⊠ *Free* ☉ *June–Aug., daily 10–7, or by appt.*

More retro 1930s and '40s than Victorian, 2nd Street—Raton's main commercial drag—also has a number of handsome old buildings. The pride and joy of the neighborhood is the **Shuler Theater** (⊠ 131 N. 2nd St.), a 1915 European rococo–style structure whose lobby contains WPA murals depicting local history. The Shuler is one of the few remaining stages where all sets, curtains, and scenery are hand-operated with hemp rope and wooden pulleys. On weekdays between 8 and 5 the staff will happily take you on a free tour.

Southern California may have its HOLLYWOOD sign, but northeastern New Mexico has its RATON **sign**—and this neon-red beauty is completely accessible. From the north end of 3rd Street, head west on Moulton Avenue to Hill Street and follow signs along the twisting road to the parking area at Goat Hill. Here you can walk around the sign, take in 270-degree views of the countryside, or picnic while contemplating the history of Raton Pass—the original Santa Fe Trail ran up Goat Hill clear into Colorado.

★ ☉   **Sugarite Canyon State Park,** a gem of a park near the Colorado state line, has some of the state's best hiking, camping, wildflower viewing, fishing, and bird-watching ("sugarite" is a corruption of the Comanche word *chicorica,* meaning "an abundance of birds," and is pronounced shug-ur-*eet*). The road to Sugarite twists and turns high up into the canyon to Lake Maloya, a trout-stocked body of water from which a spillway carries overflow down into the canyon. From its 7,500-foot elevation hills rise up the eastern and western canyon walls where miners once dug for ore; you can still see gray slag heaps and remnants of the coal camp, which thrived here from 1910 to 1940, along portions of the park road near the visitor center (the former coal-camp post office) and down near the base of the canyon. The center contains exhibits on the mining legacy, and from here you can hike 1½ mi to the original camp.

Hikes elsewhere in the park range from the easy ½ mi Grande Vista Nature Trail to the pleasant 4 mi jaunt around Lake Maloya to the challenging Opportunity Trail. "Caprock" is the name given to the park's striking basaltic rock columns, which were formed millions of years ago when hot lava from a nearby volcano created the 10- to 100-foot-thick rocks. Climbing is permitted on these sheer cliffs, although it's not recommended for the faint of heart or the claustrophobic. ⊠ *NM 526, 7 mi northeast of Raton via NM 72* ☎ *505/445–5607* ⊕ *www.emnrd. state.nm.us* 🖅 *$4 per vehicle* ⊗ *Daily 6 AM–9 PM.*

Where to Stay & Eat

$$–$$$$ ✕ **The Icehouse.** A historic 1909 icehouse is the setting for this restaurant serving steaks and seafood. The high-ceiling brick structure is accented with lots of old wood, historic photos of the icehouse in its working days, and more photos of the many celebrities who've dined here. If a memorable steak is what you're after, the prime Angus cuts are prepared to perfection by chef and co-owner Bill Ratliff. ⊠ *945 S. 2nd St., just south of downtown* ☎ *505/445–2339* ▭ *AE, DC, MC, V* ⊗ *Closed Sun. Nov.–May 1.*

$–$$$ ✕ **Sweet Shop Restaurant.** Don't be put off by the plain storefront; you can feel pampered at this restaurant, whose antiques and collectibles exude a sense of history and a pleasant nostalgia for Pappas, the Greek candy maker who founded the place in the 1920s. It's no longer a sweet shop, but it does serve familiar American fare, like Alaskan king crab legs, porterhouse steak, shrimp fettuccine, and a few surf-and-turf combos. ⊠ *1201 S. 2nd St.* ☎ *505/445–9811* ▭ *AE, D, DC, MC, V* ⊗ *Closed Sun. in winter.*

¢ ✕ **The Bakery and Coffee Shop.** Also known as Eva's Bakery, this cheerful sit-down bakery across from the Shuler Theater has fabulous chocolate-cake doughnuts and oatmeal-raisin cookies—as well as a regular crowd of old-timers who gather here to keep up with town gossip. Breakfast burritos, chile fries, burgers, and frito pies are big sellers. ⊠ *134 N. 2nd St.* ☎ *505/445–3781* 🍴 *Reservations not accepted* ▭ *No credit cards* ⊗ *Closed Sun. No dinner.*

$$$$ ▦ **Vermejo Park Ranch.** This breathtaking 588,000-acre property, the heart of the famous 2 million acre Maxwell Land Grant, includes a private hunting and fishing resort. Here you can stay in rustic yet luxurious accommodations; hunt for bison, elk, turkey, and mule deer; skeet shoot; horseback ride; and fish among the property's 21 lakes and countless rivers. The impressive main lodge houses a dining room, bar, gift shop, and guest services desk; a second lodge houses guests in 15 rooms and has its own private chef, dining room, and bar (room rates here include all meals, as well as activities like horseback riding and fishing). There's no TV on the premises, nor are there hot tubs, swimming pools, or a golf course—this place is all about returning to the land. Media mogul Ted Turner owns the ranch and his attention to land and animal stewardship is both remarkable, and evident. ⬠ *Drawer E, Raton 87740* ☎ *505/445–3097* 🖷 *505/445–0545* ⊕ *www.vermejoparkranch.com* 🛏 *15 rooms* ♿ *Restaurant, hiking, horseback riding, bar, shop, meeting rooms* ▭ *AE, D, DC, MC, V* 🍴 *AI.*

$–$$ ▦ **Holiday Inn Express.** If you prefer modern rather than rustic lodgings, this is the place for you. Clean rooms, fine views of Johnson Mesa and the vast grasslands, and a location south of downtown are all draws here. An extensive continental breakfast buffet is included, as are snacks in the lobby from 4 to 8. ⊠ *101 Card Ave., I–25, Exit 450, 87740* ☎ *505/ 445–1500 or 800/465–4329* 🖷 *505/445–7650* 🛏 *50 rooms* ♿ *In-room data ports, pool, hot tub, laundry facilities, no-smoking rooms* ▭ *AE, D, DC, MC, V* 🍴 *CP.*

$ 🏨 **Best Western Sands.** Some of the good-size rooms at this charming, rather kitschy 1950s-style motel have refrigerators, and all have coffeemakers, queen or king beds, and TVs with premium cable. The Sands provides free transportation to and from Raton's bus depot and Amtrak station. ⊠ *300 Clayton Rd., NM 87–U.S. 64, 87740* ☎ *505/445–2737 or 800/528–1234* 🖷 *505/445–4053* 🛏 *50 rooms* ⌂ *Restaurant, some refrigerators, cable TV, in-room data ports, pool, hot tub, playground, business services, no-smoking rooms* 🖃 *AE.*

★ **$** 🏨 **Hearts Desire Inn Bed & Breakfast.** Gregarious host Barbara Riley, who grew up on a ranch south of Springer, has filled the rooms of her inn with Victorian antiques and collectibles (many for sale). This 1885 former boardinghouse is steps from downtown dining and the historic district. The top-floor hunting-and-fishing-theme suite has a full kitchen, TV and VCR, and two twin beds. In addition to what is likely the best breakfast in town, snacks are served in the evening. ⊠ *301 S. 3rd St., 87740* ☎ *505/445–1000* 🛏 *5 rooms, 1 suite* ⌂ *Some kitchenettes, some in-room VCRs* 🖃 *MC, V* ⍑ *BP.*

� **Sugarite Canyon State Park.** Arrive early for the best choice among the fully developed sites at either of this park's two campgrounds, Lake Alice and Soda Pocket. Be sure to follow park warnings regarding the resident brown bears at Soda Pocket. ⊠ *NM 526, 6 mi northeast of Raton* 🖂 *HCR 63, Box 386, 87740* ☎ *505/445–5607, 877/664–7787 reservations* ⊕ *www.emnrd.state.nm.us* ⌂ *Flush toilets, full hookups, dump station, drinking water, showers, picnic tables, electricity* 🛏 *41 tent and RV sites, 12 with hookups* 🖾 *$10 camping, $4 additional each for electric and water hookups* 🖃 *No credit cards.*

Nightlife & the Arts

Shuler Theater (⊠ 131 N. 2nd St. ☎ 505/445–4746) presents late-summer concerts, Music from Angel Fire (a program that brings world-class chamber music to various venues in northern New Mexico), and productions by the Creede Repertory Theater. Children's theater, local college productions, and traveling dance, folk dance, and vocal evenings are scheduled throughout the year. For the better part of this century, locals have popped into the rollicking **White House Saloon** (⊠ 133 Cook Ave. ☎ 505/445–9992) for drinks after work and late into the evening. If you get hungry, the adjoining restaurant serves well-prepared steaks and seafood from 6 to 9. No credit cards are accepted.

Sports & the Outdoors

Raton's playground is **Sugarite Canyon State Park.** Sugarite's alpine **Lake Maloya** (⊠ NM 526, 10 mi northeast of Raton ☎ 505/445–5607) is generously stocked with rainbow trout. The profusion of wildflowers and flocks of bluebirds make the lake a joy to hike around. Boating and ice-fishing are popular as well.

Shopping

Hattie Sloan, proprietor of the **Heirloom Shop** (⊠ 132 S. 1st St. ☎ 505/445–8876), was one of the key figures involved in the restoration of Historic First Street. Hattie knows her antiques and has packed her highly browsable shop with beautiful selections, from rhinestone necklaces to quilts, china, and linens. Given the quality of some of the merchandise, the prices at **Santa Fe Trail Traders** (✉ 100 S. 2nd St. ☎ 505/445–2888 or 800/286–6975) are reasonable. Items include earrings, sand paintings, dream catchers, Nambé hand-cast bowls, Navajo rugs old and new, beadwork, and kachinas (many by well-known artists).

Rubin's Family Clothiers (✉ 113 S. 2nd St. ☎ 505/445–9492) sells Pendleton shirts, woolen skirts, and well-made shoes. Its owners, Kathryn and Leon Rubin, can tell you a thing or two about local history—their store has been in the family for almost a century. You can enter **Solano's Boot & Western Wear** (✉ 101 S. 2nd St. ☎ 505/445–2632) a city slicker and exit a cowboy or cowgirl. The enormous space, an experience as much as a store, is full of fashionable, practical Western garb. Check out the collection of cowboy hats.

**┌ EN
  ROUTE**

To reach Capulin from Raton, skip U.S. 64 and instead take **NM 72** past Sugarite Canyon State Park, a stunning road that climbs up over Johnson Mesa, from which you have amazing 100 mi views north over the mesa into the plains of eastern Colorado. It's bare and flat up here, as though you're driving across a table straddling the Colorado–New Mexico border. About halfway across the mesa (15 mi from Raton), note the **old stone church** to your right, which was built by the early farmsteaders and has since been abandoned—it's a beautiful, lonely little building with a presence that illustrates the life of solitude the mesa's settlers must have endured.

Farther along on the right, a **historical marker** details the 1908 discovery of Folsom Man by George McJunkin, which established the existence of indigenous inhabitants in the area dating back some 10,000 years. The road trails down the eastern side of the mesa and leads into tiny Folsom. Here make a right turn south on NM 325 to reach Capulin Volcano, 6 mi away.

Capulin

❻ *46 mi east of Raton via NM 72 and NM 325.*

Tiny Capulin has a gas station, a campground, and—well—little else. If you're in luck—and in season—lunch will be on at the delightful **Capulin Country Store** (➪ *see below*), which in addition to fine food sells crafts and gifts (like candlesticks made of elk antlers and dolls sewn from old quilts), snacks, maps, and cold drinks.

From the crest of **Capulin Volcano National Monument,** elevation 8,182 feet, you can see four states: Colorado, New Mexico, Texas, and

WORD OF MOUTH

"Capulin Volcano National Monument is a conical shaped dormant/extinct volcano. You can drive your car up the slope to the rim and look down into the middle. I'm not sure if you are allowed to hike into the middle. It is a smallish volcano, only several hundred yards across at the top."
                                    –KE1TH

"My son was at Capulin just last Friday. He hiked into the crater."
                                    –sharrin

Oklahoma. To the southeast is the vast section of the Santa Fe Trail that includes the Cimarron Cutoff; to the west are the snowcapped Sangre de Cristo Mountains. Unlike much of the dry surrounding territory, Capulin has enough water to support an oasis of trees, shrubs, and wildflowers. A narrow 2-mi paved road (no trailers, towed vehicles, bicycles, or pedestrians allowed) leads to the rim of the volcano; from there you can walk the final ⅕ mi into the extinct, and rather uninteresting, crater vent. (An easy-to-hike 1-mi trail circles the rim, so you can see it from different angles.) The cone of Capulin (the word is Spanish for "chokecherry"; these bushes are scattered across the area) rises more than 1,300 feet from its base. The visitor center has books, a brief video about the site, and interpretive exhibits. On busy summer weekends, you may have a short wait to enter the paved road. ⊠ *NM 325, 3 mi north of Capulin off U.S. 64* ☎ *505/278–2201* ⊕ *www.nps.gov/cavo* ⊡ *$5 per vehicle* ⊙ *Late May–early Sept., daily 7:30–6:30; early Sept.–late May, daily 8–4.*

Where to Eat

¢–$ ✕ **Capulin Country Store.** From May to the end of November, seven days a week, lunch is the big meal (and big deal) of the day at the Capulin Country Store, where Jenny Lee Pugh sets the tables with chicken-fried steak with mashed potatoes, the volcano burger (smothered in chili and cheese), and excellent desserts. Sunday dinner buffets served on holiday weekends only are not to be missed, as the ranchers who drive from miles in every direction will tell you. Lunch happens from 11 to 3, and the store shuts down at 5. ⊠ *U.S. 64 at NM 325* ☎ *505/278–3900* ⊛ *Reservations not accepted* ⊟ *AE* ⊙ *No lunch Nov.–Apr.*

▌ EN ROUTE   If you decide to skip Clayton and drive back west to Cimarron, take U.S. 64 west via Raton, which passes through ranch country underneath the biggest, bluest skies imaginable. Antelope herds graze alongside cattle. This is the classic West, with old windmills jutting into the sky of the rimrock country. The 29-mi stretch from Capulin passes through the **Raton-Clayton volcano field,** where the cones of quiet volcanos break the flat, green landscape.

Clayton

❼ *43 mi east of Capulin on U.S. 64–87, 83 mi east of Springer on U.S. 56.*

Clayton, which lies flat on the high prairie at an elevation of 5,000 feet, seemingly grew up out of nothing. Downtown is sleepy and sunny, with the old-fashioned retro-veneer typical of little western towns. It's nowhere near an interstate and so lacks the scads of ubiquitous chain properties found in Las Vegas and Raton; mom-and-pop-owned shops dominate. The town bills itself as the carbon-dioxide capital of the world, but the carbon dioxide here isn't hanging in the air but rather underground, embedded in sandstone southwest of town. Cattle graze on the many ranches around Clayton.

The friendly locals here may look at you cockeyed when they learn you've come to sightsee, but Clayton does have a few notable landmarks. The 1892 **Eklund Hotel Dining Room & Saloon,** whose splendid Victorian dining room has crystal chandeliers, apricot tufted-velvet booths, gilt-flocked wallpaper, and marble fireplaces is quite a draw in Clayton. The hunting-lodge atmosphere in the saloon is quite different but no less authentic, with a large raw-rock fireplace, wooden booths, mounted game heads, and historic photos and clippings of Clayton's past. The town's most famous historical character, the notorious train robber Black Jack Ketchum, was hanged just out front in 1901. His last words were "I had breakfast in Clayton, but I'll have dinner in hell!" Put your boot up on the brass rail at the bar (won in a poker game) and order a cold one.

★ ☼ More than 500 fossilized dinosaur tracks can be observed along the ½-mi wooden **Dinosaur Trackway at Clayton Lake State Park,** making this one of the few sites of its kind in the world. The tracks, estimated to be 100 million years old, were made when the area was the shore of a prehistoric sea. Eight species of dinosaurs, vegetarian and carnivorous, lived here. The sparkling lake that gives the state park its name is ideal for camping, hiking, and fishing. ⊠ *NM 370, 12 mi north of Clayton* ☏ *505/374–8808* ⊕ *www.emnrd.state.nm.us/nmparks* ⊠ *$4 per vehicle* ⊙ *Daily 6 AM–9 PM.*

There are few better places in New Mexico to soak in wide-open prairie vistas, clear skies, and fresh air than in the 136,000-acre **Kiowa National Grasslands.** One section of the grasslands is near Clayton and spreads east into Oklahoma and Texas. The other is about 80 mi west of Clayton, closer to Springer, south of U.S. 56. In the section near Clayton, if you look carefully, you can see ruts made by the wagons that crossed on the Old Santa Fe Trail. The land was drought-stricken during the Dust Bowl of the 1920s and '30s, when homesteaders abandoned their farms. After that, the government purchased the land and rehabilitated it to demonstrate that it could be returned to the tall grassland native to the region.

For an enjoyable loop drive through the grasslands, head east out of Clayton on U.S. 56; at NM 406 head north to just past Seneca, to where NM 406 makes a sharp turn to the east. Take the county gravel road west 3 mi and north 1 mi, noting the interpretive sign about the Santa Fe Trail. Continue a little farther north to the green gate that leads to the trail (following the limestone markers), where you can see ancient wagon ruts. Except for the occasional house or windmill, the view from the trail is not much different from what the pioneers saw. ⊠ *Off U.S. 56, north and south of Clayton* ⊡ *Administrative office: 714 Main St., Clayton 88415* ☏ *505/374–9652* ⊠ *Free.*

Where to Stay & Eat

★ $–$$ ✕⊡ **Eklund Hotel Dining Room & Saloon.** The renovated rooms of this rustic beauty of a building are comfortable and elegant, and each has custom-made furniture and a modern-but-period-style bathroom. Friendly staff help get you situated and will happily tell you about the hotel's history and things to do in the area. American standards and Southwestern fare are served in the dining room and saloon ($–$$). Old West elegance and the house specialty—hand-cut steaks—please locals and visitors alike. ⊠ *15 Main St.* ☏ *505/374–2551 or 877/355–8631* ⊟ *505/*

374–2500 ⊕ *www.theeklund.com* ⚡ *26 rooms* ⚥ *Some in-room hot tubs, cable TV, no-smoking rooms* ⊟ *MC, V* ⦿ *CP.*

$ ⊡ **Best Western Kokopelli Lodge.** Locals have long used this Southwestern-style Best Western to house out-of-town guests, where the rooms are spacious and pets are allowed (by prior arrangement only). ⊠ *702 S. 1st St., 88415* ☎ *505/374–2589 or 800/392–6691* ⬛ *505/374–2554* ⚡ *44 rooms* ⚥ *Pool, some pets allowed* ⊟ *AE, D, DC, MC, V* ⦿ *CP.*

Cimarron

⑧ *108 mi from Clayton via U.S. 56/412 west to Springer, I–25 north, and NM 58 west; 42 mi southwest of Raton on U.S. 64.*

As you approach Cimarron from the south or east, you can't help but notice a massive, greyish-white pinnacle perched atop the mountain at the northwest edge of town. Known as the **Tooth of Time**, it indicated to Santa Fe Trail travelers that their journey was nearing an end, for Santa Fe was only seven days away by wagon. Today the Tooth of Time is the emblem of the Philmont Scout Ranch, where 25,000 Boy Scouts assemble each summer.

In a land that was once home to Jicarilla Apaches and Utes, Cimarron later became a refuge for gamblers and outlaws and a stopping point for soldiers, gold seekers, and mountain men. (Its name means "untamed" in Spanish.) Founded in the early 1840s, it was the home of land baron Lucien Maxwell. These days, with a population around 900, it's a sleepy little town with some fine old buildings, and a good base from which to do some great fishing on the Cimarron River or in the various rivers flowing through Valle Vidal. It's common to see deer grazing on the edge of town—and look out for elk if you're driving at dusk or after dark. They are huge and hitting one can be deadly.

With 27 bullet holes in the tin dining-room ceiling, resident ghosts profiled on the TV show *Unsolved Mysteries,* and a guest book signed by Jesse James, the **St. James Hotel** (⊠ NM 21 at 17th St. ☎ 505/376–2664 or 800/748–2694 ⊕ www.stjamescimarron.com) epitomizes the Wild West. Every notable outlaw of the late 19th century is said to have visited the place. Chef to presidents Lincoln and Grant, Frenchman Henri Lambert opened the St. James first as a saloon in 1872 and then eight years later developed it into a hotel. The lobby is filled with western Victoriana: overstuffed sofas; stuffed heads of bison, elk, deer, and bear on the walls; and fringe on the lamp shades. Tours of the hotel, offered between 10 and 4, Monday–Saturday, are $2.

★ The workers who toiled inside the sturdy stone building that holds the **Old Mill Museum** once processed 300 barrels of flour a day for the Maxwell Ranch and the Jicarilla Apache reservation. Now the mill houses four floors of vintage photos, clothing, tools, and memorabilia depicting life in Colfax County from the 1860s into the 20th century. ⊠ *220 W. 17th St., 1 block north of St. James Hotel* ☎ *505/376–2417* ⬛ *$2* ⊙ *Late May–early Sept., Mon.–Wed., Fri., and Sat. 9–5, Sun. 1–5; early Sept–late May, Sat. 9–5 and Sun. 1–5.*

The largest scouting venue in the world, 137,000-acre **Philmont Scout Ranch** hosts nearly 30,000 Boy Scouts every summer—on any given day about 3,000 of them are out plying the property's miles of rugged trails. Phillips Petroleum magnate and Boy Scouts of American benefactor Waite Phillips established the mountainous ranch. The museums of the Philmont Scout Ranch include **Villa Philmonte,** the restored 1927 Spanish-Mediterranean summer home of Waite Phillips, furnished with European and Southwestern antiques and Native American and Southwestern art. Tours of the mansion are conducted in July and August. Scouting cofounder Ernest Thompson Seton donated most of the holdings of the **Philmont Museum & Seton Memorial Library,** among them New Mexican art and artifacts and books on natural history and the history of the Southwest. ⊠ *NM 21, 4 mi south of Cimarron* ☎ *505/376–2281* ☞ *Museum free, villa tour $4* ⊙ *Museum Sept.–May, weekdays 8–5; June–Aug., daily 8–6. Villa tours July and Aug., daily 8–11 and 12:30–4:30; by appt. rest of yr.*

Costumed reenactments at **Kit Carson Museum** demonstrate 19th-century life on what was then the Maxwell Land Grant, but is now part of the incredible Philmont Ranch. Exhibits include a working horno oven, blacksmith shop, and the Maxwell Trading Post—stocked as it might have been during Santa Fe Trail days. Period crafts are also demonstrated. ⊠ *NM 21, 11 mi south of Cimarron in Rayado* ☎ *505/376–4621* ☞ *Free* ⊙ *June–Aug., daily 8–5.*

OFF THE BEATEN PATH
★

VALLE VIDAL – One of New Mexico's great scenic routes heads northwest from U.S. 64 toward the town of Costillo (44 mi north of Taos on NM 522), affording great opportunities for sighting elk, deer, wild turkeys, and many other birds. The roughly 80-mi dirt road requires several hours of driving to complete—although it's okay for non–four-wheel-drive vehicles in summer and fall (assuming there hasn't been a major rainfall in a couple days and you're comfortable driving on some pretty rough roads). The trip passes through high-mountain grasslands, ponderosa, aspen, and sandstone cliffs. The fishing (season is July–December) in Valle Vidal is mighty fine—the native Rio Grande cutthroat trout is found only in the rivers here—and there are two campgrounds, Cimarron and McCrystal. The western section of the road is closed May through June for elk-calving season, and the eastern section is closed to protect the elks January through March. ⊠ *Off U.S. 64, turnoff is 8 mi east of Cimarron* ☎ *505/758–6200.*

Where to Stay & Eat

★ ¢–$ ✕ **Colfax Tavern.** Also known as Cold Beer, New Mexico, this little red roadhouse continues a tradition from the Prohibition era. An ongoing card game, excellent green-chile burgers, Shiner Bock (a beloved beer from Shiner, Texas) on tap, spaghetti Monday, brisket Wednesday, Saturday-night dances, and a winter *Jeopardy!* tournament are among the joint's trademarks. Visitors can walk into this hangout and feel right at home. Wear your cowboy boots. ⊠ *U.S. 64, 11 mi east of Cimarron, Colfax* ☎ *505/376–2229* ⚠ *Reservations not accepted* ▭ *MC, V.*

$ ✕▥ **St. James Hotel.** Lace curtains and Victorian-era antiques adorn 12 of the rooms here (there are also 10 modern but less distinctive motel rooms). The lodgings aren't particularly luxurious (or soundproofed), and there's a bit of a chill in the air—but that's just what you'd expect in an allegedly haunted hotel. The restaurant ($–$$$), with a ceiling full of bullet holes from the old days, serves steaks and pastas, and the café (¢–$$) serves American and Mexican standards. ⊠ *NM 21 at 17th St., 87714* ☎ *505/376–2664 or 800/748–2694* 🖷 *505/376–2623* ⊕ *www. stjamescimarron.com* ⇌ *21 rooms, 1 suite* ⚒ *Restaurant, café, lounge* 🖃 *AE, MC, V.*

★ **$–$$** 🏨 **Casa del Gavilan.** On the Santa Fe Trail and directly below the Tooth of Time, this 1912 white adobe compound (the name means "house of the hawk") on 225 acres is a romantic hideaway of the first order. The original owner, industrialist J. J. Nairn, used to entertain artists and other creative types here, and writer Zane Grey wrote "Knights of the Range" while he was holed up here. The rooms here are furnished with Southwestern antiques and artworks by the likes of Frederick Remington and Charles Stewart, and the 12-foot ceilings with huge pine vigas (support beams) lend an airy feel to the massive adobe walls. Breakfasts, which are fabulous, should be taken on the patio when the weather permits. ⊠ *NM 21, 6 mi south of Cimarron* ⌕ *Box 518, 87714* ☎ *505/376–2246 or 800/428–4526* 🖷 *505/376–2247* ⊕ *www.casadelgavilan.com* ⇌ *5 rooms* ⚒ *No room TVs, no smoking* 🖃 *D, MC, V* ⬩◎⬩ *BP.*

Shopping

Just off the main highway to the north is a street of historic buildings and a few shops. The **Cimarron Art Gallery** (⊠ 337 E. 9th St. ☎ 505/376–2614) sells Southwestern odds, ends, and artifacts, and there's a 1930s soda fountain that serves sodas, ice-cream cones, and coffee drinks. **Blue Moon Eclectics** (⊠ 333 E. 9th St. ☎ 505/376–9040) has locally made arts and crafts as well as some Navajo and Zuni jewelry.

EN ROUTE One of the most breathtaking stretches of highway in the state is U.S. 64 west from Cimarron through **Cimarron Canyon State Park** (☎ 505/377–6271 ⊕ www.emnrd.state.nm.us/nmparks ⌑ $4 per vehicle). The road passes through a steep and lush canyon banked by 400-foot crenellated granite palisades. Paralleling the road is the sparkling Cimarron River, which is known for its superb trout fishing. Wildlife (including elk, deer, and bear), granite cliff formations, a natural spring, an abandoned mine, and a visitor center are also draws. There's a campground beneath the pines, too, with spaces for RVs (no hookups) and tents, picnic tables, and pit toilets. West of Cimarron Canyon State Park, U.S. 64 passes over a high bald ridge, from which you'll be awarded a magnificent view over **Eagle Nest Lake,** the Moreno Valley, and the eastern slope of the Sangre de Cristo Mountains in the distance. Continue down through Eagle Nest Lake village toward Angel Fire. Then make a left turn (south) onto NM 434, which passes little Black Lake and offers one final view of the valley before narrowing sharply and plummeting into dark, deep, ponderosa pine–shrouded Guadalupita Canyon. Drive slowly: the road twists and turns and crosses several one-lane bridges over Coyote Creek.

The Rincon Mountains rise to 9,500 feet to the west of NM 434, and to the east (a left turn off the highway) you can stop for a ramble at

Tapetes de Lana

THERE ARE FEW FAIRY-TALE STORIES of revitalized rural economies in America. Tapetes de Lana is one of them.

Tapetes de Lana ("wool tapestry" in Spanish) started as a vocational training program for weavers in Las Vegas in 1998 with a small grant and the sheer determination of its founder, Carla Gomez. Gomez had supported herself and her three children with her weaving for years and wanted to extend the skill to her community in the hopes that others could do the same rather than leave the area to find work or take minimum wage jobs in one of the large national chain stores that have begun to populate the area.

What started out as a small group of women working in an old, one-room schoolhouse on the outskirts of Las Vegas has blossomed—considerably. Gomez now runs two weaving centers (one on the Las Vegas plaza, the other in the center of Mora), oversees 40 employees, and is supervising the construction of a spinning mill, theater arts complex, and commercial kitchen on the Mora property.

The weaving centers offer more than the promise of a new economic base in these relatively sleepy areas—they also represent a revitalization of a traditional art form that in many areas of the country is dying out entirely. Weaving has been a mainstay in New Mexico since 1598, when Don Juan de Oñate brought Spanish Colonists and churro sheep from Spain. Despite struggling to stay vital since the late 1800s, New Mexico's weavers retain a reputation for high-quality, uniquely beautiful products. Tapetes de Lana has become an essential component of that living tradition.

And the result of all this industriousness? Gorgeous, handwoven shawls, scarves, rugs, and heirloom jerga blankets. Custom-made pillows, coasters, and yarns are available. Silk and alpaca, mohair, wool, and chenille textiles all hang gracefully from the walls and racks in the studios. Weavers study and practice their skills in the same studio where the work is sold.

When you're in Las Vegas or Mora, stop and visit the bustling shops and studios of Tapetes de Lana. You're witnessing rural revitalization in action.

Coyote Creek State Park (☎ 505/387–2328 ✒ $4), which also has exceptionally good trout fishing and some campsites. South of Coyote Creek State Park on NM 434, you'll pass through tiny, insular **El Turquillo.** Here the highway widens as it opens into a broad sunny valley—to the east you'll spy the red-rock cliffs that form the face of Black Mesa, the land barrier between here and the eastern grasslands. As you come around a bend in NM 434 heading from El Turquillo toward Mora, behold the Sangre de Cristo range, specifically the east side of **Trampas and Truchas peaks,** from an angle few tourists ever see. Just before Mora and the intersection with NM 518 is an intricate network of irrigation ditches that farmers employ to keep this region so fertile.

Mora

◉ *72 mi south from Cimarron on U.S. 64 west to Eagle Nest Lake and NM 434 south via Angel Fire; 30 mi northwest of Las Vegas on NM 518; 85 mi northeast of Santa Fe via High Road to Taos north to Peñasco and then NM 518 south.*

Originally settled in 1835 by land grantees, Mora was seen by the Mexican government as a buffer between their territory and encroaching Americans. The town grew rapidly from the get-go, but refused to give up loyalty to Mexico when the U.S. troops took over in 1846. Battles for control of the area raged for more than a year, until the U.S. finally gained the upper hand on its new territory. One hundred years ago, Mora was a bustling center of commerce and politics, and was known as the "bread basket" of New Mexico because of its incredible production of wheat and grains. The wide, curbed streets and building fronts, though in need of restoration, attest to the town's past importance.

Today Mora is a small, still mostly Hispanic farming village where you can get gas, pick up snacks at the supermarket, and get your bearings. There are a couple of restaurants on the main road if a New Mexican meal is what you need. **Tapetes de Lana,** the local weaving collaborative, has a spacious studio and shop on the corner of NM 518 and NM 434, where you can purchase beautiful handwoven textiles and help support the local economy and culture. If you've got animal-loving kids with you, stop by **Victory Ranch,** a working 1,100-acre alpaca farm. You can pet and feed the high-altitude–loving creatures as well as visit the gift shop for Peruvian-made hats, sweaters, and mittens. The ranch is handicapped-accessible. ✉ *NM 434, 1 mi north of NM 518* ☎ *505/387–2254* ⊕ *www.victoryranch.com* ✉ *$2* ☉ *Thurs.–Mon. 10–4.*

6

At the junction of NM 434 and NM 518, make a right and head a couple of miles north to **Cleveland Roller Mill,** a fixture in Mora Valley, which served as the region's main flour mill in the late 1800s. Milling demonstrations are held over the Labor Day Millfest, and in summer you can visit the artists' cooperative, where local artisans sell their sculpture, weaving, jewelry, and other crafts. ✉ *NM 518* ☎ *505/387–2645* ✉ *$2* ☉ *Weekends, late May–late Oct., daily 10–3.*

EN ROUTE From Cleveland Roller Mill you can either return via NM 518 to Las Vegas (about 30 mi) or continue north on NM 518 over the gorgeous eastern face of the Sangre de Cristo range. You'll eventually come to Peñasco, on the High Road to Taos, from which you can either go south to Santa Fe or north to Taos. **The drive from Mora to Peñasco** offers spectacular mountain views, and passes by old farmsteads and adobe hamlets slowly being worn down by the wind and weather.

★ As you head south on NM 518 toward Las Vegas, be sure to stop in the **La Cueva Historic District.** Among the buildings here, which date to the 1850s, is a stone-walled mill that supplied flour to the soldiers of Fort Union. Pioneer rancher Vicente Romero's mill also supplied power to the area until 1950; at what is now called the Salman Ranch, you can pick raspberries early to mid-fall, or buy fresh berries, raspberry jam

288 < **Northeastern New Mexico**

and vinegar, and dried flowers and herbs at the original La Cueva Ranch Store (open 9–5). Brilliantly colored wildflower gardens, and homemade tamales, burgers, and raspberry sundaes served at the café (11–4) draw families out for weekend excursions. The historic district's San Rafael Church, dating from the 1870s, is also worth a look. Call ahead for raspberry-picking hours. ⊠ *NM 518 at NM 442, 10 mi south of Mora, 20 mi north of Las Vegas* ☎ *505/387-2900* ⊗ *Closed Mon.*

NORTHEASTERN NEW MEXICO ESSENTIALS

AIR TRAVEL

The two closest airports to northeastern New Mexico are Albuquerque (ABQ) and Amarillo, Texas (AMA). Albuquerque is closer to Las Vegas, Cimarron, Mora, and Springer. Amarillo is closer to Clayton, Capulin, Santa Rosa, and Tucumcari. Raton is about equidistant from both.

🛪 **Regional Airports Great Lakes Aviation** ☎ 800/554-5111 ⊕ www.greatlakesav.com. **Mesa Airlines** ☎ 800/637-2247. **Rio Grande Air** ☎ 877/435-9742.

🛪 **Airports Albuquerque International Sunport** ⊠ 2200 Sunport Blvd. SE, Albuquerque ☎ 505/842-4366 ⊕ www.cabq.gov/airport. **Amarillo International Airport** ⊠ 10801 Airport Blvd. (take I-40 to Airport Blvd. exit), Amarillo, TX ☎ 806/335-1671.

BUS TRAVEL

Texas, New Mexico & Oklahoma Coaches makes daily runs between Albuquerque and Raton and between Taos and Raton, with stops in Las Vegas, Springer, Cimarron, and Maxwell.

🛪 **Texas, New Mexico & Oklahoma Coaches** ☎ 505/445-9071 in Raton, 800/231-2222.

CAR TRAVEL

Interstate 25 is the main route into northeastern New Mexico from Santa Fe. U.S. 64 heads east into the region from Taos and west into the region from Oklahoma. U.S. 56/412 heads west from Oklahoma toward Springer, where it connects with I–25. From I–40, take either of two very scenic routes into the northeast: U.S. 84 from west of Santa Rosa, or NM 3 from west of Vaughn.

EMERGENCIES

In case of emergency dial 911.

🛪 **Hospital Alta Vista Regional Hospital** ⊠ 1235 8th St., Las Vegas ☎ 505/425-6751.

🛪 **Pharmacies Walgreens** ⊠ 620 Mills Ave., Las Vegas ☎ 505/425-3317. **Wal-Mart** ⊠ 2609 7th St., Las Vegas ☎ 505/425-5242.

VISITOR INFORMATION

🛪 **Cimarron Chamber of Commerce** ⊠ 104 N. Lincoln Ave., 87740 ☎ 505/376-2417 ⊕ www.cimarronnm.com. **Clayton Chamber of Commerce** ⊠ 1103 S 1st St., 88415 ☎ 505/374-9253 or 800/390-7858 ⊕ www.claytonnewmexico.org. **Las Vegas Chamber of Commerce** ⊠ 727 Grand Ave. ⑃ Box 128, 87701 ☎ 505/425-8631 or 800/832-5947 ⊕ www.lasvegasnewmexico.com. **New Mexico Department of Tourism** ⊕ www.nenewmexico.com. **Raton Chamber of Commerce** ⊠ 100 Clayton Rd., 87740 ☎ 505/445-3689 or 800/638-6161 ⊕ www.raton.com. **Springer Chamber of Commerce** ⊠ 606 Maxwell St., 87747 ☎ 505/483-2998.

Southeastern New Mexico

INCLUDING WHITE SANDS NATIONAL
MONUMENT & TEXAS'S GUADALUPE MOUNTAINS

WORD OF MOUTH

"We spent several days in Roswell, doing all the Roswell things including a few hours at the UFO Museum. I even bought an alien yard gnome as a souvenir."

—alfisol

" If you go in summer the white sand [of White Sands National Monument] gets really really HOT. In the area, there's Ruidoso to visit and Lincoln County of Billy the Kid lore. There are also horse races in Ruidoso, which are kind of fun. However, it's a pretty bleak drive from Albuquerque."

—jayne1973

Revised by
Georgia
de Katona

AWASH WITH GEOLOGICAL CONTRAST, the landscapes of southeastern New Mexico shift before your eyes as you drive from one area to the next. Parched red earth sparsely dotted with scrub oak turns into miles of white gypsum dunes at White Sands National Monument. Making the 19-mi drive to Cloudcroft (8,600 feet) from Alamogordo will double your altitude, and take you into the cool mountain air of the heavily forested Lincoln National Forest. Curious, large-eared mule deer wander amid the juniper and pines, as well as among sand dunes near the Pecos River farther east. The seemingly monotonous Chihuahuan desert holds the underground wonderland of Carlsbad Caverns, the hulking El Capitán peak, and, in Guadalupe Mountains National Park, pure, bubbling streams, pine laden basins, and prickly cactus. Sure, the terms "vast" and "desolate" are regularly applied to this area, but they're misleading, and only true until you look a bit closer at the amazing region you've wandered into.

For all its beauty, the area seems understandably harsh to strangers. Spanish settlers quickly bypassed the region in the late 1500s, in favor of the more friendly environs around the Rio Grande in the western and northern portions of New Mexico. Yet in this very region—at Black Water Draw near what is now Portales and Clovis—evidence of some of the earliest inhabitants of North America has been found. Artifacts discovered in the region prove that primitive hunters and gatherers lived here as long as 11,000 years ago, alongside fantastic creatures like the woolly mammoth.

Native Americans lived here for hundreds of years before encroachment by the Spanish, and later the Americans. Though Hispanic settlers had established a few scattered communities, the area was primarily the homeland of Mescalero Apaches. In the mid-1800s Fort Sumner and Fort Stanton were erected to offer protection for miners and American settlers during intensified skirmishes with local tribes. Near Ruidoso, in what is left of their traditional homeland in the Sacramento Mountains, the Mescalero Apaches now own a luxury resort and ski area that attract tens of thousands of visitors annually.

The grasslands in southeastern New Mexico came to be ruled by cattle kings like John Chisum in the late 1800s. The baby-faced outlaw Billy the Kid (Henry McCarty) became a living legend here during the infamous Lincoln County War, waged by rival entrepreneurs in 1872. He wasn't the only outlaw to make his mark on the territory, however; in the now-vanished town of Seven Rivers, between Carlsbad and Artesia, shoot-outs were said to be so common around the turn of the century that it was claimed "you could read your newspaper by the light of the gunfire." Things calmed down—a bit—once the discovery of oil and other valuable minerals brought miners to the area in the early 1900s.

Today, southeastern New Mexico retains a delicious feeling of wildness. The nearest interstate is generally as far as 200 mi away, and with no lights from strip malls or urban sprawl, the stargazing here is a treat for

GREAT ITINERARIES

You can explore a cross section of the southeast's attractions in three days by moving quickly. If you start your trip from El Paso, Texas, swing through Guadalupe Mountains and Carlsbad Caverns national parks first. If you're dropping down from Albuquerque, reverse the itinerary and make cities such as Ruidoso and Roswell your first stops before traveling on to the national parks.

IF YOU HAVE 3 DAYS

It's best to start from the gateway of El Paso, Texas, and make **Guadalupe Mountains National Park ①** your first rest stop. Just north of the mountains, over the New Mexico state line, is **Carlsbad Caverns National Park ②**. Take the Big Room Tour in the late morning or early afternoon, and in warmer months, be sure to catch the spectacular evening bat exodus out of the cave's mouth. Afterward you can overnight in 🏨 **Carlsbad ④**. On the morning of Day 2, stop by Living Desert Zoo and Gardens State Park before heading north to **Roswell ⑤** to learn about alleged alien visitors at the International UFO Museum and Research Center and view the impressive collections of the Roswell Museum and Art Center, including the Goddard rocketry display and paintings by Southwestern artists. Push on to overnight in 🏨 **Lincoln ⑩**. You awaken in a town of 70, where the ghosts of past gunslingers loom large. Make time for some outdoor activities in the mountains surrounding **Ruidoso ⑫**. A ski resort is open in winter and horse racing takes place at Ruidoso Downs in summer. Arrange your schedule so you have at least an hour for **White Sands National Monument ⑮**, which is open in summer until 9.

IF YOU HAVE 5 DAYS

Spend most of your first day at **Guadalupe Mountains National Park ①** in Texas. At McKittrick Canyon are three trails of varying lengths. On your first evening, view the bat flight at **Carlsbad Caverns National Park ②** and spend the night there.

On the morning of Day 2, return to Carlsbad Caverns to take the Natural Entrance Route into the depths of the cavern, after which you can loop through the interior, and then take the Big Room Tour. That afternoon visit Living Desert Zoo and Gardens State Park in 🏨 **Carlsbad ④**. In the evening consider strolling some of the scenic walkways along the Pecos River at the Lake Carlsbad Recreation Area.

On Day 3 drive north on U.S. 285 to **Roswell ⑤**, where you can stop at the Roswell Museum and Art Center and International UFO Museum and Research Center. Continue to 🏨 **Lincoln ⑩** on U.S. 70/380 west and take in a bit of the Wild West before settling down for the night at one of the B&Bs there. Spend Day 4 perusing the museums and galleries of 🏨 **Ruidoso ⑫** and Ruidoso Downs. Spend the night at Inn of the Mountain Gods, or at one of the many nice inns in Ruidoso. On Day 5, swing through **Cloudcroft ⑯** before examining the space ware at the New Mexico Museum of Space History in **Alamogordo ⑭**. Close your day and finish up the last roll of film at **White Sands National Monument ⑮**.

7

the expert and novice alike. Cloudcroft has one of the largest solar observatories in the world, the National Solar Observatory, because of the clarity of the skies and the absence of typical light pollution—Alamogordo, which lies at the base of the mountains, uses special lights to minimize glare. Of course, the area's seeming proximity to the heavens is what's made it the subject of an ongoing debate among UFO believers for almost 60 years: what was it, exactly, that fell from the sky over Roswell that night in July of 1947?

Exploring Southeastern New Mexico

The wildly rugged Guadalupe and Sacramento mountain ranges cut through the south-central portion of the state, dividing the Pecos River valley to the east from the Mesilla River valley to the west. Make the Carlsbad Caverns National Park and White Sands National Monument on opposite sides of these mountains a top priority: they are truly among the world's greatest natural wonders.

Timing

Winters tend to be gentle in the desert regions, but between May and early September blistering heat is not uncommon. Even the mountainous areas can be uncomfortably warm during a hot spell. Plan summer outdoor excursions for early morning or late afternoon. Spring is cooler, but it's often accompanied by blustery, dust-laden winds. One of the best times to visit is between September and early November, when skies are clear blue and the weather is usually balmy. The mountains typically get plenty of snow in the winter months, though the roads are well-maintained and navigable, and the snow wonderfully powdery and dry.

About the Restaurants

Leave the fancy duds at home—you're unlikely to find a formal dining room to strut into. Casual dress reigns supreme in this part of the world. Although much of southeastern New Mexico is cowboy country, where thick steaks and barbecue make the meal, good Mexican food can be found fairly easily.

About the Hotels

Southeastern New Mexico has any number of solid, reliable chain motels to choose from if that's what suits you, but you can also choose from a luxury resort, numerous quaint cabins, and several charming and beautiful bed-and-breakfasts in the Sacramento Mountains. These private facilities serve some of the tastiest food in the region and can offer amenities like therapeutic massage, horseback riding, and guided fishing and hiking tours.

WHAT IT COSTS				
$$$$	**$$$**	**$$**	**$**	**¢**
RESTAURANTS over $30	$23–$30	$16–$22	$10–$15	under $10
HOTELS over $250	$176–$250	$121–$175	$70–$120	under $70

Restaurant prices are per person for a main course at dinner. Hotel prices are for two people in a standard double room in high season, excluding 10%–12% tax.

IF YOU LIKE

CAVING

Most people think only of the world-famous Carlsbad Caverns when they visit southeastern New Mexico. But the entire area is riddled with hundreds of smaller caves that attract numerous "inner space" explorers. You probably need to link up with a reputable caving organization and receive at least some training in order to gain access to many of these underground frontiers. But the spelunking adventure is more than worth it.

FISHING & HIKING

Fishing, hiking, and boating on the Pecos River and in Brantley Lake State Park are among the popular activities in southeastern New Mexico. Conchas and Santa Rosa lakes are man-made lakes whose blue, blue waters stand in stark contrast to the sparse vegetation surrounding them, and Santa Rosa Lake is a wonderful place to spot cormorants. Except on certain lakes operated by the Mescalero Apaches, who charge separate fees and set their own catch limits, you'll need a fishing license. Clerks at most sporting-goods shops can inform

you of fishing regulations, which can vary. If you're hiking, be aware that trails in arid and even mountainous regions seldom have water available. Always carry water with you if you plan an excursion of more than a mile. Before you pack simply a purifier, call the administrators of the area in which you'll be hiking and find out about water sources. You might have to pack in all the water you need.

PECOS DIAMOND HUNTING

You can find your own version of treasure near the Pecos River in the Roswell and Artesia areas by participating in a popular local hobby known as Pecos diamond hunting. U.S. Bureau of Land Management staff and friendly locals will give you tips about where to go to find these quartz crystals, which are unique (in all the world), and found only in this area. It's perfectly legal on public land to pick up Pecos diamonds, which can range in color from translucent white to pink to orange. These "diamonds," usually elongated, are "double terminated" with facets forming points at each end.

THE SOUTHEAST CORNER

Some folks refer to the southeast as "Little Texas." Geographically and culturally it does indeed seem an extension of its neighbor to the east: you'll find the easy smiles and small-town graciousness of the neighbor state in great abundance. The biggest attraction—Carlsbad Caverns National Park—is just above the Texas state line. Cattle and sheep still roam miles of arid pastures, much the way they have for well over a century. During the past two decades a steady migration of newer residents—many of them retirees leaving crowded metropolitan areas for wide-open spaces and clean air—has added significantly to the population and to the availability of such staples as espresso.

Southeastern
New Mexico

Guadalupe Mountains National Park

★ ❶ *U.S. 62/180, 110 mi northeast of El Paso, Texas; 40 mi southwest of Carlsbad Caverns National Park.*

The Guadalupes, as they're called, pop right up out of the desert and the magnificent El Capitán peak, in particular, is visible for miles in all directions. These mountains provide sanctuary for a surprising variety of wildlife, including scores and scores mule deer and the occasional mountain lion. Fossils left over from an ancient sea are part of a geological terrain popular with students and researchers. The relative lack of water has kept the foothills and canyons from being developed, and the park itself doesn't ever seem to suffer from crowds.

This national park is relatively new, created by Congress in 1966 and formally established in 1972. The 5,632-acre heart of the park was given to the federal government by the Wallace Pratt family. Pratt had worked as a geologist for Humble Oil, later known as Exxon, when he first viewed and later acquired the wildly beautiful McKittrick Canyon area of the park in 1921. Most of the remaining acreage was added in a purchase of 70,000 acres from the J. C. Hunter Ranch.

Pull into the **visitor center** to view exhibits and a slide show that will give you a quick introduction to what this 86,416-acre park is all about. You can see panoramic vistas and glimpses of wildflowers, but photos simply can't do the park justice. Better to explore this territory yourself on some of the 80 mi of hiking trails, which include everything from short excursions to grueling treks. The short but rewarding Smith Spring Trail leads to a spring and small waterfall; the more challenging, 8½-mi Permian Reef has views down into the green chasm of McKittrick Canyon and is a real treat for geology buffs. The Pine Springs trailhead offers a number of appealing options at various levels of difficulty—if you really want a workout, set aside about eight hours for the steep climb up Guadalupe Peak, where you can see sheer, exposed cliffs and breathtaking views of desert plains below.

About 1 mi northeast of the visitor center, turn west off U.S. 62/180 to see the **Pinery Butterfield Station Ruins.** This was one of the rest stops along the old Butterfield Overland Mail Coach route in the mid-1800s, which carried passengers between St. Louis and San Francisco. Signs along the paved ⅔-mi round-trip trail identify such high desert plants as sotol, Apache plume, yucca, and sumac. Ruins of the old stagecoach stop are piled slabs of native limestone, stabilized but not restored. About 2 mi northeast of the visitor center, west off U.S. 62/180, is the **Frijole Ranch History Museum,** where antique saddles and ranching artifacts from the Guadalupe Mountains area are on display.

The **McKittrick Canyon** gate is open from 8 to 4:30 daily in winter months and from 8 to 6 when daylight saving time is in effect. In this day-use area you can hike almost 1 mi on a nature loop in the wide mouth of the canyon, where signs explain the area's geologic and biological history. From here, you also can take a 4½-mi round-trip excursion to the Pratt Lodge (now vacant), which was built entirely—including the roof—of native stone in the 1930s by the area's original owner, oilman Wallace Pratt. The building usually stays closed, although volunteers sometimes staff it during prime fall foliage season from mid-October through mid-November, when the canyon's oak and bigtooth maple trees turn brilliant hues of yellow, orange, and red (call first if you're planning to visit the lodge). Another option is a 6¾-mi round-trip to the Grotto picnic area. Turn west off U.S. 62/180 6 mi northeast of the visitor center and travel 4 mi to McKittrick Canyon Visitor Center, where the trails begin. ⊠ *Guadalupe Mountains National Park, off U.S. 62/180 55 mi southwest of Carlsbad and 110 mi northeast of El Paso* ☞*HC60, Box 400, Salt Flat, TX 79847* ☎*915/ 828–3251* ⊠ *$3 hiking fee at any trailhead.*

Camping

⚠ **Dog Canyon Campground.** This campground is remote and a little tricky to find, but well worth the effort. On the north side of Guadalupe National Park, it can be accessed by turning west on County Road 408 off U.S. 62/180, about 9 mi south of Carlsbad. Drive 23 mi on this county road; then turn south on NM 137. Travel 43 mi through Lincoln National Forest until the road dead-ends just at the park boundary, at the New Mexico–Texas state line. Here, you'll find a well-maintained camping area in a coniferous forest, with hiking trails nearby. ⊠ *Guadalupe Mountains National Park, off Rte. 137, 65 mi southwest of Carlsbad* ☎ *505/981– 2418* ⚖ *Flush toilets, drinking water, picnic tables, public telephone, ranger station* ⊠ *4 RV sites, 9 tent sites* ⊠ *$8* ⊟ *AE, D, MC, V.*

⚠ **Pine Springs Campground.** You'll be snuggled amid piñon and juniper trees at the base of a tall mountain peak at this site behind the Guadalupe Mountains National Park visitor center. Wood and charcoal fires are prohibited, although camp stoves are allowed. Shade here can be a bit sparse in the intense summer heat, but fall weather makes for fantastic camping. Advance reservations are accepted for group sites only. ⊠ *Guadalupe Mountains National Park, off U.S. 62/180* ☎ *915/828– 3251* ⚖ *Flush toilets, drinking water, picnic tables, public telephone, ranger station* ⊠ *20 tent sites, 18 RV sites, 1 wheelchair-accessible site, 2 group sites* ⊠ *$8* ⊟ *AE, D, MC, V.*

Carlsbad Caverns National Park

❷
Fodor'sChoice
★
167 mi east of El Paso, Texas, on U.S. 62/180, 320 mi southeast of Albuquerque.

Year after year visitors come to Carlsbad Caverns National Park by the hundreds of thousands. They come to view the outstanding array of subterranean chambers, where the fantastic, dazzling rock formations have names like Hall of the White Giant, the Kings Palace, the Devils Den, the Caveman, and Iceberg Rock.

The park is in the Chihuahuan Desert, which extends north from Mexico into southwestern Texas and southeastern New Mexico. Pictographs near the main cave entrance indicate that pre-Columbian peoples took shelter here more than 1,000 years ago, though archaeologists doubt they ventured far inside. It wasn't until the 19th century that nearby settlers rediscovered the caverns, after seeing smokelike swirling columns of bats leaving the caverns each night to feed on insects. Area caves were mined for bat dung, which was used as fertilizer, but only one person was interested in the caves for more than guano. Cowboy Jim White was fascinated by their topography and spent two decades exploring them. In the early 1920s White finally secured a photographer, Ray Davis, to bear witness to his extravagant claims about the caverns' amazing underground environment. Davis's photos sparked interest in the caverns, and White turned tour operator, taking people down 170 feet in a bucket left over from the days of bat guano mining. The federal government got wind of this natural wonder, and in 1923 President Calvin Coolidge designated the caverns a national monument; in 1930 the area was upgraded to the status of national park.

Carlsbad Caverns' formation began 250 million years ago, when the 300-mi-long Capitán Reef stretched around the edge of the warm, shallow sea that once covered this region. The sea evaporated and the reef was buried until a few million years ago, when a combination of erosion and earthquakes brought parts of it back above ground. Rainwater seeping down through the reef's cracks gradually enlarged them into cavities, which eventually collapsed, forming huge rooms. For eons the evaporated limestone deposited on the cave ceilings grew into great hanging stalactites, which in turn dripped onto the floor. In time massive stalagmites grew up to meet them, and other more fragile formations such as cave pearls, draperies, popcorn, and lily pads resulted.

No matter how tempting it is to touch the cave's walls and jutting rock formations as you walk through—don't. This can't be said often or strongly enough. Oil from the human hand forms a type of waterproofing that inhibits the natural water seepage. And please don't leave the guided pathways; if you do, you not only risk serious injury but can damage the cave. Guides will tell you the rules, but we're telling you first. Respect the caves; they are living organisms.

The temperature inside Carlsbad Caverns remains at a constant 56°F. It's damp, so bring a sweater and comfortable shoes with rubber soles—because of the moisture, the paved walkways can get slippery. The caverns are well lighted, and park rangers provide assistance and information. Exhibits at the visitor center describe park history and geology and the lives of bats. You can eat aboveground at the visitor center or at an underground lunchroom. ⊠ *Carlsbad Caverns National Park, 3225 National Parks Hwy., Carlsbad 88220* ☎ *505/785–2232 recorded information and direct contact, 800/967–2283 reservations (central National Park Service number)* ⊕ *www.nps.gov/cave* ⊠ *General entrance $6, audio guide $3 additional; see individual cave descriptions below for additional fees and hrs of operation* ☉ *Visitor center late May–mid-Aug., daily 8–7; mid-Aug.–late May, daily 8–5.*

There are two self-guided routes into Carlsbad Cavern: the **Natural Entrance Route and the Big Room Route.** An audio guide featuring commentary from park rangers is available at numbered stops along both of these trails. If you take the Natural Entrance Route, you can proceed on foot along a paved walkway that winds into the caverns' depths for about a mile, passing through underground rooms and descending slowly to a depth of about 750 feet. It takes about one hour to complete; the trail can be slick and the grades are fairly steep, so be prepared for a strenuous hike. The Big Room Route is less difficult. A high-speed elevator from the visitor center carries you down 750 feet to an underground lunchroom where you can begin your exploration. This mile-long route also takes about an hour to walk. A portion of the main cavern is accessible to visitors using wheelchairs. In both cases you can visit the Big Room, large enough to hold 14 football fields; the highest part of the ceiling reaches 255 feet. ⊠ *Combined ticket to Natural Entrance Route and Big Room Route $6 ☉ Natural Entrance Route late May–mid-Aug., daily 8:30–3:30, last entry to caverns; mid-Aug.–May, daily 8:30–2, last entry to caverns. Big Room Route late May–mid-Aug., daily 8:30–5, last elevator down; mid-Aug.–late May, daily 8:30–3:30, last elevator down.*

A third option for exploring the caverns is the ranger-led **Kings Palace Tour** through the Kings Palace, the Queens Chamber, the Papoose Room, and the Green Lake Room. The tour covers about a mile, descends into the deepest part of the caverns open to the public—830 feet below the desert floor—and includes an uphill 80-foot climb on a switchback trail. It takes about 1½ hours to complete. ⊠ *$8, in addition to $6 general entrance fee to caverns ☉ Daily, call for tour times.*

A few other **off-trail tours** are available within Carlsbad Caverns. Lefthand Tunnel is in an undeveloped part of the caverns and contains clear pools and ancient reef fossils. Lower Cave, billed as a "moderately strenuous" tour, involves climbs on 50 feet of vertical ladders. Children younger than six are not allowed on this tour. The Hall of the White Giant is a strenuous tour that requires squirming long distances on your hands and knees through tight passageways into a remote chamber with glistening white formations. The tour of "wild" Spider Cave takes you through the park's backcountry and involves tight crawlways, avoid both Hall of the White Giants and Spider Cave if you're at all claustrophobic. Reservations are essential for the special tours. The minimum age for visitors to the Hall of the White Giant and the Spider Cave is 12. ☎ *505/785–2232, 800/967–2283 reservations ⊠ In addition to general entrance fee to cavern: Lefthand Tunnel $7, Lower Cave $20, Hall of the White Giant $20, Spider Cave $20 ☉ Lefthand Tunnel, daily at 9 AM; Lower Cave, weekdays at 1; Hall of the White Giant, Sat. at 1; Spider Cave, separate from main cavern; general caverns entrance fee not required, Sun. at 1.*

Slaughter Canyon Cave, 25 mi from the main cavern, is much less accessible. Millions of years old, the cave was discovered by Tom Tucker, a local goatherd, in 1937. The cave consists primarily of a 1,140-foot-long corridor with numerous side passages. The total extent of the surveyed passage is 1¾ mi, and the lowest point is 250 feet below the surface. Outstanding formations include the Christmas Tree, the Monarch, the Tear Drop, and the China Wall.

Rangers lead groups of 25 on a two-hour lantern tour of the cave. Children under age six are not permitted. The cave temperature is a constant 62°F, and the humidity is a clammy 90%. You need to bring along your own flashlight, hiking boots or good walking shoes with heavy treads (sneakers aren't recommended), and drinking water. Photographs are permitted, but no tripod setups are allowed because the group moves along at a relatively brisk pace. Slaughter Canyon Cave is not for the casual tourist—it requires being in very good physical condition and it is long enough to satisfy those fascinated by caves. It *is* a great adventure if you want to experience what cave exploration is really like, that is, caves minus paved pathways and electric lighting.

Make reservations at least a day ahead of your visit; in summer it's recommended you reserve a place on the lantern tour at least two weeks ahead. The last few miles of the road to the cave are gravel, which means you have to slow to about 25 mph. The mouth is also at the end of a ½-mi path up a 500-foot rise, so allow yourself sufficient time to complete the drive and climb or you might arrive late for the tour. ☏ *505/ 785–2232, 800/967–2283 reservations* ✉ *$15* ⊙ *Tours late May–early Sept., daily at 10 and 1; early Sept.–late May, weekends at 10.*

The newest discovery in Carlsbad Caverns National Park is **Lechuguilla Cave,** the deepest limestone cave in the United States. Scientists began mapping the cave network in 1986, and though they've located more than 112 mi of caverns extending to a depth of more than 1,600 feet, much more of this area along the park's northern border remains to be investigated. Lechuguilla is not open to the public, but an exhibit describing it can be viewed at the visitor center.

★ Every evening, just about sunset, between late May and mid-October, Mexican free-tailed bats swirl by the tens of thousands out of the cavern's entrance to scout for flying insects. Watching the nightly **bat flights** has been one of the greatest attractions at Carlsbad Caverns since 1929. (Scientists have yet to figure out how a bat hanging upside down in a dark cave knows when the sun has set outside.) The population of bats varies even daily but is estimated to be several hundred thousand. Collectively the bats consume more than 3 tons of bugs per night. Prior to the exodus, which begins at dusk, a park ranger gives an informative talk about these much-maligned creatures. The time of the bat flights varies (though they're usually around sunset), so ranger lectures are flexible as well; the time is posted at the visitor center. The bats leave for the warmer climates of Mexico sometime in October. ✉ *Bat Flight Amphitheater, near visitor center* ✉ *Free.*

The scenic 9½-mi **Walnut Canyon Desert Drive** begins ½ mi from the visitor center. It travels along the top of a ridge to the edge of Rattlesnake Canyon and back down through upper Walnut Canyon to the main entrance road. The backcountry scenery on this one-way gravel loop is stunning; go late in the afternoon or early in the morning to enjoy the full spectrum of changing light and dancing colors. You might also spot some of the many inquisitive mule deer that inhabit the park. The self-guided, partially wheelchair-accessible Desert Nature Walk, about ½ mi long, begins near the cavern's entrance.

Trees shade the picnic and recreation area at **Rattlesnake Springs**, near the Black River—but don't let the name scare you; you wouldn't find any more rattlesnakes here than at any other similar site in the Southwest. A favorite of bird-watchers, the springs were a source of water for Native Americans hundreds of years ago. Today it's the main source of water for the park. Overnight camping and parking are not allowed, though you'll find free admission and access to shaded picnic tables as well as some fine bird-watching.

Camping

Backcountry camping is by permit only in Carlsbad Caverns National Park; free permits can be obtained at the visitor center, where you can also pick up a map of areas closed to camping. You'll need to hike to campsites. There are no vehicle or RV camping areas in the park.

Nearby Brantley Lake State Park (in the town of Carlsbad) and Dog Canyon Campground (in Guadalupe Mountains National Park) in Lincoln National Forest have camping facilities. Commercial sites can be found in White's City and Carlsbad.

Sports & the Outdoors

BIRD-WATCHING From turkey vultures to golden eagles, more than 200 species of birds have been identified in Carlsbad Caverns National Park. The best place to bird-watch in the park, and one of the state's best bird-watching areas, is Rattlesnake Springs. Ask for a checklist at the visitor center and then start looking for red-tailed hawks, red-winged blackbirds, white-throated swifts, northern flickers, pygmy nuthatches, yellow-billed cuckoos, roadrunners, mallards, American coots, and green- and blue-winged teal.

HIKING Hiking in Carlsbad Caverns National Park can be exhilarating—the desert terrain is stark and awe-inspiring—but few trails are marked. A topographical map, available at the visitor center bookstore, is helpful for finding some of the old ranch trails. Permits aren't required except for overnight backpacking. Bring water; there's none available. No pets or guns are permitted.

White's City

❸ *7 mi east of Carlsbad Caverns National Park on NM 7, at junction with U.S. 62/180.*

At the turnoff from the highway to Carlsbad Caverns, the one-road, family-owned town of White's City contains motels, restaurants, a saloon, a campground, a grocery store, a post office, a gas station, souvenir shops, a museum, and a water park for guests staying in one of the town's two motels—all along a simple, Western-style boardwalk. The town is one of the few that's privately owned in the country. The owners, the White family, live in a cluster of homes above the hotel properties.

Early-American memorabilia and artifacts—antique dolls and doll-houses, guns and rifles, music boxes, old cars, and a 6,000-year-old mum-mified Native American (or so the sign says)—fill the homespun **Million Dollar Museum.** Thirty-two mostly German dollhouses made between the late 19th and mid-20th centuries are also on display. ⊠ *21 Carlsbad Caverns Hwy., off White's City boardwalk* ☎ *505/785–2291* ⊠ *$3* ⊙ *Mid-May–mid-Sept., daily 7 AM–10 PM; mid-Sept.–mid-May, daily 7–6.*

Where to Stay & Eat

$–$$ ✕ **Velvet Garter Restaurant and Saloon.** Steaks, chicken, seafood, and Mex-ican food are served in a room decorated with pictures from the Old West, some period antiques, and Western kitsch. You won't find gòur-met meals here, but it's a decent enough place to eat if you don't want to drive 20 mi north to Carlsbad. ⊠ *26 Carlsbad Caverns Hwy.* ☎ *505/ 785–2291* ⊟ *AE, D, MC, V.*

¢ ✕ **Jack's.** For a rib-sticking, huge breakfast before heading off to the cav-erns this fast-food joint will do the job. The restaurant shares an adobe-style building with the Velvet Garter Restaurant. Grab a booth and order eggs, a burger, Mexican food, or pizza. ⊠ *26 Carlsbad Caverns Hwy.* ☎ *505/785–2291* ⊟ *No credit cards.*

$ 🏠 **Best Western Cavern Inn.** This Territorial-style, two-story motor inn just outside the entrance leading to Carlsbad Caverns has rooms with Southwestern decor. Under the same ownership next door is the hacienda-style Best Western Guadalupe Inn, with the same rates (it has 42 rooms) and Southwestern furnishings. Many tour groups and families stay at both hotels, which share facilities. All guests are free to use the water park, open May through September, that features two 150-foot water-slides along with a pirate ship with squirting cannons. The high-desert landscaping includes piñon pines, ocotillo cacti, and yucca plants. Mule deer often amble down from their protected haven at Carlsbad Caverns National Park. ⊠ *17 Carlsbad Caverns Hwy., look for large registra-tion sign on south side of road, 88268* ☎ *505/785–2291 or 800/228– 3767* 🖷 *505/785–2283* ⊕ *www.whitescity.com/* ⇝ *63 rooms* ♤ *Cable TV, in-room data ports, pool, spa, playground, some pets allowed (fee)* ⊟ *AE, D, DC, MC, V* ꙍ *BP.*

Lincoln National Forest

Access via NM 137, turn southwest off U.S. 285 12 mi northwest of Carlsbad; U.S. 82 west from Artesia; U.S. 70 west from Roswell; U.S. 82 east from Alamogordo; U.S. 70 east from Tularosa; and U.S. 380 east from Carrizozo. Numerous other gravel or dirt roads lead into the forest.

Covering 1.1 million acres of Eddy, Otero, Chaves, and Lincoln coun-ties, this magnificent forest encompasses two distinct regions: the arid lower elevations near Carlsbad, and the towering pines and mountain peaks of the Ruidoso area. The piñon and juniper of the southernmost region stretches through the Guadalupe Mountains to connect with the Carlsbad Caverns and Guadalupe Mountains national parks. The for-est land has many caves, some of which can be accessed with a free per-mit available at the Guadalupe Ranger District.

Call or visit the **Guadalupe Ranger District** (☎ 505/885–4181 ⊠ Federal Bldg., Room 159, 114 S. Halagueno St., Carlsbad) for permit information.

These caves are not developed, so be prepared for primitive conditions. The only private development you can find other than scattered ranches is at **Queen** (49 mi southwest of Carlsbad, on NM 137). This site consists of a small mobile-home community, restaurant, store, gas station, and church camp. This forested area is hugely popular with hunters lured by ample populations of mule deer.

★ You almost have to see **Sitting Bull Falls** to believe that a cascading, 150-foot-tall waterfall flowing into beautiful, crystal clear pools exists in southeastern New Mexico. It's no mirage—and you can even swim in the waters of this oasis. A 1-mi hike from the parking lot over a paved trail takes you to a desert riparian area lush with ferns, watercress, and cottonwoods. At the parking lot, the forest service provides rock ramadas for picnics. There are viewing decks and restrooms, and 16-mi of hiking trails lace the area. The park is open for day use only. If you want to camp overnight, drive southwest on NM 137 until you reach the New Mexico–Texas state line and Dog Canyon Campground in Guadalupe Mountains National Park. During extreme drought conditions, call first to make sure the area hasn't been closed. ⊠ *From Carlsbad take U.S. 285 north about 12 mi, then turn west on NM 137 for 27 mi* ☎ *505/ 885–4181* ⊒ *$5 per vehicle, free Wed.* ⊙ *Apr.–Sept., daily 8:30–6; Oct.–Mar., daily 8:30–5.*

The northernmost portion of the Lincoln forest, surrounding the resort community of Ruidoso, is a more traditional sanctuary, with snowy mountain peaks, lakes, and gurgling mountain streams. Developers have capitalized on this beauty, so the forest is interspersed with cabins, resorts, church camps, condos, and ski runs. Still, there are miles of pristine wilderness, many of which can be accessed by hiking trails.

More than 25 camping areas are scattered throughout Lincoln National Forest. Although fishing lakes and streams are available on private, municipal, or tribal lands, there's very little opportunity for the sport on these public forest lands. To obtain more information about hiking, camping, hunting, and other recreation, contact the forest service's main headquarters in Alamogordo. ☎ *505/434–7200.*

Carlsbad

④ *27 mi northeast of Carlsbad Caverns National Park, east on NM 7 and north on U.S. 60/180; 20 mi north of White's City on U.S. 62/180.*

Carlsbad, population 25,000, lies along the Pecos River and has 2¾ mi of beaches and riverside pathways—an example of the contrasts to be found in this desert region. The Territorial-style town square, a block from the river, encircles a Pueblo-style courthouse designed by famed New Mexican architect John Gaw Meem, who designed many of the buildings on the University of New Mexico campus in Albuquerque, and who was a major player in the development of the "Santa Fe Style." Some of the city's most elegant homes occupy quiet residential areas along the riverbanks.

A boat parade and evening fireworks attract thousands of visitors to the Lake Carlsbad Recreation Area for July 4 festivities. The hugely popu-

★ lar **Christmas on the Pecos** (☎ 505/887–6516 ⊕ www.christmasonthepecos. com) has dazzling Christmas displays decorating backyards and lots along a 2½-mi stretch on the Pecos River. Tremendous demand has created multiple tours nightly from Thanksgiving to New Year's Eve (excluding Christmas Eve). Internet ticket sales are year-round. Prices for boat tours vary ($10 Sunday–Thursday, $15 Friday and Saturday; half-length tours are $5 per person, inquire about tour times). The night breeze blowing across the water can be chilly, so dress warmly.

Boats leave from the **Pecos River Village** (✉ 710 N. Muscatel Ave.), once an amusement park and now a convention center.

The **Carlsbad Museum and Arts Center** houses Pueblo pottery, Native American artifacts, and early cowboy and ranch memorabilia along with exhibitions of contemporary art. The real treasure, though, is the McAdoo Collection, with works by painters of the Taos Society of Artists. ✉ 418 W. Fox St. ☎ 505/887–0276 ✇ Free ⊙ Mon.–Sat. 10–5.

★ ℃ Atop Ocotillo Hills on the northwest edge of Carlsbad, the **Living Desert Zoo and Gardens State Park** has plants and animals native to the Chihuahuan Desert. The Desert Arboretum has hundreds of exotic cacti and succulents, and the Living Desert Zoo—more a reserve than a traditional zoo—is home to mountain lions, deer, elk, wolves, buffalo, rattlesnakes, and other indigenous species. Nocturnal exhibits and dioramas let you peek in on the area's nighttime wildlife. Though there are shaded rest areas, restrooms, and water fountains, in hot weather it's best to visit during the early morning or early evening, when it's cooler. In May, the Living Desert hosts the four-day Annual Mescal Roast and Mountain Spirit Dances demonstrated by members of the Mescalero Apache tribe. The *Mescalero,* which means "mescal makers," depended for centuries on the revered desert plant, mescal, for food. ✉ 1504 Miehls Dr., off U.S. 285 ☎ 505/887–5516 ✇ $5 ⊙ Late May–early Sept., daily 8–8; early Sept.–late May, daily 9–5; last admission 1½ hrs before closing.

Where to Stay & Eat

¢–$ ✗ **Bamboo Garden Restaurant.** It may surprise you to find there is decent Chinese food to be found in cowboy country. Kung Pao chicken, a dish with vegetables and peanuts stir-fried in chile pepper sauce, is among the highlights, but there are plenty of standard favorites like sweet-and-sour pork and cashew shrimp. The buffet is reasonably priced, though the food tends to be bland, so it's best to order off the menu. Surroundings are pleasant but not elegant, with posters of Asia and sweet-faced ceramic Buddhas placed around the room. ✉ 1511 N. Canal St. ☎ 505/ 887–5145 ▤ MC, V ⊙ Closed Mon.

¢–$ ✗ **Lucy's Mexicali Restaurant & Entertainment Club.** "The best margaritas and hottest chile in the world" is the motto of this family-owned restaurant. The claim may be a bit of a stretch, but you'll find all the New Mexican standards prepared here, along with some not-so-standard items such as chicken fajita burritos, Tucson-style chimichangas, and brisket *carnitas* (beef brisket or chicken sautéed with chiles and seasonings). Low-fat and fat-free Mexican dishes and a good number of microbrews are served—or try Lucy's original Mexicali beer with a slice of orange. Live entertainment is offered most weekends. ⊠ *701 S. Canal St.* ☎ *505/887–7714* ▭ *AE, D, DC, MC, V.*

¢–$ ✕ **Red Chimney Pit Barbeque.** If you hanker for sweet-and-tangy barbe-cue, this homey, log cabin–style spot is the place for you. Sauce from an old family recipe is slathered on chicken, pork, beef, turkey, and ham here; fried catfish is tasty, as is the fried okra. Service is notoriously in-different, but you're here for the barbecue and it's well worth the wait. Hours are 4:30–8:30. ⊠ *817 N. Canal St.* ☎ *505/885–8744* ▭ *MC, V* ☉ *Closed weekends and holidays.*

★ ¢ ✕ **Blue House Bakery & Cafe.** Morning glories greet you at the front fence, the pretty blue Queen Anne–style house beckons, and the aromas com-ing from within are irresistible. Fabulous coffee and baked goods, and high quality, fresh ingredients in the food make the Blue House a de-light. Turkey avocado sandwiches, Southwest chicken salad, and chicken gumbo are just a few of the tasty goods you'll find on the ever-chang-ing lunch menu. ⊠ *609 N. Canyon Rd.* ☎ *505/628–0555* ▭ *No credit cards* ☉ *No dinner. No lunch on Sat.*

★ $ ▥ **Best Western Stevens Inn.** Etched glass and carved wooden doors add a touch of elegance to this motel, where prints of Western landscapes decorate the spacious rooms. Prime rib and steaks are served in the evening at the motel's Flume Room Restaurant and Coffee Shop, which opens at 5:30 AM daily. ⊠ *1829 S. Canal St., Box 580, 88220* ☎ *505/887–2851 or 800/730–2851* 🖷 *505/887–6338* ⊕ *www.carlsbadnm.com* ↵ *222 rooms* ⚫ *Restaurant, some kitchenettes, some microwaves, some refrigerators, cable TV, some in-room data ports, pool, wading pool, hot tub, bar, playground, laundry facilities, Internet, meeting rooms, airport shuttle, some pets allowed (fee), no-smoking rooms* ▭ *AE, D, DC, MC, V* ⦿ *BP.*

★ ¢–$ ▥ **Ocatillo Inn.** One mile from the municipal airport, this inn surrounds a landscaped patio with a pool and a sundeck about as large as an air-craft hangar. The contemporary rooms are spacious and comfortable, and the staff is friendly and accommodating. The café serves free, full continental breakfasts to guests, and the bar has a truly impressive se-lection of tequilas—worth sampling if you've never experienced a true, sipping tequila. ⊠ *3706 National Parks Hwy., 88220* ☎ *505/887–2861 or 800/321–2861* 🖷 *505/887–2861* ⊕ *www.ocotilloinn.com* ↵ *120 rooms* ⚫ *Restaurant, cable TV, pool, hot tub, bar, shop, laun-dry service, airport shuttle, some pets allowed, no-smoking rooms* ▭ *AE, D, DC, MC, V* ⦿ *CP.*

¢ ▥ **Carlsbad Super 8.** This three-story motel, 2 mi from the regional air-port and one block from Carlsbad's convention center, has rooms in desert colors with generic furnishings and coffeemakers. Outdoor grills are available, and nearby is a fast-food restaurant that's open 24 hours. The outdoor pool is heated. ⊠ *3817 National Parks Hwy., 88220* ☎ *505/887–8888, 800/800–8000 central reservations* 🖷 *505/885–0126* ↵ *60 rooms* ⚫ *Some microwaves, some refrigerators,* *cable TV, pool, hot tub, some pets allowed (fee), no-smoking rooms* ▤ *AE, D, DC, MC, V* ¶ CP.

¢ 🖫 **Continental Inn.** This inn is south of Carlsbad, about 30 minutes from Carlsbad Caverns. The simple rooms have typical matching curtains and bedspreads in Southwestern patterns. The small grounds have tidy gardens with rose bushes. ⊠ *3820 National Parks Hwy., 88220* ☎ *505/ 887–0341 or 877/887–0341* 🖶 *505/885–1186* 🌫 *57 rooms, 3 suites* ♻ *Some microwaves, some refrigerators, cable TV, pool, airport shuttle, some pets allowed, no-smoking rooms* ▤ *AE, D, DC, MC, V* ¶ CP.

🔺 **Brantley Lake State Park.** Thirteen miles north of Carlsbad, the campground in this state park is shaded with Afghan pines, Mexican elders, and desert plants. Some camping and picnic sites have views of the 3,000-acre lake and dam—an inviting haven in this upper Chihuahuan desert region. Swimming is allowed (although there's no lifeguard), along with boating and fishing for largemouth bass, bluegill, crappie, and walleye pike. ⊠ *U.S. 285, Box 2288, 88221* ☎ *505/457–2384, 877/664– 7787 reservations* 🖶 *505/457–2385* ♻ *Grills, flush toilets, 3 full hookups, 48 partial hookups, dump station, drinking water, showers, fire grates, picnic tables, electricity, public telephone, ranger station, play area, swimming (lake)* 🌫 *51 RV sites, unlimited primitive sites* 🎟 *$5 day use, full hookup $18, partial hookup $14, primitive sites $8* ▤ *No credit cards.*

🔺 **Carlsbad RV Park & Campgrounds.** This tree-filled, full-service campground inside the city limits has level gravel sites and an indoor swimming pool. Camping cabins with heating and air-conditioning are available, as are phone hookups and a meeting room. Reservations are recommended in summer. A professional RV service center where repairs can be made is next door. ⊠ *4301 National Parks Hwy., 88220* ☎ *505/885–6333* 🖶 *505/885–0784* ⊕ *www.carlsbadrvpark.com* ♻ *Grills, laundry facilities, flush toilets, full hookups, partial hookups, dump station, drinking water, showers, picnic tables, electricity, public telephone, general store, play area, swimming (pool)* 🌫 *96 RV sites, 41 tent sites* 🎟 *Full hookup $22, partial hookup $21, tent sites $17* ▤ *MC, V.*

Nightlife & the Arts

Like many other small towns, Carlsbad tends to fold up at night—you're pretty much limited to special events and the lounge circuit. **Lucy's Mexicali Restaurant & Entertainment Club** (☎ 505/887–7714) has bands on the weekend. On Saturday, popular country-and-western bands play at the **Silver Spur Lounge** (☎ 505/887–2851) in the Best Western Stevens Inn, a favored local hangout where dancing takes place all week long.

Artesia

36 mi north of Carlsbad on U.S. 285, 40 mi south of Roswell on U.S. 285, 110 mi west of Alamogordo on U.S. 82.

Artesia got its name from artesian wells that were dug here in the late 1800s to tap the abundant water supply just below the ground's surface. The region's subterranean bounty includes more than water, however; oil and gas were discovered here in the 1920s, and today there are more than 20,000 oil and 4,000 natural-gas wells in the area. Pumping jacks cover the dunes and fields to the east. The Navajo Oil Refinery, alongside U.S. 285, is a major employer for this city of about 12,000.

A Federal Law Enforcement Training Center took over the abandoned campus of a private liberal arts college here in 1989, and thousands of law-enforcement employees from agencies such as the U.S. Bureau of Land Management and U.S. Customs Service now train at its driving and shooting ranges. Other than grabbing a meal, there isn't a great deal going on here. On football-season Fridays you can't miss the array of orange banners and bulldog emblems touting the local high-school team, the Bulldogs, in this highly sports-conscious town.

Artesia is a quick 38 mi drive north of Carlsbad. The two inns listed below, as well as the restaurants, are arguably good reasons to make the drive. They stand out as gems in a little town that doesn't generally draw much tourism.

Where to Stay & Eat

★ ¢–$ ✕ **La Fonda.** This Mexican restaurant is a great place to stop on your way to or from Carlsbad Caverns; as well as tasty Mexican food, it has a gorgeous interior with a trickling fountain and greenery, and wonderfully friendly service. Try the house special, the Guadalajara, for a palate-pleasing blend of seasoned beef, cheese, and guacamole served on a corn tortilla. Combination plates also are favorites, try the chiles rellenos alongside cheese enchiladas, tacos with sides of *refritos* (refried pinto beans), and rice, and top it all off with a sopaipilla (puffy fried bread) and honey. ⊠ *210 W. Main St.* ☎ *505/746–9377* ▭ *AE, D, MC, V.*

★ ¢–$ ✕ **The Wellhead Restaurant & Brewpub.** After a long day of exploring, this is the place to come for tasty food and tasty beer brewed right on the premises. The super-friendly staff love to talk about beer and the great old building they're in. Pub favorites like burgers and fried catfish are no disappointment. The green chile can be added to anything and it's *tasty.* Their house root beer is a surefire bet for kids and adults alike; and be sure to save room for dessert. ⊠ *332 W. Main St.* ☎ *505/746–0640* ⊕ *www.thewellhead.com* ▭ *A, D, MC, V.*

★ $ ▥ **The Heritage Inn.** You'll find this lovely inn in a 1905 building in the heart of Artesia's historic business district. The high-ceilinged rooms are beautifully furnished with Colonial-style furniture, and the inn manages to be stately and elegant without being the least bit stuffy. The friendly staff can arrange tours for you, and will happily answer questions about the area. La Fonda and the Wellhead are across the street. ⊠ *209 W. Main St., 88210* ☎ *866/207–0222 or 505/748–2552* ⊕ *www. artesiaheritageinn.com* ↻ *11 rooms* ♿ *Internet access, a/c, health club access* ▭ *A, D, MC, V* ⫶❂⫶ *CP.*

★ ¢–$ ▥ **Adobe Rose.** What started out as the art studio for the College of Artesia in the '60s has been reimagined and re-created to be an amazingly relaxing and comfortable B&B. Thick adobe walls keep the spacious rooms cool, and the lush grounds have verandas to relax on throughout the heat of the day. Custom-made lodgepole pine furniture and some antiques help make this feel like you've landed in your own private hacienda. ⊠ *1614 N. 13th St., 88210* ☎ *888/909–7673 or 505/748–*

3082 ⊕ *www.adoberosenm.com* ⟳ *4 rooms* ⬠ *Computer/Internet access, laundry, cable, refrigerators* ⊟ *A, D, MC, V* ⦾ *CP.*

▌ EN
  ROUTE

For a closer look at the farms and dairies of the Pecos Valley, veer northeast off the main highway (U.S. 285) just north of Artesia and take Alt. U.S. 285. This 40-mi route meanders through quaint farming villages of Lake Arthur, Dexter, and Hagerman and will rejoin the main highway at Roswell.

To view one of the valley's little-known but fascinating attractions, turn east onto Hatchery Road in Dexter. One mile down you'll find the **Dexter National Fish Hatchery & Technology Center** (✉ 7116 Hatchery Rd., Dexter ☎ 505/734–5910), a facility with the noble mission of studying, propagating, and possibly salvaging endangered species of warmwater fish like the pike minnow (once known as the Colorado squawfish, and once common to the Colorado River). You can view live exhibits and read all about the center's activities at a small visitor center on-site. A guide will accommodate tour groups if requests are made in advance.

Roswell

⑤ *40 mi north of Artesia on U.S. 285; 205 mi southeast of Albuquerque, south on I–25 and east on U.S. 380; 78 mi southwest of Fort Sumner, via NM 20 and U.S. 285.*

The true character of Roswell has been largely obscured over the last few decades by the brouhaha over UFOs. Rather than a hotbed of extraterrestrial activity, Roswell is in reality a simple, conservative city with an economy based on manufacturing, agriculture, oil, and gas. The population of around 50,000 grew out of a farming community founded in the fertile Pecos Valley about a century ago; artesian wells still provide the water used to irrigate crops like alfalfa, hay, and cotton. Residents may sigh over the fact that visitors only come here in search of spaceships—but they've also learned to have fun with it, and to cash in on the tourist trade.

★ ⓒ Depending on your point of view, the **International UFO Museum and Research Center** will either seem like a display of only-in-America kitsch or a real opportunity to examine UFO documentation and other phenomena involving extraterrestrials. This homespun nonprofit facility is surprisingly low-tech—some of the displays look like they've seen previous duty on B-movie sets (the museum is, coincidentally, inside an old movie house). The blowups of newspaper stories about the 1947 Roswell crash, its fallout, and 1950s UFO mania make interesting reading, and you can view the videotaped recollections of residents who say they saw the crash firsthand. Dummies used in movies about the Roswell incident are also on exhibit. The gift shop sells all manner of souvenirs depicting wide-eyed extraterrestrials, along with books and videos. Though some of the exhibits are whimsical, the portion of the museum devoted to research accumulates serious written collections and investigations of reported UFOs. The museum has purchased an entire city block between 7th and 8th streets on N. Main Street to house their new facility. Plans are still in the works for this major facility upgrade. ✉ *114*

CLOSE UP

UFO Over Roswell

OF ALL THE SIGHTINGS of Unidentified Flying Objects in the world, it's the one that took place more than 50 years ago outside Roswell, New Mexico, that remains most credible in people's minds. Rumors of alien bodies and silenced witnesses are the real-life happenings that inspired fantastical entertainment like the TV series *The X-Files* and *Roswell*. The most likely reason so many people refuse to dismiss the Roswell Incident is the undisputed fact that in July 1947 *something* fell from the sky.

On July 8, 1947, officers at Roswell Army Airfield announced to the *Roswell Daily Record* that the military had retrieved wreckage of a UFO nearby. The next day Army Air Force officials retracted the story, saying it was in fact a weather balloon that had crashed. Over the years, theories of a cover-up and suspicions that the military had also recovered alien bodies linked the town of Roswell with aliens as strongly as Loch Ness is with its monster. Backing up the alien-bodies theory is the testimony of people like mortician Glen Dennis, who today works with Roswell's International UFO Museum and Research Center. He maintains that a nurse at the military hospital passed him sketches of aliens and that the military called him in 1947 to ask odd questions about embalming bodies.

In the 1990s a flood of information, including books like *UFO Crash at Roswell* and accounts from

eyewitnesses who claim they were silenced, rekindled the conspiracy theories. The air force responded in 1994 with a report revealing that fragments mistaken for a flying saucer came not from a weather balloon but from an air force balloon used in the top-secret Project Mogul. The true nature of the balloon had to be concealed in 1947 because its purpose was to monitor evidence of Soviet nuclear tests.

As this new explanation didn't address the alien-bodies issue, the air force issued a 231-page report, "The Roswell Report, Case Closed," in 1997. This document explains that from 1954 to 1959, life-size dummies were used in parachute drop experiments. That this time frame postdates the 1947 Roswell Incident is immaterial to the air force, which claims people have simply confused dates in their memories.

The holes in every story, whether from the military or eyewitnesses, have allowed the Roswell UFO legend to mushroom extravagantly. It now incorporates tales of captured aliens (alive and dead) that further feed our imaginations, thanks in part to the capitalizing media. You can see depictions of slender, doe-eyed aliens, known as the "Grays," all over storefronts and souvenir shops in Roswell. These spooky, diminutive creatures might even be called the New Mexico version of leprechauns, with only the rare treasure seeker truly hoping to encounter one.

7

N. Main St. ☎ *505/625–9495* ⊕ *www.iufomrc.com* ✉ *Free; $2 donation requested* � *Daily 9–5.*

Roswell's **UFO Festival** (☎ 505/625–9495 ⊕ www.dfn.com/festival/) takes place during the first weekend in July. Tickets for lectures about UFOs, science-fiction writers' workshops, and films are $20. The street festival is free and has vendors and events such as alien-costume competitions.

The impressive **Roswell Museum and Art Center** often gets overlooked in favor of alien hoopla, but it contains a good collection of Southwestern artists, including works by Georgia O'Keeffe, Henriette Wyeth, Peter Hurd, and the recently deceased El Paso native Luis Jiménez. The extensive Rogers Aston Collection has displays of Plains Indian artifacts and Spanish armor. Robert H. God-

dard's collection exhibits the inventions and journals of the rocketry genius, who conducted some of his early experiments near Roswell. The **Robert H. Goddard Planetarium,** which is part of the museum, is open only occasionally; generally on holiday weekends and for celestial events—call ahead for the schedule. ⊠ *100 W. 11th St.* ☎ *505/624–6744* ⌨ *Free* ☉ *Mon.–Sat. 9–5, Sun. 1–5.*

The lakes at **Bottomless Lakes State Park** were created when an ancient sea that covered the area 240 million years ago evaporated, leaving behind salt and gypsum deposits. Those deposits then slowly dissolved with accumulations of rain, and ceilings collapsed into sinkholes. Scuba divers, boaters, and swimmers now take advantage of the crystal clear, spring-fed water. The main Lea Lake facility has a bathhouse with modern showers and restrooms, and paddleboats and paddleboards can be rented from late May to early September. A visitor center has exhibits of park history, geology, and geography; during the peak season, interpretive lectures are given in the evenings. ⊠ *Off U.S. 380, 12 mi east of Roswell, turn south on NM 409 and continue 3 mi* ☎ *505/624–6058* ⌨ *$5 per vehicle* ☉ *Daily 6 AM–9 PM (day use); visitor center daily 9–6 late May–early Sept., daily 8–5 early Sept.–late May.*

From the viewing platforms along the 8½-mi self-guided tour at the **Bitter Lake National Wildlife Refuge,** you can watch for snow geese, sandhill cranes, and other exotic birds, along with more familiar species. ⊠ *4065 Bitter Lakes Rd.; from Roswell, head north on U.S. 285, then turn east on Pine Lodge Rd. for 7 mi* ☎ *505/622–6755* ⌨ *Free* ☉ *Daily dawn–dusk.*

Where to Stay & Eat

¢–$$ ✕ **Cattle Baron.** Grilled meats, seafood, and spicy sauces are the order of the day at this restaurant, including prime rib and chicken baked with jalapeño-flavored gravy. The dark-wood furnishings here are offset by big windows and a skylight. The ingredients at the salad bar are fresh and the salads ample. ⊠ *1113 N. Main St.* ☎ *505/622–2465* ▭ *AE, D, DC, MC, V.*

¢–$ ✕ **El Toro Bravo.** Next to the International UFO Museum and Research Center, this Mexican restaurant achieves a Latin flair with matador paintings, piñatas, and wrought-iron wall lamps. Owner Artie Acevas uses family recipes in the preparation of ethnic favorites such as fajitas, enchiladas, tacos, and burritos. Cold beer and wine help cool the delicious fire of the spicy dishes. ⊠ *102 S. Main St.* ☎ *505/622–9280* ☰ *AE, D, MC, V.*

$ ▣ **Best Western Sally Port Inn & Suites.** The red-tile roof and white walls of this motel match those of the nearby New Mexico Military Institute, which inspired the name Sally Port—a passageway in military quarters. The standard rooms are large, and there are executive suites with business-oriented amenities. The staff is friendly and professional. ⊠ *2000 N. Main St., 88220* ☎ *505/622–6430* 🖷 *505/623–7631* 🛏 *99 rooms, 25 suites ⚭ Restaurant, some in-room hot tubs, cable TV, in-room data ports, indoor pool, gym, hair salon, hot tub, sauna, meeting rooms, some pets allowed (fee), no-smoking rooms* ☰ *AE, D, MC, V* ⚑ *BP.*

¢–$ ▣ **Ramada Limited.** Large, contemporary rooms and convenient access to U.S. 70 are draws here. The decor is Southwestern style throughout, and amenities include an outdoor heated pool and a parking lot big enough to accommodate large RVs and trucks. ⊠ *2803 W. 2nd St., 88220* ☎ *505/623–9440* 🖷 *505/622–9708* 🛏 *58 rooms ⚭ Cable TV, pool, meeting room, airport shuttle, some pets allowed* ☰ *AE, MC, V* ⚑ *CP.*

⚠ **Bottomless Lakes State Park.** Lea Lake, 90 feet deep, is the only lake of the group where swimming is allowed. In summer, you can rent paddleboards and paddleboats for a small fee. The lakes stand in stark contrast to the hot, unshaded surroundings, although the campgrounds do have sheltered picnic tables. Rainbow Trout are stocked in Devil's Inkwell during the winter months. ⊠ *Off U.S. 380, 12 mi east of Roswell, turn south on NM 409 and continue 3 mi* ☎ *877/664–7787 ⚭ Grills, flush toilets, pit toilets, full hookups, partial hookups (electric and water), dump station, drinking water, showers, picnic tables, electricity, public telephone, ranger station, play area, swimming (lake)* 🛏 *32 RV sites, 27 tent sites* ▣ *$5 day use, tent sites $10, partial hookup $14, full hookup $18* ☰ *No credit cards.*

EAST-CENTRAL OUTPOSTS

Vast herds of pronghorn (commonly, but erroneously, called antelope) graze alongside roadways in this wide-open area, known as the Eastern Plains of New Mexico. When rains have been generous to this usually parched region, green grass and wildflowers adorn the rolling hills; ordinarily, however, the grasslands struggle to survive the burning heat of the New Mexico summer and take on a golden-brown hue. The many miles of uninhabited prairie create a convenient cattle range, helping the many ranchers in this area continue a century-old tradition.

People in these agricultural and oil communities are busy making a living, so you won't find many touristy stops or shops along the highways. The purity of the rural life seen here is part of its charm, though. A note of caution: pay attention to winter snow storm warnings. You don't want to get caught in the blinding, blizzardlike conditions that can create huge drifts of snow.

Portales

❻ *From Roswell, take U.S. 285 north 5 mi and U.S. 70 east 92 mi. Or, if you want a nice drive through sand dunes and rural farmland, from Artesia, take U.S. 82 east 65 mi to Lovington and SR 206 north to Portales 109 mi.*

Along with neighboring Clovis, this farming and ranching community bills itself as the world's top producer of Valencia peanuts, a specialty crop ideally suited to red, sandy soil. In October, Portales hosts a peanut festival where nuts are sold in raw form or cooked up in candies and other delicacies. Portales also is home to Eastern New Mexico University, a four-year college.

Ⓒ The nation's largest **windmill collection** is found on Portales's Kilgore Street (you can't miss it). Resident Bill Dalley has collected the 85 windmills in his own backyard. Since he's the past president of the International Windmillers' Trade Fair Association, meetings of the group are sometimes conducted here.

In the early 1930s, archaeologists in eastern New Mexico unearthed remnants of prehistoric animals like mammoths, camels, and saber-tooth tigers. More important, this was the first site in the contiguous United States that provided conclusive evidence that humans lived here at least 11,300 years ago. The culture and artifacts associated with these earliest inhabitants take their name from the nearby city of Clovis. The **Black Water Draw Museum** contains photographs of early excavations, along with artifacts from Clovis, Folsom, and later Native American civilizations. The museum looks a little lonely on the side of U.S. 70, 8 mi northeast of Portales, but its interior is cheerful, with informative, well-presented exhibits and a "touch and feel" table for children.

★ The **Black Water Draw Archaeological Site** remains active and is open at regular hours to visitors in summer and on weekends in spring and fall. Self-guided tours on developed trails are well worth the effort for the privilege of viewing work in progress at a major archaeological site. Stay strictly on the trails, which offer options of ¾-mi or ½-mi round trips with about 20 different interpretive stops with signs describing vegetation and geology (the wildflowers following spring rains can be spectacular). On hot days, wear a hat, use sunscreen, and carry water for these excursions. An exhibit building offers a fascinating look at ongoing excavations of prehistoric animal bones, and an ancient, hand-dug well can be viewed near the exhibit building. ⊠ *West side of NM 467, 5 mi north of Portales, turn at Mile Marker 5* ☎ *505/356–5235* ⊕ *www.enmu.edu/academics/excellence/museums/blackwater-draw/index.shtml* ⊡ *Site and museum $3* ⊙ *Museum late May–early Sept., Mon.–Sat. 10–5, Sun. noon–5; museum early Sept.–late May, Tues.–Sat. 10–5, Sun. noon–5. Site June–Aug. and Nov.–Mar., daily 9–5; Sept., Oct., Apr., and May, weekends 9–5.*

Where to Stay & Eat

★ ¢–$$ ✕ **Cattle Baron.** This Portales steak house in the heart of cattle country was the founding establishment for the popular chain that now extends into Roswell, Ruidoso, and Las Cruces. Prime rib is the specialty, and the trademark salad bar doesn't disappoint with its fresh greens, crisp veggies, and homemade soups. The interior is decorated with plenty of wooden accents and skylights. ⊠ *1600 S. Ave. D* ☎ *505/356–5587* ⊟ *AE, D, DC, MC, V.*

¢–$$ ✕ **Mark's Restaurant & Catering.** Tasty breakfast omelets, steaks, and sandwiches attract the hungry college crowd from nearby Eastern New Mexico University. Try the house specialty, a chicken-fried steak dinner. This diner-style hangout has a fun atmosphere. The tables are inlaid with tile, the chairs are covered with brightly colored vinyl, and there are a few exotic parrot decorations. All food is prepared fresh. ⊠ *1126 W. 1st St., across from airplane display next to Eastern New Mexico University* ☎ *505/359–0857* ⊟ *D, MC, V.*

¢ 🏨 **Super 8.** Decorated with contemporary furnishings and pastel colors, this motel has large rooms and bathrooms. It's one of the nicest lodging options in the city and offers convenient access to Portales businesses and Eastern New Mexico University. ⊠ *1805 W. 2nd St., 88130* ☎ *505/ 356–8518* 🖷 *505/359–0431* 🛏 *45 rooms* ♿ *Cable TV, hot tub* ⊟ *AE, D, DC, MC, V* 🍽 *CP.*

⚠ **Oasis State Park.** Sand dunes, huge cottonwood and elm trees, and the refreshing air from the 3-acre lake make this state park seem like an oasis. Especially pleasurable activities here include hiking, bird-watching (especially in winter), fishing, and camping. Horseback riding is allowed, although swimming and boating are not. Six miles north of Portales via U.S. 70 and NM 467. ⊠ *Off NM 467, 6 mi north of Portales* ☎ *505/356–5331, 877/665–7787 reservations* ♿ *Grills, flush toilets, pit toilets, partial hookups (electric and water), dump station, drinking water, showers, picnic tables, electricity, ranger station, play area* 🛏 *13 RV sites, 10 tent sites* 🏷 *$5 day use, $10 tent sites, $14 for electrical hookups, $18 for electrical and water hookups* ⊟ *No credit cards.*

Fort Sumner

❼ *70 mi northwest of Black Water Draw Museum, north on U.S. 70 and west on U.S. 60/84; 85 mi northeast of Roswell, north on U.S. 285 and northeast on NM 20; 159 mi southeast of Albuquerque, east on I–40 and south on U.S. 84*

Besides its historic significance as one of the area's earliest military outposts and the place where Billy the Kid was killed, the town of Fort Sumner is known for its air park, where NASA launches balloons used in scientific research. Nearby Sumner Lake provides irrigation for area farms and ranches, as well as boating and fishing opportunities. In June the De Baca County Chamber of Commerce hosts the annual Old Fort Days here, with living-history demonstrations and mock shoot-outs.

Artifacts and photographs at **Fort Sumner State Monument** illustrate the history of the fort, which was established in 1862 on the east bank of the Pecos River. From 1863 to 1868 it was the headquarters for a disastrous attempt to force the Navajo people and some Apache bands—after their defeat on various battlefields in the Southwest—to farm the inhospitable land. Natural disasters destroyed crops, wood was scarce, and even the water from the Pecos proved unhealthy. Those who survived the harsh treatment and wretched conditions (3,000 didn't) were returned to reservations elsewhere in 1868. The post was then sold and converted into a large ranch. This is the same ranch where, in 1881, Sheriff Pat Garrett gunned down Billy the Kid. The Kid is now buried in a nearby cemetery, where his headstone is secured in a barred cage (this was erected after the headstone was stolen three times and later recovered). ⊠ *Billy the Kid Rd.; from town of Fort Sumner, head east on U.S. 60/84 and south on Billy the Kid Rd., parts of which are signed NM 212* ☎ *505/355–2573* ⊞ *$3* ◷ *Wed.–Mon. 8:30–5.*

The small **Old Fort Sumner Museum,** next to Fort Sumner, has displays about Billy the Kid and ranch life. ⊠ *Billy the Kid Rd.* ☎ *505/355–2942* ⊞ *$3.50* ◷ *Daily 9–5; hrs can vary, call ahead to verify.*

Ⓒ The **Billy the Kid Museum** houses 17,000 square feet of exhibits about the young scofflaw, as well as antique wagon trains, guns, household goods, and other artifacts of the frontier era. ⊠ *1601 Sumner Ave., U.S. 60/84* ☎ *505/355–2380* ⊞ *$4* ◷ *Mid-May–Sept., daily 8:30–5; Oct.–Dec. and mid-Jan.–mid-May, Mon.–Sat. 8:30–5, Sun. 11–5.*

At **Sumner Lake State Park** you can boat, fish, camp, picnic, hike, sightsee, swim, and water-ski. ⊠ *10 mi north of Fort Sumner on U.S. 84, then west on NM 203 for 6 mi* ☎ *505/355–2541* ⊞ *Day use $5 per vehicle.*

Where to Stay

⚠ **Sumner Lake State Park.** The choices at this popular recreational site range from primitive, shoreline camping with no facilities to developed or partially developed sites. Shading in this desert location varies. ⊠ *10 mi north of Fort Sumner on U.S. 84, then west on NM 203 for 6 mi* ☎ *505/355–2541, 877/665–7787 reservations* ⚭ *Grills, flush toilets, pit toilets, partial hookups (electric and water), dump station, drinking water, showers, fire grates, picnic tables, electricity, ranger station, play area, swimming (lake)* ⇆ *40 developed sites, 18 sites with partial hookup, 50 primitive sites* ⊞ *Tent sites $8; extra $4 fee for water and electrical hookups* ☰ *No credit cards.*

EN ROUTE

To continue touring southeastern New Mexico, the easiest route (132 mi) is to backtrack to Roswell via Highway 20 to U.S. 285 and head west on U.S. 70/380 toward Lincoln County. Look for the pronghorns grazing alongside roadways in the flat eastern plains, which is an ideal habitat for these delicate creatures. Sometimes after a summer rain has made grasses and flowers bloom you'll find more than 100 pronghorn grazing along a short stretch of road.

A more adventurous route (178 mi) to Lincoln County would be a loop west from Fort Sumner on U.S. 60. At the town of Vaughn head south on U.S. 54 and travel through the southernmost region of Cibola National Forest to the fringes of the Lincoln National Forest. These areas are mountainous but semiarid, as evidenced by sparse hillsides dotted with brush and junipers. On this route you pass through **Corona,** near where the Roswell UFO is said to have crashed. No signs designate the site. At Carrizozo head east on U.S. 380. You pass the towns of Capitan and Lincoln before you reach U.S. 70. Cut back west on U.S. 70 to get to San Patricio.

Santa Rosa

❽ *32 mi north of Fort Sumner on U.S. 84, at I–40; 117 mi east of Albuquerque on I–40.*

A charming little town loaded with history, Santa Rosa also has the only body of water in the state—the Blue Hole—where divers can obtain deep water certification. That spot, along with the Pecos River and other natural bodies of water, were created by ancient sinkholes in the bedrock that drew early peoples and animals as far back as the time of woolly mammoths.

Spanish explorer Francisco Vázquez de Coronado is said to have settled the quaint village of **Puerto de Luna,** 10 mi south of Santa Rosa on NM 91, back in 1541, and the area has been a crossroads of settlers, travelers, and the railroad ever since. The bypassing of Santa Rosa, when Route 66 was replaced by I–40, has clearly impacted the town, although it maintains more vitality and economic activity than many of the towns along the route in this part of the state. There is a real pride among Santa Rosa's residents, and traditions of the town's deep Hispanic roots are still apparent.

About 8,000 diving permits are issued per year for folks who strap on tanks and plunge into the 80-foot-deep artesian spring–fed pool at the **Blue Hole** (✉ Blue Hole Rd.; turn south off Rte. 66 onto Lake Dr.; turn left onto Blue Hole Rd. just past Park Lake ☎ 505/472–3763).

Stella Salazar runs the dive shop (☎ 505/472–3370) adjacent to the Blue Hole; hours are generally restricted to the weekends, although the pool is open 24/7. Tanks, air, weight belts, and a few other basics are available there.

The folks from **Sandia Snorkel** (☎ 505/247–8632) in Albuquerque are out at the Hole every second weekend. The shop staff is full of helpful information about diving certification and the conditions of the pool (which remains a constant 62°F year-round). Cliff diving is great fun here, as is snorkeling and coming face to face with the many koi and goldfish who've been deposited here over the years.

Santa Rosa Lake State Park is 7 mi north of town and offers fishing, camping, and access to waterskiing and other water sports. The man-made lake was created to keep the flooding of the Pecos River under control, and it's become a resting spot for many different birds, including a number of gorgeous cormorants.

Where to Stay & Eat

¢–$$ ✕ **Lake City Diner.** In a charming old bank building on the corner of Route 66 and 4th Street, this bright, clean restaurant serves some of the best food in the region on *either* side of the Pecos. Fairly traditional dishes are notable because the ingredients are so fresh; you'll find rib-eye steak, chicken Milanesa, and a mouthwatering green-chile chicken enchilada casserole. Mixed green salads are a delight in an area where "greens" often means iceberg lettuce. Desserts, such as the chocolate espresso cake, are a must. ⊠ *101 4th St. (at Rte. 66)* ☎ *505/472–5253* ▭ *AE, MC, V* ☉ *Dinner only, 4–9.*

¢–$ ✕ **The Comet II Drive-In &Restaurant.** Expect authentic, spicy, and satisfying New Mexican food here, such as the enchiladas and famed PDL (Puerto de Luna) chile, made from the chiles grown in the village of the same name 10 mi south of town. Burgers, steaks, and seafood dishes are also available for the faint of heart. Cozy booths and walls covered with pictures of local history make this quasi-Mexican café a fun and casual place to go. ⊠ *217 Parker Ave., at Rte. 66* ☎ *505/472–3663* ▭ *A, D, DC, MC, V* ☉ *Closed Mon.*

¢–$ ✕ **Western BBQ Restaurant.** At the Santa Rosa Campground on the east side of town, this spot serves fine baby back ribs and a delectable peach cobbler—they'll even deliver right to your campsite. It's open only for dinner (5–8). ⊠ *2136 Historic Rte. 66* ☎ *505/472–3126 or 888/898– 1999* ▭ *A, D, DC, MC, V.*

★ $ ▦ **La Quinta Inn.** Perched on a high point in Santa Rosa, overlooking the valley, this motel offers the nicest stay in town, with many amenities and a spa—which is a nice way to finish a day spent in the car. ⊠ *1701 Historic Rte. 66, 88435* ☎ *505/472–4800* ▤ *505/472–8809* ⬋ *60 rooms* ⚭ *Indoor pool, Internet access, video library, irons, hair dryers, in-room microwave and refrigerator, indoor pool, coin laundry* ▭ *AE, D, DC, MC, V.*

⚠ **Santa Rosa Lake State Park.** For travelers wanting to do some fishing, this reservoir and campground is a quick and easy drive just north of Santa Rosa. Aside from fishing, waterskiing and boating are permitted, and there are numerous hiking trails. Weather in spring and fall is almost ideal at about 70°F, although summer tends to be at least 90°F. Beautiful, glossy black cormorants can be spotted on the shores and provide a real treat for bird-watchers. Reservations are allowed but are not generally necessary, even in spring. ⚭ *76 developed sites, 25 with electricity. Restrooms, showers, picnic tables* ⊠ *7 mi north of Santa Rosa via NM 91, Box 384, Santa Rosa, 88433* ☎ *505/472–3110* ⊕ *www. emnrd.state.nm.us/EMNRD/parks/santarosa.htm* ▧ *$5 day entry fee; $8–$18 for camping (tent sites, RV sites with electric, sewage, or both)* ⚓ *877/664–7787* ▭ *A, D, DC, MC, V.*

Tucumcari

❾ *59 mi east of Santa Rosa on I–40.*

Tucumcari is a tumble-down little town with intriguing early- to mid-20th-century architecture. Neat little houses on quiet, tree-shaded streets can keep you peeking around corners and down new streets for quite awhile. Along Route 66—the main, and only, route through town—you'll find low-slung motels in various stages of use and disuse, restaurants, markets, gas stations, curios stores, and, of course, *neon*. As hard as this town tries to develop itself economically, it's those neon signs and the still-living, old-time businesses that keep it alive.

The biggest attraction beyond the miles of neon and the Blue Swallow Motel is the **Mesalands Community College Dinosaur Museum,** where marvelous full-size bronze dinosaur skeletons are on display. This area was a hotbed of Triassic activity, when dinosaurs emerged in their development, and there are species here—like the Struthiomimus—that you won't find anywhere else in the world. The skeletons are cast in the local foundry, and they *are* touchable. ⊠ *222 E. Laughlin, follow signs off Rte. 66* ☎ *505/461–3466* ✉ *$5.50; children 5–11 $3* ⊙ *Tues.–Sat., Mar. 1–Labor Day, 10–6; Labor Day–Feb., noon–5.*

Where to Stay & Eat

¢–$$ ✕ **Del's.** The huge, fiberglass bull perched on the sign makes this landmark easy to find. Del's has been serving Route 66 travelers since 1956 with American and Mexican food. Eggs, pancakes, and bacon fill the breakfast menu, and hand-cut steaks keep customers returning. Windows all around make for great nighttime neon viewing. ⊠ *1202 E. Tucumcari Blvd./Rte. 66* ☎ *505/461–1740* ☐ *MC, V.*

¢–$ ✕ **Rubee's Diner.** From breakfast to dinner, what you'll get at Rubee's is a square meal. Huevos rancheros in the morning come with fresh green lettuce, tomatoes, and some of the tastiest panfried potatoes around. Eggs are cooked exactly the way you ask. The red chile is rich—loaded with beef—and not spicy. Burritos, burgers, and a basic BLT are also available. ⊠ *605 W. Tucumcari Blvd./Rte. 66* ☎ *505/461–1463* ☐ *No credit cards.*

¢ ▦ **Blue Swallow Motel.** Here it is: the retro motor court of your dreams. Built in 1939, the glowing neon, the tidy grounds, the spotlessly clean rooms furnished with vintage and antique furniture, and the abundant charm of Bill and Terri, the proprietors, all come together in one neat, feel-good package. The Blue Swallow is a landmark and a genuine pleasure for an overnight. The rooms are not the super-size, super-modern ones you get at the chains down the road, but that just isn't what this place is all about. Arrive before sunset if you can and take a seat at a table on the front lawn; the views of the western sky exploding with color are not to be missed. There is a feeling of camaraderie among the guests here—many of whom are diligently following Route 66 in its entirety—that lends a real sweetness to an already unique experience. ⊠ *Rte. 66, 88401* ☎ *505/461–9849* 🖶 *505/461–9905* ⊕ *www. blueswallowmotel.com* 🛏 *11 rooms* ♦ *Wireless Internet, phones, cable TV, 100% Refrigerated Air (the neon sign says so!)* ☐ *AE, D, MC, V* ⊙ *Nov. and Feb.*

HEADING TO HIGH COUNTRY

From the hub city of Roswell, U.S. 70 shoots out of the flatlands west toward mountain peaks. The route's slow climb in elevation is apparent beginning near San Patricio. Here, in an area known as the Hondo Valley, the shrubs and scattered forest dotting the otherwise naked hillsides provided inspiration for many of the late artist Peter Hurd's stunning landscapes.

Onward and upward, the pines thicken and grow taller. The Rio Ruidoso (Spanish for "river of noisy water") dances alongside the highway as the air grows cooler and fragrant. It's easy to imagine this majestic land as it was when outlaws, Native Americans, merchants, ranchers, and lawmen battled each other for control of the frontier; you can contemplate the stillness by taking a solitary horseback ride or hike on a wilderness trail, or by lake fishing on reservation land controlled by the Mescalero Apaches. Near the town of Ruidoso, there are more modern diversions, like skiing, shopping, horse racing, and casino gambling.

Lincoln

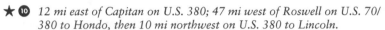

★ ⑩ *12 mi east of Capitan on U.S. 380; 47 mi west of Roswell on U.S. 70/380 to Hondo, then 10 mi northwest on U.S. 380 to Lincoln.*

It may not be as well known as Tombstone, Arizona, or Deadwood, South Dakota, but Lincoln ranks right up there with the toughest of the tough old towns of the Old West. Mellowing with age, the notorious one-street town has become a National Historic Landmark and a state monument. Its well-preserved museums and historic houses at one time were managed by the state and Ruidoso's Hubbard Museum of the American West, but there's ongoing discussion about placing all the attractions under state management. As of this writing, nothing definitive has happened, and a single ticket ($6) still grants entry to all attractions, whether they're private or state-owned (you can purchase the ticket at Historic Lincoln Center, Tunstall Store Museum, or Lincoln County Courthouse Museum).

The violent, gang-style Lincoln County War consumed this region between 1878 and 1881, as two factions, the Tunstall-McSween and the Murphy-Dolan groups, clashed over lucrative government contracts to provide food for the U.S. Army at Fort Stanton and area Native American reservations. The local conflict made national news, and President Hayes ordered Lew Wallace, governor of New Mexico, to settle the conflict. One of the more infamous figures to emerge from the bloodshed was a short, slight, sallow young man with buck teeth, startling blue eyes, and curly reddish-brown hair called Billy the Kid.

He is said to have killed 21 men (probably an exaggeration), including Lincoln County's sheriff William Brady—for whose murder he was convicted in 1881 and sentenced to hang. Billy managed to elude the gallows, however; on April 28, 1881, though manacled and shackled, he made a daring escape from the old Lincoln County Courthouse, gunning down two men and receiving cheers from townspeople who supported his group, the Tunstall-McSweens. Three months later a posse led by Sheriff Pat Garrett tracked

> **WORD OF MOUTH**
>
> "Drive over to Lincoln. It's pretty much a ghost town and is the site of a famous jail escape involving Billy the Kid. I know it's not Native American or necessarily spiritual, but there's just something about the place that draws me back every time I go. Tour the old courthouse, where the escape and shootout took place, and walk around the old buildings."   –Jayne1973

down Billy at a home in Fort Sumner, surprised him in the dark, and finished him off with two clean shots. One of the West's most notorious gunmen, and ultimately one of its best-known folk legends, was dead at age 21.

The **Historic Lincoln Center,** on the eastern end of town, serves as an information center and has a 12-minute video about Lincoln and exhibits devoted to Billy the Kid, the Lincoln County War, cowboys, Apaches, and Buffalo Soldiers, African-American cavalry troops who earned a sterling reputation as fierce protectors of Western frontiers. The center's guides and attendants dress in period costumes and lead a walking tour through town on the hour, vividly describing each building's role as a setting in the Lincoln County War. ☒ *Main St./U.S. 380; far eastern end of Lincoln, on south side of Rd.* ☎ *505/653–4025* ✉ *$6 pass grants access to all historic buildings* � *Daily 8:30–4:30.*

Lincoln was first settled by Spanish settlers in the 1840s. The short, round **Torreon** fortress served as protection from Apache raids in those days; it came in handy during the Lincoln County War, too.

José Montaño ran a saloon and boardinghouse within his **Montaño Store** for more than 30 years after the Civil War. Governor Lew Wallace stayed here when trying to arrange a meeting with Billy the Kid. Today, displayed writings in both English and Spanish describe the history of the site. ☒ *Main St./U.S. 380; on east end of town, south side of Rd.* ☎ *No phone* ✉ *$6 pass grants access to all historic buildings* ☉ *Daily 9–4:30.*

Dr. Wood's House was once occupied by a country doctor specializing in treatments for chest ailments. The doctor's house is filled with pre-1920s furnishings along with books, instruments, and pharmaceutical supplies from his era. ☒ *Main St./U.S. 380; on north side of highway, midway between Historic Lincoln Center and Tunstall Store Museum* ☎ *No phone* ✉ *$6 pass grants access to all historic buildings* ☉ *Daily 9–4:30.*

Nothing has changed much at the **Tunstall Store Museum** since the days of the Old West. When the state of New Mexico purchased the store in 1957, boxes of stock dating from the late 19th and early 20th centuries were discovered here, still unused. The clothes, hardware, butter churns, kerosene lamps, and other items are displayed in the store's original cases. ☒ *Main St./U.S. 380; located about midway through town on north side of Rd.* ☎ *505/653–4049* ✉ *$6 pass grants access to all historic buildings* ☉ *Daily 9–4:30.*

The **Lincoln County Courthouse Museum** is the building from which Billy the Kid made his famous escape. You can walk in the room where Billy was imprisoned and view a hole in the wall that just might have been caused by the gun he fired during his escape. Display cases contain historical documents, including one of Billy's handwritten, eloquent letters to Governor Lew Wallace, defending his reputation. The Lincoln State Monument office is here. ☒ *Main St./U.S. 380; on far west side of town, south side of Hwy.* ☎ *505/653–4372* ✉ *$6 pass grants access to all historic buildings* ☉ *Daily 8:30–4:30.*

When church services, weddings, funerals, and other regularly scheduled functions are not taking place here, Lincoln's historic **Iglesia de San Juan Bautista** originally built in 1887 can be viewed free. The tiny church was built and restored entirely from local materials. Roof beams and other wood elements including *latillas* (small branches laid on top of larger, rounded wood beams known as vigas) were dragged by oxcart from the nearby Capitan Mountains. ⊠ *Main St./U.S. 380; on south side of highway between Montaño Store and Lincoln County Courthouse Museum* ☎ *505/257–7067* ☒ *Free* ☉ *Daily 8:30–4:30.*

Where to Stay & Eat

☾ **$–$$** ✕⊞ **Wortley Hotel.** It's easy to imagine this hotel as it was during the days of the Lincoln County War—especially since owner Tim Hagaman presides over the property in period costume. Rebuilt after a fire in 1935, the original inn was where Deputy U.S. Marshal Bob Ollinger ate his last meal at noontime on April 28, 1881. After hearing gunfire from the courthouse down the street, he ran outside—only to meet up with one of Billy the Kid's bullets during the outlaw's famous escape. These days, there isn't much action here, but there's plenty of charm—enjoy it while sitting in a rocker on the wooden porch—and the prices are a bargain. In the (¢–$) **Wortley Dining Room** (☎ 505/653–4438), open daily 8–6, the town's frontier heritage is honored with a menu featuring Western chow (beef, pork, and chicken) with salad greens from local gardens and fruit grown in nearby orchards. Reservations are required for steak dinners, served at 6. ⊠ *U.S. 380, 88338* ☎ *505/653–4300 or 877/967–8539* ☒ *505/653–4686* ⊕ *www.wortleyhotel.com* ⋑ *7 rooms* △ *Restaurant; no a/c, no room phone, no room TVs* ⊟ *AE, MC, V; restaurant, no credit cards* ☉ *Hotel and restaurant open by reservation only Nov.–Apr.*

★ **$** ✕⊞ **Ellis Store Country Inn.** In 1850 this B&B was a modest two-room adobe in a territory where settlers and Mescaleros clashed; during the Lincoln County War, Billy the Kid was known to frequent the place. These days, rooms in the main house are decorated with antiques. Behind the main house is the Mill House, which has four guest rooms and a large common room and is ideal for families. Casa Nueva has two suites with reproduction antiques and a country-French feeling. Owner Jinny Vigil, who's won *New Mexico* magazine's chef-of-the-month award more than once, cooks six-course gourmet meals in the evening, which are served in a wood-panel dining room. The breakfasts could stir even the most avid sleeper, and the lush, well-manicured garden is becoming increasingly popular for June weddings. ⊠ *U.S. 380, Mile Marker 98* ⌂ *Box 15, 88338* ☎ *505/653–4609 or 800/653–6460* ☒ *505/653–4610* ⊕ *www.ellisstore.com* ⋑ *10 rooms (4 share 2 baths), 2 suites* △ *Restaurant, fans; no a/c, no room phones, no room TVs, no smoking* ⊟ *AE, D, DC, MC, V* ⦿ *BP.*

▮
OFF THE
BEATEN
PATH
★ **$–$$**

✕⊞ **TINNIE SILVER DOLLAR –** Just 2 mi east of the NM 70 turnoff to Ruidoso is the little town of Tinnie and this real find of a restaurant. The food at the Silver Dollar is more than worth the drive (it is owned by the well-run, local Cattle Baron chain), and if you're in need of a place to stay, they have two well-appointed guest suites available. Aside from enjoying a really fine meal of traditional favorites like filet mignon, rack of lamb, lobster tail, or chicken piccata, you can relax knowing that you're supporting a business with a mission: the Silver Dollar's profits go to support the Second Chance Boys' Ranch, an on-site program geared to help neglected boys between the ages of 10 and 16 regain self-esteem and learn the skills they need to make good life choices. Their Sunday champagne brunch is a favorite that draws folks from miles around. Ask about the haunted mirror and the building's ghost. ⊠ *NM 70, 88351* ☎ *505/653–4425* ⊕ *www.tinniesilverdollar.com* ⤳ *2 suites* ⚉ *Jacuzzi tubs, satellite TV, Internet* ▭ *AE, D, DC, MC, V.*

San Patricio

⓫ *14 mi south of Lincoln, 45 mi west of Roswell on U.S. 70/380.*

Ranchers, farmers, artists, and others who appreciate the pastoral pleasures of the Hondo Valley live in San Patricio and the nearby villages of Tinnie and Hondo. The Rio Ruidoso flows into the Rio Hondo here, providing a watery boon to farmers and wildlife alike. During the harvest, fresh cider and produce are sold at roadside stands.

★ The late artist Peter Hurd lived in the Hondo Valley on the Sentinel Ranch, which is still owned by his son, Michael Hurd, whose paintings are also displayed in the gallery. The **Hurd–La Rinconada Gallery** displays Peter's landscapes and portraits. The artist is famous for Western scenes but gained some notice when a portrait he painted of Lyndon B. Johnson displeased the president, who refused to hang it in the White House. Also on display are the works of Hurd's late wife, Henriette Wyeth (Andrew Wyeth's sister). Michael is an amiable host who has established an international reputation with a series of paintings he calls "The Road West," his vision of the lonely desert scenery surrounding his home. Michael's sister Carole Hurd Rogers and her husband, Peter Rogers, also an artist, live near the ranch as well. Paintings by Jamie Wyeth, father Andrew Wyeth, and grandfather N. C. Wyeth round out the impressive collection at the gallery. Signed reproductions and some original paintings are for sale. ⊠ *U.S. 70, Mile Marker 281* ☎ *505/653–4331* ⊕ *www. wyethartists.com* ☯ *Mon.–Sat. 9–5.*

Where to Stay

★ $$–$$$ ⊡ **Hurd Ranch Guest Homes.** Modern and Western furnishings and paintings, sculpture, and Native American artifacts decorate the adobe casitas on the Sentinel Ranch. Peter Hurd made them available to friends and to customers who needed accommodations while he painted their portraits. The rooms have washing machines and dryers, fully equipped kitchens, and fireplaces. The newest one is named after actress Helen Hayes, who was a family friend and frequent visitor. A wing of the Hurd–La Rinconada Gallery has a spacious apartment with an enclosed patio for rent. Facilities also are available for weddings and conferences. ⊠ *Off U.S. 70, turn south toward San Patricio at Mile Marker 281, 20 mi east of Ruidoso* ◌ *Box 100, 88348* ☎ *505/653–4331 or 800/658– 6912* ▤ *505/653–4218* ⤳ *5 casitas, 1 suite* ⚉ *Some in-room hot tubs, kitchens, microwaves, refrigerators, cable TV, in-room VCRs, laundry facilities* ▭ *AE, D, MC, V.*

Ruidoso

⑫ *20 mi west of San Patricio on U.S. 70*

A sophisticated year-round resort town on the eastern slopes of the pine-covered Sacramento Mountains, Ruidoso retains a certain rustic charm. Shops, antiques stores, bars, and restaurants line its main street, and in winter, skiers flock to nearby Ski Apache. In summer, Ruidoso is a paradise for outdoors lovers seeking respite from the blazing heat of lower elevations.

Ruidoso Downs is so close to Ruidoso you won't realize it's a separate township, but its Ruidoso Downs Racetrack and museums are the area's huge draws. The summer horse-racing season keeps the 9,800 or so permanent residents entertained after the snow and ski bunnies disappear.

Ruidoso Downs Racetrack & Casino, the self-proclaimed Home of the World's Richest Quarter Horse Race, has a fabulous mountain vista as the setting for cheering the ponies. On Labor Day the track is the site of the All-American Quarter Horse Futurity, with a total purse of as much as $2.5 million. Twenty percent of revenues from the **Billy the Kid Casino,** with some 300 slot machines, boosts purses for the races. Casino gambling allowed at horse racing tracks is credited with reviving the sport in New Mexico by attracting quality horses and competition. The casino is decorated with murals suggesting nearby historic Lincoln, where Billy the Kid once hung out. The facility offers year-round, full-card simulcasting from the nation's largest tracks. ⊠ *U.S. 70, Ruidoso Downs* ☎ *505/378–4431* ⊕ *www.ruidosodownsracing.com* 🖃 *Racetrack open seating $3.50, reserved seating $5 and up; Turf Club $10, higher on special weekends* ⊙ *Racing late May–early Sept., Thurs.–Sun. and Mon. holidays, post time 1 PM. Casino Sat.–Thurs. 11–11, Fri. noon–midnight.*

★ ⊙ About ½ mi east of the racetrack you can pay further respects to horses at the **Hubbard Museum of the American West.** The museum houses the **Anne C. Stradling Collection** of more than 10,000 artworks and objects related to the horse—paintings, drawings, and bronzes by master artists; saddles from Mexico, China, and the Pony Express; carriages and wagons; a horse-drawn grain thresher; and clothing worn by Native Americans and cowboys. The **Racehorse Hall of Fame** celebrates accomplished horses and jockeys and screens rare and contemporary video footage. Activities at the children's interactive center include pony rides, horse demonstrations, and puzzles. Youngsters can don Old West attire and have their photos taken in a jockey outfit. In front of the museum is a bronze sculpture of eight galloping horses—*Free Spirits at Noisy Water.* Aside from being beautiful, the monument represents a minor feat of engineering, since of the eight horses only nine hooves actually touch the ground. ⊠ *U.S. 70 E, Ruidoso Downs* ☎ *505/378–4142* 🖃 *$6* ⊙ *Daily 9–5.*

The **Mescalero Apache Indian Reservation,** bordering Ruidoso to the west, is inhabited by more than 2,500 Mescalero Apaches, most of whom work in tourism-related enterprises. One of the state's most elegant resorts, the Apache-owned and -operated **Inn of the Mountain Gods** has become a major destination point for visitors from all over the country. Also on the reservation are a general store, a trading post, and a museum where a 12-minute video about life on the reservation is screened. Regular talks are also given on the history and culture of the Mescalero Apaches. There are campsites here (with hookups at Silver and Eagle lakes only) and picnic areas. Ritual dances are occasionally performed for the public, the most colorful of which is on July 4. *Tribal Office ⊠ 106 Central Mescalero Ave., off U.S. 70, Mescalero ☎ 505/671–4494 ⊠ Free ☉ Reservation and tribal museum weekdays 8–4:30.*

WORD OF MOUTH

"Before you trek across the state, you should stay in the Ruidoso area and enjoy what is has to offer. I like Ruidoso. There's some fun shopping, some arts and crafts. There is a resort there called the Inn of the Mountain Gods—casino, interesting building, but very new-age."   –Tandoori_Girl

🕙 Built in 1868 by Captain Paul Dowlin, **Dowlin's Historic Old Mill** is the oldest building in Ruidoso and has had a variety of past lives: as a grist mill, saw mill, a bean thrasher, a blacksmith shop, a general store, and perhaps as the local spot to buy moonshine during the days of prohibition. This is one of the few remaining water wheels in the West still in operation. ⊠ *641 Sudderth Dr. ☎ 505/257–2811 ⊠ Free.*

Where to Stay & Eat

$–$$ ✕ **Café Rio.** Eclectic international is the easiest way to describe this bright, fun restaurant. There simply isn't any other place in Ruidoso to find jambalaya, spanakopita, a delicious array of Greek soups (the kale soup is a real find), or hand-tossed pizzas that have made fans all over the West. The selection of microbrew beer is as satisfying as the food. ⊠ *2547 Sudderth Dr. ☎ 505/630–1612 ⊟ No credit cards ☉ Closed after Thanksgiving (for 2–3 wks) and after Easter (for 1 wk).*

$–$$ ✕ **Weber's Grill.** This happening place is kid-friendly and operated by the Sierra Blanca Brewing Co. An adobe brick fireplace and wooden ceilings help create a cozy, mountain cabin atmosphere. Try some of the excellent microbrews served at the copper-top bar—the nut brown ale is particularly good—while sampling pizzas or steaks and seafood. ⊠ *441 Mechem Dr., NM 48 ☎ 505/257–9559 ⊟ AE, D, MC, V ☉ Closed Tues.*

¢–$$ ✕ **Cattle Baron.** This southern New Mexico franchise serves steaks, scampi, and more exotic dishes such as mustard-grilled pork chops, while offering the chance to graze at a generous salad bar. Succulent prime rib is the house specialty. Ample greenery and tile floors add a pleasant country ambience. ⊠ *657 Sudderth Dr. ☎ 505/257–9355 ⊟ AE, D, DC, MC, V.*

¢ ✕ **Lincoln County Grill.** The locals come here for quick service and good inexpensive food. Step up to the counter to order hearty Texas chili, old-fashioned hamburgers, or chicken-fried steak. At breakfast you can grab eggs served with fluffy, homemade "Lincoln County" biscuits.

Vinyl-covered tables are decorated with old coffee, tea, and tobacco tin images. This is a great stop for families in a hurry and on a budget. ⊠ *2717 Sudderth Dr.* ☎ *505/257–7669* ⊟ *AE, MC, V.*

$$–$$$ ✕⊞ **Inn of the Mountain Gods.** There is nothing run-of-the-mill about this **Fodor's**Choice beautifully designed hotel and resort. The luxurious rooms and com-★ mon areas are decorated with contemporary Southwestern flourishes and nods to the inn's Mescalero Apache ownership. Stunning bronze crown dancer sculptures are found at the entrance to the resort, which includes a 38,000-square-foot casino with 1,000 slot machines. The views here are stunning; many windows overlook a serene lake and (in winter) the nearby snow-crusted mountain peak of Sierra Blanca. Big game hunts, a championship golf course, guided fishing trips, wedding facilities, excellent food; it's all here. This resort is more Aspen in feel than southeastern New Mexico—with all the graciousness and none of the pretense. ⊠ *287 Carrizo Canyon Rd., Box 269, 88340* ☎ *800/545–9011 or 505/464–7777* ⊕ *www.innofthemountaingods.com* ☞ *273 rooms* ⌂ *2 restaurants, cable TV with movies, 18-hole golf course, pool, lake, exercise equipment, boating, fishing, mountain bikes, hiking, horseback riding, downhill skiing, 3 bars, lounge, piano bar, sports bar, casinos, concert hall, nightclub, piano, concierge, Internet, convention center, meeting rooms, no-smoking rooms* ⊟ *AE, D, DC, MC, V.*

★ **$$–$$$** ⊞ **Hawthorn Suites Conference & Golf Resort.** This luxury resort is next door to a top-rated New Mexico golf course (The Links at Sierra Blanca) and to the Ruidoso Convention Center. A dramatic, inlaid kiva fireplace looms majestically over the lobby; the huge pool, enclosed within a two-story atrium, is Ruidoso's largest. A complimentary full breakfast is served in a dining area that has views of the surrounding golf links and mountains. Most rooms have extensive views of meadows, pine trees, or the golf course; soft yellow interiors with wood furnishings complete the feel of cozy luxury. ⊠ *107 Sierra Blanca Dr., 88345* ☎ *505/258–5500 or 866/211–7727* ⊟ *505/258–2419* ⊕ *www.ruidosohawthorn.com* ☞ *117 rooms* ⌂ *Dining room, picnic area, IDD phones, some in-room hot tubs, some kitchens, microwaves, refrigerators, cable TV with movies, in-room VCRs, in-room data ports, 18-hole golf course, golf privileges, 4 tennis courts, pro shop, indoor pool, gym, hot tub, massage, bicycles, mountain bikes, hiking, lobby lounge, babysitting, playground, laundry facilities, Internet, business services, convention center, meeting rooms, free parking, some pets allowed, no-smoking floors* ⊟ *AE, D, DC, MC, V* ⭥⭥ *BP.*

★ **$$–$$$** ⊞ **Riverside Cottages.** These cozy cabins snuggled amid tall pines right next to a bubbling stream are billed as a romantic getaway for couples. The cabins combine neo-rustic decor (lots of wood and plaid) with modern amenities like indoor hot tubs and gas fireplaces. They're just across the Rio Ruidoso from the Ruidoso Lodge Cabins, which are operated by the same owners (Judy and Kurt Wilkie). Kitchenettes are stocked with cooking utensils and dishes. Since privacy is highly valued at this particular site, neither visitors nor children are allowed here. ⊠ *Office, 300 N. Main St., 88345* ☎ *505/257–2548 or 800/497–7402* ⊕ *www. ruidoso.net/river* ☞ *8 cabins* ⌂ *In-room hot tubs, kitchenettes, microwaves, refrigerators, cable TV, in-room VCRs, fishing, hiking; no room phones, no kids* ⊟ *D, MC, V.*

$–$$ 📺 **Black Bear Lodge.** Tucked into the secluded tall pines of the Upper Canyon, each of this inn's four spacious rooms has its own Jacuzzi, wood-panel ceiling, and fireplace; an off-site casita with kitchen and two bedrooms also is available. Owner Carol Olson, who re-created the property from a 1930s-era restaurant, has created a great room that has all the coziness of a family room. Privacy is emphasized above communal gatherings here, and you're on your own for breakfast (although breakfast items, as well as homemade cookies and other snacks, are stocked in the common area refrigerator). ⊠ *428 Main Rd., 88345* 🕾 *505/257–1459* 🖷 *505/630–8310* ⊕ *www.blackbearruidoso.com* 🛏 *4 rooms, 1 casita* ⚬ *BBQs, fans, in-room hot tubs, some kitchens, some microwaves, some refrigerators, cable TV with movies, in-room VCRs, some laundry facilities, Internet, meeting rooms, free parking, no-smoking rooms; no room phones* 🖃 *AE, D, MC, V* ⋈ *CP.*

★ **$$–$$$** 📺 **Ruidoso Lodge Cabins.** In the heart of Ruidoso's gorgeous, tree-filled Upper Canyon, owners Judy and Kurt Wilkie oversee a placid retreat of renovated 1920s, knotty-pine abodes. The immaculate one- and two-bedroom cabins are adorned with Western and Southwestern decor. Some have hot tubs, and all have fireplaces and decks with gas grills offering serene views. The cabins are fully equipped with kitchen utensils and dishes. You can trout fish here, right along the Rio Ruidoso, but you must arrange for your own gear. Hiking trails lead off the property through the pine forest. ⊠ *300 Main St., 88345, Take Sudderth Dr. north from U.S. 70 through downtown Ruidoso; continue west through Upper Canyon, where Sudderth turns into Main St.* 🕾 *505/257–2510 or 800/ 950–2510* ⊕ *www.ruidosolodge.com* 🛏 *10 cabins* ⚬ *Some in-room hot tubs, kitchenettes, microwaves, refrigerators, cable TV, in-room VCRs, fishing, hiking; no room phones* 🖃 *D, MC, V.*

$–$$ 📺 **Shadow Mountain Lodge.** Designed for couples, this lodge in the Upper Canyon has suites with fireplaces. Other amenities include hair dryers and irons. The front veranda views tall pines and the landscaped gardens; there's also a gazebo where you can take a relaxing soak in the hot tub. Separate cabins all have wood paneling and ample privacy. ⊠ *107 Main Rd., 88345* 🕾 *505/257–4886 or 800/441–4331* 🖷 *505/257–2000* ⊕ *www.shadowmountainlodge.com* 🛏 *19 suites, 4 cabins* ⚬ *Some in-room hot tubs, some kitchenettes, some microwaves, refrigerators, cable TV, in-room VCRs, in-room data ports, outdoor hot tub, laundry facilities* 🖃 *AE, D, DC, MC, V.*

☾ **$** 📺 **Sierra Blanca Cabins.** Log cabin–style abodes tucked between the pines alongside the Rio Ruidoso offer a gorgeous outdoor setting within walking distance of downtown shops and other attractions. This is an affordable option for families. Discounts are offered for area food outlets and ski rentals. Each cabin has a fireplace, outdoor grill, and picnic area. ⊠ *217 Country Club Rd., west on Sudderth Dr. to Country Club Rd., 88345* 🕾 *505/257–2103 or 866/262-2103* ⊕ *www.sierrablancacabins.com* 🛏 *12 cabins* ⚬ *Fans, kitchenettes, cable TV, playground, some pets allowed (fee); no a/c in some rooms* 🖃 *AE, D, MC, V.*

$ 📺 **Swiss Chalet Inn.** With a sweeping view of the forest, this property is 16 mi from the Ski Apache slopes. Common spaces have Swiss and German touches such as cowbells, an alpenhorn, and cuckoo clocks, but otherwise, guest-room decor is basic with some painted headboards and furnishings. The cozy bar, which has a small fireplace, is a convivial place to decompress after a day of skiing. On the walkways and decks facing the forest, you can relax near the fragrant pines. ⊠ *1451 Mechem Dr., 88345* ☎ *505/258–3333 or 800/477–9477* 🖷 *505/258–5325* ⊕ *www. sciruidoso.com* ➥ *82 rooms* ⚲ *Cable TV, in-room data ports, indoor pool, hot tub, sauna, hiking, bar, laundry facilities, meeting rooms, some pets allowed (fee), no-smoking rooms* ⊟ *AE, D, DC, MC, V* ⟦◯⟧ *CP.*

Nightlife & the Arts

A 514-seat venue hosting top-tier performances from jazz musicians to international ballet dancers can be found in the **Spencer Theater for the Performing Arts** (⊠ NM 220, north of NM 48 ☎ 505/336–4800 or 888/818–7872, 505/336–0055 box office, 800/905–3315 ticket orders ⊕ www.spencertheater.com). The white, templelike building looms majestically amid mountain vistas just north of Ruidoso and is one of the state's cultural icons. Tickets run $20–$55, and free tours are given Tuesday and Thursday beginning at 10. Local children sometimes act in special free summer performances; outdoor summer music concerts are also offered.

Sports & the Outdoors

Run by the Mescalero Apaches on 12,003-foot Sierra Blanca, **Ski Apache** (⊠ Ski Run Rd./NM 532 ☎ 505/336–4356, 505/257–9001 snow report ⊕ www.skiapache.com) has powder skiing for all skill levels on 55 trails and 750 acres. One of Ski Apache's distinctions is its high mountain elevation surrounded by desert. This unique climate can produce heavy snowfall (averaging more than 15 feet each winter) followed by days of pleasant, sunny weather. With the largest lift capacity in New Mexico, this huge resort can transport more than 16,500 people hourly. Ski Apache also has the state's only gondola. The season typically runs from Thanksgiving through Easter, and the snowmaking system is able to cover a third of the trails. Lift operations are open daily from 8:45 to 4; the ski area charges adults $40 for full-day lift tickets and $28 for children 12 and under. Slightly higher fees apply for certain dates, including the week between December 26 and January 1, and special weekends in January and February. Snowboarding is allowed on all trails. Families should check out the Kiddie Korral Program for children ages four to six. Although there are no overnight accommodations at the resort, day lodges have two cafeterias, three snack bars, and outdoor grills. From Ruidoso take NM 48 6 mi, and turn west on NM 532 for 12 mi.

Capitan

22 mi north of Ruidoso on NM 48, 12 mi west of Lincoln on U.S. 380.

Capitan is famous as the birthplace and final home of Smokey Bear, the nation's symbol of wildfire prevention. The original bear concept was created in 1944, and the poster bear is still seen in public service announcements issued by the Ad Council. After a devastating 1950 forest fire in the Capitan Mountains, a bear cub was found badly burned and clinging to a tree. Named Smokey after the poster bear, he lived in the National Zoo in Washington until his death in 1976, when he was returned home for burial.

Displays at the **Smokey Bear Historical Park** visitor center explain forest-fire prevention and fire ecology. A theater with informational films is offered at the 3-acre park, which also contains a picnic area. Capitan's original train depot is adjacent to the museum and gift shop. The site hosts special events for youngsters, such as an Easter egg hunt, Halloween night, and Smokey's Christmas at the Park. ⊠ *118 Smokey Bear Blvd., off NM 380* ☎ *505/354–2748* 🎫 *$2* ☉ *Daily 9–5.*

Where to Eat

★ ¢–$ ✕ **Greenhouse Café.** Within this historic building that was once a hotel, you can sample creative dishes such as orange-coconut chicken, or Pacific dumplings, and savor organic salad greens grown right next door in a hydroponic (without soil) greenhouse. A tiny back porch patio is available for outdoor dining. Try the bread pudding even if you don't think you're a fan; you may develop a new favorite dessert. You may have to stand in line for a hugely popular Sunday brunch, served 9–11; dinner only, otherwise. Reservations are suggested. ⊠ *103 Lincoln Ave.* ☎ *505/354–6025* ▤ *MC, V* ☉ *Closed Mon. and Tues.*

Carrizozo

⑬ *37 mi northwest of Capitan on U.S. 380, 58 mi north of Alamogordo on U.S. 54.*

Back when railroad crews began using this site as a supply center, the community that rose up was named after *carrizo*, the reedlike grass growing in the area. The extra "-zo" appeared when the carrizo grew so thick a ranch foreman added it to the town's name for emphasis. The ranching community incorporated in 1907 and in 1912 became the county seat of Lincoln County. About 1,000 residents live in this charming, isolated town at the junction of U.S. 54 and U.S. 380.

The **Sierra Blanca Brewing Co.,** modestly hidden on a back street of Carrizozo, is the largest brewery in New Mexico (and officially among the top 120 highest-producing breweries in the nation), with a maximum capacity of 4,500 beer barrels annually. The high-tech brewing process is reflected in the smooth taste of creations such as pale ale and the amusingly named Roswell Alien Amber Ale. You can sample some of the brews on-site, as well as organic ginger ale and root beer. Free tours also are offered. ⊠ *503 12th St.* ☎ *505/648–6606* ☉ *Free tours daily 9–4.*

Near Carrizozo is the **Valley of Fires Recreation Area** operated by the Bureau of Land Management. According to Native American legend a volcanic eruption about 1,000 years ago created a valley of fire here. When the lava cooled, a dark, jagged landscape remained. A ¾-mi trail penetrates the lava-flow area, which looks like a *Star Trek* backdrop and covers 44 mi (it's 5-mi wide in some places). Crevices and bowls trapping precious water nurture ocotillo and blooming cactus, creating natural landscaping along the well-maintained trail. The visitor center has a gift shop with souvenirs and books. Caving is allowed with the proper permits. ⊠ *U.S. 380, 4 mi west of Carrizozo* ☎ *505/648–2241* ⊡ *$3 per individual, $5 per carload* ⊙ *Information center daily 8–4.*

Where to Stay & Eat

¢ ✕ **Outpost Bar & Grill.** Rural restaurants in southern New Mexico have a long-standing rivalry over who makes the best green-chile hamburgers in the region. Many fans will tell you that the winner is right here—and many will tell you this is the best one found *anywhere*. Besides cooking awesome burgers, this bar and grill has a wacky hunting-lodge decor full of animal heads, snakeskins, and painted cow skulls. The massive antique wooden bar is the centerpiece of the establishment. ⊠ *U.S. 54 S* ☎ *505/648–9994* ⊟ *No credit cards.*

¢ ⊞ **Rainbow Inn.** This small rural motel has quite a few pleasant amenities—many of which are unusual for its price range: each room has a remote-control TV, a refrigerator, and a microwave, along with immaculate contemporary furnishings. ⊠ *Intersection of U.S. 308 and U.S. 54* ⌖ *Box 873, Carrizozo 88301* ☎ *505/648–4006* 🖷 *505/648–2989* ✉ *onecoyote@tularosa.com* ↩ *14 rooms, 3 cabins* ⌂ *Microwaves, refrigerators, cable TV, in-room data ports* ⊟ *AE, D, DC, MC.*

¢ ⊞ **Sands RV Park & Motel.** The nicely maintained, modern rooms here have extras including access to satellite television. An RV park ($10) with extra-wide spaces and full hookups and showers is also on the premises. ⊠ *U.S. 54 S* ⌖ *Box 873, Carrizozo 88301* ☎☎ *505/648–2989* ↩ *11 rooms, 21 RV sites* ⌂ *Microwaves, refrigerators, some cable TV, laundry facilities, some pets allowed* ⊟ *AE, D, MC, V.*

⚲ **Valley of Fires Recreation Area.** This small campground sits atop an island of sandstone surrounded by lava. Continuous improvements, such as paving and updated facilities, are being made. ⊠ *U.S. 380, 4 mi west of Carrizozo* ☎ *505/648–2241* ⌂ *Grills, flush toilets, pit toilets, partial hookups (electric and water), dump station, drinking water, showers, fire grates, picnic tables, electricity, public telephone, ranger station* ↩ *20 RV sites with partial hookups, 5 tent sites* ⊡ *Primitive camping $5, developed camping $7, RV sites $11.*

EN ROUTE
★ ☾

Twenty-eight miles south of Carrizozo, take CR B-30 east off U.S. 54 and in 5 mi you come to **Three Rivers Petroglyph Site,** one of the Southwest's most comprehensive and fascinating examples of prehistoric rock art. The 21,000 sunbursts, lizards, birds, hand prints, plants, masks, and other symbols are thought to represent the nature-worshipping religion of the Jornada Mogollon people, who lived in this region between AD 900 and 1400. Symbols were pinpointed and identified through the extensive work of two members of the Archaeological Society of New Mexico's Rock Art Recording Field School. Fragrant desert creosote and mesquite can be found here, along with cacti that blossom brilliantly in early summer. A rugged trail snakes for 1 mi, and from its top you can see the Tularosa Basin to the west and the Sacramento Mountains to the east. A short trail leads to a partially excavated prehistoric village. You can camp at the site, and there are 10 covered shelters with picnic tables, barbecue grills, restrooms, and water. ⊠ *CR B-30 east off U.S. 54* ☎ *505/525–4300* ⊡ *$3 per vehicle.*

Alamogordo

⑭ *58 mi south of Carrizozo on U.S. 54, 46 mi southwest of Ruidoso; 68 mi northeast of Las Cruces on U.S. 70.*

Defense-related activities are vital to the town of Alamogordo and to Otero County, which covers much of the Tularosa Basin desert. Look up and you might see the dark, bat-shape outline of a Stealth fighter swooping overhead—Holloman Air Force Base is home to these high-tech fighter planes. Many residents work at White Sands Missile Range, where the nation's first atomic bomb exploded at Trinity Site on July 12, 1945. If you find U.S. 70 closed temporarily, it's due to test launches (locals have grown accustomed to this). South of Alamogordo huge military exercises involving both U.S. and foreign troops are conducted at the Fort Bliss Military Reservation along Route 54. It's not all that surprising that flying objects can be mistaken for Unidentified Flying Objects in this state.

The multistory structure that houses the **New Mexico Museum of Space History** gleams metallic gold when the sun hits it at certain angles. The facility formerly known as the Space Center underwent a name change in 2001, partially to avoid confusion with its famous counterpart of the same name in Houston. Its centerpiece is the **International Space Hall of Fame**, into which astronauts and other space-exploration celebrities are routinely inducted. A simulated red Mars landscape is among the indoor exhibits. Outside, the **Stapp Air and Space Park** displays a rocket sled from the 1950s and other space-related artifacts. The scenic **Astronaut Memorial Garden** has a view of White Sands National Monument. The **Clyde W. Tombaugh IMAX Dome Theater and Planetarium** screens films and presents planetarium and laser light shows. Weeklong annual space-shuttle camps for children take place from the first week in June through the first week in August. ✉ *At top of NM 2001, from U.S. 70 take Indian Wells Rd. to Scenic Dr.; from U.S. 54 take Florida Ave. to Scenic Dr.* ☎ *505/437–2840 or 877/333–6589* ✏ *Museum $3, IMAX ticket prices vary, beginning at $6 but depending on show; call for additional pricing information* ☉ *International Space Hall of Fame daily 9–5. Tombaugh IMAX Dome Theater and Planetarium late May–early Sept., shows daily on the hr 10–5, with evening shows Fri. and Sat. at 6 and 7. Early Sept.–late May, shows daily on the hr 11–5 with evening shows Fri. and Sat. at 6 and 7.*

If there's a train buff in your family, the **Toy Train Depot** in Alamogordo's Alameda Park is a must-see. Here, a narrow-gauge train rumbles along a 2½-mi track, and a depot, built in 1898, displays elaborate toy train layouts in five rooms. There are live steam engines on display, and you can hear real whistles and rumbles from nearby heavy freight trains (the attraction is only 50 yards from the Union Pacific main line). If you make advance reservations, you can take a guided tour of the abandoned Alamogordo and Sacramento Railway roadbed and trestles. ✉ *1991 N. White Sands Blvd., Alameda Park* ☎ *505/437–2855* ✏ *Train $4, displays $3* ☉ *Wed.–Sun. noon–5.*

Tasty nuts are the crop at **Eagle Ranch Pistachio Groves and Heart of the Desert Vineyards,** where you can buy pistachios baked into cranberry biscotti, pistachio-filled chocolate candies, and the nuts themselves, as well as the wines being produced in the proprietary winery. Linger in the coffee shop or art gallery. George and Marianne Schweers own the family farm here, which has been growing pistachios—an unusual crop for New Mexico—since 1972. The ranch has 12,000 pistachio trees and is the largest such grove in the state; a vineyard was planted in 2003 and is now producing wines. Ask for permission at the store to camp at the picnic area—there's no charge for self-contained vehicles. ⊠ *7288 NM 54/70, 4 mi north of White Sands Mall, Alamogordo* ☎ *800/432-0999* ⊕ *www.eagleranchpistachios.com* ⊑ *Farm tours free* ☉ *Mon.–Sat. 8–6, Sun. 9–6. Farm tours daily late May–early Sept. at 10 and 1:30, early Sept.–late May, weekdays at 1:30.*

ⓒ ⓮ **White Sands National Monument** encompasses 145,344 acres of the largest
Fodor's Choice deposit of gypsum sand in the world, where shifting sand dunes reach
★ 60 feet high. The monument, one of the few landforms recognizable from space, has displays in its **visitor center** that describe how the dunes were (and are continually) formed from gypsum crystals originating at a dry lake bed called Lake Lucero, where winds and erosion break down the crystals into fine particles of sand. A 17-minute introductory video at the visitor center is very helpful if you intend to hike among the dunes. There are also a gift shop, snack bar, and bookstore.

A 16-mi round-trip car ride takes you into this eerie wonderland of gleaming white sand. You can climb to the top of the dunes for a photograph, then tumble or surf down on a sled sold at the visitor center. As you wade barefoot in the gypsum crystals you notice the sand is not hot, and there's even moisture to be felt a few inches below the surface. Gypsum is one of the most common minerals on earth and is finer than the silica sand on beaches. A walk on the 1 mi **Big Dune Trail** will give you a good overview of the site; other options are the 4¾-mi **Alkali Flat Trail** and the 600-yard **Boardwalk.** The **Nature Center in the Dunes** museum has exhibits and other information that includes interpretive displays with depictions of animals and plant life common to the dunes, along with illustrations of how the dunes shift through time. The center usually is open during regular hours, but is staffed by volunteers (so it sometimes closes unexpectedly). Call first to make sure it's open. The picnic area has shaded tables and grills. Backpackers' campsites are available by permit, obtainable at the visitor center, but there aren't any facilities. Once a month from May to September, White Sands celebrates the full moon by remaining open until 11, allowing you to experience the dunes by lunar light. Call for information and reservations for monthly auto caravans to **Lake Lucero,** the source of the gypsum sand deposit. Rangers lead tours daily at sunset. ⊠ *Off U.S. 70, 15 mi southwest of Alamogordo, Holloman AFB* ☎ *505/479-6124* ⊕ *www.nps.gov/whsa* ⊑ *$3* ☉ *Late May–early Sept., daily 7 AM–9 PM; visitor center 8–7. Early Sept.–late May, daily 7 AM–dusk; visitor center 8–5.*

OFF THE BEATEN PATH

WHITE SANDS MISSILE RANGE MUSEUM & MISSILE PARK – Here you can see outdoor displays of more than 50 rockets and missiles along with indoor exhibits honoring historic contributions of scientists including rocketry genius and inventor Werner Von Braun. The museum also contains accounts of early Native American inhabitants who occupied the surrounding Tularosa Basin. A newer display is an exhibit building with a cutout of the interior of the V-2 missile. ⊠ *White Sands Missile Range, turn east off U.S. 70, 45 mi southwest of Alamogordo or 25 mi northeast of Las Cruces; take access road 5 mi to gate and stop for visitor's pass; you must have current driver's license and insurance to enter, as well as photo identification for all passengers* ☎ *505/678–8824* ▨ *Free* ⊙ *Museum weekdays 8–4, weekends 10–3; Missile Park daily dawn–dusk.*

Where to Stay & Eat

¢–$ ✕ **Compass Rose.** Patterned after a Bavarian-style tavern, this unusual establishment has wooden bench seating and cozy surroundings along with selections of cheese, meat, bread, and salads. Hot sandwiches and stews also are served, and you can eat on an outdoor patio during balmy weather. The tasty food is a change of pace from Southwestern fare. ⊠ *2203 E. 1st St.* ☎ *505/434–9633* ▤ *AE, D, MC, V.*

¢–$ ✕ **Margo's.** *Chalupas* (beans, meat, and cheese served on crisp tortillas) is the specialty Mexican dish at family-owned Margo's. In winter *menudo*, made of hominy and tripe, is served hot and steaming. The Southwestern decor includes colorful blankets. ⊠ *504 1st St.* ☎ *505/434–0689* ▤ *AE, D, MC, V.*

¢ ▥ **Days Inn.** Clean, contemporary rooms with standard furnishings are the order of the day at this chain hotel across the street from three restaurants. There's a bar next door. ⊠ *907 S. White Sands Blvd., 88310* ☎ *505/437–5090* ▦ *505/434–5667* ▱ *40 rooms* △ *Microwaves, refrigerators, cable TV with movies, pool, gym, no-smoking rooms* ▤ *AE, D, DC, MC, V* ⋔ *CP.*

⚠ **Alamogordo Roadrunner Campground.** Motel-style amenities, such as a lounge and a recreation room, are available at this facility. There are also inviting patches of green lawn and trees where you can pitch your tent. ⊠ *412 24th St., 1 block east of U.S. 70/54* ☎ *505/437–3003 or 877/437–3003* ⊕ *www.roadrunnercampground.com* △ *Grills, laundry facilities, flush toilets, full hookups, showers, picnic tables, general store, play area, swimming (pool)* ▱ *67 RV sites, 10 tent sites, 2 cabins* ▨ *RV sites $24–$29, tent sites $19, cabins $35* ▤ *MC, V.*

Cloudcroft

⑯ *19 mi east of Alamogordo on U.S. 82.*

Cloudcroft was established in 1898 when the El Paso–Northeastern Railroad crew laid out the route for the Cloud Climbing Railroad. The natural beauty and business possibilities for creating a getaway from the blistering summer heat in the valley below were obvious and plans were quickly made for a mountaintop resort. You can still see the Mexican Canyon trestle from this era as you drive NM 82 to the west of town.

This incredibly steep, twisty and scenic drive links Cloudcroft to the desert basin below and gains 4,700 feet in elevation during its 30-mi stretch.

"9,000 feet above stress level" is one way this sweet little mountain town promotes itself these days, and from its perch high above the Tularosa desert valley the town lives up to the claim. Flowers and ponderosa and other greenery give the air an incredible mountain fragrance, and the boardwalks lining the main street, Burro Avenue, lend the town an Old West atmosphere that comes across as more charming than contrived. Despite a significant influx of retirees and big-city expats over the past few years, the town has held onto its country friendliness.

> **WORD OF MOUTH**
>
> "You might want to spend all your time in southern New Mexico. The weather will be cooler, and the aspens should be turning gold in the mountains around Cloudcroft and Ruidoso."   –ElendilPickle

People you don't know will stop and chat with you. Get used to it and enjoy; this kind of sweetness seems all too rare these days.

There are two festivals that bookend the warm season here, and a number of others in between. Mayfest happens over Memorial Day and Aspencade is held the first weekend of October. The July Jamboree, and a Labor Day weekend fiesta are two more events held, along with street dances and melodramas that most of the residents seem to participate in. Festivals typically include arts and crafts booths and all sorts of perfectly delectable munchies.

Cloudcroft has the southernmost ski area in the U.S., although it is a very small operation and only open during years when snow is abundant (it brings about 89 inches a year on average). It's a nice place for beginner skiers to get their snow legs. Contact the Chamber of Commerce for season info and ticket prices.

Ⓒ The **National Solar Observatory–Sacramento Peak,** 20 mi south of Cloudcroft on the Sunspot Highway at elevation 9,200 feet, is designated for observations of the sun. The observatory, established in 1947, has four telescopes, including a 329-foot Vacuum Tower that resembles a pyramid. One observation point has a majestic view of White Sands and the Tularosa Basin. During the day you can inspect the telescopes on a self-guided tour and watch live filtered television views of the sun. Interactive displays at the visitor center allow you to, among other activities, make infrared fingerprints. The community of Sunspot, home of the observatory, is an actual working community of scientists—not a tourist attraction—so you should stay within areas designated for visitors. ⊠ *Sunspot Hwy., Sunspot* ☎ *505/434-7000* ⊕ *www.nso.edu.* ⊠ *Visitor center $2, self-guided tours free* ⊙ *Visitor center, daily May–Oct. 10–6; self-guided tours 2; Nov.–Apr., call for hrs.*

The headquarters of the **Lincoln National Forest Sacramento Ranger District** (⊠ 61 Curlew St., off U.S. 82 ☎ 505/682-2551) has maps showing area hiking trails.

**EN
ROUTE**

Two miles south of Cloudcroft on NM 24, take Forest Road 64 (paved) to **Nelson Canyon Vista Trail** for a well-marked walking trail with absolutely breathtaking views of White Sands. This walk among the shade of tall trees is made all the more sweet if you've recently spent time down in the blazing summer heat of the Tularosa desert.

Where to Stay & Eat

¢–$$ ╳ **Western Cafe.** Locals jokingly refer to the regular morning gatherings here as "the old men's club," where all the latest happenings in Cloudcroft are discussed at great length, and sometimes with great passion. Come in as you are (this place is casual personified) and get ready for great big helpings of local favorites such as chicken-fried steak. Don't ask for pepper encrusted ahi here: this is basic, rib-sticking Western food served in a simple, no-frills room where the wood tables and chairs and paneled walls may remind you of your grandparents' living room. The bar next door is great if you require more than water and sodas, and it serves a number of good microbrews, like the amusingly named "Arrogant Bastard Ale." ⊠ *304 Burro Ave.* ☎ *505/682–2445, 505/682–9910 bar* ▭ *No credit cards.*

$–$$ ╳ **Dave's Pinecone Café.** Savory bratwurst as well as some of the tastiest, juiciest burgers around are the draw here. Noteworthy is the enormous Mongrel Burger, a 1-pound cheeseburger topped with grilled onions and jalapeños. The ice-cream and fudge shop on premises is worth a stop if you're in need of rich and creamy coldness or super-rich chocolate truffles. ⊠ *Pine Stump Mall, 300 Burro Ave.* ☎ *505/682–2127* ▭ *AE, D, MC, V.*

$–$$ ╳ **Gallo's.** With their brightly colored interior and papel picado banners hanging from the ceiling you might think you've wandered into Mexico. Basic American food and a nice assortment of Mexican favorites are served. Start your day with huevos rancheros, or stop in just to snack on tasty fresh salsas, guacamole, and chips. ⊠ *306 Burro Ave.* ☎ *505/682–2448* ▭ *AE, D, MC, V.*

★ $$–$$$$ ╳▣ **The Lodge.** The imposing Bavarian style architecture of the Lodge, with its tower and dramatic details, has drawn all sorts of notable characters over the years, including Judy Garland, Clark Gable, and even the Mexican revolutionary Pancho Villa. The outside looks like an Alpine lodge, but the interior, with its dark-wood furnishings and plush carpeted stairways, seems to have come right from a Gothic novel. Rooms are furnished with period antiques, comforters, and ceiling fans. Rebecca's restaurant serves delicious Continental cuisine (the crab is amazing; never mind that you're in the mountains of a landlocked state) in a beautiful room that is full of sunlight during the day and romantically lighted with candles at night. Rebecca is the ghost of a chambermaid apparently murdered by her lumberjack lover in the 1930s in the hotel—and she's reputedly quite playful. The downside of the Lodge is the wide variance in service and cleanliness; generally service is wonderful and the rooms lovely, and it is a gorgeous, historic property. If you're not satisfied with your accommodations at check-in, simply ask for another room. Affiliated with the Lodge is the off-premises **Lodge Pavilion,** a rustic nine-room B&B, as well as a private, historic

7

"minilodge," the **Retreat Suites,** which has three one-bedroom suites and one two-bedroom suite. ✉ *1 Corona Pl., Box 497, 88317* ☎ *505/ 682–2566 or 800/395–6343* 🖶 *505/682–2715* ⊕ *www.thelodgeresort. com* 📞 *59 rooms* ⚴ *Restaurant, some in-room hot tubs, some kitchens, some microwaves, some refrigerators, some in-room data ports, 9-hole golf course, pool, gym, outdoor hot tub, sauna, spa, croquet, horseshoes, volleyball, cross-country skiing, snowmobiling, lounge, some pets allowed (fee), no-smoking floors; no a/c in some rooms* 💳 *AE, D, DC, MC, V.*

For cabin rental information, call the Cloudcroft Chamber of Commerce, or try **Cabins at Cloudcroft** (☎ 505/682–2396, 800/248–7967 within New Mexico ⊕ www.cloudcroftnm.com). Rates are $75–$170 for one- to four-bedroom cabins.

★ **$–$$** 🏨 **RavenWind Bed & Breakfast.** Morning dew on sparkling grass and the fragrant scent of a juniper forest greet visitors awakening in sublime isolation at RavenWind (22 mi southeast of Cloudcroft). The 75-acre ranch owned by transplanted upstate New Yorkers Russ and Elaine Wright was built in 2000 specifically to create a refuge where people can rest and renew themselves—or hike, mountain bike, and explore to your heart's content. You have your choice of a separate, secluded two-bedroom house (where children are welcome) or rooms in the main lodge, which has wooden porches and native rock walls. RavenWind is popular with horse owners, who can transport and then board their animals in stables ($15 daily per horse). For some real pampering, or to work out the kinks from the busy life you left behind, Russ is a licensed therapeutic massage therapist. No kids in main lodge. ✉ *1234 Hwy. 24, Weed 88354* ☎ *505/687–3073* 🖶 *505/687–2039* ⊕ *www.ravenwindranch.com* 📞 *2 rooms, 1 2-bedroom house* ⚴ *BBQs, some kitchens, microwaves, some refrigerators, cable TV with movies, in-room VCRs, in-room data ports, exercise equipment, outdoor hot tub, massage, spa, bicycles, hiking, horseback riding, babysitting, laundry facilities; no a/c in some rooms, no smoking* 💳 *No credit cards* 🍴 *MAP.*

$ 🏨 **Cloudcroft Hotel and Mall.** If you'd like to be in the thick of things, or just want to park your car and spend your time strolling around town, this is the hotel for you. You're within walking distance of dining and nightlife, shopping, and outdoor activities. The nine spacious rooms have ceiling fans (fine for the cooler temperatures at this altitude) and clawfoot tubs. Two suites overlook Burro Avenue and have balconies. Gallo's, a restaurant in the attached shopping arcade, offers room service to guests. ✉ *306 Burro Ave., 88317* ☎ *505/682–3414* ⊕ *www.cloudcrofthotel. com* ⚴ *Some kitchenettes* 💳 *AE, D, MC, V* 🍴 *CP.*

🛖 **Deer Spring RV Park.** You can savor the forested surroundings and shade in this sanctuary far removed from any major community. The site has full hookups and pull-through parking. ✉ *2112 Rio Penasco Rd., off NM 130, about 12 mi east of Cloudcroft, Mayhill 88339* ☎ *505/687–3464* ✉ *deerspring@pvtnetworks.net* 📞 *60 RV sites* ⚴ *Recreation room, laundry facilities* 🖼 *$18* 💳 *No credit cards* ◷ *Closed Nov.–Mar.*

SOUTHEASTERN NEW MEXICO ESSENTIALS

AIR TRAVEL

Albuquerque International Sunport is 380 mi north of Carlsbad and 295 mi north of Roswell. El Paso International Airport in Texas is the main gateway to southern New Mexico. The major airlines with scheduled service to the airport are America West, American, Continental, Delta, Frontier, and Southwest. *See* Air Travel *in* New Mexico Essentials for national airline phone numbers.

The municipal airports in Carlsbad and Roswell have daily shuttle-flight service on Mesa Airlines. Roswell is southeastern New Mexico's major flight hub, offering the most daily flights and scheduling options.

🚹 Airlines **Mesa Airlines** ☎ 800/637-2247 ⊕ www.mesa-air.com.
🚹 Airports **Albuquerque International Sunport** ⊠ 2200 Sunport Blvd. SE, Albuquerque ☎ 505/842-4366. **El Paso International Airport** ⊠ 6701 Convair Dr., El Paso, TX ☎ 915/772-4271. **Sierra Blanca Regional Airport** ⊠ 1 Airport Rd., Ruidoso ☎ 505/336-8111.

CAR TRAVEL

To get to Roswell and other points in southeastern New Mexico, drive east from Albuquerque on I–40 for about 60 mi, exit on U.S. 285 heading south, and continue 140 mi to Roswell. From Roswell take U.S. 285 to Carlsbad, about 75 mi away (320 mi from Albuquerque). From El Paso, Texas, take U.S. 62/180 east and north 154 mi to Carlsbad Caverns (187 mi to Carlsbad).

The major highway south through southeastern New Mexico is U.S. 285, accessible from I–40 at the Clines Corner exit, 59 mi east of Albuquerque. If you're destined for Roswell or Carlsbad from southwestern New Mexico, the best route is U.S. 70 east from Las Cruces or U.S. 62/180 east from El Paso, Texas.

The quality of the roadways in southeastern New Mexico varies widely, particularly in remote rural areas. Drive with caution on the region's narrow highways, which particularly in mountainous areas have no shoulders. On minor roadways, even if paved, be alert for curves, dips, and steep drop-offs.

EMERGENCIES

In case of emergency dial 911.

Some Walgreens pharmacies in Roswell, Carlsbad, and other southeastern communities have late-night or 24-hour pharmacies. Wal-Mart and large grocery chain stores including Albertson's also have pharmacies.

🚹 Hospitals **Carlsbad Medical Center** ⊠ 2430 W. Pierce, Carlsbad ☎ 505/887-4100. **Dr. Dan Trigg Memorial Hospital** ⊠ 301 E. Miel de Luna, Tucumcari ☎ 505/461-7000. **Eastern New Mexico Medical Center** ⊠ 405 W. Country Club Rd., Roswell ☎ 505/622-8170. **Guadalupe County Hospital** ⊠ 535 Lake Dr., Santa Rosa ☎ 505/472-3417.
🚹 Pharmacies **Bob's Budget Pharmacy** ⊠ 511 South 2nd St., Tucumcari ☎ 505/461-1200. **Route 66 Pharmacy** ⊠ 1128 Rte. 66, Santa Rosa ☎ 505/472-5666.

VISITOR INFORMATION

🛈 **Alamogordo Chamber of Commerce** ✉ 1301 N. White Sands Blvd., 88310 ☎ 505/437-6120 or 800/826-0294 ⊕ www.alamogordo.com. **Capitan Chamber of Commerce** ✆ Box 441, 88316 ☎ 505/354-2273. **Carlsbad Chamber of Commerce** ✉ 302 S. Canal St., 88220 ☎ 505/887-6516 ⊕ www.chamber.caverns.com. **Carrizozo Chamber of Commerce** ✆ Box 567, 88301 ☎ 505/648-2732. **Cloudcroft Chamber of Commerce** ✆ Box 1290, 88317 ☎ 505/682-2733 ⊕ www.cloudcroft.net. **Lincoln State Monument** ✉ U.S. 380 ✆ Box 36, 88338 ☎ 505/653-4372. **Portales Chamber of Commerce** ✉ 100 S. Ave. A, 88130 ☎ 505/356-8541 or 800/635-8036. **Roswell Chamber of Commerce** ✉ 131 W. 2nd St. ☎ 505/623-5695 or 877/849-7679 ⊕ www.roswellnm.org. **Ruidoso Valley Chamber & Visitor Center** ✉ 720 Sudderth Dr., 88345 ☎ 505/257-7395 ⊕ www.ruidoso.net/chamber. **Santa Rosa Visitor Information Center** ✉ 486 Historic Rte. 66, 88435 ☎ 505/472-3763 ⊕ www.santarosanm.org. **Tucumcari/Quay County Chamber of Commerce** ✉ 404 W. Rte. 66, 88401 ☎ 505/461-1694 ⊕ www.tucumcarinm.com.

Southwestern New Mexico

INCLUDING EL PASO, TEXAS & CIUDAD JUÁREZ, MEXICO

WORD OF MOUTH

"On the last day [of our trip] we made a side trip to the Very Large Array, a group of huge radio telescopes about 45 minutes west of Socorro. If you saw the movie *Contact* with Jodie Foster, you saw them—very impressive, gleaming white, 8 stories tall against a blue sky."

—beach_dweller

"We stayed only one night in El Paso and didn't have time to do anything but we concluded that the next time we would stay longer and start with a day trip to Juárez using the Border Jumper trolley."

—Pat2003

Updated by
Georgia
de Katona

CALLING SOUTHWESTERN NEW MEXICO A "BORDERLAND" may seem a bit obvious, but it is one in the broadest possible sense. The proximity of Mexico is inescapable as you travel through the region, but so is the delicious blend of the people whose cultures have met and mingled in this area since long before there was a border. Southwestern New Mexico is a trove of diversity, from the scenery, to the people and their cultures, to the food.

Historically, the lack of an international border didn't mean the area was without intense struggles. For centuries this region has been populated by peoples of various "nations" struggling to control and keep it. The Apaches and the Spaniards chased and harassed each other for three centuries, until the westward push of Americans threatened the existence of both of those cultures. By the mid-1800s the Apaches had been mostly subdued and moved onto reservations, the territory was appropriated by the United States, and the struggles shifted to those between lawmen and outlaws. It wasn't called the "Wild West" for nothing.

El Paso (The Pass) is so named because of its positioning in the natural pathway of the Spanish march northward through the area more than 400 years ago. Cabeza de Vaca led the first Spanish expedition into the area in 1593. Five years later Juan de Oñate brought 500 Spanish colonists from Mexico across the Rio Grande into what is now New Mexico. Trade between the northern Spanish colonial outposts and old Mexico followed El Camino Real (The Royal Road, named in honor of the Spanish monarchy for whom the colonies were established), a route that essentially ran parallel to the Rio Grande. The 100-mi stretch of the Camino Real from Las Cruces to San Marcial became known as Jornada del Muerto (Journey of Death, or Dead Man's Walk, depending on whom you're asking for translation) because it veered away from the Rio Grande (the only water source) and straight into Apache territory.

El Paso, Texas, is the region's largest city and most convenient gateway, but the hub of southern New Mexico is Las Cruces (The Crosses, so named because of the number of people buried in the area due to hardship and Apache attacks). With a population of about 75,000 (and growing quickly), Las Cruces is bordered to the east by the jagged and beautiful Organ Mountains. Sunset often colors the jagged peaks a brilliant magenta, called "Las Cruces purple," and they are depicted endlessly by local painters and photographers. Nearby, Old Mesilla once served as the Confederate territorial capital of New Mexico and Arizona.

The incredible, irrigated lushness in the fertile Mesilla Valley would surprise the hard-pressed Spanish settlers who passed through the area 400 years ago. Miles of green fields and orchards track the path of the Rio Grande from north of El Paso to north of Las Cruces, with water from the huge Elephant Butte reservoir irrigating some of the country's most prolific pecan and chile pepper farms. New Mexico's largest body of water, Elephant Butte Lake, is a mecca for water sports and fishing. Nearby, you can soak in natural hot springs and enjoy laid-back, small-town New Mexico in Truth or Consequences. The Bosque del Apache National Wildlife Refuge is a resting place for millions of migrating birds each year. Whether you're a bird enthusiast or not, it is quite a treat to

GREAT ITINERARIES

Allow yourself plenty of time to get from town to town and to explore once you get there. There are old mining towns to visit, tasty chili to be tried, and lovely shaded forest trails to wander. If you normally stay in chain hotels, try a night or two in a cozy, rural B&B. Don't hesitate to stop in at a little café that beckons or to ask locals what they enjoy doing. El Paso, Texas, is listed here because its proximity and size make it a natural gateway.

IF YOU HAVE 3 DAYS

Spend the first day exploring the old Spanish missions of ⬚⬚ **El Paso ❶**. In the late afternoon head up NM 28 to **Old Mesilla ❷**, where you can easily find a delicious Mexican-style dinner and have a walk around the historic plaza and its surrounding streets. On Day 2, head out through Deming and go north on NM 180 to ⬚⬚ **Silver City ❺**. Spend the afternoon exploring the walkable downtown area and its many shops and diverse arts and crafts galleries. On Day 3, enjoy the scenic drive through the Gila and a visit to the cliff dwellings.

IF YOU HAVE 7 DAYS

Enjoy the extra time to explore the areas above. Spend Day 1 exploring

⬚⬚ **El Paso ❶** and the second day in Juárez. The morning of Day 3 can be spent in **Old Mesilla ❷**, with an afternoon trip up to White Sands to enjoy the shifting shadows of the late afternoon and the gorgeous colors on the sands and surrounding mountains as the sun sets. Spend the night back in ⬚⬚ **Las Cruces ❸**. Drive to **Silver City ❺** on Day 4 and spend the afternoon wandering around town. Spend all of Day 5 in the **Gila National Forest**, visiting the cliff dwellings, canyons, and old mining towns. Spend the night in one of the lovely mountain B&Bs or inns. On Day 6, head east from Silver City on the very scenic NM 152 on your way to **Truth or Consequences ❼** and take a good, long soak in the hot springs there. After your soak, make a point of visiting the **Bosque del Apache National Wildlife Refuge ❾** before heading a bit north to spend the night in ⬚⬚ **Socorro ❿**. On Day 7, head west on U.S. 60 from Socorro to the **Very Large Array ⓫** or simply to explore the villages along the way like Pie Town. Head back to Socorro and down I–25 to El Paso, stopping in Hatch for some green chiles to take home if time allows.

8

witness the sky fill up with enormous varieties of birds taking off or landing in the marshy area.

Outdoor enthusiasts from all over head to the Gila National Forest (pronounced "heela") and Gila Wilderness areas for access to fantastic camping and hiking and natural hot springs. Old mining towns remind you of the thousands who came here on their quest for silver, copper, and other minerals once found abundantly in the ore-rich hills. Several small museums display the region's minerals, along with fine pottery created by early indigenous inhabitants. This rugged, mountainous area, with its breathtaking vistas and seemingly endless span of trees, was home

Southwestern New Mexico

at different times to two Western legends: Geronimo and Billy the Kid. The hub of the area is Silver City, one of the great small towns of the West. Here you'll find a burgeoning art scene, numerous community festivals, and friendly locals.

Exploring Southwestern New Mexico

The Rio Grande flows through the fertile Mesilla Valley, known for its plump green chile peppers and acres of thick, shaded pecan groves. Try leaving I–10 and following the green agriculture fields along NM 28, which begins just north of El Paso and ends at Old Mesilla. The adobe shops and restaurants in Old Mesilla's historic plaza make for an easy, leisurely afternoon of wandering. They are virtually unchanged from the way they appeared a century ago. From Las Cruces, take NM 185 north through the farm valley on the route that leads to Hatch. During the fall harvest this whole valley takes on the rich scent of roasting chiles.

You could easily spend several days (or weeks) exploring the old, but still lively, mining town of Silver City and the vast Gila National Forest, which surrounds it. New Mexico's largest lake, Elephant Butte, begins at Truth or Consequences and tracks north for miles alongside I–25. The Bosque del Apache Wildlife Refuge near Socorro provides a haven

IF YOU LIKE

GALLERY HOPPING

Several southwestern New Mexico communities are reinventing themselves as art communities, and Silver City is doing it well. Once-abandoned historic buildings in the downtown area now house galleries, where compelling art can be had at reasonable prices. Old Mesilla has several very fine, long-established galleries that emphasize the area's Hispanic culture and Southwestern influences. The El Paso Museum of Art has exceptional galleries and displays, including works of the city's own "native son," widely acclaimed artist Luis Jiménez, who is noted for his fiberglass sculptures.

HOT SPRINGS

The town of Truth or Consequences is this region's best-known spot for naturally heated mineral springs, where you can soak away stress in steamy bliss at a variety of spas. But these aren't the only hot springs in southwestern New Mexico; other, more secluded spots can be found outside Silver City, and in the Gila National Forest, where you can camp and then hike to natural outdoor soaking pools. Stop in at forest service offices for information about where to find these hot spots, or pick up a guide to hot springs of the Southwest before you head out.

OUTDOOR ACTIVITIES & SPORTS

Outdoor opportunities abound in this corner of New Mexico. Elephant Butte Lake near Truth or Consequences offers world-class competition fishing for striped bass, though other varieties such as catfish are also abundant. All sorts of water sports take advantage of the lake's miles of surface. The Gila National Forest and mountains near Silver City provide a cooler environment for trout fishing or hiking, but don't expect large streams or lakes here: this forest land is drier than what you would find in higher elevations (though white-water rafting is an option in the Gila). The mountains are still immense and fun to explore, either on foot or via scenic drives. Camping is another popular activity in this area. Bird-watchers will be busy just about anywhere they go along the Rio Grande, Gila National Forest, Elephant Butte Lake, or Bosque del Apache Wildlife Refuge.

8

for countless species of birds. Heading west at Socorro on U.S. 60 to explore tiny rural villages such as Magdalena and Datil will show you more of New Mexico's charm. On the Plains of San Augustin, look for the awesome array of giant, gleaming white radio antennae that are part of the National Radio Astronomy Observatory.

Timing

Mild and sunny winters are this region's major draw. From May to September, though, it's just plain hot. Really hot. And dry. The mountain areas provide a respite, and are generally 10 degrees cooler during the day. Unless you're used to dry, intense heat, plan summer outdoor excursions for early morning or late afternoon. Wear sunscreen, sunglasses, and hats in the midday sun, and don't just carry plenty of water—drink it. Temperatures drop in the evenings, so keep light jackets or sweaters on hand. Spring is cooler, but it can bring strong, dusty winds. The weather between mid-September and early November tends to be delightful and balmy, and the sunsets and moonrises at this time are fantastic.

About the Restaurants

The cost of a meal in this area is extremely reasonable. The Mexican cuisine in the Mesilla Valley and Las Cruces rivals any in Santa Fe, and costs much less. Mexican food is an almost sure bet in this area, especially if you're a fan of the locally grown green chiles. You won't get far before you realize that BBQ joints and steak houses are almost as numerous as the Mexican restaurants. Las Cruces has several tasty ethnic food restaurants in the university district; again, generally at very reasonable prices.

About the Hotels

Whether they're historic lodgings or chain hotels, you'll find many of the accommodations in this part of the state incorporate Spanish influences in their architecture. Haciendas, mission-style buildings with tile roofs, and courtyards with fountains and gardens are everywhere here—evidence of the style first introduced by Spanish colonists more than four centuries ago.

WHAT IT COSTS				
$$$$	**$$$**	**$$**	**$**	**¢**
RESTAURANTS over $30	$23–$30	$16–$22	$10–$15	under $10
HOTELS over $250	$176–$250	$121–$175	$70–$120	under $70

Restaurant prices are per person for a main course at dinner. Hotel prices are for two people in a standard double room in high season, excluding 10%–12% tax.

BORDERLAND

Lines drawn on a map do little to divide the inhabitants of two countries and three states (New Mexico, Texas, and the Mexican state of Chihuahua) who share a history dating back some 400 years. In the small border villages of Columbus and Las Palomas, Mexico, families live and do business on both sides of the international boundary line. Las Cruces, New Mexico, and El Paso, Texas, are both growing so quickly that they seem to be near the point of merging via housing developments. Anthony is the little town between the two, with a sweet, small-town feel and a dynamic community-minded sensibility. The borderland area also draws transplants from the eastern and western United States, who come to take advantage of the mild weather and placid way of life.

You might be surprised to find U.S. Border Patrol checkpoints on all major highways leading away from the El Paso area to destinations such as Carlsbad, Deming, Truth or Consequences, and Alamogordo. Uniformed officers will simply ask your citizenship, though trained dogs sometimes circle vehicles in searches for illegal drugs. The stops are routine, and law-abiding citizens should encounter no difficulty.

El Paso, Texas

❶ *267 mi south of Albuquerque, I–25 to I–10.*

Yes, El Paso *is* in Texas—but just barely. At one time, the city along the now streamlike Rio Grande was part of the New Mexico Territory. One glance at a map will show why this area has become the transportation and business hub for southern New Mexico, as well as a destination for outdoor adventurers and history buffs. Most residents speak English and at least some Spanish, and the mix of Native American, Spanish, and American cultures is evident in the art and music, architecture, and cuisine.

In April 1598 Spanish explorer Don Juan de Oñate dubbed the entire Rio Grande Valley Paso del Rio del Norte ("the pass through the river of the north")—from which El Paso derives its name. Oñate was so grateful that the expedition of about 500 ragged colonists had reached the Rio Grande that he ordered his people to don their best clothes for a feast of thanksgiving—a celebration that preceded the arrival of the pilgrims in Massachusetts by nearly a quarter century. On that feast day, April 30, Oñate issued a formal proclamation of *La Toma,* claiming the land for the King of Spain.

El Paso lies between the southern end of the Rockies and the northern terminus of Mexico's Sierra Madre, making it a major stopping point on the southern route west during the California gold rush. In 1850 the downtown area was sparsely settled, with a dirt trail leading to the Rio Grande. Eight years later there was an established roadway populated with adobe homes and businesses, and not long after that San Jacinto Plaza became the official town square. The arrival of the railroad in 1888 sealed El Paso's fate as a vital, vibrant city of the west.

Many of El Paso's downtown buildings date from the early 20th century, built by the regionally famous architect Henry C. Trost. His firm, Trost and Trost, designed more than 300 buildings in the area and his fondness for the variations on the regional style informs the pillars and stained glass of the grandiose Camino Real Paso del Norte to the sturdy, reinforced concrete of the Mills Building. Trost's influences were many—from local adobe to Frank Lloyd Wright—and he received much acclaim for his buildings at the University of Texas at El Paso. Based on Bhutanese structures, the campus buildings have an almost monastic design. Unfortunately, many downtown gems like the historically protected Plaza Hotel (one of Conrad Hilton's first hotels) stand empty. Hotels during the 1950s were often full, sometimes with Hollywood stars and the wealthy heading for a cheap and easy divorce in Ciudad Juárez, just across the border. Adding to the town's bravado were live alligators in the plaza pond (a sculpture of writhing alligators has replaced the real reptiles, which ended their residency in the 1960s).

The **El Paso Museum of Arts** has an American collection including works of Southwest artists Tom Lea, Frederic Remington, Henrietta Wyeth, and native son Luis Jiménez. The museum also has the enormous Samuel Kress collection with European art from the 13th to 18th centuries. Striking religious art can be found in the Spanish Viceroyal section and in the room full of Mexican folk *retablos* (pictures of saints and religious scenes painted on wooden tablets). Drawings and prints by masters like Picasso, Goya, and Rivera, and works by contemporary artists, round out the collection. ⊠ *1 Arts Festival Plaza* ☎ *915/532–1707* ⊕ *www. elpasoartmuseum.com* ☒ *Free* ⊙ *Tues.–Sat. 9–5, Sun. noon–5.*

Magoffin Home State Historical Park has a Territorial-style adobe homestead near downtown El Paso erected in 1875 by an early El Paso pioneer, Joseph Magoffin, and occupied by the Magoffin family for 110 years. The city of El Paso grew out of Magoffinsville, a town started by this prominent and powerful family whose influence in the area is vast. The original furnishings of the house remain, including an imposing 13-foot-tall half-canopy bed that is part of a five-piece bedroom set purchased at the 1884 World's Fair in New Orleans. ⊠ *1120 Magoffin St., follow signs off I–10; westbound traffic takes Cotton St. exit, eastbound traffic takes Downtown exit to Kansas St.* ☎ *915/533–5147* ☒ *$3* ⊙ *Daily 9–4.*

At 24,247 acres (37 square mi), all within the city of El Paso, **Franklin Mountains State Park** is the largest urban park in the United States. The mountains overlook the Rio Grande and make up the northern end of El Paso del Norte, the gap in the mountains that has permitted travelers of all types to move north and south through this region for centuries. Miles of hiking, mountain biking, and horse trails wind through the park, which offers amazing views of the city below. Rock climbing is permitted. Limited camping is available for tents and there are five RV sites. Tours are offered on the first and third weekends of the month; call ahead to reserve a space. ⊠ *1331 McKelligon Canyon Rd.* ☎ *915/ 566–6441* ⊕ *www.tpwd.state.tx.us/spdest/findadest/parks/franklin* ☒ *$3* ⊙ *8–5.*

ⓒ Touted as the only public-accessible tram in Texas, **Wyler Aerial Tramway** provides a phenomenal view of three states, two nations, and 7,000 square mi (the tram operators are proud of this). The tram totes you up to 5,632-foot Ranger Peak, where you can marvel at the view on an observation deck. City views, as well as surrounding canyons with cacti and interesting rock formations, are breathtaking. ⊠ *1700 McKinley Ave.* ☎ *915/ 566–6622* ⊕ *www.tpwd.state.tx.us/spdest/findadest/parks/wyler_aerial tram/* ☒ *$7* ⊙ *Sun., Mon., and Thurs. noon–6, Fri. and Sat. noon–8.*

★ Around 1681, Spanish refugees from the Pueblo Revolt in and around Santa Fe established the **Mission Ysleta** (*ysleta* means "small island"). Clergy converted members of the Tigua tribe (Tiwa speakers from what is now the Isleta Pueblo, south of Albuquerque) who had accompanied the refugees on their southern flight. The thick-walled adobe structure has a remarkably small door, made so in the hopes of fending off attacks from Apaches. Like other old missions in the area, Ysleta is still an ac-

CLOSE UP

Pat Garrett, Lawman

BEST KNOWN FOR TRACKING DOWN AND KILLING the outlaw Billy the Kid near Fort Sumner, New Mexico, Pat Garrett's life after the July 13, 1881, event was relatively quiet. That is, until his own violent death near his ranch in Las Cruces some 27 years later.

Garrett, who'd been elected sheriff of Lincoln County just a year before his run-in with Billy the Kid, was subsequently named the sheriff of Doña Ana County (where Las Cruces is now the county seat). He owned a parcel of grazing land near Las Cruces—land that became the center of a dispute that resulted in his death.

Garrett had granted a lease to local rancher Wayne Brazel, allowing Brazel to graze goats on Garrett's land. When Garrett decided to sell his ranch, however, Brazel balked at relinquishing the grazing lease. On February 29, 1908, Garrett and his brother-in-law were riding together in a wagon on their way from the ranch to a meeting in Las Cruces with the buyer. Brazel met up with them and accompanied them on his own horse. At some point en route, Garrett was shot in the back of the head. In a typical turn of quirky Old West justice, Brazel confessed to killing Garrett, but was later acquitted by a jury for apparently murdering him on grounds of self-defense. Controversy surrounds this account of Garrett's death, and conspiracy theories about what really happened (and motives for the lawman's death) still abound.

A little-known bit of trivia is that, even after Garrett was buried in Las Cruces, his family still managed to have an impact on the state where he'd lived. His daughter, Elizabeth, who was born blind but became a singer and lover of music, eventually wrote New Mexico's official state song: "O Fair New Mexico," three years after statehood was achieved in 1912. The song begins with the lyrics:

"Under a sky of azure, where balmy breezes blow. Kissed by the golden sunshine, is Nuevo Mejico."

8

---

tive church. A guide from the Mission Trail Association is available to conduct free tours from Friday through Sunday, depending on church schedules. ⊠ *Old Pueblo Rd. at Zaragosa and Alameda, take Zaragosa exit off I–10, east of El Paso* ☎ *915/859–9848* ☜ *Free* ☉ *Mon.–Sat. 9–5; Sun. openings vary with church schedules.*

Adjacent to Mission Ysleta is the **Tigua Indian Reservation** (⊠ 119 S. Old Pueblo Rd. ☎ 915/859–7913), home of the oldest ethnic group in Texas. Tigua pottery, jewelry, art, and replicas of ancient Native American homes are sold here.

The **Speaking Rock Entertainment Center** (⊠ Tigua Indian Reservation, 122 Old Pueblo Rd. ☎ 915/860–7777) has mariachi music and performances, and at **Wyngs Restaurant** (☎ 915/859–3916 ☉ Closed Mon. and Tues.) you can dine on barbecue, steaks, and Mexican food or unwind in the lounge.

Socorro Mission, to the south of the Tigua Indian Reservation, is famed for its fine vigas—the carved ceiling beams that support the roof. Because it's so small, the building is used only for special occasions such as weddings and funerals. A Mission Trail Association guide conducts free tours here in the morning, Friday through Sunday, unless they conflict with services. ⊠ *328 S. Nevares Rd.* ☎ *915/859–7718* ✆ *Free* ☉ *Weekdays 9–3.*

Presidio Chapel San Elceario in San Elizario (yes, the two spellings conflict) is 6 mi south of the Socorro Mission. The 1789 Spanish fortress provided settlers protection from raiding Comanches and Apaches. After fire damaged the chapel in 1936, a bell tower and stained glass were added; the stark white facade of the church is an archetype of Southwestern church architecture. It was near this site that the expedition of Spanish explorer Don Juan de Oñate stopped to conduct a thanksgiving celebration in 1598. ⊠ *1556 San Elizario Rd.* ☎ *915/851–2333* ✆ *Free* ☉ *Daily 10–4, generally.*

The **San Elizario County Jail** is thought to have been built as a private residence in the early 1800s, but at some point the adobe building became El Paso County's first courthouse and jail. According to Pat Garrett's book Authentic Life of Billy the Kid, this is the only jail the Kid broke *into,* in order to free his friend Melquiades Segura. In the same vicinity you can find other historic structures, including Los Portales, which started as a private residence in the 1850s and later served as an area schoolhouse. ⊠ *San Elizario Plaza* ☎ *915/851–1682 San Elizario Genealogy and Historical Society* ✆ *Free guided tours of jail and plaza beginning at the Los Portales building* ☉ *Tues.–Sun. 10–2, and after hrs by special arrangement.*

The *huecos* at **Hueco Tanks State Historic Site** are the natural stone basins that hold rain water and have been used as water sources by inhabitants and travelers in this arid zone for centuries. The park is an internationally renowned mecca for rock climbers, and a big draw for pictograph lovers, with hundreds of amazing and unusual mask pictographs left by the prehistoric Jornada Mogollon people as well as newer designs left by Apache and Kiowa people. Choose among camping, picnicking, hiking, rock climbing and bouldering, bird-watching, stargazing, and petroglyph hunting. This is an easy day trip from El Paso, and well worth several days if you have the time. The number of visitors each day is limited so make reservations at least two days in advance. Take U.S. 62/180 32 mi northeast from El Paso, turn north on Ranch Road 2775; follow signs. ⊠ *6900 Hueco Tanks Rd., No. 1, El Paso, TX 79938* ☎ *512/389–8900, 915/849–6684 for next-day-only reservations* ⊕ *www.tpwd. state.tx.us/spdest/findadest/parks/hueco_tanks* ✆ *$4 per person, day use; camping $12–$16* ☉ *Oct.–Apr. daily 8–6; May–Sept. Mon.–Thurs. 8–6, Fri.–Sun. 7–7.*

At **Sunland Park Racetrack & Casino** (⊠ 101 Futurity Dr., Sunland Park ☎ 505/589–1131), races are held are Friday–Sunday and Tuesday from November through early April. Post time is 12:15 November through January and 12:55 February through April. Not just a run-of-the-mill racetrack, Sunland has a lake in the center of the track, a good restaurant, lounge, and snack bar, and live entertainment on weekends. The **casino** stays open year-round, from noon to midnight, and has 600 slot machines. Because the casino is limited in size and it's the only one in town, stakes are higher here than at most New Mexico casinos. The nickel machines are few, and the place is packed and lively during prime hours. From El Paso, take Sunland Park exit off I–25 near the northern city limits.

Where to Stay & Eat

Fodor'sChoice ★ ✕ **Café Central.** The old saw "evolve or perish" has served this restaurant well. In 1918 Café Central opened in Juárez and served alcohol (and tasty food) to the prohibition–weary masses from the United States. Once prohibition ended, the café moved north across the border and it's been part of the local scene since. Today, bold decoration, an airy courtyard, and innovative Southwestern–Asian food combine to make this urbane eatery a popular destination for the city's hip crowds. Dos Equis steamed clams, shrimp with tequila-cilantro sauce, and divine très leches cake (oh my!!) are some of the amazing possibilities on a menu that changes daily, according to availability of ingredients. Well worth the splurge. Lunch is a bit less expensive and equally tantalizing. ⊠ *Texas Tower, 109 N. Oregon St.* ☎ *915/545–2233* ⚍ *Reservations required* ⊟ *AE, D, DC, MC, V* ☺ *Closed Sun.*

☯ **$–$$$$** ✕ **Cattleman's Steakhouse.** This is pretty much in the middle of nowhere—
Fodor'sChoice 20 mi east of El Paso—but it's worth the trip, as much for the quirky
★ theme-rooms as for the terrific steaks. The mesquite-smoked barbecue and seafood on the menu are as tempting as the steaks; strict vegetarians won't find a happy meal here. Consistently voted a local favorite, the succulent steaks are so tender they almost melt in your mouth. A children's zoo, playground, lake walk, hayrides (on Sunday), and a movie set are among the numerous nonculinary diversions. Cattleman's is part of Indian Cliffs Ranch, which provided the backdrop for scenes in the movie *Courage Under Fire.* Open hours are weekdays 4:30–10, Saturday 12:30–10, and Sunday 12:30–9. ⊠ *Off I–10, Exit 49, follow signs, Fabens* ☎ *915/544–3200* ⚍ *Reservations not accepted* ⊟ *AE, D, MC, V.*

★ **$–$$$** ✕ **The State Line.** Barbecued ribs and smoked chicken are tangy and fabulous at this local favorite near the Sunland Park Racetrack. Bring an appetite, because the trimmings include generous helpings of potato salad, coleslaw, and beans. For dessert try the ultrarich brownie. Drinks are served in an outdoor courtyard, where you can wait for your table. ⊠ *1222 Sunland Park Dr., Sunland Park exit off I–10* ☎ *915/581–3371* ⚍ *Reservations not accepted* ⊟ *AE, D, DC, MC, V.*

¢ ✕ **Leo's.** The Mexican food at Leo's four El Paso locations is repeatedly voted a favorite by locals in annual newspaper polls. Enchiladas, tacos, combination plates, and fluffy sopaipillas are served in helpings that will leave you stuffed—that is, if you can elbow your way through the crowds and get a table. ⊠ *5103 Montana St.* ☎ *915/566–4972* ⊠ *5315 Hondo Pass* ☎ *915/757–9025* ⊠ *315 Mills Ave.* ☎ *915/544–1001* ⊠ *7520 Remcon Circle* ☎ *915/833–1189* ⊟ *AE, D, MC, V.*

$ ✕▨ **Camino Real Hotel, El Paso.** The grande dame of downtown hotels, the stunner here is the enormous 1912 Tiffany–designed, stained-glass

8

dome suspended above the bar. The rooms are large and airy, with marble-top desks and many antique furnishings. The Dome Restaurant ($$) offers fine dining, and brunch is popular at the more casual Azulejo (¢–$). It's in a fantastic location, across the street from the art museum and civic center, and 15 minutes from the airport. ⊠ *101 S. El Paso St., 79901* ☎ *915/534–3000 or 800/769–4300* 🖷 *915/534–3024* ⊕ *www.caminoreal.com/elpaso_i/index.html* 🖙 *359 rooms* 🖐 *2 restaurants, coffee shop, room service, cable TV with movies, pool, gym, sauna, Internet, meeting rooms, airport shuttle, parking (fee), some pets allowed (fee), no-smoking rooms* ▭ *AE, D, DC, MC, V.*

$–$$ 🖃 **Holiday Inn Sunland Park.** This Holiday Inn, on a hill with 6½ acres near Sunland Park Racetrack, has outdoor courtyards; the Southwestern-style rooms have ironing boards, hair dryers, coffeemakers. Breakfast buffets are served in the Sierra Grille Restaurant, and a Sunday brunch is available from 11 to 2. The service from the staff is attentive and noteworthy. ⊠ *900 Sunland Park Dr., 79922* ☎ *915/833–2900 or 800/658–2744* 🖷 *915/833–6338* ⊕ *www.holidayinn.com* 🖙 *178 rooms* 🖐 *Restaurant, cable TV, in-room data ports, pool, hot tub, lounge, meeting rooms* ▭ *AE, D, DC, MC, V.*

★ ♨ $ 🖃 **Hilton El Paso Airport.** Just 200 yards from the El Paso International Airport, the Hilton offers consistent comfort and convenience, with a bit more luxury than other chain hotels. Many rooms convert into two-room suites. Two restaurants on the premises provide a choice of Continental fare (Magnim) or northern Italian (Canarozzos, dinner only). The 200-foot waterslide into the pool makes this a great spot to let the kids decompress after a day of touring. ⊠ *2027 Airway Blvd., 79925* ☎ *915/778–4241* 🖷 *915/772–6871* 🖙 *272 rooms* 🖐 *2 restaurants, some in-room hot tubs, some microwaves, some refrigerators, cable TV with movies, pool, hot tub, spa, meeting rooms, airport shuttle, free parking, some pets allowed* ▭ *AE, D, DC, MC, V.*

Nightlife & the Arts

Live music happens Thursday–Saturday at the **Dome Bar** (⊠ 101 S. El Paso St. ☎ 915/534–3000) of the Camino Real Hotel. There isn't a cover and the drinks are good. The revitalized downtown area is a good area to find bars and nightclubs. Join the locals and walk around to see what's up; there are new places opening up on a regular basis.

The year's highlight for the city is the annual **Viva El Paso!** (☎ 915/478–0617), a musical celebrating El Paso's history and legendary characters with music, dance, and drama. Held Friday and Saturday nights at the McKelligon Canyon Amphitheater in the Franklin Mountains, June through late July. Tickets can be purchased at Ticketmaster ☎ 915/544–8444. This is a fun community event, good for all ages.

Shopping

El Paso is *big* on cowboy boots, and great deals on them can be found at the factory outlet stores here. Technically, you're buying discontinued and "irregular" boots, but don't let that deter your search. Unless you're maniacally detail-fixated, the boots at the **Tony Lama Factory Stores** (⊠ 5040 N. Desert Blvd. ☎ 915/581–8192 ⊠ 12151 Gateway

W ☎ 915/858–0124 ⌧ 7156 Gateway E ☎ 915/772–4327) are good-looking, well-priced, and hand-crafted in El Paso.

There are no factory outlet stores for the boots at **Rocketbuster Boots** (⌧ 115 S. Anthony St.; just across from old train station in Union Plaza district of downtown ☎ 915/541–1300); it's just the factory itself. If you've got a fair amount of cash in your pocket and a yen for personal detailing and butter-soft leather, saddle up.

If your boots were made for riding, not walking, check out **Barnett Harley-Davidson** (⌧ 8272 I–10, between Lomaland and Lee Trevino ☎ 915/592–5804 or 800/736–8173), the world's largest dealership for the famed motorcycles. New, used, and rare bikes are showcased, along with parts and accessories for the care and feeding of the bikes.

Ciudad Juárez, Mexico

Across the Rio Grande border from El Paso.

If what you want is a quick and easy Mexican experience, Juárez is worth a day's excursion. There are any number of goods to buy, and tastes to taste, but it's a border town at the very end of it, with all the good and bad that title entails. Walking across the border is easy enough, but taking the trolley makes it all so much easier and ultimately much more fun. At the end of a hot day of exploring, eating, and drinking margaritas, hopping on the trolley to take you back across the border is a welcome respite from the crowds. Avoid driving in Juárez if you can as it tends to be stressful, and parking your car is dodgy in terms of safety.

The plaza, with its lovely cathedral, and the Spanish architecture of the wealthier neighborhoods make for scenic walks among some areas of the city. The harsh reality, however, is that this is the last stop along a long route for hundreds of thousands of Latin Americans trying to get into the United States to work. And the masses are poor. Although this fact makes for fascinating intellectual musings, it doesn't necessarily make for a carefree day of touring. Poverty is ever-present—and so long as you're prepared to deal with this fact, journeying into Juárez can be a great pleasure, rendering many wonderful finds to take home.

The decade-long string of serial murders of women (more than 300 since 1993) has caused a great deal of legitimate concern. Travelers of all genders should be mindful of this and *women should not travel alone at all.*

You can park in El Paso near the Santa Fe Street bridge and walk to Juárez, or catch a ride with the **El Paso–Juárez Trolley Co.** (⌧ 1 Civic Center Plaza, El Paso ☎ 915/544–0061). The Border Jumper leaves hourly from 10 to 5. For a $12.50 ticket, you have a day's worth of transportation along the route weaving through Juárez's shopping areas and restaurants. The trolley gets you through most of the border-crossing hassles, although you may still get hung-up in some traffic. Trolleys make hourly stops at designated points, and some of the drivers will regale you with lively border tales. Juárez is a sprawling city, and not necessarily a pretty one. The trolley stops keep you moving toward the areas most worth visiting.

Juárez became an official settlement with the building of its first church, **Nuestra Señora de Guadalupe Misión** (Our Lady of Guadalupe Mission), which was completed in 1668.

The church and the **Juárez Cathedral** (⊠ At Av. 16 de Septiembre and Mariscal ☎ 52–656/611–3174 Juárez Convention & Visitor's Office, 888/654–0394 Juárez Visitor Center) next door still have an active congregation.

The downtown **Mercado** (⊠ Av. 16 de Septiembre) is where most daytrippers spend their time shopping. It's a comfortable and protected warehouse-style building where merchants have set up individual stalls.

Walk down Calle Francisco I. Madero from the mercado and you'll get to a pleasant **park** centered by a statue of Benito Juárez.

Where to Eat

¢–$ ✕ **Ajuua!** Built in the style of a *pueblito* (small pueblo), this restaurant is a popular stopover for passengers aboard the El Paso–Juárez Trolley Co. Border Jumper. The traditional Mexican dishes are reliably good, as are the margaritas. On weekend evenings, expect mariachi bands and colorfully costumed dancers to perform. It's customary to tip the mariachi's leader a dollar or two. ⊠ *162 N. Efren Ornelas, Av. Lincoln and Av. 16 de Septiembre* ☎ *52–656/616–6935* ▭ *AE, MC, V.*

Shopping

There are hundreds of shops here, but the ones catering to tourists are clear. If your Spanish is good, venturing into side streets off the trolley route can yield all sorts of treasures. Be smart about what you purchase; if it seems too good to be true, it probably is. If you're not familiar with Mexico, stick to the tourist-oriented shops and you'll have a fun day of Mexican-flavored adventure. Many stores in Juárez are closed on Sunday. Your most reliable shopping options in town are spots such as the **Mercado** (⊠ Av. 16 de Septiembre). Merchants sell wares in a labyrinth of booths carrying piñatas (papier-mâché animals stuffed with candy, or left empty for you to stuff), wooden figurines, belts, and jewelry. *Please* try your hand at bartering with the vendors! They really, really do expect you to haggle about the price and you'll look like a rube if you don't. **Avenida de Juárez** features more artisan-oriented shops where you can find hand-woven shawls or hand-embroidered *huipiles*, the traditional blouses worn by indigenous Mexican women.

Old Mesilla

★ ❷ *2 mi south of Las Cruces on NM 28.*

Historians disagree about the origins of Mesilla (called both Mesilla and Old Mesilla), which in Spanish means "little table." Some say the town occupies the exact spot that Don Juan de Oñate declared "the first pueblo of this kingdom." Don't confuse Mesilla with Mesilla Park, another little village nearby.

Many of the sturdy adobe structures abundant in this community date back as far as 150 years and are still in use today. The thick walls of the adobes in this area not only helped keep the interiors cool and comfortable during hot days, but also helped defend against attacks by Apache, who were none too excited about the influx of people into their territory.

Mesilla was established by a group of lifetime Mexican residents when the territory of New Mexico was acquired by the United States in 1848. Wishing to remain Mexican, they left Las Cruces, moved a few miles west across the new border of the Rio Grande, and established their village in Mexican territory. All this effort was for naught, because the Rio Grande not only changed its path in 1865 putting both Las Cruces and Mesilla east of the rive, but the whole area had already been annexed by the United States in 1854. Mesilla had established itself well and was the largest station between El Paso and Los Angeles on the Butterfield Stage Line, and for a time served as the Confederate territorial capital, an area that covered Arizona and western New Mexico. In 1881 the Santa Fe Railroad extended its line into Las Cruces, bypassing Mesilla and establishing Las Cruces as the area's major hub of commerce and transportation.

Mesilla has seen celebrations, weddings, bloody political battles, and the milestone trial of Billy the Kid. A Mesilla jury convicted the Kid for the murder of Matthew Brady, the sheriff of Lincoln County. The Kid was transferred to the Lincoln County Courthouse (⇨ Lincoln *in* Chapter 7) to be hanged for the crime but briefly staved off the inevitable by escaping.

Today shops, galleries, and restaurants line the cobbled streets of Old Mesilla. With a Mexican-style plaza and gazebo where many weddings and fiestas take place, the village retains the charm of bygone days. It is well worth your time to stroll around the village and the surrounding neighborhoods, where many of the adobe homes are lovingly maintained. One present-day must-see is the **San Albino Church** (⊠ Old Mesilla Plaza), an impressive adobe and stained-glass building originally established in 1851.

STAHMANN FARMS – Pecan trees cover about 4,000 acres here, at the world's largest family-owned pecan orchard. You can take a shaded drive through the trees and drop by the farm's store to sample yummy pecan products, or take a tour of the farms (2:30 in winter, 10 AM in summer). ⊠ NM 28, 8 mi south of Old Mesilla, San Miguel ☎ 505/526–8974 or 800/654–6887 ⊘ Store Mon.–Sat. 9–6, Sun. 11–5.

OFF THE
BEATEN
PATH

8

Where to Stay & Eat

★ $$–$$$$ ✕ **Double Eagle.** Chandeliers, century-old wall tapestries, and gold-leaf ceilings set the scene at this elegant restaurant inside an 1848 mansion on Old Mesilla's plaza. Some say ghosts, including one of a young man who incurred his mother's wrath by falling in love with a servant girl, haunt the property. Continental cuisine, steaks, and flambé dishes are served, formally, in the main restaurant. **Pepper's,** the adjoining Southwestern-style café, has more casual fare including chiles rellenos served with colorful tortilla chips. The Double Eagle Sunday champagne brunch is worth a stop (reservations are recommended). ⊠ *308 C. de Guadalupe* ☎ *505/523–6700* ☰ *AE, D, DC, MC, V.*

¢–$$ ✕ **Lorenzo's.** Walk into this restaurant and it's easy to imagine you're in Italy: a hand-painted mural of the Mesilla Valley decorates a wall, light floods in through windows. The warm, colorful decor, friendly service, and really good food make Lorenzo's a favorite among locals. Old Sicilian recipes are used to create the pastas, sauces, pizzas, sandwiches, and salads. An outdoor courtyard offers a relaxing spot for a leisurely lunch or dinner. ⊠ *1750 Calle de Mercado, Suite 4, near Mercado shopping center* ☎ *505/525–3170* ☰ *AE, D, MC, V.*

★ ¢–$ ✕ **La Posta.** Once a way station for the Butterfield Overland Mail and Wells Fargo stagecoaches, this restaurant in an old adobe structure has hosted many celebrities through the years, including Bob Hope and Mexican revolutionary Pancho Villa. Some of the Mexican recipes here date back more than a century; among the best menu choices are *tostadas compuestos* (red or green chile, meat, and pinto beans in tortilla shells), and enchiladas with red or green chile. Exotic birds and tropical fish inhabit the lushly planted atrium. ⊠ *2410 C. de San Albino* ☎ *505/ 524–3524* ☰ *AE, D, DC, MC, V* ⊙ *Closed Mon.*

¢ ✕ **Chope's Bar & Cafe.** It looks like a run-of-the-mill adobe building from the outside, but inside you'll find happy locals eating fiery Southwestern-style food in the restaurant and drinking ice-cold beer and tasty margaritas in the bar. It's well worth the 15-mi drive south from Old Mesilla for the food and the local flavor. No credit cards are accepted in the bar. ⊠ *NM 28, La Mesa* ☎ *505/233–9976 bar, 505/233–3420 restaurant* ☰ *MC, V.*

¢–$$ ✕▦ **Meson de Mesilla.** Folks drive from all over southern New Mexico and west Texas to enjoy this inn's Continental cuisine ($$–$$$$; reservations recommended). Dishes like fresh Atlantic salmon, chateaubriand for two, and filet mignon are standard house specials. For inn guests only, a gourmet breakfast is served in a glass-enclosed atrium. The views of the jagged Organ Mountains and lower mesas from the back patio and second-floor balcony are beautiful. In addition to the standard rooms, a separate, one-bedroom private apartment is also available. ⊠ *1803 Av. de Mesilla, 88046, Off I–10, Exit 140, and ¾ mi west into Mesilla* ☎ *505/525–9212 or 800/732–6025* 🖷 *505/527–4196* ➥ *15 rooms, 1 apartment* ⚒ *Restaurant, some refrigerators, cable TV with movies, in-room data ports, pool, lounge, some pets allowed (fee); no smoking* ☰ *AE, D, MC, V* ¶◎¶ *BP.*

The Arts

The Fountain Theater, built in 1905 by the prominent Fountain family, is the oldest continuously operating theater in New Mexico and is still owned by the family. Vaudeville acts once graced the stage; today, independent films, amateur theater, and some chamber music are featured. (⊠ 2469 C. de Guadalupe, ½ block off plaza ☎ 505/524–8287 ⊕ www. fountaintheatre.org)

Shopping

High-quality Native American jewelry and crafts are sold at surprisingly good prices in the adobe shops of **Old Mesilla Plaza.** The **Farmers Mar-**

ket offers homegrown produce such as watermelons and green chiles (in season), as well as handcrafted souvenirs and jewelry, noon–4 Sunday and 11–4 Thursday year-round. In mid-afternoon on Sunday from September to early November, you can enjoy live mariachi music here, too. **El Platero** (✉ 2350 C. de Principal ☎ 505/523–5561) offers jewelry, souvenirs, Southwestern gift items and post cards. This is also a great place to grab an ice cream or a piece of fudge to consume on the outside benches.

An interior-design firm and art gallery, **Charles Inc.** (✉ 1885 W. Boutz St., at Av. de Mesilla ☎ 505/523–1888) has an extensive collection of fine art, such as bronze and marble pieces by master stone carver Jesús Mata. Open 9–5, weekdays.

Las Cruces

❸ *45 mi north of El Paso on I–10.*

The Mesilla Valley has been populated for centuries. The Spanish passed through the region first in 1598 and continued to use the route to reach the northern territories around Santa Fe. Though the Spanish could not maintain settlements in the region at all during the 1700s, by the early 1800s people were able to move in and create hamlets that grew to become Doña Ana and, eventually, Las Cruces.

In 1848 the Treaty of Guadalupe Hidalgo ended the Mexican-American war, but rendered uncertain the sovereignty of Las Cruces. The Mesilla Valley ended up split between two nations, with the town of Mesilla on the west of the Rio Grande belonging to Mexico and Las Cruces, on the eastern banks of the river, belonging to the United States. The Gadsden Purchase in 1853 made the whole area U.S. territory and Las Cruces began its ascent as the area's power center. The railroad, irrigation, agriculture, and local ranching drove the city's growth. Much of the new city was built in the territorial and Victorian styles popular at the time. The College of Las Cruces was founded in 1880 and eventually became New Mexico State University.

Mention Las Cruces to someone today and their reply is likely to be about its status as one of the fastest growing cities in the United States—second fastest in New Mexico, behind Albuquerque. Spurred by retirees looking for sun and mild winters, the defense and commercial business at White Sands Missile Range, the increasing strength of New Mexico State University, and its proximity to the business on the border with Mexico, this city of about 75,000 people *is* growing, though it doesn't seem to be losing any of its casual charm.

Las Cruces is following the lead of many U.S. cities by pushing a major revitalization of its historic downtown. The district and its surrounding residential neighborhoods date back more than a century, and a casual walk around will show all sorts of renovation—from simple painting and planting to the restabilization of entire buildings. Museums, a performing arts center, a renovated movie theater, and new shops and some cafés are draws. A farmers' market on the weekends makes for a fun

8

way to spend a Saturday morning. It's exciting to see this kind of dedication to an older area, and the community of Las Cruces has shown remarkable dedication to the task.

Accessible real estate prices, good hospitals and schools, several golf courses, and support services for retirees are driving growth here. But not incidental to this influx is the simple fact that the locals are quite friendly. Many artists (painters, sculptors, actors, writers, metalsmiths) make their homes here not just because the surrounding area offers a perpetually inspiring palette, but also because the arts community is vital and supportive of its own. The Hispanic population in Las Cruces is comprised of descendents from the Spanish settlers as well as many Mexican immigrants; both influences add unique cultural elements to the community as well as some outstanding food. The emphasis on family is strong here, and kids are welcome just about everywhere.

Although Mesilla is listed separately, it's so close to Las Cruces that you can comfortably go back and forth to eat, shop, or enjoy a night out.

☾ The **Branigan Cultural Center** is the hub of the revitalized downtown and operates as a hub for educational activities, arts conferences, and traveling crafts exhibits. It also serves as the central contact point for other city-operated museums in the neighborhood. The **Museum of Fine Art And Culture,** open Tuesday–Friday 10–2, Saturday 9–2, next door to the Cultural Center, features works of regional artists with an eclectic mix of styles, and an emphasis on the Southwest. The **Bicentennial Log Cabin Museum** is an original structure moved from southern New Mexico's Black Range mountains, with hands-on displays that include a cider press and butter churn. Admission is free; inquire at the cultural center. The **New Mexico Railroad and Transportation Museum,** open Saturday 9–1, is in the old Santa Fe Railroad Depot several blocks west of the Cultural Center. ⊠ *Cultural Center, 500 N. Water St.* ☎ *505/ 541–2155* ▧ *Free* ☾ *Weekdays 9–5, Sat. 9–1.*

☾ The handsomely designed **New Mexico Farm and Ranch Heritage Museum** documents 3,000 years of agriculture in New Mexico and the Southwest. Visit a re-creation of a 1,200-year-old Mogollon farmhouse, based on styles built by some of the first non-nomadic people to live in what is now New Mexico. Longhorn cattle, churro sheep, and dairy cows are among the heritage breeds—descendants of animals the Spanish brought from Mexico—raised at the museum. There are also some unusual burros called Jerusalem donkeys, named for the crosslike markings on their backs. At milking times (11 and 3), you can learn about the history of dairy farming in New Mexico. Chuck-wagon cooking demonstrations are offered during special events. ⊠ *4100 Dripping Springs Rd., from Las Cruces head east on University Ave., which becomes Dripping Springs Rd.; ranch is 1½ mi east of I–25* ☎ *505/522–4100* ▧ *$3* ☾ *Mon.–Sat. 9–5, Sun. noon–5.*

Where to Stay & Eat

$–$$ ✕ **Lemongrass.** Super fresh ingredients and a truly outstanding pad thai make this airy restaurant worth your time. The food isn't traditional

Thai, with nary a trace of fish sauce or chile paste to be found, but the Americanized flavors are clean and crisp. And the wonderful freshness of ingredients can't be overstated. ⊠ *2540 El Paseo Rd., Hadley Center* ☎ *505/523–8778* ▭ *AE, D, MC, V.*

¢–$$ ✗ **Cattle Baron.** Part of a regional chain, this restaurant serves prime rib, steaks, seafood, and pastas and has a well-stocked salad bar. The plant-filled, skylighted dining room is done in brass and wood; the outdoor patio has city views. ⊠ *790 S. Telshor Blvd.* ☎ *505/522–7533* ▭ *AE, D, DC, MC, V.*

¢–$$ ✗ **Joy Luck.** With Chinese and some Hawaiian dishes on the menu, this restaurant offers some of the most varied and interesting Asian food in the region—on the dinner menu. Plum sauce is used in several of the dinner entrées, and while unusual, they are excellent. Lunch is more standard Chinese fare. ⊠ *3530 Foothills Rd.* ☎ *505/532–0157.*

¢–$ ✗ **Farley's Pub.** For a family evening out with no worries about the kids being loud or throwing their peanut shells on the floor, Farley's is the place. Choose from a huge menu of typical but tasty pub fare; peel 'n' eat shrimp, burgers and sandwiches, salads, pizzas, all sorts of appetizers, and truly decadent desserts. Pool tables make for a fun evening. ⊠ *3499 Foothills Rd. (at Nacho Dr.)* ☎ *505/522–0466* ▭ *A, D, MC, V.*

¢–$ ✗ **International Delights.** A popular place to sample specialty coffees and teas, this downtown café pipes rhythmic Middle Eastern music among its tables and outdoor patio. Order hummus, falafel, or lamb couscous here for amazingly reasonable prices (the chicken-and-lamb combo, at $11, is the most expensive item on the menu). Imported olives, pastas, rice, and other items can be purchased in the attached grocery shop. ⊠ *1245 El Paseo Rd.* ☎ *505/647–5956* ▭ *AE, D, MC, V.*

★ ¢–$ ✗ **Lorenzo's.** Convenient to New Mexico State University, the largest of Lorenzo's three Las Cruces locations re-creates the relaxed feel of an Italian country inn with ample greenery, a fountain, and large murals depicting Italian scenes. Grilled fish and chicken are served along with Sicilian sandwiches, pizzas, pastas, and salads. The smaller outlet on North Alameda Street is open only for lunch weekdays. ⊠ *University Plaza, 1753 E. University Ave.* ☎ *505/521–3505* ⊠ *3961 E. Lohman* ☎ *505/ 522–7755* ⊠ *741 N. Alameda St.* ☎ *505/524–2850* ▭ *AE, D, MC, V.*

★ ¢–$ ✗ **My Brother's Place.** *Tostadas compuestos* (a concoction of red or green chile, meat, pinto beans, and cheese in a crispy tortilla cup) and other Southwestern dishes are served with flair at this exceptional Mexican restaurant, where you can order pitchers of beer or margaritas to soothe the fire. Try an empanada (a Mexican turnover) or crème caramel flan for dessert. The upstairs lounge is a pleasant watering hole decorated with brightly colored chairs and piñatas. Several varieties of Mexican beer are served here, including Negra Modelo and Tecate. ⊠ *334 S. Main St.* ☎ *505/523–7681* ▭ *AE, D, DC, MC, V.*

¢–$ ✗ **Red Mountain Café.** This café, whose menu and decor has an international theme, serves a booming business district on the northeast side of Las Cruces. The menu includes fresh Greek salads, standard deli sandwiches, and vegetarian pita pockets stuffed with smoked cheese and hummus. ⊠ *1120 Commerce Dr., Suite A, Commerce Plaza, off Telshor Blvd.* ☎ *505/522–7584* ▭ *AE, D, MC, V.*

¢–$ ✕**Si Señor Restaurant.** Popular with businesspeople, this immaculate restaurant has spacious rooms with Southwestern paintings. Mexican entrées emphasize three distinct chile sauce types—Las Cruces green (mild and flavorful), Deming red (medium hot), and a variety known as Hatch green "smoke," which may set your hair on fire, but you'll love it if you enjoy spice. The cooks here use family recipes and locally grown green chile peppers. Friendly service and laughter abound here. It's no wonder the locals love it. ⊠ *1551 E. Amador* ☎ *505/527–0817* ⊟ *AE, D, MC, V.*

¢ ✕**Caliche's.** Order from the window at one of these hamburger stands, and then enjoy specialty hot dogs, mesquite-smoked turkey sandwiches, or prime rib–on-sourdough in your car or on the outside benches. All kinds of delectable sundaes and sodas are made here, too, using homemade, custard-style ice cream. ⊠ *590 S. Valley Dr.* ☎ *505/647–5066* ⊠ *131 N. Roadrunner Pkwy.* ☎ *505/521–1161* ⊟ *MC, V.*

¢ ✕**The Durango Bagel.** The Durango caters to a college crowd with gourmet coffee and specialty bagels like apple-walnut and cranberry-orange. Muffins, cookies, and sandwiches are also served. The interior has a few Western prints on the walls, and bright light filters through ample windows. No one minds if you linger, though they close at 2 PM. ⊠ *2460 S. Locust St.* ☎ *505/522–3397* ⊟ *No credit cards.*

¢ ✕**Mesilla Valley Kitchen.** Pull up to the counter or settle into a table at this casual, friendly little joint, where huevos rancheros, delicious sandwiches and burgers, and homemade baked goods will fill you up in short order. ⊠ *Arroyo Plaza, 2001 E. Lohman Ave.* ☎ *505/523–9311* ⊟ *AE, D, DC, MC, V.*

$–$$ ▦ **Hilton Las Cruces.** The friendly staff, comfortable rooms, and expansive views of the Mesilla Valley and Organ Mountains make this Hilton a great option, even if you're just pulling off the Interstate for the night. Rooms reflect the surrounding Chihuahuan Desert's simple beauty with prints of cacti and rustic bookcase-style entertainment centers. Each floor has its own lobby area with armchairs and coffee tables. You can often find locals swapping stories in the lounge. ⊠ *705 S. Telshor Blvd., 88011* ☎ *505/522–4300* ╗ *505/521–4707* ⊕ *www.hilton.com* ➷ *196 rooms, 7 suites △ Restaurant, room service, BBQs, some in-room hot tubs, some microwaves, some refrigerators, cable TV with movies and video games, in-room data ports, indoor pool, exercise equipment, hot tub, spa, bar, lounge, dry cleaning, Internet, some business services, convention center, meeting rooms, airport shuttle, car rental, free parking, some pets allowed (fee), no-smoking floors* ⊟ *AE, D, DC, MC, V.*

★ $–$$ ▦ **Lundeen Inn of the Arts.** This art-filled B&B is recommended almost immediately by Las Crucens as *the* place to stay in town. Architect Gerald Lundeen seamlessly joined two 1895 adobe houses to create the property; Linda, his wife, runs the impressionist gallery on the premises. Guest rooms pay homage to western artists like Georgia O'Keeffe and Frederic Remington, and are furnished with a whimsical mix of antiques and newer handcrafted pieces. The morning breakfasts might include French toast with apple-and-raisin frosting; in the evenings you can carry a glass of wine upstairs into the newly added bell tower and gaze at the stars. ⊠ *618 S. Alameda Blvd., 88005* ☎ *505/526–3326* ╗ *505/647–1334*

⊕ *www.innofthearts.com* ➪ *7 rooms, 2 suites ⚹ Cable TV, some pets allowed (fee), no-smoking rooms* ☰ *AE, D, DC, MC, V* ⏴○⏵ *BP.*

¢–$ 🏨 **Teakwood Inn & Suites.** This tidy, inexpensive establishment is near I–10 and convenient to New Mexico State University and Old Mesilla. You'll find a surprising number of luxuries for such an economical alternative, including a sauna and indoor pool, along with microwaves and refrigerators in rooms. ⊠ *2600 S. Valley Dr., 88005, Off I–10, Exit 142* ☎ *505/526–4441 or 800/829–7466* 🖷 *505/526–1980* ➪ *131 rooms ⚹ Microwaves, refrigerators, cable TV with movies, indoor pool, sauna, laundry facilities, Internet, meeting rooms, some pets allowed (fee), no-smoking rooms* ☰ *AE, D, DC, MC, V* ⏴○⏵ *CP.*

★ ⚠ **Aguirre Springs.** This exceptionally beautiful high-elevation spot is tucked alongside the towering spires of the Organ Mountains, giving you an expansive view of the Tularosa Basin. During drought conditions, fires may be restricted or prohibited. If you're fortunate enough to be here when the moon is full, make sure you catch the moonrise—you're not likely to forget it. ⊠ *Off U.S. 70, from Las Cruces take U.S. 70 northeast 12 mi; head south at road marked Aguirre Springs an additional 5 mi* ☎ *505/525–4300 ⚹ Grills, pit toilets, fire grates, fire pits, picnic tables* ➪ *54 sites* 🎫 *Free with $3 day-use fee* ⚹ *Reservations not accepted* ☰ *No credit cards.*

OFF THE
BEATEN
PATH

LA VIÑA WINERY – Head 20 mi south of Las Cruces on NM 28 and you'll find the pride of proprietors Denise and Ken Stark, and the oldest winery in New Mexico. La Viña also hosts the popular Winefest (in October) and the Jazz & Blues Fest (in April). A wide variety of wines is produced here—from a crisp viognier, to pinot noir, to white zinfandel. Tasting room, daily tours, closed Wednesday. ⊠ *4201 S. NM 28, La Union* ☎ *505/882–7632* ⊕ *www.lavinawinery.com.*

8

Nightlife & the Arts

Head over to **El Patio,** in the plaza in Old Mesilla, for some of the area's best live music. Established in 1934, this unassuming little adobe cantina is in the old office building of the Butterfield Stage Co. The cantina is open seven days a week, live music happens Wednesday–Saturday. ⊠ *2171 Calle de Parian* ☎ *505/526–9943.*

New Mexico State University (⊠ Corbett Center, University Park ☎ 505/646–4111 information center, 505/646–1420 special events office) presents lectures, concerts, and other special events. Nightly live entertainment is featured at the **Hilton Las Cruces** (⊠ 705 S. Telshor Blvd. ☎ 505/522–4300) lounge. The locally based **Tierra del Encanto Ballet Folklorico** performs folk dances of Mexico at the annual weekend **International Mariachi Festival** (☎ 505/525–1735 ⊕ www.lascrucesmariachi.org) in November.

Sports & the Outdoors

An 18-hole course that hosts men's and women's NCAA championships, **New Mexico State University Golf Course** has a full-service bar and grill in addition to the pro shop, driving range, and practice green. Greens fees for an 18-hole game are $22 weekdays, $28 weekends, slightly less for a 9-hole game. Cart rental is offered. (⊠ 3000 Champions Dr., near University Ave. and I–25 ☎ 505/646–3219).

At **Aguirre Springs,** beneath the towering spires of the Organ Mountains, hiking trails lead into the upper regions of the ponderosa pines, including **Pine Tree Trail** (4-mi loop) and **Baylor Pass National Recreation Trail** (6 mi one-way). During drought conditions fires may be restricted or prohibited. ⊠ *Off U.S. 70, from Las Cruces take U.S. 70 northeast 12 mi; head south at road marked Aguirre Springs an additional 5 mi* ☎ *505/525–4300* ≊ *$3* ☉ *Apr.–Oct., daily 8–8; Nov.–Mar., daily 8–6.*

At the **Dripping Springs Natural Area** is an abandoned mountain resort built in the 1870s and converted decades later into a sanatorium for tuberculosis patients. You can tour the now empty facility, or take a 1-mi round-trip hike on a trail following a scenic canyon (it even has a stream when it's been raining) amid mesquite and wildflowers. You might spot a few rock climbers testing their mettle on sheer rock walls jutting above you. When you reach **Hermit's Peak**—a hill where Agostini Justiniani, an Italian nobleman, lived in solitude and treated the sick during the 19th century—you can step inside the cave where he once lived, and wonder about the stories of his miraculous healing powers. This is the same hermit who lived in a cave northwest of Las Vegas, New Mexico, on what is also known as Hermit's Peak. Justiniani was found murdered at the site in 1869. This site is for day use only. ⊠ *Dripping Springs Rd., from Las Cruces head east on University Ave. 10 mi* ☎ *505/522–1219* ≊ *$3 per vehicle* ☉ *Daily 8 AM–dusk.*

Shopping

If you're in town on a Wednesday or Saturday, don't miss the **outdoor market** on North Main Street, where approximately 200 vendors sell produce, handcrafted items, and baked goods. Mingle with the locals and enjoy the scene between 8:00 and 12:30. The upscale **Glenn Cutter Gallery** (⊠ 2640 El Paseo Rd. ☎ 505/524–4300) carries paintings from regional artists like Fred Chilton, as well as fine jewelry. The small complex surrounding Glenn Cutter Gallery is developing into an arts zone with interesting contemporary work by local artists; be sure to walk around and see who's moved in and what they're showing. The only artist coop in the Las Cruces area, the **Mesilla Valley Fine Arts Gallery** (⊠ 2470 Calle de Guadalupe, southeast corner of Old Mesilla plaza ☎ 505/522–2933) has a broad range of art by 30 juried artists.

Radium Springs

❹ *13 mi north of Las Cruces on I–25.*

Fort Selden was established in 1865 to protect Mesilla Valley settlers and travelers. The flat-roofed adobe buildings at **Fort Selden State Monument** are arranged around a drill field. Several units of "Buffalo Soldiers" were stationed here. These were the acclaimed African-American cavalry troops noted for their bravery and crucial role in helping protect frontier settlers from Native American attacks and desperadoes. Native Americans thought the soldiers' hair resembled that of a buffalo and gave the regiments their name. Knowing the respect the Apaches held for the animals, the soldiers did not take offense. Buffalo Soldiers were also stationed at Fort Bayard, near Silver City, and Fort Stanton, in Lincoln County, to shield miners and travelers from attacks by Apaches.

In the early 1880s Capt. Arthur MacArthur was appointed post commander of Fort Selden. His young son spent several years on the post
and grew up to become World War II hero General Douglas MacArthur.
A permanent exhibit called "Fort Selden: An Adobe Post on the Rio
Grande" depicts the roles of officers, enlisted men, and women on the
American frontier during the Indian Wars. Camping facilities can be found
at Leasburg State Park. ⊠ *Off I–25 Radium Springs Exit 19, 13 mi north
of Las Cruces* ☎ *505/526–8911* ⊕ *www.museumofnewmexico.org*
⊠ *$3* ☯ *Wed.–Mon. 8:30–5.*

Built in 1908 Leasburg Dam retains irrigation water for Mesilla Valley
farmland and recreational water for the **Leasburg State Park.** Kayakers
and anglers enjoy boating and fishing here, and on hot days the cool
water draws dozens of swimmers. ⊠ *NM 157 west of I–25* ⊠ *Day use
$5 per vehicle* ☯ *Daily 7 AM–sunset.*

Where to Stay

⚑ **Leasburg State Park Campground.** A favorite campground for locals,
this nicely developed camping area also draws plenty of out-of-state visitors. Reservations are essential during peak times (weekends, holidays,
and summer). ⊠ *NM 157 west of I–25* ☎ *505/524–4068 reservations*
⚑ *Grills, playground, flush toilets, partial hookups (electric and water),
dump station, drinking water, showers, fire grates, fire pits, picnic tables,
electricity, public telephone, ranger station, swimming (river)* ⊅ *18 RV
sites, 6 developed tent sites, 3 primitive sites* ⊠ *$8–$14* ⊟ *No credit cards.*

Deming

60 mi west of Las Cruces on I–10.

In the late 1800s Deming was considered such a wild, out-of-control
place that Arizona outlaws were sent here (with one-way stage tickets)
as punishment. A stop on the Butterfield Stage Trail, Deming received
an economic boost when the Atchison, Topeka & Santa Fe Railway met
up with the Southern Pacific line here in 1881. Far from the wild west
town it once was, farming and small industry are now the main sources
of income for the town's roughly 15,000 residents.

**OFF THE
BEATEN
PATH**

⚑ **PANCHO VILLA STATE PARK –** Early on the morning of March 9, 1916,
Francisco "Pancho" Villa, the famed revolutionary from Mexico, crossed
into New Mexico to attack the town of Columbus and nearby Camp Furlong, a U.S. military outpost. This was the first time since the War of 1812
that the United States had experienced an armed invasion. A general who
later would be commander of Allied forces in World War I—General John
Joseph "Black Jack" Pershing—led 10,000 troops into Mexico for a grueling but futile search for Villa that lasted almost a year. This park on
the site of Camp Furlong has exhibits depicting the raid, along with a
20 minute documentary film. ⊠ *NM 11, 35 mi south of Deming, in Columbus* ☎ *505/531–2711* ⊠ *$5 per vehicle* ☯ *Visitor center daily 8–5.*

☾ **SHAKESPEARE GHOST TOWN –** In the heart of a working ranch 50 mi west
of Deming, portions of this settlement have been preserved as they were
in the town's heyday as a gold and silver mining town in the late 1800s.

8

Founded in 1856, the ghost town has been designated a National Historic Site, and original structures such as homes, saloons, and stables still stand. The Living History reenactments are staged four times a year—usually the fourth weekend of April, June, August, and October. You'll find no snack shops or other tourist amenities in Shakespeare, as owner Janaloo Hill (who grew up on the ranch, and died in May 2005) vowed not to compromise the authenticity of this genuine piece of the Old West. ⊠ 2½ mi southwest of Lordsburg, south of I–10 at Exit 22, Box 253, Lordsburg, NM 88045 ☎ 506/542–9034 ⊕ www.shakespeareghostown. com ☞ $5 ☉ Tours: Mar.–Dec., 1 or 2 weekends each month at 10 and 2, or by special appt.; call ahead for more information.

Where to Stay & Eat

★ ¢–$ ✕ **Si Señor Restaurant.** Tasty, spicy Mexican food and standard American dishes are served at this family-owned restaurant (a sister property to the Si Señor in Las Cruces). The dining experience here isn't fancy, but the food is reliably good and the prices are reasonable. ⊠ 200 E. Pine St. ☎ 505/546–3938 ☐ AE, D, MC, V.

¢ ▦ **Holiday Inn Deming.** This property offers the most luxurious lodgings in at least a 60-mi radius. It's also very accessible from the interstate (I–10). The spacious rooms have contemporary, Southwestern-style decor, and include irons and ironing boards. The on-site **Prime Rib Restaurant** (¢–$$) starts off the day with an all-you-can-eat buffet breakfast for $4.95. ⊠ Off I–10 Exit 85 east, 88031 ☎ 505/546–2661 ⊲ 116 rooms ♧ Restaurant, refrigerators, cable TV, pool, gym, bar, dry cleaning, laundry facilities, some pets allowed ☐ AE, D, DC, MC, V.

⚠ **Pancho Villa State Park Campground.** This campground on the Mexican border is a comfortable place to stop for the night. You may feel you're in the middle of nowhere, but a general store and a service station are right next door, and showers are a dream for hot, sweaty desert travelers. ⊠ NM 11, 35 mi south of Deming ☎ 505/531–2711 ♧ Grills, playground, flush toilets, partial hookups (electric and water), dump station, drinking water, showers, fire grates, fire pits, picnic tables, electricity, public telephone, ranger station ⊲ 61 RV sites, 5 primitive sites ☞ $5 day use, $10 RV sites, plus $4 for electrical hookup, tent sites $8.

GILA NATIONAL FOREST

The cliff dwellings, ghost towns, and sprawling ranches scattered among hundreds of miles of desert, forest, and jagged canyons in the Gila (pronounced "heela") are the legacy of the hearty souls who have inhabited this remote area over the centuries. The early cliff dwellers mysteriously disappeared sometime after the year 1000, leaving behind the ruins and relics of a culture replaced half a millennium later by Spanish explorers, roving bands of Apaches, and occasional trappers. In the 1800s Apache leaders including Cochise, Geronimo, and Victorio waged war against the encroaching Mexican and American settlers, and for a time the sheer ruggedness of the mountains provided refuge for them. Any hope for the Apaches retaining freedom in the area vanished when prospectors discovered the area was rich with minerals in the late 1800s. The mining boom began and the area was flooded with settlers. Scenic drives lead to several ghost towns from this era, including the old gold-mining settlement of Mogollon.

Silver City

 53 mi northwest of Deming; 115 mi northwest of Las Cruces, west on I–10 and northwest on U.S. 180.

Silver City began as a tough and lawless mining camp in 1870, and struggled for a long time to become a more respectable—and permanent—settlement. Henry McCarty spent part of his boyhood here, perhaps learning some of the ruthlessness that led to his later infamy under his nickname—Billy the Kid. Other mining towns in the area sparked briefly and then died, but Silver City eventually flourished and became the area's most populated city. Today, even though it has 12,000 residents, Silver City retains a sense of pristine, private beauty—largely due to the nearby Gila National Forest and vast Gila Wilderness.

Since the area's copper ore is now close to depleted and the huge mine nearby all but officially closed, the town's traditional population of miners is being replaced by artists, outdoor enthusiasts, and retirees looking for a slightly more bohemian community than, say, Las Cruces. Thanks to efforts of preservationists, though, Silver City's origins are evident in the many distinctive houses and storefronts of the downtown area, making it ideal for exploring by foot (buy a self-guided walking tour map and guide at the Silver City Museum shop—several are offered). A stroll through the historic downtown district will take you by many of the town's three dozen or so art galleries. Silver City has become fairly well-known for being artsy, and artists may well make up the bulk of new residents. Silver City's arts scene couldn't be more different from the one in Santa Fe. High dollar isn't king here, and arts galleries tend to feel more like friendly gathering places than the dead-serious spaces found so often farther north. A local artist said "Silver City is where art is for *the* people, not *some* people."

Festivals and community events abound in this town, and almost every month sees some sort of community event in, or close to, Silver City. In early May the **Celebration of Spring** happens downtown in the Big Ditch Park, with crafts booths, activities, and lots of frolicking in the balmy weather. This fiesta marks the opening of the city's farmer's market at Bullard and 6th Street, where locally grown produce and locally produced crafts are available. The **Silver City Blues Festival** also happens in May, in Gough Park (downtown), and locals treat it as sort of a large-scale block party where young and old dance on the grass under beautiful, starry skies. September brings the **Taste of Silver City** event where, for the price of a ticket, you can walk around downtown sampling food and treats from many participating establishments. The calendar of events and activities at ⊕ www.silvercity.org gives comprehensive information, or you can call the Silver City Main Street Project (☎ 505/534–1700) for downtown events.

In the historic district, the **Silver City Grant County Chamber of Commerce** (✉ 201 N. Hudson St. ☎ 505/538–3785 ⊕ www.silvercity.org) has an

8

information center. The Web site is up-to-date and offers an excellent calendar of events for planning your trip, in addition to all sorts of information about the city and region. If you're traveling north on NM 90, the highway turns into Hudson Street. If you're traveling on U.S. 180, it turns into Silver Heights Boulevard within the city limits and intersects Hudson Street.

NEED A BREAK?

Alotta Gelato. Made on-site, the gelato here is creamy and delicious. Flavors change regularly; espresso, chocolate hazelnut, and a very un-ordinary vanilla are regulars, as are sorbettos like raspberry and mango. They're open late if you need a night time snack. ⊠ *619 N. Bullard St.* ☎ *512/534-4995.*

The Ailman House, built in 1881, serves as headquarters for the **Silver City Museum**, whose main gallery mural of the mining and ranching community circa 1882 provides a good overview of the area's colorful history. Displays include pottery and other relics from the area's ancient (and now extinct) Mimbres and Mogollon cultures. From the museum's tower you can catch a glimpse of Silver City's three historic districts. Self-guided walking tours with maps, are sold in the museum's store, which carries Southwestern gifts and books. Free guided walking tours of the neighboring historic district are offered on Memorial Day and Labor Day. The museum also has a local-history research library. ⊠ *312 W. Broadway* ☎ *505/538-5921* ☞ *Free* ☉ *Tues.–Fri. 9–4:30, weekends 10–4.*

The **Western New Mexico University Museum** contains the world's largest permanent collection of distinctive Mimbres pottery (which has influenced modern ceramic artists around the world), as well as basketry and other artifacts. Exhibits also include the intricately decorated Casas Grandes pottery from northern Mexico. The museum's fourth floor displays photos and other memorabilia of the university. From the photo archives on the fourth floor you get a 360-degree view of Silver City. If crowds permit, check out the antique urinals in the men's restroom (ladies, ask someone to stand guard!). ⊠ *1000 W. College Ave., on campus, west end of 10th St.* ☎ *505/538-6386* ☞ *Free* ☉ *Weekdays 9–4:30, weekends 10–4.*

OFF THE BEATEN PATH

★ ☺

CITY OF ROCKS STATE PARK – One look at the spires here and you'll figure out how the area came by its name. The unusual rock formations were spewed from an ancient volcano and have been eroded over the centuries by wind and rain into the marvelous shapes there today—some more than 40 feet tall. You've got to walk through the city to fully appreciate the place—and it's a great, easy adventure to have with kids (this is one of those places where sturdy walking shoes are a *must*). The park has a visitor center, and a large developed campground ($10–$14) with 10 RV sites with water and electric hookups, 42 camping sites, picnic tables, grills, flush toilets, and showers. ⊠ *Take NM 180 northwest from Deming for 24 mi; then turn northeast onto NM 61 for 4 mi, Faywood* ☎ *505/536-2800* ☞ *Day use $5 per vehicle* ☉ *Visitor center daily 10–4.*

Where to Stay & Eat

★ ¢–$$ ✕ **Diane's Restaurant.** Fresh flowers grace the wooden tables and sunshine streams through the large windows at this cheerful bakery and eatery. Chef-owner Diane Barret's creative menu includes blackened pork loin with apple bourbon demi-glace, and a terrific rack of lamb. The sandwiches are all made with wonderfully tasty house-baked bread; if you're in the mood for something sweet, don't miss the knock-out cinnamon rolls. Imported beer and specialty wines are available. ⊠ *510 N. Bullard St.* ☎ *505/538–8722* ⊟ *AE, D, MC, V* ⊘ *Closed Mon.*

¢–$$ ✕ **Jalisco's.** The Mesa family serves up top-notch traditional Mexican food here, all based on old family recipes. Enchiladas and chiles rellenos satisfy big appetites in the cheerful dining room decorated with art from local artists. ⊠ *103 S. Bullard St.* ☎ *505/388–2060* ⊟ *MC, V* ⊘ *Closed Sun.*

¢–$ ✕ **Vicki's Eatery.** Hearty deli sandwiches like pastrami Reubens, as well as yummy vegetarian options, are served up at this lunchtime café. It can feel a bit crowded indoors—the eating area is charming but very small—try for a table on the outdoor patio in summer. ⊠ *107 W. Yankie St.* ☎ *505/388–5430* ⊟ *AE, D, MC, V* ⊘ *No dinner.*

¢ ✕ **A.I.R. Espresso, Art, Ice Cream.** A.I.R. stands for Artist-In-Residence, which is exactly what owner Jacqueline Shaw is. While painting her own masterpieces (some of which are on display), she operates this relaxed and friendly ice-cream and coffee shop, where locals lounge on the plump sofa or discuss the state of the world on the rear patio. Shaw's specialties are mochas and cappuccinos, along with hot chocolate, truffles, and toffee. Waffle cones, gourmet ice cream, frozen yogurt, and a few pastries are available. ⊠ *112 W. Yankie St.* ☎ *505/388–5952* ⊟ *D, MC, V.*

¢ ✕ **Gregorio's Kountry Kitchen.** Though small and informal, this diner serves huge helpings of Southwestern food like crunchy tacos or ground beef burritos. If you're just plain hungry and not choosy about atmosphere, drop in. The restaurant is attached to the Fashion Max building, which contains a locally owned clothing and jewelry store. ⊠ *1500 N. Hudson St.* ☎ *505/388–4512* ⊟ *MC, V* ⊘ *Closed Sun.*

$–$$$ ▤ **Bear Mountain Lodge.** Owned and operated by the Nature Conservancy, this serene, isolated haven offers luxury accommodations for birdwatchers and nature lovers. You have direct access to 178 acres of Gila National Forest land, where you can spot bird species such as the Gila woodpecker, vermilion flycatcher, and red-faced warbler. Four second-story rooms in the main lodge have views of mountains and forest land. Two downstairs lodge rooms have outdoor access to a covered porch. Four guest rooms are available in Myra's Retreat, a separate building named for the former owner, and a great space for a larger family or group. A one-room guesthouse known as the Wren's Nest has an exposed wood ceiling and its own kitchen. Hardwood floors and locally (and sustainable) handcrafted furniture add to the rustic elegance. A naturalist is available to answer questions and conduct regular activities for guests. ⊠ *Cottage San Rd., 3 mi off Alabama St., 3 mi north of Silver City, take U.S. 180 west and turn north onto Alabama, 88062* ☎ *505/538–2538* ⊕ *www.bearmountainlodge.com* ⬄ *10 rooms, 1 house* ⚐ *Some in-room hot tubs, in-room data ports, hiking, Internet; no a/c in some rooms, no TV in some rooms, no kids under 10, no smoking* ⊟ *AE, MC, V* ⍟❘ *BP.*

★ $–$$ ▤ **The Cottages.** Virgin forests, a friendly wild fox, and a lost silver mine add to the romantic allure of this inn with detached French country–style cottages and B&B-style suites. The 224-acre estate has access to miles of pristine trails including those on nearby Gila National Forest. The one-bedroom cottages are comfortably furnished and supplied with cooking utensils and staples like eggs, milk, and fresh fruit, along with snacks and frozen items for lunch or dinner. Each suite within the main house has its own private entrance, one with a private outdoor court-yard and fountain. ⊠ *2037 Cottage San Rd., Box 2562, 88062* ☎ *505/ 388–3000 or 800/938–3001* ⊕ *www.zianet.com/cottages* � *2 suites, 3 cottages* ⚬ *Some fans, cottages have a/c, in-room hot tubs, some kitchens, some kitchenettes, microwaves, refrigerators, cable TV, in-room VCRs, in-room data ports, hiking, no-smoking rooms; no kids under 12* ☰ *AE, D, MC, V* ⑩ *CP.*

$ 🏨 **Comfort Inn.** The Southwestern-style rooms at this modern chain hotel have good views of Silver City. In the evening, complimentary cook-ies and apple cider are served in the lobby. ⊠ *1060 E. NM 180, 88061* ☎ *505/534–1883, 800/228–5150 central reservations* ☒ *505/534– 0778* ➡ *52 rooms, 2 suites* ⚬ *Some in-room hot tubs, cable TV, in-door pool, laundry facilities, meeting rooms, some pets allowed (fee)* ☰ *AE, D, DC, MC, V* ⑩ *CP.*

$ 🏨 **Holiday Inn Express.** Just 2 mi from Silver City's historic downtown district, this hotel has bright, contemporary rooms with modern furni-ture. Paintings by local artists are on display in the lobby. ⊠ *1103 Su-perior St., 88061* ☎ *505/538–2525* ➡ *60 rooms* ⚬ *Refrigerators, cable TV, in-room data ports, gym, hot tub, Internet, meeting rooms, some pets allowed, no-smoking rooms* ☰ *AE, D, DC, MC, V* ⑩ *CP.*

¢–$ 🏨 **Econo Lodge Silver City.** This lodge on a mesa overlooking Silver City has economy accommodations and contemporary decor. You'll find extra touches here ordinarily associated with higher-end lodges, such as microwaves, refrigerators, a hot tub, and a gym. ⊠ *1120 NM 180 E, 88061* ☎ *505/534–1111, 800/553–2666 central reservations* ☒ *505/ 534–2222* ⊕ *www.econolodgesilvercity.com* ➡ *62 rooms* ⚬ *Mi-crowaves, refrigerators, cable TV with movies, in-room data ports, pool, gym, hot tub, laundry facilities, meeting rooms, some pets allowed (fee)* ☰ *AE, D, DC, MC, V* ⑩ *CP.*

¢–$ 🏨 **Palace Hotel.** Originally this grand two-story building was used as a bank, but it was reinvented as a hotel in 1900. News accounts at the time touted the Palace as a first-class lodging with the intimacy of a small European hotel. The New Mexico Historical Preservation Office helped to restore and reopen the hotel in 1990, which helped keep much of the historical detail intact. Some rooms have Western-style furnishings, oth-ers have neo-Victorian decor such as ruffled pillow coverings and bed skirts. The upstairs garden room is a peaceful spot for playing board games or reading. ⊠ *106 W. Broadway, 88061* ☎ *505/388–1811* ⊕ *www.zianet.com/palacehotel* ➡ *11 rooms, 7 suites* ⚬ *Cable TV; no a/c, no pets* ☰ *AE, D, DC, MC, V* ⑩ *CP.*

¢ 🏨 **Super 8.** A forest of piñon and juniper trees surrounds this two-story motel. Most of the rooms have double beds; five business minisuites have extra amenities like refrigerators. ⊠ *1040 E. U.S. 180, 88061* ☎ *505/ 388–1983, 800/800–8000 central reservations* ☒ *505/388–1983* ➡ *64* *rooms* �& *Microwaves, some refrigerators, cable TV, some in-room data ports, some pets allowed (fee)* ⊟ *AE, D, DC, MC, V* ⦿❘ *CP.*

Shopping

Shops, galleries, cafés, parks, and all sorts of building renovation make walking Silver City's downtown district a super way to explore this great little town.

A standout in any town, **Blue Dome Gallery** (⊠ 307 N. Texas St. ☎ 505/534–8671) is a real find for contemporary art collectors with an eye for fine crafts. Linda and John, the owners, make a point of knowing each of the artists they represent, and they have a real knack for spotting up-and-coming artists. Pottery is clearly a passion here, though sculpture, painting, jewelry, glass, even furniture, are well-represented and compelling. Closed Tuesday.

Hester House Candy & Gifts (⊠ 316 N. Bullard St. ☎ 505/388–1360) sells scrumptious homemade fudge, chocolates, and truffles, along with porcelain dolls, Tiffany-style lamps, wind chimes, jewelry, bath products, and garden art. The shop is open daily except Sunday.

Vendors at the **Silver City Trading Co.'s Antique Mall** (⊠ 205 W. Broadway ☎ 505/388–8989) stock antiques, collectibles, and Navajo kachina dolls; works of area artists also are displayed.

Gila National Forest

❻ *8 mi northeast of Silver City via NM 15 to Pinos Altos range and Gila Cliff Dwellings portion of Gila National Forest; 60 mi northwest of Silver City via U.S. 180 to western portions of forest. From I-25 eastern edge of forest can be accessed via NM 152: 62 mi north of Las Cruces take NM 152 west toward Hillsboro; 91 mi north of Las Cruces take NM 52 west through Winston and Chloride.*

The Gila, as it's called, covers 3.3 million acres—that's 65 mi by 100 mi—and was the first land in the nation to be set aside as "wilderness" by the U.S. Forest Service back in 1924. The area is vast and continues to feel like a great, relatively undiscovered treasure. You are unlikely to come across any crowds, even in peak summer months. Whether you're backpacking or doing day hikes, you have 1,500 mi of incredibly diverse trails to explore. Open camping is permitted throughout the forest, although there are 18 developed campgrounds (all with toilets and seven with potable water). The Gila is an outdoor lover's paradise: with seemingly endless trails to explore on mountain bikes, white-water rafting (the season usually starts in April), and fishing in rivers, lakes (three of them), and streams. Thirty percent of the forest is closed to vehicular traffic entirely, but the rest is open for touring.

The **Inner Loop Scenic Drive** snakes through 75 mi of some of the most gorgeous and scenic forest in the wilderness. The roads are paved but the sharp, narrow, and steep turns make it inadvisable for large RVs. From Silver City, take NM 15 north to Gila Cliff Dwellings National Monument. From the monument backtrack on NM 15 to NM 35 heading southeast to NM 152, which leads west back to Silver City.

The **Gila Cliff Dwellings National Monument** showcases a series of flat-roof, stone-and-mud adobe dwellings built into the shallow caves of sheer sandstone cliffs by the Mogollon (*mow-go-yone*) people some 700 years ago. The visitor center has a small museum with books and other materials about the wilderness and the Mogollon. A fairly steep trail leads to the dwellings (1 mi); there are interesting pictographs to be seen on the wheelchair-accessible Trail to the Past. ⊠ *Off NM 15, 44 mi north of Silver City* ☎ *505/536–9461 or 505/536–9344* ☒ *$3* ⊙ *Monument late May–early Sept., daily 8–6; early Sept.–late May, daily 9–4. Visitor center late May–early Sept., daily 8–5; early Sept.–late May, daily 8–4:30.*

★ U.S. 180 leads west about 50 mi from Silver City to Glenwood and the **Whitewater Canyon.** The **Catwalk** (⊠ Catwalk Rd., NM 174; turn east 5 mi off U.S. 180) is a 250-foot-long metal walkway drilled into the sides of massive rock cliffs of the breathtaking Whitewater Canyon—which is only 20 feet wide in places. It was built in 1935 as an access route so water lines could be extended 3 mi into the canyon. A number of famous outlaws, including Butch Cassidy and the Wild Bunch, have used the canyon as a hideout because of its remote, and almost inaccessible, location. You need to be in reasonably good physical condition to scramble up some steep stairways, but the 2.2-mi round-trip trail is well maintained and worth the effort—dramatic waterfalls tumbling over rocks await you. Admission is $3.

Several miles north of the Catwalk on U.S. 180 is the **Glenwood State Trout Hatchery** (⊠ U.S. 180 ☎ 505/539–2461). There are picnic tables and a fishing pond with Rocky Mountain bighorn sheep grazing nearby. East of the Glenwood State Trout Hatchery, on NM 159, is **Mogollon.** The gold-mining town, established in the 1880s, was a ghost town for many years but has been revived in the last few decades by a dozen or so residents who live there year-round. A small museum, an art gallery and a gift shop, and a café operate on the weekends. Book a stay at the Silver Creek Inn and you can spend the weekend exploring this interesting relic of the American West, as well as the breathtaking, and huge, Gila National Forest bordering it.

As you drop down into **Pinos Altos** 7 mi north of Silver City on NM 15, check out the **Log Cabin Museum** (⊠ 33 Main St., off NM 15 ☎ 505/388–1882 ☒ $1), where you'll find the structure originally built in 1865 by the pioneer George Shafer (the property is still in his family). Dusty artifacts tell the story of more than a century of occupation.

On the eastern edge of the Gila National Forest, NM 52 leads west from I–25 to **Winston** and **Chloride,** two fascinating mining towns about 35 mi northwest of Truth or Consequences. Prospectors searching for silver in the nearby ore-rich mountains founded the towns in the late 1800s; abandoned saloons and false-front buildings, and pioneer relics still remain. Though the communities are designated ghost towns, the moniker is belied by the 50 or so residents currently living in each place. ⊠ *Gila National Forest Headquarters, 3005 E. Camino del Bosque, Silver City* ☎ *505/388–8201.*

Where to Stay & Eat

¢–$$$ ✕ **Buckhorn Saloon and Opera House.** Come here to see 1860s western
Fodor's Choice decor and stay for the food—including what may be the best steak and
★ seafood in the region, with their hamburgers ranking way up on the list
as well. The bar is a friendly place to gather for a drink, and has live
folk-flavored music Wednesday–Saturday; the dining rooms are cozy and
have walls replete with photos from the last 140 years of the area's his-
tory. The property also includes the Opera House, where melodramas
are performed (on Friday and Saturday at 8), and Pinos Altos Mercan-
tile, another 1860s era business, that's now an ice-cream parlor and soda
shop. ⊠ *32 Main St., Pinos Altos, 7 mi north of Silver City on NM 15*
☎ *505/538–9911, 505/388–3848 opera house* ▤ *MC, V* ☉ *Closed
Sun. No lunch.*

¢–$ ✕ **Carmen's.** This is a great place to stop—on NM 12 just northwest of
the Gila National Forest—not just because of the spicy enchiladas and
other good Mexican dishes served, but because once you leave the ham-
let of Reserve, New Mexico (population about 300), you won't find an-
other place to eat for about 70 mi. It's sometimes closed on major
holidays. ⊠ *NM 12 at NM 435* ☎ *505/533–6990* ▤ *MC, V.*

¢ ✕ **The Chuck Wagon Cafe.** Originally built in the early 1900s, the barn-
like building that houses this comfy diner-style eatery has been every-
thing from a church to a skating rink to a wrestling arena. These days
wooden floors and cattle brands on the wall give it a down-home coun-
try feel. The tasty chicken-fried steak is the most popular item on the
menu. ⊠ *30 mi northwest of Silver City on U.S. 180* ☎ *505/535–4100*
▤ *No credit cards.*

★ $$–$$$ ▥ The **Casitas de Gila** are five private casitas ("little houses" in Span-
ish) overlooking Bear Creek, nestled on 90 acres in gorgeous Gila coun-
try. The night skies are brilliant, with countless stars twinkling, and the
swath of the Milky Way glowing brightly. Each casita has its own spot-
ting telescope or high-powered binoculars. Watching the stars from the
shared hot tub is not to be missed. Guests have access to the organic
herb garden (in season), which is super for those wanting to use the ca-
sitas' well-equipped kitchens and BBQ grills. Southwestern-style furnish-
ings, Mexican rugs, and generously appointed baths make for a perfect
getaway. The hosts offer star parties and tips on hiking in the area. On-
site art gallery. ⊠ *50 Casita Flats Rd., off Hooker Loop* ✉ *Box 325,
Gila 88038-0325* ☎ *505/535–4455* 🖷 *505/535–4456* ⊕ *www.
casitasdegila.com* ⇆ *4 1-bedroom casitas, 1 2-bedroom casita* ⚴ *Pic-
nic area, kitchens, microwaves, refrigerators, outdoor hot tub, hiking,
Internet; no room TVs* ▤ *AE, DC, MC, V* ⑩ *CP.*

OFF THE
BEATEN
PATH

$$$$

▦ **SILVER CREEK INN –** Just getting to this property in the Mogollon ghost
town is something of a thrill; the scenic and twisty mountain road that
leads here has some heart-stoppingly steep drop-offs along the way. Once
you've arrived, settle into a room at one of the original, two-story adobe
structures of this old mining town, which is now all but abandoned (pop-
ulation about 15). The 1885 Inn building has been refurbished beauti-
fully. Each of the four rooms has a private bath, and all (delicious) meals
are included in the room rate. Proprietors Kathy and Stan make some

8

outstanding pies—she's the famed pie-maker for the Pie-O-Neer café in Pie Town, and the pie recipes at the Inn are hers. Head here if you're looking for a relaxing getaway in an out-of-the-ordinary locale. The Inn is for adults 21 and over only, reservations are required, bookings are for Friday and Saturday (two-night minimum—open only on weekends). ⊠ *Take NM 180 toward Glenwood; about 4 mi north of Glenwood, turn east onto NM 159 and travel about 9 mi of steep roadway to Mogollon* ☎ *866/276–4882* ⇆ *4 rooms* ♺ *Fans; no a/c, no room phones, no room TVs* ⊟ *AE, D, MC, V* ⦿| *MAP.*

♺ **$–$$** ⊞ **Bear Creek Motel & Cabins.** Gold panning, hiking, and fishing are among the popular activities at this mountain getaway, one of the better accommodations in the Silver City area. A ponderosa pine forest surrounds the well-kept A-frame cabins, half of which have kitchens, cookware, and fireplaces. ⊠ *NM 15, 6 mi north of Silver City* ⌖ *Box 53082, Pinos Altos 88053* ☎ *505/388–4501* ⊟ *505/538–5583* ⊕ *www. bearcreekcabins.com* ⇆ *15 cabins* ♺ *BBQs, some kitchenettes, some refrigerators, in-room data ports, hiking, some pets allowed (fee); no a/c, no room TVs* ⊟ *AE, D, DC, MC, V.*

Lake Valley National Back Country Byway

★ *From Silver City: head east on U.S. 180/NM 152 to junction with NM 27. From Hatch: head west on NM 26 and north on NM 27.*

The 48-mi Lake Valley National Back Country Byway provides an exciting link to the Wild West. This remote drive (there are no gas stations)—which encompasses the stretch of NM 27 between Nutt and Hillsboro (31 mi) and then NM 152 east from Hillsboro to Truth or Consequences (17 mi)—follows part of the route taken by the Kingston Lake Valley Stage Line, which operated when this region was terrorized by Apache leaders like Geronimo and outlaw bands led by the likes of Butch Cassidy. A Lake Valley–area landmark, west of NM 27, is Cooke's Peak, where the first wagon road through the Southwest to California was opened in 1846.

Not much is going on these days in the old silver mining town of **Lake Valley**—the last residents departed in the mid-1990s—but it once was home to 4,000 people. The mine produced 2.5 million ounces of pure silver and gave up one nugget weighing several hundred pounds. Visit the schoolhouse (which later served as a saloon), walk around the chapel, the railroad depot, and some of the few remaining old homes. At the junction of NM 152 and NM 27 is another mining-era boomtown, **Hillsboro,** where gold was discovered as well as silver (about $6 million worth of the two ores was extracted). The town, slowly coming back to life with the artists and retirees who've moved in, has a small museum, some shops, restaurants, and galleries. The Hillsboro Apple Festival draws visitors from all over the state on Labor Day weekend. Street vendors sell apples and apple pies, chiles, antiques, and arts and crafts.

Caballo Lake State Park provides a winter nesting grounds for golden and bald eagles, often sighted gliding aloft as they search for prey. Fishing and water sports are popular at the lake, and hiking trails lead through the desert areas where yucca, century plants, and numerous varieties of cacti are abundant. A great time to visit is late March or early April, when prickly pears and other succulents are in bloom. ✉ *Take state park exit off I-25, about 58 mi north of Las Cruces and 16 mi south of Truth or Consequences* ☎ *505/743-3942* 🖷 *505/743-0031* 🄫 *$5 per vehicle* ☉ *Visitor center 7:30-4:30, later in summer.*

Where to Stay

★ ¢-$ 🏨 **Black Range Lodge Bed & Breakfast.** It's not quite enough to merely describe this lodge as "built from the ruins of an old casino and saloon that date back to the 1880s." Although true, and yes, this getaway has sturdy log beam ceilings and rock walls, an interesting history, and an informal, rustic atmosphere that makes it nice for families—the charm here owes a lot to the care and tending, and presence, of the gently charismatic proprietors. There's an outdoor hot tub and nearby freshwater creek with a hiking trail. The "town" of Kingston—population about 30—and the surrounding area is fun to explore and fantastic by mountain bike. The rooms on the north side of the inn are nice because they have views of the mountains, rather than views into the greenhouse—though it is an amazing one. One-bedroom suites within the house have decks, indoor hot tubs, and spectacular views. Breakfasts are healthy and hearty, and the kitchen is open for you to cook in if you bring your own food. ✉ *119 Main St./NM 152* 🏚 *Star Rte. 2, Box 119, Kingston 88042* ☎ *505/895-5652* 🖷 *505/895-3326* ⊕ *www.blackrangelodge. com* 🛏 *3 rooms, 5 suites, 1 guesthouse* ⚭ *Some in-room hot tubs, some kitchens, some microwaves, some refrigerators, some cable TV with movies, outdoor hot tub, billiards, hiking, video game room, Internet, meeting rooms, some pets allowed (fee); no a/c, no smoking* ⊟ *D, MC, V* ⦿❘ *BP.*

⛺ **Caballo Lake State Park.** Three camping areas offer views of the lake, which is within walking distance of each site. Cottonwoods and other trees shade two sites; the other has desert landscaping. The tent sites ($8) are lakeside. You can stock up on goods at a grocery store, bait shop, and gasoline station 3 mi from the park. Developed sites for RVs cost $10-$14 (some have sewer). ✉ *Take state park exit off I-25, about 58 mi north of Las Cruces and 16 mi south of Truth or Consequences* ☎ *505/743-3942* 🖷 *505/743-0031* 🛏 *136 sites* ⚭ *Grills, flush toilets, full hookups, partial hookups, dump station, drinking water, showers, fire grates, fire pits, picnic tables, electricity, public telephone, ranger station, play area, swimming (lake)* 🄫 *RV sites $10-$14, tent sites $8* ⊟ *No credit cards.*

EN ROUTE

El Camino Real International Heritage Center. The beautiful, contemporary Heritage Center opened in 2005, after many years and much effort by New Mexicans to create a monument to El Camino Real. The 400-year history, and to some extent, the pre-history, of the Royal Road is the focus of the captivating exhibits here, more than the political and military struggles that happened along it. It was a vital trade route that linked ancient peoples from North America to Mesoamericans, and later linked the Spanish explorers to Mexico, Spain, Europe, Asia, and finally the United States of America. The exchange of cultural ideas, beliefs, and customs that occurred because of the extensive trade and travel along the route is amazing to consider—particularly while gazing at the stark environment it runs through. Today, this international trade route lives on in the form of the parallel-running I–25. ⊠ *30 mi south of Socorro, Exit 115, east to NM 1 frontage road, south 1.5 mi, east onto CR 1598, 2.7 mi to center* ✆ *Box 175, Socorro, NM 87801* ☎ *505/854–3600* ⊕ *www.caminorealheritage.org* ▨ *$5* ⊙ *Closed Tues.*

Truth or Consequences

❼ *72 mi north of Las Cruces on I–25, 140 mi south of Albuquerque on I–25.*

Truth or Consequences really did get its name from the game show of the same name. The show's producer, Ralph Edwards, suggested that a town adopt the name to honor the production's 10th anniversary in 1950. The community, which had been known as Hot Springs, accepted the challenge, earning national publicity for the stunt. A portion of the community rebelled, though, withdrawing from T or C (as the town is frequently called) and incorporating as Williamsburg. T or C's name is a favorite point of contention for some of the old-school residents.

Centuries ago the area's earliest inhabitants came here for relaxation and the waters' healing properties—hot water seems to be a universally appreciated healing method. In the 1930s bathhouses tapping into the soothing mineral waters were established near the downtown district. About a half dozen of those still operate at prices that are quite reasonable compared to those in other parts of the Southwest. In fact, T or C bills itself as the "most affordable spa town in America." Facilities are clean but tend to the modest, and many offer therapeutic treatments like massage, Reiki, and reflexology. The most upscale of the hot spring facilities is the Sierra Grande Lodge & Spa, which occupies a historic downtown building.

Hay-Yo-Kay Hot Springs has seven naturally flowing pools, including one that, at 10 feet by 20 feet, is the largest in the hot-springs district. The standard price for the hot baths is $5.50 per person for a half-hour soak. Massage, Reiki, and reflexology therapists are on call for varying fees. Packages are available; for instance a soak and a 50-minute massage cost $65. The property also includes three two-bedroom condominiums (ideal for housing small group retreats) with kitchens, refrigerators, microwaves, cable TV, in-room VCRs, and barbecues (standard rates of $65–$95 nightly). Those staying on the property have unlimited free access to the pools. Closed Monday and Tuesday. ⊠ *300 Austin Ave.* ☎ *505/894–2228* 🖷 *505/894–2506* ▤ *AE, D, DC, MC, V.*

At the **Geronimo Springs Museum** you can visit an authentic, well-maintained miner's log cabin that was transported from the nearby Gila National Forest; view the giant skull of a woolly mammoth, and inspect early Mimbres, Tularosa, Alma, and Hohokam pottery. The farm and ranch section has tools used by early settlers. ⊠ *211 Main St.* ☎ *505/894–6600* ▨ *$3* ⊙ *Mon.–Sat. 9–5.*

CLOSE UP

Space Tourism

IT MAY SEEM HARD TO IMAGINE as you gaze into the infinite blue of New Mexico's sky near White Sands Missile Range and Alamogordo, but some day, and perhaps sooner than later, those wispy contrails you see lingering from rocket engines may be the residue of vehicles carrying tourists into Earth's orbit—and beyond.

In October 2005 the missile range hosted the first of a series of annual events known as the X-Prize Cup Exhibition aimed at enabling private industry to become involved in economical space travel. Funded through a private foundation, the exhibition bestows annual awards of $10 million to the winner of each competition, from among competing (nongovernment backed) teams of experts worldwide. The mission of the X Prize Foundation is to spur innovation in space and related technologies, and to create low-cost space vehicles capable of (eventually) carrying civilian passengers into space.

Competing space vehicles must have the ability to lift three people up and beyond Earth's gravity to a height of 62.5 mi. The feat then must be repeated with the same vehicle within two weeks, to demonstrate reliability and economic feasibility associated with quick turnaround.

With an eye on the potential of both the X-Prize competition and space tourism that could result from development of a successful vehicle, New Mexico has obtained a permit for a commercial spaceport license for a remote, unpopulated area near the western edge of the missile range. State tourism officials expect the X-Prize competition itself to become a major attraction luring thousands of visitors annually to watch launches of competing space vehicles as they reach for the sky.

8

Where to Stay & Eat

¢–$$$ ✕ **Los Arcos Restaurant and Bar.** Steaks and seafood are the draws at this adobe-style establishment, whose Southwestern decor comes complete with a cactus garden. Homemade soups, desserts, and freshly baked bread add to the aromas and the cheery ambience. ⊠ *1400 N. Date St.* ☎ *505/ 894–6200* ▭ *AE, D, MC, V* ⊘ *No lunch.*

¢ ✕ **Santa Fe Diner.** A copper rooster and mission bells decorate the dining room here, where waitresses are likely to call you "honey." Locals come here when they're not in the mood for anything fancier than a reliably good sandwich, hamburger, or fried catfish dinner. ⊠ *2205 N. Date St.* ☎ *505/894–1660* ▭ *AE, D, MC, V.*

$–$$$$ ✕▣ **Sierra Grande Lodge & Spa.** There's something here that's not like
Fodor's Choice the others. This is *by far* the most elegant dining and lodging option in
★ T or C. In a 1937 building in downtown T or C, this inn feels like a secluded retreat because of the massive boulders surrounding its mission-style architecture. The airy rooms have hardwood floors, four-poster beds,

and serene prints on the walls. Soak in an outdoor or indoor kiva-style hot tub swirling with steamy water from natural, underground hot springs; massages, facials, and other holistic body therapies are available by appointment. In the restaurant ($–$$$), where tables are dressed with white linen and fresh flowers, and where one wall is adorned with a 1917 stained-glass mural of Elephant Butte Dam, you can dine on rack of lamb, free-range chicken stuffed with artichoke, or olive-crusted salmon (the owner of the lodge also runs an acclaimed New York City restaurant, Raoul's). ⊠ *501 McAdoo St., 87901* ☎ *505/894–6976* 🖷 *505/894–6999* ⊕ *www.sierragrandelodge.com* 🛏 *16 rooms, 1 suite* ☖ *Restaurant, some in-room hot tubs, cable TV, in-room VCRs, hot tub, outdoor hot tub; no smoking* ☰ *AE, D, MC, V* ⦿ *CP.*

¢ 🏨 **Best Western Hot Springs Inn.** Large rooms and modern furnishings make this lodge a restful haven. The inviting pool comes in handy on hot summer days. A steak house is next door. The staff cheerfully provides all manner of complimentary amenities, from shaving cream to sewing kits. ⊠ *2270 N. Date St., 87901, off I–25 Exit 79* ☎ *800/528–1234 or 505/894–6665* 🛏 *40 rooms, 1 suite* ☖ *Kitchens, microwaves, refrigerators, cable TV, in-room data ports, pool, Internet, some pets allowed* ☰ *AE, D, DC, MC, V* ⦿ *CP.*

¢ 🏨 **Charles Motel & Bath House.** This is the most bohemian of T or Cs hotels, and certainly one of the most inexpensive. The Charles is a favorite among artists and healers who espouse all sorts of interesting and unorthodox approaches to health. The therapies practiced here include massage, reflexology, Reiki, and ayurvedic science. Costs depend on the treatment and its length, but $5 will buy you an hour-long soak in one of the nine indoor soaking tubs fed from natural hot springs ($4 for a half hour). For $8 (and a reservation) you can soak in one of two outdoor Jacuzzis up on the roof. The huge (400 square foot) guest rooms, many of which have kitchenettes, have so much extra space you can easily imagine settling in for months rather than days; in fact, excellent weekly rates are offered. ⊠ *601 Broadway, 87901* ☎ *800/317–4518 or 505/894–7154* ⊕ *www.charlesspa.com* 🛏 *20 rooms* ☖ *Some kitchenettes, some microwaves, some refrigerators, cable TV with movies, outdoor hot tubs, spa, shop, meeting room, some pets allowed (fee)* ☰ *AE, D, MC, V.*

Shopping

Paintings and sculpture by contemporary local artists can be found at the **Rio Bravo Gallery Fine Art Inc.** (⊠ 110 E. Broadway Ave. ☎ 505/894–0572), open Wednesday–Saturday 10–5, Sunday noon–5.

Elephant Butte

❽ *5 mi east of Truth or Consequences on NM 51.*

★ More than a million people each year visit **Elephant Butte Lake State Park,** whose 36,500-acre lake is New Mexico's largest. A world-class competition lake for bass fishing, it also offers catfish, pike, and crappie fishing year-round. Boaters come here in droves, and when the wind picks up so do the windsurfers. Special events include an April balloon festival and July drag-boat racing. The lake, known as Elephant Butte Reservoir, was created in 1916 by **Elephant Butte Dam,** a concrete structure 306 feet high and 1,674 feet long. The stretch of the Rio Grande below the dam is stocked with trout during colder months; these fish attract anglers as well as many species of waterfowl, including raptors. The lake level is dependent on the water conditions in the state, which fluctuate wildly. It's best to check the conditions before you plan a vacation around the lake.

The state park straddles Elephant Butte Lake and the Rio Grande east of I–25 for about 50 mi (from south of Fort Craig to just north of Truth or Consequences). To take a **scenic drive** from Truth or Consequences, head east on NM 51, turn north at NM 179 for about 2 mi, head southeast on NM 195, and take a loop drive of about 5 mi to Elephant Butte Dam. At the end of the dam turn north for overlooks of the lake and a view of the rocky elephant-shape island formation that inspired the name of the reservoir. To visit the **Dam Site Recreation Area** turn west on NM 177, where you'll find a terraced picnic area with striking views and tall shade trees. A private concessionaire operates a restaurant, lounge, marina, and cabins. ⊠ *3 mi north of Truth or Consequences* ☏ *505/744–5421* 🗐 *$5 per vehicle.*

Where to Stay & Eat

¢–$ ✕ **Hodges Corner Restaurant.** Owner Ray Hodges believes in hearty food and lots of it—so if you're in the mood for a heaping plate of thick barbecued pork ribs, cube steak, or deep-fried fish, this is the place for you. Late in the day, the ultracasual dining area is usually filled with hungry anglers who've stopped to relax and chow down after a day of fishing. Come in earlier in the day to buy a bucket of home-fried chicken to take with you to the lake. ⊠ *915 NM 195* ☏ *505/744–5626* ▤ *D, MC, V.*

$ ✕▣ **Elephant Butte Inn.** The mesa-top property feels like a resort and has panoramic views of the lake. Get a lake-view room if you can and enjoy the huge, lush lawn that seems to disappear into the water. Rooms have either two queen-size beds or one king-size bed, and all have irons, hair dryers, and coffeemakers. The Ivory Tusk Tavern & Restaurant (¢–$$) serves standard fare including hamburgers, and steak and seafood platters. ⊠ *NM 195* ⌂ *Box E, Elephant Butte 87935* ☏ *505/744–5431* 🖨 *505/744–5044* 🛏 *44 rooms, 4 suites* ⌕ *Restaurant, some microwaves, some refrigerators, cable TV, 2 tennis courts, pool, hiking, lounge, meeting rooms, some pets allowed (fee)* ▤ *AE, D, MC, V* ⏍ *CP.*

¢–$ ▣ **Dam Site Resort.** The lodgings at this resort are a fun step back in time. The lodge was built in 1911 for the dam's administration and engineering offices. The "cabins" are quaint, neo-pueblo, stucco structures built by the Civilian Conservation Corps in the 1940s. The resort has been established as an official historic district, and the restoration of the buildings is top-notch. The lodge operates as a B&B and is furnished with many period antiques. The spacious covered porch overlooks the marina. The cabins are an experience in retro-chic, and all have views of the lake, and kitchenettes (you must furnish utensils, plates, etc.). The bar-restaurant (¢–$) serves steaks, seafood, and sandwiches–and some excellent margaritas. On weekends between about Easter and Labor Day, dance bands play blues or rock on the outdoor patio, which also has a bar. ⊠ *77B Engle Star Rte., 87901, 5 mi east of 3rd St. light in Truth* or *Consequences* ☎ *505/894–2073* 🖶 *505/894–0776* 🛏 *16 cabins* ⚭ *Restaurant, some kitchenettes, lake, dock, windsurfing, boating, jet skiing, marina, waterskiing, fishing, lounge, playground, some pets allowed; no a/c in cabins, no room phones, no room TVs* ☰ *AE, D, MC, V* ⊕ *www.damsiteresort.com* ¶◯¶ *BP in lodge.*

⚠ **Dam Site Recreation Area.** At night, campfires flicker along the beaches of the many sandy coves of Elephant Butte Lake. There are developed and primitive campsites, many of them delightfully secluded. Sites without hookups are first come–first served, sites with hookups can be reserved. ✉ *3 mi north of Truth or Consequences* ☎ *877/664–7787 for reservations, 505/744–5923 for information* ⊕ *www.nmparks.com* ⚭ *Restaurant, grills, playground, flush toilets, pit toilets, partial hookups (electric and water), dump station, drinking water, showers, fire grates, fire pits, picnic tables, electricity, public telephone, ranger station, swimming (lake)* 🛏 *127 developed sites, several hundred primitive or partially developed tent sites* 🏷 *$8–$14.*

Sports & the Outdoors

The **Dam Site Recreation Area Marina** (✉ 77B Engle Star Rte., 5 mi east of 3rd St. traffic light in Truth or Consequences ☎ 505/894–2041) rents runabouts, ski boats, and pontoon boats late May–early September. The vessels cost between $20 and $45 hourly ($110 and $220 daily). A $250 deposit is required for use of any boat.

⌐ EN ROUTE Heading north on I–25 there are two interesting places to stop. The first one is **Fort Craig National Historic Site.** Fort Craig was established after the New Mexico Territory became part of the United States to prevent raids by the Apache and Navajo peoples and to secure the trade routes within the region. The growth of Socorro and what is now Truth or Consequences can be traced to the protection the fort provided between 1854 and the mid-1880s, when it was decommissioned. Battles west of the Mississippi River during the American Civil War were relatively rare, but in 1862 the Confederate army crossed the Rio Grande and headed to Valverde, north of Fort Craig, with the goal of cutting off the fort from the Union military headquarters in Santa Fe. Confederate forces first were sent into retreat but later won a few battles and made the Union forces withdraw. The Rebels later occupied Santa Fe for a few months. Today, signs describe the various buildings and solitary life at the outpost, where only a couple of masonry walls and numerous foundations remain. Historic markers are very informative, however, and a well-maintained gravel trail winds among the ruins. The roads to Fort Craig, which is about 40 mi south and east of Socorro, can become hard to pass during rainy weather. During the closest weekend to significant dates of February 21 and 22, historical reenactors re-create the Civil War Battle of Valverde and even "capture" the nearby city of Socorro in a grand finale. ✉ *Off I–25 San Marcial Exit 124, follow signs from exit for about 10 mi* ☎ *505/835–0412* 🏷 *Free* ◷ *Daily dawn–dusk.*

Hundreds of different types of birds, including snow geese, cranes, falcons, and eagles, can be spotted from viewing platforms and directly ★❾ through your car window at the popular **Bosque del Apache National Wildlife Refuge.** Besides serving as a rest stop for migrating birds, the Bosque del Apache also shelters mule deer, turkeys, quail, and other wildlife. Photo opportunities abound on the 15-mi auto loop tour; you can also hike through arid shrub land or bike through the refuge or take a van tour. October and November are the months the cottonwoods show their colors. In winter months, the refuge echoes with the haunting cries of whooping cranes flocking for the evening. Snow geese are so thick on lakes at times that shores are white with feathers washed ashore. Whether you're a bird-watcher or not, it is well worth bringing binoculars or a spotting scope to get some idea of how many varieties of birds land here (377 species have been spotted since 1940). The Festival of the Cranes in mid-November draws thousands of people. ⊠ *1001 NM 1, off I–25 San Marcial Exit 124 for northbound traffic and Exit 139 for southbound traffic, San Antonio* ☎ *505/835–1828* ⌨ *$3 per vehicle* ☉ *Refuge daily dawn–dusk; visitor center weekdays 7:30–4, weekends 8–4:30; tour road open Apr.–Sept., closed Oct.–Mar. for roosting birds.*

Socorro

⑩ *72 mi north of Truth or Consequences; 77 mi southwest of Albuquerque, south on I–25 and west on U.S. 60.*

The town of Socorro, population about 9,000, traces its roots back to the earliest Spanish expeditions into New Mexico when explorer Juan de Oñate established a permanent settlement along the Rio Grande in 1598. Native Americans provided corn for the expedition, inspiring Oñate to give the community a name that means succor, or help. The San Miguel Mission church was established in 1628, but Spanish settlement was virtually erased during the Pueblo Revolt of 1680 and did not reestablish itself until 1816. If not for this early and lengthy period of dormancy in the area, the city might have been the capital New Mexico; with a prime location in a large, fertile valley, amid then-thriving pueblos, abundant water sources, and tremendous mineral wealth.

Socorro's business district now occupies historic buildings that surround its square, which has a park with a gazebo and a plaque commemorating the arrival of Juan de Oñate. The town's claim to fame is the highly regarded New Mexico Institute of Mining and Technology (New Mexico Tech) founded in 1893. The institution's original special ties were chemistry and metallurgy, but along with scientific research now there are programs in medicine, engineering, and business.

More than 2,500 minerals and fossils are on display at the **New Mexico Bureau of Geology and Mineral Resources Mineral Museum,** among them samples from the area's ore-rich mining districts of Magdalena, Hansonburg, Santa Rita, and Tyrone. Many rocks here, from glittering pyrite to the deep-blue azurite, have exotic colors like those of tropical fish. Special tours can be arranged. ⊠ *New Mexico Institute of Mining and Technology, 801 Leroy Pl., from I–25 Exit 150, follow signs to institute* ☎ *505/835–5140* ⌨ *Free* ☉ *Weekdays 8–5, weekends 10–3. Closed weekends during academic holidays.*

Only a monument remains at **Trinity Site,** where the world's first atomic bomb exploded, on July 16, 1945. The resulting crater has been filled in, but the test site and monument are open for public viewing two days of the year. The McDonald ranch house, where the first plutonium core for the bomb was assembled, can be toured on those days. ⊠ *5 mi south of U.S. 380. Turn east at San Antonio exit off I–25, 10 mi south of Socorro. Drive 12 mi east on U.S. 380 and turn south onto paved road, NM 525, for 5 mi until route dead-ends at Stallion Gate. Visitors (everyone must present photo ID) will be met at gate off U.S. 380 and allowed to drive 17 mi east to site* ☎ *505/678–1134* ▣ *Free* ⊗ *1st Sat. of Apr. and Oct., gate opens 8–2.*

Where to Stay & Eat

¢ ✕ **La Pasadita.** Wander off the main drag into this place and you'll realize that it's a well-kept secret among locals. The New Mexican food here is really good, and really inexpensive. Don't be put off by the lack of charm on the outside; order at the counter, sit down at a table, and wait for the friendly staff to bring you a plate of their wonderful food. The burrito plate with red chile is big and mouthwatering, and the combo plates are H-U-G-E. Don't miss what may be the very best sopaipillas in all of New Mexico—light, flaky, and soooo good with honey. They close at 6, so if you're looking for dinner, go early. ⊠ *230 Garfield St., turn onto Garfield from southwest corner of Plaza, restaurant is a few blocks on left* ☎ *505/835–3696* ▭ *No credit cards.*

¢ ✕ **Socorro Springs Brewing Co.** This microbrewery and restaurant is housed in a renovated adobe building off the plaza and is almost always full of happy locals drinking good beer and eating excellent calzones, thin crust pizzas, home made soups, and big, fresh salads. It's hard to go wrong here, unless you're in a hurry. "Hurry" isn't on this menu, though the service is friendly. Good breakfasts, too, but no beer served in the morning! ⊠ *1012 N. California St.* ☎ *505/838–0650* ▭ *A, D, DC, MC, V.*

$ ▦ **Holiday Inn Express.** A favorite of groups and small conventions that otherwise might have limited options in such a remote area, this haven offers condensed versions of some of the luxuries of larger resorts. You can expect the chain's usual quality and contemporary, modern flourishes in standard rooms; a friendly staff rounds out an easy stay. ⊠ *1100 California NE, 87801* ☎ *505/838–0556* ▤ *505/838–0598* ◆ *120 rooms* △ *Microwaves, refrigerators, cable TV with movies, in-room data ports, pool, gym, hot tub, laundry facilities, meeting rooms, some pets allowed (fee)* ▭ *AE, D, DC, MC, V* ▯◯▯ *CP.*

¢–$ ▦ **Super 8.** Southwestern pastel colors and prints of adobe architecture and pottery decorate this establishment's rooms, most of which have microwaves and refrigerators. K-Bob's, a franchise restaurant specializing in steaks, is next door. ⊠ *1121 Frontage Rd., I–25 Exit 150, 87801* ☎ *505/835–4626, 800/800–8000 central reservations* ▤ *505/835–3988* ◆ *86 rooms* △ *Cable TV, pool, hot tub* ▭ *AE, D, MC, V* ▯◯▯ *CP.*

HEADING WEST ON U.S. 60

Maybe you're a traveler who prefers to stay off the beaten path, and venture to places you've never even heard of. If you're in the mood to take the slow road and encounter an authentic Western America decades removed from today's franchise operations, head west on old NM 60 out of Socorro and keep going—as far as the Arizona border if you like. The speed limit is 55 mph, there's not a chain restaurant within 200 mi, and the scenery hasn't changed much for 50 years.

This long, often lonely highway opened in 1917 as the first numbered auto route to cross the United States. Called the Ocean to Ocean Highway, U.S. 60 ran from Norfolk, Virginia, to Los Angeles. Earlier in the 20th century it was a "hoof highway," the route of cattle drives from Springerville, Arizona, to Magdalena, New Mexico. Walk into any café along this dusty roadside and you're still likely to be greeted by a blue-eyed cowboy in spurs fresh from tending to ranch business.

People really ranch here, much the way they have for more than 100 years—prior to the era of homesteaders and ranchers, the Apaches ruled and weren't much inclined to allow ranching or settlements of any kind. Livestock production and timber are still the leading industries. U.S. 60 takes you through the heart of Catron County, New Mexico's largest county by area, and least populated by square mile. Notoriously politically incorrect and proud of it, this is a place where Confederate flags fly and animal trophies are considered high art.

After you've headed as far west as Quemado, you can make an interesting loop by continuing north on NM 36 to NM 117, which skirts the east side of El Malpais National Monument (⇨ Chapter 5), eventually hooking up with I–40 east of Grant. To get to Albuquerque take I–40 east.

8

Magdalena

27 mi west of Socorro on U.S. 60.

Magdalena, population 300, enjoyed its heyday about a hundred years ago as a raucous town of miners and cowboys. It was once the biggest livestock shipping point west of Chicago. The Atchison, Topeka & Santa Fe Railway built a spur line from Socorro in 1885 to transport timber, wool, cattle, and ore. Lead, zinc, silver, copper, and gold all were mined in the area, but now there are more ghosts than miners.

The town took its name from Mary Magdalene, protector of miners, whose face is supposedly visible on the east slope of Magdalena Peak, a spot held sacred by the Native Americans of the area. To get a feel for the place, walk down to the Atchison, Topeka & Santa Fe Railway depot, now the town hall and library. Across the street is the Charles Ilfeld Warehouse, where the company's motto, "wholesalers of everything," is a reminder of the great trade empire of the late 19th century.

Although there are arts festivals in spring and fall, the biggest event of the year in Magdalena is the **Magdalena Old Timers Reunion** (☎ 505/854–3365), held for three days in early July. The festival, which draws about 5,000 and has the biggest parade in New Mexico after the State Fair's, began quietly 30 years ago. With the end of cattle drives and the shutdown of the rail spur in the early 1970s, cowboys began returning at the same time each year to greet each other and reminisce. Over the past three decades, the reunion has grown into an event-packed weekend including both kids' and adult rodeos, Western swing dances on Friday and Saturday nights, a fiddling contest, a barbecue dinner, and an authentic chuckwagon cook-off. The parade takes place Saturday morning, and the crowned reunion queen must be at least 60 years old. Most events are held at the Magdalena Fairgrounds, and admission is free. The deserted **Old Kelly Mine** (⊠ Kelly Rd. off U.S. 60 ☎ No phone), 4 mi south of town, is reputed to be haunted, and during the Old Timers Reunion a 7K race finishes here (it begins in the village).

Where to Stay & Eat

¢–$ ✕ **Magdalena Cafe.** Hearty lunch fare including roast beef, burgers, hot sandwiches, homemade pie, Mexican pineapple cake, and delicious milk shakes are served on red-and-white checkered tablecloths here. There's also a $6.95 all-you-can-eat salad bar. Plans are in the works for the café to move across from the Marshall's office in late summer 2006. Keep your eyes open as you drive through town. ⊠ *U.S. NM 60, across from Trail's End Supermarket* ☎ *505/854–2696* ⊟ *No credit cards* ⊘ *No dinner.*

¢ ⊞ **Western Bed & Breakfast Motel & RV Park.** To inspire dreams of riding the range, rooms of knotty pine are set off with Western paintings and Native American artifacts, and some have Victorian-style flowered upholstery and matching art. Locally handmade quilts and Mexican textiles decorate the walls. The facility was a maternity hospital for the region in the 1920s. There are also 13 RV sites with full hookups ($20; weekly and monthly rates available). ⊠ *U.S. NM 60, town center, 87835* ☎ *505/854–2417* ⊟ *505/854–3217* ⊲₽ *6 rooms, 13 RV sites* & *Microwaves, refrigerators, some cable TV with movies, some pets allowed (fee), hot tub* ⊟ *AE, D, DC, MC, V* ⊠ *BP.*

Shopping

Histories of some of the notable buildings in Magdalena and a guide for a walking tour are available on ⊕ www.magdalena-nm.com. It's fun to have the print-out of the walking tour while exploring the shops and cafés.

Blue Canyon Gallery (⊠ NM 60 ☎ 888/854–8337) carries photographs, pottery, paintings, and artwork by area artists.

EN
ROUTE
★ ⑪

With its 27 glistening-white 80-foot radio-telescope antennae arranged in patterns, the **Very Large Array** is a startling sight when spotted along the Plains of San Augustin. The complex's dish-shaped "ears," each weighing 230 tons, are tuned in to the cosmos. The array is part of a series of facilities that compose the National Radio Astronomy Observatory. The antennas, which provided an impressive backdrop for the movie *Contact,* based on the Carl Sagan book, form the largest, most advanced radio telescope in the world. The telescope chronicles the birth and death of stars and galaxies from 10 to 12 billion light-years away. Hundreds of scientists from around the world travel to this windy, remote spot to research black holes, colliding galaxies, and exploding stars, as well as to chart the movements of planets. Visitors are permitted to stroll right up to the array on a self-guided walking tour that begins at the unstaffed visitor center. Staff members emphasize that their work does *not* involve a search for life on other planets. ⊠ *Off U.S. 60, 23 mi west of Magdalena* ☎ *505/835–0424 Socorro County Chamber of Commerce* 💷 *Free* ⊙ *Daily 8:30–dusk.*

Datil

36 mi west of Magdalena on U.S. 60.

More a crossroads than a town, Datil is named for the datelike fruit that once grew wild here.

Where to Stay & Eat

¢ ✕🏨 **Eagle Guest Ranch.** At the Datil's main intersection sits this hotel and restaurant, which is a good—as well as the only—reason to stop here. Since the Eagle opened in the 1920s, it has had various incarnations. roadside store, café, lounge, and dance hall. These days, the dark-panel restaurant (¢–$$) serves mainly beef dishes, as well as pies made from recipes that are more than a half-century old. The guest rooms are low-end affairs, but if you're in need of accommodations in a place this remote, you have to think like an Old West traveler: "When you're at the Last Chance Hotel, you don't look for luxury." ⊠ *U.S. 60 at NM 12* 🖂 *Box 68, 87821* ☎ *505/772–5612 BLM office open weekdays* 🛆 *Restaurant, cable TV; no a/c, no room phones* 🚭 *8 rooms* 🖃 *AE, D, DC, MC, V* ⊙ *Rooms only available Fri. and Sat. nights, restaurant closed Sun.*

🏕 **Datil Well Campground.** The well for which this campground is named was once an important stop on cattle drives. Along the ridges west of the campground there's a 3-mi trail through piñon-juniper and ponderosa pine woodlands, with overlooks of the San Augustin Plains and surrounding mountains. Several sites have been converted to pull-throughs for large RVs. ⊠ *At intersection of U.S. NM 60 and NM 12, go left on NM 12 (south) 5 mi* ☎ *505/835–0412* 🛆 *Grills, pit toilets, drinking water, fire pits, picnic tables* 🚭 *22 sites* 💷 *$5* 🖃 *No credit cards.*

Pie Town

21 mi west of Datil on U.S. 60.

During the 1930s and '40s, it was said that the best pie in New Mexico was served at a little café in Pie Town, a homesteading community west of the Continental Divide. Cowboys on cattle drives and tourists heading to California spread stories of the legendary pies. Thanks to the still-operational Pie-O-Neer Cafe, the tradition of great pie in this part of the world is alive and well.

Pie Town's reputation can be traced to 1922 when World War I veteran Clyde Norman came from Texas and filed a mining claim on the Hound Pup Lode. Gold mining didn't go as well as he'd hoped, but he began selling kerosene and gasoline, as well as doughnuts he'd brought from Magdalena in his Model T. Eventually he learned to bake pies with dried apples, which were an immediate success. Spanish American War veteran Harmon L. Craig, who made a great sourdough, arrived in 1923 or '24, and the two went into partnership. The post office granted the place the name Pie Town in 1927.

Craig bought Norman out in 1932. He ran the mercantile end while his wife, Theodora Baugh, and her two daughters took over the pie baking. Nowadays aficionados can dig in at the annual Pie Festival, held on the second weekend in September, with pie-eating and pie-baking contests, horny-toad races, and hot-air balloon flights.

Where to Eat

★ ¢–$ ✕ **Pie-O-Neer Cafe.** "Life goes on and days go by. That's why you should stop for pie." Such is the motto of one of New Mexico's most legendary roadside stops. Owner Kathy Knapp serves meals, including excellent green-chile cheeseburgers, from mid-morning through early evening, but pie is her stock in trade. She keeps these delicious varieties on hand: apple, cherry, peach, coconut cream, lemon meringue, and banana cream. Her best sellers are the apple and the more rarely made oatmeal-pecan. On some Sunday afternoons, local talent drops by for guitar strumming. Kathy is also one of the proprietors at the lovely Silver Creek Inn in Mogollon. ⊠ *U.S. 60* ☎ *505/772–2711* ⊟ *AE, D, MC, V.*

Quemado

22 mi west of Pie Town on U.S. 60.

Quemado (pronounced kay-*ma*-dough) means "burnt" in Spanish, and the town is supposedly named for a legendary Apache chief who burned his hand in a campfire. The bustling village, which contains several motels and cafés, is busiest in fall, when it is a favorite base for deer hunters. **Quemado Lake,** about 20 mi south of town on NM 32 and NM 103, is a man-made fishing and hiking area where it's not unusual to spot herds of elk.

⌐ OFF THE BEATEN PATH

LIGHTNING FIELD – The sculptor Walter De Maria created *Lightning Field,* a work of land art composed of 400 stainless-steel poles of varying heights (the average is 20 feet, although they create a horizontal plane) arranged in a rectangular grid over 1 mi by ½ mi of flat, isolated terrain. Groups of up to six people are permitted to stay overnight between May 1 and October 31—the only way you can experience the artwork—at a rustic on-site 1930s cabin (the fee ranges from $110 to $135 per person, although those who can afford it are asked to pay up to $300 per person to help cover actual expenses of providing visitor meals and transportation). Dia Center for the Arts administers *Lightning Field,* shuttling visitors from Quemado to the sculpture, which is on private land to the northeast. Thunder and lightning storms are most common from July to mid-September; book way ahead for visits during this time. If you're lucky, you'll see flashes you'll never forget (though lightning isn't required for the sculpture to be stunning in effect). ⌂ *Box 2993, Corrales 87048* ☎ *505/898–3335 Corrales office and reservations, 505/773–4560 Quemado shuttle* ☐ *505/898–3336* ⚲ *Reservations essential* ☉ *Closed Nov.–Apr.*

Where to Stay & Eat

¢–$$ ✕ **Snuffy's Steak House.** On the road to Quemado Lake, this true Western bar serves steaks, burgers, and Mexican food. The enchiladas aren't bad, but this is more a place to soak up local color than eat fine cuisine. There's an antique bar, and the walls are plastered with pictures of homesteaders and folks with their fish and wild-game trophies. Snuffy's is open for breakfast on weekends and for early dinner (until 8) on Friday and Saturday. ⊠ *NM 103* ☎ *505/773–4672* 🖃 *MC, V* ⊗ *No dinner Sun.–Thurs.*

¢ ✕🖾 **Largo Motel.** With plain, comfortable rooms, the Largo is as good a motel as you're going to find to wash off the trail dust and find a night's rest. The Largo has the best café in town (¢–$$), a busy little spot known for homemade corn tortillas and biscuits, gravy, and chicken-fried steak, and excellent red-and-green chile on Mexican food dishes. The Navajo tacos are famous. They serve "a real full plate," too. Above the spacious booths are mounted trophies (the owner is a hunting guide). ⊠ *U.S. NM 60 on west side of town, 87829* ☎ *505/773–4686* 🛏 *6 rooms* 🖃 *MC, V.*

△ **Quemado Lake Campgrounds.** Six campgrounds surround Quemado Lake, providing convenient access to hiking trails or lake fishing for stocked rainbow trout. ⊠ *20 mi south of Pie Town on NM 32 and NM 103* ☎ *505/773–4678* ⚒ *Grills, pit toilets, partial hookups (electric and water), dump station, drinking water, fire grates, fire pits, picnic tables* 🛏 *Unlimited primitive sites, 60 developed sites, 16 sites with partial hookups* 🚐 *RV sites $15, tent sites $10, primitive sites are free* 🖃 *No credit cards.*

SOUTHWESTERN NEW MEXICO ESSENTIALS

AIR TRAVEL

El Paso International Airport is the main gateway to southern New Mexico. The major airlines with scheduled service to the airport are America West, American, Continental, Delta, Frontier, and Southwest. Albuquerque International Sunport is 210 mi north of Las Cruces. *See* Air Travel *in* New Mexico Essentials for national airline phone numbers.

🚩 Airports **Albuquerque International Sunport** ⊠ 2200 Sunport Blvd. SE, Albuquerque ☎ 505/842–4366. **El Paso International Airport** ⊠ 6701 Convair Dr., El Paso, TX ☎ 915/772–4271.

BUS TRAVEL

Texas, New Mexico & Oklahoma Coaches provides bus service throughout southwestern New Mexico (though not Silver City). Silver Stage Lines provides shuttle service to Las Cruces and Silver City from El Paso International Airport. Las Cruces Shuttle Service makes regular runs daily between El Paso International Airport and Las Cruces, Deming, and Silver City. Roadrunner City Bus operates public buses in Las Cruces.

🚩 **Las Cruces Shuttle Service** ☎ 505/525–1784 ⊕ www.lascrucesshuttle.com. **Roadrunner City Bus** ☎ 505/525–2500. **Silver Stage Lines** ☎ 800/522–0162. **Texas, New Mexico & Oklahoma Coaches** ☎ 505/524–8518 in Las Cruces, 800/231–2222 for all other destinations ⊕ www.tnmo.com.

CAR RENTAL

You can rent a car from one of the national agencies at either Albuquerque International Airport or El Paso International Airport. Auto dealerships in some communities rent cars. Hertz has an office at the Las Cruces Hilton. *See* Car Rental *in* New Mexico Essentials for national rental agency phone numbers.

CAR TRAVEL

Two major interstates travel through southwestern New Mexico, I–10 from west to east and I–25 from north to south. U.S. 70 connects Las Cruces to Alamogordo and the southeast. From Albuquerque, the drive is about two hours to Truth or Consequences, three hours to Las Cruces. Silver City can be accessed from minor highways leading off I–10 and I–25. From Las Cruces, I–10 leads south to El Paso.

The quality of the region's roadways varies widely, particularly in remote rural areas. Drive with caution on the narrow highways, which particularly in mountainous areas have no shoulders. On minor roadways, even if paved, be alert for curves, dips, and steep drop-offs. If you veer too far into unexplored territory with primitive, unpaved roads, make sure you have a vehicle with high clearance and four-wheel drive, such as an SUV.

EMERGENCIES

In an emergency, dial 911.

Some Walgreens pharmacies in El Paso, Texas, and in Las Cruces stay open late or are open 24 hours. Wal-Mart and large supermarket chains such as Albertson's also have pharmacies.

🏥 Hospitals **Gila Regional Medical Center** ✉ 1313 E. 32nd St., Silver City ☎ 505/538-4000. **Memorial Medical Center** ✉ 2450 S. Telshor Blvd., Las Cruces ☎ 505/522-8641. **Socorro General Hospital** ✉ 1202 NM 60 W, Socorro ☎ 505/835-1140.

🏥 Pharmacies **Albertson's Pharmacy** ✉ 1956 Hwy. 180 E, Silver City ☎ 505/388-1909. **Walgreens Pharmacy** ✉ 1300 El Paseo Rd., Las Cruces ☎ 505/525-8708.

PASSPORTS & VISAS

On a day trip into Mexico, citizens of the United States and Canada need only carry a government-issue photo ID as documentation, but it's always a good idea also to have a valid passport or certified copy of a birth certificate, especially since there is now a fair amount of confusion at different checkpoints as to whether or not passports, or merely ID cards, are *actually* required, due to increased security measures along the border. Citizens of other countries must have a valid passport to enter.

ENTERING MEXICO Mexico has one of the strictest policies about children entering the country. Though it's not always checked for, all children, including infants, must have proof of citizenship for travel to Mexico. All children up to age 18 traveling with a single parent must also have a notarized letter from the other parent stating that the child has his or her permission to leave the home country. If the other parent is deceased or the child has only one legal parent, a notarized statement saying so must also be provided.

If you're visiting for less than 72 hours and are not traveling past a border town like Ciudad Juárez and into the country's interior, you're not required to obtain a tourist card (free). You do not have to buy Mexican auto insurance if you're only traveling to Mexico for the day. Be sure the insurance you do have covers you if you drive your vehicle across the border. If you do not own your car outright, you'll need a letter from your car loan lender stating you have their permission to take the vehicle into Mexico. If you're caught transporting a gun into Mexico, you can be jailed indefinitely.

🚹 **Mexican Consulate (New Mexico)** ✉ 1610 4th St. NW, Albuquerque ☎ 505/242-7566 ⊕ www.embassyofmexico.org.

TOURS

El Paso–Juárez Trolley Co. has daily guided tours into Juárez, Mexico, for a $12.50 fee. Call for schedules and rates for special tours to the old Spanish missions of El Paso, Texas. Around and About Tours specializes in El Paso, Texas; Ciudad Juárez, Mexico; and tours of several days or a week into southern New Mexico. Volunteers from El Paso Mission Trail Association lead groups of at least 10 people on visits to the old Spanish missions of the El Paso area. A donation of at least $2.50 per person is requested.

🚹 **Around and About Tours** ✉ 6716 Mesa Grande Ave., El Paso, TX ☎ 915/833-2650. **El Paso–Juárez Trolley Co.** ✉ 1 Civic Center Plaza, El Paso, TX ☎ 915/544-0062. **El Paso Mission Trail Association** ✉ 1 Civic Center Plaza, El Paso, TX ☎ 800/351-6024.

TRAIN TRAVEL

Amtrak serves El Paso and Deming, New Mexico, on the *Sunset Limited*, which operates between Los Angeles, New Orleans, and Florida.

🚹 **Amtrak** ✉ Union Station, 700 San Francisco St., El Paso, TX ☎ 800/872-7245 ⊕ www.amtrak.com.

VISITOR INFORMATION

🚹 **El Paso Convention & Tourism Department** ✉ 1 Civic Center Plaza, 79901 ☎ 915/534-0600 or 800/351-6024 ⊕ www.visitelpaso.com. **Las Cruces Convention & Visitors Bureau** ✉ 211 Water St., 88001 ☎ 505/541-2444 or 800/343-7827 ⊕ www.lascrucescvb.org. **Mesilla Visitor's Center** ✉ 2340 Avenida de Mesilla, 88046 ☎ 505/647-9698 ⊕ www.oldmesilla.org. **Silver City Grant County Chamber of Commerce** ✉ 201 N. Hudson St., 88061 ☎ 505/538-3785 ⊕ www.silvercity.org. **Truth or Consequences/ Sierra County Chamber of Commerce** ✉ 400 W. 4th St., 87901 ☎ 505/894-3536 ⊕ www.truthorconsequencesnm.net.

UNDERSTANDING
NEW MEXICO

NEW MEXICO AT A GLANCE

Fast Facts

Nickname: Land of Enchantment
Capital: Santa Fe
Motto: It Grows As It Goes
State song: *O, Fair New Mexico*
State bird: Roadrunner
State flower: Yucca
State tree: Piñon pine
Administrative divisions: 33 counties
Entered the Union: January 6, 1912, the 47th state

Population: 1.9 million
Population density: 15.4 people per square mi
Ethnic groups: White 45%; Latino 42%; native American 10%; black 2%; Asian 1%
Religion: Unaffiliated 42%; Catholic 37%; Protestant 20%; other 1%

Geography & Environment

Land area: 121,356 square mi
Natural resources: Beryllium, coal, copper ore, manganese ore, natural gas, perlite, petroleum, potash, salt, tin concentrates, uranium ore
Natural hazards: Floods, landslides, wildfires
Environmental issues: Water shortages from drought and water rights adjudications, as well as water pollution from bacteria and man-made pollutants; development demanding open space and scarce water resources

I think New Mexico was the greatest experience from the outside world that I have ever had.
—D. H. Lawrence

[Sun-bleached bones] were most wonderful against the blue/that blue that will always be there as it is now after all man's destruction is finished.
—Georgia O'Keeffe, on desert skies of New Mexico

Economy

GSP: 55.4 billion
Per capita income: $25,541
Unemployment: 5.4%
Work force: 910,500
Major industries: Chemicals, electrical equipment, food processing, high-tech manufacturing, military, mineral processing, mining, ordnance, ranching,
Agricultural products: Cattle, chiles, dairy products, onions, piñon nuts, pinto beans, potatoes, sheep

Did You Know?

• Think alien legends in Roswell are only for kooks? Count among those kooks former Energy Secretary and state governor Bill Richardson, who wrote in 2004, "the mystery surrounding this crash has never been adequately explained."

• The mean altitude of the entire state of New Mexico is more than a mile above sea level. At 7,000 feet above sea level, Santa Fe is the highest capital city in the United States.

CHILE TIME

CHILE PEPPERS, WHICH HAVE BEEN locally grown since ancient times, are a defining ingredient of New Mexican cuisine. Combined with corn tortillas, beans, tomatoes, and potatoes, chiles bind together the New Mexico that for centuries sustained indigenous people, the Spanish, and subsequent arrivals. A dedicated fan will travel any distance—down any highway—in pursuit of a great chile sauce (which is referred to in these parts as simply "chile"). From Chope's south of Las Cruces to M&J's Sanitary Tortilla Factory in Albuquerque and JoAnn's Ranch-o-Casados in Española (to name a few classic hot spots), the pursuit of the most flavorful—but not necessarily the hottest—chile remains a personal quest akin to proving one's honor.

When Christopher Columbus set out across the ocean in 1492, he was seeking a sea route to the lucrative spice trade of Asia. Instead, he stumbled onto the New World, where he tasted chiles. He took some back to Spain, and from there they spread around the world on trade routes, transforming the cuisines of Spain, Portugal, Italy, Hungary, North Africa, India, Nepal, Tibet, and China. In addition to their distinction as some of the world's favorite spices, chiles are some of the oldest: they're believed to have originated 10,000 years ago in the Amazon region of South America, near the area of Brazil and Bolivia.

How chiles first arrived in New Mexico is the subject of debate. Some believe the Spanish introduced them to the Pueblo Indians on their travels north from Mexico. Others say they were grown in New Mexico centuries prior to the arrival of the Spanish, having been introduced through trade with the peoples of Mexico and South America. It's interesting to note that chiles aren't used in the traditional ceremonies among the Pueblo Indians as corn is—although red and green chile dishes are served at all feasts and ceremonies.

The source of the chile's heat is the chemical capsaicin, found in the pepper's heart and membrane. The seeds themselves are not hot, but they absorb capsaicin from their contact with the heart and membrane. In addition to providing a culinary delight to chile lovers, capsaicin has been used medicinally since prehistoric times; it's thought to prevent blood clots and heart attacks, and has been found to hinder cholesterol absorption. Low in fat and high in vitamins A and C and beta-carotene, it also speeds up metabolism and helps digestion. New Mexican old-timers have been known to spread chile on arthritic limbs; and newer topical creams made from capsaicin have become available in pharmacies. These chile-based products bring pain relief because of the chemical effect capsaicin has on the brain. When you eat chile, or even touch it, endorphins (the "hormones of pleasure") are released in the brain. So, the same chemical reaction that produces "chile addiction" also blunts pain.

The green variety of chile, generically called "Hatch" (for the New Mexico town that produces the bulk of the state's crop), is the commercially developed type known as New Mexico 6–10 and the Big Jim. The best red chiles are said to be grown from the old stock cultivated in Chimayó and other high mountain villages of the north—Española, Dixon, Velarde, and Peñasco.

By far the state's most important vegetable crop, New Mexico chiles are grown on 30,000 acres, mostly in Luna and Doña Ana counties. Sixty percent of the nation's chile crop comes from the Land of Enchantment. Since 1980 chile consumption has doubled in the United States, much of it going into salsa, which in the 1990s surpassed ketchup to become the country's most popular condiment.

From mid-August through the fall, the New Mexican air is scented with the warm, enticing fragrance of chiles roasting outdoors in large, wire, propane-fired cages. Around State Fair time in September, people head for their favorite roadside stand to buy a sack of fresh-roasted green chiles. Once stored in the freezer, they're used all winter long, in stews, enchiladas, salsas, and burritos.

As the season progresses into October, it's time to buy a red chile ristra, a string of chiles, to hang full, heavy and sweet, near the front door, a sign of warmth and welcome. It's said the ristra brings good luck—and it certainly is convenient to have the makings of soul-warming red-chile salsa right at hand.

—Sharon Niederman

A LAND APART

ALMOST EVERY NEW MEXICAN HAS A TALE or two to tell about being perceived as a "foreigner" by the rest of the country. There's the well-documented case of the Santa Fe man who tried to purchase tickets to the 1996 Olympic Games in Atlanta, only to be shuffled over to the department handling international requests. Even the U.S. Postal Service occasionally returns New Mexico–bound mail to its senders for insufficient "international" postage.

Though annoying to residents, such cases of mistaken identity are oddly apt (keep an ear open to how often New Mexicans themselves refer to their state, one of the nation's poorest, as a Third World country). New Mexico is, in many ways, an anomaly: it has its own cuisine, architecture, fashion, and culture, all of these an amalgam of the designs and accidents of a long and intriguing history. In prehistoric times indigenous peoples hunted game in New Mexico's mountains and farmed along its riverbanks. Two thousand years ago Pueblo Indians began expressing their reverence for the land through flat-roofed earthen architecture, drawings carved onto rocks, and rhythmic chants and dances. The late-16th and early-17th centuries brought the Spanish explorers who, along with the Franciscan monks, founded Santa Fe as a northern capital of the empire of New Spain, a settlement that was contemporaneous with the Jamestown colony of Virginia.

Although the Spanish brutally enslaved and mistreated the Native Americans, during the course of several hundred years tolerance has grown and traditions have commingled. Pueblo Indians passed on the use of chiles, beans, and corn, and the Spanish shared their skill at metalwork, influencing the Native American jewelry that has become symbolic of the region. The Spanish also shared their architecture, which itself had been influenced by 700 years of Arab domination of Spain, and the acequia method of irrigation still in use in the villages of northern New Mexico.

The last of the three main cultures to make their mark was that of the Anglo (any nonindigenous, non-Hispanic person in New Mexico is considered an Anglo—even groups who don't normally identify with the Anglo-Saxon tradition). Arriving throughout the 19th century, Anglos mined the mountains for gold, other precious metals, and gemstones and uncovered vast deposits of coal, oil, and natural gas. Their contributions to New Mexican life include the railroad, the highway system, and—for better or worse—the atomic bomb.

The resulting mélange of cultures has produced a character that's uniquely New Mexican: Spanish words are sprinkled liberally through everyday English parlance; Spanish itself, still widely spoken in the smaller villages, contains numerous words from the Pueblo Indian dialects. Architectural references and culinary terms in particular tend to hew to the original Spanish: you can admire the vigas and bancos that adorn the restaurant where you can partake of posole or sopaipilla.

But beyond the linguistic quirks, gastronomic surprises, and cultural anomalies that make New Mexico unique, there remains the most distinctive feature of all—the landscape. At once subtle and dramatic, the mountains and mesas seem almost surreal as they glow gold, terracotta, and pink in the clear, still air of the high desert. The shifting clouds overhead cast rippling shadows across the land, illuminating the delicate palette of greens, grays, and browns that contrast with a sky that can go purple or dead black or eye-searingly blue in a matter of seconds. It's a landscape that has inspired writers (such as D. H. Lawrence and Willa Cather), painters (such as Georgia O'Keeffe and Peter Hurd), and countless poets, dreamers, filmmakers, and assorted creative spirits for centuries.

Indeed, watching the ever-changing sky is something of a spectator sport here, especially during the usual "monsoons" of summer. So regular that you could almost set your watch by them, the thunderheads start to gather in late afternoon, giving visual warning before the inevitable downpour. In the meantime, the sky dazzles with its interplay of creamy-white clouds edged by charcoal, sizzling flashes of lightning, and dramatic shafts of light shooting earthward from some ethereal perch.

The mountains absorb and radiate this special illumination, transforming themselves daily according to the whims of light and shadow. The very names of the major ranges attest to the profound effect their light show had on the original Spanish settlers. The Franciscan monks named the mountains to the east of Santa Fe *Sangre de Cristo,* or "blood of Christ," because of their tendency to glow deep red at sunset. To the south, east of Albuquerque, the Sandia Mountains ("watermelon" in Spanish) also live up to their colorful name when the sun sets. Georgia O'Keeffe once joked about the Pedernal mesa in the Jemez range, "It's my private mountain, it belongs to me. God told me if I painted it enough, I could have it."

The awe-inspiring beauty of the landscape renders New Mexico's tag lines more than just marketing clichés. The state is truly a "Land of Enchantment," and Santa Fe is indeed "the City Different." Surrounded by mind-expanding mountain views and filled with sinuous streets that promote foot over car traffic, Santa Fe welcomes with characteristic adobe warmth. Rapid growth and development have prompted many local residents to worry about becoming too much like "everywhere else," but the surfeit of trendy restaurants, galleries, and boutiques that tout regional fare and wares, both authentic and artificial, are still distinctly Santa Fean. Commercialism notwithstanding, Santa Fe's deeply spiritual aura affects even nonreligious types in surprising ways, inspiring a reverence probably not unlike that which inspired the Spanish monks to name it the City of Holy Faith. (Its full name is La Villa Real de la Santa Fe de San Francisco de Asís, or the Royal City of the Holy Faith of St. Francis of Assisi.) A kind of mystical Catholicism blended with ancient Native American lore and beliefs flourishes throughout northern New Mexico in tiny mountain villages that have seen little change through the centuries. Tales of miracles, spontaneous healings, and spiritual visitations thrive in the old adobe churches that line the High Road that leads north of Santa Fe to Taos.

* * *

IF SANTA FE IS SPIRITUAL, sophisticated, and occasionally snobby, Taos, 65 mi away, is very much an outpost despite its relative proximity to the capital. Compared with Santa Fe, Taos is smaller, feistier, quirkier, tougher, and very independent. Taoseños are a study in diverse convictions, and most anyone will share his or hers with you if you lend an ear. Rustic and comfortably unpretentious, the town contains a handful of upscale restaurants with cuisines and wine lists as innovative as what you might find in New York. It's a haven for aging hippies, creative geniuses, cranky misanthropes, and anyone else who wants a good quality of life in a place that accepts new arrivals without a lot of questions—as long as they don't offend longtime residents with their city attitudes.

Sixty miles south of Santa Fe, Albuquerque adds another distinctive perspective to the mix. New Mexico's only big city by most standards, it shares many traits with cities its size elsewhere: traffic, noise, crime, and sprawl. But what sets it apart is its dogged determination to remain a friendly small town, a place where pedestrians still greet one another as they pass and where downtown's main street is lined with angle parking (a modern-day version of the hitching post). Old Town, a congenial district whose authentic historical appeal is tempered by the unabashed pursuit of the tourist buck, is a typical example of how traditional small-town New Mexico flourishes amid a larger, more demanding economy without sacrificing the heart and soul of the lifestyle. San Felipe de Neri Catholic Church, built in 1793, is still attended by local worshippers.

The unifying factor among these and other towns and the terrain around them is the appeal of the land and the people. From the stunning natural formations of Carlsbad Caverns to the oceanic sweep of the "badlands" north of Santa Fe, it's the character of the residents and respect for the land that imbue New Mexico with its enchanted spirit. First-time visitors discover the unexpected pleasures of a place where time is measured not only by linear calculations of hours, days, weeks, and years but also by the circular sweep of crop cycles, gestation periods, the rotation of generations, and the changing of seasons.

Summer is traditionally the high season, when the arts scene explodes with gallery openings, performances at Santa Fe's open-air opera house, and a variety of festivals and celebrations. In autumn the towering cottonwoods that hug the riverbanks turn gold, days are warm and sunny, and the nights are crisp. Those beehive-shape kiva fireplaces get a workout in winter, a time when life slows down to accommodate occasional snowstorms, and the scent of aromatic firewood like piñon and cedar fill the air like an earthy incense.

Even after you leave, New Mexico will sneak into your consciousness in unexpected ways. As much a state of mind as it is a geographic entity, a place where nature can be glimpsed simultaneously at its most fragile and most powerful, New Mexico truly is a land of enchantment.

—Nancy Zimmerman

GLOSSARY

Perhaps more than any other region in the United States, New Mexico has its own distinctive cuisine and architectural style, both heavily influenced by Native American, Spanish-colonial, Mexican, and American frontier traditions. The brief glossary that follows explains terms used frequently in this book. As befits a land occupied—in several senses of the word in some cases—by so many diverse peoples, the use of accents on place and other names is a tricky matter. For some people, among them many Hispanic residents, accents are a matter of identification and pride—Rio Grande, for instance, represents more clearly the linguistic origins of the current name of the river that runs so grandly through the state. On the other hand, though including the accent for Picurís Pueblo or Jémez Pueblo might be linguistically accurate, it's also a reminder of the Spanish conquest of Pueblo Native Americans. ("I couldn't care less whether you use accents or not—I don't," said a woman at the governor's office of Jemez Pueblo when asked whether having an accent above the first "e" in the pueblo's name would be more accurate.)

In general in this book we've applied accents when they're part of an official place or other name. Signs for and official documents of Española, for instance, tend to have a tilde above the "n" in the city's name. On the other hand, though the names of Capulin Volcano and the city of Raton are sometimes written Capulín Volcano and Ratón, we have not employed the accents because New Mexican residents rarely do. A generally workable solution, this strategy does lead to some apparent inconsistencies (Picurís Pueblo; Jemez Pueblo), an illustration of the conflicting cultural sentiments still at play within New Mexico.

Art & Architecture
Adobe: A brick of sun-dried earth and clay, usually stabilized with straw; a structure made of adobe.

Banco: A small bench, or banquette, often upholstered with handwoven textiles, that gracefully emerges from adobe walls.

Bulto: Folk-art figures of a santo (saint), usually carved from wood.

Camposanto: A graveyard.

Capilla: A chapel.

Casita: Literally "small house," this term is generally used to describe a separate guesthouse.

Cerquita: A spiked, wrought-iron, rectangular fence, often marking grave sites.

Corbel: An ornately carved, decorative wooden bracket set between posts and beams.

Coyote fence: A type of wooden fence that surrounds many New Mexico homes; it comprises branches, usually from cedar or aspen trees, arranged vertically and wired tightly together.

Equipal: Pigskin-and-cedar furniture from Jalisco, Mexico, these chairs have rounded backs and bases rather than legs.

Farolito: Small votive candles set in paperbag lanterns, farolitos are popular at Christmastime. The term is used in northern New Mexico only. People in Albuquerque and points south call the lanterns *luminarias*, which in the north is the term for the bonfires of Christmas Eve.

Heishi: Shell jewelry.

Hornos: Outdoor domed ovens.

Kiva: A ceremonial room, rounded and built at least partially underground, used by Native Americans of the Southwest. Entrance is gained from the roof.

Kiva fireplace: A corner fireplace whose round form resembles that of a kiva.

Latilla: Small pole, often made of aspen, used as a lath in a ceiling.

Nicho: A built-in shelf cut into an adobe or stucco wall.

Placita: A small plaza.

Portal: A porch or large covered area adjacent to a house.

Pueblo Revival (also informally called Pueblo-style): Most homes in this style, modeled after the traditional dwellings of the Southwest Pueblo Indians, are cube or rectangle shaped. Other characteristics are flat roofs, thick adobe or stucco walls, small windows, rounded corners, and viga beams.

Retablo: Holy image painted on wood or tin.

Santero: Maker of religious images.

Territorial style: This modified Pueblo style evolved in the late 19th century when New Mexico was still a U.S. territory. The Territorial home incorporates a broad central hallway and entryway and adds wooden elements, such as window frames, in neoclassical style; some structures have pitched (often corrugated or flat metal) rather than flat roofs, and brick copings.

Terrones adobes: Adobe cut from the ground rather than formed from mud.

Viga: Horizontal roof beam made of logs, usually protruding from the side of the house.

Flora & Fauna

Cholla: A term for various species of spiny cactus, which grow irregular branches with clustered berries.

Collared peccary: Known also as javelina hogs, these piglike animals are aggressive and highly protective of their young. They're commonly found in the mountains of southwestern New Mexico.

Creosote: Rare desert rain enhances the strong, medicinelike fragrance of this somewhat scraggly plant common to arid regions. Nicknamed greasewood for its oily resins, creosote produces evergreen leaves and small yellow or green flowers.

Desert horned lizard: Called horned or horny toads by locals, this species has a flattened body and rows of tiny spikes that resemble formidable armor.

Desert tarantula: It's a rare but startling sight to see thousands of large, dark tarantulas skittering across New Mexico highways after a heavy rain. With a leg span of up to 4 inches, this cousin of tropical spiders can look terrifying. It rarely bites, and its venom usually produces only a mild swelling on human skin.

El lobo: The Spanish term for the Mexican gray wolf once common in New Mexico but no longer found in the wild. Efforts are being made to reintroduce this genetically unique species to its original home range.

Jackrabbit: Tall, rangy, and graceful, this long-eared rabbit can sprint and hop at astonishing speeds.

Juniper: A shrub or tree, common to arid regions, with a waxy covering that retains moisture.

Kangaroo rat: This nocturnal rodent is a master of water conservation, as well as leaping, which helps it evade predators. Its kidneys expel very little water, and its body can convert a meal of dry seeds to moisture.

Lechuguilla: This fleshy desert plant has daggerlike leaves and tall stalks of yellow flowers.

Mesquite: Thorny branches and bean pods distinguish this common range plant, technically a small tree, which grows in thickets.

Mexican freetail bat: These bats are harmless to humans, except for the rare rabid individual. The half million bats living in Carlsbad Caverns during summer months can consume 3 tons of insects in one night.

Mountain lion: Solitary and stealthy, the mountain lion long has been a legend of the Old West. Habitats are disappearing, making remaining wildernesses of New Mexico a refuge for the creature.

Mule deer: The long ears of this timid deer explain the name. The animal thrives in virtually every corner of New Mexico, from forests to sand dunes.

Ocotillo: This common desert plant grows in clusters of thorny branches capped by red, tubular blossoms.

Piñon pine: These robust pines found in mountains and foothills throughout the Southwest survive drought through taproots that plunge as deep as 40 feet into the soil. The resinous wood produces fragrant scents from Santa Fe fireplaces, while tasty piñon nuts garnish foods.

Prickly pear cactus: The fleshy, rounded pads of this common cactus inspired its nickname "elephant ears."

Pronghorn: Look alongside roadways for a flash of white from the rear of this delicate creature, often incorrectly called an antelope. Pronghorns roam in bands and prefer open rangeland.

Quail: Highly tolerant of dry weather, this sociable bird generally is found in a covey, which tries to sneak out of danger by running through the cover of brush. The birds take wing in short bursts of flight.

Raptor: A bird of prey, such as a hawk or owl.

Roadrunner: The crested head and speckled feathers of this desert dweller can be seen making mad dashes across or alongside New Mexico highways. The fearless fowl eats lizards and snakes. Its curiosity is well known to state residents, who sometimes find themselves face-to-face with a roadrunner peering through a window.

Sagebrush: This greenish-gray shrub carpets much of northern New Mexico, blooms with small yellow flowers, and smells slightly like the herb sage (to which it is not related). It's often collected, dried, and bundled into incense sticks or potpourri.

Soaptree yucca: White flowers adorn the broomsticklike protrusions of this plant, New Mexico's state flower.

Tamarisk: Imported from overseas, the tamarisk (or salt cedar) is a small evergreen found choking waterways throughout the Southwest. The non-native plant is a major nuisance, sucking up precious moisture and providing very little benefit as animal habitat.

Texas madrone: The reddish, smooth bark of this unusual evergreen gives it the nickname "lady's legs." The tree dresses up with urn-shape white-and-pink flowers and red fruit. A relic of the last ice age, this variety is found only in isolated regions of west Texas and southeastern New Mexico. Look for it at Guadalupe Mountains National Park.

Vinegaroon: You'll know it when you see it. This dark, whip-tail scorpion appears fearsome at up to 3 inches long. It waves wicked-looking pincers and sprays an acid that reeks of vinegar. Yet, it's harmless to humans—unlike some of its more venomous cousins.

Western diamondback: This rattlesnake is usually found coiled under shady bushes or lounging in cool cave entrances. Watch your step.

MENU GUIDE

Aguacate: Spanish for avocado, the key ingredient of guacamole.

Albóndigas: Meatballs, usually cooked with rice in a meat broth.

Bizcochitos: Buttery cookies flavored with cinnamon and anise seeds and served typically at Christmas but available throughout the year.

Bolsa del pobre: A seafood and vegetable dish; a specialty from Colima.

Burrito: A warm flour tortilla wrapped around meat, beans, and vegetables and smothered in chile and cheese; many New Mexicans also love breakfast burritos (filled with any combination of the above, along with eggs and, typically, bacon or sausage and potatoes).

Calabacitas: Summer squash, usually served with corn, chiles, and other vegetables.

Carne adovada: Red chile–marinated pork (or, occasionally, chicken).

Chalupa: A corn tortilla deep-fried in the shape of a bowl, filled with pinto beans (sometimes meat), and topped with cheese, guacamole, sour cream, lettuce, tomatoes, and salsa.

Chicharrones: Fried pork rinds.

Chilaquiles: Often served at breakfast, this casserolelike dish consists of small pieces of fried tortillas baked with red or green chiles, bits of chicken or cheese, and sometimes eggs.

Chile relleno: A large green chile pepper peeled, stuffed with cheese or a special mixture of spicy ingredients, dipped in batter, and fried.

Chiles: New Mexico's infamous hot peppers, which come in an endless variety of sizes and in various degrees of hotness, from the thumb-size jalapeño to the smaller and often hotter serrano. They can be canned or fresh, dried or cut up into salsa.

Most traditional New Mexican dishes are served either with green, red, or both types of chiles (ask for "Christmas" when indicating to your server that you'd like both red and green). Famous regional uses for green chile include green chile stew (usually made with shredded pork), green chile cheeseburgers, and green chile-and-cheese tamales.

Chili: A stewlike dish with Texas origins that typically contains beans, beef, and red chile.

Chimichanga: The same as a burrito only deep-fried and topped with a dab of sour cream or salsa. (The chimichanga was allegedly invented in Tucson, Arizona.)

Chipotle: A dried smoked jalapeño with a smoky, almost sweet, chocolaty flavor.

Chorizo: Well-spiced Spanish sausage, made with pork and red chiles.

Enchilada: A rolled or flat corn tortilla filled with meat, chicken, seafood, or cheese, an enchilada is covered with chile and baked. The ultimate enchilada is made with blue Native American corn tortillas. New Mexicans order them flat, sometimes topped with a fried egg.

Fajitas: A Tex-Mex dish of grilled beef, chicken, fish, or roasted vegetables and served with peppers, onions, and pico de gallo, served with tortillas; traditionally known as arracheras.

Flauta: A tortilla filled with cheese or meat and rolled into a flutelike shape ("flauta" means flute) and lightly fried.

Frijoles refritos: Refried beans, often seasoned with lard or cheese.

Frito Pie: Originally from Texas but extremely popular in New Mexican diners and short-order restaurants, this savory, humble casserole consists of Fritos snack chips layered with chile, cheese, green onions, and pinto beans.

Guacamole: Mashed avocado, mixed with tomatoes, garlic, onions, lemon juice, and chiles, used as a dip, a side dish, or a topping.

Hatch: A small southern New Mexico town in the Mesilla Valley, known for its outstanding production and quality of both green and red chile. The "Hatch" name often is found on canned chile food products.

Huevos rancheros: New Mexico's answer to eggs Benedict—eggs doused with chile and sometimes melted cheese, served on top of a corn tortilla (they're best with a side order of chorizo).

Nopalitos: The pads of the prickly pear cactus, typically cut up and served uncooked in salads or baked or stir-fried as a vegetable side dish. (The tangy-sweet, purplish-red fruit of the prickly pear are often used to make juice drinks and margaritas.)

Pan de cazón: Grilled shark with black beans and red onions on a tortilla; a specialty from Campeche.

Posole: Resembling popcorn soup, this is a sublime marriage of lime, hominy, pork, chile, garlic, and spices.

Quesadilla: A folded flour tortilla filled with cheese and meat or vegetables and warmed or lightly fried so the cheese melts.

Queso: Cheese; an ingredient in many Mexican and southwestern recipes (cheddar or jack is used most commonly in New Mexican dishes).

Ristra: String of dried red chile peppers, often used as decoration.

Salsa: Finely chopped concoction of green and red chile peppers, mixed with onion, garlic, and other spices.

Sopaipilla: Puffy deep-fried bread that's similar to Navajo fry bread (found in Arizona and western New Mexico); it's served either as a dessert with honey drizzled over it or savory as a meal stuffed with pinto beans or meat.

Taco: A corn or flour tortilla served either soft, or baked or fried and served in a hard shell; it's then stuffed with vegetables or spicy meat and garnished with shredded lettuce, chopped tomatoes, onions, and grated cheese.

Tacos al carbón: Shredded pork cooked in a mole sauce and folded into corn tortillas.

Tamale: Ground corn made into a dough, often filled with finely ground pork and red chiles; it's steamed in a corn husk.

Tortilla: A thin pancake made of corn or wheat flour, a tortilla is used as bread, as an edible "spoon," and as a container for other foods. Locals place butter in the center of a hot tortilla, roll it up, and eat it as a scroll.

Trucha en terra-cotta: Fresh trout wrapped in corn husks and baked in clay.

Verde: Spanish for "green," as in chile verde (a green chile sauce).

New Mexico Essentials

PLANNING TOOLS, EXPERT INSIGHT, GREAT CONTACTS

There are planners, and there are those who fly by the seat of their pants. We happily place ourselves among the planners. Our writers and editors try to anticipate all the issues you may face before and during any journey, and then they do their research. This section is the product of their efforts. Use it to get excited about your trip to New Mexico, to inform your travel planning, or to guide you on the road should the seat of your pants start to feel threadbare.

GETTING STARTED

We're really proud of our Web site: Fodors. com is a great place to begin any journey. Scan Travel Wire for suggested itineraries, travel deals, restaurant and hotel openings, and other up-to-the-minute info. Check out Booking to research prices and book plane tickets, hotel rooms, rental cars, and vacation packages. Head to Talk for on-the-ground pointers from travelers who frequent our message boards. You can also link to loads of other travel-related resources.

▌RESOURCES

ONLINE TRAVEL TOOLS

Check out the New Mexico Home page (⊕ www.state.nm.us) for information on state government, and for links to state agencies on doing business, working, learning, living, and visiting in the Land of Enchantment. A terrific general resource for just about every kind of recreational activity is ⊕ www.gorp.com; just click on the New Mexico link under "Destinations," and you'll be flooded with links to myriad topics, from wildlife refuges to ski trips to backpacking advice. Check the site of the New Mexico Film Office (⊕ www.nmfilm.com) for a list of movies shot in New Mexico as well as links to downloadable clips of upcoming made-in-New Mexico movies. A wide range of reviews and links to dining, culture, and services in Albuquerque and Santa Fe is available at ⊕ www.citysearch. com and ⊕ http://cityguide.aol.com, and ⊕ www.999dine.com is a site that sells steeply discounted meal certificates to dozens of top restaurants in Albuquerque, Santa Fe, and Taos. Visit ⊕ www. farmersmarketsnm.org for information on the dozens of great farmers' markets around the state, and see ⊕ www.nmwine. com for tours and details related to the region's burgeoning wine-making industry.

ALL ABOUT NEW MEXICO

Safety Transportation Security Administration (TSA) ⊕ www.tsa.gov

Time Zones Timeanddate.com ⊕ www. timeanddate.com/worldclock can help you figure out the correct time anywhere.

Weather Accuweather.com ⊕ www. accuweather.com is an independent weather-forecasting service with good coverage of hurricanes. **Weather.com** ⊕ www.weather.com is the Web site for the Weather Channel.

Other Resources CIA World Factbook ⊕ www.odci.gov/cia/publications/factbook/index.html has profiles of every country in the world. It's a good source if you need some quick facts and figures.

VISITOR INFORMATION

The New Mexico Department of Tourism can provide general information on the state, but you'll find more specific and useful information by consulting the local chambers of commerce, tourism offices, and convention and visitors bureaus in individual communities throughout the state (⇨ See individual chapter Essentials).

Statewide Information New Mexico Department of Tourism ☎ 505/827-7400, 800/733-6396 Ext. 0643 ⊕ www.newmexico.org. **Indian Pueblo Cultural Center** ☎ 505/843-7270, 800/766-4405 outside New Mexico ⊕ www.indianpueblo.org.

National Forests USDA Forest Service, Southwestern Region ☎ 505/842-3292, 877/864-6985 for fire restrictions and closures ⊕ www.fs.fed.us/r3.

■ THINGS TO CONSIDER

GEAR

Typical of the Southwest, temperatures can vary considerably from sunup to sundown. Generally, you should **pack for warm days and chilly nights** from spring through fall, but this is a huge state with a tremendous range of elevations, so the most important thing is to check local weather conditions before you leave home and pack accordingly. In April for instance, you may need to pack for nighttime lows in the 20s and daytime highs in the 60s in Taos, but daytime highs in the 80s and nighttime lows in the 50s in Las Cruces. Any time of year pack at least a few warm outfits and a jacket; in winter pack very warm clothes—coats, parkas, and whatever else your body's thermostat and your ultimate destination dictate. Sweaters and jackets are also needed in summer at higher elevations, because though days are warm, nights can dip well below 50°F. And **bring comfortable shoes**; you're likely to be doing a lot of walking.

Typical of the Southwest and southern Rockies, temperatures can vary considerably in North-Central New Mexico from sunup to sundown. Generally, you should **pack for warm days and chilly nights** from late spring through early fall, and for genuinely nippy days and freezing nights in winter if you're headed to Taos and Santa Fe (Albuquerque runs about 10 to 15 degrees warmer). Because temperatures vary greatly even within this relatively compact area, it's important to check local weather conditions before you leave home and pack accordingly. In April for instance, you may need to pack for nighttime lows in the 20s and daytime highs in the 60s in Taos, but daytime highs in the low 80s and nighttime lows in the 40s in Albuquerque. Any time of year pack at least a few warm outfits and a jacket; in winter pack very warm clothes—coats, parkas, and whatever else your body's thermostat and your ultimate destination dictate. Sweaters and jackets are also needed in summer at higher elevations, because though days are warm, nights can dip well below 50°F. And **bring comfortable shoes**; you're likely to be doing a lot of walking.

New Mexico is one of the most informal and laid-back areas of the country, which for many is part of its appeal. Probably no more than three or four restaurants in the entire state enforce a dress code, even for dinner, though men are likely to feel more comfortable wearing a jacket in the major hotel dining rooms, and anyone wearing tennis shoes may feel out of place.

The Western look has, of course, never lost its hold on the West, though Western-style clothes now get mixed with tweed jackets, for example, for a more conservative, sophisticated image. You can wear your boots and big belt buckles in even the best places in Santa Fe, Taos, or Albuquerque, but if you come strolling through the lobby of the Eldorado Hotel looking like Hopalong Cassidy, you'll get some funny looks.

Bring skin moisturizer; even people who rarely need this elsewhere in the country can suffer from dry and itchy skin in New Mexico. And **bring sunglasses** to protect your eyes from the glare of lakes or ski slopes. High altitude can cause headaches and dizziness, so check with your doctor about medication to alleviate symptoms. Sunscreen is a necessity. When planning even a short day trip, especially if there's hiking or exercise involved, always pack a bottle or two of water—it's very easy to become dehydrated in New Mexico.

PASSPORTS & VISAS

PASSPORTS

We're always surprised at how few Americans have passports—only 25% at this writing. This number is expected to grow in coming years, when it becomes impossible to reenter the United States from trips to neighboring Canada or Mexico without one. Remember this: a passport verifies both your identity and nationality—a great reason to have one.

PACKING 101

Why do some people travel with a convoy of huge suitcases yet never have a thing to wear? How do others pack a duffle with a week's worth of outfits *and* supplies for every contingency? We realize that packing is a matter of style, but there's a lot to be said for traveling light. These tips help fight the battle of the bulging bag.

MAKE A LIST. In a recent Fodor's survey, 29% of respondents said they make lists (and often pack) a week before a trip. You can use your list to pack and to repack at the end of your trip. It can also serve as record of the contents of your suitcase—in case it disappears in transit.

THINK IT THROUGH. What's the weather like? Is this a business trip? A cruise? Going abroad? In some places dress may be more or less conservative than you're used to. As you create your itinerary, note outfits next to each activity (don't forget accessories).

EDIT YOUR WARDROBE. Plan to wear everything twice (better yet, thrice) and to do laundry along the way. Stick to one basic look—urban chic, sporty casual, etc. Build around one or two neutrals and an accent (e.g., black, white, and olive green). Women can freshen looks by changing scarves or jewelry. For a week's trip, you can look smashing with three bottoms, four or five tops, a sweater, and a jacket.

BE PRACTICAL. Put comfortable shoes atop your list. (Did we need to say this?) Pack lightweight, wrinkle-resistent, compact, washable items. (Or this?) Stack and roll clothes, so they'll wrinkle less. Unless you're on a guided tour or a cruise, select luggage you can readily carry. Porters, like good butlers, are hard to find these days.

CHECK WEIGHT AND SIZE LIMITATIONS. In the United States you may be charged extra for checked bags weighing more than 50 pounds. Abroad some airlines don't allow you to check bags over 60 to 70 pounds, or they charge outrageous fees for every excess pound—or bag. Carry-on size limitations can be stringent, too.

CHECK CARRY-ON RESTRICTIONS. Research restrictions with the TSA. Rules vary abroad, so check them with your airline if you're traveling overseas on a foreign carrier. Consider packing all but essentials (travel documents, prescription meds, wallet) in checked luggage. This leads to a "pack only what you can afford to lose" approach that might help you streamline.

RETHINK VALUABLES. On U.S. flights, airlines are liable for only about $2,800 per person for bags. On international flights, the liability limit is around $635 per bag. But items like computers, cameras, and jewelry aren't covered, and as gadgetry regularly goes on and of the list of carry-on no-no's, you can't count on keeping things safe by keeping them close. Although comprehensive travel policies may cover luggage, the liability limit is often a pittance. Your home-owner's policy may cover you sufficiently when you travel—or not.

LOCK IT UP. If you must pack valuables, use TSA-approved locks (about $10) that can be unlocked by all U.S. security personnel.

TAG IT. Always tag your luggage; use your business address if you don't want people to know your home address. Put the same information (and a copy of your itinerary) inside your luggage, too.

REPORT PROBLEMS IMMEDIATELY. If your bags—or things inside them—are damaged or go astray, file a written claim with your airline *before leaving the airport*. If the airline is at fault, it may give you money for essentials until your luggage arrives. Most lost bags are found within 48 hours, so alert the airline to your whereabouts for two or three days. If your bag was opened for security reasons in the United States and something is missing, file a claim with the TSA.

U.S. passports are valid for 10 years. You must apply in person if you're getting a passport for the first time; if your previous passport was lost, stolen, or damaged; or if your previous passport has expired and was issued more than 15 years ago or when you were under 16. All children under 18 must appear in person to apply for or renew a passport. Both parents must accompany any child under 14 (or send a notarized statement with their permission) and provide proof of their relationship to the child.

There are 13 regional passport offices, as well as 7,000 passport acceptance facilities in post offices, public libraries, and other governmental offices. If you're renewing a passport, you can do so by mail. Forms are available at passport acceptance facilities and online.

The cost to apply for a new passport is $97 for adults, $82 for children under 16; renewals are $67. Allow six weeks for processing, both for first-time passports and renewals. For an expediting fee of $60 you can reduce this time to about two weeks. If your trip is less than two weeks away, you can get a passport even more rapidly by going to a passport office with the necessary documentation. Private expediters can get things done in as little as 48 hours, but charge hefty fees for their services.

■ TIP➔ Before your trip, make two copies of your passport's data page (one for someone at home and another for you to carry separately). Or scan the page and e-mail it to someone at home and/or yourself.

U.S. Passport Information U.S. Department of State ☎ 877/487-2778 ⊕ http://travel. state.gov/passport.

U.S. Passport & Visa Expediters A. Briggs Passport & Visa Expeditors ☎ 800/806-0581 or 202/464-3000 ⊕ www.abriggs.com. **American Passport Express** ☎ 800/455-5166 or 603/559-9888 ⊕ www. americanpassport.com. **Passport Express** ☎ 800/362-8196 or 401/272-4612 ⊕ www. passportexpress.com. **Travel Document Systems** ☎ 800/874-5100 or 202/638-3800

⊕ www.traveldocs.com. **Travel the World Visas** ☎ 866/886-8472 or 301/495-7700 ⊕ www.world-visa.com.

TRIP INSURANCE

What kind of coverage do you honestly need? Do you even need trip insurance at all? Take a deep breath and read on.

We believe that comprehensive trip insurance is especially valuable if you're booking a very expensive or complicated trip (particularly to an isolated region) or if you're booking far in advance. Who knows what could happen six months down the road? But whether or not you get insurance has more to do with how comfortable you are assuming all that risk yourself.

Comprehensive travel policies typically cover trip-cancellation and interruption, letting you cancel or cut your trip short because of a personal emergency, illness, or, in some cases, acts of terrorism in your destination. Such policies also cover evacuation and medical care. Some also cover you for trip delays because of bad weather or mechanical problems as well as for lost or delayed baggage. Another type of coverage to look for is financial default— that is, when your trip is disrupted because a tour operator, airline, or cruise line goes out of business. Generally you must buy this when you book your trip or shortly thereafter, and it's only available to you if your operator isn't on a list of excluded companies.

If you're going abroad, consider buying medical-only coverage at the very least. Neither Medicare nor some private insurers cover medical expenses anywhere outside of the United States besides Mexico and Canada (including time aboard a cruise ship, even if it leaves from a U.S. port). Medical-only policies typically reimburse you for medical care (excluding that related to pre-existing conditions) and hospitalization abroad, and provide for evacuation. You still have to pay the bills and await reimbursement from the insurer, though.

Trip Insurance Resources

INSURANCE COMPARISON SITES		
Insure My Trip.com	800/487-4722	www.insuremytrip.com
Square Mouth.com	800/240-0369	www.quotetravelinsurance.com
COMPREHENSIVE TRAVEL INSURERS		
Access America	866/807-3982	www.accessamerica.com
CSA Travel Protection	800/873-9855	www.csatravelprotection.com
HTH Worldwide	610/254-8700 or 888/243-2358	www.hthworldwide.com
Travelex Insurance	888/457-4602	www.travelex-insurance.com
Travel Guard International	715/345-0505 or 800/826-4919	www.travelguard.com
Travel Insured International	800/243-3174	www.travelinsured.com
MEDICAL-ONLY INSURERS		
International Medical Group	000/628-4664	www.imglobal.com
International SOS	215/942-8000 or 713/521-7611	www.internationalsos.com
Wallach & Company	800/237-6615 or 504/687-3166	www.wallach.com

Expect comprehensive travel insurance policies to cost about 4% to 7% of the total price of your trip (it's more like 12% if you're over age 70). A medical-only policy may or may not be cheaper than a comprehensive policy. Always read the fine print of your policy to make sure that you are covered for the risks that are of most concern to you. Compare several policies to make sure you're getting the best price and range of coverage available.

■ TIP→ OK. You know you can save a bundle on trips to warm-weather destinations by traveling in rainy season. But there's also a chance that a severe storm will disrupt your plans. The solution? Look for hotels and resorts that offer storm-hurricane guarantees. Although they rarely allow refunds, most guarantees do let you rebook later if a storm strikes.

BOOKING YOUR TRIP

Unless your cousin is a travel agent, you're probably among the millions of people who make most of their travel arrangements online. But have you ever wondered just what the differences are between an online travel agent (a Web site through which you make reservations instead of going directly to the airline, hotel, or car-rental company), a discounter (a firm that does a high volume of business with a hotel chain or airline and accordingly gets good prices), a wholesaler (one that makes cheap reservations in bulk and then re-sells them to people like you), and an aggregator (one that compares all the offerings so you don't have to)? Is it truly better to book directly on an airline or hotel Web site? And when does a real live travel agent come in handy?

ONLINE

You really have to shop around. A travel wholesaler such as Hotels.com or Hotel-Club.net can be a source of good rates, as can discounters such as Hotwire or Priceline, particularly if you can bid for your hotel room or airfare. Indeed, such sites sometimes have deals that are unavailable elsewhere. They do, however, tend to work only with hotel chains (which makes them just plain useless for getting hotel reservations outside of major cities) or big airlines (so that often leaves out upstarts like jetBlue and some foreign carriers like Air India). Also, with discounters and wholesalers you must generally prepay, and everything is nonrefundable. And before you fork over the dough, be sure to check the terms and conditions, so you know what a given company will do for you if there's a problem and what you'll have to deal with on your own.

■ TIP➜ To be absolutely sure everything was processed correctly, confirm reservations made through online travel agents, discounters, and wholesalers directly with your hotel before leaving home.

Booking engines like Expedia, Travelocity, and Orbitz are actually travel agents, albeit high-volume, online ones. And airline travel packagers like American Airlines Vacations and Virgin Vacations—well, they're travel agents, too. But they may still not work with all the world's hotels.

An aggregator site will search many sites and pull the best prices for airfares, hotels, and rental cars from them. Most aggregators compare the major travel-booking sites such as Expedia, Travelocity, and Orbitz; some also look at airline Web sites, though rarely the sites of smaller budget airlines. Some aggregators also compare other travel products, including complex packages—a good thing, as you can sometimes get the best overall deal by booking an air-and-hotel package.

WITH A TRAVEL AGENT

If you use an agent—brick-and-mortar or virtual—you'll pay a fee for the service. And know that the service you get from some online agents isn't comprehensive. For example Expedia and Travelocity don't search for prices on budget airlines like jetBlue, Southwest, or small foreign carriers. That said, some agents (online or not) *do* have access to fares that are difficult to find otherwise, and the savings can more than make up for any surcharge.

A knowledgeable brick-and-mortar travel agent can be a godsend if you're booking a cruise, a package trip that's not available to you directly, an air pass, or a complicated itinerary including several overseas flights. What's more, travel agents that specialize in a destination may have exclusive access to certain deals and insider information on things such as charter flights. Agents who specialize in types of travelers (senior citizens, gays and lesbians, naturists) or types of trips (cruises, luxury travel, safaris) can also be invaluable.

Online Booking Resources

AGGREGATORS	
Kayak	www.kayak.com; also looks at cruises and vacation packages.
Mobissimo	www.mobissimo.com
Qixo even travel insurance.	www.qixo.com; also compares cruises, vacation packages, and
Sidestep travel deals.	www.sidestep.com; also compares vacation packages and lists
Travelgrove	www.travelgrove.com; also compares cruises and packages.
BOOKING ENGINES	
Cheap Tickets	www.cheaptickets.com; a discounter.
Expedia	www.expedia.com; a large online agency that charges a booking fee for airline tickets.
Hotwire	www.hotwire.com; a discounter.
lastminute.com	www.lastminute.com; specializes in last-minute travel; the main site is for the U.K., but it has a link to a U.S. site.
Luxury Link	www.luxurylink.com; has auctions (surprisingly good deals) as well as offers on the high-end side of travel.
Onetravel.com and packages.	www.onetravel.com; a discounter for hotels, car rentals, airfares,
Orbitz	www.orbitz.com; charges a booking fee for airline tickets, but gives a clear breakdown of fees and taxes before you book.
Priceline.com	www.priceline.com; a discounter that also allows bidding.
Travel.com	www.travel.com; allows you to compare its rates with those of other booking engines.
Travelocity	www.travelocity.com; charges a booking fee for airline tickets, but promises good problem resolution.
ONLINE ACCOMMODATIONS	
Hotelbook.com	www.hotelbook.com; focuses on independent hotels worldwide
Hotel Club	www.hotelclub.net; good for major cities worldwide.
Hotels.com	www.hotels.com; a big Expedia-owned wholesaler that offers rooms in hotels all over the world.
Quikbook	www.quikbook.com; offers "pay when you stay" reservations that let you settle your bill at check out, not when you book.
OTHER RESOURCES	
Bidding For Travel	www.biddingfortravel.com; a good place to figure out what you can get and for how much before you start bidding on, say, Priceline.

A top-notch agent planning your trip to Russia will make sure you get the correct visa application and complete it on time; the one booking your cruise may get you a cabin upgrade or arrange to have bottle of champagne chilling in your cabin when you embark. And complain about the surcharges all you like, but when things don't work out the way you'd hoped, it's nice to have an agent to put things right.

■ **TIP→** Remember that Expedia, Travelocity, and Orbitz are travel agents, not just booking engines. To resolve any problems with a reservation made through these companies, contact them first.

There isn't a great advantage to using a travel agent to book a trip to New Mexico, as this is a region that's most often visited by independent travelers, and relatively few companies offer package deals and major tours. You'll generally have as much luck using online travel sites, such as Expedia.com and Orbitz.com, to book airfare, car rentals, and hotels as you would using a travel agent.

Agent Resources American Society of Travel Agents ☎ 703/739-2782 ⊕ www.travelsense. org.

■ ACCOMMODATIONS

With the exceptions of Santa Fe and Taos, two rather upscale tourist-driven destinations with some of the higher lodging rates in the Southwest, New Mexico has fairly low hotel prices. Albuquerque is loaded with chain hotels, and four or five new ones seem to open each year, further saturating the market and driving down prices. During busy times or certain festivals (the Balloon Fiesta in Albuquerque, some of the art markets and events in Taos and Santa Fe), it can be extremely difficult to find a hotel room, and prices can be steep. Check to make sure there's not a major event planned for the time you're headed to New Mexico, and book well ahead if so. New Mexico Central Reservations offers good deals at a number of properties throughout the state, but you'll find an even bigger selection (and often better deals) by checking the usual major travel sites, such as ⊕ www.expedia.com. You'll be charged a hotel tax, which varies among towns and counties, throughout New Mexico.

Most hotels and other lodgings require you to give your credit-card details before they will confirm your reservation. If you don't feel comfortable e-mailing this information, ask if you can fax it (some places even prefer faxes). However you book, get confirmation in writing and have a copy of it handy when you check in.

If you book through an online travel agent, discounter, or wholesaler, you might even want to confirm your reservation with the hotel before leaving home—just to be sure everything was processed correctly.

Be sure you understand the hotel's cancellation policy. Some places allow you to cancel without any kind of penalty—even if you prepaid to secure a discounted rate—if you cancel at least 24 hours in advance. Others require you to cancel a week in advance or penalize you the cost of one night. Small inns and B&Bs are most likely to require you to cancel far in advance. Most hotels allow children under a certain age to stay in their parents' room at no extra charge, but others charge for them as extra adults; find out the cutoff age for discounts.

■ **TIP→** Assume that hotels operate on the European Plan (EP, no meals) unless we specify

---

WORD OF MOUTH

Did the resort look as good in real life as it did in the photos? Did you sleep like a baby, or were the walls paper thin? Did you get your money's worth? Rate hotels and write your own reviews in Travel Ratings or start a discussion about your favorite places in Travel Talk on www.fodors. com. Your comments might even appear in our books. Yes, you, too, can be a correspondent!

that they use the Breakfast Plan (**BP**, with full breakfast), Continental Plan (**CP**, continental breakfast), Full American Plan (**FAP**, all meals), Modified American Plan (**MAP**, breakfast and dinner) or are all-inclusive (**AI**, all meals and most activities).

Reservations New Mexico Central Reservations ☎ 800/466-7829 ⊕ www.nmtravel. com.

APARTMENT & HOUSE RENTALS

Some parts of New Mexico are popular for short- and long-term vacation rentals, such as Santa Fe, Taos, and Ruidoso. See the book's individual regional chapters for rental listings in these locations.

BED & BREAKFASTS

B&Bs in New Mexico run the gamut from rooms in locals' homes to grandly restored adobe or Victorian homes. Rates in Santa Fe and Taos tend to be high; they're a little lower in Albuquerque and rival those of chain motels in the outlying areas. Good deals can be found in southern New Mexico as well. See the book's individual chapters for names of local reservation agencies.

Reservation Services Bed & Breakfast.com ☎ 512/322-2710 or 800/462-2632 ⊕ www. bedandbreakfast.com also sends out an online newsletter. **Bed & Breakfast Inns Online** ☎ 615/868-1946 or 800/215-7365 ⊕ www. bbonline.com. **BnB Finder.com** ☎ 212/432-7693 or 888/547-8226 ⊕ www.bnbfinder.com. **New Mexico Bed and Breakfast Association** ☎ 800/661-6649 ⊕ www.nmbba.org.

HOME EXCHANGES

With a direct home exchange you stay in someone else's home while they stay in yours. Some outfits also deal with vacation homes, so you're not actually staying in someone's full-time residence, just their vacant weekend place.

Exchange Clubs Home Exchange.com ☎ 800/877-8723 ⊕ www.homeexchange. com; $59.95 for a 1-year online listing. **Home-Link International** ☎ 800/638-3841 ⊕ www. homelink.org; $80 yearly for Web-only membership; $125 includes Web access and 2 cata-

---

10 WAYS TO SAVE

1. Join "frequent guest" programs. You may get preferential treatment in room choice and/or upgrades in your favorite chains.

2. Call direct. You can sometimes get a better price if you call a hotel's local toll-free number (if available) rather than a central reservations number.

3. Check online. Check hotel Web sites, as not all chains are represented on all travel sites.

4. Look for specials. Always inquire about packages and corporate rates.

5. Look for price guarantees. For overseas trips, look for guaranteed rates. With your rate locked in you won't pay more, even if the price goes up in the local currency.

6. Look for weekend deals at business hotels. High-end chains catering to business travelers are often busy only on weekdays; to fill rooms they often drop rates dramatically on weekends.

7. Ask about taxes. Verify whether local hotel taxes are included in quoted rates. In some places taxes can add 20% or more to your bill.

8. Read the fine print. Watch for add-ons, including resort fees, energy surcharges, and "convenience" fees for such things as unlimited local phone service you won't use or a free newspaper in a language you can't read.

9. Know when to go. If your destination's high season is December through April and you're trying to book, say, in late April, you might save money by changing your dates by a week or two. Ask when rates go down, though: if your dates straddle peak and non-peak seasons, a property may still charge peak-season rates for the entire stay.

10. Weigh your options (we can't say this enough). Weigh transportation times and costs against the savings of staying in a hotel that's cheaper because it's out of the way.

10 WAYS TO SAVE

1. Nonrefundable is best. If saving money is more important than flexibility, then nonrefundable tickets work, but you'll pay dearly if you change your plans.

2. Comparison shop. Web sites and travel agents can have different arrangements with the airlines and offer different prices for exactly the same flights.

3. Beware those prices. Many airline Web sites—and most ads—show prices without taxes and surcharges. Don't buy until you know the full price.

4. Stay loyal. Stick with one or two frequent-flier programs (many airlines allow you to assign miles earned to an airline partner's frequent-flier program). You'll rack up free trips faster and you'll accumulate more quickly the perks that make trips easier.

5. Watch those ticketing fees. Surcharges are usually added when you buy your ticket anywhere but on an airline Web site. (That includes by phone—even if you call the airline directly—and paper tickets regardless of how you book).

6. Check early and often. Start looking for cheap fares up to a year in advance. Keep looking until you find a price you like.

7. Don't work alone. Some Web sites have tracking features that will e-mail you immediately when good deals are posted.

8. Jump on the good deals. Waiting even a few minutes might mean paying more.

9. Be flexible. Look for departures on Tuesday, Wednesday, and Thursday, typically the cheapest days to travel. Check on prices for departures at different times and to and from alternative airports.

10. Weigh your options. What you get can be as important as what you save. A cheaper flight might have a long layover or it might land at a secondary airport, where ground transportation costs may be higher.

logs. **Intervac U.S.** ☎ 800/756-4663 ⊕ www.intervacus.com; $78.88 for Web-only membership; $126 includes Web access and a catalog.

HOSTELS

Hostels offer bare-bones lodging at low, low prices—often in shared dorm rooms with shared baths—to people of all ages, though the primary market is young travelers, especially students. Most hostels serve breakfast; dinner and/or shared cooking facilities may also be available. In some hostels you aren't allowed to be in your room during the day, and there may be a curfew at night. Nevertheless, hostels provide a sense of community, with public rooms where travelers often gather to share stories. Many hostels are affiliated with Hostelling International (HI), an umbrella group of hostel associations with some 4,500 member properties in more than 70 countries. Other hostels are completely independent and may be nothing more than a really cheap hotel.

Membership in any HI association, open to travelers of all ages, allows you to stay in HI-affiliated hostels at member rates. One-year membership is about $28 for adults; hostels charge about $10–$30 per night. Members have priority if the hostel is full; they're also eligible for discounts around the world, even on rail and bus travel in some countries.

Several New Mexico communities have hostels, including Albuquerque, Cedar Crest (on the Turquoise Trail, near Albuquerque), Cloudcroft, Cuba, Oscuro (south of Carrizozo), Santa Fe, Taos, Truth or Consequences, and Tucumcari. **Hostelling International—USA** ☎ 301/495-1240 ⊕ www.hiusa.org.

▌AIRLINE TICKETS

Most domestic airline tickets are electronic; international tickets may be either electronic or paper. With an e-ticket the only thing you receive is an e-mailed receipt citing your itinerary and reservation and ticket numbers. The greatest advantage of an e-ticket is that if you lose your receipt, you can simply print out another copy or ask the airline to do it for you at check-in. You usually pay a surcharge (up to $50) to get a paper ticket, if you can get one at all. The sole advantage of a paper ticket is that it may be easier to endorse over to another airline if your flight is canceled and the airline with which you booked can't accommodate you on another flight.

■ TIP→ Discount air passes that let you travel economically in a country or region must often be purchased before you leave home. In some cases you can only get them through a travel agent.

The least expensive airfares to New Mexico are priced for round-trip travel and must usually be purchased in advance. Because the discount airline Southwest serves Albuquerque and El Paso, fares from these cities to airports served by Southwest are often 20% to 40% less than to other airports (whether or not you actually fly Southwest, as competing airlines often match Southwest's fares). For instance, it's almost always cheaper to fly from Hartford, Providence, or Baltimore (all served by Southwest) to Albuquerque than from Boston, New York, or Washington. Airlines generally allow you to change your return date for a fee; Southwest Airlines is, again, the exception—they allow you to change your return date or cancel your flight for no fee, although you'll have to pay any higher fare if the flight you rebook costs more than your original one.

▮ RENTAL CARS

When you reserve a car, ask about cancellation penalties, taxes, drop-off charges (if you're planning to pick up the car in one city and leave it in another), and surcharges (for being under or over a certain age, for additional drivers, or for driving across state or country borders or beyond a specific distance from your point of

10 WAYS TO SAVE

1. Beware of cheap rates. Those great rates aren't so great when you add in taxes, surcharges, and insurance.

2. Rent weekly. Weekly rates are usually better than daily ones. Even if you only want to rent for five or six days, ask for the weekly rate; it's virtually always cheaper than the daily rate for that period of time.

3. Don't forget the locals. Price local companies as well as the majors.

4. Airport rentals can cost more. Airports often add surcharges, which you can sometimes avoid by renting from an agency whose office is just off airport property.

5. Wholesalers can help. Investigate wholesalers, which don't own fleets but rent in bulk from firms that do, and which frequently offer better rates (note that you must usually pay for such rentals before leaving home).

6. Look for rate guarantees. With your rate locked in, you won't pay more, even if the price goes up in the local currency.

7. Fill up farther away. Avoid higher gas costs by filling the tank at a station well away from where you plan to turn in the car—avoid pricey gas stations near airports.

8. Pump it yourself. Don't prepay for the tank of gas that's in the car when you rent it unless you plan to do a lot of driving. Even then, it's cheaper to pump it yourself.

9. Get all your discounts. Find out whether a credit card you carry or organization or frequent-renter program to which you belong has a discount program. And confirm that such discounts really are a deal. You can often do better with special weekend or weekly rates offered by a rental agency.

10. Check out packages. Adding a car rental onto your air/hotel vacation package may be cheaper than renting a car separately.

Car Rental Resources

AUTOMOBILE ASSOCIATIONS		
American Automobile Association	315/797-5000	www.aaa.com; most contact with the organization is through state and regional members.
National Automobile Club	650/294-7000	www.thenac.com; membership open to CA residents only.
LOCAL AGENCIES		
Enterprise	800/325-8007	www.enterprise.com
Sears	800/527-0770	www.sears.com
Thrifty	800/367-2277	www.thrifty.com
MAJOR AGENCIES		
Alamo	800/462-5266	www.alamo.com
Avis	800/230-4898	www.avis.com
Budget	800/527-0700	www.budget.com
Hertz	800/654-3131	www.hertz.com
National Car Rental	800/227-7368	www.nationalcar.com

rental). All these things can add substantially to your costs. Request car seats and extras such as GPS when you book.

Rates are sometimes—but not always—better if you book in advance or reserve through a rental agency's Web site. There are other reasons to book ahead, though: for popular destinations, during busy times of the year, or to ensure that you get certain types of cars (vans, SUVs, exotic sports cars).

■ TIP→ Make sure that a confirmed reservation guarantees you a car. Agencies sometimes overbook, particularly for busy weekends and holiday periods.

You really need a car to explore most of New Mexico—even in cities like Albuquerque and Santa Fe, it's easiest to get around with a car. All the major car-rental agencies are represented at Albuquerque's and El Paso's airports, and you can also find a limited number of car-rental agencies in other communities throughout the state.

Rates at Albuquerque's airport begin at around $23 a day and $140 a week for an economy car with air-conditioning, automatic transmission, and unlimited mileage;

although you should expect to pay more during busier times. The same car in El Paso typically goes for about the same or even a bit less, again depending on the time of year. If you want to explore the backcountry, consider renting an SUV, which will cost you about $40 to $60 per day and $200 to $400 per week, depending on the size of the SUV and the time of year. Dollar in Albuquerque has a fleet of smaller SUVs, still good on dirt roads and with much better mileage than larger ones, and they often run extremely reasonable deals, as low as $175 a week. You can save money by renting at a nonairport location, as you then are able to avoid the hefty (roughly) 10% in extra taxes charged at airports.

CAR-RENTAL INSURANCE

Everyone who rents a car wonders whether the insurance that the rental companies offer is worth the expense. No one—including us—has a simple answer. It all depends on how much regular insurance you have, how comfortable you are with risk, and whether money is an issue.

If you own a car and carry comprehensive car insurance for both collision and liability, your personal auto insurance will probably cover a rental, but read your policy's fine print to be sure. If you don't have auto insurance, then you should probably buy the collision- or loss-damage waiver (CDW or LDW) from the rental company. This eliminates your liability for damage to the car. Some credit cards offer CDW coverage, but it's usually supplemental to your own insurance and rarely covers SUVs, minivans, luxury models, and the like. If your coverage is secondary, you may still be liable for loss-of-use costs from the car-rental company (again, read the fine print). But no credit-card insurance is valid unless you use that card for *all* transactions, from reserving to paying the final bill.

■ TIP→ Diners Club offers primary CDW coverage on all rentals reserved and paid for with the card. This means that Diners Club's company—not your own car insurance—pays in case of an accident. It doesn't mean that your car-insurance company won't raise your rates once it discovers you had an accident.

You may also be offered supplemental liability coverage; the car-rental company is required to carry a minimal level of liability coverage insuring all renters, but it's rarely enough to cover claims in a really serious accident if you're at fault. Your own auto-insurance policy will protect you if you own a car; if you don't, you have to decide whether you are willing to take the risk.

U.S. rental companies sell CDWs and LDWs for about $15 to $25 a day; supplemental liability is usually more than $10 a day. The car-rental company may offer you all sorts of other policies, but they're rarely worth the cost. Personal accident insurance, which is basic hospital-ization coverage, is an especially egregious rip-off if you already have health insurance.

■ TIP→ You can decline the insurance from the rental company and purchase it through a third-party provider such as Travel Guard (⊕ www.travelguard.com)—$9 per day for $35,000 of coverage. That's sometimes just under half the price of the CDW offered by some car-rental companies.

■ GUIDED TOURS

Guided tours are a good option when you don't want to do it all yourself. You travel along with a group (sometimes large, sometimes small), stay in prebooked hotels, eat with your fellow travelers (the cost of meals sometimes included in the price of your tour, sometimes not), and follow a schedule. But not all guided tours are an if-it's-Tuesday-this-must-be-Belgium experience. A knowledgeable guide can take you places that you might never discover on your own, and you may be pushed to see more than you would have otherwise. Tours aren't for everyone, but they can be just the thing for trips to places where making travel arrangements is difficult or time-consuming (particularly when you don't speak the language). Whenever you book a guided tour, find out what's included and what isn't. A "land-only" tour includes all your travel (by bus, in most cases) in the destination, but not necessarily your flights to and from or even within it. Also, in most cases prices in tour brochures don't include fees and taxes. And remember that you'll be expected to tip your guide (in cash) at the end of the tour.

Recommended Companies New Mexico Guides Association ☎ 505/988-8022 ⊕ www.nmguides.com.

TRANSPORTATION

A tour bus or car is the best way to take in the entire state. Public transportation options do exist in some metropolitan areas, but they are not very convenient for visitors. City buses and taxi service are available only in a few larger communities such as Albuquerque, Santa Fe, and Las Cruces. Don't expect to find easy transportation for rural excursions.

■ TIP➡ Ask the local tourist board about hotel and local transportation packages that include tickets to major museum exhibits or other special events.

■ BY AIR

To reach New Mexico by air, you have two primary options: if you're visiting central or northern New Mexico, it's best to fly into Albuquerque, and if you're headed to the southern part of the state, El Paso may make more sense. However, El Paso is smaller and served by far fewer flights, so depending on where you're flying from, it can still be easier to fly into Albuquerque than El Paso even when visiting the southern part of the state. Some visitors to Taos and northeastern New Mexico may also want to consider flying into Denver, which is an hour or two farther than Albuquerque but receives a high number of direct domestic and international flights. A few smaller airports in New Mexico (Santa Fe, Farmington) also receive very limited commercial flights. From Albuquerque airport, ground transportation is available throughout North-Central New Mexico, and commuter air service is available to Farmington, Hobbs, Carlsbad, Roswell, and a few other communities around the state. El Paso has ground transportation to Las Cruces. Although Albuquerque and El Paso have small, clean, and user-friendly airports, they also have relatively few direct flights compared with larger cities around the country. With a few exceptions, travelers coming from the East Coast and to a certain extent the West Coast have to connect through other airports to fly into Albuquerque and, especially, El Paso.

Flying time between Albuquerque and Los Angeles is 2 hours for direct flights (available only on Southwest Airlines) and 3½ to 4 when connecting through another airport; Chicago, 2 hours and 45 minutes; New York, 4½ hours for direct flights (available only on Continental Airlines) and 5½ to 6½ when connecting through another airport; Dallas, 1 hour and 45 minutes.

Airlines & Airports Airline and Airport Links.com ⊕ www.airlineandairportlinks.com has links to many of the world's airlines and airports.
Airline Security Issues Transportation Security Administration ⊕ www.tsa.gov has answers for almost every question that might come up.

AIRPORTS

The major gateway to New Mexico is Albuquerque International Sunport (ABQ), which is 65 mi southwest of Santa Fe, 130 mi south of Taos, and 180 mi southeast of Farmington. Some travelers to Chama, Raton, and Taos prefer to fly into Denver (four to five hours' drive), which has far more direct flights to the rest of the country than Albuquerque—it's a scenic drive, too.

The gateway to southern New Mexico is El Paso International Airport (ELP), 50 mi southeast of Las Cruces, 160 mi southeast of Silver City, 135 mi southwest of Ruidoso, and 160 mi southwest of Carlsbad. The flight between El Paso and Albuquerque takes 50 minutes. The state's easternmost side can also be accessed via major airports in Texas, including Lubbock (170 mi east of Roswell) and Amarillo (105 mi northeast of Clovis).

■ TIP➡ Long layovers don't have to be only about sitting around or shopping. These days they can be about burning off vacation calo-

FLYING 101

Flying may not be as carefree as it once was, but there are some things you can do to make your trip smoother.

MINIMIZE THE TIME SPENT STANDING LINE. Buy an e-ticket, check in at an electronic kiosk, or—even better—check in on your airline's Web site before leaving home. Pack light and limit carry-on items to only the essentials.

ARRIVE WHEN YOU NEED TO. Research your airline's policy. It's usually at least an hour before domestic flights and two to three hours before international flights. But airlines at some busy airports have more stringent requirements. Check the TSA Web site for estimated security waiting times at major airports.

GET TO THE GATE. If you aren't at the gate at least 10 minutes before your flight is scheduled to take off (sometimes earlier), you won't be allowed to board.

DOUBLE-CHECK YOUR FLIGHT TIMES. Do this especially if you reserved far in advance. Schedules change, and alerts may not reach you.

DON'T GO HUNGRY. Ask whether your airline offers anything to eat; even when it does, be prepared to pay.

GET THE SEAT YOU WANT. Often, you can pick a seat when you buy your ticket on an airline Web site. But it's not guaranteed; the airline could change the plane after you book, so double-check. You can also select a seat if you check in electronically. Avoid seats on the aisle directly across from the lavatories. Frequent fliers say those are even worse than back-row seats that don't recline.

GOT KIDS? GET INFO. Ask the airline about its children's menus, activities, and fares. Sometimes infants and toddlers fly free if they sit on a parent's lap, and older children fly for half price in their own seats. Also inquire about policies involving car seats; having one may limit seating options.

Also ask about seat-belt extenders for car seats. And note that you can't count on a flight attendant to produce an extender; you may have to ask for one when you board.

CHECK YOUR SCHEDULING. Don't buy a ticket if there's less than an hour between connecting flights. Although schedules are padded, if anything goes wrong you might miss your connection. If you're traveling to an important function, consider departing a day early.

BRING PAPER. Even when using an e-ticket, always carry a hard copy of your receipt; most airports now require a boarding pass to get past security.

COMPLAIN AT THE AIRPORT. If your baggage goes astray or your flight goes awry, complain before leaving the airport. Most carriers require that you file a claim immediately.

BEWARE OF OVERBOOKED FLIGHTS. If a flight is oversold, the gate agent will usually ask for volunteers and offer some sort of compensation for taking a different flight. If you're bumped from a flight *involuntarily*, the airline must give you some kind of compensation if an alternate flight can't be found within one hour.

KNOW YOUR RIGHTS. If your flight is delayed because of something within the airline's control (bad weather doesn't count), the airline must get you to your destination on the same day, even if they have to book you on another airline and in an upgraded class. Read the Contract of Carriage, which is usually buried on the airline's Web site.

BE PREPARED. The Boy Scout motto is especially important if you're traveling during a stormy season. To quickly adjust your plans, program a few numbers into your cell: your airline, an airport hotel or two, your destination hotel, your car service, and/or your travel agent.

ries. Check out ⊕ www.airportgyms.com for lists of health clubs that are in or near many U.S. and Canadian airports.

Airport Information **Albuquerque International Sunport** ☎ 505/244-7700 ⊕ www.cabq.gov/airport. **Denver International Airport** ☎ 303/342-2000 ⊕ www.flydenver.com. **El Paso International Airport** ☎ 915/780-4749 ⊕ www.elpasointernationalairport.com.

Municipal Airports **Cavern City Air Terminal (CNM), Carlsbad** ☎ 505/887-6858. **Four Corners Regional Airport (FMN), Farmington** ☎ 505/599-1285. **Grant County Airport (SVC), Silver City area** ☎ 505/388-4554. **Roswell Municipal Airport (ROW)** ☎ 505/624-6700. **Santa Fe Municipal Airport (SAF)** ☎ 505/955-2908. **Sierra Blanca Regional Airport (SRR), Ruidoso area** ☎ 505/336-8111.

GROUND TRANSPORTATION

From the terminal at Albuquerque Airport, it's 5 to 20 minutes by car to get anywhere in town. Taxis, available at clearly marked stands, charge about $10 to $25 for most trips from the airport to around Albuquerque. Sun Tran Buses stop at the sunburst signs every 30 minutes; the fare is $1. Some hotels provide shuttle service to and from the airport. Airport Shuttle and Sunport Shuttle both cost less than $10 to most downtown locations.

Shuttle buses between the Albuquerque International Sunport and Santa Fe take about 1 hour and 20 minutes and cost about $20 to $25 each way. Shuttle service runs from Albuquerque to Taos and nearby ski areas; the ride takes 2¾ to 3 hours and costs $40–$50. In southern New Mexico there are daily trips between El Paso International Airport and Las Cruces (1 hour), Deming (2½ hours), and Silver City (3½ hours); the trip costs $35–$55 each way. There's also Greyhound bus service between Albuquerque International Sunport and many New Mexico towns and cities; fares are considerably less than those charged by the shuttle services listed here.

TRANSFERS BETWEEN AIRPORTS **Around Albuquerque** **Airport Shuttle** ☎ 505/765-1234. **Sun Tran Bus** ☎ 505/843-9200 ⊕ www.cabq.gov/transit. **Sunport Shuttle** ☎ 505/883-4966 or 866/505-4966 ⊕ www.sunportshuttle.com **Between Albuquerque & Santa Fe** **Sandia Shuttle Express** ☎ 505/474-5696 or 888/775-5696 ⊕ www.sandiashuttle.com. **Santa Fe Shuttle** ☎ 505/243-2300 or 888/833-2300. **Between Albuquerque & Taos** **Faust's Transportation** ☎ 505/758-3410 or 888/830-3410 ⊕ www.newmexiconet.com/trans/faust/faust.html. **Between El Paso & Southern New Mexico Destinations** **Las Cruces Shuttle Service** ☎ 505/525-1784 or 800/288-1784 ⊕ www.lascrucesshuttle.com.

FLIGHTS

Most major domestic airlines provide service to the state's main airport in Albuquerque; just over the border in Texas (near Las Cruces and Carlsbad), El Paso International Airport is served by American, Southwest, Delta, Continental, Frontier, Northwest, United, and US Airways. The state is also served by a few regional carriers. Mesa Airlines offers shuttle flights between Albuquerque and Farmington, Colorado Springs, Roswell, Hobbs, and Carlsbad. Great Lakes Airlines flies from Denver to both Farmington and Santa Fe and from Albuquerque to Silver City and Clovis (and then from Clovis on to Amarillo, Texas). Frontier Airlines flies daily from Denver to El Paso and Albuquerque. Skywest Airlines, a subsidiary of Delta, flies between Albuquerque and Salt Lake City.

■ BY BUS

Bus service on Texas, New Mexico & Oklahoma Coaches, affiliated with Greyhound Lines, is available to Alamogordo, Albuquerque, Carlsbad, Clovis, El Paso (TX), Farmington, Gallup, Grants, Las Cruces, Las Vegas, Raton, Roswell, Santa Fe, Taos, and several other towns and cities. Las Cruces Shuttle Service can get you from Silver City to Deming, Las Cruces, and El Paso.

Greyhound offers the **North America Discovery Pass,** which allows unlimited travel in the United States (and certain parts of Canada and Mexico) within any 7-, 15-, 30-, or 60-day period ($283–$645, depending on length of the pass). You can also buy similar passes covering different areas (America and Canada, the West Coast of North America, the East Coast of North America, Canada exclusively), and international travelers can purchase international versions of these same passes, which offer a greater variety of travel periods and cost considerably less. Greyhound also has senior-citizen, military, children's, and student discounts, which apply to individual fares and to the Discovery Pass.

Approximate standard sample one-way fares (based on 7-day advance purchase—prices can be 10% to 50% higher otherwise), times, and routes (note that times vary greatly depending on the number of stops) on major carriers: Albuquerque to Santa Fe, 70 minutes, $15; Albuquerque to Taos, 3 hours, $30; Albuquerque to Las Cruces, 4–5 hours, $25; Albuquerque to Ruidoso, 6½ hours, $40; Denver to Santa Fe, 9–10 hours, $50; Dallas to Las Cruces, 14–16 hours, $65; Oklahoma City to Albuquerque, 11–12 hours, $70; Tucson to Las Cruces, 5–7 hours, $55; and Phoenix to Albuquerque, 9–10 hours, $60.

Bus Information Greyhound/Texas. New Mexico & Oklahoma Coaches ☎ 800/231-2222 ⊕ www.tnmo.com. **Las Cruces Shuttle Service** ☎ 505/525-1784 or 800/288-1784 ⊕ www.lascrucesshuttle.com.

▌ BY CAR

A car is a basic necessity in New Mexico, as even the few cities are challenging to get around strictly using public transportation. Distances are considerable, but you can make excellent time on long stretches of interstate and other four-lane highways with speed limits of up to 75 mph. If you wander off major thoroughfares, slow down. Speed limits here generally are only 55 mph, and for good reason. Many such roadways have no shoulders; on many twisting and turning mountain roads speed limits dip to 25 mph. For the most part, the scenery you'll take in while driving makes the drive a form of sightseeing in itself.

Interstate 40 runs east–west across the middle of the state. Interstate 10 cuts across the southern part of the state from the Texas border at El Paso to the Arizona line, through Las Cruces, Deming, and Lordsburg. Interstate 25 runs north from the state line at El Paso through Albuquerque and Santa Fe, then angles northeast to the Colorado line through Raton.

U.S. highways connect all major cities and towns in the state with a good network of paved roads—many of the state's U.S. highways, including large stretches of U.S. 285 and U.S. 550, have four lanes and high speed limits. You can make nearly as good time on these roads as you can on interstates. State roads are mostly paved two-lane thoroughfares, but some are well-graded gravel. Roads on Native American lands are designated by wooden, arrow-shape signs and you'd best adhere to the speed limit; some roads on reservation or forest land aren't paved. Even in cities, quite a few surface streets are unpaved and often bumpy and narrow—Santa Fe, for instance, has a higher percentage of dirt roads than any other state capital in the nation.

Morning and evening rush-hour traffic is light in most of New Mexico, although it can get a bit heavy in Albuquerque. Keep in mind also that from most cities in New Mexico, there are only one or two main routes to Albuquerque, so if you encounter an accident or some other delay on a major thoroughfare into Albuquerque (or even Santa Fe), you can expect significant delays. It's a big reason to leave early and give yourself extra time when attempting to drive to Albuquerque to catch a plane.

Airline Resources

MAJOR AIRLINES		
Alaska Airlines	800/252-7522 or 206/433-3100	www.alaskaair.com
American Airlines	800/433-7300	www.aa.com
ATA	800/435-9282 or 317/282-8308	www.ata.com
Continental Airlines	800/523-3273 for U.S. and Mexico reservations, 800/231-0856 for international reservations	www.continental.com
Delta Airlines	800/221-1212 for U.S. reservations, 800/241-4141 for international reservations	www.delta.com
jetBlue	800/538-2583	www.jetblue.com
Northwest Airlines	800/225-2525	www.nwa.com
Southwest Airlines	800/435-9792	www.southwest.com
Spirit Airlines	800/772-7117 or 586/791-7300	www.spiritair.com
United Airlines	800/864-8331 for U.S. reservations, 800/538-2929 for international reservations	www.united.com
US Airways	800/428-4322 for U.S. and Canada reservations, 800/622-1015 for international reservations	www.usairways.com
SMALLER AIRLINES		
Frontier	800/432-1359	www.frontierairlines.com
Great Lakes Airlines	800/554-5111	www.greatlakesav.com
Mesa Airlines	800/637-2247	www.mesa-air.com
Skywest Airlines	435/634-3000	www.skywest.com

Parking is plentiful and either free or inexpensive in most New Mexico towns, even Albuquerque and Santa Fe. During busy times, however, such as summer weekends, parking in Santa Fe, Taos, Ruidoso, and parts of Albuquerque can be tougher to find.

Here are some common distances and approximate travel times between Albuquerque and several popular destinations, assuming no lengthy stops and averaging the 65 to 75 mph speed limits: Santa Fe is 65 mi and about an hour; Taos is 135 mi and about 2½ hours; Farmington is 185 mi and 3 hours; Gallup is 140 mi and 2 hours; Amarillo is 290 mi and 4 hours; Denver is 450 mi and 6–7 hours; Oklahoma City is 550 mi and 8–9 hours; Moab is 290 mi and 6–7 hours; Flagstaff is 320 mi and 4½ hours; Phoenix is 465 mi and 6½ to 7½ hours; Silver City is 230 mi and 3½–4 hours; Las Cruces is 225 mi and 3½ hours; Ruidoso is 190 mi and 3 hours; Carlsbad is 280 mi and 4½–5 hours; El Paso is 270 mi and 4 hours; Dallas is 650 mi and 10–11 hours; and San Antonio is 730 mi and 11–12 hours.

GASOLINE

There's a lot of high, dry, lonesome country in New Mexico—it's possible to go 50 or 60 mi in some of the less-populated areas between gas stations. For a safe trip **keep your gas tank full.** Self-service gas stations are the norm in New Mexico, though in some of the less-populated regions you can find stations with full service. The cost of unleaded gas at self-service stations in New Mexico is close to the U.S. average, but it's usually 10¢ to 20¢ more per gallon in Santa Fe, Taos, and certain spots off the beaten path.

ROAD CONDITIONS

Arroyos (dry washes or gullies) are bridged on major roads, but lesser roads often dip down through them. These can be a hazard during the rainy season, late June–early September. Even if it looks shallow, **don't try to cross an arroyo filled with water**—it may have an axle-breaking hole in the middle. Wait a little while, and it will drain off almost as quickly as it filled. If you stall in a flooded arroyo, get out of the car and onto high ground if possible. In the backcountry, never drive (or walk) in a dry arroyo bed if the sky is dark anywhere upstream. A sudden thunderstorm 15 mi away could send a raging flash flood down a wash in a matter of minutes.

Unless they are well graded and graveled, **avoid unpaved roads in New Mexico when they are wet.** The soil contains a lot of caliche, or clay, which gets slick when mixed with water. During winter storms roads may be shut down entirely; call the State Highway Department for road conditions.

At certain times in fall or spring, New Mexico winds can be vicious for large vehicles like RVs. Driving conditions can be particularly treacherous in passages through foothills or mountains where wind gusts are concentrated.

New Mexico has a high incidence of drunk driving and uninsured motorists. Factor in the state's high speed limits, many winding and steep roads, and eye-popping scenery, and you can see how important it is to drive as alertly and defensively as possible. On the plus side, major traffic jams are a rarity even in cities—and recent improvements to the state's busiest intersection, the I–40/I–25 interchange in Albuquerque, has helped to reduce rush-hour backups there. Additionally, a major highway widening and improvement along U.S. 285/84, north of Santa Fe, has also greatly smoothed the flow and speed of traffic up toward Taos.

Road Conditions State Highway Department ☎ 800/432–4269 ⊕ www.nmshtd.state.nm. us.

ROADSIDE EMERGENCIES

In the event of a roadside emergency, call 911. Depending on the location, either the New Mexico State Police or the county sheriff's department will respond. Call the city or village police department if you encounter trouble within the limits of a municipality. Indian reservations have tribal police headquarters, and rangers assist travelers within U.S. Forest Service boundaries.

▮ BY TRAIN

Amtrak's *Sunset Limited,* from Orlando, Florida, to Los Angeles, stops in El Paso, Texas; Deming; and Lordsburg on Tuesday, Thursday, and Saturday eastbound, and Monday, Thursday, and Saturday westbound. Amtrak's *Southwest Chief,* from Chicago to Los Angeles via Kansas City, stops in Raton, Las Vegas, Lamy (near Santa Fe), Albuquerque, and Gallup daily.

In summer 2006 the City of Albuquerque launched the state's first-ever commuter train line, the **New Mexico Rail Runner Express.** As of this writing, service is from Bernalillo south through the city of Albuquerque, continuing south through Los Lunas to the suburb of Belén, covering a distance of about 50 mi. The second and final phase of the project, expected to be completed by late 2008, will extend the service north to Santa Fe.

Amtrak offers a **North America rail pass** that gives you unlimited travel within the United States and Canada within any 30-

day period ($999 peak, $709 off-peak), and several kinds of **USA Rail passes** (for non-U.S. residents only) offering unlimited travel for 15 to 30 days. Amtrak also has senior-citizen, children's, disability, and student discounts, as well as occasional deals that allow a second or third accompanying passenger to travel for half price or even free. The **Amtrak Vacations** program customizes entire vacations, including hotels, car rentals, and tours.

Sample one-way fares on the *Sunset Limited* are $140 to $180 from Los Angeles to El Paso, and $100 to $150 from San Antonio, Texas, to Deming. Sample one-way fares on the *Southwest Chief* are $140 from Chicago to Lamy; $40 Denver to Las Vegas; and $60 Albuquerque to Los Angeles.

The *New Mexico Rail Runner Express* was running only on weekdays as of this writing, but it's expected to add weekend service by 2007. Tickets cost $2 for any one-way ride on the system. **Amtrak** ☎ 800/872-7245 ⊕ www.amtrak. com. **New Mexico Rail Runner Express** ☎ 505/245-7245 ⊕ www.nmrailrunner.com.

▌FOR INTERNATIONAL TRAVELERS

DRIVING

Driving in the United States is on the right. Speed limits are posted in miles per hour (usually between 55 mph and 70 mph). Watch for lower limits in small towns and on back roads (usually 30 mph to 40 mph). Most states require front-seat passengers to wear seat belts; many states require children to sit in the back seat and to wear seat belts. In major cities morning rush hour is between 7 and 10 AM; afternoon rush hour is between 4 and 7 PM. To encourage carpooling, some freeways have special lanes, ordinarily marked with a diamond, for high-occupancy vehicles (HOV)—cars carrying two people or more.

Highways are well paved. Interstates—limited-access, multilane highways designated with an "I–" before the number—are fastest. Interstates with three-digit numbers circle urban areas, which may also have other limited-access expressways, freeways, and parkways. Tolls may be levied on limited-access highways. U.S. and state highways aren't necessarily limited-access, but may have several lanes.

Gas stations are plentiful. Most stay open late (24 hours along major highways and in big cities) except in rural areas, where Sunday hours are limited and where you may drive for long stretches without a refueling opportunity. Along larger highways, roadside stops with restrooms, fast-food restaurants, and sundries stores are well spaced. State police and tow trucks patrol major highways. If your car breaks down on an interstate, pull onto the shoulder and wait for help, or have your passengers wait while you walk to an emergency phone (available in most states). If you carry a cell phone, dial *55, noting your location on the small green roadside mileage marker.

ELECTRICITY

The U.S. standard is AC, 110 volts/60 cycles. Plugs have two flat pins set parallel to each other.

EMERGENCIES

For police, fire, or ambulance, dial 911 (0 in rural areas).

EMBASSIES

Contacts Australia (☎ 202/797-3000 ⊕ www.austemb.org). **Canada** (☎ 202/682-1740 ⊕ www.canadianembassy.org). **United Kingdom** (☎ 202/588-7800 ⊕ www.britainusa.com).

HOLIDAYS

New Mexico is an exceptional destination at Christmastime. In Santa Fe and Taos there are excellent chances for snow to put you in the holiday mood—but it's usually in moderation and at tolerable temperatures. Farolitos (paper-bag lanterns) line sidewalks and the roofs of adobe buildings. Similar scenes are repeated throughout most of New Mexico, reflecting traditions dating back several centuries. In a nationally recognized Christmas tour at Carlsbad, home owners provide several miles of brightly lighted backyard displays for the benefit of evening boat cruises along the Pecos River.

MAIL

You can buy stamps and aerograms and send letters and parcels in post offices. Stamp-dispensing machines can occasionally be found in airports, bus and train stations, office buildings, drugstores, and convenience stores. U.S. mail boxes are stout, dark blue steel bins; pickup schedules are posted inside the bin (pull down the handle to see them). Parcels weighing more than a pound must be mailed at a post office or at a private mailing center.

Within the United States a first-class letter weighing 1 ounce or less costs 39¢; each additional ounce costs 24¢. Postcards cost 24¢. A 1-ounce airmail letter to most countries costs 84¢, an airmail postcard costs 75¢; a 1-ounce letter to Canada or Mexico costs 63¢, a postcard 55¢.

To receive mail on the road, have it sent c/o General Delivery at your destination's main post office (use the correct five-digit ZIP code). You must pick up mail in person within 30 days, with a driver's license or passport for identification.

Contacts DHL (☎ 800/225–5345 ⊕ www.dhl.com). **Federal Express** (☎ 800/463–3339 ⊕ www.fedex.com). **Mail Boxes, Etc./The UPS Store** (☎ 800/789–4623 ⊕www.mbe.com). **United States Postal Service** (⊕ www.usps.com).

PASSPORTS & VISAS

Visitor visas aren't necessary for citizens of Australia, Canada, the United Kingdom, or most citizens of European Union countries coming for tourism and staying for fewer than 90 days. If you require a visa, the cost is $100, and waiting time can be substantial, depending on where you live. Apply for a visa at the U.S. consulate in your place of residence; check the U.S. State Department's special Visa Web site for further information.

Visa Information Destination USA (⊕ www.unitedstatesvisas.gov).

PHONES

New Mexico's area code is 505, although there's talk of adding a new 575 area code to parts of the state in the next few years. Numbers consist of a three-digit area code and a seven-digit local number. Within many local calling areas you dial only the seven digits; in others you dial "1" first and all 10 digits—just as you would for calls between area-code regions. The same is true for calls to numbers prefixed by "800," "888," "866," and "877"—all toll free. For calls to numbers prefixed by "900" you must pay—usually dearly.

For international calls, dial "011" followed by the country code and the local number. For help, dial "0" and ask for an overseas operator. Most phone books list country codes and U.S. area codes. The country code for Australia is 61, for New Zealand 64, for the United Kingdom 44. Calling Canada is the same as calling within the United States, whose country code, by the way, is 1.

For operator assistance, dial "0." For directory assistance, call 555–1212 or occasionally 411 (free at many public phones). You can reverse long-distance charges by calling "collect"; dial "0" instead of "1" before the 10-digit number.

Instructions are generally posted on pay phones. Usually you insert coins in a slot (usually 25¢–50¢ for local calls) and wait for a steady tone before dialing. On long-distance calls the operator tells you how much to insert; prepaid phone cards, widely available in various denominations, can be used from any phone. Follow the directions to activate the card (there's usually an access number, then an activation code), then dial your number.

CELL PHONES

The United States has several GSM (Global System for Mobile Communications) networks, so multiband mobiles from most countries (except for Japan) work here. Unfortunately, it's almost impossible to buy a pay-as-you-go mobile SIM card in the U.S.—which allows you to avoid roaming charges—without also buying a phone. That said, cell phones with pay-as-you-go plans are available for well under $100. The cheapest ones with decent national coverage are the GoPhone from Cingular and Virgin Mobile, which only offers pay-as-you-go service.

Contacts Cingular (☎ 888/333–6651 ⊕ www.cingular.com). **Virgin Mobile** (☎ No phone ⊕ www.virginmobileusa.com).

■ COMMUNICATIONS

INTERNET

Since the early 2000s, the number of accommodations throughout the state offering Wi-Fi or wired high-speed Internet, if not in room then at least in common areas or business centers, has increased dramatically. In most of New Mexico, it's the exception rather than the rule to find a hotel or inn that doesn't offer this service. However, in smaller communities, you're more likely to encounter properties that have only dial-up Internet capacity. If it's important to you, check ahead. In the larger cities and primary tourist destinations in the region, you can find at least one or two coffeehouses or cafés with computer terminals that have Internet access as well as a library. Restaurants, coffeehouses, and bars with Wi-Fi have also become quite common throughout the state.

Cybercafes ⊕ www.cybercafes.com lists over 4,000 Internet cafés worldwide.

■ EATING OUT

New Mexico is justly famous for its distinctive cuisine, which utilizes ingredients and recipes common to Mexico, the Rockies, the Southwest, and the West's Native American communities. Most longtime residents like their chile sauces and salsas with some fire—in the Santa Fe, Albu-

querque, and Las Cruces areas, chile is sometimes celebrated for its ability to set off smoke alarms. Most restaurants offer a choice of red or green chile with one type typically being milder than the other. If you want both kinds with your meal, when your server asks you if you'd like "red or green," reply "Christmas." If you're not used to spicy foods, you may find even the average chile served with chips to be quite a lot hotter than back home—so proceed with caution. Excellent barbecue and steaks also can be found throughout New Mexico, with other specialties being local game (especially elk) and trout. The restaurants we list are the cream of the crop in each price category. Properties indicated by a ✕▣ are lodging establishments whose restaurant warrants a special trip.

MEALS & MEALTIMES

Statewide, many kitchens stop serving around 8 PM, so **don't arrive too late** if you're looking forward to a leisurely dinner. Unless otherwise noted, the restaurants listed in this guide are open daily for lunch and dinner.

PAYING

Credit cards are widely accepted at restaurants in major towns and cities and even most smaller communities, but in the latter places, you may occasionally encounter smaller, independent restaurants that are cash only. For guidelines on tipping *see* Tipping *below*.

RESERVATIONS & DRESS

Regardless of where you are, it's a good idea to make a reservation if you can. In some places (Hong Kong, for example), it's expected. We only mention them specifically when reservations are essential (there's no other way you'll ever get a table) or when they are not accepted. For popular restaurants, book as far ahead as you can (often 30 days), and reconfirm as soon as you arrive. (Large parties should always call ahead to check the reservations policy.) We mention dress only when men

WORD OF MOUTH

Was the service stellar or not up to snuff? Did the food give you shivers of delight or leave you cold? Did the prices and portions make you happy or sad? Rate restaurants and write your own reviews in Travel Ratings or start a discussion about your favorite places in Travel Talk on ⊕ www.fodors.com. Your comments might even appear in our books. Yes, you, too, can be a correspondent!

are required to wear a jacket or a jacket and tie.

Online reservation services make it easy to book a table before you even leave home. OpenTable covers most states, including 20 major cities, and has limited listings in Canada, Mexico, the United Kingdom, and elsewhere. DinnerBroker has restaurants throughout the United States as well as a few in Canada.
OpenTable ⊕ www.opentable.com. **Dinner-Broker** ⊕ www.dinnerbroker.com.

WINES, BEER & SPIRITS

Like many other states, New Mexico has some fine microbreweries, with the most prominent producer, Sierra Blanca Brewing Co., found in the unlikely and highly remote location of Carrizozo, in south-central New Mexico—Sierra Blanca's excellent beers are served throughout the state. New Mexico also has a growing number of wineries, some of them producing first-rate vintages. Franciscan monks first planted their vines here before moving more successfully to northern California, and the state's winemaking industry has really taken off since the late '90s. The New Mexico Wine Growers Association provides extensive information on the many fine wineries around the state as well as details on several prominent wine festivals.
New Mexico Wine Growers Association ☎ 866/494-6366 ⊕ www.nmwine.com.

■ ELECTRICITY

Consider making a small investment in a universal adapter, which has several types of plugs in one lightweight, compact unit. Most laptops and mobile phone chargers are dual voltage (i.e., they operate equally well on 110 and 220 volts), so require only an adapter. These days the same is true of small appliances such as hair dryers. Always check labels and manufacturer instructions to be sure. Don't use 110-volt outlets marked FOR SHAVERS ONLY for high-wattage appliances such as hair dryers.
Steve Kropla's Help for World Traveler's ⊕ www.kropla.com has information on electrical and telephone plugs around the world.
Walkabout Travel Gear ⊕ www.walkabouttravelgear.com has a good coverage of electricity under "adapters."

■ HOURS OF OPERATION

Although hours differ little in New Mexico from other parts of the United States, some businesses do keep shorter hours here than in more densely populated parts of the country. In particular, outside of the larger towns in New Mexico, it can be hard to find shops and restaurants open past 8 or 9 in the evening. Within the state, businesses tend to keep later hours in Albuquerque, Las Cruces, and Santa Fe than in rural areas.

Most major museums and attractions are open daily or six days a week (with Monday or Tuesday being the most likely day of closing). Hours are often shorter on Saturday and especially Sunday, and a handful of museums in larger cities stay open late one or two nights a week, usually Tuesday, Thursday, or Friday. New Mexico's less populous areas also have quite a few smaller museums—historical societies, small art galleries, highly specialized collections—that open only a few days a week, and sometimes only by appointment during slow times. It's always a good idea to call ahead if you're planning to go out of your way to visit a smaller museum.

Banks are usually open weekdays from 9 to 3 or a bit later and some Saturday mornings, the post office from 8 to 5 or 6 weekdays and often on Saturday mornings. Shops in urban and touristy areas, particularly in indoor and strip malls, typically open at 9 or 10 daily and stay open until anywhere from 6 PM to 10 PM on weekdays and Saturday, and until 5 or 6 on Sunday. Hours vary greatly, so call ahead when in doubt.

On major highways and in densely populated areas you can usually find at least one or two supermarkets, drugstores, and gas stations open 24 hours, and in Albuquerque, you can find a smattering of all-night fast-food restaurants, diners, and coffeehouses. Bars and discos stay open until 1 or 2 AM.

▌ MONEY

In New Mexico, Santa Fe is by far the priciest city: meals, gasoline, and motel rates are all significantly higher in the state's capital. Overall travel costs in Santa Fe, including dining and lodging, typically run 30% to 50% higher than in any other New Mexico city. Taos, too, can be a little expensive because it's such a popular tourist destination, but you have more choices for economizing there than in Santa Fe. Lodging and dining throughout much of the rest of the state are a genuine bargain. Depending on the establishment, $7 can buy you a savory Mexican dinner in Farmington, Old Mesilla, or Silver City. As the state's largest metropolitan area, Albuquerque has a full range of price choices.

CREDIT CARDS

Throughout this guide, the following abbreviations are used: **AE**, American Express; **D**, Discover; **DC**, Diners Club; **MC**, MasterCard; and **V**, Visa.

It's a good idea to inform your credit-card company before you travel, especially if you're going abroad and don't travel internationally very often. Otherwise, the credit-card company might put a hold on your card owing to unusual activity—not a good thing halfway through your trip. Record all your credit-card numbers—as well as the phone numbers to call if your cards are lost or stolen—in a safe place, so you're prepared should something go wrong. Both MasterCard and Visa have general numbers you can call (collect if you're abroad) if your card is lost, but you're better off calling the number of your issuing bank, since Master-Card and Visa usually just transfer you to your bank; your bank's number is usually printed on your card.

Reporting Lost Cards American Express ☏ 800/992-3404 in U.S., 336/393-1111 collect from abroad ⊕ www.americanexpress.com. **Diners Club** ☏ 800/234-6377 in U.S., 303/799-1504 collect from abroad ⊕ www.dinersclub.com. **Discover** ☏ 800/347-2683 in U.S., 801/902-3100 collect from abroad ⊕ www.discovercard.com. **MasterCard** ☏ 800/622-7747 in U.S., 636/722-7111 collect from abroad ⊕ www.mastercard.com. **Visa** ☏ 800/847-2911 in U.S., 410/581-9994 collect from abroad ⊕ www.visa.com.

TRAVELER'S CHECKS & CARDS

Some consider this the currency of the cave man, and it's true that fewer establishments accept traveler's checks these days. Nevertheless, they're a cheap and secure way to carry extra money, particularly on trips to urban areas. Both Citibank (under the Visa brand) and American Express issue traveler's checks in the United States, but Amex is better known and more widely accepted; you can also avoid hefty surcharges by cashing Amex checks at Amex offices. Whatever you do, keep track of all the serial numbers in case the checks are lost or stolen.

American Express now offers a stored-value card called a Travelers Cheque Card, which you can use wherever American Express credit cards are accepted, including ATMs. The card can carry a minimum of $300 and a maximum of $2,700, and it's a very safe way to carry your funds. Although you can get replacement funds in

24 hours if your card is lost or stolen, it does-n't really strike us as a very good deal. In addition to a high initial cost ($14.95 to set up the card, plus $5 each time you "reload"), you still have to pay a 2% fee for each purchase in a foreign currency (similar to that of any credit card). Further, each time you use the card in an ATM you pay a transaction fee of $2.50 on top of the 2% transaction fee for the conversion—add it all up and it can be considerably more than you would pay when simply using your own ATM card. Regular traveler's checks are just as secure and cost less. **American Express** ☎ 888/412-6945 in U.S., 801/945-9450 collect outside U.S. to add value or speak to customer service ⊕ www.americanexpress.com.

▌TAXES

The standard state gross receipts tax rate is 5%, but municipalities and counties enact additional charges at varying rates. Even with additional charges, you will encounter no sales tax higher than 7%.

▌TIME

New Mexico and a small portion of west Texas (including El Paso) observe moun-tain standard time, switching over with most of the rest of the country to daylight saving time in the spring through fall. In New Mexico, you'll be two hours behind New York and one hour ahead of Arizona (except during daylight saving time, which Arizona does not observe) and California.

▌TIPPING

The customary tipping rate for taxi driv-ers is 15%–20%, with a minimum of $2; bellhops are usually given $2 per bag in lux-ury hotels, $1 per bag elsewhere. Hotel maids should be tipped $2 per day of your stay. A doorman who hails or helps you into a cab can be tipped $1–$2. You should also tip your hotel concierge for services ren-dered; the size of the tip depends on the dif-ficulty of your request, as well as the quality of the concierge's work. For an ordinary

dinner reservation or tour arrangements, $3–$5 should do; if the concierge scores seats at a popular restaurant or show or performs unusual services (getting your laptop repaired, finding a good pet-sitter, etc.), $10 or more is appropriate.

Waiters should be tipped 15%–20%, though at higher-end restaurants, a solid 20% is more the norm. Many restaurants add a gratuity to the bill for parties of six or more. Ask what the percentage is if the menu or bill doesn't state it. Tip $1 per drink you order at the bar, though if at an upscale establishment, those $15 martinis might warrant a $2 tip.

TIPPING GUIDELINES FOR NEW MEXICO	
Bartender	$1 to $5 per round of drinks, depending on the number of drinks
Bellhop	$1 to $5 per bag, depending on the level of the hotel
Hotel Concierge	$5 or more, if he or she per-forms a service for you
Hotel Doorman	$1–$2 if he helps you get a cab
Hotel Maid	1$–$3 a day (either daily or at the end of your stay, in cash)
Hotel Room-Service Waiter	$1 to $2 per delivery, even if a service charge has been added
Porter at Airport or Train Station	$1 per bag
Skycap at Airport	$1 to $3 per bag checked
Taxi Driver	15%–20%, but round up the fare to the next dollar amount
Tour Guide	10% of the cost of the tour
Valet Parking Attendant	$1–$2, but only when you get your car
Waiter	15%–20%, with 20% being the norm at high-end restau-rants; nothing additional if a service charge is added to the bill

INDEX

428 < Index